Audi Automotive Repair Manual

John S Mead

Models covered:
Audi 5000S (including Wagon) and 5000S Turbo
131 cu in (2144 cc), 136 cu in (2226 cc) &
141 cu in (2309 cc)

Does not cover Quattro or Diesel engine versions

1117 – 1Q2

ABCDE
FGHIJ

Haynes Publishing Group
Sparkford Nr Yeovil
Somerset BA22 7JJ England

Haynes Publications, Inc
861 Lawrence Drive
Newbury Park
California 91320 USA

Acknowledgements

Thanks are due to the Champion Sparking Plug Company Limited who supplied the illustrations showing the spark plug conditions. Certain other illustrations are the copyright of Volkswagenwerk AG, and are used with their permission. Thanks are also due to Mr. John Day of JP and S Day, South Lea Garage, South Molton, Devon, England for the loan of the project car, to Swallowdale Motors, Seaton, Devon, England for technical assistance, to Sykes-Pickavant Limited who provided some of the workshop tools, and to all those people at Sparkford who helped in the production of this manual.

© **Haynes Publishing Group 1986, 1989**

A book in the **Haynes Automotive Repair Manual Series**

Printed by J.H. Haynes & Co., Ltd. Sparkford Nr. Yeovil, Somerset BA22 7JJ, England

ISBN 1 85010 569 3

Library of Congress Catalog Card Number 88-83190

Contents

Audi 100 CD – UK

Audi 100 Avant CD – UK

About this manual

Its aim

The aim of this manual is to help you get the best value from your vehicle. It can do so in several ways. It can help you decide what work must be done (even should you choose to get it done by a garage), provide information on routine maintenance and servicing, and give a logical course of action and diagnosis when random faults occur. However, it is hoped that you will use the manual by tackling the work yourself. On simpler jobs it may even be quicker than booking the car into a garage and going there twice, to leave and collect it. Perhaps most important, a lot of money can be saved by avoiding the costs a garage must charge to cover its labour and overheads.

The manual has drawings and descriptions to show the function of the various components so that their layout can be understood. Then the tasks are described and photographed in a step-by-step sequence so that even a novice can do the work.

Its arrangement

The manual is divided into thirteen Chapters, each covering a logical sub-division of the vehicle. The Chapters are each divided into Sections, numbered with single figures, eg 5; and the Sections into paragraphs (or sub-sections), with decimal numbers following on from the Section they are in, eg 5.1, 5.2, 5.3 etc.

It is freely illustrated, especially in those parts where there is a detailed sequence of operations to be carried out. There are two forms of illustration: figures and photographs. The figures are numbered in sequence with decimal numbers, according to their position in the Chapter – eg Fig. 6.4 is the fourth drawing/illustration in Chapter 6. Photographs carry the same number (either individually or in related groups) as the Section or sub-section to which they relate.

There is an alphabetical index at the back of the manual as well as a contents list at the front. Each Chapter is also preceded by its own individual contents list.

References to the 'left' or 'right' of the vehicle are in the sense of a person in the driver's seat facing forwards.

Unless otherwise stated, nuts and bolts are removed by turning anti-clockwise, and tightened by turning clockwise.

Vehicle manufacturers continually make changes to specifications and recommendations, and these, when notified, are incorporated into our manuals at the earliest opportunity.

Whilst every care is taken to ensure that the information in this manual is correct, no liability can be accepted by the authors or publishers for loss, damage or injury caused by any errors in, or omissions from, the information given.

Introduction to the Audi 100, 200 and 5000

The 'new' Audi 100 was announced in October 1982 with the 200 version becoming available in early 1984. The North American version, the Audi 5000, was launched in 1983.

All models feature startling new advances in automotive design and technology, foremost among these being the meticulous attention to aerodynamic shape. With a drag coefficient (Cd) of 0.30 for the Audi 100, these cars are of a design which is amongst the most aerodynamically efficient in their class.

In addition to aerodynamic excellence, all models offer a comprehensive package of standard and optional equipment features.

The model range is extensive and offers a choice of trim, Saloon or Estate (Avant) body styles, four or five-cylinder engines, and four or five-speed gearbox or automatic transmission. Full instrumentation is provided, together with electric windows, central locking, on-board computer, extensive audio system, and power steering, according to model. UK models are available with carburettor, fuel injection or fuel injection with turbocharger engines. North American models are available with fuel injection or fuel injection with turbocharger engines.

Audi 5000S Wagon – USA

Audi 5000S – USA

General dimensions, weights and capacities

Dimensions
Overall length:

Audi 100	4792 mm (188.8 in)
Audi 200	4808 mm (189.4 in)
Audi 5000	4894 mm (192.8 in)
Overall width	1814 mm (71.5 in)
Overall height (unladen)	1428 mm (56.2 in) approximately

Ground clearance (laden):

Saloon models	133 mm (5.2 in)
Avant models	140 mm (5.5 in)
Vehicles with self-levelling suspension	187 mm (7.3 in)
Wheelbase	2687.5 mm (105.8 in)
Front track	1468 mm (57.8 in)
Rear track	1469 mm (57.8 in)
Turning circle (between walls)	11500 mm (453.1 in) approximately

Weights*
Kerb weight:

Saloon models:

55 kW engine	1090 kg (2403 lb)
66 kW engine	1090 kg (2403 lb)
74 kW engine	1145 kg (2524 lb)
85 kW engine	1250 kg (2756 lb)
100 kW engine	1210 kg (2668 lb)
101 kW engine	1250 kg (2756 lb)
134 kW engine	1300 kg (2866 lb)

Avant models:

55 kW engine	1130 kg (2491 lb)
66 kW engine	1140 kg (2513 lb)
85 kW engine	1290 kg (2844 lb)
100 kW engine	1260 kg (2778 lb)
101 kW engine	1290 kg (2844 lb)

Add 15 kg (33 lb) for automatic transmission on five-cylinder engines. Add 25 kg (55 lb) for automatic transmission on four-cylinder engines

Gross vehicle weight:
    Saloon models:
        55 and 66 kW engine .... 1640 kg (3616 lb)
        74 kW engine .... 1645 kg (3627 lb)
        85 kW engine .... 1800 kg (3969 lb)
        100 kW engine .... 1710 kg (3770 lb)
        101 kW engine .... 1800 kg (3969 lb)
        134 kW engine .... 1790 kg (3946 lb)
    Avant models:
        55 and 66 kW engine .... 1680 kg (3704 lb)
        85 kW engine .... 1840 kg (4057 lb)
        100 kW engine .... 1760 kg (3880 lb)
        101 kW engine .... 1840 kg (4057 lb)
Maximum roof rack load .... 75 kg (165 lb)
Maximum towing weight (12% gradient):
    Saloon models:
        55 and 66 kW engines .... 1150 kg (2535 lb)
        74 kW engine:
            Manual gearbox .... 1300 kg (2866 lb)
            Automatic transmission .... 1400 kg (3087 lb)
        85 kW engine:
            Manual gearbox .... 1200 kg (2646 lb)
            Automatic transmission .... 1300 kg (2866 lb)
        100 kW engine:
            Manual gearbox .... 1500 kg (3307 lb)
            Automatic transmission .... 1600 kg (3528 lb)
        101 and 134 kW engines:
            Manual gearbox .... 1400 kg (3087 lb)
            Automatic transmission .... 1500 kg (3307 lb)
    Avant models:
        55 and 66 kW engines .... 1100 kg (2425 lb)
        74 kW engine:
            Manual gearbox .... 1200 kg (2646 lb)
            Automatic transmission .... 1300 kg (2866 lb)
        85 kW engine:
            Manual gearbox .... 1150 kg (2535 lb)
            Automatic transmission .... 1250 kg (2756 lb)
        100 kW engine:
            Manual gearbox .... 1400 kg (3087 lb)
            Automatic transmission .... 1500 kg (3307 lb)
        101 kW engine:
            Manual gearbox .... 1350 kg (2976 lb)
            Automatic transmission .... 1450 kg (3197 lb)

On North American models the weights are given on a Safety Compliance Sticker located on the left-hand side door jam

Capacities

Engine oil:
    Four-cylinder engines with filter change .... 3.0 litre; 5.3 Imp pt; 3.2 US qt
    Four-cylinder engines without filter change .... 2.5 litre; 4.4 Imp pt; 2.6 US qt
    Five-cylinder engines with filter change .... 4.5 litre; 7.9 Imp pt; 4.8 US qt
    Five-cylinder engines without filter change .... 4.0 litre; 7.0 Imp pt; 4.2 US qt
    Difference between MIN and MAX marks on dipstick .... 1.0 litre; 1.8 Imp pt; 1.1 US qt
Cooling system (including heater):
    Four-cylinder engines .... 7.0 litre; 12.3 Imp pt; 7.4 US qt
    Five-cylinder engines .... 8.1 litre; 14.2 Imp pt; 8.5 US qt
Fuel tank:
    All models .... 80 litre; 17.6 Imp gal; 21.1 US gal
Manual gearbox:
    013 .... 2.0 litre; 3.5 Imp pt; 2.1 US qt
    014 .... 1.7 litre; 3.0 Imp pt; 1.8 US qt
    016 .... 2.6 litre; 4.5 Imp pt; 2.7 US qt
    093 .... 2.3 litre; 4.0 Imp pt; 2.4 US qt
Automatic transmission:
    089 gearbox ATF (total) .... 6.0 litre; 10.6 Imp pt; 6.3 US qt
    089 gearbox ATF (service) .... 3.0 litre; 5.3 Imp pt; 3.2 US qt
    089 final drive .... 0.75 litre; 1.3 Imp pt; 0.8 US qt
    087 gearbox ATF (total) .... 6.0 litre; 10.6 Imp pt; 6.3 US qt
    087 gearbox ATF (service .... 3.0 litre; 5.3 Imp pt; 3.2 US qt
    087 final drive .... 0.7 litre; 1.2 Imp pt; 0.7 US qt
Combined hydraulic system:
    Power-assisted steering and brake servo unit .... 1.6 litre; 2.8 Imp pt; 1.7 US qt
    Power-assisted steering, brake servo unit and self-levelling
    suspension .... 2.7 litre; 4.7 Imp pt; 2.8 US qt

Jacking, towing and wheel changing

Jacking

To change a roadwheel, first remove the spare wheel and jack from the left-hand side of the luggage compartment and remove the tool kit from the rear panel. With the car on firm level ground apply the handbrake and chock the wheel diagonally opposite the one to be changed. Using the tools provided, remove the hub cap where necessary, then loosen the wheel bolts half a turn. Locate the lifting arm of the jack beneath the reinforced seam of the side sill panel directly beneath the wedge shaped depression nearest to the wheel to be removed. Turn the jack handle until the base of the jack contacts the ground directly beneath the sill, then continue to turn the handle until the wheel is free of the ground. Unscrew the wheel bolts and remove the wheel. On light alloy wheels prise off the centre trim cap and press it into the spare wheel.

Locate the spare wheel on the hub, then insert and tighten the bolts in diagonal sequence. Lower the jack and fully tighten the bolts. Refit the hub cap where necessary, remove the chock and relocate the tool kit, jack and wheel in the luggage compartment.

Note that certain models are equipped with a space saving temporary spare wheel which is smaller and lighter than an ordinary wheel and is only intended for temporary use over short distances.

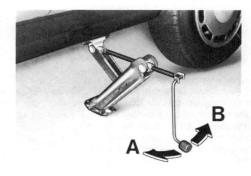

Vehicle jack in position. Turn handle in direction 'A' to raise and 'B' to lower

Spare wheel and tool kit location on Saloon models

Spare wheel and tool kit location on Avant models

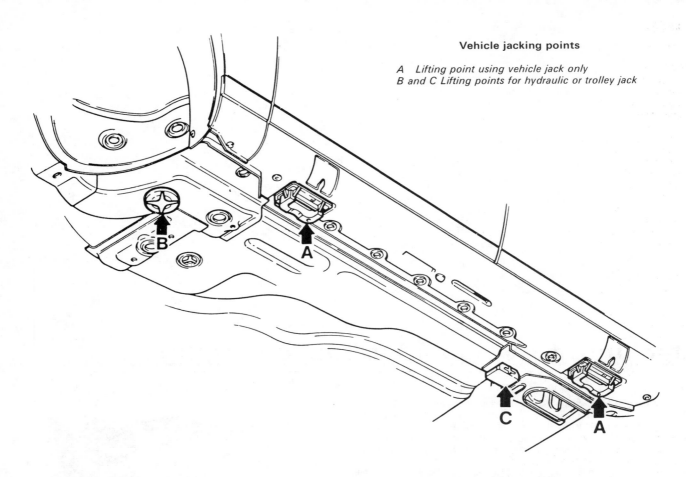

Vehicle jacking points

A   Lifting point using vehicle jack only
B and C Lifting points for hydraulic or trolley jack

With this type of wheel in place, do not exceed 50 mph (80 km/h), and avoid full throttle acceleration, heavy braking and fast cornering.

When jacking up the car with a trolley jack, position the jack beneath the reinforced plate behind the front wheel (see illustration) or beneath the reinforced seam at the rear of the side sill panel. Use the same positions when supporting the car with axle stands. *Never jack up the car beneath the suspension or axle components, the sump, or the gearbox.*

Towing

Towing eyes are fitted to the front and the rear of the vehicle and a tow line should not be attached to any other points. It is preferable to use a slightly elastic tow line, to reduce the strain on both vehicles, either by having a tow line manufactured from synthetic fibre, or one which is fitted with an elastic link.

When towing, the following important precautions must be observed:

(a) *Turn the ignition key of the vehicle being towed, so that the steering wheel is free (unlocked)*

(b) *Remember that when the engine is not running the brake servo will not operate, so that additional pressure will be required on the brake pedal after the first few applications*

(c) *On vehicles with automatic transmission, ensure that the gear selector lever is at N. Do not tow faster than 30 mph (50 kph), or further than 30 miles (50 km) unless the front wheels are lifted clear of the ground.*

Buying spare parts and vehicle identification numbers

Buying spare parts

Spare parts are available from many sources, Audi have many dealers throughout the country and other dealers, accessory stores and motor factors will also stock Audi spare parts. Our advice regarding spare parts sources is as follows:

Officially appointed vehicle main dealers: This is the best source of parts which are peculiar to your vehicle and are otherwise not generally available (eg, complete cylinder heads, internal transmission components, badges, interior trim etc). It is also the only place at which you should buy parts if your vehicle is still under warranty. To be sure of obtaining the correct parts it will always be necessary to give the storeman your vehicle's engine and chassis number, and if possible to take the 'old' part along for positive identification. Remember that many parts are available on a factory exchange scheme – any parts returned should always be clean! It obviously makes good sense to go straight to the specialists on your vehicle for this type of part for they are best equipped to supply you.

Other dealers and auto accessory shops – These are often very good places to buy materials and components needed for the maintenance of your car (eg, oil filters, spark plugs, bulbs, fan belts, oils and greases, touch-up paint, filler paste etc). They also sell general accessories, usually have convenient opening hours, charge lower prices and can often be found not far from home.

Motor factors – Good factors will stock all of the more important components which wear out relatively quickly (eg, clutch components, pistons, valves, exhaust systems, brake cylinders/pipes/hoses/seals/shoes and pads etc). Motor factors will often provide new or reconditioned components on a part exchange basis – this can save a considerable amount of money.

Vehicle identification numbers

Modifications are a continuing and unpublicised process in vehicle manufacture. Spare parts manuals and lists are compiled on a numerical basis, the individual vehicle numbers being essential for correct identification of the component required.

The vehicle identification plate is located on the right-hand side of the engine compartment front panel on UK models, or on the inside of the luggage compartment lid on North American models. The vehicle identification number is also located on the bottom left-hand side of the windscreen on North American models and is visible from the outside.

The engine number is stamped on the left-hand side of the cylinder block.

The manual gearbox number is stamped on the right-hand side of the gearbox, above the drive flange.

The automatic transmission number is stamped inside the torque converter housing, but the transmission type number is on the top of the gear casing.

Vehicle identification plate on UK models

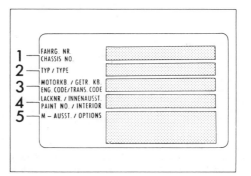

Vehicle identification label on North American models

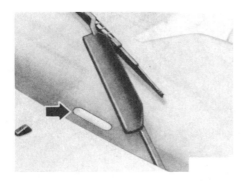

Vehicle identification number on North American models, viewed through the windscreen

The engine number

Use of English

As this book has been written in England, it uses the appropriate English component names, phrases, and spelling. Some of these differ from those used in America. Normally, these cause no difficulty, but to make sure, a glossary is printed below. In ordering spare parts remember the parts list may use some of these words:

English	American	English	American
Accelerator	Gas pedal	Locks	Latches
Aerial	Antenna	Methylated spirit	Denatured alcohol
Anti-roll bar	Stabiliser or sway bar	Motorway	Freeway, turnpike etc
Big-end bearing	Rod bearing	Number plate	License plate
Bonnet (engine cover)	Hood	Paraffin	Kerosene
Boot (luggage compartment)	Trunk	Petrol	Gasoline (gas)
Bulkhead	Firewall	Petrol tank	Gas tank
Bush	Bushing	'Pinking'	'Pinging'
Cam follower or tappet	Valve lifter or tappet	Prise (force apart)	Pry
Carburettor	Carburetor	Propeller shaft	Driveshaft
Catch	Latch	Quarterlight	Quarter window
Choke/venturi	Barrel	Retread	Recap
Circlip	Snap-ring	Reverse	Back-up
Clearance	Lash	Rocker cover	Valve cover
Crownwheel	Ring gear (of differential)	Saloon	Sedan
Damper	Shock absorber, shock	Seized	Frozen
Disc (brake)	Rotor/disk	Sidelight	Parking light
Distance piece	Spacer	Silencer	Muffler
Drop arm	Pitman arm	Sill panel (beneath doors)	Rocker panel
Drop head coupe	Convertible	Small end, little end	Piston pin or wrist pin
Dynamo	Generator (DC)	Spanner	Wrench
Earth (electrical)	Ground	Split cotter (for valve spring cap)	Lock (for valve spring retainer)
Engineer's blue	Prussian blue	Split pin	Cotter pin
Estate car	Station wagon	Steering arm	Spindle arm
Exhaust manifold	Header	Sump	Oil pan
Fault finding/diagnosis	Troubleshooting	Swarf	Metal chips or debris
Float chamber	Float bowl	Tab washer	Tang or lock
Free-play	Lash	Tappet	Valve lifter
Freewheel	Coast	Thrust bearing	Throw-out bearing
Gearbox	Transmission	Top gear	High
Gearchange	Shift	Torch	Flashlight
Grub screw	Setscrew, Allen screw	Trackrod (of steering)	Tie-rod (or connecting rod)
Gudgeon pin	Piston pin or wrist pin	Trailing shoe (of brake)	Secondary shoe
Halfshaft	Axleshaft	Transmission	Whole drive line
Handbrake	Parking brake	Tyre	Tire
Hood	Soft top	Van	Panel wagon/van
Hot spot	Heat riser	Vice	Vise
Indicator	Turn signal	Wheel nut	Lug nut
Interior light	Dome lamp	Windscreen	Windshield
Layshaft (of gearbox)	Countershaft	Wing/mudguard	Fender
Leading shoe (of brake)	Primary shoe		

General repair procedures

Whenever servicing, repair or overhaul work is carried out on the car or its components, it is necessary to observe the following procedures and instructions. This will assist in carrying out the operation efficiently and to a professional standard of workmanship.

Joint mating faces and gaskets

Where a gasket is used between the mating faces of two components, ensure that it is renewed on reassembly, and fit it dry unless otherwise stated in the repair procedure. Make sure that the mating faces are clean and dry with all traces of old gasket removed. When cleaning a joint face, use a tool which is not likely to score or damage the face, and remove any burrs or nicks with an oilstone or fine file.

Make sure that tapped holes are cleaned with a pipe cleaner, and keep them free of jointing compound if this is being used unless specifically instructed otherwise.

Ensure that all orifices, channels or pipes are clear and blow through them, preferably using compressed air.

Oil seals

Whenever an oil seal is removed from its working location, either individually or as part of an assembly, it should be renewed.

The very fine sealing lip of the seal is easily damaged and will not seal if the surface it contacts is not completely clean and free from scratches, nicks or grooves. If the original sealing surface of the component cannot be restored, the component should be renewed.

Protect the lips of the seal from any surface which may damage them in the course of fitting. Use tape or a conical sleeve where possible. Lubricate the seal lips with oil before fitting and, on dual lipped seals, fill the space between the lips with grease.

Unless otherwise stated, oil seals must be fitted with their sealing lips toward the lubricant to be sealed.

Use a tubular drift or block of wood of the appropriate size to install the seal and, if the seal housing is shouldered, drive the seal down to the shoulder. If the seal housing is unshouldered, the seal should be fitted with its face flush with the housing top face.

Screw threads and fastenings

Always ensure that a blind tapped hole is completely free from oil, grease, water or other fluid before installing the bolt or stud. Failure to do this could cause the housing to crack due to the hydraulic action of the bolt or stud as it is screwed in.

When tightening a castellated nut to accept a split pin, tighten the nut to the specified torque, where applicable, and then tighten further to the next split pin hole. Never slacken the nut to align a split pin hole unless stated in the repair procedure.

When checking or retightening a nut or bolt to a specified torque setting, slacken the nut or bolt by a quarter of a turn, and then retighten to the specified setting.

Locknuts, locktabs and washers

Any fastening which will rotate against a component or housing in the course of tightening should always have a washer between it and the relevant component or housing.

Spring or split washers should always be renewed when they are used to lock a critical component such as a big-end bearing retaining nut or bolt.

Locktabs which are folded over to retain a nut or bolt should always be renewed.

Self-locking nuts can be reused in non-critical areas, providing resistance can be felt when the locking portion passes over the bolt or stud thread.

Split pins must always be replaced with new ones of the correct size for the hole.

Special tools

Some repair procedures in this manual entail the use of special tools such as a press, two or three-legged pullers, spring compressors etc. Wherever possible, suitable readily available alternatives to the manufacturer's special tools are described, and are shown in use. In some instances, where no alternative is possible, it has been necessary to resort to the use of a manufacturer's tool and this has been done for reasons of safety as well as the efficient completion of the repair operation. Unless you are highly skilled and have a thorough understanding of the procedure described, never attempt to bypass the use of any special tool when the procedure described specifies its use. Not only is there a very great risk of personal injury, but expensive damage could be caused to the components involved.

Tools and working facilities

Introduction

A selection of good tools is a fundamental requirement for anyone contemplating the maintenance and repair of a motor vehicle. For the owner who does not possess any, their purchase will prove a considerable expense, offsetting some of the savings made by doing-it-yourself. However, provided that the tools purchased are of good quality, they will last for many years and prove an extremely worthwhile investment.

To help the average owner to decide which tools are needed to carry out the various tasks detailed in this manual, we have compiled three lists of tools under the following headings: *Maintenance and minor repair, Repair and overhaul,* and *Special.* The newcomer to practical mechanics should start off with the *Maintenance and minor repair* tool kit and confine himself to the simpler jobs around the vehicle. Then, as his confidence and experience grow, he can undertake more difficult tasks, buying extra tools as, and when, they are needed. In this way, a *Maintenance and minor repair* tool kit can be built-up into a *Repair and overhaul* tool kit over a considerable period of time without any major cash outlays. The experienced do-it-yourselfer will have a tool kit good enough for most repair and overhaul procedures and will add tools from the *Special* category when he feels the expense is justified by the amount of use to which these tools will be put.

It is obviously not possible to cover the subject of tools fully here. For those who wish to learn more about tools and their use there is a book entitled *How to Choose and Use Car Tools* available from the publishers of this manual.

Maintenance and minor repair tool kit

The tools given in this list should be considered as a minimum requirement if routine maintenance, servicing and minor repair operations are to be undertaken. We recommend the purchase of combination spanners (ring one end, open-ended the other); although more expensive than open-ended ones, they do give the advantages of both types of spanner.

Combination spanners - 10, 11, 12, 13, 14 & 17 mm
Adjustable spanner - 9 inch
Spark plug spanner (with rubber insert)
Spark plug gap adjustment tool
Set of feeler gauges
Brake bleed nipple spanner
Screwdriver - 4 in long x $^1/_4$ in dia (flat blade)
Screwdriver - 4 in long x $^1/_4$ in dia (cross blade)
Combination pliers - 6 inch
Hacksaw (junior)
Tyre pump
Tyre pressure gauge
Oil can
Fine emery cloth (1 sheet)
Wire brush (small)
Funnel (medium size)

Repair and overhaul tool kit

These tools are virtually essential for anyone undertaking any major repairs to a motor vehicle, and are additional to those given in the *Maintenance and minor repair* list. Included in this list is a comprehensive set of sockets. Although these are expensive they will be found invaluable as they are so versatile - particularly if various drives are included in the set. We recommend the ½ in square-drive type, as this can be used with most proprietary torque wrenches. If you cannot afford a socket set, even bought piecemeal, then inexpensive tubular box spanners are a useful alternative.

The tools in this list will occasionally need to be supplemented by tools from the *Special* list.

Sockets (or box spanners) to cover range in previous list
Reversible ratchet drive (for use with sockets)
Extension piece, 10 inch (for use with sockets)
Universal joint (for use with sockets)
Torque wrench (for use with sockets)
'Mole' wrench - 8 inch
Ball pein hammer
Soft-faced hammer, plastic or rubber
Screwdriver - 6 in long x $^5/_{16}$ in dia (flat blade)
Screwdriver - 2 in long x $^5/_{16}$ in square (flat blade)
Screwdriver - 1$^1/_2$ in long x $^1/_4$ in dia (cross blade)
Screwdriver - 3 in long x $^1/_8$ in dia (electricians)
Pliers - electricians side cutters
Pliers - needle nosed
Pliers - circlip (internal and external)
Cold chisel - $^1/_2$ inch
Scriber
Scraper
Centre punch
Pin punch
Hacksaw
Valve grinding tool
Steel rule/straight-edge
Allen keys
Selection of files
Wire brush (large)
Axle-stands
Jack (strong trolley or hydraulic type)
Splined key (for cylinder head bolts)

Special tools

The tools in this list are those which are not used regularly, are expensive to buy, or which need to be used in accordance with their manufacturers' instructions. Unless relatively difficult mechanical jobs are undertaken frequently, it will not be economic to buy many of these tools. Where this is the case, you could consider clubbing together with friends (or joining a motorists' club) to make a joint purchase, or borrowing the tools against a deposit from a local garage or tool hire specialist.

The following list contains only those tools and instruments freely available to the public, and not those special tools produced by the vehicle manufacturer specifically for its dealer network. You will find occasional references to these manufacturers' special tools in the text of this manual. Generally, an alternative method of doing the job without the vehicle manufacturers' special tool is given. However, sometimes, there is no alternative to using them. Where this is the case and the relevant tool cannot be bought or borrowed, you will have to entrust the work to a franchised garage.

> Valve spring compressor
> Piston ring compressor
> Balljoint separator
> Universal hub/bearing puller
> Impact screwdriver
> Micrometer and/or vernier gauge
> Dial gauge
> Stroboscopic timing light
> Dwell angle meter/tachometer
> Universal electrical multi-meter
> Cylinder compression gauge
> Lifting tackle
> Trolley jack
> Light with extension lead

Buying tools

For practically all tools, a tool factor is the best source since he will have a very comprehensive range compared with the average garage or accessory shop. Having said that, accessory shops often offer excellent quality tools at discount prices, so it pays to shop around.

Remember, you don't have to buy the most expensive items on the shelf, but it is always advisable to steer clear of the very cheap tools. There are plenty of good tools around at reasonable prices, so ask the proprietor or manager of the shop for advice before making a purchase.

Care and maintenance of tools

Having purchased a reasonable tool kit, it is necessary to keep the tools in a clean serviceable condition. After use, always wipe off any dirt, grease and metal particles using a clean, dry cloth, before putting the tools away. Never leave them lying around after they have been used. A simple tool rack on the garage or workshop wall, for items such as screwdrivers and pliers is a good idea. Store all normal wrenches and sockets in a metal box. Any measuring instruments, gauges, meters, etc, must be carefully stored where they cannot be damaged or become rusty.

Take a little care when tools are used. Hammer heads inevitably become marked and screwdrivers lose the keen edge on their blades from time to time. A little timely attention with emery cloth or a file will soon restore items like this to a good serviceable finish.

Working facilities

Not to be forgotten when discussing tools, is the workshop itself. If anything more than routine maintenance is to be carried out, some form of suitable working area becomes essential.

It is appreciated that many an owner mechanic is forced by circumstances to remove an engine or similar item, without the benefit of a garage or workshop. Having done this, any repairs should always be done under the cover of a roof.

Wherever possible, any dismantling should be done on a clean, flat workbench or table at a suitable working height.

Any workbench needs a vice: one with a jaw opening of 4 in (100 mm) is suitable for most jobs. As mentioned previously, some clean dry storage space is also required for tools, as well as for lubricants, cleaning fluids, touch-up paints and so on, which become necessary.

Another item which may be required, and which has a much more general usage, is an electric drill with a chuck capacity of at least $5/16$ in (8 mm). This, together with a good range of twist drills, is virtually essential for fitting accessories such as mirrors and reversing lights.

Last, but not least, always keep a supply of old newspapers and clean, lint-free rags available, and try to keep any working area as clean as possible.

Spanner jaw gap comparison table

Jaw gap (in)	Spanner size
0.250	1/4 in AF
0.276	7 mm
0.313	5/16 in AF
0.315	8 mm
0.344	11/32 in AF; 1/8 in Whitworth
0.354	9 mm
0.375	3/8 in AF
0.394	10 mm
0.433	11 mm
0.438	7/16 in AF
0.445	3/16 in Whitworth; 1/4 in BSF
0.472	12 mm
0.500	1/2 in AF
0.512	13 mm
0.525	1/4 in Whitworth; 5/16 in BSF
0.551	14 mm
0.563	9/16 in AF
0.591	15 mm
0.600	5/16 in Whitworth; 3/8 in BSF
0.625	5/8 in AF
0.630	16 mm
0.669	17 mm
0.686	11/16 in AF
0.709	18 mm
0.710	3/8 in Whitworth; 7/16 in BSF
0.748	19 mm
0.750	3/4 in AF
0.813	13/16 in AF
0.820	7/16 in Whitworth; 1/2 in BSF
0.866	22 mm
0.875	7/8 in AF
0.920	1/2 in Whitworth; 9/16 in BSF
0.938	15/16 in AF
0.945	24 mm
1.000	1 in AF
1.010	9/16 in Whitworth; 5/8 in BSF
1.024	26 mm
1.063	11/16 in AF; 27 mm
1.100	5/8 in Whitworth; 11/16 in BSF
1.125	11/8 in AF
1.181	30 mm
1.200	11/16 in Whitworth; 3/4 in BSF
1.250	11/4 in AF
1.260	32 mm
1.300	3/4 in Whitworth; 7/8 in BSF
1.313	15/16 in AF
1.390	13/16 in Whitworth; 15/16 in BSF
1.417	36 mm
1.438	17/16 in AF
1.480	7/8 in Whitworth; 1 in BSF
1.500	11/2 in AF
1.575	40 mm; 15/16 in Whitworth
1.614	41 mm
1.625	15/8 in AF
1.670	1 in Whitworth; 11/8 in BSF
1.688	111/16 in AF
1.811	46 mm
1.813	113/16 in AF
1.860	11/8 in Whitworth; 11/4 in BSF
1.875	17/8 in AF
1.969	50 mm
2.000	2 in AF
2.050	11/4 in Whitworth; 13/8 in BSF
2.165	55 mm
2.362	60 mm

Safety first!

Regardless of how enthusiastic you may be about getting on with the job at hand, take the time to ensure that your safety is not jeopardized. A moment's lack of attention can result in an accident, as can failure to observe certain simple safety precautions. The possibility of an accident will always exist, and the following points should not be considered a comprehensive list of all dangers. Rather, they are intended to make you aware of the risks and to encourage a safety conscious approach to all work you carry out on your vehicle.

Essential DOs and DON'Ts

DON'T rely on a jack when working under the vehicle. Always use approved jackstands to support the weight of the vehicle and place them under the recommended lift or support points.

DON'T attempt to loosen extremely tight fasteners (i.e. wheel lug nuts) while the vehicle is on a jack — it may fall.

DON'T start the engine without first making sure that the transmission is in Neutral (or Park where applicable) and the parking brake is set.

DON'T remove the radiator cap from a hot cooling system — let it cool or cover it with a cloth and release the pressure gradually.

DON'T attempt to drain the engine oil until you are sure it has cooled to the point that it will not burn you.

DON'T touch any part of the engine or exhaust system until it has cooled sufficiently to avoid burns.

DON'T siphon toxic liquids such as gasoline, antifreeze and brake fluid by mouth, or allow them to remain on your skin.

DON'T inhale brake lining dust — it is potentially hazardous (see *Asbestos* below)

DON'T allow spilled oil or grease to remain on the floor — wipe it up before someone slips on it.

DON'T use loose fitting wrenches or other tools which may slip and cause injury.

DON'T push on wrenches when loosening or tightening nuts or bolts. Always try to pull the wrench toward you. If the situation calls for pushing the wrench away, push with an open hand to avoid scraped knuckles if the wrench should slip.

DON'T attempt to lift a heavy component alone — get someone to help you.

DON'T rush or take unsafe shortcuts to finish a job.

DON'T allow children or animals in or around the vehicle while you are working on it.

DO wear eye protection when using power tools such as a drill, sander, bench grinder, etc. and when working under a vehicle.

DO keep loose clothing and long hair well out of the way of moving parts.

DO make sure that any hoist used has a safe working load rating adequate for the job.

DO get someone to check on you periodically when working alone on a vehicle.

DO carry out work in a logical sequence and make sure that everything is correctly assembled and tightened.

DO keep chemicals and fluids tightly capped and out of the reach of children and pets.

DO remember that your vehicle's safety affects that of yourself and others. If in doubt on any point, get professional advice.

Asbestos

Certain friction, insulating, sealing, and other products — such as brake linings, brake bands, clutch linings, torque converters, gaskets, etc. — contain asbestos. *Extreme care must be taken to avoid inhalation of dust from such products since it is hazardous to health.* If in doubt, assume that they *do* contain asbestos.

Fire

Remember at all times that gasoline is highly flammable. Never smoke or have any kind of open flame around when working on a vehicle. But the risk does not end there. A spark caused by an electrical short circuit, by two metal surfaces contacting each other, or even by static electricity built up in your body under certain conditions, can ignite gasoline vapors, which in a confined space are highly explosive. Do not, under any circumstances, use gasoline for cleaning parts. Use an approved safety solvent.

Always disconnect the battery ground (−) cable *at the battery* before working on any part of the fuel system or electrical system. Never risk spilling fuel on a hot engine or exhaust component.

It is strongly recommended that a fire extinguisher suitable for use on fuel and electrical fires be kept handy in the garage or workshop at all times. Never try to extinguish a fuel or electrical fire with water.

Torch (flashlight in the US)

Any reference to a "torch" appearing in this manual should always be taken to mean a hand-held, battery-operated electric light or flashlight. It DOES NOT mean a welding or propane torch or blowtorch.

Fumes

Certain fumes are highly toxic and can quickly cause unconsciousness and even death if inhaled to any extent. Gasoline vapor falls into this category, as do the vapors from some cleaning solvents. Any draining or pouring of such volatile fluids should be done in a well ventilated area.

When using cleaning fluids and solvents, read the instructions on the container carefully. Never use materials from unmarked containers.

Never run the engine in an enclosed space, such as a garage. Exhaust fumes contain carbon monoxide, which is extremely poisonous. If you need to run the engine, always do so in the open air, or at least have the rear of the vehicle outside the work area.

If you are fortunate enough to have the use of an inspection pit, never drain or pour gasoline and never run the engine while the vehicle is over the pit. The fumes, being heavier than air, will concentrate in the pit with possibly lethal results.

The battery

Never create a spark or allow a bare light bulb near a battery. They normally give off a certain amount of hydrogen gas, which is highly explosive.

Always disconnect the battery ground (−) cable *at the battery* before working on the fuel or electrical systems.

If possible, loosen the filler caps or cover when charging the battery from an external source (this does not apply to sealed or maintenance-free batteries). Do not charge at an excessive rate or the battery may burst.

Take care when adding water to a non maintenance-free battery and when carrying a battery. The electrolyte, even when diluted, is very corrosive and should not be allowed to contact clothing or skin.

Always wear eye protection when cleaning the battery to prevent the caustic deposits from entering your eyes.

Mains electricity (household current in the US)

When using an electric power tool, inspection light, etc., which operates on household current, always make sure that the tool is correctly connected to its plug and that, where necessary, it is properly grounded. Do not use such items in damp conditions and, again, do not create a spark or apply excessive heat in the vicinity of fuel or fuel vapor.

Secondary ignition system voltage

A severe electric shock can result from touching certain parts of the ignition system (such as the spark plug wires) when the engine is running or being cranked, particularly if components are damp or the insulation is defective. In the case of an electronic ignition system, the secondary system voltage is much higher and could prove fatal.

Routine maintenance

Maintenance is essential for ensuring safety and desirable for the purpose of getting the best in terms of performance and economy from your car. Over the years the need for periodic lubrication has been greatly reduced if not totally eliminated. This has unfortunately tended to lead some owners to think that because no such action is required, the items either no longer exist, or will last forever. This is certainly not the case; it is essential to carry out regular visual examination as comprehensively as possible in order to spot any possible defects at an early stage before they develop into major expensive repairs.

The following service schedules are a list of the maintenance requirements and the intervals at which they should be carried out, as recommended by the manufacturers. Where applicable these procedures are covered in greater detail throughout this Manual, near the beginning of each Chapter.

Engine and underbody component locations (2.2 litre Audi 100 with fuel injection)

1	Fusebox	9	Radiator cooling fan	15	Air cleaner
2	Brake master cylinder reservoir	10	Power-assisted steering drivebelt adjuster	16	Fuel metering distributor
3	Idle stabilisation valve	11	Warm-up valve	17	Windscreen and headlamp washer reservoir
4	Ignition coil	12	Engine oil dipstick	18	Fuel filter
5	Battery	13	Distributor	19	Throttle valve housing
6	Power-assisted steering hydraulic oil reservoir	14	Cold start valve	20	Vehicle identification plate
7	Suspension strut upper mounting				
8	Cooling system expansion tank				

18

Front underbody view

1 Horns
2 Anti-roll bar clamp
3 Driveshaft constant velocity joint
4 Anti-roll bar-to-track control arm mounting
5 Track control arm inner mounting
6 Subframe mounting
7 Gearbox mounting
8 Exhaust front pipe
9 Exhaust intermediate silencer
10 Windscreen and headlamp washer reservoir
11 Alternator
12 Oil filter
13 Engine oil drain plug

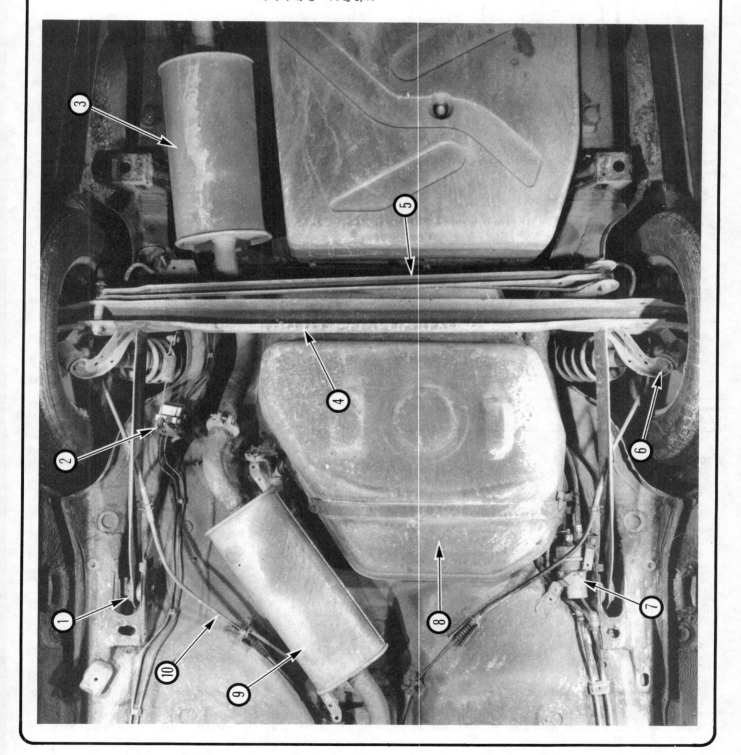

Rear underbody view

1 Trailing arm mounting
2 Brake pressure regulator
3 Tailpipe silencer
4 Rear axle beam
5 Panhard rod
6 Rear shock absorber lower
   mounting
7 Fuel pressure accumulator
8 Fuel tank
9 Main silencer
10 Handbrake cable

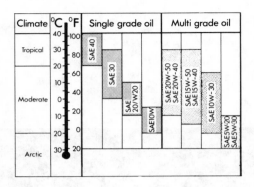

Engine oil viscosity chart

Every 250 miles (400 km) or weekly – whichever occurs first

Engine, cooling system, suspension and brakes
Check the engine oil level and top up, if necessary (Chapter 1, Sec 2 or 30)
Check the coolant level and top up, if necessary (Chapter 2, Sec 2)
Check the oil level in the power-assisted steering reservoir and top up, if necessary (Chapter 10, Sec 2)
Check the brake fluid level in the master cylinder reservoir and top up, if necessary (Chapter 9, Sec 2)

Lights and wipers
Check the operation of the horn, and all lights, wipers and washers
Check and if necessary, top up the washer reservoirs

Tyres
Check the tyre pressures (Chapter 10, Sec 30)
Visually examine the tyres for wear or damage (Chapter 10, Sec 30)

Every 10 000 miles (15 000 km) or 12 months – whichever occurs first

Engine
Renew the engine oil and filter – including the turbo filter, if applicable (Chapter 1, Sec 2 or 30)
Visually check the engine for oil leaks and for the security and condition of all related components and attachments (Chapter 1, Sec 2)

Cooling system
Check the hoses, hose clips and visible joint gaskets for leaks and any signs of corrosion or deterioration (Chapter 2, Sec 2)
Check and if necessary top up the cooling system and have the antifreeze strength checked (Chapter 2, Secs 2 and 6)

Fuel and exhaust system
Visually check the fuel pipes and hoses for security, chafing, leaks and corrosion (Chapter 3, Sec 2)
Check the fuel tank for leaks and any signs of damage and corrosion (Chapter 3, Sec 2)
Check the operation of the accelerator cable and linkage. (Chapter 3, Sec 2)
Check and if necessary adjust the idle speed and CO settings (where applicable) (Chapter 3, Sec 11)
Renew the additional oil filter on Turbo models
Check the exhaust system for corrosion, leaks and security (Chapter 3, Sec 2)

Ignition system
Clean and adjust the spark plugs. Renew if necessary (Chapter 4, Sec 9)
Check and if necessary adjust the ignition timing (where applicable) (Chapter 4, Secs 6 and 7 or 15)
Clean the distributor cap, HT leads and coil tower (Chapter 4, Secs 5 and 9)

Clutch
Check the operation of the clutch and clutch pedal
Check the clutch adjustment on cable operated clutches (Chapter 5, Sec 2)

Manual gearbox
Visually check for oil leaks around the joint faces and oil seals (Chapter 6, Sec 2)
Check and if necessary top up the gearbox oil (Chapter 6, Sec 2)

Automatic transmission
Visually check for oil leaks around the joint faces and oil seals (Chapter 7, Sec 2)
Check the fluid level and top up if necessary (Chapter 7, Sec 2)
Check the final drive fluid level and top up if necessary (Chapter 7, Sec 2)

Driveshafts
Check the driveshaft constant velocity joints for wear or damage and check the rubber gaiters for condition (Chapter 8, Sec 2)

Braking system
Check visually all brake pipes, hoses and unions for corrosion, chafing, leakage and security (Chapter 9, Sec 2)
Check and, if necessary, top up the brake fluid (Chapter 9, Sec 2)
Check the brake servo vacuum hose for condition and security (where applicable) (Chapter 9, Sec 22)
Check the operation of the hand and footbrake (Chapter 9, Sec 2)
Check the front brake pads for wear, and the discs for condition (Chapter 9, Sec 2)
Check the rear brake shoes or pads for wear and the drums or discs for condition (Chapter 9, Sec 2)

Electrical system
Check and if necessary top up the battery
Check the condition and security of all accessible wiring connectors, harnesses and retaining clips
Check the operation of all electrical equipment and accessories (lights, indicators, horn, wipers etc)
Check and adjust the operation of the screen washer, tailgate washer and headlamp washer and if necessary, top up the reservoirs
Clean the battery terminals and smear with petroleum jelly
Have the headlamp alignment checked, and if necessary, adjusted
Check and if necessary renew or adjust the alternator drivebelt (Chapter 12, Sec 7)

Suspension, steering, wheels and tyres
Check and if necessary renew or adjust the power-assisted steering pump drivebelt (where applicable) (Chapter 10, Sec 27)
Check the front and rear suspension struts for fluid leaks (Chapter 10, Sec 2)
Check the condition and security of the steering gear, steering and suspension joints, and rubber gaiters (Chapter 10, Sec 2)
Check the front wheel toe setting (Chapter 10, Sec 29)
Check and adjust the tyre pressures (Chapter 10, Sec 30)
Check the tyres for damage, tread depth and uneven wear (Chapter 10, Sec 30)
Inspect the roadwheels for damage (Chapter 10, Sec 30)
Check the tightness of the wheel bolts
Check, and if necessary, top up the power-assisted steering oil (where applicable) (Chapter 10, Sec 2)

Bodywork
Carefully inspect the paintwork for damage and the bodywork for corrosion (Chapter 11, Sec 2)
Check the condition of the underseal (Chapter 11, Sec 2)
Oil all hinges, door locks and the bonnet release mechanism with a few drops of light oil

Every 20 000 miles (30 000 km) or 24 months – whichever occurs first

In addition to the items listed in the 10 000 mile (15 000 km) service, carry out the following

Engine
Check and if necessary adjust the valve clearances (where applicable) and renew the valve cover gaskets (Chapter 1, Sec 17 or 46)
Check the timing belt tension (Chapter 1, Sec 18)

Cooling system
Drain the system, flush and refill with fresh antifreeze (Chapter 2, Secs 3, 4, 5 and 6)

Fuel system
Renew the air cleaner element (Chapter 3, Sec 2)
Renew the fuel filter (Chapter 3, Sec 2)

Ignition system
Renew the spark plugs (Chapter 4, Sec 9)

Automatic transmission
Drain the transmission fluid, clean the oil pan and strainer and renew the gasket. Refill with fresh fluid (Chapter 7, Sec 3)

Braking system
Renew the brake fluid (Chapter 9, Sec 17)

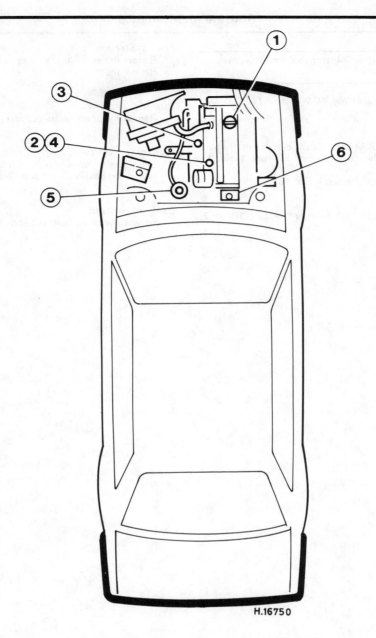

H.16750

Recommended lubricants and fluids

Component or system	Lubricant type or specification
Engine (1)	API SF multigrade engine oil of viscosity to suit the operating climatic conditions (see viscosity chart)
Manual gearbox (2)	Gearbox oil API GL4, SAE 80W or 80W/90 hypoid
Automatic transmission (3)	Dexron type automatic transmission fluid
Automatic transmission final drive (4)	Gearbox oil API GL5, SAE 90 hypoid
Power-assisted steering, hydraulic brake servo and self-levelling suspension (5)	Volkswagen/Audi hydraulic oil part No AOE 041 020 10 or ARAL hydraulic oil 1010
Brake and clutch fluid (6)	FMVSS 116 DOT 3 or 116 DOT 4

Note: *The above are general recommendations only. Lubrication requirements vary from territory to territory and depend on vehicle usage. If in doubt, consult the operator's handbook supplied with the vehicle, or your nearest dealer.*

Conversion factors

Length (distance)

Inches (in)	X	25.4	= Millimetres (mm)	X	0.0394 = Inches (in)
Feet (ft)	X	0.305	= Metres (m)	X	3.281 = Feet (ft)
Miles	X	1.609	= Kilometres (km)	X	0.621 = Miles

Volume (capacity)

Cubic inches (cu in; in³)	X	16.387	= Cubic centimetres (cc; cm³)	X	0.061 = Cubic inches (cu in; in³)
Imperial pints (Imp pt)	X	0.568	= Litres (l)	X	1.76 = Imperial pints (Imp pt)
Imperial quarts (Imp qt)	X	1.137	= Litres (l)	X	0.88 = Imperial quarts (Imp qt)
Imperial quarts (Imp qt)	X	1.201	= US quarts (US qt)	X	0.833 = Imperial quarts (Imp qt)
US quarts (US qt)	X	0.946	= Litres (l)	X	1.057 = US quarts (US qt)
Imperial gallons (Imp gal)	X	4.546	= Litres (l)	X	0.22 = Imperial gallons (Imp gal)
Imperial gallons (Imp gal)	X	1.201	= US gallons (US gal)	X	0.833 = Imperial gallons (Imp gal)
US gallons (US gal)	X	3.785	= Litres (l)	X	0.264 = US gallons (US gal)

Mass (weight)

Ounces (oz)	X	28.35	= Grams (g)	X	0.035 = Ounces (oz)
Pounds (lb)	X	0.454	= Kilograms (kg)	X	2.205 = Pounds (lb)

Force

Ounces-force (ozf; oz)	X	0.278	= Newtons (N)	X	3.6 = Ounces-force (ozf; oz)
Pounds-force (lbf; lb)	X	4.448	= Newtons (N)	X	0.225 = Pounds-force (lbf; lb)
Newtons (N)	X	0.1	= Kilograms-force (kgf; kg)	X	9.81 = Newtons (N)

Pressure

Pounds-force per square inch (psi; lbf/in²; lb/in²)	X	0.070	= Kilograms-force per square centimetre (kgf/cm²; kg/cm²)	X	14.223 = Pounds-force per square inch (psi; lbf/in²; lb/in²)
Pounds-force per square inch (psi; lbf/in²; lb/in²)	X	0.068	= Atmospheres (atm)	X	14.696 = Pounds-force per square inch (psi; lbf/in²; lb/in²)
Pounds-force per square inch (psi; lbf/in²; lb/in²)	X	0.069	= Bars	X	14.5 = Pounds-force per square inch (psi; lbf/in²; lb/in²)
Pounds-force per square inch (psi; lbf/in²; lb/in²)	X	6.895	= Kilopascals (kPa)	X	0.145 = Pounds-force per square inch (psi; lbf/in²; lb/in²)
Kilopascals (kPa)	X	0.01	= Kilograms-force per square centimetre (kgf/cm²; kg/cm²)	X	98.1 = Kilopascals (kPa)

Torque (moment of force)

Pounds-force inches (lbf in; lb in)	X	1.152	= Kilograms-force centimetre (kgf cm; kg cm)	X	0.868 = Pounds-force inches (lbf in; lb in)
Pounds-force inches (lbf in; lb in)	X	0.113	= Newton metres (Nm)	X	8.85 = Pounds-force inches (lbf in; lb in)
Pounds-force inches (lbf in; lb in)	X	0.083	= Pounds-force feet (lbf ft; lb ft)	X	12 = Pounds-force inches (lbf in; lb in)
Pounds-force feet (lbf ft; lb ft)	X	0.138	= Kilograms-force metres (kgf m; kg m)	X	7.233 = Pounds-force feet (lbf ft; lb ft)
Pounds-force feet (lbf ft; lb ft)	X	1.356	= Newton metres (Nm)	X	0.738 = Pounds-force feet (lbf ft; lb ft)
Newton metres (Nm)	X	0.102	= Kilograms-force metres (kgf m; kg m)	X	9.804 = Newton metres (Nm)

Power

Horsepower (hp)	X	745.7	= Watts (W)	X	0.0013 = Horsepower (hp)

Velocity (speed)

Miles per hour (miles/hr; mph)	X	1.609	= Kilometres per hour (km/hr; kph)	X	0.621 = Miles per hour (miles/hr; mph)

Fuel consumption*

Miles per gallon, Imperial (mpg)	X	0.354	= Kilometres per litre (km/l)	X	2.825 = Miles per gallon, Imperial (mpg)
Miles per gallon, US (mpg)	X	0.425	= Kilometres per litre (km/l)	X	2.352 = Miles per gallon, US (mpg)

Temperature

Degrees Fahrenheit = (°C x 1.8) + 32   Degrees Celsius (Degrees Centigrade; °C)   = (°F - 32) x 0.56

It is common practice to convert from miles per gallon (mpg) to litres/100 kilometres (l/100km), where mpg (Imperial) x l/100 km = 282 and mpg (US) x l/100 km = 235

Fault diagnosis

Introduction

The vehicle owner who does his or her own maintenance according to the recommended schedules should not have to use this section of the manual very often. Modern component reliability is such that, provided those items subject to wear or deterioration are inspected or renewed at the specified intervals, sudden failure is comparatively rare. Faults do not usually just happen as a result of sudden failure, but develop over a period of time. Major mechanical failures in particular are usually preceded by characteristic symptoms over hundreds or even thousands of miles. Those components which do occasionally fail without warning are often small and easily carried in the vehicle.

With any fault finding, the first step is to decide where to begin investigations. Sometimes this is obvious, but on other occasions a little detective work will be necessary. The owner who makes half a dozen haphazard adjustments or replacements may be successful in curing a fault (or its symptoms), but he will be none the wiser if the fault recurs and he may well have spent more time and money than was necessary. A calm and logical approach will be found to be more satisfactory in the long run. Always take into account any warning signs or abnormalities that may have been noticed in the period preceding the fault – power loss, high or low gauge readings, unusual noises or smells, etc – and remember that failure of components such as fuses or spark plugs may only be pointers to some underlying fault.

The pages which follow here are intended to help in cases of failure to start or breakdown on the road. There is also a Fault Diagnosis Section at the end of each Chapter which should be consulted if the preliminary checks prove unfruitful. Whatever the fault, certain basic principles apply. These are as follows:

Verify the fault. This is simply a matter of being sure that you know what the symptoms are before starting work. This is particularly important if you are investigating a fault for someone else who may not have described it very accurately.

Don't overlook the obvious. For example, if the vehicle won't start, is there petrol in the tank? (Don't take anyone else's word on this particular point, and don't trust the fuel gauge either!) If an electrical fault is indicated, look for loose or broken wires before digging out the test gear.

Cure the disease, not the symptom. Substituting a flat battery with a fully charged one will get you off the hard shoulder, but if the underlying cause is not attended to, the new battery will go the same way. Similarly, changing oil-fouled spark plugs for a new set will get you moving again, but remember that the reason for the fouling (if it wasn't simply an incorrect grade of plug) will have to be established and corrected.

Don't take anything for granted. Particularly, don't forget that a 'new' component may itself be defective (especially if it's been rattling round in the boot for months), and don't leave components out of a fault diagnosis sequence just because they are new or recently fitted. When you do finally diagnose a difficult fault, you'll probably realise that all the evidence was there from the start.

Electrical faults

Electrical faults can be more puzzling than straightforward mechanical failures, but they are no less susceptible to logical analysis if the basic principles of operation are understood. Vehicle electrical wiring exists in extremely unfavourable conditions – heat, vibration and chemical attack – and the first things to look for are loose or corroded connections and broken or chafed wires, especially where the wires pass through holes in the bodywork or are subject to vibration.

All metal-bodied vehicles in current production have one pole of the battery 'earthed', ie connected to the vehicle bodywork, and in nearly all modern vehicles it is the negative (–) terminal. The various electrical components – motors, bulb holders etc – are also connected to earth, either by means of a lead or directly by their mountings. Electric current flows through the component and then back to the battery via the bodywork. If the component mounting is loose or corroded, or if a good path back to the battery is not available, the circuit will be incomplete and malfunction will result. The engine and/or gearbox are also earthed by means of flexible metal straps to the body or subframe; if these straps are loose or missing, starter motor, generator and ignition trouble may result.

Assuming the earth return to be satisfactory, electrical faults will be due either to component malfunction or to defects in the current supply. Individual components are dealt with in Chapter 12. If supply wires are broken or cracked internally this results in an open-circuit, and the easiest way to check for this is to bypass the suspect wire temporarily with a length of wire having a crocodile clip or suitable connector at each end. Alternatively, a 12V test lamp can be used to verify the presence of supply voltage at various points along the wire and the break can be thus isolated.

If a bare portion of a live wire touches the bodywork or other earthed metal part, the electricity will take the low-resistance path thus formed back to the battery: this is known as a short-circuit. Hopefully a short-circuit will blow a fuse, but otherwise it may cause burning of the insulation (and possibly further short-circuits) or even a fire. This is why it is inadvisable to bypass persistently blowing fuses with silver foil or wire.

Spares and tool kit

Most vehicles are supplied only with sufficient tools for wheel changing; the *Maintenance and minor repair* tool kit detailed in *Tools and working facilities,* with the addition of a hammer, is probably sufficient for those repairs that most motorists would consider attempting at the roadside. In addition a few items which can be fitted without too much trouble in the event of a breakdown should be carried. Experience and available space will modify the list below, but the following may save having to call on professional assistance:

Spark plugs, clean and correctly gapped
HT lead and plug cap – long enough to reach the plug furthest from the distributor
Distributor rotor
Drivebelt(s) – emergency type may suffice
Spare fuses
Set of principal light bulbs
Tin of radiator sealer and hose bandage
Exhaust bandage
Roll of insulating tape
Length of soft iron wire
Length of electrical flex
Torch or inspection lamp (can double as test lamp)
Battery jump leads
Tow-rope
Ignition waterproofing aerosol
Litre of engine oil
Sealed can of hydraulic fluid
Emergency windscreen
Worm drive clips
Tube of filler paste

If spare fuel is carried, a can designed for the purpose should be used to minimise risks of leakage and collision damage. A first aid kit and a warning triangle, whilst not at present compulsory in the UK, are obviously sensible items to carry in addition to the above.

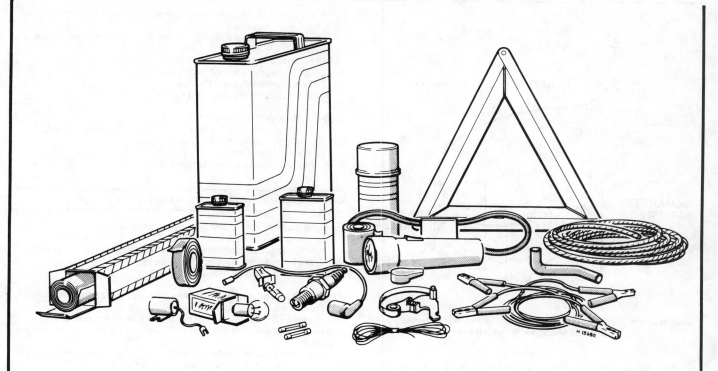

Carrying a few spares can save a long walk

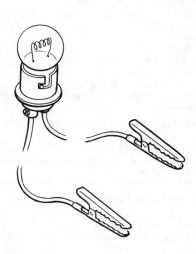

Simple test lamp is useful for tracing electrical faults

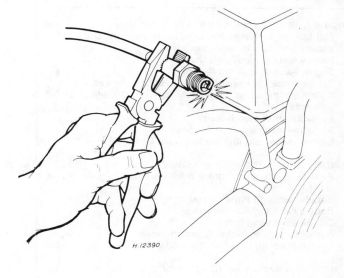

Crank engine and check for a spark. Note use of insulated tool

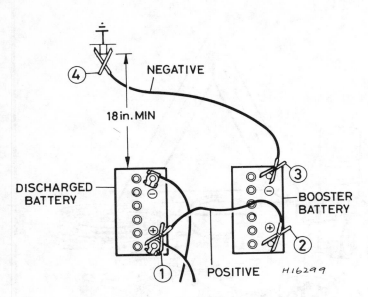

Jump start lead connections for negative earth vehicles – connect leads in order shown

When touring abroad it may be advisable to carry additional spares which, even if you cannot fit them yourself, could save having to wait while parts are obtained. The items below may be worth considering:

Clutch and throttle cables
Cylinder head gasket
Alternator brushes
Tyre valve core

One of the motoring organisations will be able to advise on availability of fuel etc in foreign countries.

Engine will not start

Engine fails to turn when starter operated
Flat battery (recharge, use jump leads, or push start)
Battery terminals loose or corroded
Battery earth to body defective
Engine earth strap loose or broken
Starter motor (or solenoid) wiring loose or broken
Automatic transmission selector in wrong position, or inhibitor switch faulty
Ignition/starter switch faulty
Major mechanical failure (seizure)
Starter or solenoid internal fault (see Chapter 12)

Starter motor turns engine slowly
Partially discharged battery (recharge, use jump leads, or push start)
Battery terminals loose or corroded
Battery earth to body defective
Engine earth strap loose
Starter motor (or solenoid) wiring loose
Starter motor internal fault (see Chapter 12)

Starter motor spins without turning engine
Flat battery
Starter motor pinion sticking on sleeve
Flywheel gear teeth damaged or worn
Starter motor mounting bolts loose

Engine turns normally but fails to start
Damp or dirty HT leads and distributor cap (crank engine and check for spark)
No fuel in tank (check for delivery at carburettor)

Excessive choke (hot engine) or insufficient choke (cold engine) – carburettor engines only
Fouled or incorrectly gapped spark plugs (remove, clean and regap)
Other ignition system fault (see Chapter 4)
Other fuel system fault (see Chapter 3)
Poor compression (see Chapter 1)
Major mechanical failure (eg camshaft drive)

Engine fires but will not run
Insufficient choke (cold engine) – carburettor engines only
Air leaks at carburettor or inlet manifold
Fuel starvation (see Chapter 3)
Other ignition fault (see Chapter 4)

Engine cuts out and will not restart

Engine cuts out suddenly – ignition fault
Loose or disconnected LT wires
Wet HT leads or distributor cap (after traversing water splash)
Coil or condenser failure (check for spark)
Other ignition fault (see Chapter 4)

Engine misfires before cutting out – fuel fault
Fuel tank empty
Fuel pump defective or filter blocked (check for delivery)
Fuel tank filler vent blocked (suction will be evident on releasing cap)
Carburettor needle valve sticking – carburettor engines only
Carburettor jets blocked (fuel contaminated)
Other fuel system fault (see Chapter 3)

Engine cuts out – other causes
Serious overheating
Major mechanical failure (eg camshaft drive)

Engine overheats

Ignition (no-charge) warning light illuminated
Slack or broken drivebelt – retension or renew (Chapter 12)

Ignition warning light not illuminated
Coolant loss due to internal or external leakage (see Chapter 12)
Thermostat defective
Low oil level
Brakes binding
Radiator clogged externally or internally
Electric cooling fan not operating correctly
Engine waterways clogged
Ignition timing incorrect or automatic advance malfunctioning
Mixture too weak

Note: *Do not add cold water to an overheated engine or damage may result*

Low engine oil pressure

Gauge reads low or warning light illuminated with engine running
Oil level low or incorrect grade
Defective gauge or sender unit
Wire to sender unit earthed
Engine overheating
Oil filter clogged or bypass valve defective
Oil pressure relief valve defective
Oil pick-up strainer clogged
Oil pump worn or mountings loose
Worn main or big-end bearings

Note: *Low oil pressure in a high-mileage engine at tickover is not necessarily a cause for concern. Sudden pressure loss at speed is far more significant. In any event, check the gauge or warning light sender before condemning the engine.*

Engine noises

Pre-ignition (pinking) on acceleration
Incorrect grade of fuel
Ignition timing incorrect
Distributor faulty or worn
Worn or maladjusted carburettor (where applicable)
Excessive carbon build-up in engine

Whistling or wheezing noises
Leaking vacuum hose
Leaking carburettor or manifold gasket (where applicable)
Blowing head gasket

Tapping or rattling
Incorrect valve clearances
Worn valve gear
Worn timing belt
Broken piston ring (ticking noise)

Knocking or thumping
Unintentional mechanical contact (eg fan blades)
Worn drivebelt
Peripheral component fault (generator, water pump etc)
Worn big-end bearings (regular heavy knocking, perhaps less under load)
Worn main bearings (rumbling and knocking, perhaps worsening under load)
Piston slap (most noticeable when cold)

Chapter 1 Engine

Refer to Chapter 13 for specifications and information on 1987 and later models

Contents

Specifications

Part A – four-cylinder engines
General

Code letters	DR,DS
Capacity	1781 cc (108.6 cu in)
Power output:	
Code DR	55 kW (75 bhp)
Code DS	66 kW (90 bhp)
Bore	81.0 mm (3.19 in)
Stroke	86.4 mm (3.40 in)
Compression ratio:	
Code DR	8.75 : 1
Code DS	10.0 : 1

Cylinder compression

Compression pressure (warm engine, throttle open):	
Code DR	7.0 bar (102 lbf/in²)
Code DS	7.5 bar (110 lbf/in²)
Maximum pressure difference between cylinders	3.0 bar (44 lbf/in²)

Firing order

1-3-4-2 (No 1 at timing belt end)

Crankshaft

Needle spigot bearing fitted depth	1.5 mm (0.059 in)
Endplay:	
New	0.07 to 0.17 mm (0.003 to 0.007 in)
Wear limit	0.25 mm (0.010 in)
Maximum main bearing running clearance	0.17 mm (0.007 in)
Main bearing journal diameter:	
Standard size	53.96 to 53.98 mm (2.1244 to 2.1252 in)
1st undersize	53.71 to 53.73 mm (2.1145 to 2.1154 in)
2nd undersize	53.46 to 53.48 mm (2.1047 to 2.1055 in)
3rd undersize	53.21 to 53.23 mm (2.0949 to 2.0957 in)
Big-end bearing journal diameter:	
Standard size	47.76 to 47.79 mm (1.8803 to 1.8815 in)

1st undersize	47.51 to 47.53 mm (1.8705 to 1.8712 in)
2nd undersize	47.26 to 47.29 mm (1.8606 to 1.8618 in)
3rd undersize	47.01 to 47.03 mm (1.8508 to 1.8516 in)
Maximum journal ovality	0.03 mm (0.0012 in)

Pistons and rings

Piston-to-bore clearance:

| New | 0.03 mm (0.0012 in) |
| Wear limit | 0.07 mm (0.0028 in) |

Ring-to-groove clearance:

| New | 0.02 to 0.05 mm (0.0008 to 0.0020 in) |
| Wear limit | 0.15 mm (0.0059 in) |

Piston size:

	Piston diameter	Bore diameter
Standard size	80.98 mm (3.1882 in)	81.01 mm (3.1894 in)
1st oversize	81.23 mm (3.1980 in)	81.26 mm (3.1992 in)
2nd oversize	81.48 mm (3.2079 in)	81.51 mm (3.2091 in)

Cylinder bore:

| Maximum ovality | 0.08 mm (0.003 in) |

Piston ring end gap clearance (ring 15 mm/0.6 in from bottom of bore):

Compression rings:

| New | 0.30 to 0.45 mm (0.012 to 0.018 in) |
| Wear limit | 1.0 mm (0.040 in) |

Scraper rings:

| New | 0.25 to 0.50 mm (0.01 to 0.02 in) |
| Wear limit | 1.0 mm (0.040 in) |

Connecting rods

| Maximum endplay | 0.37 mm (0.015 in) |

Big-end bearing running clearance:

| New | 0.015 to 0.062 mm (0.0006 to 0.0024 in) |
| Wear limit | 0.12 mm (0.0047 in) |

Camshaft

| Maximum endplay | 0.15 mm (0.006 in) |
| Maximum run-out | 0.01 mm (0.0004 in) |

Valves

Valve clearances:

Engine warm:

| Inlet | 0.20 to 0.30 mm (0.008 to 0.012 in) |
| Exhaust | 0.40 to 0.50 mm (0.016 to 0.020 in) |

Engine cold:

Inlet	0.15 to 0.25 mm (0.006 to 0.010 in)
Exhaust	0.35 to 0.45 mm (0.014 to 0.018 in)
Adjusting shim thickness	3.00 to 4.25 mm (0.118 to 0.167 in) in increments of 0.05 mm (0.002 in)

Valve stem diameter:

| Inlet | 7.97 mm (0.3138 in) |
| Exhaust | 7.95 mm (0.3129 in) |

Valve head diameter:

| Inlet | 38.0 mm (1.497 in) |
| Exhaust | 33.0 mm (1.300 in) |

Valve length:

Inlet	98.70 mm (3.8858 in)
Exhaust	98.50 mm (3.8779 in)
Valve seat angle	45°

Valve guides:

Maximum valve rock (measured at head):

| Inlet | 1.0 mm (0.039 in) |
| Exhaust | 1.3 mm (0.051 in) |

Valve timing at 1.0 mm lift /0 mm clearance:

		Engine code	
	DR	DS (up to August 85)	DS (from August 85)
Inlet opens BTDC	1°	1°	3°
Inlet closes ABDC	37°	37°	33°
Exhaust opens BBDC	42°	42°	41°
Exhaust closes ATDC	2°	2°	5°

Cylinder head

Minimum height (between faces)	132.6 mm (5.220 in)
Maximum gasket face distortion	0.1 mm (0.004 in)
Valve seat angle	45°

Intermediate shaft
Endplay .... 0.25 mm (0.010 in)

Lubrication system
Oil pressure (minimum at 2000 rpm – engine hot) .... 2.0 bar (29 lbf/in²)
Oil pump gear backlash .... 0.05 to 0.20 mm (0.002 to 0.008 in)
Oil pump gear endplay (maximum) .... 0.15 mm (0.006 in)

Part B – Five-cylinder engines
General
Code letters:
  UK models:
    1.9 .... WH
    2.0 .... KP
    2.2 .... KG, WC
    2.3 .... KU
  North American models:
    2.2 .... WU, WK, KH
    2.3 .... KZ
Capacity:
  1.9 .... 1921 cc (117.2 cu in)
  2.0 .... 1994 cc (121.6 cu in)
  2.2 .... 2144 cc (130.7 cu in)
  2.3 .... 2226 cc (135.7 cu in)
Power output:
  1.9 .... 74 kW (96.2 bhp)
  2.0 .... 85 kW (115 bhp)
  2.2 litre:
    Code WC .... 100 kW (130 bhp)
    Code KG .... 134 kW (174.2 bhp)
    Code WU .... 74.5 kW (100 bhp)
    Code KH, WK .... 104.4 kW (140 bhp)
  2.3 litre:
    Code KU .... 101 kW (131.3 bhp)
    Code KZ .... 82 kW (110 bhp)
Bore:
  1.9 and 2.2 .... 79.5 mm (3.13 in)
  2.0 and 2.3 .... 81.0 mm (3.19 in)
Stroke:
  1.9 and 2.0 .... 77.4 mm (3.05 in)
  2.2 and 2.3 .... 86.4 mm (3.40 in)
Compression ratio:
  1.9 .... 10.0 : 1
  2.0 .... 10.0 : 1
  2.2:
    KG .... 8.8 : 1
    WC .... 9.3 : 1
    WU .... 8.2 : 1
    KH, WK .... 8.3 : 1
  2.3:
    KU .... 10.0 : 1
    KZ .... 8.5 : 1

Cylinder compression
Compression pressure (warm engine, throttle open):
  1.9 and 2.0 .... 10 to 14 bar (145 to 203 lbf/in²)
  2.2:
    Code WC and KG .... 10 to 14 bar (145 to 203 lbf/in²)
    Code WU, KH* and WK* .... 8 to 11 bar (116 to 159.5 lbf/in²)
  2.3:
    Code KU and KZ* .... 8 to 11 bar (116 to 159.5 lbf/in²)
Minimum pressures:
  1.9 and 2.0 .... 8.0 bar (116 lbf/in²)
  2.2:
    Code WC and KG .... 8.0 bar (116 lbf/in²)
    Code WU, KH* and WK* .... 6.5 bar (94.25 lbf/in²)
  2.3:
    Code KU and KZ* .... 6.5 bar (94.25 lbf/in²)
Maximum pressure difference between cylinders:
  1.9, 2.0 and 2.2 (code WC and KG) .... 3.0 bar (43.5 lbf/in²)
  2.2 (code WU, KH, WK) and 2.3 .... 2.0 bar (29 lbf/in²)
* Approximate values for North American engines

Firing order
Firing order .... 1-2-4-5-3 (No 1 at timing belt end)

Crankshaft

Needle spigot bearing fitted depth .... 5.5 mm (0.217 in)
Endplay:
  New .... 0.07 to 0.18 mm (0.003 to 0.007 in)
  Wear limit .... 0.25 mm (0.010 in)
Maximum main bearing running clearance .... 0.16 mm (0.006 in)
Main bearing journal diameter:
  Standard size .... 57.96 to 57.98 mm (2.2819 to 2.2827 in)
  1st undersize .... 57.71 to 57.73 mm (2.2720 to 2.2728 in)
  2nd undersize .... 57.46 to 57.48 mm (2.2622 to 2.2629 in)
  3rd undersize .... 57.21 to 57.23 mm (2.2524 to 2.2532 in)
Big-end bearing journal diameter:
  Standard size .... 45.96 to 45.98 mm (1.8094 to 1.8102 in)
  1st undersize .... 45.71 to 45.73 mm (1.7996 to 1.8004 in)
  2nd undersize .... 45.46 to 45.48 mm (1.7898 to 1.7906 in)
  3rd undersize .... 45.21 to 45.23 mm (1.7799 to 1.7807 in)
Maximum journal ovality .... 0.03 mm (0.0012 in)

Pistons and rings

Piston-to-bore clearance:
  New .... 0.03 mm (0.0012 in)
  Wear limit .... 0.07 mm (0.0028 in)
Ring-to-groove clearance:
  New .... 0.02 to 0.08 mm (0.0008 to 0.0032 in)
  Wear limit .... 0.1 mm (0.004 in)
Piston size:

	Piston diameter	Bore diameter
1.9 and 2.2:		
Standard size	79.48 mm (3.1291 in)	79.51 mm (3.1303 in)
1st oversize	79.73 mm (3.1389 in)	79.76 mm (3.1402 in)
2nd oversize	79.98 mm (3.1488 in)	80.01 mm (3.1500 in)
3rd oversize	80.48 mm (3.1685 in)	80.51 mm (3.1697 in)
2.0 and 2.3:		
Standard size	80.98 mm (3.1882 in)	81.01 mm (3.1894 in)
1st oversize	81.23 mm (3.1980 in)	81.26 mm (3.1992 in)
2nd oversize	81.48 mm (3.2079 in)	81.51 mm (3.2091 in)

Cylinder bore:
  Maximum ovality .... 0.08 mm (0.003 in)
Piston ring end gap clearance (ring 15 mm/0.6 in from bottom of bore):
  New .... 0.25 to 0.50 mm (0.010 to 0.020 in)
  Wear limit .... 1.0 mm (0.040 in)

Connecting rods

Maximum endplay .... 0.4 mm (0.016 in)
Big-end bearing running clearance:
  New .... 0.015 to 0.062 mm (0.0006 to 0.0024 in)
  Wear limit .... 0.12 mm (0.0047 in)

Camshaft

Maximum endplay .... 0.15 mm (0.006 in)

Valves

Valve clearances .... See 1.8 litre four-cylinder engine
Valve stem diameter:
  Inlet .... 7.97 mm (0.3138 in)
  Exhaust .... 7.95 mm (0.3129 in)
Valve head diameter:
  Inlet .... 38.0 mm (1.4961 in)
  Exhaust .... 33.0 mm (1.2992 in)
Valve length:
  Inlet .... 91.0 mm (3.5827 in)
  Exhaust .... 90.8 mm (3.5748 in)
Valve seat angle .... 45°
Valve guides:
  Maximum valve rock (measured at head):
    Inlet .... 1.0 mm (0.039 in)
    Exhaust .... 1.3 mm (0.051 in)
Valve timing at 1.0 mm lift/0 mm clearance:

	Engine code*				
	WH	**KP**	**KG**	**WC**	**KU**
Inlet opens BTDC	10°	1°	4°	0°	0°
Inlet closes ABDC	36°	37°	36°	51°	41°
Exhaust opens BBDC	45°	37°	42°	40°	40°
Exhaust closes ATDC	3°	1°	6°	10°	1°

*Data for North American engines not available at time of writing

Cylinder head
Minimum height (between faces) .... 132.75 mm (5.2264 in)
Maximum gasket face distortion .... 0.1 mm (0.004 in)
Valve seat angle .... 45°

Lubrication system
Oil pressure (minimum at 2000 rpm – engine hot) .... 2.0 bar (29 lbf/in²)

All engines
Torque wrench settings

	Nm	lbf ft
Part A – four-cylinder engines		
Cylinder head bolts:		
Stage 1	40	30
Stage 2	60	44
Stage 3	Tighten further by half a turn (180°)	
Engine to transmission	55	41
Engine mounting bracket to cylinder block:		
M8 bolts	25	18
M10 bolts	45	33
Engine mountings to mounting bracket	35	26
Timing belt covers	10	7.4
Timing belt tensioner	45	33
Intermediate shaft gear retaining bolt	80	59
Crankshaft pulley to gear	20	15
Crankshaft gear to crankshaft	200	148
Camshaft gear to camshaft	80	59
Camshaft bearing cap nuts	20	15
Valve cover to cylinder head	10	7.4
Main bearing cap bolts	65	48
Big-end bearing cap nuts:		
Stage 1	30	22
Stage 2	Tighten further by one quarter turn (90°)	
Intermediate shaft sealing flange	25	18
Front oil seal housing	20	15
Rear oil seal housing	10	7.4
Flywheel or driveplate to crankshaft	100	74
Oil filter housing to cylinder block	25	18
Oil pump to crankcase	20	15
Oil pump cover to body	10	7.4
Sump to crankcase	20	15
Oil drain plug	30	22
Part B – five-cylinder engines		
Cylinder head bolts:		
Stage 1	40	30
Stage 2	60	44
Stage 3	Tighten further by half a turn (180°)	
Engine to transmission:		
M8 bolts	20	15
M10 bolts	45	33
M12 bolts	60	44
Engine mounting bracket to cylinder block:		
M8 bolts	25	18
M10 bolts	45	33
Engine mountings to mounting bracket	45	33
Timing belt covers	10	7.4
Water pump to engine	20	15
Crankshaft pulley to crankshaft (using tool 2079 – see text)	350	258
Camshaft gear to camshaft	80	59
Camshaft bearing cap nuts	20	15
Valve cover to cylinder head	10	7.4
Main bearing cap bolts	65	48
Big-end bearing cap nuts:		
Flat-sided nuts	50	37
Notched-sided nuts:		
Stage 1	30	22
Stage 2	Tighten further by one quarter turn (90°)	
Rear oil seal housing	10	7.4
Oil pump to block:		
Short bolts and stud	10	7.4
Long bolts	20	15
Oil intake pipe to crankcase	10	7.4
Idler pulley to oil pump	10	7.4
Oil pump backplate	10	7.4

Torque wrench settings (contd)

	Nm	lbf ft
Oil pressure relief valve	40	30
Oil filter housing to block (Turbo models)	70	52
Oil feed and return pipe flanges (Turbo models)	25	18
Oil cooler hose union nuts (Turbo models)	40	30
Sump to crankcase	25	18
Oil drain plug	40	30

PART A – FOUR-CYLINDER ENGINES

1 General description

The engine is of four-cylinder, in-line overhead camshaft type mounted conventionally at the front of the car. The crankshaft is of five-bearing type and the centre main bearing shells incorporate flanged or separate thrust washers to control crankshaft endfloat (endplay). The camshaft is driven by a toothed belt from the crankshaft sprocket, and the belt also drives the intermediate shaft which is used to drive the distributor, oil pump and the fuel pump. The valves are operated from the camshaft through bucket type tappets, and valve clearances are adjusted by the use of shims located in the top of the tappets.

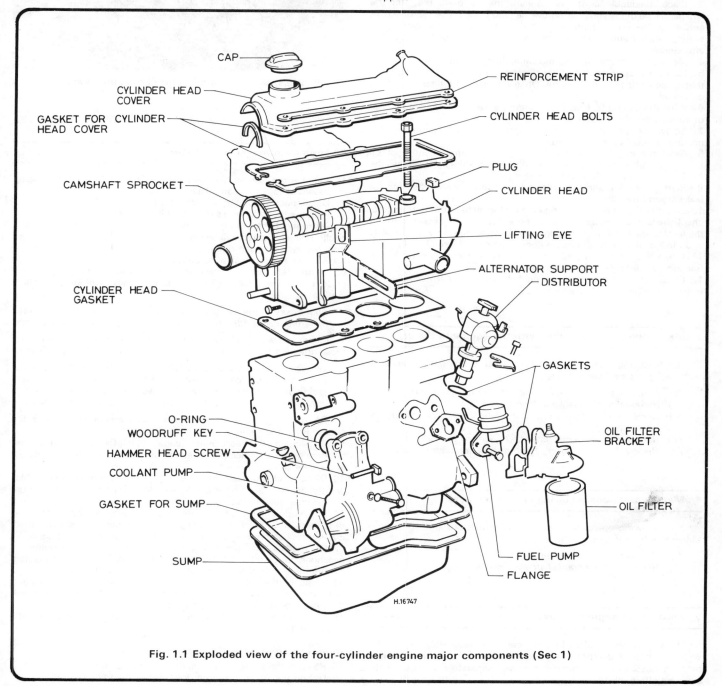

Fig. 1.1 Exploded view of the four-cylinder engine major components (Sec 1)

The engine has a full-flow lubrication system from a gear type oil pump mounted in the sump, and driven by an extension of the distributor which is itself geared to the intermediate shaft. The oil filter is of the cartridge type, mounted on the left-hand side of the cylinder block.

2 Maintenance and inspection

1   At the intervals given in Routine Maintenance at the beginning of this manual, carry out the following service operations on the engine.
2   Visually inspect the engine joint faces, gaskets and seals for any sign of oil or water leaks. Pay particular attention to the areas around the valve cover, cylinder head and sump joint faces. Rectify any leaks by referring to the appropriate Sections of this Chapter.
3   Place a suitable container beneath the oil drain plug on the left-hand side of the sump. Unscrew the plug using a spanner or socket and allow the oil to drain. Inspect the condition of the drain plug sealing washer and renew it if necessary. Refit and tighten the plug after draining.
4   Move the container rearwards, beneath the oil filter.
5   Using a strap wrench or filter removal tool, slacken the filter and then unscrew it from the engine. Once removed, the filter should be discarded.
6   Wipe the mating face on the oil filter bracket and lubricate the seal of a new filter using clean engine oil.
7   Screw the filter into position and tighten it firmly by hand only. Do not use any tools for tightening.
8   Refill the engine with the specified grade and quantity of oil through the filler on the valve cover (photo), until the level reaches the MAX mark on the oil level dipstick.
9   Start the engine and run it for a few minutes while checking for leaks around the filter.
10 Switch off, and after allowing time for the oil to return to the sump, check the level on the dipstick once more. Top up as necessary to bring the level to the MAX mark, noting that the difference between the MIN and MAX marks on the dipstick is approximately 1.0 litre (1.76 Imp pt).
11 Check and if necessary adjust the valve clearances, as described in Section 17, and renew the valve cover gasket.
12 Check the tension of the timing belt and adjust if necessary, as described in Section 18, paragraph 22.

3 Major operations possible with the engine in the car

The following operations can be carried out without having to remove the engine from the car:

(a) Removal and servicing of the cylinder head and camshaft
(b) Removal of the timing belt and gears
(c) Removal of the flywheel or driveplate (after first removing the transmission)
(d) Removal of the sump (after first lowering the subframe)
(e) Removal of the oil pump, pistons and connecting rods

4 Major operations requiring engine removal

The following operations can only be carried out after removal of the engine from the car:

(a) Removal of the intermediate shaft
(b) Removal of the crankshaft and main bearings

5 Methods of engine removal

The engine can be lifted from the car either separately, or together with the manual gearbox. On automatic transmission models, it is recommended that the engine is removed separately because of the extra weight involved.

2.8 Fill the engine with oil through the filler on the valve cover

6 Engine – removal and refitting

1   Remove the bonnet, as described in Chapter 11 and stand it on cardboard or rags in a safe place.
2   Disconnect the battery negative lead.
3   Remove the radiator, as described in Chapter 2.
4   Disconnect the wiring from the rear of the alternator – where a cooling duct is fitted it will be necessary to disconnect the bypass hose from the cylinder head outlet and remove the duct first.
5   Remove the air cleaner, as described in Chapter 3.
6   Identify all fuel and vacuum hoses using masking tape, then disconnect those affecting engine removal. These will include, where applicable:

Fuel hoses to the fuel pump and filter, vacuum hoses to the inlet manifold, carburettor, distributor and emission control equipment

7   Identify all wiring for location using masking tape, then disconnect those affecting engine removal. These will include, where applicable:

Wiring to the oil pressure switch, temperature sender, distributor, coil, inlet manifold preheater, gearchange indicator switch, carburettor bypass and cut-off valve and air channel heating, automatic choke, thermotime valve and overrun control valve

8   On manual gearbox models, disconnect the clutch cable from the release lever and cable bracket.
9   Disconnect the accelerator cable (Chapter 3), throttle and accelerator pedal cables (automatic transmission – Chapters 3 and 7), and choke cable (Chapter 3).
10 Disconnect the hose from the inlet manifold (where applicable) and the heater hoses from the bulkhead. Also disconnect the hose from the cylinder head outlet.
11 On models with air conditioning, remove the compressor as described in Chapter 11, leaving the refrigerant hoses connected. Secure the compressor to one side, without straining the hoses.
12 On models with power-assisted steering, remove the pump, as described in Chapter 10, but leave the hydraulic pipes connected. Secure the pump to one side without straining the hoses.
13 Remove the right-hand engine mounting cover plate, and disconnect the exhaust front pipe at the manifold flange. Also detach the front pipe at the transmission bracket.
14 Slacken the engine left and right-hand mountings. Disconnect the engine earth strap.

Removing engine without transmission

15 Remove the starter motor, as described in Chapter 12.
16 Unbolt the cover plate from the front of the transmission.

17 On automatic transmission models, unscrew the torque converter-to-driveplate bolts, while holding the starter ring gear stationary with a screwdriver. It will be necessary to rotate the engine to position the bolts in the starter aperture using a socket on the crankshaft pulley bolt.

18 Connect a hoist and take the weight of the engine. The hoist should be positioned centrally over the engine.

19 Support the weight of the transmission with a trolley jack.

20 Unscrew the engine-to-transmission bolts, noting the position of any brackets or cable supports.

21 Unscrew the engine mounting bracket-to-engine bolts, and swing the mounting brackets forward, clear of the engine.

22 Lift the engine slightly, and pull it forward off the transmission. On automatic transmission models, make sure that the torque converter remains fully engaged with the transmission splines.

23 Manipulate the engine as necessary, and lift it from the engine compartment. Lower the engine to the floor, and if necessary remove the engine rear plate (photo).

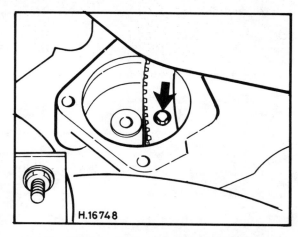

Fig. 1.2 Automatic transmission torque converter-to-driveplate retaining bolt (arrowed) viewed through starter aperture (Sec 6)

6.23 Removing the engine rear plate

Removing engine with manual transmission attached

24 Disconnect the wiring to the reversing light switch and release the cable clip. Remove the earth strap.

25 Disconnect the exhaust front pipe-to-intermediate pipe joint, and remove the front pipe from the car.

26 Disconnect the driveshafts from the transmission flanges, with reference to Chapter 8.

27 Disconnect the gearchange linkage at the shift rods, with reference to Chapter 6.

28 Unscrew the retainer, and disconnect the speedometer cable from the differential cover.

29 Support the transmission with a trolley jack.

30 Undo the bolts securing the transmission to its support, and unbolt and remove the support from the subframe.

31 Connect a hoist and take the weight of the engine. The hoist should be positioned near the front of the engine, so that the engine and transmission will hang at a steep angle.

32 Lift the engine and move it forwards, then lower the trolley jack and lift the engine and transmission from the engine compartment; turning it as necessary to clear the body. Lower the engine and gearbox to the ground when the unit is clear of the car.

33 If necessary, separate the transmission from the engine by removing the starter motor, transmission cover plate, and engine-to-transmission attachment bolts. Remove the engine rear plate after separation.

Refitting

34 Refitting is a reversal of the removal procedure, but smear the manual transmission input shaft and release bearing face with molybdenum disulphide grease before fitting. Ensure that all the engine and transmission mountings are fitted free of tension, and tighten all nuts and bolts to the specified torque. Refit, and where applicable adjust, all engine related components and systems with reference to the Chapters concerned. Ensure that the engine is filled with oil, and that the cooling system is topped up before starting the engine.

7 Engine dismantling – general

1 If possible position the engine on a bench or strong table for the dismantling procedure. Two or three blocks of wood will be necessary to support the engine in an upright position.

2 Cleanliness is most important, and if the engine is dirty, it should be cleaned with paraffin before commencing work.

3 Avoid working with the engine directly on a concrete floor, as grit presents a real source of trouble.

4 As parts are removed, clean them in a paraffin bath. However, do not immerse parts with internal oilways in paraffin as it is difficult to remove, usually requiring a high pressure hose. Clean oilways with nylon pipe cleaners.

5 It is advisable to have suitable containers to hold small items according to their use, as this will help when reassembling the engine and also prevent possible losses.

6 Always obtain complete sets of gaskets when the engine is being dismantled, but retain the old gaskets with a view to using them as a pattern to make a replacement if a new one is not available.

7 When possible, refit nuts, bolts, and washers in their location after being removed, as this helps to protect the threads and will also be helpful when reassembling the engine.

8 Retain unserviceable components in order to compare them with the new parts supplied.

8 Ancillary components – removal and refitting

1 If the engine has been removed from the car for major overhaul or repair, the following externally mounted ancillary components can now be removed. The removal sequence need not necessarily follow the order given:

Water pump (Chapter 2)
Inlet and exhaust manifolds (Chapter 3)
Fuel pump (Chapter 3)
HT leads and spark plugs (Chapter 4)
Oil filter cartridge (Section 2 of this Chapter)
Distributor (Chapter 4)
Dipstick
Alternator (Chapter 12)
Engine mountings (Section 28 of this Chapter)

2 Refitting is essentially a reversal of the removal sequence, with reference to the Sections and Chapters indicated.

9 Cylinder head and camshaft – removal

Note: *If the engine is still in the car, first carry out the following operations:*

(a) *Disconnect the battery negative lead*
(b) *Drain the cooling system*
(c) *Remove the alternator*
(d) *Remove the inlet and exhaust manifolds*
(e) *Remove the HT leads and spark plugs*
(f) *Disconnect all wiring, cables and hoses*
(g) *Disconnect the exhaust downpipe from the exhaust manifold*

1 Unscrew the nuts and lift off the upper timing cover, using an Allen key where necessary (photo).
2 Unscrew the nuts and lift off the valve cover, together with the reinforcement strips and gaskets (photos).
3 Unbolt the outlet elbows and remove the gaskets, if necessary (photos).
4 Using a socket on the crankshaft pulley bolt, turn the engine so that the piston in No 1 cylinder is at TDC on its compression stroke. The notch in the crankshaft pulley must be in line with the arrow on the lower timing cover (photo), and both No 1 cylinder valves must .be

9.2A Removing the reinforcement strips ...

9.2B ... and valve cover

9.2C Removing the valve cover front gasket ...

9.2D ... and rear plug

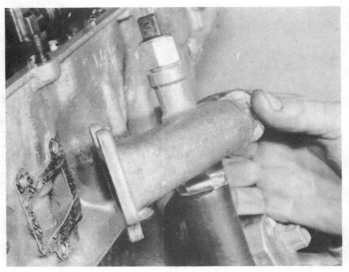

9.3A Removing the cylinder head side outlet ...

9.3B ... and rear outlet

9.4 Crankshaft pulley notch aligned with TDC arrow on the lower timing cover

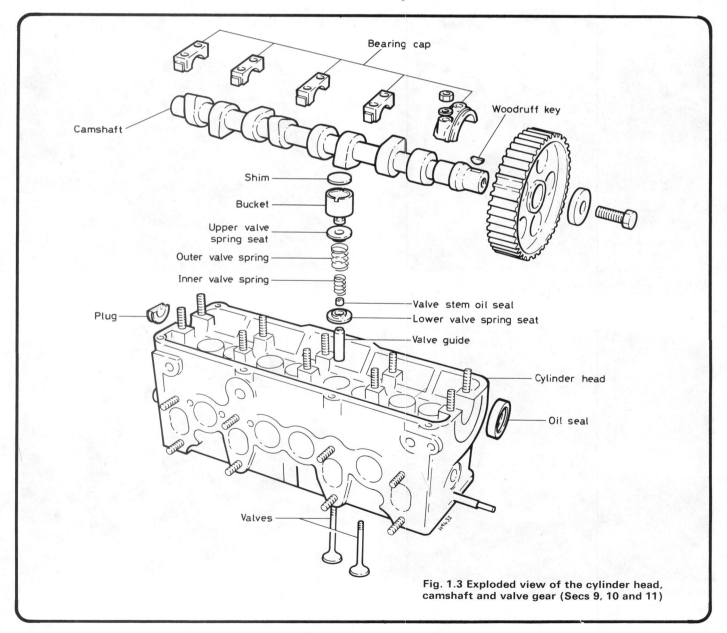

Fig. 1.3 Exploded view of the cylinder head, camshaft and valve gear (Secs 9, 10 and 11)

Bearing cap

Camshaft

Woodruff key

Shim

Bucket

Upper valve spring seat

Outer valve spring

Inner valve spring

Valve stem oil seal

Lower valve spring seat

Valve guide

Plug

Cylinder head

Oil seal

Valves

closed (ie cam peaks away from the tappets). The notch on the rear of the camshaft gear will also be in line with the top of the timing belt rear cover.

5   Loosen the nut on the timing belt tensioner and, using an open-ended spanner, rotate the eccentric hub anti-clockwise to release the belt tension.

6   Remove the timing belt from the camshaft gear and tensioner and move it to one side while keeping it in firm contact with the intermediate and crankshaft gears. *The intermediate gear must not be moved, otherwise the ignition timing will be lost and the lower timing cover will have to be removed.*

7   Unscrew the nut and remove the timing belt tensioner.

8   Unscrew the bolt securing the timing belt rear cover to the cylinder head.

9   Using a splined key, unscrew the cylinder head bolts a turn at a time in reverse order to that shown in Fig. 1.7.

10 With all the bolts removed lift the cylinder head from the block. If it is stuck, tap it free with a wooden mallet. *Do not insert a lever into the gasket joint.*

11 Remove the cylinder head gasket.

10 Camshaft and tappets – removal

Note: *If the engine is still in the car, first carry out the following operations:*

   (a) *Disconnect the battery negative lead*
   (b) *Disconnect the wiring, cables and hoses which cross the engine valve cover – remove the air cleaner*
   (c) *Remove the alternator/water pump drivebelt*

1   Follow paragraphs 1 to 6 of Section 9, excluding paragraph 3.

2   Unscrew the centre bolt from the camshaft gear while holding the gear stationary with a bar through one of the holes.

3   Withdraw the gear from the camshaft and extract the Woodruff key (photos).

4   Unscrew the nuts from bearing caps 1, 3 and 5. Identify all the caps for position then remove caps 1, 3 and 5 (photos).

5   Loosen the nuts on bearing caps 2 and 4 evenly until all valve spring tension has been released, then remove the caps.

6   Lift out the camshaft and discard the oil seal (photo).

10.3A Removing the camshaft gear

10.3B Woodruff key location in camshaft

10.4A Removing No 3 camshaft bearing cap ...

10.4B ... and No 1 bearing cap

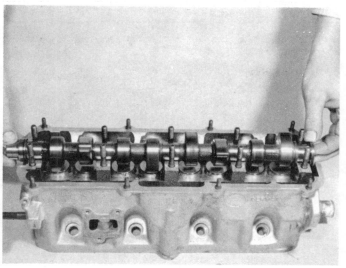

10.6 Removing the camshaft

10.7 Removing a tappet, together with its shim

7   Have ready a board with eight pegs on it, or alternatively use a box with internal compartments, marked to identify cylinder number and whether inlet or exhaust or position in the head, numbering from the front of the engine. As each tappet is removed (photo), place it on the appropriate peg, or mark the actual tappet to indicate its position. *Note that each tappet has a shim (disc) fitted into a recess in its top. This shim must be kept with its particular tappet.*

11 Valves – removal and renovation

1   With the cylinder head removed, as previously described, the valve gear can be dismantled as follows. Because the valves are recessed deeply into the top of the cylinder head, their removal requires a valve spring compressor with long claws or the use of some ingenuity in adapting other types of compressor.
2   Have ready a board with holes in it, into which each valve can be fitted as it is removed, or have a set of labelled containers so that each valve and its associated parts can be identified and kept separate. Inlet valves are Nos. 2-4-5-7, Exhaust valves are Nos 1-3-6-8, numbered from the timing belt end of the engine.
3   Compress each valve spring until the collets can be removed (photo). Take out the collets, release the spring compressor and remove it.
4   Remove the valve spring cover, the outer and inner spring and the valve (photos).
5   Prise off the valve stem seals, or pull them off with pliers and discard them, then lift off the valve spring seat and place it with its valve (photos).
6   Examine the heads of the valves for pitting and burning, paying particular attention to the heads of the exhaust valves. The valve seats should be examined at the same time. If the pitting on the valve and seat is only slight, the marks can be removed by grinding the seats and valves together with coarse and then fine grinding paste. Where bad pitting has occurred, it will be necessary to have the valve seat re-cut and either use a new valve, or have the valve re-faced. Exhaust valves must not be re-faced, but ground in by hand only.
7   Scrape away all carbon from the valve head and valve stem. Carefully clean away every trace of grinding paste, taking care to leave none in the ports, or in the valve guides. Wipe the valves and valve seats with a paraffin soaked rag and then with a clean dry rag.

11.3 Compress the valve springs and remove the collets

11.4A Removing the valve spring cover ...

11.4B ... outer valve spring

11.4C ... inner valve spring ...

11.4D ... and the valve

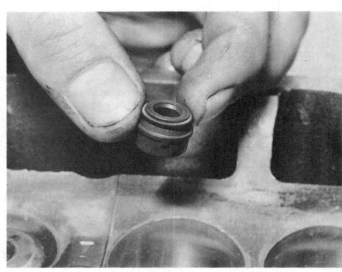

11.5A Removing the valve stem seal ...

11.5B ... and valve spring seat

12 Cylinder head – examination and renovation

1 Check the cylinder head for distortion, by placing a straight-edge across it at a number of points, lengthwise, crosswise and diagonally and measuring the gap beneath it with feeler gauges. If the gap exceeds the limit given in the Specifications, the head must be re-faced by a workshop which is equipped for this work. Re-facing must not reduce the cylinder head height below the minimum dimension given in the Specifications.

2 Examine the cylinder head for cracks. If there are minor cracks of not more than 0.5 mm (0.020 in) width between the valve seats, or at the bottom of the spark plug holes, the head can be re-used, but a cylinder head cannot be repaired or new valve seat inserts fitted.

3 Check the valve guides for wear. First clean out the guide and then insert the stem of a new valve into the guide. Because the stem diameters are different, ensure that only an inlet valve is used to check the inlet valve guides, and an exhaust valve for the exhaust valve guides. With the end of the valve stem flush with the top of the valve guide, measure the total amount by which the rim of the valve head can be moved sideways. If the movement exceeds the maximum amount given in the Specifications, new guides should be fitted, but this is a job for an Audi dealer or specialist workshop.

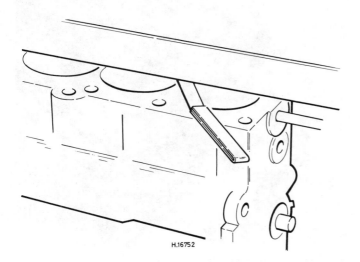

Fig. 1.4 Checking the cylinder head for distortion using a straight-edge and feeler blade (Sec 12)

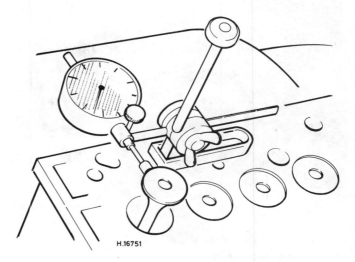

Fig. 1.5 Checking valve gear wear by measuring valve movement using a dial gauge (Sec 12)

13 Camshaft and bearings – examination and renovation

1   Examine the camshaft for signs of damage or excessive wear. If either the cam lobes or any of the journals have wear grooves, a new camshaft must be fitted.
2   With the camshaft fitted in its bearings, but with the bucket tappets removed so that there is no pressure on the crankshaft, measure the endplay of the camshaft, which should not exceed the limit given in the Specifications.
3   The camshaft bearings are part of the cylinder head and cannot be renewed. The bearing clearance is very small and the clearances can only be checked with a dial gauge. *If there is excessive looseness in the camshaft bearings, do not attempt to decrease it by grinding or filing the bottoms of the bearing caps.*

14 Valves – refitting

1   Locate the valve spring seats over the guides, then press a new seal on the top of each valve guide. A plastic sleeve should be provided with the valve stem seals, so that the seals are not damaged when the valves are fitted.
2   Apply oil to the valve stem and the stem seal. Fit the plastic sleeve over the top of the valve stem and insert the valve carefully. Remove the sleeve after inserting the valve. If there is no plastic sleeve, wrap a piece of thin adhesive tape around the top of the valve stem, so that it covers the recess for the collets and prevents the sharp edges of the recess damaging the seal. Remove the tape after fitting the valve.
3   Fit the inner and outer valve springs, then the valve spring cover. If renewing springs, they must only be renewed as a pair on any valve.
4   Fit the spring compressor and compress the spring just enough to allow the collets to be fitted. If the spring is pressed right down there is a danger of damaging the stem seal.
5   Fit the collets, release the spring compressor slightly and check that the collets seat properly, then remove the compressor.
6   Tap the top of the valve stem with a soft-headed hammer to ensure that the collets are seated.
7   Repeat the procedure for all the valves.

15 Camshaft and tappets – refitting

1   Fit the bucket tappets to their original positions; the adjustment shims on the top of the tappets must be fitted so that the lettering on them is downwards. Lubricate the tappets and the camshaft journals.
2   Lay the camshaft into the lower half of its bearings so that the lowest point of the cams of No 1 cylinder are towards the tappets, and fit the bearing caps in their original positions, making sure that they are the right way round before fitting them over the studs.
3   Fit the nuts to bearing cap Nos 2 and 4 and tighten them in diagonal sequence until the camshaft fully enters its bearings.
4   Fit the nuts to bearing caps Nos 1, 3 and 5, then tighten all the nuts to the specified torque in diagonal sequence (photo).
5   Smear a little oil onto the sealing lip and outer edge of the camshaft oil seal, then locate it open end first in the cylinder head No 1 camshaft bearing cap (photo).
6   Using a metal tube, drive the seal squarely into the cylinder head until flush with the front of the cylinder head – *if the seal is driven in further, it will block the oil return hole.*
7   Fit the Woodruff key in its groove and locate the gear on the end of the camshaft.
8   Fit the centre bolt and spacer and tighten the bolt to the specified torque while holding the gear stationary with a bar through one of the holes (photo).
9   Turn the camshaft gear and align the rear notch with the top of the timing belt rear cover.

15.4 Tightening the camshaft bearing cap nuts

15.5 Installing the camshaft oil seal

15.8 Tightening the camshaft gear centre bolt

10 Without disturbing the intermediate gear setting, and keeping the timing belt in firm contact with the intermediate gear and crankshaft gear, locate the timing belt on the camshaft gear and tensioner. The crankshaft must be positioned with No 1 cylinder at TDC. If the position of the intermediate gear is in doubt, it must be checked with reference to Section 18.

11 Turn the timing belt tensioner clockwise and tension the timing belt until it can just be twisted 90° with the thumb and index finger midway between the camshaft and intermediate gears. Tighten the nut to secure the tensioner.

12 Check and, if necessary, adjust the valve clearances, as described in Section 17.

13 Refit the valve cover and reinforcement strips, together with new gaskets and seals, and tighten the nuts.

14 Refit the upper timing belt cover and tighten the nuts.

15 If the engine is in the car, reverse the preliminary procedures given in Section 10.

16 Cylinder head and camshaft – refitting

1 Check that the top of the block is perfectly clean, then locate a new gasket on it with the words OBEN – TOP facing upward (photos).

2 Check that the cylinder head face is perfectly clean. Place two long rods or pieces of dowel in two cylinder head bolt holes at opposite ends of the block, to position the gasket and give a location for fitting the cylinder head. Lower the head on to the block (photo), remove the guides and insert the bolts and washers. Do not use jointing compound on the cylinder head joint.

3 Tighten the bolts using the sequence shown in Fig. 1.7 in the three stages given in the Specifications to the specified torque (photo).

4 Insert and tighten the bolt securing the timing belt rear cover to the cylinder head.

5 Refit the timing belt tensioner and fit the nut finger tight.

6 Follow paragraphs 9 to 14 inclusive of Section 15.

7 Refit the outlet elbow, together with a new gasket, and tighten the bolts.

8 If the engine is in the car, reverse the preliminary procedures given in Section 9.

17 Valve clearances – checking and adjustment

1 Valve clearances are adjusted by inserting the appropriate thickness shim to the top of the tappet. Shims are available in thicknesses from 3.00 to 4.25 mm (0.118 to 0.167 in) in increments of 0.05 mm (0.002 in).

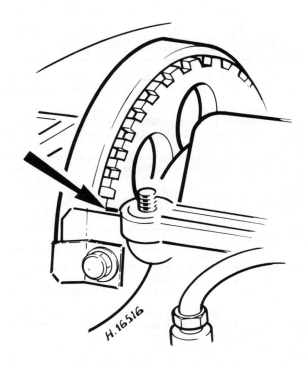

Fig. 1.6 Camshaft gear TDC mark aligned with the top of the timing belt rear cover (Sec 15)

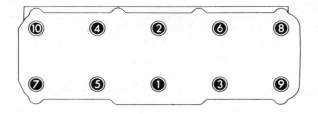

Fig. 1.7 Cylinder head bolt tightening sequence (Sec 16)

16.1A Locate the new cylinder head gasket on the block ...

16.1B ... with the OBEN – TOP words uppermost

16.2 Lowering the cylinder head into place

16.3 Tightening the cylinder head bolts

2   Adjust the valve clearances for the initial setting-up after fitting a new camshaft, or grinding in the valves with the engine cold. The valve clearances should be re-checked after 620 miles (1000 km), with the engine warm, and the coolant over 35°C (95°F).

3   Remove the valve cover after removing the upper timing cover.

4   Fit a spanner to the crankshaft pulley bolt and turn the crankshaft until the highest points of the cams for one cylinder are pointing upwards and outwards at similar angles. Use feeler gauges to check the gap between the cam and the tappet and record the dimension.

5   Repeat the operation for all four cylinders and complete the list of clearances. Valves are numbered from the timing belt end of the engine. Inlet valves are Nos 2-4-5-7, exhaust valves are Nos 1-3-6-8.

6   Where any tolerances exceed those given in the Specifications, remove the existing shim by placing a cranked dowel rod with a suitably shaped end between two tappets with the rod resting on the edge of the tappets (photo). With the piston for the relevant cylinder at TDC compression, lever against the camshaft to depress the tappets sufficiently to remove the shim(s) from the top of the tappet(s). Do not over depress the tappets so that the valves touch the pistons. Note that each tappet incorporates notches in its upper rim so that a small screwdriver or similar tool can be used to remove the shim (photos).

17.6A Using a cranked dowel rod to depress the tappets

17.6B Removing a shim from a tappet (tappet removed)

17.6C Notches in tappet (arrowed) for shim removal

17.7 The thickness (in mm) engraved on the underside of the tappet shim

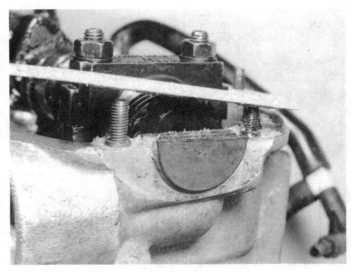

17.9 Fitting a new valve cover gasket and rear plug

7   Note the thickness of the shim (engraved on its underside), and calculate the shim thickness required to correct the clearance (photo). If the clearance is too large, a thicker shim is required, and a smaller shim is needed when there is insufficient clearance.
8   Provided they are not worn or damaged, shims which have been removed can be re-used in other positions if they are of the correct thickness.
9   Refit the valve cover and upper timing cover, together with new gaskets, after checking and adjusting the valve clearances (photo).

18 Timing belt and gears – removal and refitting

Note: If the engine is still in the car, first carry out the following operations:

   (a) Disconnect the battery negative lead
   (b) Remove the power-assisted steering pump drivebelt on models so equipped, as described in Chapter 10
   (c) Remove the alternator, as described in Chapter 12

1   Unscrew the nuts and lift off the upper timing cover, using an Allen key where necessary.
2   Unbolt and remove the pulley from the water pump (photo).
3   Using a socket on the crankshaft pulley bolt, turn the engine so that the piston in No 1 cylinder is at TDC (top dead centre) on its compression stroke. The notch in the crankshaft pulley must be in line with the arrow on the lower timing cover, and both No 1 cylinder valves must be closed (ie cam peaks away from the tappets).
4   If it is required to remove the crankshaft gear, loosen the centre bolt now. Hold the crankshaft stationary with a wide-bladed screwdriver in the starter ring gear (starter motor removed) or engage top gear and apply the handbrake if the engine is still in the car.
5   With the TDC marks aligned unbolt the crankshaft pulley from the gear (photo).
6   Unbolt and remove the lower timing cover (photo).
7   Loosen the nut on the timing belt tensioner and, using an open-ended spanner, rotate the eccentric hub anti-clockwise to release the belt tension (photo).
8   Remove the timing belt from the crankshaft, camshaft and intermediate gears, and from the tensioner.

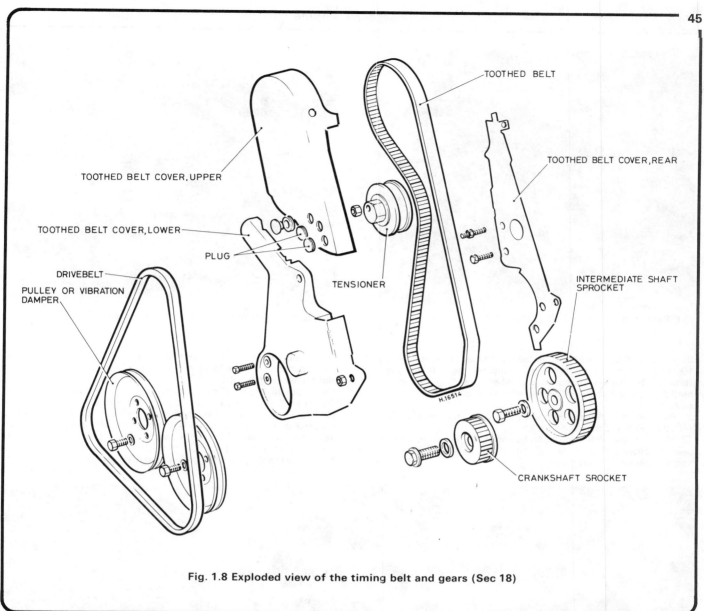

TOOTHED BELT

TOOTHED BELT COVER, UPPER

TOOTHED BELT COVER, REAR

TOOTHED BELT COVER, LOWER

PLUG

DRIVEBELT

PULLEY OR VIBRATION DAMPER

TENSIONER

INTERMEDIATE SHAFT SPROCKET

H.16514

CRANKSHAFT SROCKET

Fig. 1.8 Exploded view of the timing belt and gears (Sec 18)

18.2 Removing the water pump pulley

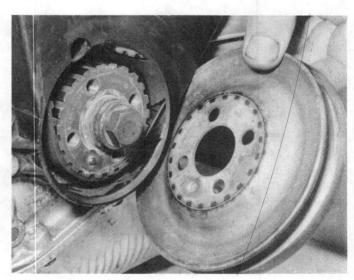

18.5 Removing the crankshaft pulley

18.6 Removing the lower timing cover

18.7 Turn the tensioner anti-clockwise to release the belt tension

9   Unscrew the nut and remove the timing belt tensioner (photo).
10 Unscrew the centre bolt and withdraw the intermediate gear (photo). Remove the Woodruff key. When loosening the centre bolt, hold the gear stationary with a socket and bar on the rear timing cover bolt.
11 Remove the centre bolt and withdraw the crankshaft gear (photos). Remove the Woodruff key.
12 Unscrew the centre bolt from the camshaft gear while holding the gear stationary with a bar through one of the holes. Withdraw the gear and remove the Woodruff key.

13 Unbolt and remove the rear timing cover.
14 Commence refitting by locating the rear timing cover on the engine and tightening the bolts.
15 Locate the Woodruff key and camshaft gear on the camshaft, insert the centre bolt and washer, and tighten the bolt.
16 Locate the Woodruff key and crankshaft gear on the crankshaft, coat the threads of the centre bolt with a liquid locking agent, then insert the bolt with its washer and tighten it while holding the crankshaft stationary (photo).
17 Locate the Woodruff key and intermediate gear on the intermediate

18.9 Removing the timing belt tensioner

18.10 Removing the gear from the intermediate shaft

18.11A Unscrew the centre bolt ...

18.11B ... and withdraw the crankshaft gear

18.16 Tightening the crankshaft gear centre bolt

18.17 Tightening the intermediate shaft gear centre bolt

18.20 Crankshaft pulley TDC notch aligned with the indentation in the intermediate gear (arrowed)

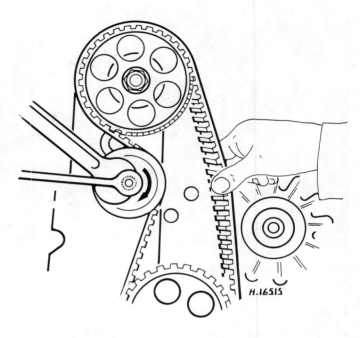

Fig. 1.9 Checking timing belt tension (Sec 18)

Turn tensioner clockwise until belt can just be twisted through 90°

shaft, then insert the centre bolt and washer, and tighten the bolt (photo).
18 Refit the timing belt tensioner and fit the nut finger tight.
19 Make sure that the notch on the rear of the camshaft gear is aligned with the top of the timing belt rear cover.
20 Temporarily fit the crankshaft pulley to the gear then, with No 1 piston at TDC, turn the intermediate gear so that the indentation is aligned with the notch in the pulley (photo). If the distributor has not been disturbed the rotor arm will point in the direction of No 1 distributor cap segment.
21 Locate the timing belt on the gears and tensioner, turn the tensioner clockwise to pretension the timing belt, and check that the TDC marks are still correctly aligned.
22 Turn the tensioner clockwise until the timing belt can just be twisted 90° with the thumb and index finger midway between the camshaft and intermediate gears. Tighten the nut to secure the tensioner.
23 Remove the crankshaft pulley, fit the lower timing cover, and tighten the bolts.
24 Refit the crankshaft pulley and tighten the bolts.
25 Locate the pulley on the water pump and tighten the bolts.
26 Refit the upper timing cover and tighten the nuts.
27 If the engine is in the car, reverse the preliminary procedures given at the beginning of this Section.

19 Flywheel/driveplate – removal and refitting

Note: *If the engine is still in the car, first carry out the following operations:*

(a) On manual gearbox models, remove the gearbox (Chapter 6), and clutch (Chapter 5)
(b) On automatic transmission models, remove the automatic transmission (Chapter 7)

1 The flywheel/driveplate bolts are offset to ensure correct refitting. Unscrew the bolts while holding the flywheel/driveplate stationary (photos).
2 Lift the flywheel.driveplate from the crankshaft (photo). If removing a driveplate note the location of the shim and spacer.
3 Refitting is a reversal of removal, but coat the threads of the bolts with a liquid locking agent before inserting them and tightening them

19.1A Removing the flywheel bolts

19.1B Using a bar and angle iron to hold the flywheel stationary

19.2 Removing the flywheel

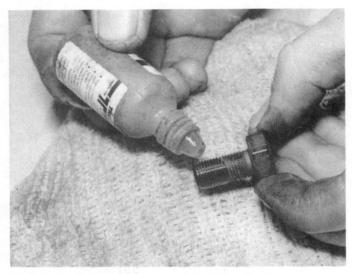

19.3 Apply a liquid locking agent to the flywheel bolts

Fig. 1.10 Automatic transmission driveplate showing location of spacer (1) and shim (2) (Sec 19)

to the specified torque (photo). If a replacement driveplate is to be fitted, its position must be checked and adjusted if necessary. The distance from the rear face of the block to the torque converter *mounting face* on the driveplate (Fig. 1.11) must be between 30.5 and 32.1 mm (1.20 and 1.26 in). If necessary, remove the driveplate and fit a spacer behind it to achieve the correct dimension.

20 Intermediate shaft – removal and refitting

1 Remove the distributor (Chapter 4), and the fuel pump (Chapter 3).
2 Remove the timing belt and intermediate gear, as described in Section 18.
3 Remove the two bolts from the sealing flange, take off the sealing flange and the O-ring (photos).
4 Withdraw the intermediate shaft from the block (photo).
5 With the flange removed, the oil seal can be removed (photo). Fit a new seal with its open face towards the engine and use a block of

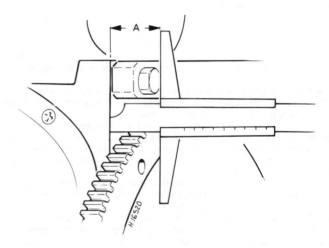

Fig. 1.11 Checking the driveplate-to-block dimension 'A' (Sec 19)

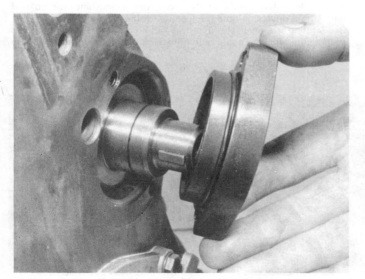

20.3A Removing the intermediate shaft sealing flange ...

20.3B ... and O-ring

20.4 The intermediate shaft

20.5 Levering out the intermediate shaft oil seal from the flange

wood to drive the seal in flush. Oil the lips of the seal before fitting the sealing flange.

6 Refitting is a reversal of removal, but fit a new O-ring and check that the shaft endplay does not exceed the amount given in the Specifications. Refer to Section 18 when refitting the timing belt and intermediate gear, and to Chapters 3 and 4 when refitting the fuel pump and distributor.

21 Sump – removal and refitting

Note: *If the engine is still in the car, first carry out the following operations:*

(a) *Jack up the front of the car and support it on axle stands*
(b) *Support the weight of the engine with a hoist*
(c) *Unbolt and remove the transmission front cover*
(d) *Drain the engine oil*
(e) *Unscrew the subframe front bolts and lower the subframe*

1 Unbolt and remove the sump, using an Allen key where necessary. Remove the dipstick.
2 Remove the gasket.
3 Refitting is a reversal of removal, but use a new gasket without adhesive (photo), and tighten the bolts evenly to the specified torque.

22 Crankshaft oil seals – renewal

Front oil seal

1 Remove the timing belt and crankshaft gear, as described in Section 18.
2 If an extractor tool is available the seal may be renewed without removing the housing, otherwise unbolt and remove the housing (including the relevant sump bolts) and remove the gasket (photo). If the sump gasket is damaged while removing the housing it will be necessary to remove the sump and fit a new gasket. However, refit the sump *after* fitting the housing.
3 Drive the old seal out of the housing then dip the new seal in

21.3 Locating a new sump gasket on the block

22.2 Removing the crankshaft front oil seal housing

engine oil and drive it into the housing with a block of wood or a socket until flush (photo). Make sure that the closed end of the seal is facing outwards.

4   Fit the housing, together with a new gasket, and tighten the bolts evenly in diagonal sequence.

5   Refit the crankshaft gear and timing belt, as described in Section 18.

Rear oil seal

6   Remove the flywheel or driveplate, as described in Section 19.

7   Follow paragraphs 2 to 4 inclusive (photo).

8   Refit the flywheel or driveplate, as described in Section 19.

23 Oil pump – removal, examination and refitting

1   Remove the sump, as described in Section 21.

2   Using an Allen key, unscrew the socket-headed bolts and withdraw the oil pump and strainer from the cylinder block (photo).

3   Remove the two hexagon-headed bolts from the pump cover and lift off the cover (photo).

4   Bend up the metal rim of the filter plate so that it can be removed

22.3 Using a socket to fit a new crankshaft front oil seal

22.7 Removing the crankshaft rear oil seal housing

23.2 Removing the oil pump and strainer

23.3 Removing the oil pump cover

23.4 Oil pump filter screen

and take the filter screen out (photo). Clean the screen thoroughly with paraffin and a brush.

5   Clean the pump casing, cover and gears.

6   Check the backlash of the gears with a feeler gauge (photo) and, with a straight-edge across the end face of the pump, measure the endplay of the gears (photo). Examine the pump cover grooves worn by the ends of the gears, which will effectively increase the endplay of the gears. If the wear on the pump is beyond the specified limits a new pump should be fitted.

7   Fill the pump housing with engine oil then reassemble and refit it using a reversal of the removal and dismantling procedure. Refer to Section 21 when refitting the sump.

24 Pistons and connecting rods – removal and dismantling

1   Remove the cylinder head (Section 9), timing belt (Section 18) and oil pump (Section 23).

2   Mark each connecting rod and cap in relation to its cylinder and position.

3   Turn the crankshaft so that No 1 piston is at the bottom of its bore, then unscrew the nuts and remove the big-end bearing cap (photo).

4   Using the handle of a hammer, push the piston and connecting rod out of the top of the cylinder. Put the bearing cap with its connecting rod and make sure that they both have the cylinder number marked on them. If any of the bearing shells become detached while removing the connecting rod and bearing cap, ensure that they are placed with their matching cap or rod.

5   Repeat the procedure given in paragraphs 3 and 4 to remove the remaining pistons and connecting rods.

6   Before removing the pistons from the connecting rods, if necessary, mark the connecting rods to show which side of them is towards the front of the engine. The casting marks on the rod and cap face towards the front of the engine (photo).

7   Remove the circlips from the grooves in the gudgeon pin holes and push the pin out enough for the connecting rod to be removed (photo). Do not remove the pins completely unless new ones are to be fitted, to ensure that the pin is not turned end for end when the piston is refitted. If the pin is difficult to push out, heat the piston by immersing it in hot water.

8   New bushes can be fitted to the connecting rods, but as they need to be reamed to size after fitting, the job is best left to an Audi agent.

9   Using old feeler gauges, or pieces of rigid plastic inserted behind the piston rings, carefully ease each ring in turn off the piston. Lay the rings out so that they are kept the right way up and so that the top ring

23.6A Checking the oil pump gear backlash ...

23.6B ... and endplay

24.3 Removing a big-end cap

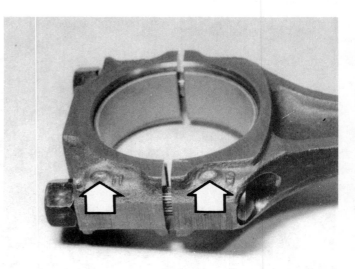

24.6 The casting marks (arrowed) which must face the front of the engine

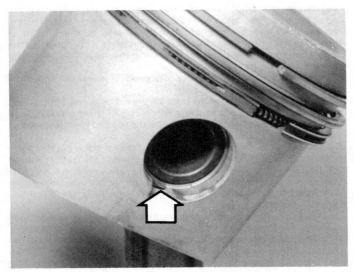

24.7 Location of a gudgeon pin circlip (arrowed) in the piston

can be identified. Carefully scrape the rings free of carbon and clean out the ring grooves on the pistons, using a piece of wood or a piece of broken piston ring.

25 Pistons and cylinder bores – examination

1   Examine the pistons and the bores for obvious signs of damage and excessive wear. If they appear to be satisfactory, make the following checks.

2   Measure the piston diameter at a position 15 mm (0.60 in) from the lower edge of the skirt and at 90° to the axis of the piston (Fig. 1.12) and compare this with the information in the Specifications.

3   Push a piston ring into the cylinder bore and use a piston to push the ring down the bore so that it is square in the bore and about 15 mm (0.6 in) from the bottom of the cylinder. Measure the ring cap using a feeler gauge (photo). If the gap is above the top limit, look for obvious signs of bore wear, or if a new piston ring is available, measure the gap when a new piston ring is fitted to the bore.

4   To measure the bore diameter directly a dial gauge with an internal measuring attachment is required. If one is available, measure each bore in six places and compare the readings with the wear limit given. Bore diameter should be measured 10 mm (0.4 in) from the top of the bore, 10 mm (0.4 in) from the bottom and at the mid-point. At each of the three stations, measure in-line with the crankshaft and at right angles to it. If the bores are worn beyond the limit, they will need to be rebored and new pistons fitted.

5   If one bore is oversize, all four must be rebored and a new set of pistons fitted, otherwise the engine will not be balanced. Connecting rods must only be fitted as complete sets and not be replaced individually.

6   Fit the rings to the pistons and use a feeler gauge to measure the gap between the piston ring and the side of its groove (photo). If the gap is beyond the wear limit, it is more likely that it is the piston groove rather than the ring which has worn, and either a new piston or a proprietary oversize ring will be required. If new piston rings are fitted the wear ridge at the top of the cylinder bore must be removed, or a stepped top ring used.

Fig. 1.12 Checking the piston diameter (Sec 25)

26 Pistons and connecting rods – reassembly and refitting

1   Heat each piston in hot water, then insert the connecting rod and push in the pin until central. Make sure that the casting marks on the connecting rod and the arrow on the piston crown (photo) are facing the same way, then refit the circlips.

2   Before refitting the piston rings, or fitting new rings, check the gap of each ring in turn in its correct cylinder bore using a piston to push

25.3 Checking the piston ring gap

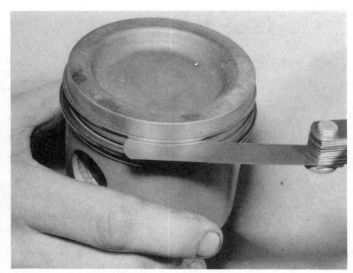

25.6 Checking the piston ring-to-groove clearance

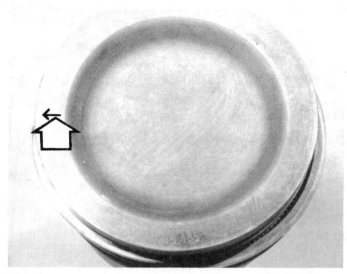
26.1 The arrow on the piston crown (arrowed) must face the front of the engine

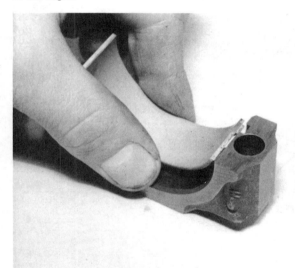
26.5 Fit the bearing shells so that the tang engages the recess in the cap and rod

the ring down the bore, as described in the previous Section. Measure the gap between the ends of the piston ring, using feeler gauges. The gap must be within the limits given in the Specifications.

3   If the piston ring gap is too small, carefully file the piston ring end until the gap is sufficient. Pistons rings are very brittle, so handle them carefully.

4   When fitting piston rings, look for the word TOP etched on one side of the ring and fit this side so that it is towards the piston crown. The outer recessed edge on the centre ring must face the gudgeon pin.

5   Unless the big-end bearing shells are known to be almost new, it is worth fitting a new set when reassembling the engine. Clean the connecting rods and bearing caps thoroughly and fit the bearing shells so that the tang on the bearing engages in the recess in the connecting rod, or cap, and the ends of the bearing are flush with the joint face (photo).

6   To refit the pistons, first space the joints in the piston rings so that they are at 120° intervals. Oil the rings and grooves generously and fit a piston ring compressor over the piston.

7   Oil the cylinder bores and insert the pistons (photo) with the arrow on the piston crown pointing towards the front of the engine. Make sure that the relevant crankpin is at its furthest point from the cylinder.

8   When the piston is pushed in flush with the top of the bore, oil the two bearing halves and the crankshaft journal and guide the connecting rod half-bearing on to the crankpin.

9   Fit the big-end bearing cap, complete with shell, and tighten the nuts to the specified torque wrench setting (photo).

10 Rotate the crankshaft to ensure that everything is free, before fitting the next piston and connecting rod.

11 Using feeler gauges between the machined face of each big-end bearing, and the machined face of the crankshaft web, check the endplay, which should not exceed the maximum amount given in the Specifications.

12 Refit the oil pump (Section 23), timing belt (Section 18), and cylinder head (Section 16).

27 Crankshaft – removal, examination and refitting

1   With the engine removed from the car, remove the pistons and connecting rods, as described in Section 24.

2   Reassemble the big-end bearings to their matching connecting rods to ensure correct refitting.

3   Remove the crankshaft oil seals complete with housings, as described in Section 22.

4   Check that each main bearing cap is numbered for position.

5   Remove the bolts from each bearing cap in turn, then remove the caps and lift out the crankshaft (photos).

6   If the bearings are not being renewed, ensure that each half-bearing shell is identified so that it is put back in the same place

26.7 Fitting the piston and connecting rods

26.9 Tightening the big-end cap nuts

27.5A Removing a crankshaft main bearing cap

27.5B Removing the crankshaft

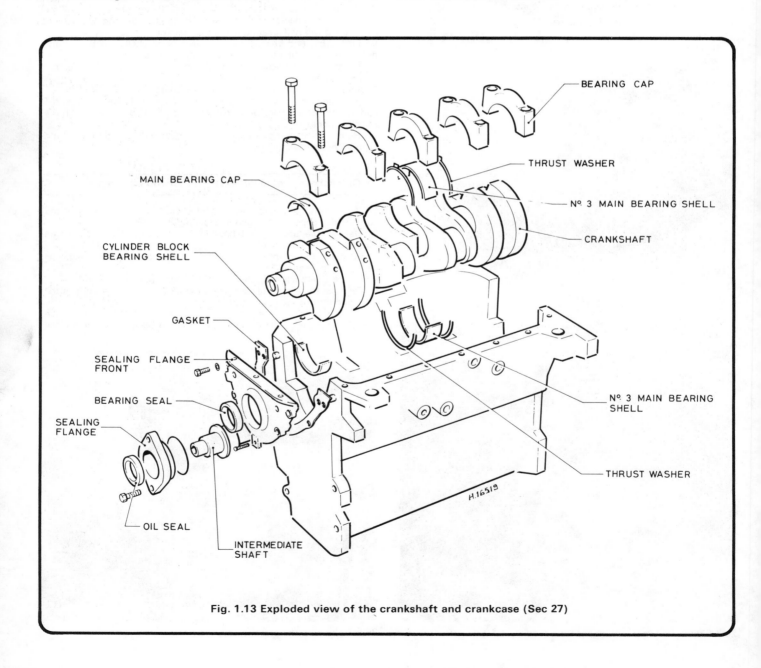

BEARING CAP

THRUST WASHER

MAIN BEARING CAP

Nº 3 MAIN BEARING SHELL

CRANKSHAFT

CYLINDER BLOCK
BEARING SHELL

GASKET

SEALING FLANGE
FRONT

BEARING SEAL

SEALING
FLANGE

Nº 3 MAIN BEARING
SHELL

THRUST WASHER

OIL SEAL

INTERMEDIATE
SHAFT

H.16519

Fig. 1.13 Exploded view of the crankshaft and crankcase (Sec 27)

from which it was removed. This also applies to the thrust washers if fitted – see paragraph 7. If the engine has done a high mileage and it is suspected that the crankshaft requires attention, it is best to seek the opinion of an Audi dealer or crankshaft re-finishing specialist for advice on the need for regrinding. Unless the bearing shells (and thrust washers if applicable) are known to be almost new, it is worth fitting a new set when the crankshaft is refitted. If available, Plastigage may be used to check the running clearance of the existing bearings (photo).

7   Clean the crankcase recesses and bearing caps thoroughly and fit the bearing shells so that the tang on the bearing engages in the recess in the crankcase or bearing cap. Make sure that the shells fitted to the crankcase have oil holes, and that these line up with the drillings in the bearing housings. The shells fitted to the bearing caps do not have oil holes, with the exception of No 4 bearing cap which does. Note that the bearing shells of the centre bearing (No 3) may either be flanged to act as thrust washers, or may have separate thrust washers. These should be fitted oil groove outwards as shown. Fit the bearing shells so that the ends of the bearing are flush with the joint face (photos).

8   Oil the bearings and journals, then locate the crankshaft in the crankcase.

9   Fit the main bearing caps (with centre main bearing thrust washers if applicable) in their correct positions.

27.6 Using Plastigage to check the crankshaft journal clearances

27.7A Fitting the flanged type centre main bearing to the cap

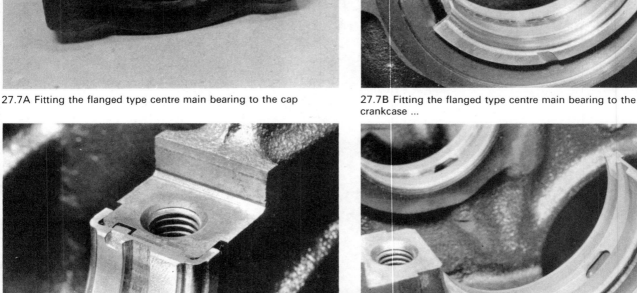

27.7B Fitting the flanged type centre main bearing to the crankcase ...

27.7C ... ensuring that the ends of the bearing are flush with the joint face

27.7D Fitting the alternative type centre main bearing to the crankcase ...

27.7E ... together with the thrust washers

27.10 Tightening the main bearing cap bolts

10 Fit the bolts to the bearing caps and tighten the bolts of the centre cap to the specified torque (photo), then check that the crankshaft rotates freely.

11 Working out from the centre, tighten the remaining bearing caps in turn, checking that the crankshaft rotates freely after each bearing has been tightened.

12 Check that the endplay of the crankshaft is within specification, by inserting feeler gauges between the crankshaft and the centre bearing thrust face/washer while levering the crankshaft first in one direction and then in the other (photo).

13 The rear end of the crankshaft carries a needle roller bearing (photo) which supports the front end of the gearbox input shaft. Inspect the bearing for obvious signs of wear and damage. If the gearbox has been removed and dismantled, fit the input shaft into the bearing to see if there is excessive clearance. If the bearing requires renewing, insert a hook behind the bearing and pull it out of the end of the crankshaft. Install the new bearing with the lettering on the end of the bearing outwards. Press it in until the end of the bearing is 1.5 mm (0.059 in) below the face of the flywheel flange (photo).

14 Fit new crankshaft oil seals (Section 22) then refit the pistons and connecting rods, as described in Section 26.

27.12 Checking the crankshaft endplay

27.13A Location of the spigot needle roller bearing in the end of the crankshaft

27.13B Checking the spigot bearing fitted position

28 Engine mountings – removal and refitting

1   Jack up the front of the car and support it on stands.
2   Support the engine under the sump using a trolley jack.
3   Undo the bolts securing the mounting to the body, and the through-bolt and nut securing the mounting to the engine support brackets. If working on the right-hand mounting it will be necessary to remove the cover plate to gain access to the mounting.
4   Raise the engine slightly, then remove the mountings from their locations.
5   Refitting is a reversal of removal.

PART B – FIVE-CYLINDER ENGINES

29 General description

The engine is of five-cylinder, in-line, overhead camshaft type, mounted conventionally at the front of the car. The crankshaft is of six-bearing type and the No 4 (from front) main bearing shells incorporate flanged thrust washers to control crankshaft endfloat (endplay). The camshaft is driven by a toothed belt from the crankshaft sprocket, and the belt also drives the water pump mounted on the left-hand side of the block. A gear on the rear of the camshaft drives the distributor, and on carburettor models the camshaft also drives the fuel pump.

The valves are operated from the camshaft through bucket type tappets, and valve clearances are adjusted by the use of shims located in the top of the tappets, or self-adjusting with hydraulic tappets.

The engine has a full-flow lubrication system. A gear and crescent type oil pump is mounted on the front of the crankshaft. The oil filter is of the cartridge type, mounted on the right-hand side of the cylinder block.

30 Maintenance and inspection

1   Refer to Section 2 of this Chapter, with the following exceptions:

   (a) The oil drain plug is located on the right-hand side of the sump, and the oil filter is located on the right-hand side of the cylinder block (photos)
   (b) Valve clearance adjustment is not necessary on engines with hydraulic tappets
   (c) The timing belt adjustment procedure is contained in Section 47
   (d) On Turbo models there is an additional oil filter for the turbocharger

31 Major operations possible with the engine in the car

The following operations can be carried out without having to remove the engine from the car:

   (a) Removal and servicing of the cylinder head and camshaft
   (b) Removal of the timing belt and gears
   (c) Removal of the flywheel or driveplate (after first removing the transmission)
   (d) Removal of the sump (after first lowering the subframe)
   (e) Removal of the oil pump
   (f) Removal of the pistons and connecting rods

32 Major operations requiring engine removal

The following operation can only be carried out after removal of the engine from the car:

   Removal of crankshaft and main bearings

33 Method of engine removal

The engine must be disconnected from the transmission, then lifted from the car.

34 Engine – removal and refitting

All models except Turbo

1   Remove the bonnet, as described in Chapter 11 and stand it on cardboard or rags in a safe place.
2   Disconnect the battery negative lead.
3   Remove the radiator, as described in Chapter 2.
4   Remove the radiator grille and the front bumper upper trim strip, as described in Chapter 11.
5   Remove the distributor cap and plug leads.
6   Refer to Chapter 3, and remove the air cleaner and, where applicable, the air intake hoses at the front of the engine.
7   Refer to Chapter 10 and remove the power-assisted steering pump, but leave the hydraulic pipes connected. Secure the pump to one side without straining the hoses.
8   On models equipped with air conditioning, remove the compressor, as described in Chapter 11, leaving the refrigerant hoses connected. Secure the compressor to one side without straining the hoses.

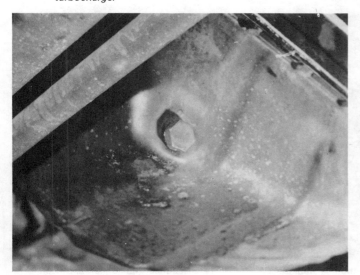

30.1A Engine oil drain plug ...

30.1B ... and oil filter location

9   Identify all wiring for location using masking tape, then disconnect those affecting engine removal. These include, where applicable:

Wiring to the oil pressure switches (photo), temperature sender (photo), distributor (photo), coil, gearchange indicator, warm-up valve, thermo-switches, idle stabiliser (photo), thermotime switch, cold start valve (photo), throttle switch (photo), intake temperature sender, ignition timing sender, rpm sender, automatic choke, inlet manifold preheater, and additional emission control components (see Chapter 3)

10   On fuel injection models, slacken the hose clips and lift away the complete idle stabiliser valve and hose assembly (photos).

11   Working clockwise around the engine, disconnect all coolant and heater hoses and pipes which affect engine removal (photo).

12   Refer to Chapter 3, and disconnect the accelerator cable.

13   On automatic transmission models, refer to Chapters 3 and 7, disconnect the throttle and accelerator pedal cables and linkage.

14   On fuel injection models, slacken the clip and withdraw the air duct from the throttle valve housing (photo).

15   Identify all fuel and vacuum hoses using masking tape, then disconnect those affecting engine removal. These will include, where applicable:

Carburettor models: *Fuel line at fuel pump, return line at return valve, vacuum pipes at vacuum reservoir, econometer, and distributor*

Fuel injection models: *Fuel hoses at the metering distributor (photo), cold start valve (photo) and warm-up valve (photo), vacuum hoses at warm-up valve, econometer, throttle valve housing (photo) and distributor (photo), also any additional emission control components (see Chapter 3)*

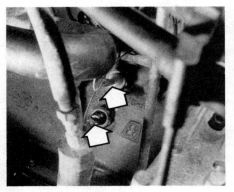

34.9A Disconnect the wiring at the oil pressure switches (arrowed) ...

34.9B ... temperature sender ...

34.9C ... distributor ...

34.9D ... idle stabiliser ...

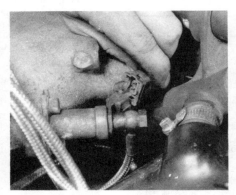

34.9E ... cold start valve

34.9F ... and throttle switch

34.10A Slacken the hose clips and cable clamp (arrowed) ...

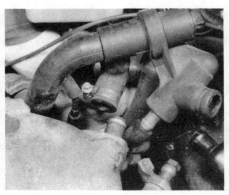

34.10B ... and remove the idle stabiliser assembly

34.11 Disconnect the coolant and heater hoses and pipes

34.14 Withdraw the air duct from the throttle valve housing

34.15A Disconnect the fuel hoses at the metering distributor ...

34.15B ... cold start valve ...

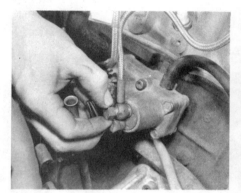

34.15C ... and warm-up valve

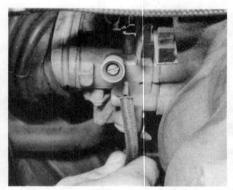

34.15D Disconnect the vacuum hoses at the throttle valve housing ...

34.15E ... and distributor

16 Disconnect the earth braid at the rear of the valve cover.
17 Refer to Chapter 12 and remove the alternator and starter motor.
18 Disconnect the exhaust front pipe at the manifold and transmission bracket (photo).
19 Remove the engine front mounting, and the body-mounted bracket (photo).
20 On automatic transmission models, unscrew the torque converter-to-driveplate bolts, while holding the starter ring gear stationary with a screwdriver. It will be necessary to rotate the engine to position the bolts in the starter aperture, using a socket on the crankshaft pulley. bolt.
21 Using an Allen key, unscrew the nuts and lift off the timing belt upper cover. Recover the distance pieces.
22 Disconnect the clutch cable from the release lever and left-hand

34.18 Disconnect the exhaust front pipe at the manifold

34.19 Remove the engine front mounting

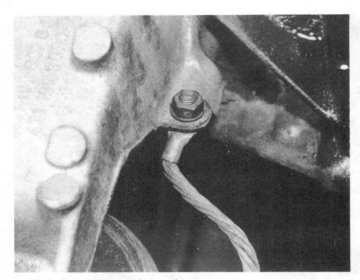

34.22 Disconnect the engine earth strap

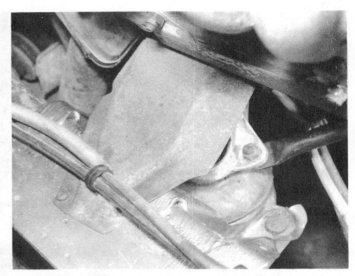

34.23 Remove the engine mounting cover plate

engine mounting (where applicable) and disconnect the engine earth strap from the mounting (photo).

23 Remove the cover plate over the right-hand engine mounting (photo).

24 Connect a hoist and take the weight of the engine. The hoist should be positioned centrally over the engine.

25 Support the weight of the transmission with a trolley jack.

26 Unscrew the engine-to-transmission bolts, noting the position of any brackets or cable supports.

27 Unscrew the engine mounting bracket-to-mounting through-bolts (photo), then lift the engine slightly and remove the left-hand mounting bracket (photo).

28 Lift the engine and pull it off the transmission. On automatic transmission models, make sure that the torque converter remains fully engaged with the transmission splines.

29 Manipulate the engine as necessary, and lift it from the engine compartment, then lower the unit to the floor (photo).

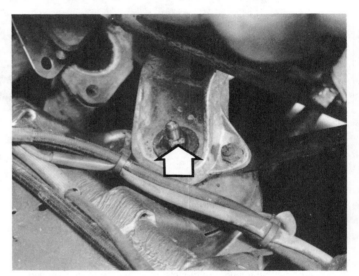

34,27A Unscrew the engine mounting through-bolts (arrowed) ...

34.27B ... then remove the left-hand mounting bracket

34.29 Removing the engine

Turbo models

30 Carry out the operations described in paragraphs 1 to 5.
31 Refer to Chapter 11 and remove the front bumper.
32 Refer to Chapter 10 and remove the power-assisted steering pump, but leave the hydraulic pipes connected. Secure the pump to one side without straining the hoses.
33 Disconnect the wiring at the thermo-switch.
34 Disconnect the wiring at the thermotime switch, oil pressure switches and warm-up valve.
35 Detach the warm-up valve vacuum hose, then undo the two bolts and move the valve to one side.
36 On automatic transmission models, disconnect the transmission pushrod at the bellcrank lever.
37 Disconnect the wiring connectors for the engine speed sender, reference mark sender, and knock sensor at the bulkhead bracket.
38 Disconnect the wiring at the distributor and ignition coil.
39 Remove the injector cooling fan duct over the valve cover.
40 Disconnect the injector cooling fan wiring, then remove the fan assembly.
41 Remove the engine speed and reference mark sender support bracket.
42 Disconnect the engine earth strap at the left-hand engine mounting.
43 Detach the coolant and heater hoses at the coolant pipe, then remove the pipe from the engine.
44 Disconnect the vacuum hose at the cruise control system.
45 Disconnect the wiring connectors at the cold start valve and idle stabiliser switch.
46 Unscrew the earth lead and bracket at the throttle linkage relay.
47 Detach the vacuum hose at the electronic ignition control unit and at the gearchange indicator.
48 Remove the cold start valve from the manifold, leaving the fuel line connected.
49 Disconnect the cruise control linkage pushrod and accelerator cable at the throttle valve housing. Release the cable from its supports.
50 Disconnect the throttle valve switch wiring connector, and release the wiring from the cable clips.
51 Remove the air temperature sensor from the throttle valve housing. Seal the manifold opening, and cover the sensor with a protective cap.
52 Disconnect the wiring at the injector cooling fan thermo-switch in

the waste gate heat deflector plate. Release the wiring from the cable clips.
53 Firmly pull each injector out of the cylinder head, with fuel hose still attached, then move all the fuel lines and injectors clear of the engine.
54 Slacken the clips and remove the air duct from the airflow sensor and intake tube.
55 Unclip the air cleaner cover and remove it, complete with the intake tube.
56 Remove the connecting hose from the intercooler to the throttle body.
57 Disconnect the idle stabilizer hose at the intercooler, remove the hose between intercooler and turbo, then remove the intercooler.
58 Disconnect the exhaust front pipe at the turbo unit flange.
59 Remove the cover plate over the right-hand engine mounting.
60 Disconnect the exhaust corrugated branch pipe at the front pipe flange.
61 Disconnect the exhaust front pipe at the intermediate pipe flange and transmission support, then remove the pipe from the car.
62 From under the car, remove the alternator air duct.
63 Remove the alternator adjustment and mounting bolts, lift the unit away, and support it clear of the engine with the wiring still attached.
64 Undo the starter motor bolts, withdraw the starter, and support it clear of the engine with the wiring still attached.
65 Unscrew the oil cooler hoses at the oil filter housing.
66 On models equipped with air conditioning, remove the compressor, as described in Chapter 11, leaving the refrigerant hoses connected. Secure the compressor to one side without straining the hoses, then remove the compressor bracket.
67 On automatic transmission models, unscrew the torque converter-to-driveplate bolts while holding the starter ring gear stationary with a screwdriver. It will be necessary to rotate the engine to position the bolts in the starter aperture, using a socket on the crankshaft pulley bolt.
68 Connect a hoist and take the weight of the engine. The hoist should be positioned centrally over the engine.
69 Support the weight of the transmission with a trolley jack.
70 Unscrew the engine-to-transmission bolts noting the position of any brackets or cable supports.
71 Unscrew the engine mounting bracket-to-mounting through-bolts, then remove the left-hand mounting bracket.

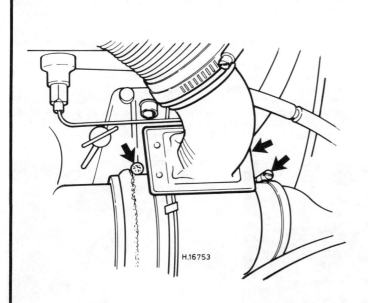

Fig. 1.14 Injector cooling fan attachments – Turbo models (Sec 34)

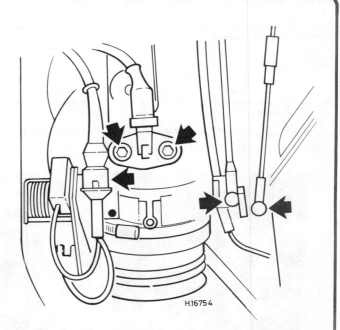

Fig. 1.15 Air temperature sensor, throttle valve switch and cruise control attachments at the throttle valve housing – Turbo models (Sec 34)

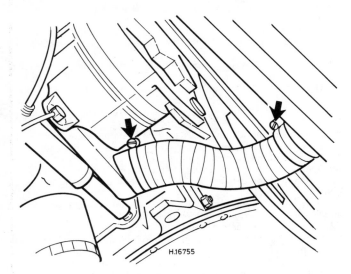

Fig. 1.16 Alternator air duct location and attachments –
Turbo models (Sec 34)

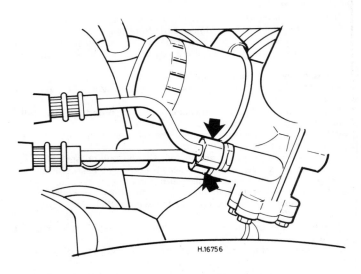

Fig. 1.17 Oil cooler hose connections at the oil filter
housing (Sec 34)

72 Lift the engine and pull it off the transmission. On automatic
transmission models, make sure that the torque converter remains fully
engaged with the transmission splines.
73 Manipulate the engine as necessary and lift it from the engine
compartment, then lower the unit to the floor.

Refitting – all models
74 Refitting is a reversal of the removal procedure, but smear the
manual transmission input shaft and release bearing face with
molybdenum disulphide grease before fitting. Ensure that all the
engine and transmission mountings are fitted free of strain, and tighten
all nuts and bolts to the specified torque. Refit, and where applicable
adjust, all engine related components and systems with reference to
the Chapters concerned. Ensure that the engine is filled with oil and
that the cooling system is topped up before starting the engine.

35 Engine dismantling – general

Refer to Section 7 of this Chapter.

36 Ancillary components – removal and refitting

Refer to Section 8 of this Chapter, with the following exception:
Oil filter cartridge (Section 30 of this Chapter)

37 Camshaft and tappets – removal

Note: *If the engine is still in the car, first carry out the following
operations:*

   (a) *Disconnect the battery negative lead*
   (b) *On carburettor models remove the air cleaner and fuel pump
       (Chapter 3)*
   (c) *Remove the distributor (Chapter 4)*
   (d) *Remove the upper radiator cowl*
   (e) *Remove the alternator, air conditioning and power-assisted
       steering drivebelts as applicable (Chapter 12, 11 and 10
       respectively)*
   (f) *Disconnect all relevant wiring, cables and hoses*
   (g) *On Turbo models remove the injector cooling fan duct over
       the valve cover, the cruise control linkage and the intercooler
       (Chapter 3)*

1   Unscrew the nuts and lift off the valve cover, together with the
reinforcement strips and gaskets. Note the location of the HT lead
holder.
2   Using an Allen key, unscrew the nuts and lift off the timing belt
upper cover. Recover the distance pieces (photos).
3   Using a socket on the crankshaft pulley bolt, turn the engine so that
the piston in No 1 cylinder is at TDC on its compression stroke. The
notch in the crankshaft pulley must be in line with the pip on the timing
belt lower cover (photo), or the pointer on the oil pump housing –
alternatively the O mark (TDC) on the flywheel/driveplate must be

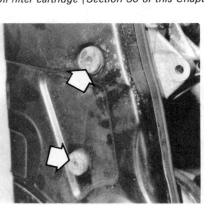

37.2A Unscrew the timing belt cover nuts
(arrowed) and remove the cover ...

37.2B ... then remove the distance pieces
(arrowed)

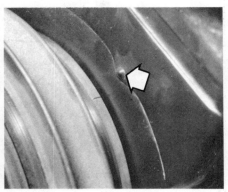

37.3 Notch on crankshaft pulley aligned
with pip on timing belt lower cover
(arrowed)

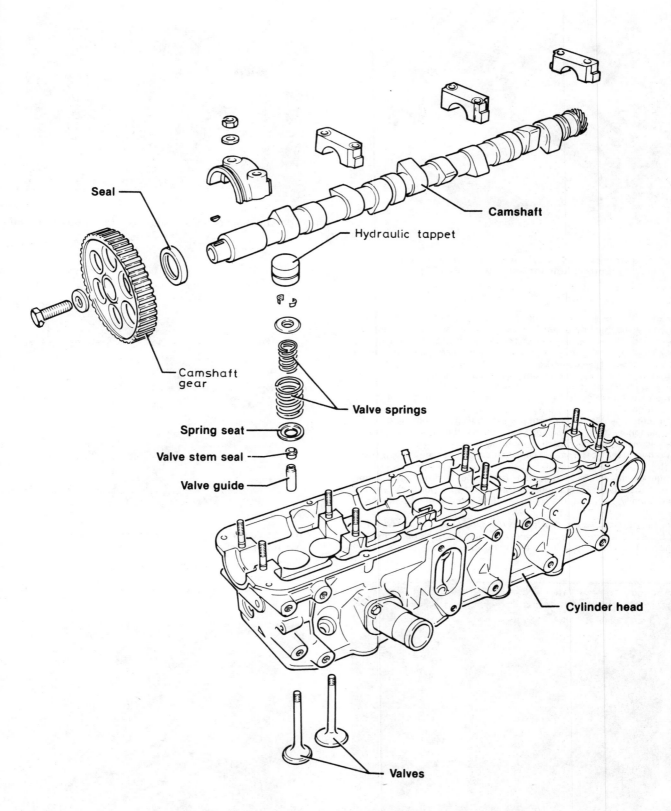

Seal

Camshaft

Hydraulic tappet

Camshaft
gear

Valve springs

Spring seat

Valve stem seal

Valve guide

Cylinder head

Valves

Fig. 1.18 Exploded view of the cylinder head and valve gear (Sec 37)

Fig. 1.19 Crankshaft pulley notch aligned with pointer on oil pump housing – arrowed (Sec 37)

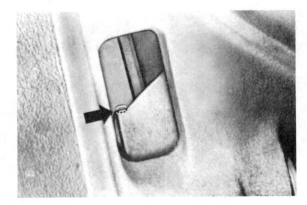

Fig. 1.20 Flywheel O mark aligned with bellhousing pointer (Sec 37)

aligned with the pointer in the bellhousing aperture. Both No 1 cylinder valves must be closed (ie cam peaks away from the tappets) and the indentation on the rear of the camshaft gear in line with the upper surface of the valve cover gasket (temporarily refit the gasket and valve cover, if necessary).

4 Loosen the water pump mounting and adjustment bolts and rotate the pump clockwise to release the tension on the timing belt.

5 Remove the timing belt from the camshaft gear and move it to one side (photo).

6 Unscrew the centre bolt from the camshaft gear while holding the gear stationary with a bar through one of the holes or using a wide-bladed screwdriver, as shown in Fig. 1.22.

7 Withdraw the gear from the camshaft and extract the Woodruff key (photo).

8 Check that each bearing cap has its number stamped on it; if not, make an identifying mark to ensure that each cap is put back where it was originally. Note that the caps are offset and can only be fitted one way round.

9 *It is important that the camshaft is removed exactly as described so that there is no danger of it becoming distorted.* Loosen one of the nuts on bearing cap No 2 about two turns and then loosen the diagonally

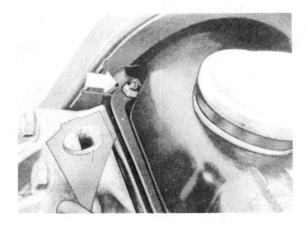

Fig. 1.21 Camshaft gear indentation (arrowed) aligned with upper surface of valve cover gasket (Sec 37)

37.5 Removing the timing belt from the camshaft gear. Belt marked to show fitted running direction

Fig. 1.22 Using a wide-bladed screwdriver to hold the camshaft gear stationary (Sec 37)

37.7 Camshaft gear Woodruff key (arrowed)

37.10 Removing the camshaft

37.11 Removing a tappet

opposite nut on bearing cap No 4 about two turns. Repeat the operations on the other nut of bearing cap No 2 and bearing cap No 4. Continue the sequence until the nuts are free, then remove them. Loosen and remove the nuts of bearing caps Nos 1 and 3 using a similar diagonal sequence.

10 Lift the bearing caps off and lift the camshaft out (photo). Discard the oil seal.

11 Withdraw each tappet in turn (photo) and mark its position (1 to 10 numbering from the timing belt end of the engine) using adhesive tape or a box with divisions. Take care to keep the adjustment shims with their respective tappets (where fitted). On engines with hydraulic tappets, store the tappets upside down once they have been removed from the engine.

38 Cylinder head removal – engine in car

All models except Turbo

1 Disconnect the battery negative lead.
2 Drain the cooling system, as described in Chapter 2.
3 Remove the radiator grille (Chapter 11) and the upper radiator cowl.

4 Remove the air cleaner, as described in Chapter 3, and the front intake ducts on fuel injection models.
5 Refer to Chapter 12 and remove the alternator drivebelt.
6 On models equipped with air conditioning, remove the compressor, as described in Chapter 11, leaving the refrigerant hoses connected. Secure the compressor to one side without straining the hoses.
7 Refer to Chapter 10 and remove the power-assisted steering pump, but leave the hydraulic pipes connected. Secure the pump to one side without straining the hoses.
8 Remove the radiator top hose and any heater hose connections or clips likely to impede cylinder head removal.
9 Identify all fuel and vacuum hoses using masking tape and disconnect those affecting cylinder head removal. These will include, where applicable:

Carburettor models: Fuel lines at fuel pump, return line at return valve, vacuum pipes at vacuum reservoir, econometer and distributor
Fuel injection models: Fuel hoses at the metering distributor (photo), cold start valve (photo) and warm-up valve (photo), vacuum hoses at econometer, throttle valve housing and distributor as well as any additional emission control components (see Chapter 3)

38.9A Disconnect the fuel lines at the metering distributor ...

38.9B ... cold start valve ...

38.9C ... and warm-up valve

10 Identify all wiring for location using masking tape, then disconnect those affecting cylinder head removal. These will include, where applicable:

Wiring to temperature sender (photo), distributor, coil, gearchange indicator, thermo-switches, idle stabiliser, thermotime switch, cold start valve, throttle switch (photo), intake temperature sender, automatic choke, inlet manifold preheater and additional emission control components (see Chapter 3)

11 Pull off the spark plug HT leads, remove the HT lead holder from the valve cover and remove the leads and distributor cap (photo).
12 On fuel injection models, slacken the hose clips and lift away the complete idle stabiliser valve and hose assembly (photo).
13 Refer to Chapter 3 and disconnect the accelerator cable and, where applicable, the cruise control linkage.
14 On automatic transmission models refer to Chapters 3 and 7 and disconnect the throttle and accelerator pedal cables and linkage.
15 Disconnect the earth braid at the rear of the valve cover.
16 On fuel injection models, slacken the clip and withdraw the air duct from the throttle valve housing.
17 Disconnect the exhaust front pipe at the manifold and transmission bracket.

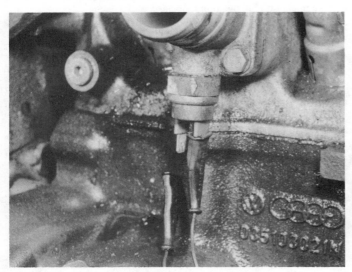

38.10A Disconnect the wiring at the temperature sender and ...

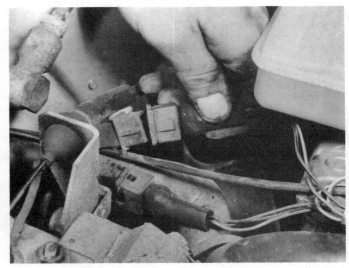

38.10B ... throttle switch

38.11 Removing the distributor cap and leads

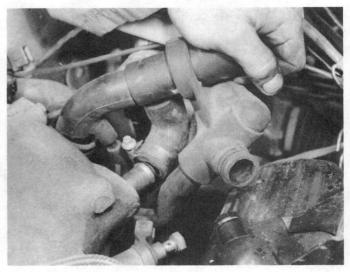

38.12 Removing the idle stabiliser valve assembly

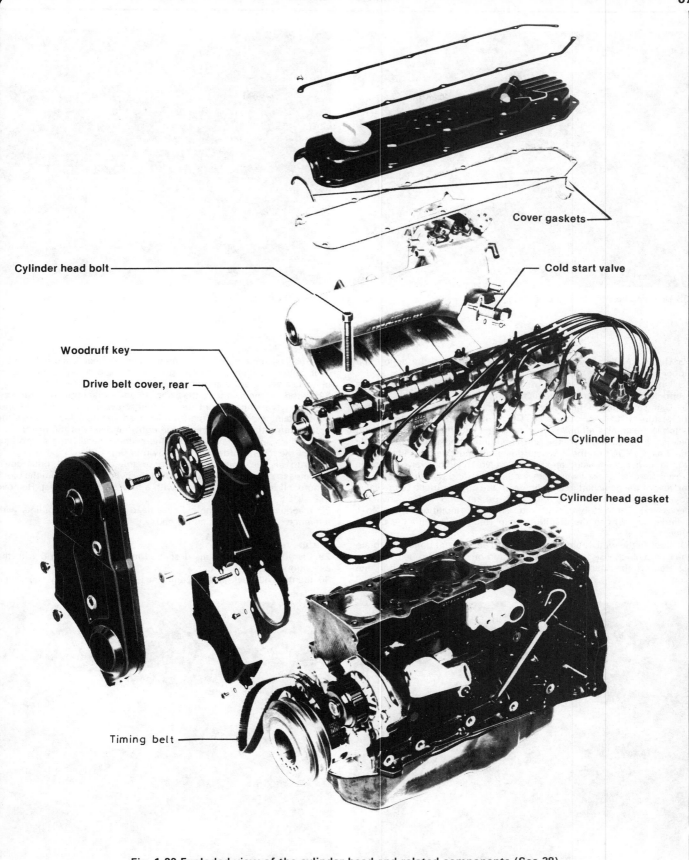

Cover gaskets

Cylinder head bolt

Cold start valve

Woodruff key

Drive belt cover, rear

Cylinder head

Cylinder head gasket

Timing belt

Fig. 1.23 Exploded view of the cylinder head and related components (Sec 38)

38.18 Removing the timing belt upper cover

38.19 Lift off the valve cover and reinforcement strips

18 Using an Allen key, unscrew the nuts and lift off the timing belt upper cover. Remove the distance pieces (photo).
19 Unscrew the nuts and lift off the valve cover, together with the reinforcement strips and gaskets (photo).
20 Using a socket on the crankshaft pulley bolt, turn the engine so that the piston in No 1 cylinder is at TDC on its compression stroke. The notch in the crankshaft pulley must be in line with the pip on the timing belt lower cover or the pointer on the oil pump housing – alternatively the 0 mark (TDC) on the flywheel/driveplate must be aligned with the pointer in the bellhousing aperture. Both No 1 cylinder valves must be closed (ie cam peaks away from the tappets) and the indentation on the rear of the camshaft gear in line with the upper surface of the valve cover gasket (temporarily refit the gasket and valve cover, if necessary). The distributor rotor arm should be pointing to the No 1 cylinder segment in the distributor cap (temporarily refit the cap to check).
21 Loosen the water pump mounting and adjustment bolts, and rotate the pump clockwise to release the tension on the timing belt.
22 Remove the timing belt from the camshaft gear and move it to one side.

23 Unscrew the centre bolt from the camshaft gear while holding the gear stationary with a bar through one of the holes or using a wide bladed screwdriver, as shown in Fig. 1.22.
24 Withdraw the gear from the camshaft and extract the Woodruff key.
25 Using two nuts locked together, unscrew the timing belt upper cover retaining stud from the cylinder head (photo). Also remove the bolt securing the inner cover to the right-hand side of the head.
26 Using a splined key, unscrew the cylinder head bolts a turn at a time in the reverse order to that shown in Fig. 1.25.
27 With all the bolts removed, ease the timing belt inner cover forwards to clear the camshaft, and lift the cylinder head from the block (photo). If it is stuck, tap it free with a hide or plastic mallet. Remove the gasket.
28 If required, remove the cylinder head ancillary components with reference to the Chapters concerned.

Turbo models
29 Carry out the operations described in paragraphs 1 to 8 with the exception of paragraph 4.
30 Identify all fuel and vacuum hoses using masking tape, and

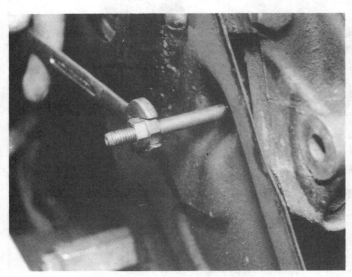

38.25 Unscrew the timing belt cover retaining stud

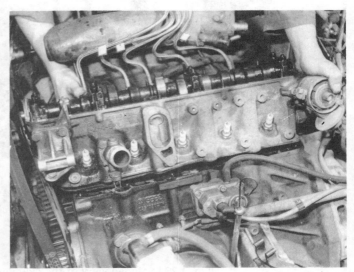

38.27 Removing the cylinder head

disconnect those affecting cylinder head removal. These will include, where applicable:

Fuel hoses at the metering distributor, cold start valve and warm-up valve, vacuum hoses at cruise control, econometer, throttle valve housing, and distributor, also any additional emission control components (see Chapter 3)

31 Identify all wiring for location using masking tape, and disconnect those affecting cylinder head removal. These will include, where applicable:

Wiring to temperature sender, distributor, coil, gearchange indicator, thermo-switch, idle stabliser, thermotime switch, cold start valve, throttle valve switch and injector cooling fan thermo-switch, also any additional emission control components (see Chapter 3)

32 Refer to Chapter 3 and disconnect the accelerator cable and the cruise control linkage.
33 On automatic transmission models refer to Chapters 3 and 7 and disconnect the throttle and accelerator pedal cables and linkage.
34 Pull off the spark plug HT leads, remove the HT lead holder from the valve cover, and remove the leads and distributor cap.
35 Remove the injector cooling fan duct over the valve cover.
36 Remove the air temperature sensor from the throttle valve housing. Seal the manifold opening, and cover the sensor with a protective cap.
37 Slacken the clips, and remove the air duct from the airflow sensor and intake tube.
38 Unclip the air cleaner cover and remove it complete with the intake tube.
39 Remove the connecting hose from the intercooler to the throttle body.
40 Disconnect the idle stabiliser hose at the intercooler, remove the hose between intercooler and turbo, then remove the intercooler.
41 Disconnect the exhaust front pipe at the turbo unit flange.
42 Disconnect the exhaust corrugated branch pipe at the front pipe flange.
43 Release the exhaust front pipe at the transmission bracket.
44 Disconnect any additional oil and water pipes to the turbo or related components likely to impede removal. The turbo and manifolds remain attached to the cylinder head during removal.
45 Carry out the remaining operations as described in paragraphs 18 to 28 inclusive.

39 Cylinder head removal – engine on bench

The procedure for removing the cylinder head with the engine on the bench is similar to that for removal when the engine is in the car, with the exception of disconnecting the controls and services. Refer to Section 38 and follow the procedure given as applicable.

40 Valves – removal and renovation

1 Remove the camshaft and tappets, as described in Section 37, and the cylinder head, as described in Section 38 or 39.
2 Follow the procedure given in Section 11, – inlet valves are 2-4-5-7-9 and exhaust valves are 1-3-6-8-10, numbered from the timing belt end of the engine.
3 *Note that on certain engines sodium filled exhaust valves are used for reasons of heat dissipation. If any of these valves are renewed, the old valves must be rendered safe by removing the sodium before discarding the valve. This is a potentiallly dangerous operation and must only be carried out by an Audi dealer.*

41 Cylinder head – examination and renovation

Refer to Section 12 of this Chapter.

42 Camshaft and bearings – examination and renovation

1 Refer to Section 13 of this Chapter.
2 Check that the oil spray jets located in the top of the cylinder head direct spray at 90° to the camshaft.

Fig. 1.24 Correct position of the oil spray jets (arrowed) in the cylinder head (Sec 42)

3 On engines equipped with hydraulic tappets, renew any tappets that were noisy in service. To check the tappets with the engine installed, run the engine until the cooling fan operates at least once. Increase the engine speed to 2500 rpm for two minutes, then return it to idling speed. Any tappets which are now still noisy should be renewed.

43 Valves – refitting

Refer to Section 14 of this Chapter.

44 Cylinder head – refitting

1 Check that the top of the block is perfectly clean, then locate a new gasket on it with the part number or TOP marking facing upward (photos).
2 Check that the cylinder head face is perfectly clean. Insert two long rods, or pieces of dowel into the cylinder head bolt holes at opposite ends of the block, to position the gasket and to give a location for fitting the cylinder head. Lower the head on to the block, remove the guide dowels and insert the bolts and washers. Do not use jointing compound on the cylinder head joint (photo).

44.1A Locate a new gasket on the block ...

44.1B ... with the part number uppermost ...

44.2 ... then lower the cylinder head onto the block

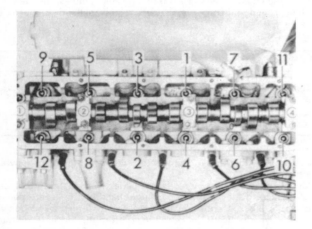

Fig. 1.25 Cylinder head tightening sequence (Sec 44)

3   Tighten the bolts using the sequence shown in Fig. 1.25 in the three stages given in the Specifications to the specified torque.

4   Secure the timing belt inner cover to the cylinder head (where applicable), with the bolt on the right-hand side and the upper cover retaining stud (photo).

5   Fit the Woodruff key in its groove and locate the gear on the end of the camshaft (photo).

6   Fit the centre bolt and spacer and tighten the bolt to the specified torque while holding the gear stationary with a bar through one of the holes, or using a wide-bladed screwdriver as shown in Fig. 1.22.

7   Turn the camshaft gear and align the rear indentation with the upper surface of the valve cover gasket (temporarily locate the gasket on the head).

8   Check that No 1 piston is at TDC with the O mark on the flywheel aligned with the pointer in the bellhousing aperture. The notch in the crankshaft pulley will also be in line with the pointer on the oil pump housing or timing belt lower cover.

9   Locate the timing belt on the crankshaft, camshaft and water pump gears, turn the water pump anti-clockwise to pre-tension the belt, then check that the TDC timing marks are still aligned.

10 With the upper radiator cowl removed (if engine is in the car) use a

44.4 Timing belt inner cover stud and retaining bolt locations (arrowed)

44.5 Refit the camshaft gear

screwdriver, to turn the water pump anti-clockwise and tension the timing belt until it can just be twisted 90° with the thumb and index finger midway between the camshaft and water pump gears. Tighten the water pump mounting and adjustment bolts when the adjustment is correct (photo).

11 Refit the cylinder head ancillary components with reference to the Chapters concerned.

12 If the engine is in the car, carry out the operations in reverse order described in Section 38, paragraphs 1 to 19 for all models except Turbo and paragraphs 29 to 45 for Turbo models.

13 Adjust the valve clearances, as described in Section 46, on completion, except on engines with hydraulic tappets.

45 Camshaft and tappets – refitting

1 Fit the bucket tappets in their original positions – the adjustment shims on the top of the tappets must be fitted so that the lettering on them is downwards (photos). Lubricate the tappets and the camshaft journals.

2 Lay the camshaft into the lower half of its bearings so that the lowest point of the cams of No 1 cylinder are towards the tappets, then fit the bearing caps in their original positions, making sure that they are the right way round before fitting them over the studs (photo).

3 Fit the nuts to bearing caps Nos 2 and 4 and tighten them in diagonal sequence until the camshaft fully enters its bearings.

4 Fit the nuts to bearing caps 1 and 3, then tighten all the nuts to the specified torque in diagonal sequence.

5 Smear a little oil onto the sealing lip and outer edge of the camshaft oil seal, then locate it open end first in the cylinder head and No 1 camshaft bearing cap.

6 Using a metal tube drive the seal squarely into the cylinder head until flush with the front of the cylinder head – *do not drive it in further otherwise it will block the oil return hole.*

7 Carry out the operations described in paragraphs 5 to 10 inclusive of Section 44.

8 Refit the timing belt upper cover.

9 Check and if necessary adjust the valve clearances, as described in Section 46.

10 Refit the valve cover and reinforcement strips, together with the HT lead holder, new gaskets and seals and tighten the nuts.

11 If the engine is in the car, reverse the preliminary procedures given in Section 37.

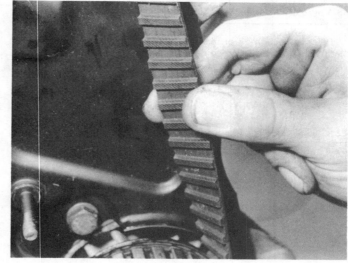

44.10 Checking timing belt tension

45.1A Refit the tappets to their original locations ...

45.1B ... and fit the shims with their size marking towards the tappet

45.2 Fitting the camshaft bearings

46 Valve clearances – checking and adjustment

Refer to Section 17 of this Chapter. The procedure is identical to that for the four-cylinder engine with the following exceptions:

 (a) It is not necessary to remove the timing belt cover
 (b) From the timing belt end of the engine the inlet valves are numbered 2-4-5-7-9, and the exhaust valves 1-3-6-8-10
 (c) It is not necessary to adjust the valve clearances on engines with hydraulic tappets

47 Timing belt and gears – removal and refitting

Note: *If the engine is still in the car, first carry out the following operations:*

 (a) Disconnect the battery negative lead
 (b) Remove the radiator grille, ventilation grille and upper radiator cowl

 (c) Remove the alternator, air conditioning and power-assisted steering drivebelts as applicable (Chapters 12, 11 and 10 respectively)
 (d) On Turbo models remove the intercooler (Chapter 3)

1   Using Audi tool 2084 lock the vibration damper on the front of the crankshaft stationary, then using Audi tool 2079 loosen the centre bolt. The bolt is tightened to a high torque and it is recommended that these tools are used if at all possible.
2   Carry out the operations described in paragraphs 2 to 7 of Section 37, but remove the timing belt upper and lower covers.
3   Unscrew the centre bolt and withdraw the vibration damper, together with the crankshaft gear and timing belt.
4   On later 1.9 litre engines remove the idler pulley by undoing the bolt and withdrawing the pulley using a puller (Figs. 1.27 and 1.28).
5   Locate the timing belt on the crankshaft gear, then refit the gear and vibration damper, followed by the idler pulley (where applicable) (photo).
6   Coat the threads of the centre bolt with a liquid locking agent then insert the bolt and tighten it while holding the crankshaft stationary. *Note that the torque wrench setting given for this bolt is only*

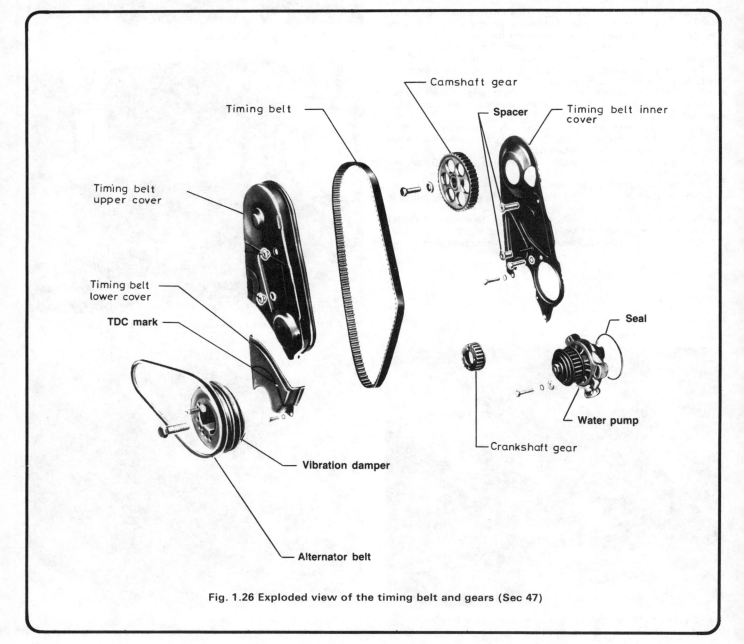

Fig. 1.26 Exploded view of the timing belt and gears (Sec 47)

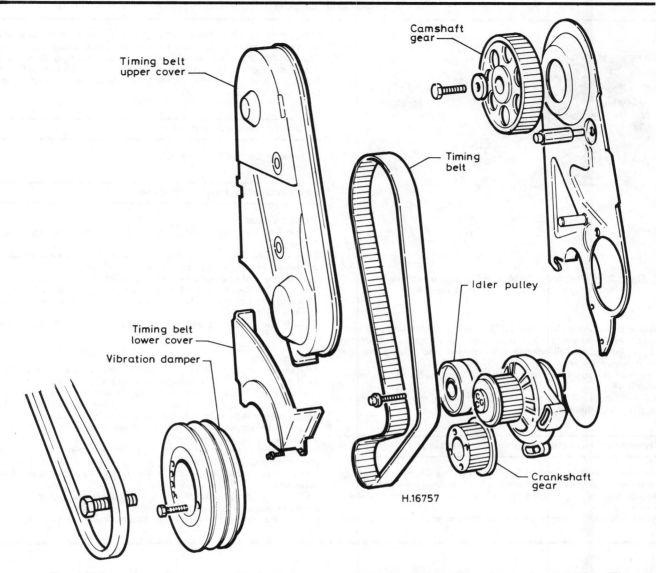

Camshaft gear

Timing belt upper cover

Timing belt

Timing belt lower cover

Idler pulley

Vibration damper

Crankshaft gear

H.16757

Fig. 1.27 Exploded view of the timing belt, gears and idler pulley fitted to later 1.9 litre engines (Sec 47)

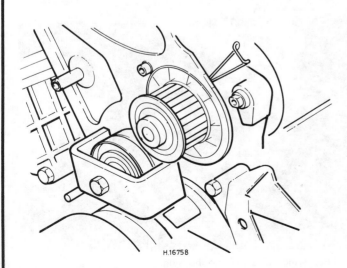

H.16758

Fig. 1.28 Using a puller to remove the idler pulley – 1.9 litre engines (Sec 47)

47.5 Refitting the crankshaft gear and vibration damper

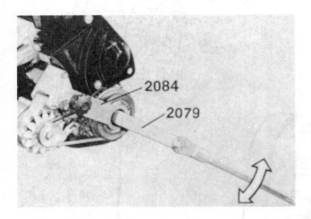

Fig. 1.29 Using tools 2084 and 2079 to unscrew the vibration damper centre bolt (Sec 47)

applicable when using Audi tool 2079. If you are not using this tool tighten the bolt to at least the specified torque, and have an Audi dealer check its tightness. (The special tool increases the leverage of the standard torque wrench).

7   Carry out the operations described in paragraphs 5 to 10 inclusive of Section 44.
8   If the engine is still in the car, reverse the preliminary procedures at the beginning of this Section.

48 Flywheel/driveplate – removal and refitting

1   The procedure is as given in Section 19 of this Chapter. However, the retaining bolts may not be offset so the flywheel/driveplate and crankshaft should be marked in relation to each other before separation.
2   When refitting a driveplate note that the raised pip must face the

torque converter. If a replacement driveplate is to be fitted, its position must be checked and adjusted if necessary. The distance from the rear face of the block to the torque converter *mounting face* on the driveplate (Fig. 1.30) must be between 17.2 and 18.8 mm (0.667 and 0.740 in). If necessary, remove the driveplate and fit a spacer behind it to achieve the correct dimension.

49 Sump – removal and refitting

Refer to Section 21 of this Chapter.

50 Crankshaft oil seals – renewal

Front oil seal
1   Remove the timing belt and crankshaft gear, as described in Section 47.
2   If an extractor tool is available the seal may be renewed without removing the oil pump, otherwise refer to Section 51. It is also recommended that Audi tool 2080, together with a guide sleeve, be used to install the new seal. Dip the seal in engine oil before fitting, and if the old seal has scored the crankshaft, position the new seal on the unworn surface.
3   Refit the crankshaft gear and timing belt, as described in Section 47.

Rear oil seal
4   Remove the flywheel or driveplate, as described in Section 48.
5   If an extractor tool is available the seal may be renewed without removing the housing, otherwise unbolt and remove the housing (including the two sump bolts) and remove the gasket (photo). If the sump gasket is damaged while removing the housing it will be necessary to remove the sump and fit a new gasket. However, refit the sump *after* fitting the housing.
6   Drive the old seal out of the housing, then dip the new seal in engine oil and drive it into the housing with a block of wood or a socket, until flush. Make sure that the closed end of the seal is facing outwards.
7   Fit the housing, together with a new gasket, and tighten the bolts evenly in diagonal sequence.
8   Refit the flywheel or driveplate, as described in Section 48.

Fig. 1.30 Torque converter-to-cylinder block dimension checking faces – check in two places for average (Sec 48)

50.5 Removing the rear oil seal housing

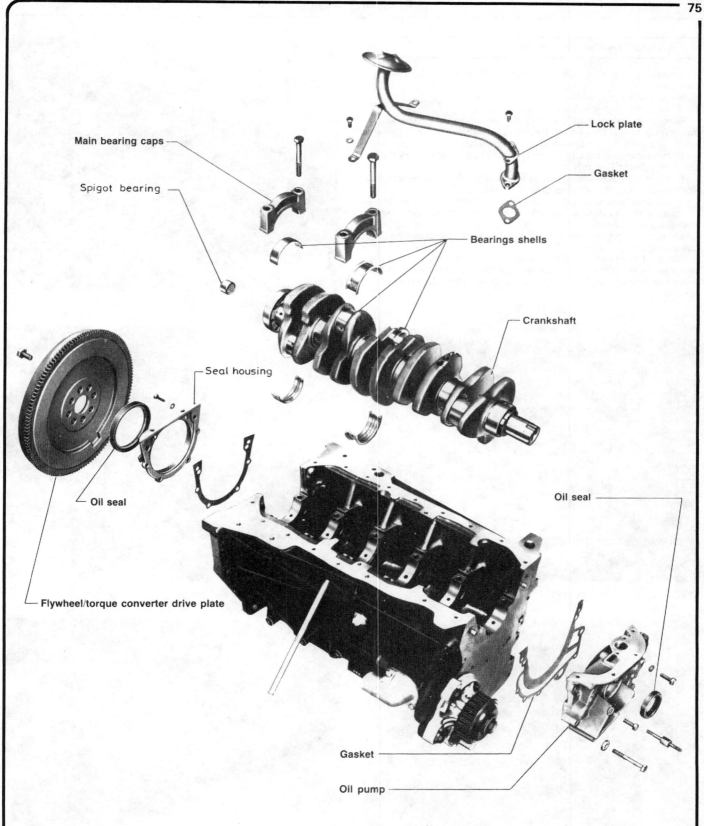

Main bearing caps

Spigot bearing

Lock plate

Gasket

Bearings shells

Crankshaft

Seal housing

Oil seal

Oil seal

Flywheel/torque converter drive plate

Gasket

Oil pump

Fig. 1.31 Exploded view of the crankshaft, main bearings and oil pump (Secs 50, 51 and 55)

51 Oil pump – removal, examination and refitting

1   Remove the timing belt and crankshaft gear, as described in Section 47.
2   Remove the sump, with reference to Section 49.
3   Remove the timing belt inner cover.
4   Remove the two bolts securing the oil intake pipe stay to the crankcase (photo). Knock back the tabs of the lockplate on the intake pipe flange, remove the bolts and the intake pipe.
5   Remove the bolts securing the oil pump (photo) and take off the oil pump and gasket (photo).
6   Remove the countersunk screws securing the pump backplate and lift the backplate off, exposing the gears (photo).
7   Check that there is a mark on the exposed face of the gears and if not, make a mark to show which side of the gears is towards the engine before removing them.
8   Unscrew the pressure relief valve and remove the plug, sealing ring, spring and plunger (photo).
9   Clean all the parts thoroughly and examine the pump casing and backplate for signs of wear or scoring. Examine the pressure relief valve plunger and its seating for damage and wear and check that the spring

51.4 Oil intake pipe and stay attachments (arrowed)

51.5A Remove the oil pump retaining bolts ...

51.5B ... and withdraw the pump

51.6 Removing the oil pump backplate

51.8 Removing the pressure relief valve components

is not damaged or distorted. Clean the gears for damage and wear. New gears may be fitted, but they must be fitted as a pair (photo).

10 Prise out the oil seal from the front of the pump (photo). Oil the lip of the new seal, enter the seal with its closed face outwards and use a block of wood to tap the seal in flush. If there is any scoring on the crankshaft in the area on which the lip of the seal bears, the seal may be pushed to the bottom of its recess so that the lip bears on an undamaged part of the crankshaft.

11 Reassemble the pump by fitting the gears and the backplate. The inner gear has its slotted end towards the crankshaft and although the outer gear can be fitted either way round, it should be fitted the same way round as it was before removal. Some gears have a triangle stamped on them and this mark should be towards the pump backplate (photo).

12 Refit the oil pump, together with a new gasket, making sure that the slot on the inner gear engages the dog on the crankshaft.

13 Insert the bolts and tighten them in diagonal sequence to the specified torque.

14 Fit the oil intake pipe, together with a new gasket, tighten the bolts, and bend the lockplate tabs onto the flange bolts (photo).

15 Refit the timing belt inner cover, sump (Section 49), and timing belt and crankshaft gear (Section 47).

52 Pistons and connecting rods – removal and dismantling

Refer to Section 24 of this Chapter. Removal of the cylinder head is described in Section 38, and the timing belt in Section 47. Instead of removing the oil pump, remove the sump, as described in Section 49, then unbolt the oil intake pipe, as described in Section 51.

53 Pistons and cylinder bores – examination

Refer to Section 25 of this Chapter.

54 Pistons and connecting rods – reassembly and refitting

Refer to Section 26 of this Chapter. With the pistons fitted, refit the oil intake pipe, together with a new gasket, tighten the bolts, and bend the lockplate tabs onto the flange bolts. Refitting of the sump is described in Section 49, the timing belt in Section 47 and the cylinder head in Section 44.

51.9 Examine the oil pump parts for wear or damage

51.10 Removing the front oil seal from the pump

51.11 Triangle mark (arrowed) on pump gear must face the backplate

51.14 Bend up the locktabs to secure the intake pipe bolts

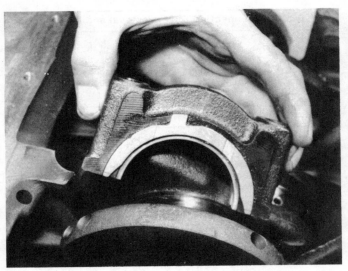

55.3A Crankshaft main bearing cap showing flanged thrust washers

55.3B Checking crankshaft endplay at No 4 main bearing

55 Crankshaft – removal, examination and refitting

1   With the engine removed from the car, remove the pistons and connecting rods, as described in Section 52. Keep the big-end bearings with their matching connecting rods to ensure correct refitting.
2   Remove the oil pump (Section 51) and rear oil seal complete with housing (Section 50).
3   Follow the procedure in Section 27 of this Chapter, paragraphs 4 to 13 inclusive (photos) but note the following exceptions:

   (a)   The flanged main bearing shells or thrust washers are fitted to main bearing No 4 (from the front of the engine)
   (b)   The needle roller bearing in the rear of the crankshaft must be pressed in to a depth of 5.5 mm (0.217 in) below the face of the flange

4   Fit the oil pump and rear oil seal housing complete with new seals, as described in Sections 51 and 50 respectively.
5   Refit the pistons and connecting rods, as described in Section 54.

56 Engine mountings – removal and refitting

1   Refer to Section 28 of this Chapter, but note that an additional snubber type front mounting is used on the five-cylinder engine. To remove the front mountings, first remove the alternator (Chapter 12), then undo the bolts and lift the mounting away. The mounting support, or snubber cup, is attached with bolts through the front body panel. Access to the nuts behind entails removal of the front bumper assembly (Chapter 11).

PART C – ALL ENGINES

57 Fault diagnosis – engine

Symptom	Reason(s)
Engine fails to start	Discharged battery Loose battery connection Loose or broken ignition leads Moisture on spark plugs, distributor cap, or HT leads Incorrect spark plug gap Cracked distributor cap or rotor arm Dirt or water in carburettor (where applicable) Empty fuel tank Faulty fuel pump Faulty starter motor Low cylinder compression Other fuel or ignition system fault (see Chapters 3 and 4)
Engine idles erratically	Intake manifold air leak Leaking cylinder head gasket Worn camshaft lobes Faulty fuel pump Incorrect valve clearances Loose crankcase ventilation hoses Idling adjustments incorrect Uneven cylinder compressions Other fuel or ignition system fault (see Chapters 3 and 4)
Engine misfires	Spark plug gap incorrect Faulty coil, condenser or transistorised ignition component (as applicable) Dirt or water in carburettor (where applicable) Burn out valve Leaking cylinder head gasket Distributor cap cracked Incorrect valve clearances Uneven cylinder compressions Idling adjustments incorrect Other fuel or ignition system fault (see Chapters 3 and 4)
Engine stalls	Idling adjustments incorrect Intake manifold air leak Ignition timing incorrect
Excessive oil consumption	Worn pistons and cylinder bores Valve guides and valve stem seals worn Oil leaking from crankshaft oil seals, valve cover gasket etc Other fuel or ignition system fault (see Chapters 3 and 4)
Engine backfires	Idling adjustments incorrect Ignition timing incorrect Incorrect valve clearances Intake manifold air leak Sticking valve Other fuel or ignition system fault (see Chapters 3 and 4)
Engine lacks power	Incorrect ignition timing Incorrect spark plug gap Low cylinder compression Excessive carbon build up in engine Air filter choked Other fuel or ignition system fault (see Chapters 3 and 4)

Chapter 2 Cooling system

Refer to Chapter 13 for information on 1987 and later models

Contents

Specifications

System type .... Pressurized radiator and expansion tank, belt driven water pump, thermostatically controlled electric cooling fan

Filler cap opening pressure .... 1.2 to 1.35 bar (17 to 19 lbf/in²)

Thermostat
Start-to-open temperature:
  Four-cylinder engines .... 85°C (185°F)
  Five-cylinder engines .... 87°C (188°F)
Fully open temperature:
  Four-cylinder engines .... 106°C (221°F)
  Five-cylinder engines .... 102°C (216°F)
Stroke (minimum) .... 7.0 mm (0.27 in)

Electric cooling fan thermoswitch operating temperatures
Switches on:
  All engines except five-cylinder for North America .... 93° to 98°C (199° to 208°F)
  Five-cylinder engines for North America .... 88° to 93°C (190° to 199°F)
Switches off:
  All engines except five-cylinder for North America .... 88° to 93°C (190° to 199°F)
  Five-cylinder engines for North America .... 82° to 86°C (180° to 186°F)

Antifreeze
Type .... Ethylene glycol with corrosion inhibitor
Concentration for protection down to: **Percent antifreeze by volume**
  -25°C (-14°F) 40
  -30°C (-22°F) 45
  -35°C (-31°F) 50

Torque wrench settings

	Nm	lbf ft
Radiator mountings (except five-cylinder upper support)	20	14
Radiator mountings (five-cylinder upper support)	10	7
Electric cooling fan and shroud	10	7
Air deflector shrouds	10	7
Thermo-switch	25	18
Water pump to engine	20	14
Water pump to housing (four-cylinder)	10	7
Water pump pulley (four-cylinder)	20	14
Thermostat cover	10	7
Cylinder head rear outlet (four-cylinder)	10	7

1 General description

The cooling system is of the pressurized, pump assisted, thermo-syphon type, and includes a front mounted (four-cylinder), or side mounted (five-cylinder) radiator, a water pump driven by an external V-belt on four-cylinder engines, or by the timing belt on five-cylinder engines, an electric cooling fan, and a remote expansion tank. The cooling system thermostat is located in the water pump housing on four-cylinder engines, and in the inlet on the left-hand side of the cylinder block on five-cylinder engines.

The system functions as follows. With the engine cold, the thermostat is shut and the water pump forces the water through the internal passages then via the bypass hose (and heater circuit if turned on) over the thermostat capsule and to the water pump inlet again.

This circulation of water cools the cylinder bores, combustion surfaces and valve seats. However, when the coolant reaches the predetermined temperature, the thermostat begins to open. The coolant now circulates through the top hose to the top of the radiator. As it passes through the radiator matrix it is cooled by the inrush of air when the car is in forward motion, supplemented by the action of the electric cooling fan when necessary. Finally the coolant is returned to the water pump via the bottom hose and through the open thermostat.

The electric cooling fan is controlled by a thermo-switch located in the bottom of the radiator. Water temperature is monitored by a sender unit in the cylinder head.

Note: *The electric cooling fan will operate when the temperature of the coolant in the radiator reaches a predetermined level even if the engine is not running. Therefore extreme caution should be exercised when working in the vicinity of the fan blades.*

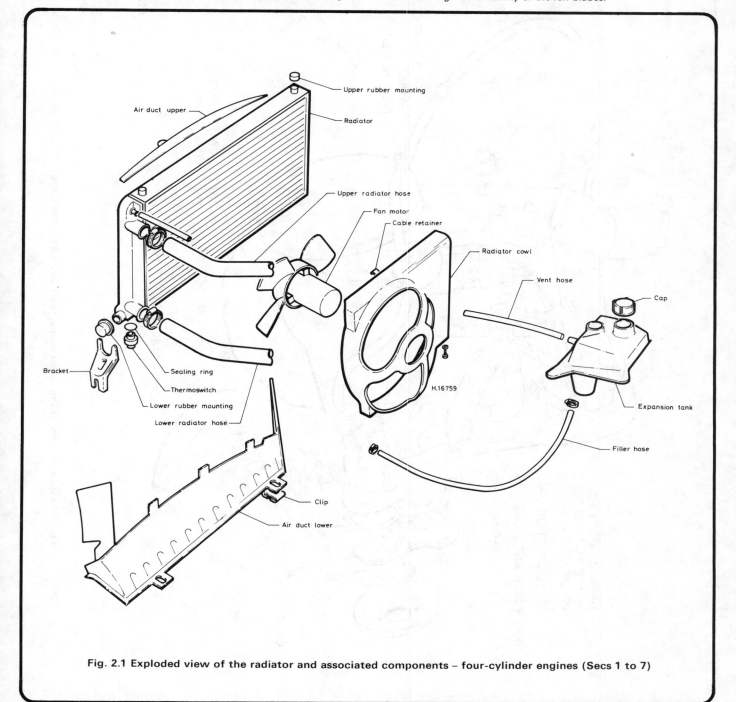

Fig. 2.1 Exploded view of the radiator and associated components – four-cylinder engines (Secs 1 to 7)

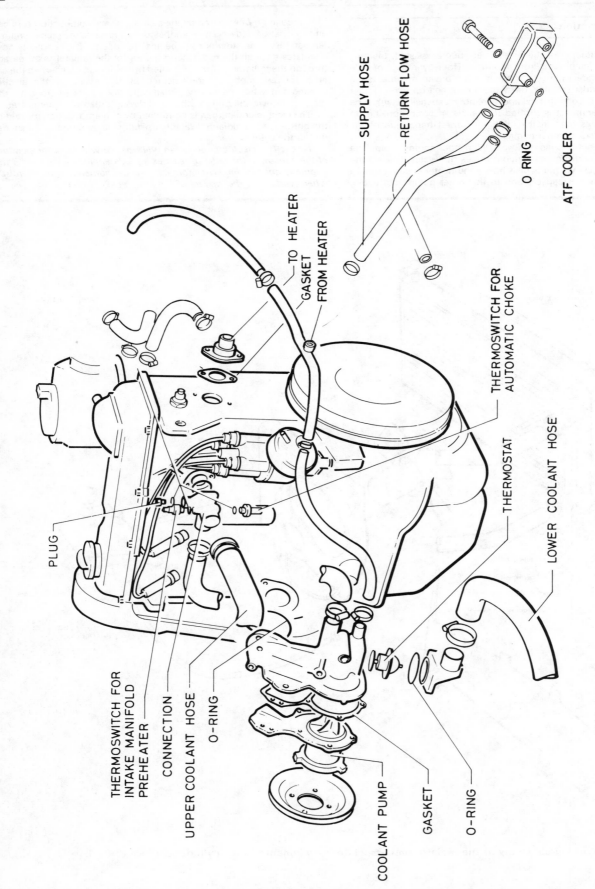

SUPPLY HOSE

RETURN FLOW HOSE

O RING

ATF COOLER

TO HEATER

GASKET

FROM HEATER

THERMOSWITCH FOR
AUTOMATIC CHOKE

THERMOSTAT

LOWER COOLANT HOSE

PLUG

THERMOSWITCH FOR
INTAKE MANIFOLD
PREHEATER

CONNECTION

UPPER COOLANT HOSE

O-RING

COOLANT PUMP

GASKET

O-RING

Fig. 2.2 Exploded view of the water pump, thermostat and hose layout – four-cylinder engines (Secs 1 to 11)

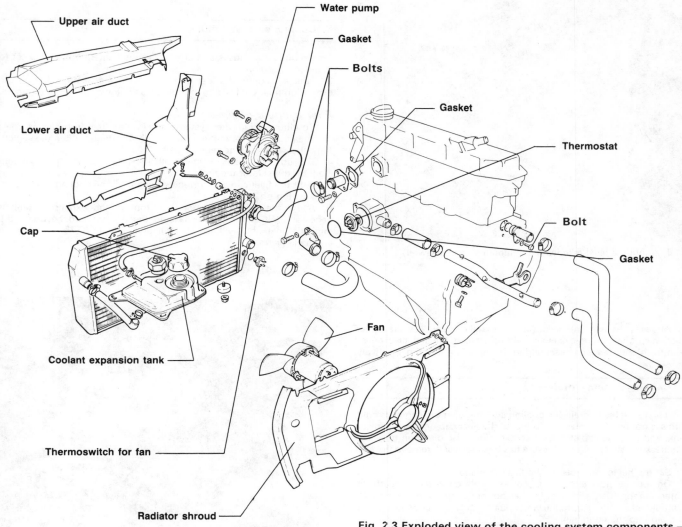

Fig. 2.3 Exploded view of the cooling system components –
five-cylinder models (Secs 1 to 11)

2 Maintenance and inspection

1   Check the coolant level in the system weekly and, if necessary, top up with a water and antifreeze mixture until the level is up to the mimumum mark indicated on the expansion tank (photos). Check the level with the engine switched off, and only top up when the engine is cold. (If the engine is warm the level may be slightly higher). With a sealed type cooling system, topping-up should only be necessary at very infrequent intervals. If this is not the case and frequent topping-up is required, it is likely that there is a leak in the system. Check all hoses and joint faces for any staining or actual wetness, and rectify if necessary. If no leaks can be found it is advisable to have the system pressure tested, as the leak could possibly be internal.

2   At the service intervals given in Routine Maintenance at the beginning of this manual, carefully inspect all the hoses, hose clips and visible joint gaskets of the system for cracks, corrosion, deterioration or leakage. Renew any hoses and clips which are suspect, and also renew any gaskets, if necessary.

3   At the same service interval, check the condition of the alternator and water pump drivebelt on four-cylinder engines. Renew the belt if there is any sign of cracking or fraying and also check, and if necessary adjust, the drivebelt tension. These procedures are covered in Chapter 12.

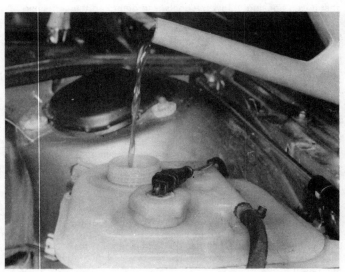

2.1A Top up the expansion tank ...

2.1B ... until the level reaches the minimum mark (arrowed)

4   At less frequent intervals (approximately every 2 years – see Section 6), the cooling system should be drained, flushed, and refilled with fresh antifreeze, as described in Sections 3, 4 and 5 respectively.

3   Cooling system – draining

1   It is preferable to drain the cooling system when the engine is cold. If this is not possible, place a cloth over the filler cap on the expansion tank, and turn the cap slowly in an anti-clockwise direction to relieve the pressure. When all the pressure has been released, remove the filler cap.
2   Set the heater controls on the facia to warm.
3   On four-cylinder engines, place a suitable container beneath the water pump, then disconnect the bottom hose and heater/inlet manifold return hoses from the water pump housing. Allow the coolant to drain into the container.
4   On five-cylinder engines, place a suitable container beneath the hose connections on the left-hand side of the engine. Unscrew the bolt securing the heater return pipe to the cylinder block, then disconnect the pipe from the hose. Also disconnect the radiator bottom hose at the thermostat housing. Allow the coolant to drain into the container.
5   On four-cylinder engines, slacken the thermotime switch located on the cylinder head outlet housing, after disconnecting the wiring plug.

4   Cooling system – flushing

1   After some time the radiator and engine waterways may become restricted or even blocked with scale or sediment. When this occurs the coolant will appear rusty and dark in colour and the system should then be flushed. In severe cases, reverse flushing may also be required.
2   Drain the cooling system, as described in Section 3.
3   Disconnect the top hose from the radiator, insert a hose in the radiator and allow water to circulate through the matrix and out of the bottom of the radiator until it runs clear.
4   Insert the hose in the expansion tank and allow the water to run through the supply hose.
5   In severe cases of contamination remove the radiator, invert it, and flush it with water until it runs clear.
6   To flush the engine and heater, insert a hose in the top hose and allow the water to circulate through the system until it runs clear from the return hose.
7   The use of chemical cleaners should only be necessary as a last

resort, and the regular renewal of antifreeze should prevent the contamination of the system.

5   Cooling system – filling

1   Reconnect all hoses and check that the heater controls are set to the warm position.
2   Pour a mixture of water and antifreeze (see Section 6) into the expansion tank until full, then proceed as follows according to model.

Four-cylinder engines
3   Continue filling the system until water free from air bubbles emerges from the thermotime switch (photo), then tighten the switch. Refit the switch wiring plug.
4   Top up the expansion tank until the level reaches the minimum mark on the side of the tank.
5   Refit the filler cap and run the engine until the cooling fan cuts in, then switch off.
6   Allow the engine to cool then top up the expansion tank if necessary. When the engine is cold the level should be up to the minimum mark, but will rise approximately 20 mm (0.75 in) when the engine is warm.

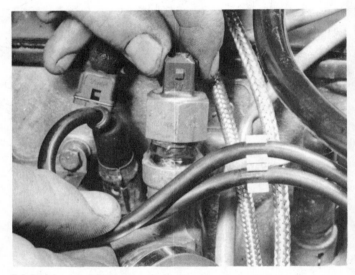

5.3 Purging air from the cooling system by slackening the thermotime switch (four-cylinder engines)

Five-cylinder engines
7   Start the engine and add coolant as necessary until the level remains constant, then refit the expansion tank filler cap.
8   Allow the engine to run until the cooling fan cuts in, then switch off.
9   When the engine is cool, top up the expansion tank until the level reaches the minimum mark on the side of the tank. The level will rise approximately 20 mm (0.75 in) when the engine is warm.

6   Antifreeze mixture

1   The cooling system is filled at the factory with an antifreeze mixture which contains a corrosion inhibitor. The antifreeze mixture prevents freezing, raises the boiling point of the coolant and so delays the tendency of the coolant to boil, while the corrosion inhibitor reduces corrosion and the formation of scale. For these reasons the cooling system should be filled with antifreeze all the year round.

2 Any good quality antifreeze is suitable, providing it is of the ethylene glycol type and also contains corrosion inhibitors. Do not use an antifreeze preparation based on methanol, because these mixtures have the disadvantage of being inflammable, together with a high rate of evaporation.

3 The concentration of antifreeze should be adjusted to give the required level of protection selected from the table given in the Specifications.

4 When topping-up the cooling system always use the same mixture of water and antifreeze which the system contains. Topping-up using water only will gradually reduce the antifreeze concentration and lower the level of protection against both freezing and boiling.

5 At the beginning of the winter season, check the coolant for antifreeze concentration and add pure antifreeze if necessary.

6 Antifreeze mixture should not be left in the system for longer than its manufacturers' recommendation, which does not usually exceed two years. At the end of this time drain the system and refill with fresh mixture. **Note:** *Do not use engine antifreeze in the screen washer system as it will cause damage to the vehicle paintwork. Screen washer antifreeze is available from most accessory shops.*

7 Radiator – removal, inspection, cleaning and refitting

1 Disconnect the battery negative terminal.
2 Drain the cooling system, as described in Section 3.

Four-cylinder engines

3 Slacken the clips and disconnect the top and bottom hoses and expansion tank hoses at the radiator.
4 Disconnect the wiring at the electric cooling fan and at the thermo-switch.

5 Undo the lower mounting bracket retaining bolts and remove the brackets.
6 Disengage the radiator from its upper mountings, then lift the unit, complete with cooling fan and cowl, upwards and out of the engine compartment.
7 If necessary unbolt the cooling fan and cowl from the radiator, then unscrew the nuts and separate the fan and motor from the cowl.

Five-cylinder engines

8 Undo the retaining screws and remove the radiator upper cowl (photo).
9 Slacken the clips and disconnect the top and bottom radiator hoses and the expansion tank hoses.
10 Disconnect the wiring at the electric cooling fan and at the thermo-switch (photo).
11 From under the car, undo the bolts securing the air deflector cowl to the radiator, and the nut securing the lower mountings to their brackets (photo).
12 Undo the upper mounting nuts and lift the radiator, complete with cooling fan and cowl, upwards and out of the engine compartment (photos).
13 If necessary unbolt the cooling fan and cowl from the radiator, then unscrew the nuts and separate the fan and motor from the cowl.

All models

14 Radiator repair is best left to a specialist, although minor leaks can be stopped using a proprietary coolant additive. Clear the radiator matrix of flies and small leaves with a soft brush or by hosing.
15 Reverse flush the radiator, as described in Section 4 and renew the hoses and clips if they are damaged or have deteriorated.
16 Refitting is a reversal of removal, and fill the cooling system as described in Section 5. If the thermo-switch is removed, fit a new sealing washer when refitting it.

7.8 Undo the retaining screws (arrowed) and remove the radiator upper cowl (five-cylinder engines)

7.10 Disconnect the wiring plug (arrowed) at the electric cooling fan (five-cylinder engines)

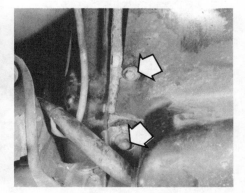

7.11 Radiator lower mounting and air deflector retaining nuts – arrowed (five-cylinder engines)

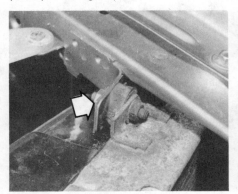

7.12A Radiator upper mounting ...

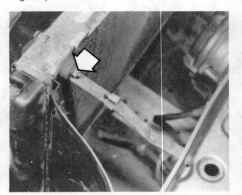

7.12B ... and upper mounting stay (five-cylinder engines)

7.12C Radiator removal (five-cylinder engines)

8 Thermostat – removal, testing and refitting

1   On four-cylinder engines the thermostat is located in the bottom of the water pump housing, but on five-cylinder engines it is located behind the water pump on the left-hand side of the cylinder block.

2   To remove the thermostat first drain the cooling system, as described in Section 3.

3   Unbolt and remove the thermostat cover, and remove the sealing ring (photos).

4   Prise the thermostat from its housing (photo).

5   To test whether the unit is serviceable, suspend it with a piece of string in a container of water. Gradually heat the water and note the temperatures at which the thermostat starts to open and is fully open. Remove the thermostat from the water and check that it is fully closed when cold. Renew the thermostat if it fails to operate in accordance with the information given in the Specifications.

6   Clean the thermostat housing and cover faces, and locate a new sealing ring on the cover (four-cylinder engines). On five-cylinder engines, fit a new sealing ring to the thermostat and fit the thermostat in its housing (photo).

7   Fit the thermostat cover and tighten the bolts evenly.

8   Fill the cooling system, as described in Section 5.

8.3A Removing the thermostat cover (four-cylinder engines)

8.3B Thermostat cover and sealing ring (four-cylinder engines)

8.3C Thermostat cover removal (five-cylinder engines)

8.4 Removing the thermostat (four-cylinder engines)

8.6 Fit a new sealing ring to the thermostat (five-cylinder engines)

9.4 Hose connections at the rear of the water pump housing (four-cylinder engines)

9.6A Water pump assembly removal (four-cylinder engines)

9.6B Water pump housing sealing ring (four-cylinder engines)

9 Water pump – removal and refitting

1 Drain the cooling system, as described in Section 3.

Four-cylinder engines

2 Remove the alternator and drivebelt, as described in Chapter 12.

3 Unbolt the pulley from the water pump drive flange.

4 Loosen the clips and disconnect the hoses from the rear of the water pump housing (photo).

5 Unscrew the nut and remove the special bolt retaining the lower timing cover to the water pump assembly.

6 Unbolt the water pump assembly from the cylinder block and remove the sealing ring (photos).

7 Unscrew the bolts and remove the water pump from its housing using a mallet to break the seal. Remove the gasket.

Five-cylinder engines

8 Remove the alternator drivebelt, as described in Chapter 12, and where fitted the air conditioning compressor drivebelt, as described in Chapter 11.

9 Remove the power steering pump, leaving the hoses connected, and place it to one side. Refer to Chapter 10 if necessary.

10 Using an Allen key where necessary, unscrew the nuts and lift off the timing belt outer cover.

11 Slacken but do not remove the bolt securing the camshaft gear to the camshaft. Hold the gear stationary during removal using a screwdriver engaged with one of the teeth and resting against the belt cover retaining stud.

12 Set the engine on TDC compression for No 1 cylinder (refer to Chapter 1 if necessary).

13 Slacken the water pump mounting and adjustment bolts, again using an Allen key where necessary, and rotate the pump to release the tension on the timing belt. Slip the timing belt off the water pump and camshaft gears. **Do not** turn the camshaft or crankshaft with the timing belt removed.

14 Unscrew the camshaft gear retaining bolt and withdraw the gear.

15 Undo the bolts securing the water pump and timing belt inner cover to the engine.

16 Lift off the timing belt inner cover, then withdraw the water pump and remove the sealing ring (photo).

Fig. 2.4 Using a wide-bladed screwdriver to hold the camshaft gear stationary (Sec 9)

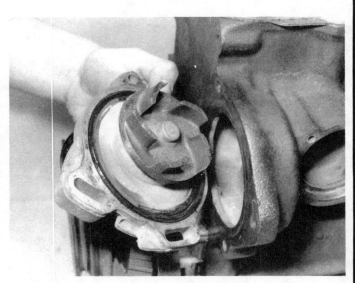

9.16 Removing the water pump and sealing ring (five-cylinder engines)

All models

17 If the water pump is faulty, renew it, as individual components are not available. Clean the mating faces of the water pump, cylinder block, and pump housing (four-cylinder engines).

18 Refitting is a reversal of the removal procedure, but use a new sealing ring or gasket as applicable. On five-cylinder engines check that the camshaft and crankshaft are still on TDC compression for No 1 cylinder and correctly tension the timing belt using the procedures described in Chapter 1.

19 Refit the power steering pump, air conditioning compressor, and alternator drivebelts as applicable with reference to Chapter 10, 11 and 12 respectively.

20 Fill the cooling system, as described in Section 5, on completion.

10 Cooling fan thermo-switch – testing, removal and refitting

1   If the thermo-switch located in the bottom of the radiator develops a fault, it is most likely to fail open circuit. This will cause the fan motor to remain stationary even though the coolant reaches the operating temperature.

2   To test the thermo-switch for an open circuit fault, disconnect the wiring and connect a length of wire or suitable metal object between the two terminals in the wiring plug. The fan should operate (even without the ignition switched on) in which case the thermo-switch is proved faulty and must be renewed.

3   To remove the thermo-switch first drain the cooling system, as described in Section 3.

4   Disconnect the battery negative terminal.

5   Disconnect the wiring, then unscrew the thermo-switch from the radiator and remove the sealing washer.

6   To check the operating temperature of the thermo-switch, suspend it in a pan of water so that only the screwed end of the switch is immersed and the electrical contacts are clear of the water. Either connect an ohmmeter between the switch terminals, or connect up a battery and bulb in series with the switch. With a thermometer placed in the pan, heat the water and note the temperature at which the switch contacts close, so that the ohmmeter reads zero, or the bulb lights. Allow the water to cool and note the temperature at which the switch contacts open. Discard the switch and fit a new one if the operating temperatures are not within the specified limits.

7   Refitting is a reversal of removal, but always fit a new sealing washer. Fill the cooling system, as described in Section 5.

11 Coolant temperature sender unit – removal and refitting

1   The temperature sender unit is located on the rear of the cylinder head. To remove it, first drain half of the cooling system, with reference to Section 3.

2   Disconnect the wiring and unscrew the sender unit from the connector or cylinder head, as applicable. Remove the sealing washer(s).

3   Refitting is a reversal of removal, but always renew the washer(s). Top up the cooling system, with reference to Section 5.

12 Fault diagnosis – cooling system

Symptom	Reason(s)
Overheating	Low coolant level
	Faulty pressure cap
	Thermostat sticking shut
	Drivebelt broken (four-cyl)
	Open circuit thermo-switch
	Faulty cooling fan motor
	Clogged radiator matrix
	Retarded ignition timing
Slow warm-up	Thermostat sticking open
	Short circuit thermo-switch
Coolant loss	Deteriorated hose
	Leaking water pump or cooling system joints
	Blown cylinder head gasket
	Leaking radiator
	Leaking core plugs

Chapter 3
Fuel, exhaust and emission control systems

Refer to Chapter 13 for specifications and information on 1987 and later models

Contents

Specifications

Part A – 1.8 and 1.9 litre carburettor models

Air cleaner
Type .... Renewable paper element; automatic air temperature control

Fuel pump
Type .... Mechanical, diaphragm, operated by eccentric on intermediate shaft or camshaft

Operating pressure:
    1.8 litre engine .... 0.2 to 0.25 bar (2.9 to 3.6 lbf/in²)
    1.9 litre engine .... 0.35 to 0.40 bar (5.1 to 5.8 lbf/in²)

Carburettor 1.8 litre – 1B3

Application ....
Carburettor type ....

Engine code DR
Single choke downdraught, automatic choke

Jets and settings:

	Manual gearbox	Automatic transmission
Venturi diameter	24	24
Main jet	X112.5	X110
Air correction jet with emulsion tube	90	90
Idle fuel/air jet	47.5/130	47.5/130
Auxiliary fuel/air jet	37.5/130	37.5/130
Float needle valve diameter	1.75 mm	1.75 mm
Part throttle enrichment valve	0.50	0.50
Pump injection tube diameter	0.40 mm	0.40 mm
Injection capacity	0.75 to 1.05 cc/stroke	0.75 to 1.05 cc/stroke
Choke valve gap:		
Stage 1	2.15 to 2.45 mm	1.95 to 2.25 mm
Stage 2	2.85 to 3.15 mm	2.85 to 3.15 mm
Fast idle speed	3400 to 3800 rpm	3400 to 3800 rpm
Automatic choke identification	251	250
Idle speed	700 to 800 rpm	700 to 800 rpm
CO content	0.5 to 1.5%	0.5 to 1.5%

Carburettor 1.8 litre – 2E2

Application ....
Carburettor type ....

Engine code DS
Twin choke downdraught, automatic choke

Jets and settings:

	Stage 1	Stage 2
Venturi diameter	22 mm	26 mm
Main jet	X105	X120
Air correction jet with emulsion tube diameter	1.0 mm	1.0 mm
Idle fuel/air jet	40	–
Full throttle enrichment valve diameter	–	1.25 mm
Pump injection tube diameter	0.35 mm	–
Injection capacity	0.95 to 1.25 cc/stroke	–
Choke valve gap	2.15 to 2.45 mm	4.55 to 4.85 mm
Fast idle speed	2800 to 3200 rpm	
Automatic choke cover identification	258	
Idle speed	700 to 800 rpm	
CO content	0.5 to 1.5%	

Carburettor 1.9 litre – Keihin

Application ....
Carburettor type ....

Engine code WH
Twin choke downdraught, automatic choke

Jets and settings:

	Manual gearbox		Automatic transmission	
	Stage 1	*Stage 2*	*Stage 1*	*Stage 2*
Venturi diameter	22 mm	28 mm	22 mm	28 mm
Main jet	120	165	120	150
Idling jet	50	90	50	90
Air correction jet	80	110	80	110
Idling air jet	120	1.5	120	1.5
Float needle valve diameter	2.8 mm	–	2.8 mm	–
Pump injection tube diameter	0.35 mm	–	0.35 mm	–
Enrichment valve diameter	50 mm	–	60 mm	–
Fast idle speed	3500 rpm		3500 rpm	
Injection capacity	0.7 to 0.94 cc/stroke		0.7 to 0.94 cc/stroke	
Choke valve gap	5.45 to 5.75 mm		5.45 to 5.75 mm	
Throttle valve gap:				
Starting gap	1.2 to 1.4 mm		1.4 to 1.6 mm	
Idling gap	0.53 to 0.67 mm		0.63 to 0.77 mm	
Idle speed	700 to 800 rpm		700 to 800 rpm	
CO content	0.5 to 1.5%		0.5 to 1.5%	

Fuel octane rating

Engine code DR	91 RON (two-star)
Engines codes DS and WH	98 RON (four-star)

Torque wrench settings

	Nm	lbf ft
Fuel tank mountings	25	18
Fuel pump	20	15
Inlet manifold	25	18
Carburettor	10	7.4
Inlet manifold preheater	10	7.4
Exhaust manifold	25	18
Exhaust pipe flanges and clamps	25	18

Part B – 2.0, 2.2 and 2.3 litre fuel injection models

General

System type .... Bosch K or KE-Jetronic continuous injection system (CIS), turbocharged on certain 2.2 litre models

System pressure .... 4.7 to 5.4 bar (68 to 78 lbf/in²)

Adjustment data

Idle speed	750 to 850 rpm
CO content:	
UK models	0.5 to 1.5%
North American models:	
Engine codes WU, WK, KH	0.3 to 1.2%
Engine code KZ	0.3 to 3.0%

Fuel octane rating

UK models	98 RON (four-star)
North American models	91 RON (lead-free)

Torque wrench settings

	Nm	lbf ft
Fuel tank mountings	25	18
Thermotime switch	15	11
Fuel metering distributor screws	3.5	2.5
Pressure relief valve	25	18
Airflow meter	3.5	2.5
Cold start valve	3.5	2.5
Turbocharger to manifold	60	44
Waste gate to manifold	25	18
Oil supply and return lines to turbocharger	25	18
Exhaust manifold	30	22
Exhaust front pipe to turbocharger	35	26
Exhaust pipe flanges and clamps	25	18
Inlet manifold	25	18

PART A – 1.8 AND 1.9 LITRE CARBURETTOR MODELS

1 General description

The fuel system consists of a centrally mounted fuel tank, mechanical fuel pump, and single or twin choke downdraught carburettor.

The air cleaner is of the automatic air temperature control type, and contains a disposable paper element.

The exhaust system is in four sections, comprising twin front pipes and main and intermediate silencers. The system is bolted to a cast iron manifold at the front, and suspended on flexible rubber mountings throughout its length.

Warning: *Many of the procedures in this Chapter entail the removal of fuel pipes and connections which may result in some fuel spillage. Before carrying out any operation on the fuel system refer to the precautions given in Safety First! at the beginning of this Manual and follow them implicity. Petrol is a highly dangerous and volatile liquid and the precautions necessary when handling it cannot be overstressed.*

2 Maintenance and inspection

1   At the intervals given in Routine Maintenance at the beginning of this Manual, carry out the following service operations to the fuel system components.
2   With the car raised on a vehicle lift, or securely supported on axle stands carefully inspect the fuel pipes, hoses and unions for chafing, leaks and corrosion. Renew any pipes that are severely pitted with corrosion or in any way damaged. Renew any hoses that show signs of cracking or other deterioration.
3   Examine the fuel tank for leaks, particularly around the fuel gauge sender unit, and for signs of corrosion or damage.
4   Check condition of exhaust system, as described in Section 13.
5   From within the engine compartment, check the security of all fuel

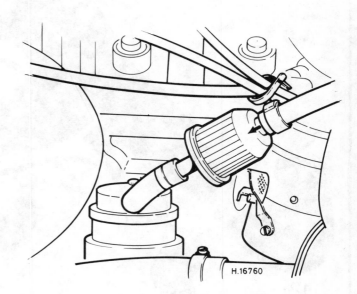

Fig. 3.1 Fuel filter location showing direction of fitting (Sec 2)

hose attachments and inspect the fuel hoses and vacuum hoses for kinks, chafing or deterioration.
6   Renew the air cleaner element and check the operation of the air cleaner automatic temperature control, as described in Section 4.
7   Check the operation of the accelerator linkage and lubricate the linkage, cable and pedal pivot with a few drops of engine oil.
8   Renew the fuel filter by slackening the clips and disconnecting the fuel lines at the filter. Fit the new filter, ensuring that the arrows on the filter body face the direction of fuel flow. Tighten the fuel line clips securely.
9   Check the carburettor idle speed and CO adjustment, as described in Section 11.

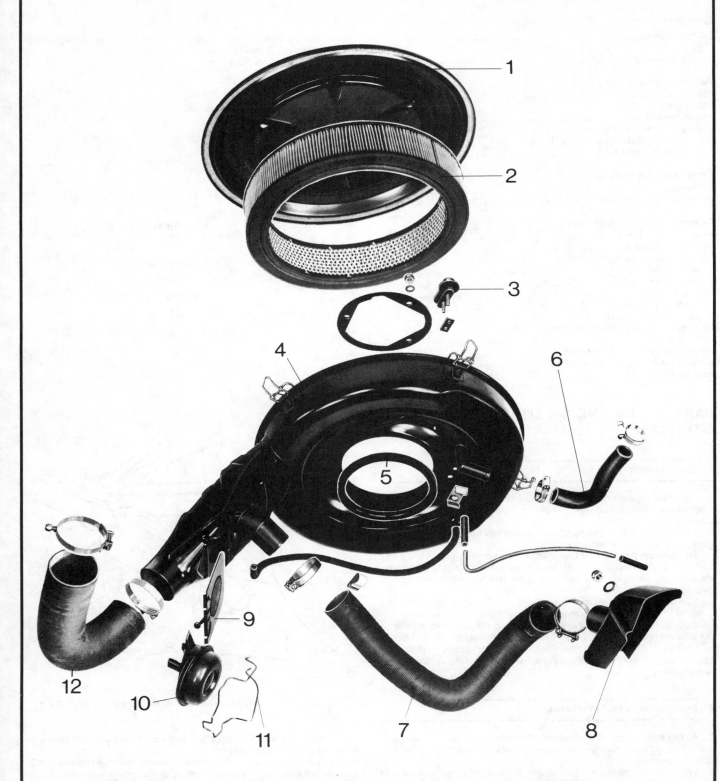

Fig. 3.2 Air cleaner assembly and automatic air temperature components – typical (Secs 3 and 4)

1 Air cleaner cover	4 Air cleaner housing	7 Preheating hose	10 Vacuum unit
2 Filter element	5 Seal	8 Warm air duct	11 Spring clip
3 Thermostatic control valve	6 Crankcase breather hose	9 Regulator flap	12 Cold air duct

3 Air cleaner – removal and refitting

Element renewal

1 Remove the two screws (where fitted), and spring back the air cleaner cover retaining clips.
2 Lift off the cover, noting its fitted direction, and take out the element. Renew the element if it is dirty or has exceeded its service life.
3 Cover the carburettor intake and wipe out the inside of the air cleaner body.
4 Refit the element and secure the air cleaner cover in place.

Air cleaner assembly

5 Remove the element, as previously described.
6 Slacken the clips and disconnect the intake hoses and breather hoses.
7 Undo the retaining nut or bolt and lift up the air cleaner body, noting its fitted position.
8 Disconnect the vacuum hoses, noting their locations, and remove the air cleaner from the car.
9 Refitting is the reverse sequence to removal.

4 Automatic air temperature control – checking

1 The air cleaner is equipped with a temperature and load sensitive intake air preheating device, comprising a temperature regulator, vacuum unit, and flap valve. According to air temperature and engine load, the system operates to admit cold air or hot air regulated by the position of the flap valve. The operation of the components can be checked as follows according to model.

1.8 litre engines

2 Remove the air cleaner, as described in Section 3, but leave the vacuum hoses connected at this stage.
3 Disconnect the hose from the notched brass connection on the temperature regulator, and check that the flap valve can be heard to open and close as suction is applied to the hose. If this is not the case, check the condition and security of the vacuum hoses, and check that the flap valve is not binding. If the flap valve still does not operate under suction, check the temperature regulator as follows.
4 For this check the ambient air temperature must not be above 20°C (68°F).
5 Lay the air cleaner on a suitable place in the engine compartment and connect the notched brass connection on the temperature regulator to the carburettor, using a long length of vacuum hose.
6 Start the engine and allow it to idle, the flap valve should be in the open position.
7 Disconnect the vacuum hose between the carburettor and regulator at the carburettor end. The flap valve must return to its at rest position after a maximum of 20 seconds.
8 Remake the original connections and refit the air cleaner on completion of the checks.

1.9 litre engines

9 With the engine cold, disconnect the air cleaner cold air intake and observe the position of the flap valve through the intake. Use a mirror if necessary. The flap valve should be open to admit cold air into the air cleaner.
10 Disconnect the vacuum hose from the temperature regulator to the vacuum unit at the temperature regulator. Disconnect the vacuum hose from the temperature regulator to the carburettor at the carburettor, and connect the hose from the vacuum unit to this outlet.
11 Start the engine and allow it to idle. Observe the flap valve which should be positioned to admit hot air into the air cleaner, Pull the hose off the vacuum unit and check that the flap valve now closes off the hot air supply. If the flap valve does not function as described, check the vacuum hose, and if satisfactory the vacuum unit is faulty.
12 Remake the original connections on completion of the checks.
13 To check the temperature regulator, make sure that the vacuum unit is operating correctly, as previously described, and that the engine is cold. Remove the cold air intake at the air cleaner.
14 Start the engine and allow it to idle.
15 Disconnect the hose at the vacuum unit, and check that vacuum can be felt at the hose. The flap valve should be open to allow cold air to enter the air cleaner.

16 Refit the hose to the vacuum unit and check that the flap valve moves to shut off the cold air supply. Now pull the hose of the vacuum unit and check that the flap valve instantly shuts off the hot air supply. Note that if the engine starts to warm up during these checks the flap valve may not move to the fully open or fully closed positions.
17 Remake the original connections on completion of the checks.

5 Fuel pump – removal and refitting

1 The fuel pump is located on the left-hand side of the engine and is operated by an eccentric on the intermediate shaft (four-cylinder engines), or camshaft (five-cylinder engines). The pump is a sealed unit and cannot be dismantled for servicing or repair.
2 Disconnect the battery negative lead.
3 Slacken the clamps and disconnect the fuel lines at the pump. Plug the fuel lines after disconnection.
4 Undo the two bolts and remove the pump. Remove the rubber seal and flange.
5 To check the pump operation, reconnect the feed pipe to the pump and operate the pump lever. If the pump is operating correctly a regular spurt of fuel should be ejected from the pump outlet as the lever is operated. Use a suitable container to collect the ejected fuel, and only carry out this test in a well ventilated area.
6 Refit the pump using a reversal of the removal procedure. Renew the rubber seal and flange if damaged, and fit the flange with its gasket face towards the engine.

6 Fuel tank – removal and refitting

1 Removal of the fuel tank should be undertaken when the tank is almost empty, as a drain plug is not provided. Alternatively, use a syphon or hand pump to remove the fuel, but ensure that this, and the fuel tank removal operations, are carried out in a well ventilated area.
2 Raise the rear of the car and support it on stands. Do not position the car over an inspection pit.
3 Disconnect the battery negative lead.
4 Remove the cover over the fuel gauge sender unit beneath the luggage compartment lining.
5 Mark the positions of the supply, return, and vent pipes at the sender unit and disconnect them.
6 Disconnect the fuel gauge wiring plug at the sender unit.
7 Slacken the filler pipe-to-tank hose clip and detach the filler pipe. Disconnect the vent and overflow hoses at the tank connectors.
8 Undo the screw securing the filler pipe to the body just inside the filler flap, and withdraw the filler pipe.
9 Support the tank on a trolley jack with interposed block of wood.
10 Remove the tank retaining straps, lower the tank, and remove it from under the car.
11 If the tank is contaminated with sediment or water, remove the gauge sender unit, as described in Section 7, and swill the tank out with clean fuel. If the tank is damaged or leaks, it should be repaired by specialists, or alternatively renewed. **Note:** *Do not, under any circumstances, solder or weld a fuel tank, for safety reasons.*
12 Refitting is a reversal of removal, but ensure that the vent pipe at the sender unit is laid on the top of the tank and secured with adhesive tape, and that the fuel lines are retained by their clips.

7 Fuel gauge sender unit – removal and refitting

1 Disconnect the battery negative lead.
2 Remove the cover over the sender unit beneath the luggage compartment lining.
3 Mark the positions of the supply, return and vent pipes at the sender unit and disconnect them. Disconnect the lead at the wiring terminal.
4 Using two crossed screwdrivers, turn the locking ring anti-clockwise, then withdraw the sender unit and float. Remove the sealing ring.
5 Refitting is a reversal of removal, but use a new sealing ring and ensure that the unit is positioned with the wiring terminal facing forwards. Secure the vent pipe with adhesive tape to the top of the tank, and secure the fuel lines with their retaining clips.

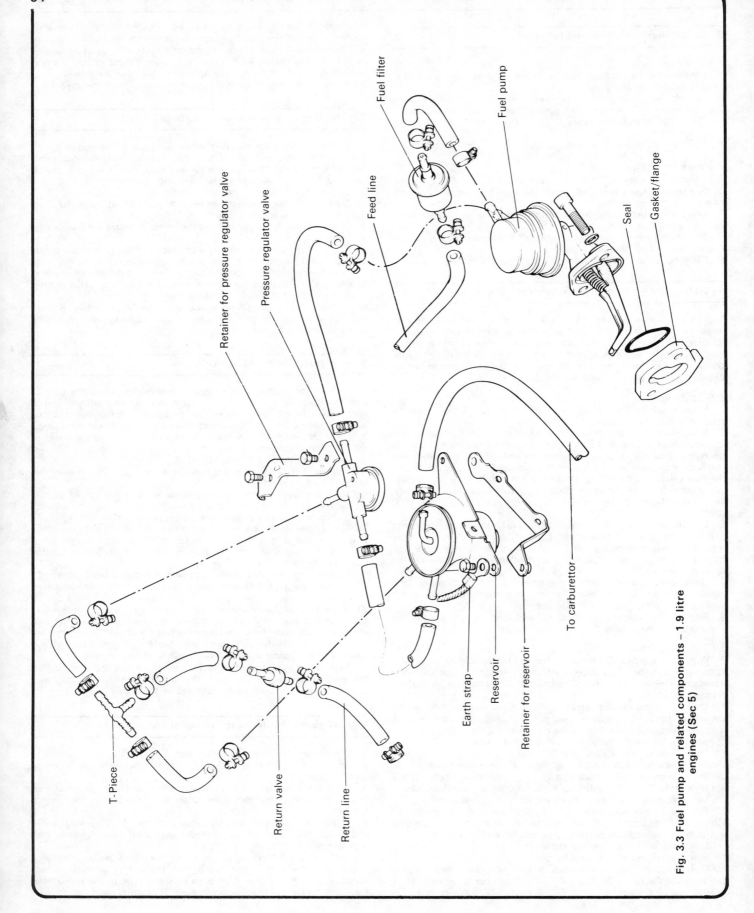

Fig. 3.3 Fuel pump and related components – 1.9 litre engines (Sec 5)

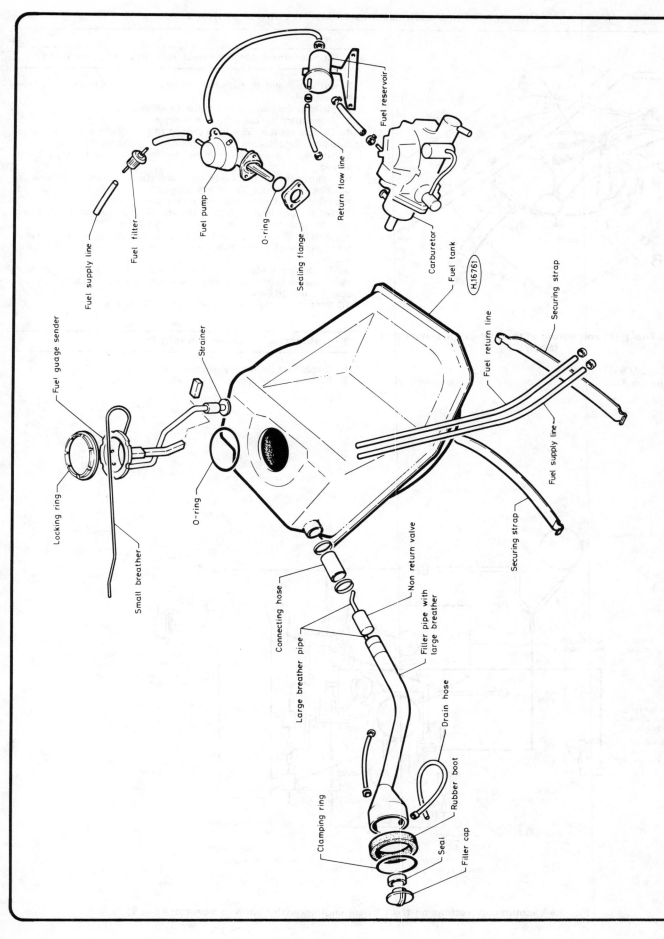

Fuel supply line

Fuel filter

Fuel pump

O-ring

Sealing flange

Return flow line

Fuel reservoir

Carburetor

Fuel tank

Fuel guage sender

Strainer

H.16761

Locking ring

O-ring

Small breather

Fuel return line

Securing strap

Fuel supply line

Securing strap

Connecting hose

Large breather pipe

Non return valve

Filler pipe with large breather

Drain hose

Clamping ring

Rubber boot

Seal

Filler cap

Fig. 3.4 Fuel tank, fuel gauge sender unit and related components – 1.8 litre engines (Secs 6 and 7)

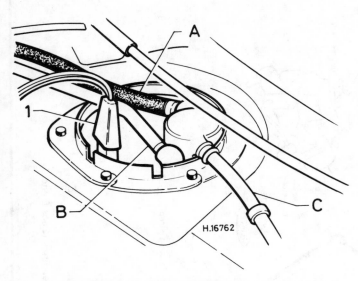

Fig. 3.5 Fuel lines and wiring at the fuel gauge sender unit (Sec 7)

A   Supply line
B   Return line
C   Breather
1   Sender unit wiring

8   Accelerator cable – removal, refitting and adjustment

1   On automatic transmission models refer to Chapter 7 where necessary.
2   Refer to Section 3 and remove the air cleaner.
3   Disconnect the cable from the engine.
4   Disconnect the cable from the top of the accelerator pedal or the automatic transmission, as applicable, and withdraw the cable.
5   Refitting is a reversal of removal, but make sure that the cable is not kinked.
6   Adjustment of the cable on automatic transmission models is described in Chapter 7. On manual gearbox models, first disconnect the cable from the throttle lever on the carburettor.
7   Set the accelerator pedal to the idle position so that the distance from the stop on the floor to the pedal is 60.0 mm (2.36 in).
8   With the throttle lever in its idling position, reconnect the cable and take up the slack in the cable. Insert the clip in the nearest groove to the bracket.
9   To check the adjustment, fully depress the accelerator pedal and check that the distance between the throttle lever and stop is no more than 1.0 mm (0.04 in).
10 Refit the air cleaner with reference to Section 3.

9   Carburettor – removal and refitting

1   Disconnect the battery negative lead.
2   Remove the air cleaner, as described in Section 3.

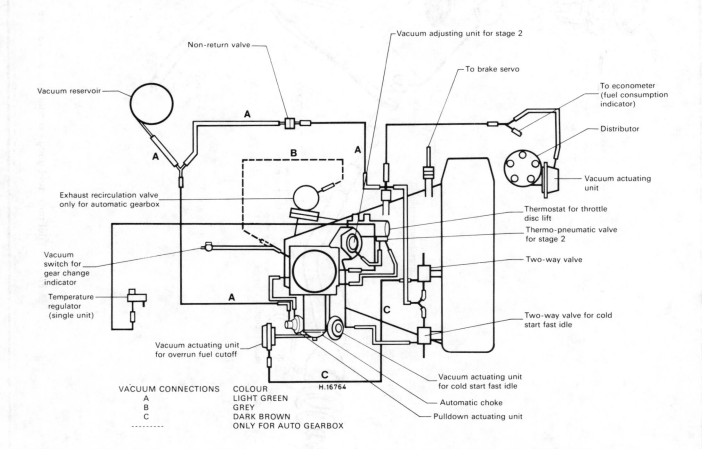

VACUUM CONNECTIONS   COLOUR
          A   LIGHT GREEN
          B   GREY
          C   DARK BROWN
-------   ONLY FOR AUTO GEARBOX

Fig. 3.6 Vacuum connections on the 1.9 litre engines with Keihin carburettor (Sec 9)

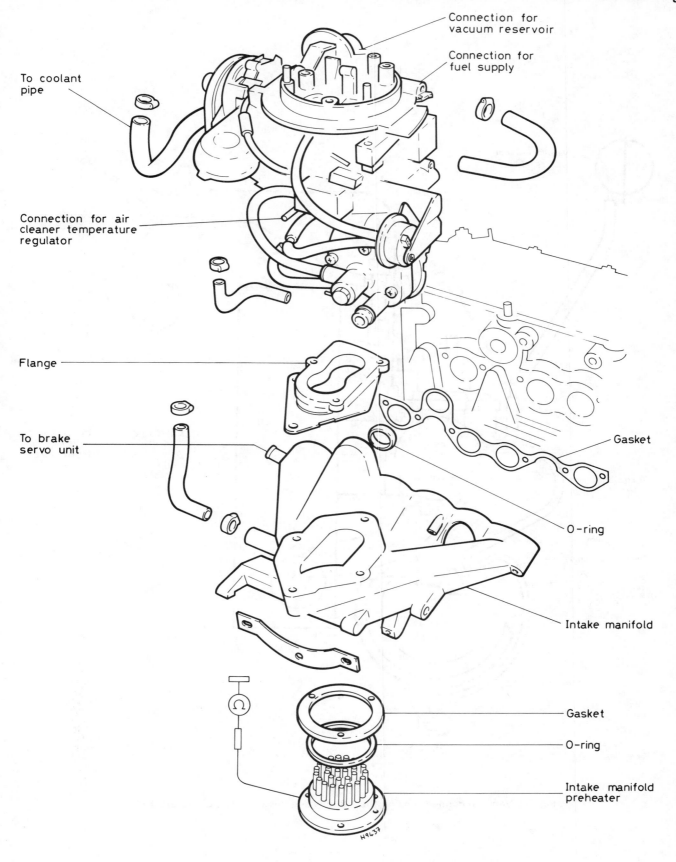

Connection for
vacuum reservoir

Connection for
fuel supply

To coolant
pipe

Connection for air
cleaner temperature
regulator

Flange

To brake
servo unit

Gasket

O-ring

Intake manifold

Gasket

O-ring

Intake manifold
preheater

H9637

Fig. 3.7 Inlet manifold and carburettor components – 1.8 litre engines (Sec 9)

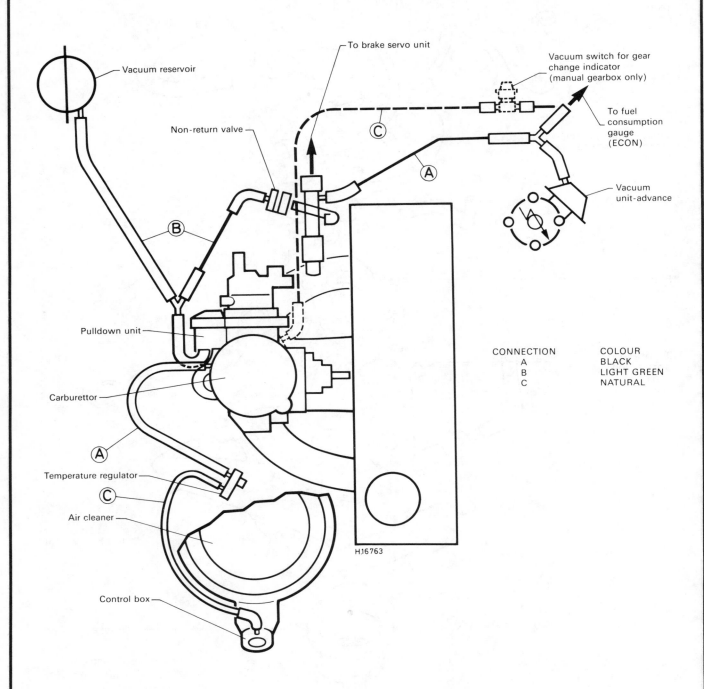

Fig. 3.8 Vacuum connections on the 1.8 litre engines with 1B3 carburettor (Sec 9)

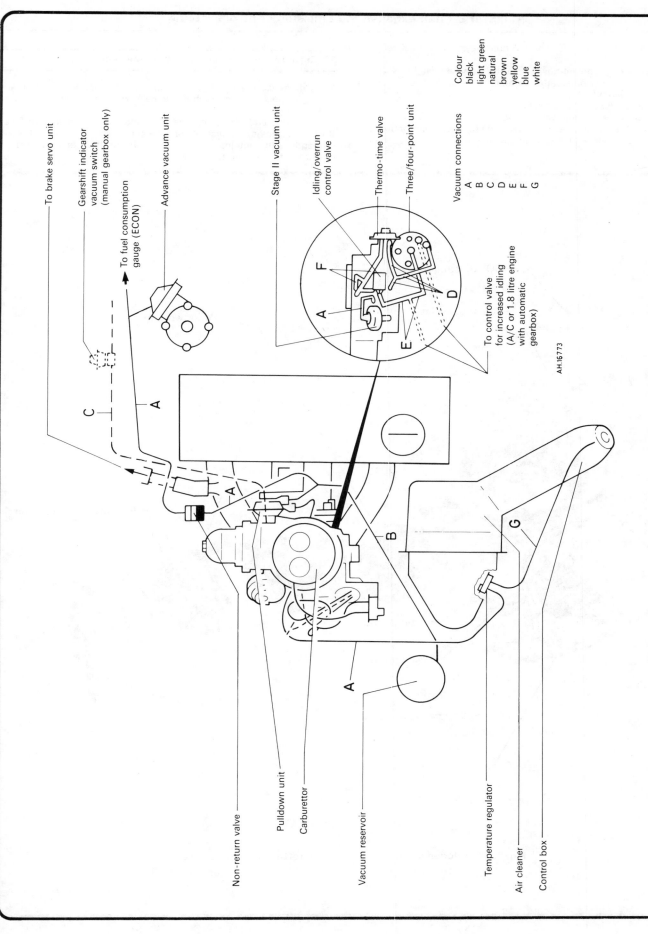

To brake servo unit

Gearshift indicator vacuum switch (manual gearbox only)

To fuel consumption gauge (ECON)

Advance vacuum unit

Stage II vacuum unit

Idling/overrun control valve

Thermo-time valve

Three/four-point unit

Vacuum connections
A
B
C
D
E
F
G

Colour
black
light green
natural
brown
yellow
blue
white

To control valve for increased idling (A/C or 1.8 litre engine with automatic gearbox)

AH.16773

Non-return valve

Pulldown unit

Carburettor

Vacuum reservoir

Temperature regulator

Air cleaner

Control box

Fig. 3.9 Vacuum connections on the 1.8 litre engines with 2E2 carburettor (Sec 9)

3   Drain half of the coolant from the cooling system, with reference to Chapter 2.
4   Disconnect the coolant hoses from the automatic choke.
5   As applicable, disconnect the wiring from the automatic choke and fuel cut-off solenoid.
6   Disconnect the accelerator cable.
7   Disconnect the fuel and vacuum hoses.
8   Unscrew the through-bolts or nuts, and lift the carburettor from the inlet manifolds. Remove the insulating flange gasket.

10 Carburettor – dismantling and reassembly

1   With the carburettor removed from the inlet manifold, as described in the previous Section, wash it externally with a suitable solvent and allow to dry.
2   Dismantle and reassemble the carburettor, with reference to Figs. 3.10 to 3.19, having first obtained a repair set of gaskets. Before dismantling the automatic choke, note the position of the cover in relation to the carburettor cover.

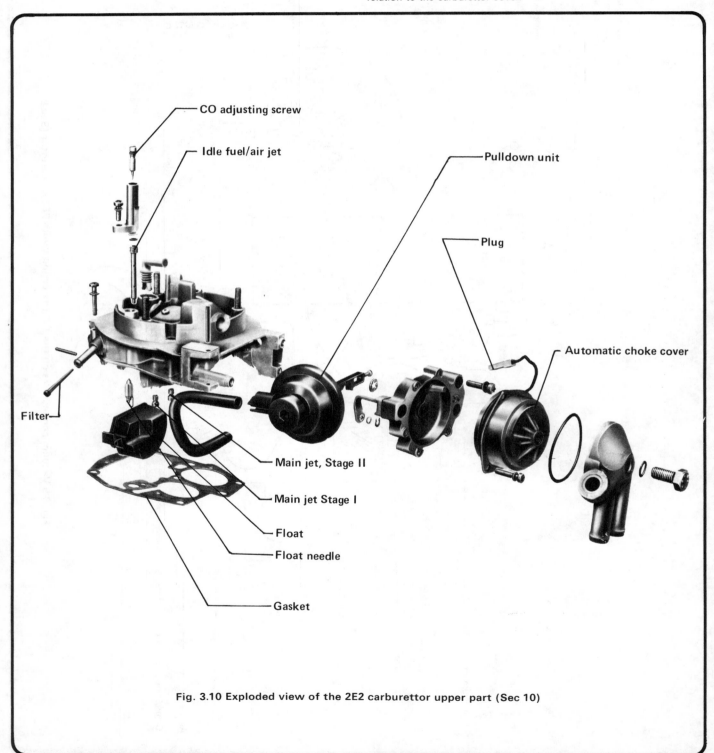

Fig. 3.10 Exploded view of the 2E2 carburettor upper part (Sec 10)

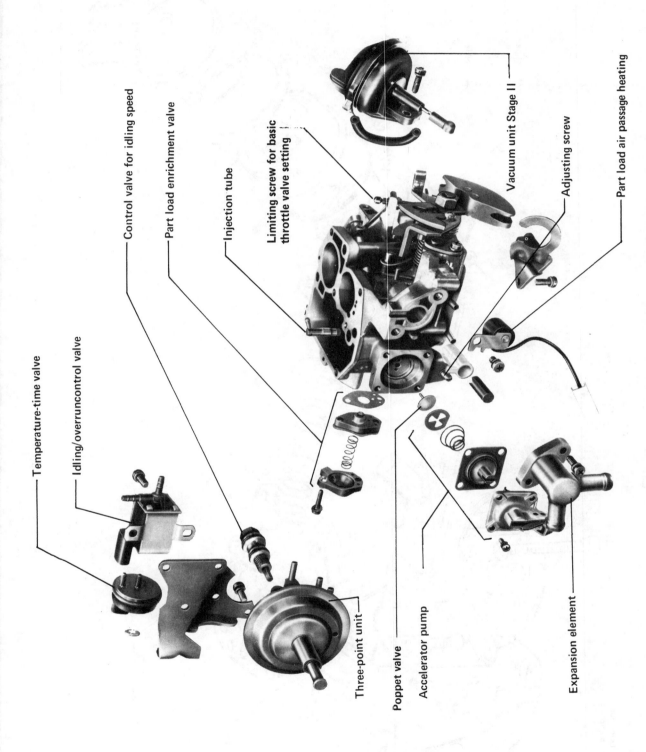

Temperature-time valve

Idling/overruncontrol valve

Control valve for idling speed

Part load enrichment valve

Injection tube

Limiting screw for basic throttle valve setting

Vacuum unit Stage II

Adjusting screw

Part load air passage heating

Three-point unit

Poppet valve

Accelerator pump

Expansion element

Fig. 3.11 Exploded view of the 2E2 carburettor lower part (Sec 10)

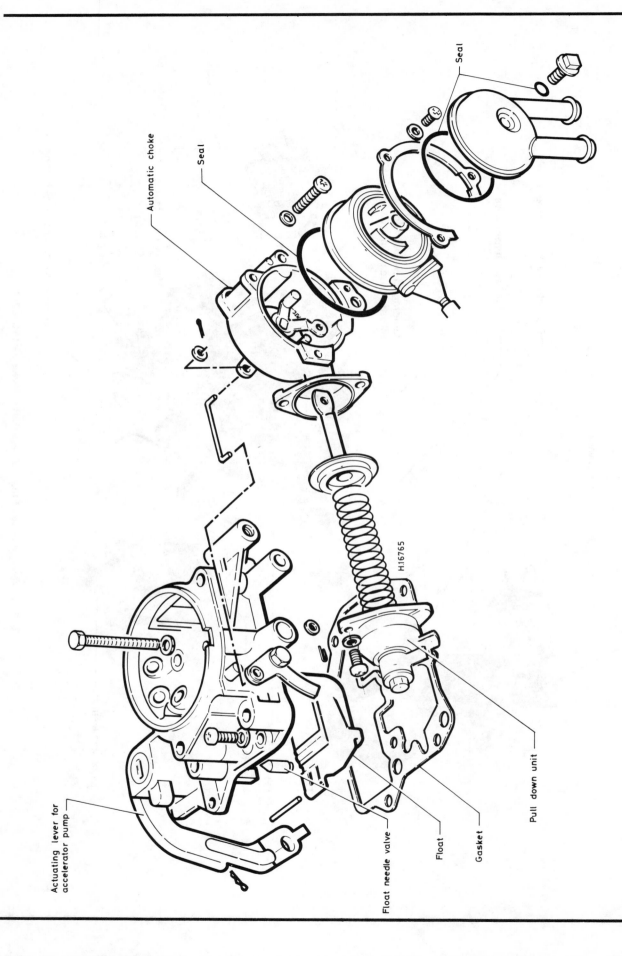

Automatic choke

Seal

Seal

H.16765

Actuating lever for accelerator pump

Float needle valve

Float

Gasket

Pull down unit

Fig. 3.12 Exploded view of the Keihin carburettor upper part (Sec 10)

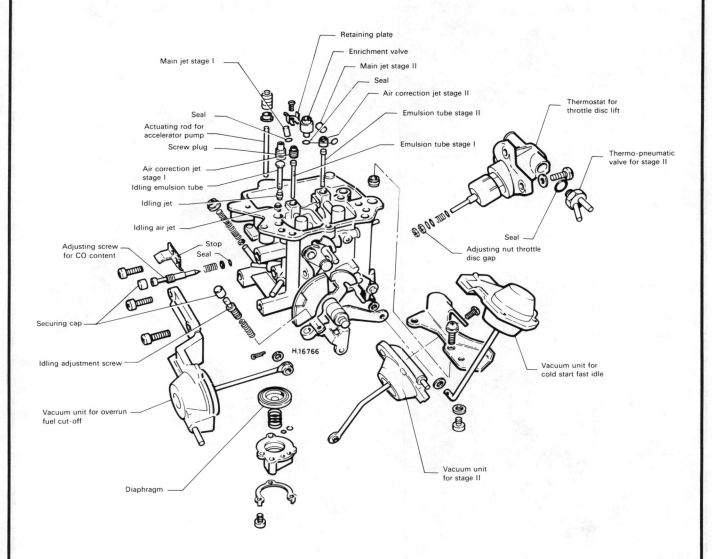

Retaining plate

Enrichment valve

Main jet stage I

Main jet stage II

Seal

Air correction jet stage II

Emulsion tube stage II

Seal

Actuating rod for accelerator pump

Screw plug

Emulsion tube stage I

Air correction jet stage I

Idling emulsion tube

Idling jet

Idling air jet

Thermostat for throttle disc lift

Thermo-pneumatic valve for stage II

Seal

Adjusting nut throttle disc gap

Adjusting screw for CO content

Stop

Seal

Securing cap

Idling adjustment screw

Vacuum unit for overrun fuel cut-off

Vacuum unit for cold start fast idle

H.16766

Diaphragm

Vacuum unit for stage II

Fig. 3.13 Exploded view of the Keihin carburettor lower part (Sec 10)

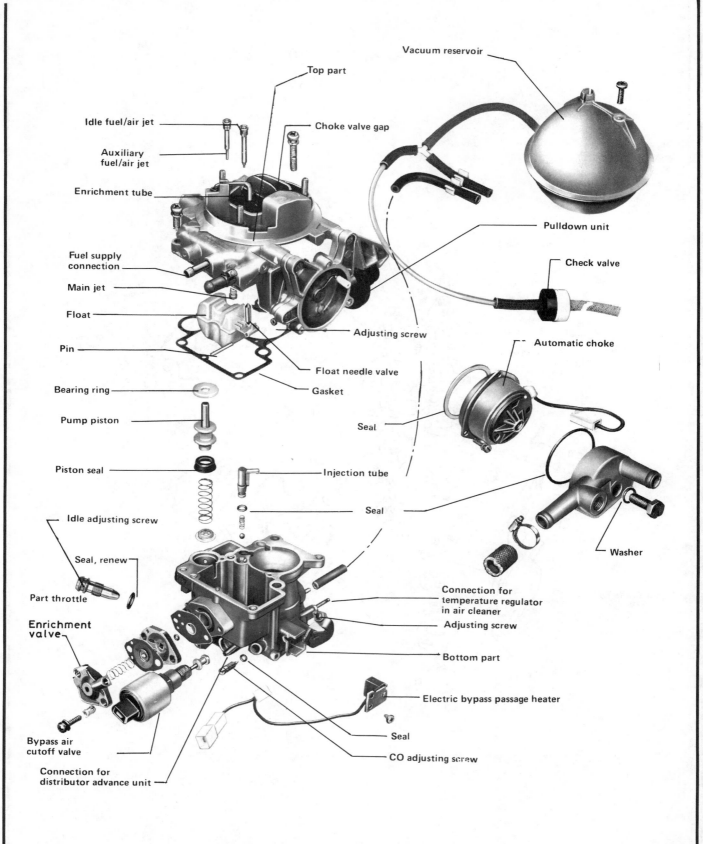

Idle fuel/air jet

Auxiliary fuel/air jet

Enrichment tube

Fuel supply connection

Main jet

Float

Pin

Bearing ring

Pump piston

Piston seal

Idle adjusting screw

Seal, renew

Part throttle

Enrichment valve

Bypass air cutoff valve

Connection for distributor advance unit

Top part

Choke valve gap

Adjusting screw

Float needle valve

Gasket

Injection tube

Seal

Connection for temperature regulator in air cleaner

Adjusting screw

Bottom part

Electric bypass passage heater

Seal

CO adjusting screw

Vacuum reservoir

Pulldown unit

Check valve

Automatic choke

Seal

Washer

Fig. 3.14 Exploded view of the 1B3 carburettor (Sec 10)

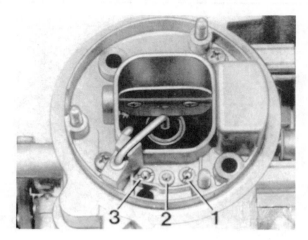

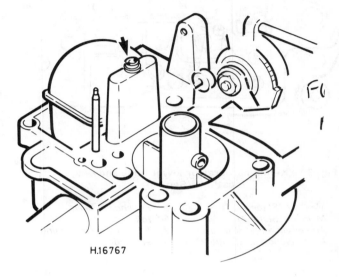

Fig. 3.15 1B3 carburettor upper body showing jet locations (Sec 10)

1 Idle fuel/air jet
2 Air correction jet and emulsion tube
3 Auxiliary fuel/air jet

H.16767

Fig. 3.16 1B3 carburettor upper body (inverted) showing main jet location – arrowed (Sec 10)

Fig. 3.17 2E2 carburettor upper body showing jet locations (Sec 10)

1 Idle fuel/air jet (beneath CO adjustment screw guide tube)
2 Air correction jet and emulsion tube (do not remove) – Stage 1
3 Air correction jet and emulsion tube (do not remove) – Stage 2

Fig. 3.18 2E2 carburettor upper body (inverted) showing jet locations (Sec 10)

1 Main jet (Stage 1)
2 Main jet (Stage 2)
3 Full load enrichment feed pipe
4 Progression feed pipe (Stage 2)

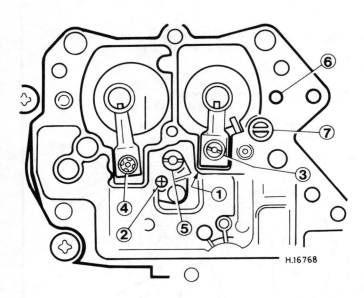

Fig. 3.19 Keihin carburettor lower body showing jet locations (Sec 10)

1   Main jet (Stage 1)   5   Enrichment valve
2   Main jet (Stage 2)   6   Idling air jet
3   Air correction jet (Stage 1) 7   Idling jet (below idling
4   Air correction jet (Stage 2)   emulsion tube)

3   Before removing the respective jets note their locations and note that the air correction jet on the 1B3 and 2E2 carburettor types cannot be removed.
4   When dismantled, clean the various components with petrol and blow dry with an air line. Do not probe or clean out the jets and apertures with wire or any other similar implement as this will damage the machined surfaces.
5   Inspect the various components for signs of wear and damage and renew any parts where necessary.
6   The following checks and adjustments should be made during the assembly of each carburettor type. Do not overtighten the jets and fastenings.

1B3 carburettor
7   To check the fuel cut-off valve, apply 12 volts to the terminal and earth the body. With the valve pin depressed approximately 3 to 4 mm (0.12 to 0.16 in), the core must be pulled in.
8   When inserting the accelerator pump piston seal, press it towards the opposite side of the vent drilling. The piston retaining ring must be pressed flush into the carburettor body.
9   When refitting the enrichment tube check that its setting clearance, a in Fig. 3.20, which is measured between the upper choke valve face and the bottom end of the tube is as specified.
10 The thermo-switches may be checked with an ohmmeter. Their resistance should be 0 ohms when the temperature is below 33°C (91°F).

Keihin carburettor
11 When refitting the emulsion tubes, note that on the stage 1 tube the bore is at the top, and on the Stage 2 tube the bore is at the bottom.

2E2 carburettor
12 When refitting the injection tube it must be correctly positioned so that fuel is sprayed in line with the recess, shown in Fig. 3.21.

All models
13 When the carburettor is reassembed and refitted, refer to Section 11 for the necessary adjustments.

Fig. 3.20 1B3 carburettor enrichment tube setting clearance (Sec 10)

a = 0.7 to 1.3 mm (0.027 to 0.051 in)

Fig. 3.21 2E2 carburettor injection tube direction (Sec 10)

11 Carburettor – adjustments

Idling speed (1B3 carburettor)
1   Run the engine to normal operating temperature and switch off all electrical components.
2   Disconnect the crankcase ventilation hose at the air cleaner and plug the hose.
3   Make sure that the automatic choke is fully open, otherwise the throttle valve linkage may still be on the fast idle cam.
4   On models with automatic transmission it is important that the accelerator cable adjustment is correct as described in Section 8, and in Chapter 7.
5   Connect a tachometer to the engine, then start the engine and let it idle. Check that the idling speed is as given in the Specifications – note that the radiator fan must not be running. If necessary, turn the idling adjusting screw in or out until the idling speed is correct (Fig. 3.22).
6   The CO adjustment screw is covered with a tamperproof cap which must be removed in order to adjust the mixture. However, first make sure that current regulations permit its removal (Fig. 3.23).
7   If an exhaust gas analyser is available, connect it to the exhaust system, then run the engine at idling speed and adjust the screw to

Fig. 3.22 1B3 carburettor idle adjusting screw – arrowed
(Sec 11)

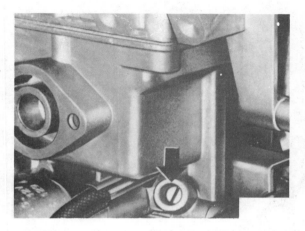

Fig. 3.23 1B3 carburettor CO adjusting screw – arrowed
(Sec 11)

give the specified CO content percentage. Alternatively, as a temporary measure, adjust the screw to give the highest engine speed, then readadjust the idling speed if necessary.

8 After making the adjustment, fit a new tamperproof cap, and reconnect the crankcase ventilation hose.

Fast idling speed (1B3 carburettor)

9 With the engine at normal operating temperature and switched off, connect a tachometer and remove the air cleaner.

10 Fully open the throttle valve, then turn the fast idle cam and release the throttle valve so that the adjustment screw is positioned on the highest part of the cam (Fig. 3.24).

11 Without touching the accelerator pedal, start the engine and check that the fast idling speed is as given in the Specifications. If not, turn the adjustment screw on the linkage as necessary. If a tamperproof cap is fitted renew it after making the adjustment.

Choke pull-down system (1B3 carburettor)

12 Remove the air cleaner cover, as described in Section 3.

13 Half open the throttle valve then completely close the choke valve.

14 Without touching the accelerator pedal, start the engine.

15 Close the choke valve by hand and check that resistance is felt over the final 4 mm (0.16 in) of travel. If no resistance is felt there may be a leak in the vacuum connections or the pull-down diaphragm may be broken.

16 Further checking of the system requires the use of a vacuum pump and a gauge, therefore this work should be entrusted to your Audi dealer.

Choke valve gap (1B3 carburettor)

17 The choke valve gap measurement and adjustment points are shown in Fig. 3.25 for reference purposes only; the use of a vacuum tester and gauge is required, so this task is best left to an Audi dealer.

Throttle valve basic setting (1B3 carburettor)

18 This setting is made during manufacture and will not normally require adjustment. However, if the setting has been disturbed proceed as follows.

19 First run the engine to normal operating temperature.

20 Remove the air cleaner, as described in Section 3.

21 Disconnect the vacuum advance hose at the carburettor and connect a vacuum gauge.

22 Run the engine at idling speed, then turn the idle limiting screw on the lever until vacuum is indicated on the gauge. Turn the screw out until the vacuum drops to zero, then turn it out a further quarter turn, (Fig. 3.26).

23 After making the adjustment, adjust the idle speed as described in paragraphs 1 to 8.

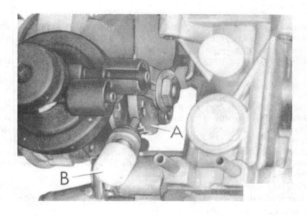

Fig. 3.24 1B3 carburettor fast idle cam (A) and adjustment
screw (B) (Sec 11)

Fig. 3.25 1B3 carburettor choke valve gap check using drill
shank (1) and adjust using socket-head bolt (2) (Sec 11)

Fig. 3.26 1B3 carburettor idle limiting screw (C) (Sec 11)

Fig. 3.27 1B3 carburettor accelerator pump adjustment
(Sec 11)

a   Locking screw   b   Cam plate

Electric bypass air heating element (1B3 carburettor)
24 Disconnect the wiring from the fuel cut-off solenoid and thermoswitch, and connect a test lamp to the heating element wire and the battery positive terminal.
25 If the lamp lights up, the heater element is in good working order.

Accelerator pump (1B3 carburettor)
26 Hold the carburettor over a funnel and measuring glass.
27 Turn the fast idle cam so that the adjusting screw is off the cam. Hold the cam in this position during the following procedure.
28 Fully open the throttle ten times, allowing at least three seconds per stroke. Divide the total quantity by ten and check that the resultant injection capacity is as given in the Specifications. If not, refer to Fig. 3.27 and loosen the cross-head screw, turn the cam plate as required, and tighten the screws.
29 If difficulty is experienced in making the adjustment, check the pump seal and make sure that the return check valve and injection tube are clear.

Automatic choke (1B3 carburettor)
30 The line on the cover must be in alignment with the dot on the automatic choke body.

Inlet manifold preheater (1B3 carburettor)
31 Using an ohmmeter between the disconnected lead and earth; check that the resistance of the preheater is between 0.25 and 0.50 ohms. If not, renew the unit.

Idling speed (Keihin carburettor)
32 The procedure is the same as for the 1B3 carburettor described in paragraphs 1 to 8 inclusive. The adjustment screws are shown in Figs. 3.28 and 3.29.

Fast idling speed (Keihin carburettor)
33 With the engine oil temperature at least 50°C (122°F), remove the air cleaner unit and pull free the vacuum hose from the vacuum fast idle unit. Start the engine and note the idle speed. Compare it with that specified and, if necessary, adjust accordingly by squeezing the adjuster lever together to reduce engine speed, or prising it open further to increase engine speed (Figs. 3.30, 3.31 and 3.32).
34 On completion reconnect the vacuum hose and refit the air cleaner unit.

Throttle valve gap adjustment (Keihin carburettor)
35 Using the shank of a twist drill, check the throttle lever valve-to-body clearance (starting gap) and compare it with the clearance specified. If the clearance is incorrect, prise open the adjuster

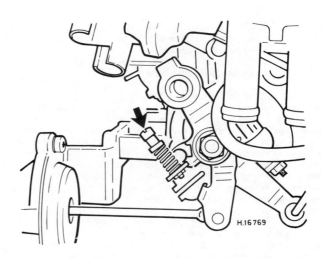

Fig. 3.28 Keihin carburettor idle adjusting screw – arrowed
(Sec 11)

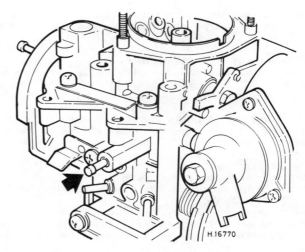

Fig. 3.29 Keihin carburettor CO adjusting screw – arrowed
(Sec 11)

Fig. 3.30 Keihin carburettor vacuum hose connection (arrowed) removed for fast idle adjustment (Sec 11)

Fig. 3.31 Keihin carburettor fast idle adjustment – compress adjuster lever to reduce speed (Sec 11)

Fig. 3.32 Keihin carburettor fast idle adjustment – prise open adjuster lever to increase speed (Sec 11)

Fig. 3.33 Keihin carburettor throttle valve starting gap measurement using twist drill (Sec 11)

Fig. 3.34 Keihin carburettor throttle valve starting gap adjustment – increase by spreading adjuster lever (Sec 11)

lever to increase the clearance or close the adjuster lever by squeezing together using suitable pliers (Figs. 3.33 and 3.34).

36 To check the continuous running (idling gap) clearance, push the pullrod of the vacuum unit onto the stop, then fit a 9.5 mm diameter rod between the thermostat lever and the carburettor housing (a drill shank will suffice). Adjust the lever to suit the rod thickness, then measure the running clearance between the throttle valve and carburettor body using a gauge rod or drill shank. If adjustment is necessary to set the clearance to that specified, prise open the adjuster lever to reduce the clearance or compress the lever with pliers to enlarge the clearance (Fig. 3.35).

Choke valve gap adjustment (Keihin carburettor)

37 The choke valve gap is preset and should not normally need adjustment except when fitting a new upper carburettor body.

38 Remove the automatic choke unit cover and, using an elastic band positioned as shown (Fig. 3.36), tension the lever against the stop, then, while pressing the operating lever of the pull-down unit onto its stop, measure the choke valve gap. Compare with that specified and, if necessary, bend the stop lever apart to enlarge the gap, or squeeze it together to reduce the gap (Fig. 3.37).

39 Remove elastic band and refit the choke cover on completion.

Fig. 3.35 Keihin carburettor continuous running (idling gap) adjustment – spread adjuster lever to reduce clearance (Sec 11)

Fig. 3.36 Keihin carburettor choke valve gap adjustment (Sec 11)

Lever tensioned with elastic band – pulldown lever arrowed

Fig. 3.37 Keihin carburettor choke valve gap stop lever (arrowed) (Sec 11)

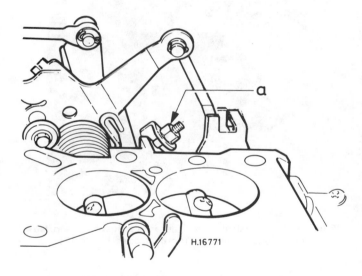

Fig. 3.38 Keihin carburettor Stage 2 basic throttle setting (Sec 11)

a   Limiting screw

Basic throttle setting – Stage 2 (Keihin carburettor)
40 The limiting screw (a in Fig. 3.38) is set during manufacture, and this setting should not be altered. If the screw is turned by mistake the correct setting can be re-established by the following method.
41 With the carburettor removed, unscrew the limiting screw until there is a gap between the end of the screw and the stop.
42 Turn the limiting screw until it just contacts the stop, then screw it in by a further half a turn. Check the idling adjustments described in paragraph 32 after refitting the carburettor.

Acclerator pump adjustment (Keihin carburettor)
43 With the carburettor removed, hold the carburettor (with its float chamber full) above a funnel and measuring jar.
44 Push the thermostat lever in the 'open' direction and push the Stage2 vacuum unit actuating rod against its stop.
45 Fit an M12 bolt between the carburettor body and the thermostat lever.
46 Open the throttle valve fully and release it slowly, taking at least three seconds to complete the operation and then repeat the cycle until

ten complete strokes have been completed. Read off the amount of fuel ejected and divide by ten to obtain the quantity delivered per stroke. Compare this with the value given in Specifications.
47 If adjustment is necessary, bend the stop accordingly, upwards if capacity is too low, downwards if capacity is too high. Ensure that there is no clearance between the lever and the operating rod. The injection duration is not adjustable. If the required capacity cannot be obtained then the accelerator pump diaphragm may well be at fault and should be renewed.

Choke pull-down system (Keihin carburettor)
48 The system can only be accurately checked using a vacuum pump and gauge; therefore this work should be entrusted to an Audi dealer.

Inlet manifold preheater (Keihin carburettor)
49 The procedure is the same as for the 1B3 carburettor described in paragraph 31.

Starting fast idle and overrun fuel cut-off two-way value (Keihin carburettor)

50 To check the operation of the valve, connect a test lamp across the two terminals of the valve, which is located on the front of the engine valve cover.

51 Start the engine and allow it to idle. The test lamp should be illuminated with the engine idling. If not, switch off the engine and connect the test lamp between the valve positive terminal and earth. The bulb should be illuminated when the ignition is switch on. If the bulb does not light up there is a wiring fault in the live feed to the valve. If the lamp does light up, switch off the ignition, disconnect the wiring to the valve, and check the resistance across the valve terminals using an ohmmeter. The resistance should be 30 to 40 ohms. If this value is not obtained, renew the two-way valve. If the resistance is satisfactory, there is likely to be a fault in the wiring between the valve wiring plug and the socket for relay No 3 in the relay plate, or in the relay itself.

Thermo-pneumatic valve (Keihin carburettor)

52 A thermo-pneumatic valve is screwed into the throttle lift thermostat to control the thermostat vacuum supply according to temperature.

53 To check the valve without removing it from the vehicle, remove the two hoses from the valve and attach a length of tubing to one of the connections on the valve. Blow down the pipe when the engine is cold and the valve should not pass any air, or very little.

54 Run the engine until it is at normal operating temperature and again blow down the pipe. With the engine hot the valve should be open and allow free passage of air.

55 Remove the piece of tubing from the valve and re-connect the vacuum pipes to it.

Idling speed (2E2 carburettor)

56 The procedure is the same as for the 1B3 carburettor described in paragraphs 1 to 8 inclusive, but check that the fast idle adjustment screw is just making contact with the diaphragm pushrod (Fig. 3.39). The adjustment screws are shown in Fig. 3.40.

Choke pull-down system (2E2 carburettor)

57 The procedure is the same as for the 1B3 carburettor described in paragraphs 12 to 16 inclusive.

Choke valve gap (2E2 carburettor)

58 To check and adjust the choke valve gap necessitates the use of a vacuum tester and gauge, and in view of this it is a task best entrusted to an Audi dealer.

Stage 2 throttle valve basic setting (2E2 carburettor)

59 This is made during manufacture and will not normally require adjustment. However if the setting has been disturbed proceed as follows. First remove the carburettor (Section 9).

60 Referring to Fig. 3.41, open the throttle valve and hold in this position by inserting a wooden rod or similar implement between the valve and the venturi.

61 Using a rubber band as shown, pre-tension the Stage 2 throttle valve locking lever, then unscrew the limiting screw to provide a clearance between the stop and limiting screw.

62 Now turn the limiting screw in so that it is just in contact with the stop. The limiting screw stop point can be assessed by inserting a piece of thin paper between the screw and stop, moving the paper as the limiting screw is tightened. With the stop point reached turn the screw in a further quarter of a turn then secure it with locking compound. Close both throttle valves then measure the locking lever clearances, A and B in Fig. 3.42. If the clearances are not as specified, bend the arm as necessary.

Fig. 3.39 2E2 carburettor diaphragm pushrod (A) and fast idle adjustment screw (B) (Sec 11)

Fig. 3.40 2E2 carburettor idle adjusting screw (A) and CO adjustment screw (B) (Sec 11)

Fig. 3.41 2E2 carburettor throttle valve basic setting showing rod to hold valve open (arrowed), lock lever (1), limiting screw (2) and stop (3) (Sec 11)

Fig. 3.42 2E2 carburettor lock lever clearance with throttle valves closed (Sec 11)

A = 0.3 to 0.5 mm (0.011 to 0.019 in)
B = 0.9 to 1.1 mm (0.035 to 0.043 in)

Accelerator pump (2E2 carburettor)
63 To check and adjust the accelerator pump necessitates the use of a vacuum pump and gauges, and in view of this the work should be entrusted to an Audi dealer.

Three-point unit (2E2 carburettor)
64 To check this, specialised test equipment is required and it should therefore be entrusted to your Audi dealer.

Idle/overrun control valve (2E2 carburettor)
65 To check this, specialised test equipment is required and it should therefore be entrusted to your Audi dealer.

Temperature time valve (2E2 carburettor)
66 To check this, specialised test equipment is required and it should therefore be entrusted to your Audi dealer.

12 Inlet and exhaust manifolds – removal and refitting

1 Partially drain the cooling system, with reference to Chapter 2.
2 Remove the air cleaner, as described in Section 3, and the carburettor, as described in Section 9.
3 Disconnect the brake servo vacuum hose.
4 Disconnect the coolant hoses at the inlet manifold.
5 Disconnect the inlet manifold preheater lead at the connector.
6 Detach the exhaust stabiliser and manifold support brackets where fitted.
7 Undo the retaining bolts and withdraw the inlet manifold.
8 Undo the exhaust front pipe-to-manifold nuts, and separate the front pipe at the flange. Recover the gasket.
9 Remove the exhaust manifold retaining nuts and withdraw the manifold. Recover the gasket.
10 Refitting is the reverse sequence to removal. Use a new gasket and tighten the retaining nuts and bolts to the specified torque.

13 Exhaust system – checking, removal and refitting

1 The exhaust system should be examined for leaks, damage and security at regular intervals (see Routine Maintenance). To do this, apply the handbrake and, in a well ventilated area, allow the engine to idle. Lie down on each side of the car in turn, and check the full length of the exhaust system for leaks whilst an assistant temporarily places a wad of cloth over the end of the tailpipe. If a leak is evident, stop the engine and use a proprietary repair kit to seal. If the leak is excessive, or damage is evident, renew the section. Check the rubber mountings for deterioration, and renew them, if necessary (photos).
2 Before doing any dismantling work on the exhaust system, wait until the system has cooled down and then saturate the fixing bolts and joints with a proprietary anti-corrosion fluid.
3 When refitting the system, new nuts and bolts should be used, and it may be found easier to cut through the old bolts with a hacksaw, rather than unscrew them.
4 When renewing any part of the exhaust system, it is usually easier to undo the manifold-to-front pipe joint and remove the complete system from the car, then separate the various pieces of the system, or cut out the defective part, using a hacksaw.
5 Refit the system a piece at a time, starting with the front pipe. Use a new joint gasket and note that it has a flanged side, the flanged side should face towards the exhaust pipe.
6 Smear all the joints with a proprietary exhaust sealing compound before assembly. This makes it easier to slide the pieces to align them and ensures that the joints will be gas tight.
7 Tighten all exhaust fastenings to the specified torque and, while doing this, twist any movable joints as necessary so that the system remains clear of the underbody, and places an equal load on all the mountings.

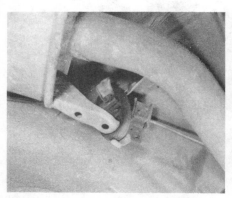

13.1A Exhaust intermediate silencer front rubber mounting ...

13.1B ... rear rubber mounting ...

13.1C ... and tail pipe mounting

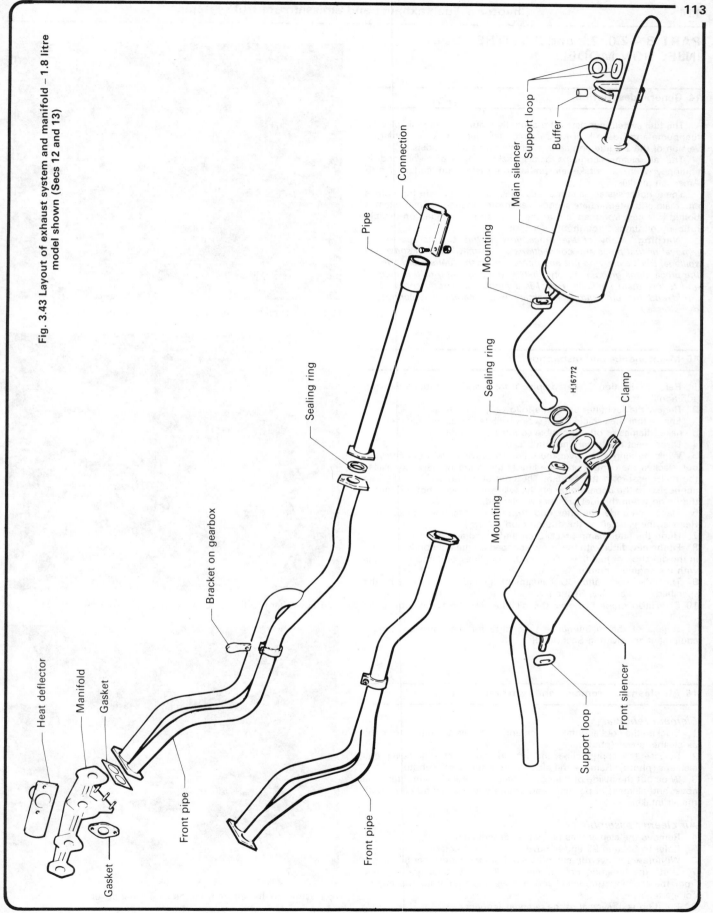

Fig. 3.43 Layout of exhaust system and manifold – 1.8 litre model shown (Secs 12 and 13)

Heat deflector

Manifold

Gasket

Gasket

Front pipe

Front pipe

Bracket on gearbox

Sealing ring

Pipe

Connection

Support loop

Buffer

Main silencer

Mounting

Sealing ring

H.16772

Clamp

Mounting

Support loop

Front silencer

PART B – 2.0, 2.2 and 2.3 LITRE FUEL INJECTION MODELS

14 General description

The fuel system consists off a centrally mounted fuel tank, electric fuel pump and Bosch K or KE-Jetronic fuel injection. A tuborcharged version of the 2.2 litre engine is available on certain models.

The air cleaner contains a disposable paper element, and is equipped with an intake air preheating system on certain North American models.

The exhaust system is in four sections, comprising twin front pipes and main and intermediate silencers according to model. The system is bolted to a cast iron manifold at the front, and suspended on flexible rubber mountings throughout its length.

Warning: *Many of the procedures in this Chapter entail the removal of fuel pipes and connections which may result in some fuel spillage. Before carrying out any operation on the fuel system refer to the precautions given in Safety First! at the beginning of this manual and follow them implicity. Petrol is a highly dangerous and volatile liquid and the precautions necessary when handling it cannot be overstressed.*

15.5 Control pressure line union (arrowed) at the warm-up valve

15 Maintenance and inspection

1   Refer to Section 2, paragraphs 1 to 7 and note the following additional items.
2   Renew the fuel filter using the following procedure.
3   Ensure that the vehicle is in a well ventilated area, and that there are no naked flames or other possible sources of ignition.
4   Disconnect the battery negative lead.
5   While holding a rag over the union to prevent fuel from spraying out, slacken the control pressure line at the warm-up valve to release the fuel pressure in the system. The control pressure line is the one connected to the upper union on the warm-up valve (photo). Tighten the union when the fuel pressure is released.
6   Place rags under the filter, and unscrew the fuel lines at each end. Recover the washers at the outlet union (photo).
7   Undo the filter clamp bracket nut and withdraw the filter.
8   Fit the new filter with the arrow stamped on the filter body pointing in the direction of fuel flow. Tighten the fuel lines, and check for leaks with the engine running.
9   The idle speed and CO adjustment should be checked at the specified intervals (see Section 23).
10 On Turbo models, renew the oil filter for the turbo lubrication circuit.
11 Details of the maintenance procedure for the emission control equipment are given in Section 38.

15.6 Fuel filter fuel line unions (A) and clamp bracket nut (B)

16 Air cleaners – removal and refitting

Element renewal
1   Slacken the cold air intake clamp and withdraw the intake from the air cleaner cover (photo).
2   Release the spring clips and lift off the air cleaner cover and element (photo). Remove the element from the cover (photo).
3   Wipe out the inside of the cover, then fit a new element. Place the cover and element in position, and secure with the spring clips. Refit the air intake.

Air cleaner assembly
4   Remove the element, as previously described.
5   Refer to Section 25 and remove the air-flow meter.
6   Withdraw the overrun cut-off valve from the air cleaner housing.
7   Undo the retaining bolt, disengage the air cleaner housing peg from the locating grommet, and remove the unit from the engine compartment.
8   Refitting is a reversal of the removal sequence.

16.1 Withdraw the intake from the air cleaner cover

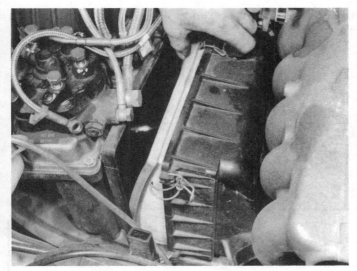

16.2A Lift off the air cleaner cover and element ...

16.2B ... and withdraw the element from the cover

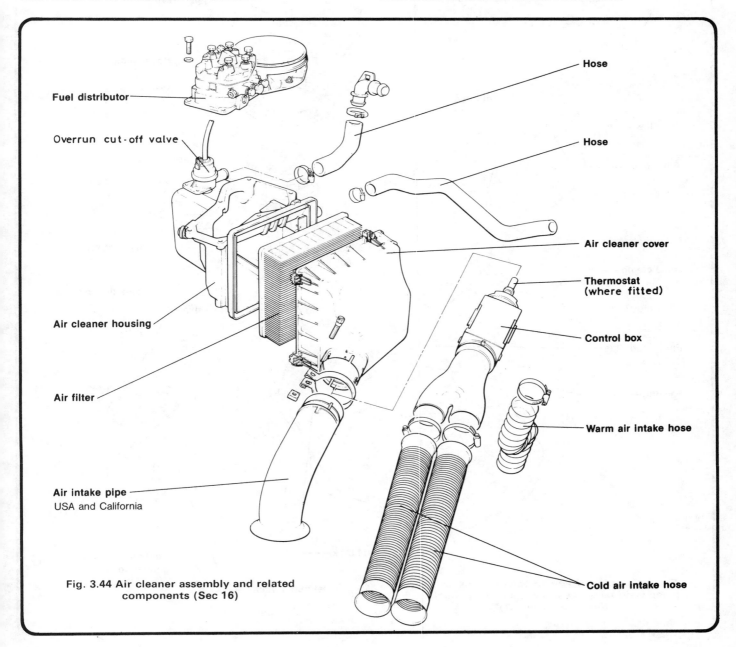

Fuel distributor

Overrun cut-off valve

Air cleaner housing

Air filter

Air intake pipe
USA and California

Hose

Hose

Air cleaner cover

Thermostat
(where fitted)

Control box

Warm air intake hose

Cold air intake hose

Fig. 3.44 Air cleaner assembly and related
components (Sec 16)

17 Automatic air temperature control – checking

1   Certain North American models are equipped with a thermostatically operated air temperature control device, located in a regulator box fitted in the air cleaner intake. The unit contains a flap valve, which can open or close a hot or cold air intake to maintain the intake air temperature within predetermined parameters.
2   To check the operation of the unit, remove the air intake ducts, then remove the regulator box from the air cleaner.
3   Hold the thermostat capsule in warm water (approximately 20°C, 68°F) for two minutes. Check that the flap valve has moved to a position where it is just shutting off the cold air intake. If necessary,

alter the thermostat position by screwing it in or out of the adjuster as required. Secure the thermostat with sealing paint after adjustment.
4   When refitting the regulator box, ensure that the rib aligns with the groove in the air cleaner cover.

18 Fuel tank – removal and refitting

Refer to Section 6 of this Chapter, but note that the fuel pump is located in the tank along with the fuel gauge sender unit. If necessary, remove the pump, as described in Section 31.

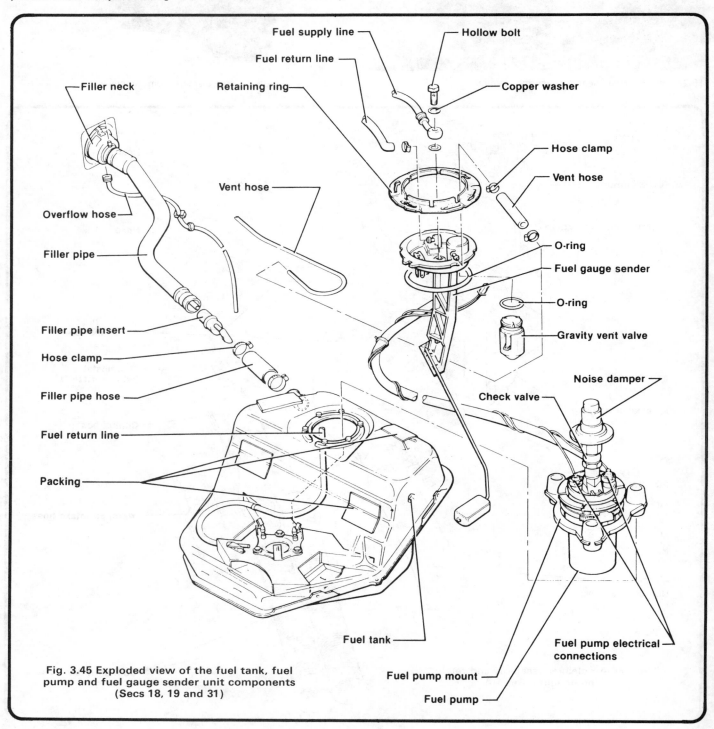

Fig. 3.45 Exploded view of the fuel tank, fuel
pump and fuel gauge sender unit components
(Secs 18, 19 and 31)

19 Fuel gauge sender unit – removal and refitting

Refer to Section 7 of this Chapter.

20 Accelerator cable – removal, refitting and adjustment

Refer to Section 8 of this Chapter, but note that it is not necessary to remove the air cleaner. The cable is secured to the lever on the throttle valve housing by a clamp bolt (photo), or ferrule.

20.1 Accelerator cable attachment at the throttle valve housing

21 Fuel injection system – general description

The Bosch KE-Jetronic fuel injection system is fitted to all fuel injected models covered by this manual. An exploded view of the main parts of the system is shown in Fig. 3.46 and the accompanying illustrations show the various subsidiary components associated with the main system.

The following paragraphs describe the system and its various elements. Later Sections describe the tests which can be carried out to ensure whether a particular unit is functioning correctly, but dismantling and repair procedure of units are not generally given because repairs are not possible.

The system measures the amount of air entering the engine and determines the amount of fuel which needs to be mixed with the air to give the correct combustion mixture for the particular conditions of engine operation. The fuel is sprayed continuously by an injection nozzle to the inlet channel of each cylinder. This fuel and air is drawn into the cylinders when the inlet valves open.

Airflow meter
1   This measures the volume of air entering the engine and relies on the principle that a circular disc, when placed in a funnel through which a current of air is passing, will rise until the weight of the disc is equal to the force on its lower surface which the air creates. If the volume of air flowing is increased and the plate were to remain in the same place, the rate of flow of air through the gap between the cone and the plate would increase and the force on the plate would increase.
2   If the plate is free to move then, as the force on the plate increases, the plate rises in the cone and the area between the edge of the plate and the edge of the cone increases, until the rate of airflow and hence the force on the plate, becomes the same as it was at the former lower

flow rate and smaller area. Thus the height of the plate is a measure of the volume of air entering the engine.
3   The airflow meter consists of an air funnel with a sensor plate mounted on a lever which is supported at its fulcrum. The weight of the airflow sensor plate and its lever are balanced by a counterweight and the upward force on the sensor plate is opposed by a plunger. The plunger, which moves up and down as a result of the variations in airflow, is surrounded by a sleeve having vertical slots in it. The vertical movement of the plunger uncovers a greater or lesser length of the slots, which meters the fuel to the injection valves.
4   The sides of the air funnel are not a pure cone because optimum operation of the engine requires a different air/fuel ratio under different conditions such as idling, part load and full load. By making parts of the funnel steeper than the basic shape, a richer mixture can be provided for at idling and full load. By making the funnel flatter than the basic shape, a leaner mixture can be provided.

Fuel supply
5   Fuel is pumped continuously while the engine is running by a roller cell pump running at constant speed; excess fuel is returned to the tank. The fuel pump is operated when the ignition switch is in the START position, but once the starter is released a switch connected to the air plate prevents the pump from operating unless the engine is running.
6   The fuel line to the fuel supply valve incorporates a filter and also a fuel accumulator. The function of the accumulator is to maintain pressure in the fuel system after the engine has been switched off and so give good hot restarting.
7   Associated with the fuel accumulator is a pressure regulator which is an integral part of the fuel metering device. When the engine is switched off, the pressure regulator lets the pressure to the injection valves fall rapidly to cut off the fuel flow through them and so prevent the engine from dieseling or running on. The valve closes at just below the opening pressure of the injector valves and this pressure is then maintained by the pressure accumulator.

Fuel distributor
8   The fuel distributor is mounted on the air metering device and is controlled by the vertical movement of the airflow sensor plate. It consists of a spool valve which moves vertically in a sleeve, the sleeve having as many vertical slots around its circumference as there are cylinders on the engine.
9   The spool valve is subjected to hydraulic pressure on the upper end and this balances the pressure on the air plate which is applied to the bottom of the valve by a plunger. As the spool valve rises and falls it uncovers a greater or lesser length of metering slot and so controls the column of fuel fed to each injector.
10 Each metering slot has a different pressure valve, which ensures that the difference in pressure between the two sides of the slot is always the same. Because the drop in pressure across the metering slot is unaffected by the length of slot exposed, the amount of fuel flowing depends only on the exposed area of the slots.

Compensation units
11 For cold starting and during warming-up, additional devices are required to adjust the fuel supply to the different fuel requirements of the engine under these conditions.

Cold start valve
12 The cold start valve is mounted in the intake manifold and sprays additional fuel into the manifold during cold starting. The valve is solenoid operated and is controlled by a thermotime switch in the engine cooling system. The thermotime switch is actuated for a period which depends upon coolant temperature, the period decreasing with rise in coolant temperature. If the coolant temperature is high enough for the engine not to need additional fuel for starting, the switch does not operate.

Warm-up regulator
13 While warming up, the engine needs a richer mixture to compensate for fuel which condenses on the cold walls of the inlet

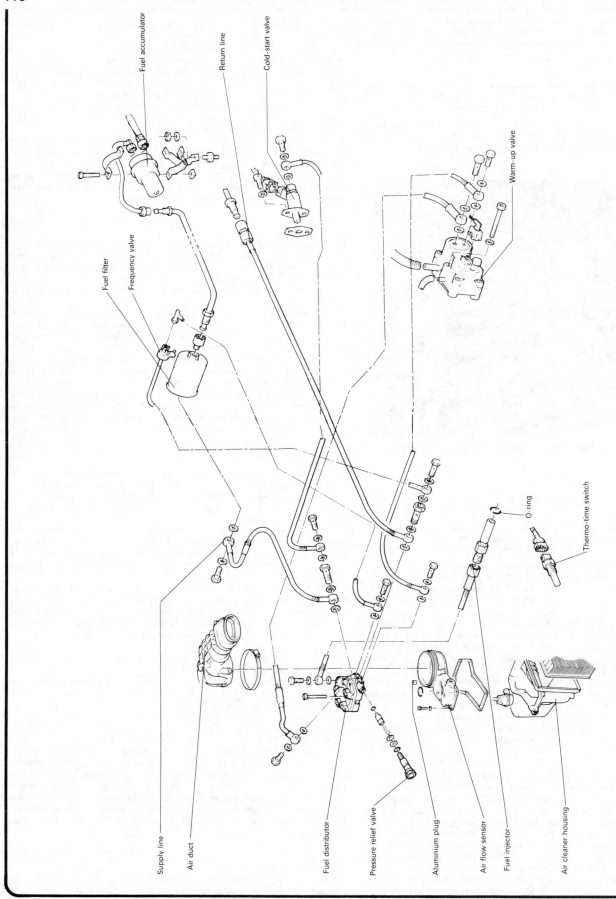

Fig. 3.46 Exploded view of the fuel injection system main components (Sec 21)

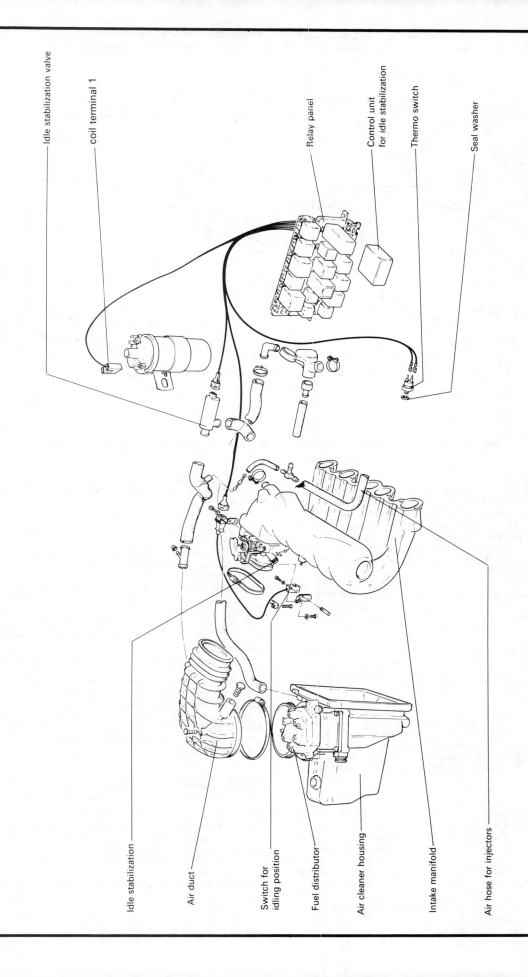

Idle stabilization valve

coil terminal 1

Relay panel

Control unit
for idle stabilization

Thermo switch

Seal washer

Idle stabilization

Air duct

Switch for
idling position

Fuel distributor

Air cleaner housing

Intake manifold

Air hose for injectors

Fig. 3.47 Layout of the idle stabilisation system (Sec 21)

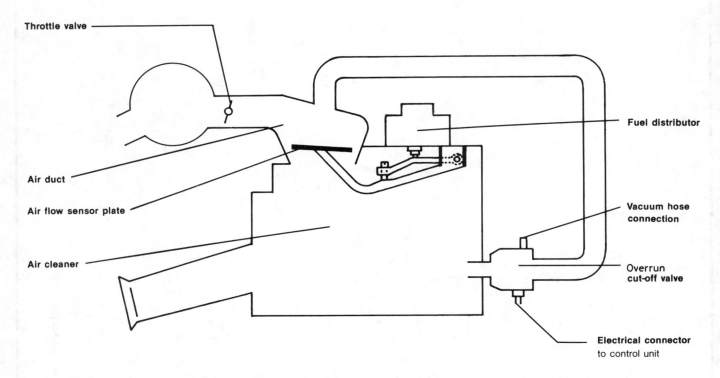

Fig. 3.48 Diagrammatic representation of the overrun fuel cut-off system (Sec 21)

manifold and cylinder walls. It also needs more fuel to compensate for power lost because of increased friction losses and increased oil drag in a cold engine. The mixture is made richer during warming up by the warm-up regulator. This is a pressure regulator which lowers the pressure applied to the control plunger of the fuel regulator during warm-up. This reduced pressure causes the airflow plate to rise higher than it would do otherwise, thus uncovering a greater length of metering slot and making the mixture richer.

14 The valve is operated by a bi-metallic strip which is heated by an electric heater. When the engine is cold the bit-metallic spring pressed against the delivery valve spring to reduce the pressure on the diaphragm and enlarge the discharge cross-section. This increase in cross-section results in a lowering of the pressure fed to the control plunger.

15 When the engine is started, the electrical heater of the bi-metallic strip is switch *ON*. As the strip warms it rises gradually until it ultimately rises free of the control spring plate and the valve spring becomes fully effective to give normal control pressure.

Idle stabilisation

16 Various sensors on the engine monitor engine speed, temperature and throttle position and transmit the information to an electronic switch unit. If the engine idle speed varies from the design speed of the switch unit, the unit operates a control valve to increase or decrease an additional air supply around the throttle valve, and maintain the idling speed at a stablised level.

Overrun cut-off

17 In the interests of fuel economy, an additional device is used to restrict the fuel supply during engine overrun.

18 The overrun cut-off valve is located on the air cleaner housing, and is controlled by a switch unit which in turn receives information from a temperature switch, and throttle valve switch. If the coolant temperature is above 30°C (86°F), the engine speed above 1400 rpm, and the throttle in the idling position, the switch unit activates the overrun cut-off valve which is then opened by vacuum. An auxiliary air channel is opened, and intake air bypasses the airflow sensor plate, and the plate then falls. Consequently the fuel supply is cut-off until the auxiliary air channel once again closes.

22 Fuel injection system – precautions and general repair information

1 Due to the complexity of the fuel injection system, and the need for special tools and test equipment, any work should be limited to the operations described in this Chapter. Other adjustments and system checks are beyond the scope of most readers, and should be left to an Audi dealer.

2 Before disconnecting any fuel lines, unions, or components, thoroughly clean the component or connection and the adjacent area.

3 Place any removed components on a clean surface and cover them with plastic sheet or paper. Do not use fluffy rags for cleaning.

4 New parts should be left packaged until immediately before they are to be fitted.

5 The system operates under pressure at all times, and care must be taken when disconnecting fuel lines. Relieve the system pressure, as described in Section 15, paragraphs 3 to 5, before disconnecting any fuel lines under pressure. Refer to the warning note in Section 14, and always work with the battery negative lead disconnected.

6 In the event of a malfunction in the system, reference should be made to the Fault Diagnosis Section at the end of this Chapter, but first make a basic check of the system hoses, connections, fuses, and relays for any obvious and immediately visible defects.

23 Idle speed and idle mixture – adjustment

1 The engine idling speed is maintained at a predetermined value by the idle stabilisation valve, and does not normally require adjustment. In the event of unsatisfactory idling, the advice of an Audi dealer should be sought. The engine idling speed cannot be adjusted without bypassing the idle stabilisation system, and this entails the use of Audi test equipment.

2 The idle mixture adjustment is carried out in conjunction with the idle speed adjustment, and special Audi test equipment is also required for this operation.

3 For reference purposes the idle speed adjustment screws are shown in the photos.

23.3A Idle speed adjustment screw (arrowed) on normally aspirated fuel injection engines ...

23.3B ... and on turbocharged engines with tamperproof cap (arrowed) in place over the screw

24.2 Disconnect the fuel lines at the fuel metering distributor

24 Fuel metering distributor – removal and refitting

1   Release the fuel pressure in the system, as described in Section 15, paragraphs 3 to 5 inclusive.
2   Mark each fuel line and its port on the distributor, then disconnect the fuel lines (photo). Recover the copper washers at each union.
3   Unscrew and remove the connection of the pressure control line to the fuel metering distributor.
4   Undo the three fuel metering distributor retaining screws.
5   Lift off the fuel metering distributor, taking care that the metering plunger does not fall out. If the plunger does fall out accidentally, clean it in fuel and then re-insert it with its chamfered end downwards.
6   Before refitting the metering distributor, ensure that the plunger moves up and down freely. If the plunger sticks, the distributor must be renewed, because the plunger cannot be repaired or replaced separately.
7   Refit the distributor, using a new sealing ring, and after tightening the screws, lock them with paint.
8   Reconnect the fuel lines to their original positions.

25 Airflow meter – removal and refitting

1   Release the fuel pressure in the system, as described in Section 15, paragraphs 3 to 5 inclusive.
2   Mark each fuel line and its port on the fuel metering distributor, then disconnect the fuel lines. Recover the copper washers at each union.
3   Unscrew and remove the connection of the pressure control line to the fuel metering distributor.
4   Slacken the clamps and remove the air intake duct.
5   Remove the bolts securing the airflow meter to the air cleaner and remove the meter, complete with fuel metering distributor.
6   The fuel metering plunger should be prevented from falling out when the fuel metering distributor is removed from the airflow meter (see previous Section).
7   Refitting is the reverse of removing, but it is necessary to use a new gasket between the airflow meter and the air cleaner.

26 Pressure relief valve – removal, servicing and refitting

1   Release the pressure in the fuel system, as described in paragraphs 3 to 5 of Section 15.
2   Unscrew the non-return valve plug and remove the plug and its sealing washer.
3   Take out the O-ring, plunger and O-ring in that order.
4   When refitting the assembly, use new O-rings and ensure that all the shims which were removed are refitted.

27 Thermo time switch – checking

1   The thermotime switch energises the cold start valve for a short time on starting and the time for which the valve is switched on depends upon the engine temperature.
2   Pull the connector off the cold start valve and connect a test lamp across the contacts of the connector.
3   Pull the high tension lead off the centre of the distributor and connect the lead to earth.
4   Operate the starter for 10 seconds and note the interval before the test lamp lights and the period for which it remains alight. Reference to the graph (Fig. 3.49) will show that at a coolant temperature of 30°C (86°F) the lamp should light immediately and stay on for two seconds.
5   The check should not be carried out if the coolant temperature is above 30°C (86°F).
6   Refit the high tension lead onto the distributor, and reconnect the lead to the cold start valve.

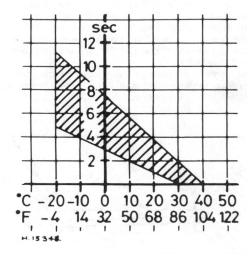

Fig. 3.49 Thermotime switch operation graph (Sec 27)

28 Cold start valve – checking

1   Ensure that the coolant temperature is below 30°C (86°F) and that the car battery is fully charged.
2   Pull the high tension lead off the centre of the distributor and connect the lead to earth.

3   Pull the connectors off the warm-up valve and the cold start valve.

4   Remove the two bolts securing the cold start valve to the inlet manifold and remove the valve, taking care not to damage the gasket.

5   With fuel line and electrical connections connected to the valve, hold the valve over a glass jar and operate the starter for 10 seconds. The cold start valve should produce an even cone of spray during the time the thermotime switch is on.

6   After completing the checks refit the valve and reconnect the leads that were disturbed.

29 Warm-up regulator – checking

1   With the engine cold, pull the connectors off the warm-up valve.

2   Connect a voltmeter across the terminals of the warm-up valve connector and operate the starter. The voltage across the terminals should be a minimum of 8.0 volts.

3   Switch the ignition OFF and connect an ohmmeter across the terminals of the warm-up valve. If the meter does not indicate a resistance of about 20 ohms, the heater coil is defective and a new valve must be fitted.

30 Airflow sensor lever and control plunger – checking

1   For the correct mixture to be supplied to the engine it is essential that the sensor plate is central in the venturi, and that its height is correct.

2   Slacken the retaining clips and remove the air intake duct. If the sensor plate appears to be off-centre, loosen its centre screw and carefully run a 0.10 mm (0.004 in) feeler gauge round the edge of the plate to centralise it, then retighten the bolt.

3   Raise the airflow sensor plate and then quickly move it to its rest position. No resistance should be felt on the downward movement; if there is resistance the airflow meter is defective and a new one must be fitted.

4   If the sensor plate can be moved downwards easily, but has a strong resistance to upward movement, the control plunger is sticking. Remove the fuel distributor (Section 24) and clean the control plunger in fuel. If this does not cure the problem, a new fuel distributor must be fitted.

5   Check the position of the airflow sensor in relation to the air cone. On all engines except code KZ, the upper edge of the plate should be flush with the bottom edge of the air cone, or a maximum of 0.5 mm (0.020 in) below it. On code KZ engines, the upper edge of the plate should be 1.75 to 2.05 mm (0.068 to 0.081 in) below the bottom edge of the air cone (Fig. 3.50).

6   Adjust the height of the plate by lifting it and bending the wire clips attaching the plate to the balance arm, but take care not to scratch or damage the surface of the air cone.

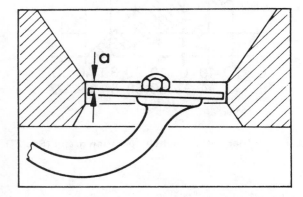

Fig. 3.50 Airflow sensor plate position relative to air cone bottom edge (Sec 30)

a = specified plate upper edge to air cone bottom edge dimension

31 Electric fuel pump – removal and refitting

1   The electric fuel pump is located in the fuel tank and is just accessible through the sender unit opening with the sender unit removed (Section 19). The pump is a sealed unit; the only replacement part available is the check valve on the fuel outlet.

2   Before removing the pump, first ensure that the car is in a well ventilated place and that there is no danger of ignition from sparks or naked flames. Disconnect the battery negative lead.

3   With the sender unit removed, release the pump from its retaining lugs and remove it from the tank.

4   To separate the pump from the sender unit, unscrew the nuts and disconnect the wiring. Remove the noise damper from the check valve and lift off the fuel line and washers.

5   The outlet check valve may be unscrewed if necessary, but the pump body must not be held in a vice. Either grip the hexagon of the valve in the vice and turn the pump by hand, or use a spanner on the valve and a strap wrench on the pump body.

6   The pump is designed to work with all its moving parts immersed in petrol and it will be damaged irreparably if it is run without being connected to the fuel system.

7   The capacity of the pump is much greater than the fuel requirement of the engine and it is unlikely that pump output will fall to a point where it is inadequate.

8   Refitting is a reversal of removal.

32 Fuel accumulator – removal and refitting

1   Jack up the rear of the car and support it on stands.

2   Release the fuel system pressure, as described in Section 15, paragraphs 3 to 5 inclusive.

3   Disconnect the fuel pipes from the fuel accumulator and catch the small amount of fuel which will be released (photo).

4   Detach and remove the fuel accumulator from its support bracket.

5   Refitting is a reversal of removal. Check for leaks on completion with the engine restarted.

33 Fuel injectors – removal and refitting

1   Release the fuel system pressure as described in Section 15, paragraphs 3 to 5 inclusive.

2   Grip the fuel line union nut and withdraw the injector by pulling up firmly until the rubber O-ring seal is released from the injector insert (photo).

3   Using two spanners, hold the injector and unscrew the fuel line union, then remove the injector.

4   Accurate checking of the injector spray pattern and leakage requires special test equipment and should be left to an Audi dealer.

5   Refitting is a reversal of removal, but lubricate the O-ring seal by moistening it with petrol before fitting. Use a spanner on top of the fuel line union nut to push the injector fully into place (photo).

34 Inlet manifold – removal and refitting

All models except Turbo

1   Disconnect the battery negative lead.

2   Undo the two bolts and remove the cold start valve.

3   Disconnect the hoses and clips, and withdraw the idle stabilisation valve from the manifold.

4   Disconnect the accelerator cable and linkage, and where fitted the cruise control linkage from the throttle valve housing.

5   Undo the clip and release the air intake duct.

6   Disconnect the vacuum and electrical connections at the manifold according to model.

7   Release the fuel lines from the manifold clips.

8   Remove the air cleaner cover, element, and air intake hoses.

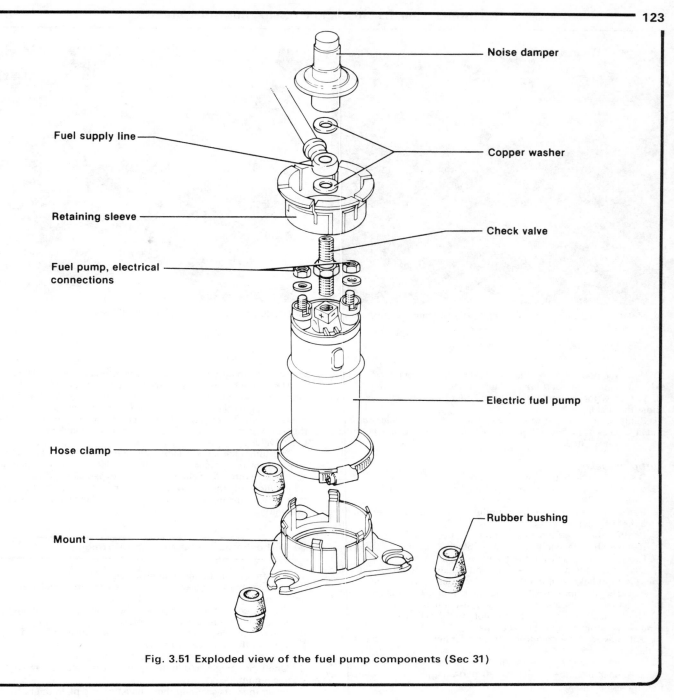

Noise damper

Fuel supply line

Copper washer

Retaining sleeve

Check valve

Fuel pump, electrical connections

Electric fuel pump

Hose clamp

Rubber bushing

Mount

Fig. 3.51 Exploded view of the fuel pump components (Sec 31)

32.3 Fuel accumulator fuel pipe connections and mounting

33.2 Withdrawing a fuel injector

33.5 Using a spanner to push a fuel injector fully home

34.9 Inlet manifold retaining bolts and exhaust manifold support brackets

34.16 Idle stabilisation valve on Turbo models

9   Undo the bolts securing the manifold to the cylinder head, and the exhaust manifold support bracket nuts (photo).
10 Withdraw the manifold from the cylinder head and remove it from under the fuel lines.
11 Refitting is a reversal of removal, but adjust the accelerator cable and linkage as described in Section 20, and Chapter 7 where automatic transmission is fitted.

Turbo models
12 Disconnect the battery negative lead.
13 Undo the clip and remove the air intake duct at the throttle valve housing.
14 Remove the air intake tube from the air cleaner, and intake duct at the airflow sensor.
15 Remove the air cleaner cover and element.
16 Remove the idle stabilisation valve, bracket, and duct (photo).
17 Release the fuel lines at the manifold clips.
18 Disconnect the accelerator cable and linkage, and where fitted the cruise control linkage at the throttle valve housing and manifold.
19 Note the locations of all electrical and vacuum connections likely to restrict removal of the manifold, and disconnect them.
20 Undo the bolts securing the manifold to the cylinder head, and the exhaust manifold support bracket nuts.
21 Withdraw the manifold from the cylinder head, and remove it from under the fuel lines.
22 Refitting is a reversal of removal, but adjust the accelerator cable and linkage as described in Section 20, and Chapter 7 where automatic transmission is fitted.

35 Turbocharger – description

2.2 litre Turbo models are equipped with an exhaust driven turbocharger, which is a device designed to increase the engine's power output without increasing exhaust emissions or adversely affecting fuel economy. It does so by utilizing the heat energy present in the exhaust gases as they exit the engine.

Basically, the turbocharger consists of two fans mounted on a common shaft. One fan is driven by the hot exhaust gases as they rush through the exhaust manifold and expand. The other pulls in fresh air and compresses it before it enters the intake manifold. By compressing the air, a larger charge can be let into each cylinder and greater power output is achieved.

The temperature of the intake air is reduced, thus increasing its density, by passing it through an intercooler mounted at the front of the engine prior to it entering the manifold.

The boost pressure generated by the turbocharger is controlled by a waste gate which opens once a predetermined pressure is achieved.

The turbocharger is lubricated by oil from the engine lubrication circuit, but an additional oil filter and an oil cooler are fitted.

On later models, the turbocharger is connected into the engine coolant circuit for cooling, and an electric coolant pump, activated by a thermo-switch, operates when the coolant temperature exceeds a preset value.

The turbocharger is a close tolerance, expensive component, and servicing or repairs should be left to a dealer service department, or specialist with turbocharger repair experience. Apart from the information in the following Sections, any other work on the turbocharger or its related components is beyond the scope of the average reader.

36 Turbocharger – removal and refitting

1   Disconnect the battery negative lead.
2   Remove the air intake duct between the intercooler and throttle valve housing.
3   Disconnect the vacuum hose, then remove the air intake duct between the air-flow sensor and intake tube.
4   Remove the air cleaner cover and filter element.
5   On North American models with water-cooled turbocharger, remove the oxygen sensor and CO measuring tube.
6   Undo the screws, and lift away the cover plate over the right-hand engine mounting.
7   Undo the nuts securing the exhaust front pipe to the turbocharger.
8   Undo the flange nuts, and disconnect the oil supply pipe at the turbocharger.
9   Disconnect the exhaust front pipe at the waste gate, intermediate pipe and transmission, and remove the pipe. Recover the gaskets.
10 Slacken the clips, and remove the air duct to the alternator.
11 Slacken the clip, and disconnect the intercooler hose from the turbocharger.
12 Undo the flange nuts, and disconnect the oil return pipe at the turbocharger.
13 On water-cooled versions, disconnect the lower coolant pipe at the union adjacent to the oil return pipe.
14 Refer to Chapter 12 and remove the alternator, then remove the alternator mounting bracket.
15 On water-cooled versions, disconnect the upper coolant pipe and the adjacent oil supply pipe.
16 Undo the nuts securing the turbocharger to the exhaust manifold, and remove the turbocharger.
17 Refitting is a reversal of removal. Check, and if necessary top up the cooling system on water-cooled versions.

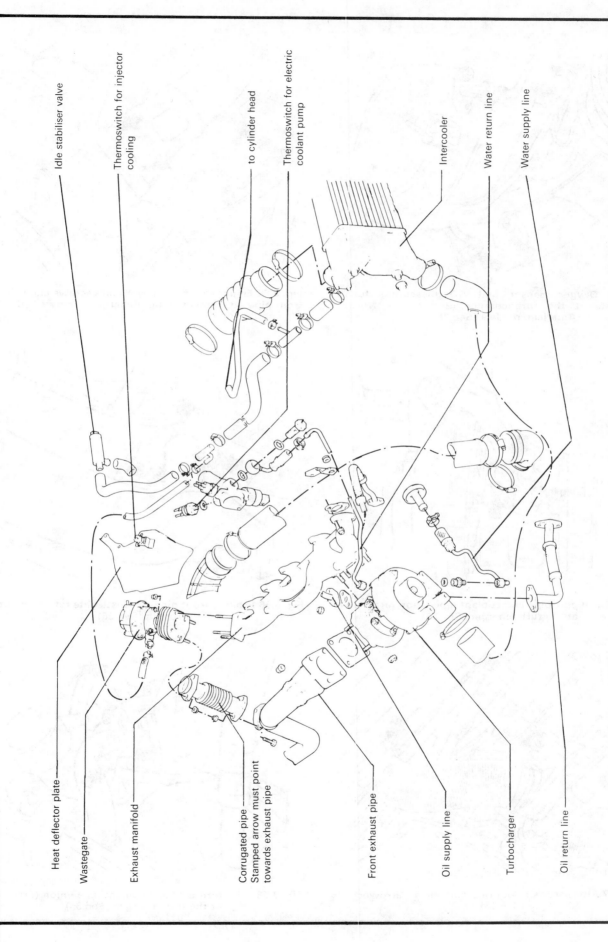

Idle stabiliser valve

Thermoswitch for injector cooling

to cylinder head

Thermoswitch for electric coolant pump

Intercooler

Water return line

Water supply line

Heat deflector plate

Wastegate

Exhaust manifold

Corrugated pipe
Stamped arrow must point towards exhaust pipe

Front exhaust pipe

Oil supply line

Turbocharger

Oil return line

Fig. 3.52 Exploded view of the water-cooled turbocharger components (Secs 35 and 36)

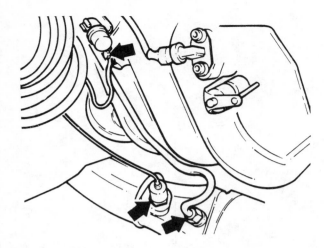

Fig. 3.53 Oxygen sensor and CO measuring tube attachments at the turbocharger (arrowed) – North American models (Sec 36)

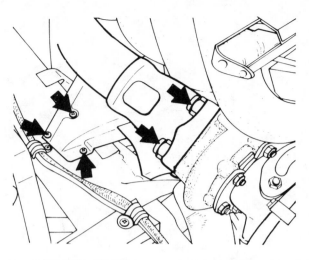

Fig. 3.54 Engine mounting cover plate screws and exhaust front pipe attachment at turbocharger – arrowed (Sec 36)

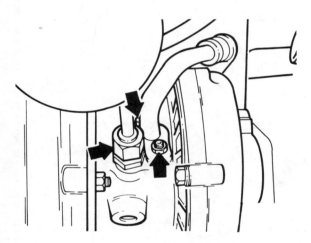

Fig. 3.55 Oil supply pipe and coolant pipe union (arrowed) at the turbocharger (Sec 36)

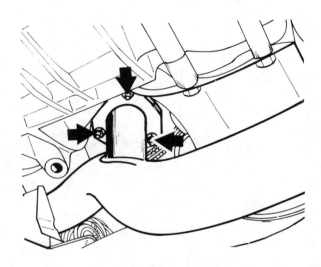

Fig. 3.56 Exhaust front pipe-to-waste gate retaining nuts – arrowed (Sec 36)

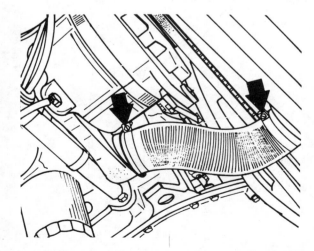

Fig. 3.57 Alternator air duct retaining clips – arrowed (Sec 36)

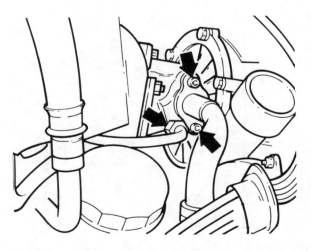

Fig. 3.58 Oil return pipe and coolant pipe union (arrowed) at the turbocharger (Sec 36)

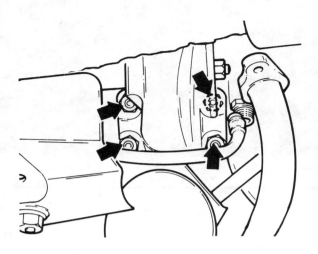

Fig. 3.59 Turbocharger retaining nuts – arrowed (Sec 36)

37 Turbo intercooler – removal and refitting

1   Remove the radiator grille, as described in Chapter 11.
2   Slacken the clips, and remove the air intake hoses and ducts at the intercooler.
3   Undo the upper and lower mountings, disengage the unit from its mounting grommets, and remove the intercooler from the car.
4   Refitting is a reversal of removal.

38 Emission control systems – general

Although careful attention to the correct ignition and mixture settings minimises the amount of harmful gases released by the exhaust system, the increasingly stringent legislation in some countries has made the introduction of additional systems necessary.

Crankcase ventilation system

Some of the products of combustion blow past the piston rings and enter the crankcase, from whence they would escape to the atmosphere if special precautions were not taken.

To prevent these gases from escaping to the atmosphere the crankcase breather is connected by a hose to the air cleaner so that the crankcase gases mix with the air/fuel mixture in the manifold and are consumed by the engine.

Exhaust gas recirculation (EGR)

The principle of the system is that some of the hot exhaust gas is ducted from the exhaust manifold to the inlet manifold where it mixes with the fuel/air mixture and again enters the cylinders. This lowers the temperature of combustion in the cylinders and reduces the oxides of nitrogen content of the exhaust.

The system is controlled by a thermostatic valve and by a vacuum valve, controlled by inlet manifold pressure, and system operation must be checked annually as a maintenance item.

Check the physical condition of the hoses of the system, looking for cracks and splits.

Run the engine and check that there are no leaks in the line from the EGR valve to the exhaust manifold.

Disconnect the yellow coloured hose from the straight connection of the temperature control valve and connect it to the T-piece on the hose to the inlet manifold. If the idling speed of the engine falls, or the engine stalls, the EGR valve is working properly. If the idle speed does not change, check that none of the hoses is blocked. If the hoses are clear the EGR valve is faulty and must be renewed.

Catalytic converter

This is only fitted to cars intended for certain North American territories and it consists of an additional component in the exhaust pipe and silencer system.

The converter contains a catalyst which induces a chemical reaction to turn the carbon monoxide and hydrocarbons in the exhaust gas into carbon dioxide and water.

The converter does not require any maintenance, but should be examined periodically for signs of physical damage.

The catalyst in the converter can be rendered ineffective by lead and other fuel additives, so it is important that only unleaded fuel is used, and that the fuel contains no harmful additives.

The catalytic converter contains a ceramic insert which is fragile and is liable to fracture if the converter is hit, or dropped.

Evaporative fuel control

To prevent fuel vapour escaping to the atmosphere, the fuel tank is vented to a charcoal canister. The fuel tank has an expansion chamber and vent lines which are arranged so that no fuel or vapour can escape even though the car may be at a very high temperature, or may be driven or parked on a very steep incline.

The vent lines are connected to a canister containing charcoal which absorbs the hydrocarbon vapours. When the engine is not running, fuel vapour collects in the charcoal canister. When the engine is running, fresh air is sucked through the canister and the vapours are drawn from the canister through the air cleaner and into the engine, where they are burnt.

Oxygen sensor system

This system consists of a sensor located in the exhaust manifold, an electronic control unit located in the right-hand front footwell, a thermo-switch relay, and frequency valve. An elapsed mileage odometer also illuminates a warning light on the instrument panel to indicate a maintenance check is required on the system.

The system controls the fuel/air mixture according to engine temperature and exhaust gas content, but will only be accurate if the basic mixture adjustments are correct.

39 Emission control systems – operating precautions

1   The efficiency and reliability of the emission control system is dependent upon a number of operating factors, and the following precautions must be observed.
2   Ensure that the fuel and ignition systems are serviced regularly and that only suitable fuel, free from harmful additives, is used.
3   Do not alter or remove any parts of the emission control system, or any controls which have been fitted to the vehicle to protect the environment.
4   Do not continue to use the car if it is misfiring, or showing any other symptoms of faulty operation of the engine.
5   Do not leave the car unattended when the engine is running, because any indications of improper operation will not be noticed and prolonged idling can cause the engine to overheat and be damaged.
6   If a catalytic converter is fitted, take care not to park the car on areas of dry grass or leaves, because the external temperature of the converter may be sufficient to ignite them.
7   Do not apply any additional undersealing or rustproofing material to the exhaust system, or anywhere very near to it, because this may lead to a fire.
8   If a catalytic converter is fitted, the car must never be pushed or towed to start it and the engine must not be turned off if the car is moving. To do so would allow unburnt fuel to enter the converter and damage it.

40 Exhaust manifold – removal and refitting

1   Disconnect the battery negative terminal.
2   On Turbo models remove the turbocharger, as described in Section 36.
3   Undo the exhaust front pipe-to-manifold nuts, and separate the front pipe at the flange. Recover the gasket.
4   On Turbo models, undo the nuts and separate the waste gate at the manifold.
5   Undo the nuts securing the manifold to the cylinder head, and the bolts securing the support brackets to the inlet manifold (photo).
6   Withdraw the manifold and recover the gaskets (photos).
7   Refitting is the reverse sequence to removal.

40.5 Exhaust manifold retaining nuts

40.6A Withdraw the manifold ...

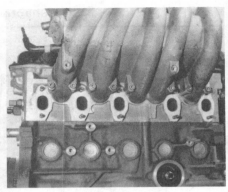

40.6B ... and recover the gaskets

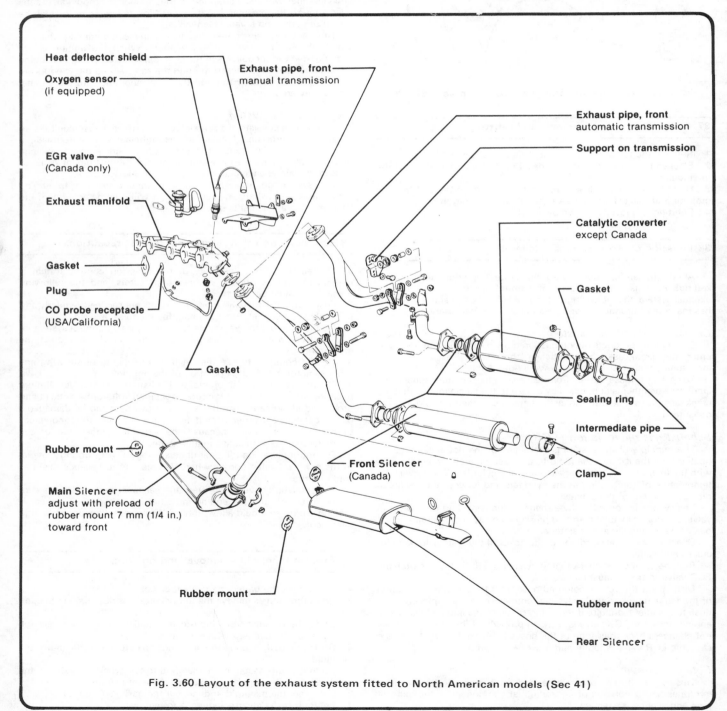

Heat deflector shield

Oxygen sensor
(if equipped)

Exhaust pipe, front
manual transmission

Exhaust pipe, front
automatic transmission

Support on transmission

EGR valve
(Canada only)

Exhaust manifold

Catalytic converter
except Canada

Gasket

Plug

Gasket

CO probe receptacle
(USA/California)

Sealing ring

Gasket

Intermediate pipe

Rubber mount

Clamp

Main Silencer
adjust with preload of
rubber mount 7 mm (1/4 in.)
toward front

Front Silencer
(Canada)

Rubber mount

Rubber mount

Rear Silencer

Fig. 3.60 Layout of the exhaust system fitted to North American models (Sec 41)

41 Exhaust system – checking, removal and refitting

The procedures are the same as described in Section 13 of this Chapter, but refer to Fig. 3.60 for an exploded view of the system fitted to North American models. Note that on Turbo models the front pipe is connected to the turbocharger, and an additional pipe connects the waste gate to the front pipe. If this pipe is renewed, the arrow must point towards the front pipe when refitting.

PART C – FAULT DIAGNOSIS – ALL ENGINES

42 Fault diagnosis – fuel system (carburettor models)

Note: *High fuel consumption and poor performance are not necessarily due to carburettor faults. Make sure that the ignition system is properly adjusted, that the brakes are not binding and that the engine is in good mechanical condition before tampering with the carburettor*

Symptom	Reason(s)
Fuel consumption excessive	Air cleaner choked, giving rich mixture Leak from tank, pump or fuel lines Float chamber flooding due to incorrect level or worn needle valve Carburettor incorrectly adjusted Idle speed too high Choke faulty (sticks on) Excessively worn carburettor
Lack of power, stalling or difficult starting	Faulty fuel pump Leak on suction side of pump or in fuel line Intake manifold or carburettor flange gaskets leaking Carburettor incorrectly adjusted Faulty choke Emission control system defect
Poor or erratic idling	Weak mixture Leak in intake manifold Leak in crankcase breather hose Leak in brake servo hose

43 Fault diagnosis – fuel system (fuel injection models)

Before assuming that a malfunction is caused by the fuel system, check the items mentioned in the special note at the start of the previous Section

Symptom	Reason(s)
Engine will not start (cold)	Fuel pump faulty Cold start valve faulty Sensor plate rest position incorrect Sensor plate and/or control plunger sticking Vacuum system leak Fuel system leak Thermotime switch remains open
Engine will not start (hot)	Faulty fuel pump Warm control pressure low Sensor plate rest position incorrect Sensor plate and/or control plunger sticking Vacuum system leak Fuel system leak Leaky injector valve(s) or low opening pressure Incorrect mixture adjustment
Engine difficult to start (cold)	Cold control pressure incorrect Cold start valve faulty Sensor plate rest position faulty Sensor plate and/or control plunger sticking Fuel system leak Thermotime switch not closing

Symptom	Reason(s)
Engine difficult to start (hot)	Warm control pressure too high or too low
	Sensor plate/control plunger faulty
	Fuel or vacuum leak in system
	Leaky injector valve(s) or low opening pressure
	Incorrect mixture adjustment
Rough idling (during warm-up period)	Incorrect cold control pressure
	Faulty idle stabilization system
	Faulty cold start valve
	Fuel or vacuum leak in system
	Leaky injector valve(s) or low opening pressure
Rough idling (engine warm)	Warm control pressure incorrect
	Faulty idle stabilization system
	Cold start valve faulty
	Sensor plate and/or control plunger sticking
	Fuel or vacuum leak in system
	Injector(s) leaking or low opening pressure
	Incorrect mixture adjustment
Engine backfiring into intake manifold	Warm control pressure high
	Vacuum system leak
Engine backfiring into exhaust manifold	Warm control pressure high
	Start valve leak
	Fuel system leak
	Incorrect mixture adjustment
Engine misfires (on road)	Fuel system leak
Engine 'runs on'	Sensor plate and or control plunger sticking
	Overrun cut-off valve faulty
Excessive petrol consumption	Fuel system leak
	Mixture adjustment incorrect
	Low warm control pressure

Chapter 4 Ignition system

Refer to Chapter 13 for specifications and information on 1987 and later models

Contents

Specifications

Part A – Transistorised coil ignition

General

System type	Hall effect transistorised coil ignition
Application	All models except Turbo

Distributor

Rotor rotation	Clockwise
Firing order:	
Four-cylinder engines	1-3-4-2 (No 1 at timing belt end)
Five-cylinder engines	1-2-4-5-3 (No 1 at timing belt end)

Coil

Primary resistance	0.52 to 0.76 ohm
Secondary resistance	2.4 to 3.5 kohm

Ignition timing

Vacuum hoses remain connected on all models

UK models:	
1.8 litre engines	17° to 19° BTDC at 700 to 800 rpm
1.9, 2.0, 2.2 and 2.3 litre engines	17° to 19° BTDC at 750 to 850 rpm
North American models:	
2.2 litre engines	
USA models	5° to 7° BTDC at 750 to 850 rpm
Canada models	2° to 4° ATDC at 750 to 850 rpm
2.3 litre engines	5° to 7° BTDC at 750 to 850 rpm

Spark plugs

Type:
  1.8 litre engines:
    Code DR .... Bosch W7D, W7DC, W7DTC*, (W8D, W8DC – short journeys only)
                                                                                  Beru 14-7D, 14-7DU, RS35, (14-8D, 14-8DU – short journeys only)
                                                                                  Champion N8Y, N7YC (N10Y, N9YC – short journeys only)

    Code DS .... Bosch W6DO, W6DTC*
                                                                                  Beru 14-6 DU
                                                                                  Champion N79Y

  1.9 litre engines:
    Code WH .... Bosch W6D, W6DC
                                                                                  Beru 14-6D, 14-6DU, RS37
                                                                                  Champion N8Y, N7YC

  2.0 litre engines:
    Code KP .... Bosch W6DO, W6DTC*
                                                                                  Beru 14-6DU, 14-5DTU*
                                                                                  Champion N79Y, N7BYC*

  2.2 litre engines:
    UK models:
      Code WC .... Bosch W6DO
                                                                                  Beru 14-6DU
                                                                                  Champion N79Y

    North American models:
      Code WU:
        For California only .... Bosch WR7DS
                                                                                  Beru RS35
                                                                                  Champion N8GY

        For all territories except California .... Bosch W7D, W7DC
                                                                                  Beru 14-7D, 14-7DU
                                                                                  Champion N8Y, N9YC

  2.3 litre engines:
    UK models:
      Code KU .... Bosch W6DC, W6DTC*
                                                                                  Beru 14-6DU, 14-6DTU*
                                                                                  Champion N7YC, N7BYC*

    North American models:
      Code KZ:
        For California only .... Bosch WR7DS, W7DTC*
                                                                                  Beru RS35, 14-7DTU*
                                                                                  Champion N8GY

        For all territories except California .... Bosch W7DC, W7DTC*
                                                                                  Beru 14-7DU, 14-7DTU*
                                                                                  Champion N9YC

*Long life versions with copper core and multiple earth electrodes

Electrode gap:
  1.8 litre engines:
    Code DR .... 0.6 to 0.8 mm (0.023 to 0.031 in)
    Code DS .... 0.8 to 0.9 mm (0.031 to 0.035 in)
  1.9 litre engines .... 0.6 to 0.8 mm (0.023 to 0.031 in)
  2.0 litre engines .... 0.7 to 0.9 mm (0.027 to 0.035 in)
  2.2 litre engines:
    UK models (code WC) .... 0.8 to 0.9 mm (0.031 to 0.035 in)
    North American models (code WU):
      USA .... 0.6 to 0.8 mm (0.023 to 0.031 in)
      Canada .... 0.7 to 0.9 mm (0.027 to 0.035 in)
  2.3 litre engines:
    UK models (code KU) .... 0.7 to 0.9 mm (0.027 to 0.035 in)
    North American models (code KZ) .... 0.7 to 0.8 mm (0.027 to 0.031 in)

Torque wrench settings	**Nm**	**lbf ft**
Spark plugs	20	15
Distributor clamp bolt/nut	15	11

Part B – all-electronic ignition
General
System type .... Hall effect all electronic ignition with microprocessor control
Application .... 2.2 litre Turbo models

Distributor
Rotor rotation .... Clockwise
Firing order .... 1-2-4-5-3 (No 1 at timing belt end)

Coil
Primary resistance .... 0.5 to 1.5 ohm
Secondary resistance:
    Type 1 .... 6.8 kohm
    Type 2 .... 7.7 kohm

Ignition timing sender
Clearance between sender head and flywheel pin .... 0.45 to 1.25 mm (0.017 to 0.049 in)

RPM sender
Clearance between sender head and flywheel ring gear teeth .... 0.51 to 1.24 mm (0.020 to 0.048 in)

Spark plugs
Type:
    UK models (code KG) .... Bosch W5D, W5DC, W6DTC
    Beru 14-5D, 14-5DU
    Champion N6Y, N6YC

    North American models (code KH, WK) .... Bosch WR7DS
    Beru RS35
    Champion N8GY

Electrode gap:
    UK models .... 0.8 to 0.9 mm (0.031 to 0.035 in)
    North American models .... 0.7 to 0.8 mm (0.027 to 0.031 in)

Torque wrench settings

	Nm	lbf ft
Spark plugs	20	15
Distributor clamp nut	15	11

PART A – TRANSISTORISED COIL IGNITION

1 General description

A transistorised coil ignition system (TCI-H) working on the Hall effect principle is used on all models except Turbo versions and comprises the battery, coil, distributor, ignition control unit, spark plugs and associated leads and wiring.

The system is divided into two circuits, low tension and high tension. The high tension (HT) circuit is similar to that of a conventional ignition system, and consists of the high tension coil windings, distributor, rotor arm, spark plugs and leads. The low tension (LT) circuit consists of the battery, ignition switch, low tension or primary coil windings, and a rotor and pick-up unit operating in conjunction with the control unit. The rotor and pick-up unit are located in the distributor, and perform the same function as the contact breaker points used in conventional systems.

The rotor is a four or five toothed wheel (one for each cylinder) which is fitted to the distributor shaft.

The pick-up unit is fitted to the distributor baseplate and basically consists of a coil and permanent magnet.

The control unit is located in the engine compartment and is an amplifier module which is used to boost the voltage induced by the pick-up coil.

When the ignition switch is on, the ignition primary circuit is energised. When the distributor rotor teeth approach the pick-up coil assembly, a voltage is induced which signals the amplifier to switch off the coil primary circuit, causing the magnetic field in the ignition coil to collapse, inducing a high voltage in the secondary windings. This is conducted to the distributor cap where the rotor arm directs it to the appropriate spark plug. A timing circuit in the amplifier module turns on the coil current again after the coil magnetic field has collapsed, and the process continues for each power stroke of the engine.

The distributor is fitted with centrifugal and vacuum advance mechanisms to control the ignition timing according to engine speed and load respectively.

2 Maintenance and inspection

1 At the intervals specified in Routine Maintenance at the beginning of this manual remove the distributor cap and thoroughly clean it inside and out with a dry lint-free rag. Examine the HT lead segments inside the cap. If the segments appear badly burnt or pitted, renew the cap. Make sure that the carbon brush in the centre of the cap is free to move and that it protrudes by approximately 3 mm (0.1 in) from its holder.

2 With the distributor cap removed, lift off the rotor arm and the protective plastic cover. Carefully apply two drops of engine oil to the centre of the cam spindle. Also lubricate the centrifugal advance mechanism by applying two drops of engine oil through one of the holes in the baseplate. Wipe away any excess oil and refit the plastic cover, rotor arm, and distributor cap.

3 Renew the spark plugs, as described in Section 9. If the spark plugs have been renewed within the service interval, clean them and reset the electrode gap, as described in Section 9.

4 Check the condition and security of all leads and wiring associated with the ignition system. Make sure that no chafing is occurring on any of the wires, and that all connections are secure, clean, and free of corrosion. Pay particular attention to the HT leads which should be carefully inspected for any sign of corrosion on their end fitting which, if evident, should be carefully cleaned away. Wipe clean the HT leads over their entire length before refitting.

3 Ignition system – precautions

1 To prevent personal injury and damage to the ignition system, the following precautions must be observed when working on the ignition system.

2 Do not attempt to disconnect any plug lead or touch any of the high tension cables when the engine is running, or being turned by the starter motor.

3 Ensure that the ignition is turned OFF before connecting or disconnecting any ignition wiring.

4 Ensure that the ignition is switched OFF before connecting or disconnecting any ignition testing equipment such as a timing light.

5 Do not connect a suppression condenser or test lamp to the coil negative terminal (1).

6 Do not connect any test appliance or stroboscopic lamp requiring a 12 volt supply to the coil positive terminal (15).

7 If the HT cable is disconnected from the distributor (terminal 4), the cable must be connected to earth and remain earthed if the engine is to be rotated by the starter motor, for example if a compression test is to be done.

8 If a high current boost charger is used, the charger output voltage must not exceed 16.5 volts and the time must not exceed one minute.

9 The ignition coil of a transistorised system must never be replaced by the ignition coil from a contact breaker type ignition system.

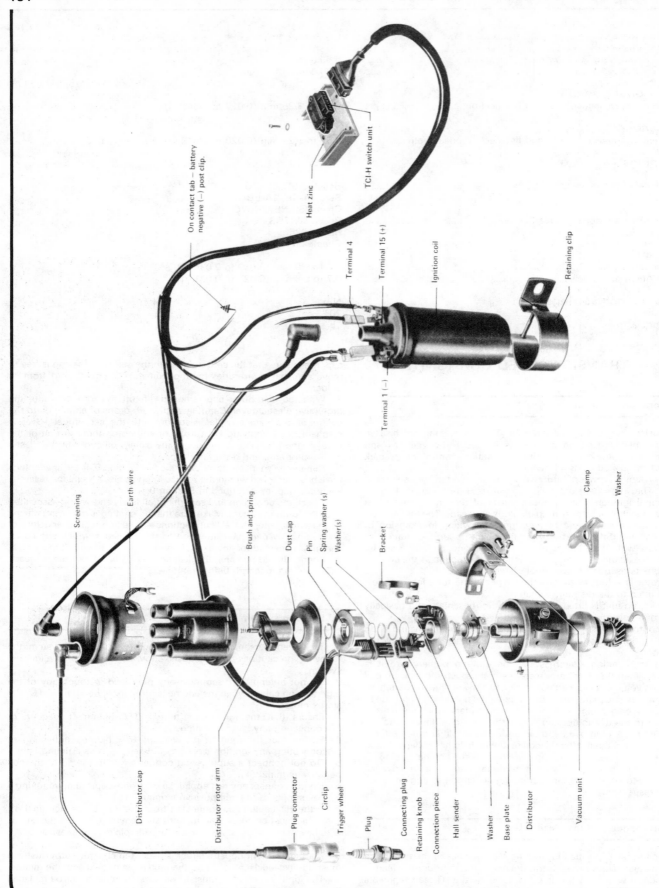

On contact tab – battery negative (–) post clip.

Heat zinc

TCI-H switch unit

Terminal 4

Terminal 15 (+)

Ignition coil

Retaining clip

Terminal 1 (–)

Screening

Earth wire

Brush and spring

Dust cap

Pin

Spring washer (s)

Washer(s)

Bracket

Clamp

Washer

Distributor cap

Distributor rotor arm

Plug connector

Circlip

Trigger wheel

Plug

Connecting plug

Retaining knob

Connection piece

Hall sender

Washer

Base plate

Distributor

Vacuum unit

Fig. 4.1 Transistorised coil ignition components (Sec 1)

10 If an electric arc welder is to be used on any part of the vehicle, the car battery must be disconnected while welding is being done.

11 If a stationary engine is heated to above 80°C (176°F) such as may happen after paint drying, or steam cleaning, the engine must not be started until it has cooled.

12 Ensure that the ignition is switched *OFF* when the car is washed.

13 Where there is a known or suspected defect in the ignition system the wiring plug at the control unit must be disconnected if the vehicle is to be towed.

14 Never substitute the standard fitting 1 kohm rotor arm (marked R1) with a different type.

15 For the purposes of radio suppression, only 1 kohm spark plug HT leads with 1 kohm to 5 kohm spark plug connectors may be used.

4 Distributor – removal and refitting

1 Pull the high tension connection from the centre of the ignition coil and remove the caps from the spark plugs (photo).

2 Release the two spring clips securing the distributor cap, then remove the distributor cap with the ignition harness attached. On models with metal screening round the top of the distributor, it is necessary to remove the bonding strap connector before the cap can be taken off (photo).

3 Turn the engine using a spanner on the crankshaft pulley bolt until the TDC mark (0) on the flywheel or driveplate is aligned with the pointer in the timing aperture. Alternatively, check that the notch on the crankshaft pulley is aligned with the TDC arrow or pip on the lower timing belt cover.

4 Check that the mark on the rear of the camshaft gear is aligned with the top of the timing belt rear cover – four-cylinder engines (Fig. 4.3), or with the upper surface of the valve cover gasket – five-cylinder engines (Fig. 4.4). In this position the distributor rotor arm contact should be aligned with the mark on the rim of the distributor body.

5 Disconnect the wiring connector at the distributor pick-up unit.

6 Note the exact position of the rotor arm, so that the distributor can be fitted with the rotor arm in the same position, and also put mating marks on the distributor mounting flange and base. By marking these

4.1 Disconnecting the spark plug HT leads (five-cylinder engines)

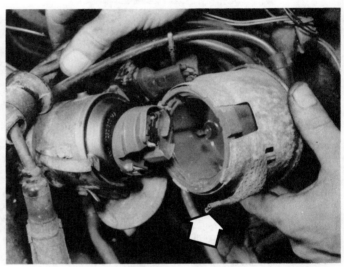

4.2 Disconnect the earth bonding strap connector (arrowed) before removing the distributor cap (five-cylinder engines)

Fig. 4.2 Flywheel TDC O mark (arrowed) aligned with pointer in timing aperture (Sec 4)

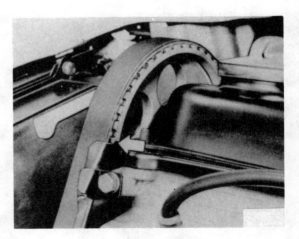

Fig. 4.3 Mark on camshaft gear (arrowed) aligned with top of timing belt rear cover – four-cylinder engines (Sec 4)

Fig. 4.4 Mark on camshaft gear (arrowed) aligned with upper surface of valve cover gasket – five-cylinder engines (Sec 4)

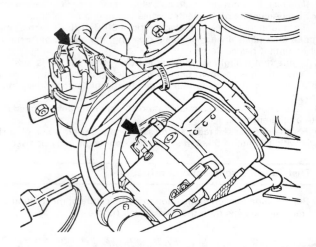

Fig. 4.5 HT lead connection at ignition coil and wiring plug location on distributor – arrowed (Sec 4)

positions and also ensuring that the crankshaft is not moved while the distributor is off, the distributor can be refitted without upsetting the ignition timing.

7   Pull the vacuum pipe(s) from the vacuum control unit, marking the position of the pipes if there is more than one.

8   Remove the nut/bolt and washer from the distributor clamp plate and take the clamp plate off. Remove the distributor and gasket (photos).

9   When refitting the distributor always renew the gasket (photo). Provided the crankshaft has not been moved, turn the rotor arm to such a position that when the distributor is fully installed and the gears mesh, the rotor will turn and take up the position which it held before removal (photo). On the four-cylinder engine if the distributor will not seat fully, withdraw the unit and use pliers to turn the oil pump driveshaft slightly, then try again.

10   Fit the clamp plate and washer, then fit the nut/bolt and tighten it.

11   Fit the distributor cap and clip it in place, then reconnect the high and low tension wires and the earth bonding strap (if fitted).

12   If the engine has been the subject of overhaul, the crankshaft has been rotated or a new distributor is being fitted, then the procedure for installing the distributor will differ according to engine; refer to Section 6.

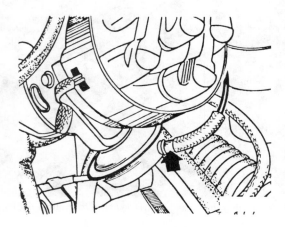

Fig. 4.6 Vacuum pipe attachment (arrowed) at distributor (Sec 4)

4.8A Remove the clamp plate and retaining bolt ...

4.8B ... then remove the distributor (five-cylinder engines)

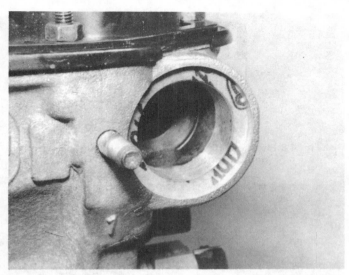

4.9A Gasket in place prior to fitting the distributor (five-cylinder engines)

4.9B Distributor fitted position with rotor arm contact (A) aligned with mark on distributor rim (B) (five-cylinder engines)

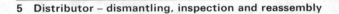

5 Distributor – dismantling, inspection and reassembly

Note: *Before commencing work check if spare parts are readily available for the distributor.*

1 Remove the distributor, as described in Section 4.
2 Pull the rotor arm off the distrubutor shaft, then lift off the plastic cover. Do not allow the cap retaining clips to touch the toothed rotor.
3 Mark the toothed rotor in relation to the distributor shaft, then prise out the retainer. Using two screwdrivers, carefully lever off the rotor and recover the locating pin.
4 Remove the retainer and washers, noting their location.
5 Remove the screws, and withdraw the vacuum unit and packing after disconnecting the operating arm.
6 Remove the retainer and washers from the baseplate, and also remove the screw securing the socket to the side of the distributor. Withdraw the pick-up unit and socket together.
7 Remove the screws and lift out the baseplate followed by the washer.
8 Clean all the components and examine them for wear and damage.
9 Inspect the inside of the distributor cap for signs of burning, or tracking. Make sure that the small carbon brush in the centre of the distributor cap is in good condition and can move up and down freely under the influence of its spring.
10 Check that the rotor arm is not damaged. Use an ohmmeter to measure the resistance between the brass contact in the centre of the rotor arm and the brass contact at the edge of the arm. The measured value of resistance should be between 0.6 and 1.4 kohms.
11 Suck on the pipe connection to the vacuum diaphragm and check that the operating rod of the diaphragm unit moves. Retain the diaphragm under vacuum to check that the diaphragm is not perforated.
12 Reassemble the distributor in the reverse order of dismantling, but apply a few drops of engine oil to the centrifugal advance weights and smear a little grease on the bearing surface of the baseplate.

6 Ignition timing – basic setting

1 If the distributor has been removed and the ignition timing disturbed, it will be necessary to reset the timing using the following static method before setting it dynamically, as described in Section 7.

Four-cylinder engines

2 Turn the engine using a spanner on the crankshaft pulley bolt until the TDC mark (O) on the flywheel or driveplate is aligned with the pointer in the timing aperture (Fig. 4.2) which is located next to the distributor.

3 Check that the mark on the rear of the camshaft gear is aligned with the top of the timing belt rear cover, as shown in Fig. 4.3. If the mark is on the opposite side of the cylinder head, turn the crankshaft forward one complete revolution, and again align the TDC mark.
4 Turn the oil pump shaft so that its lug is parallel with the crankshaft.
5 With the distributor cap removed, turn the rotor arm so that the centre of the metal contact is aligned with the mark on the rim of the distributor body.
6 Hold the distributor over its recess in the cylinder block with the vacuum unit slightly clockwise of the position shown in Fig. 4.7.
7 Insert the distributor fully. As the drivegear meshes with the intermediate shaft, the rotor will turn slightly anti-clockwise and the body can be realigned with the rotor arm to take up the final positions shown in Fig. 4.7. A certain amount of trial and error may be required for this. If the distributor cannot be fully inserted into its mounting hole, slightly reposition the oil pump driveshaft lug. Turn the distributor body until the original body-to-cylinder head marks are in alignment. Tighten the distributor clamp bolt

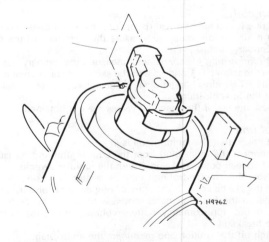

Fig. 4.7 Distributor fitted position with rotor arm aligned with notch in distributor body rim – four-cylinder engines (Sec 6)

Five-cylinder engines

8 Turn the engine using a spanner on the crankshaft pulley bolt until the TDC mark (O) is aligned with the lug in the timing aperture in the flywheel or driveplate housing.

9   Check that the mark on the rear of the camshaft gear is aligned with the upper edge of the valve cover gasket. If the mark is on the opposite side of the cylinder head, turn the crankshaft forward one complete revolution and again align the TDC mark.
10 With the distributor cap removed, turn the rotor arm so that the centre of the metal contact is aligned with the mark on the rim of the distributor body (photo 4.9B).
11 Hold the distributor over the location aperture in the rear of the cylinder head with the vacuum unit facing downwards.
12 Insert the distributor fully. As the drivegear meshes with the camshaft, the rotor will turn slightly anti-clockwise, and the body can then be realigned with the rotor arm so that the vacuum unit faces slightly to the right.
13 Fit the clamp and tighten the nut.

7 Ignition timing – dynamic setting

1   The ignition timing is adjusted dynamically with the engine at normal operating temperature, idling at the specified speed (see Chapter 3), with all electrical accessories switched off and the radiator cooling fan not running. The vacuum hose connections remain connected at the distributor.
2   The ignition timing may be checked using a digital tester connected to the TDC sensor in the flywheel or driveplate housing. However, as this equipment is not normally available to the home mechanic, the following method describes the use of a timing light.
3   Connect the timing light to the engine in accordance with the manufacturer's instructions.
4   Run the engine at idling speed and direct the timing light through the timing aperture in the flywheel or driveplate housing. The mark on the flywheel or driveplate should appear in line with the pointer or reference edge on the housing (Fig. 4.8). If adjustment is necessary, loosen the clamp and turn the distributor body until the correct position is achieved, then tighten the clamp.
5   Gradually increase the engine speed and check that the ignition advances – the centrifugal advance can be checked by pinching the vacuum hoses, and an indication of the vacuum advances can be obtained by releasing the hoses and noting that a different advance occurs.
6   After adjustment check and if necessary reset the engine idling speed, then switch off and remove the timing light.

8 Ignition system – testing

Ignition coil
1   It is rare for an ignition coil (photo) to fail, but if there is reason to suspect it, use an ohmmeter to measure the resistance of the primary and secondary circuits.
2   With the wiring disconnected, measure the primary resistance between the terminals 1 and 15 and the secondary resistance between the centre HT terminal and terminal 1. The correct resistance values are given in the Specifications.
3   Renew the coil if the specified values are not obtained.

Control unit
4   First check that the ignition coil is in order.
5   Disconnect the multi-plug from the control unit and measure the voltage between contacts 4 and 2 with the ignition switched on (Fig. 4.11). Note that the control unit may be located alongside the heater beneath the plastic cover in the engine compartment (photo), or under the carpet in the front left-hand footwell, according to model. If the voltage is not approximately battery voltage, check the wiring for possible breakage.
6   Switch off the ignition and reconnect the multi-plug.
7   Disconnect the multi-plug from the distributor and connect a voltmeter across the coil primary terminals. With the ignition switched on at least 2 volts must register, falling to zero after approximately 1 to 2 seconds. If this does not occur, renew the control unit and coil.
8   Connect a wire briefly between the centre terminal of the distributor multi-plug and earth. The voltage should rise to at least 2 volts on four-cylinder engines, and between 5 and 6 volts on five-cylinder engines, otherwise the control unit should be renewed.
9   Switch off the ignition and connect a voltmeter across the outer

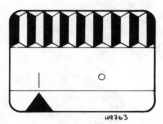

Fig. 4.8 Flywheel 18° BTDC timing mark aligned with pointer in timing aperture (Sec 7)

8.1 Ignition coil location on bulkhead (five-cylinder engines)

Fig. 4.9 Checking ignition coil primary resistance (Sec 8)

terminals of the distributor multi-plug. Switch on the ignition and check that 5 volts is registered. If not, check the wiring for possible breakage.

Pick-up unit
10 First check the ignition coil, and control unit. The following test should be made within ambient temperature extremes of 0° and 40°C (32° and 104°F).
11 Disconnect the central HT lead from the distributor cap and earth it with a bridging wire.

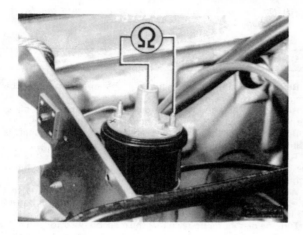

Fig. 4.10 Checking ignition coil secondary resistance (Sec 8)

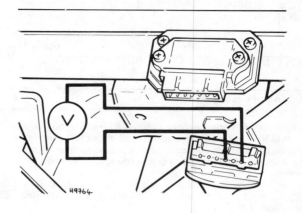

Fig. 4.11 Checking voltage at control unit plug terminals 4 and 2 (Sec 8)

8.5 Ignition control unit location alongside heater in engine compartment (five-cylinder engines)

12 Pull back the rubber grommet on the control unit and connect a voltmeter across terminals 6 and 3 (Fig. 4.12).
13 Switch on the ignition, then turn the engine slowly in the normal direction using a spanner on the crankshaft pulley bolt. The voltage should alternate between 0 to 0.7 volts, and 1.8 volts to battery voltage; if required, the distributor cap can be removed – with a full air gap 0 to 0.7 volts should register, but when the toothed rotor covers the air gap 1.8 volts to battery voltage should register.
14 If the results are not as given in paragraph 13, the pick-up unit is faulty.

9 Spark plugs and HT leads – general

1 The correct functioning of the spark plugs is vital for the correct running and efficiency of the engine. The spark plugs should be renewed at the specified intervals. However, if misfiring or bad starting is experienced in the service period, they must be removed, cleaned, and regapped.
2 The condition of the spark plugs will also tell much about the overall condition of the engine.
3 If the insulator nose of the spark plug is clean and white, with no deposits, this is indicative of a weak mixture, or too hot a plug. (A hot

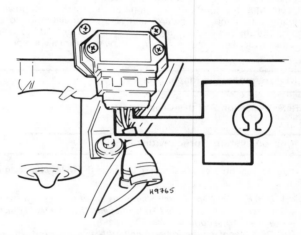

Fig. 4.12 Voltmeter connected across control unit plug terminals 6 and 3 (Sec 8)

plug transfers heat away from the electrode slowly – a cold plug transfers it away quickly).
4 If the tip and insulator nose is covered with hard black-looking deposits, then this is indicative that the mixture is too rich. Should the plug be black and oily, then it is likely that the engine is fairly worn, as well as the mixture being too rich.
5 If the insulator nose is covered with light tan to greyish brown deposits, then the mixture is correct and it is likely that the engine is in good condition.
6 If there are any traces of long brown tapering stains on the outside of the white portion of the plug, then the plug will have to be renewed, as this shows that there is a faulty joint between the plug body and the insulator, and compression is being lost.
7 Plugs should be cleaned by a sand blasting machine, which will free them from carbon more thoroughly than cleaning by hand. The machine will also test the condition of the plugs under compression. Any plug that fails to spark at the recommended pressure should be renewed.
8 The spark plug gap is of considerable importance, as, if it is too large or too small, the size of the spark and its efficiency will be seriously impaired. The spark plug gap should be set to the figure given in the Specifications at the beginning of this Chapter.
9 To set it, measure the gap with a feeler gauge, and then bend open, or close the *outer* plug electrode until the correct gap is achieved. The centre electrode should *never* be bent as this may crack the insulation and cause plug failure, if nothing worse.
10 Always tighten the spark plugs to the specified torque.

11 Note that long life spark plugs with a copper core and multiple earth electrodes are available for certain engines. If these plugs are fitted do not attempt to adjust the electrode gap by the conventional method, but renew the plug when the gap exceeds the specified amount.

PART B – ALL-ELECTRONIC IGNITION

10 General description

Turbo models are equipped with an all-electronic ignition system, which utilizes computer technology and electro-magnetic circuitry to simulate the main functions of a conventional ignition distributor, and also to locate and identify by visual warning any faults occurring in the system.

The all-electronic ignition comprises the battery, coil, distributor, ignition control unit, spark plugs, and associated sender units, cables and wiring (Fig. 4.13).

The distributor operates on the Hall effect principle and functions in the same manner as the unit used in the transistorised coil ignition described in Part A of this Chapter. The electronic control unit receives information on engine speed and load from the various sender units, and computes the most efficient ignition timing for the prevailing operating conditions. The control unit also continually monitors the operation of the system, and initiates a fault display made to visually warn the driver of any serious system fault by means of a warning lamp.

11 Maintenance and inspection

Refer to Section 2 of this Chapter.

12 Ignition system – precautions

Refer to Section 3 of this Chapter, but note the following additional items:

(a) *If a high current boost charger is used, the charger output voltage must not exceed 16.5 volts and the time used must not exceed 15 seconds*
(b) *Do not replace the ignition coil with any other type of coil*
(c) *Do not disconnect the battery with the engine running*

(d) *Do not apply a voltage to the control unit to simulate output signals*

13 Distributor – removal and refitting

1 Refer to Section 4 and carry out the operations described in paragraphs 1 to 5 inclusive.
2 Remove the bolt and washer from the distributor clamp plate, and take the clamp plate off. Remove the distributor and gasket.
3 Before refitting the distributor, ensure that the crankshaft is still positioned as described in Section 4.
4 Turn the distributor shaft as necessary so that the mark on the upper face of the toothed rotor is aligned with the notch on the rim of the distributor body (photo).
5 With a new gasket in position, hold the distributor so that the wiring socket is in approximately the 3 o'clock position, and insert the unit into its location.
6 Turn the distributor body so that the mark on the rotor and notch on the distributor body rim are once again aligned, then refit and tighten the clamp plate.
7 Refit the wiring plug, distributor cap and HT leads.

14 Distributor – dismantling, inspection and reassembly

Refer to Section 5 of this Chapter.

15 Ignition timing – adjustment

On the all-electronic ignition system, ignition timing settings are generated by the electronic control unit to suit the engine's prevailing operating conditions. Adjustment of the timing in service is therefore unnecessary, apart from ensuring that the distributor is positioned correctly initially after removal and refitting (See Section 13).

16 Ignition system – testing

Ignition coil
1 The ignition coil fitted may be either type 1 or type 2, as shown in Fig. 4.13. Identify the type being worked on before proceeding (photo).

13.4 Mark on distributor toothed rotor (A) aligned with distributor body notch (B) (five-cylinder Turbo engines)

16.1 Wiring connections at the type 2 ignition coil (five-cylinder Turbo engines)

A Terminal 1   C Terminal 4
B Terminal 15   D Power stage wiring plug

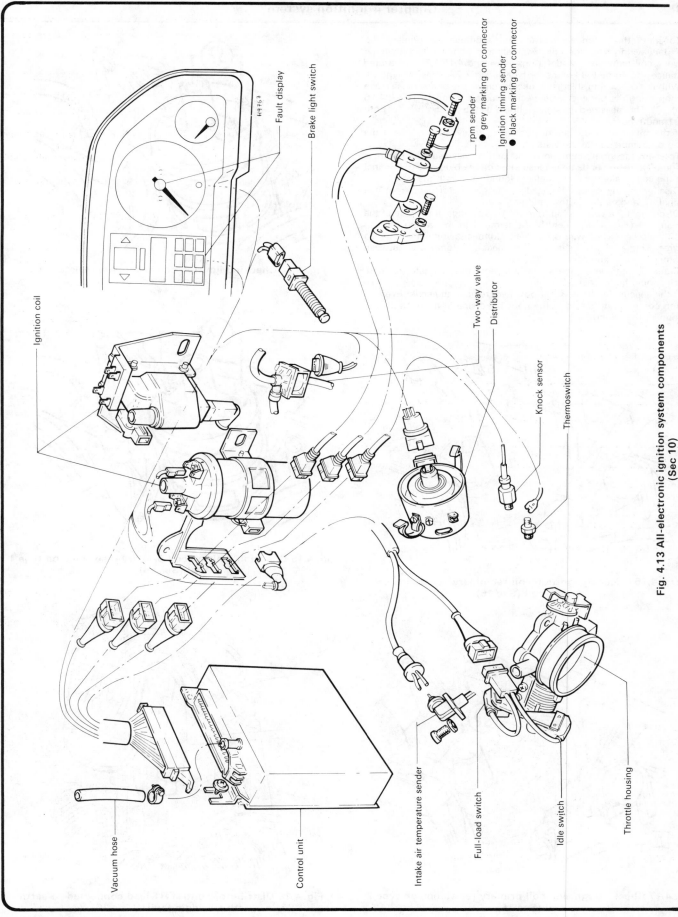

Fault display

Brake light switch

rpm sender
● grey marking on connector
Ignition timing sender
● black marking on connector

Ignition coil

Two-way valve
Distributor

Knock sensor

Thermoswitch

Fig. 4.13 All-electronic ignition system components
(Sec 10)

Vacuum hose

Control unit

Intake air temperature sender

Full-load switch

Idle switch

Throttle housing

2   To check the secondary resistance, disconnect the primary and secondary wiring from the coil terminals and connect an ohmmeter between coil terminals 1 and 4 (Figs. 4.14 and 4.15). The measured resistance should be 6.8 kohms for type 1 and 7.7 kohms for type 2.

3   With the coil wiring still disconnected, check the primary resistance by connecting the ohmmeter between terminals 1 and 15 (Figs. 4.16 and 4.17). The measured resistance should be 0.5 to 1.5 ohms for both type 1 and type 2.

4   If the specified values are not obtained, renew the coil. Refit the wiring on completion of the tests.

5   To check the ignition coil power stage, first make sure that there is no sign of corrosion or damaged insulation on the blue wire to terminal 1 on the coil. Make good any defects found, then refit the wire.

6   Disconnect the central HT lead at the distributor cap (from coil terminal 4), and earth it with a bridging wire.

7   Disconnect the wiring plug from the power stage at the side of the ignition coil (Fig. 4.19). Identify the terminal in the wiring plug to which the green/white wire is attached. Connect a voltmeter between the green/white wire and earth, and connect a bridging wire between the other terminal and earth.

8   Crank the engine on the starter and note the voltmeter reading, which should be at least 0.2 volts.

9   If the specified voltage is not obtained, remove the cover over the igntion control unit located in the right-hand side front footwell, and disconnect the wiring plug.

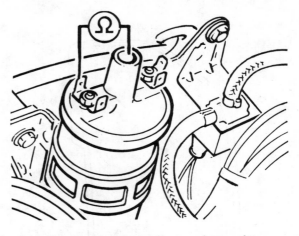

Fig. 4.14 Checking ignition coil secondary resistance on type 1 coil (Sec 16)

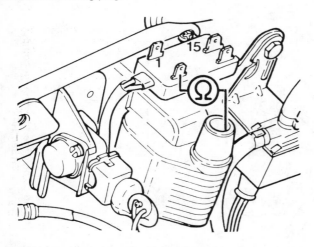

Fig. 4.15 Checking ignition coil secondary resistance on type 2 coil (Sec 16)

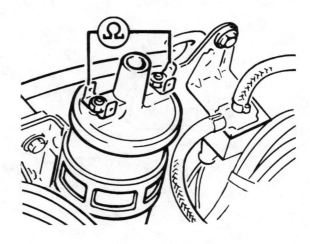

Fig. 4.16 Checking ignition coil primary resistance on type 1 coil (Sec 16)

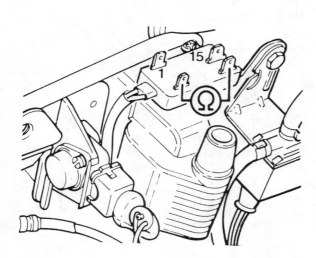

Fig. 4.17 Checking ignition coil primary resistance on type 2 coil (Sec 16)

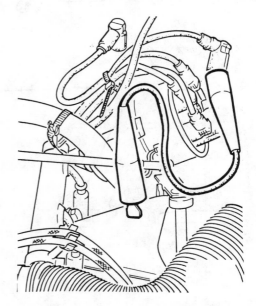

Fig. 4.18 Distributor central HT lead connected to earth with a bridging wire (Sec 16)

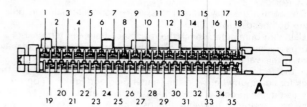

Fig. 4.20 Ignition control unit wiring plug terminal identification (Sec 16)

10 Check the continuity of the wiring between the power stage wiring plug (green/white terminal), and terminal 22 in the control unit plug (Fig. 4.20). The reading obtained should be approximately 0 ohms. The same value should be obtained when checking between terminal 2 in the control unit plug, and the other terminal in the power stage wiring plug. If these values are not obtained, check for breaks in the wiring or poor connections in the wiring plugs. If all is satisfactory, renew the ignition control unit. Reconnect all wiring on completion of the tests.

Ignition timing sender
11 Disconnect the black plug at the wiring connector support bracket on the bulkhead (Fig. 4.21).
12 Using an ohmmeter, check the resistance between terminals 1 and 2 in the wiring socket, which should be approximately 1 kohm (Fig. 4.22). If this value is not obtained, renew the ignition timing sender.
13 If the specified reading is obtained, connect the ohmmeter between terminals 1 and 3 in the wiring socket, then between terminals 2 and 3. There should be no reading on the ohmmeter in each case. If there is, renew the ignition timing sender.
14 If the test results are satisfactory so far, check for continuity in the wiring between the ignition timing sender plug and the ignition control unit plug as follows.
15 Remove the cover over the ignition control unit located in the right-hand side front footwell and disconnect the wiring plug.
16 Check the continuity of the wiring between terminal 1 in the sender plug (Fig. 4.23) and terminal 13 in the control unit plug (Fig. 4.20). Next, check the continuity between terminal 2 in the sender plug and 12 in the control unit plug, then finally terminal 3 in the sender plug and 28 in the control unit plug. The ohmmeter readings should be 0 ohms in each case. If the specified values are not obtained, there is a break in the wiring between the two plugs. If the readings are satisfactory, check the ignition timing sender fitted position, as described in Section 17. If this is correct, renew the ignition control unit. reconnect all wiring on completion of the checks.

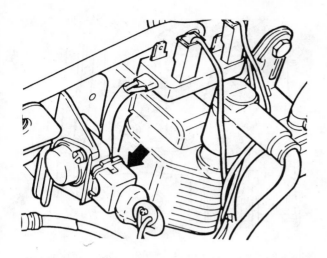

Fig. 4.19 Ignition coil power stage wiring plug – arrowed (Sec 16)

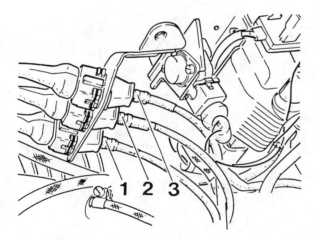

Fig. 4.21 Wiring connectors at the bulkhead support bracket (Sec 16)

1   Black plug – ignition timing sender
2   Grey plug – rpm sender
3   Red plug – knock sensor

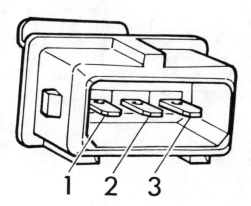

Fig. 4.22 Wiring socket terminal identification (Sec 16)

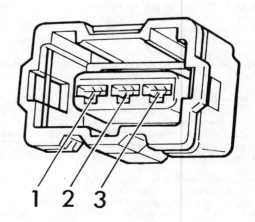

Fig. 4.23 Wiring plug terminal identification on 3-pin type (Sec 16)

RPM sender

17 Disconnect the grey plug at the wiring connector support bracket on the bulkhead (Fig. 4.21).

18 Using an ohmmeter, check the resistance between terminals 1 and 2 in the wiring socket (Fig. 4.22), which should be approximately 1 kohm. If this value is not obtained, renew the rpm sender.

19 If the test results are satisfactory, check the wiring socket, then check for continuity between the sender plug and ignition control unit plug using the procedure described in paragraphs 13 to 16. When checking continuity between the two plugs, the checks are made between sender plug terminal 1, and control unit plug terminal 29, then between terminal 2 and 11, and 3 and 28 in the sender plug and control unit plug respectively.

Air intake temperature sender

20 Pull back the cover over the air intake temperature sender on the throttle valve housing (Fig. 4.24).

21 Using an ohmmeter, check the resistance between the two sender contacts which should be between 400 and 700 ohms.

22 If the specified value is not obtained, remove the cover over the ignition control unit, located in the right-hand side front footwell, and disconnect the wiring plug.

23 Check the resistance of the wiring between terminal 23 in the control unit plug (Fig. 4.20) and contact 1 and contact 2 alternately on the intake temperature sender (Fig. 4.25). The readings obtained should be 0 ohms and 400 to 700 ohms respectively. Repeat this test between control unit plug terminal 24, and senser contacts 1 and 2 alternately. The readings should again be 0 ohms and between 400 and 700 ohms respectively. If the specified values are obtained, cut off the two wires at the intake air temperature sender (the sender will have to be renewed after doing this, as described below). Now recheck the resistance at the two sender contacts, which should be between 400 and 700 ohms. If this is the case, there is a fault in the wiring between the sender and the control unit plug which must be rectified before renewing the sender.

24 To renew the sender, first cut off the two wires at the contacts if not already done. Undo the bolts and remove the sender unit.

25 Fit the new unit and secure with the two bolts.

26 Fit the rubber cover and protective cover over the wiring, fit terminal lugs on the bared wires, and solder the wires to the two contacts. Fit the protective covers over the soldered wiring.

27 Refit the wiring plug to the control unit.

Coolant temperature sender

28 For the following check the coolant temperature must be above 20°C (68°F).

29 Disconnect the wire from the coolant temperature sender (Fig. 4.26), and measure the resistance between the sender terminal and earth using an ohmmeter. The value obtained should be 60 to 1000 ohms. If this is not the case, renew the sender.

30 If the specified resistance value is obtained, remove the cover over the ignition control unit, located in the right-hand side front footwell, and disconnect the wiring plug.

31 Check the continuity of the wiring by connecting the ohmmeter between the disconnected coolant temperature sender wire and terminal 10 of the control unit wiring plug (Fig. 4.20). The ohmmeter reading should be 0 ohms. If this value is not obtained, there is a fault in the wiring between the sender and control unit plug. If the specified value is obtained, renew the ignition control unit. Refit the wiring after completing the checks.

Idle switch and full throttle switch

32 To check the switch supply voltage, disconnect the wiring plug at the idle and full throttle switch on the throttle valve housing (Fig 4.27), and connect a voltmeter between terminal 2 of the plug and earth (Fig. 4.24). Switch on the ignition and check that approximately 12 volts is present at the wiring plug. If not, check for a fault in the wiring to the plug.

33 Check the idle switch by connecting an ohmmeter between terminals 1 and 2 of the idle switch wiring socket (Fig. 4.28). The value obtained should be 0 ohms. Now operate the throttle to activate the switch, and check that no reading is shown on the ohmmeter. If these values are not obtained, have the idle switch adjustment checked by an Audi dealer, then repeat the checks. If the specified readings are still not obtained, renew the idle switch. If the readings are satisfactory, check the full throttle switch as follows.

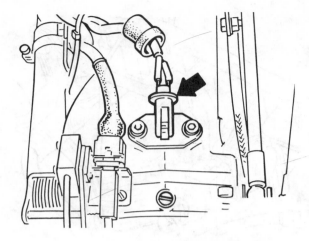

Fig. 4.24 Air intake temperature sender (arrowed) on throttle valve housing (Sec 16)

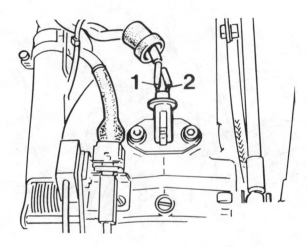

Fig. 4.25 Air intake temperature sender terminal identification (Sec 16)

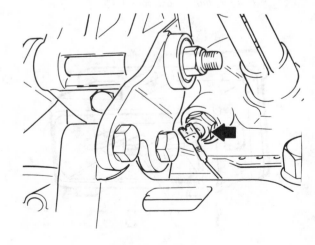

Fig. 4.26 Coolant temperature sender location – arrowed (Sec 16)

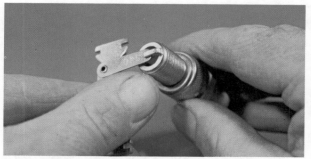

Measuring plug gap. A feeler gauge of the correct size (see ignition system specifications) should have a slight 'drag' when slid between the electrodes. Adjust gap if necessary

Adjusting plug gap. The plug gap is adjusted by bending the ground electrode inwards, or outwards, as necessary until the correct clearance is obtained. Note the use of the correct tool

Normal. Gray brown deposits, lightly coated core nose. Gap increasing by around 0.001 in (0.025 mm) per 1000 miles (1600 km). Plugs ideally suited to engine, and engine in good condition

Carbon fouling. Dry, black, sooty deposits. Will cause weak spark and eventually misfire. Fault: over-rich fuel mixture. Check: carburetor mixture settings, float level and jet sizes; choke operation and cleanliness of air filter. Plugs can be re-used after cleaning

Oil fouling. Wet, oily deposits. Will cause weak spark and eventually misfire. Fault: worn bores/piston rings or valve guides; sometimes occurs (temporarily) during running-in period. Plugs can be re-used after thorough cleaning

Overheating. Electrodes have glazed appearance, core nose very white — few deposits. Fault: plug overheating. Check: plug value, ignition timing, fuel octane rating (too low) and fuel mixture (too weak). Discard plugs and cure fault immediately

Electrode damage. Electrodes burned away; core nose has burned, glazed appearance. Fault: pre-ignition. Check: as for 'Overheating' but may be more severe. Discard plugs and remedy fault before piston or valve damage occurs

Split core nose (may appear initially as a crack). Damage is self-evident, but cracks will only show after cleaning. Fault: pre-ignition or wrong gap-setting technique. Check: ignition timing, cooling system, fuel octane rating (too low) and fuel mixture (too weak). Discard plugs, rectify fault immediately

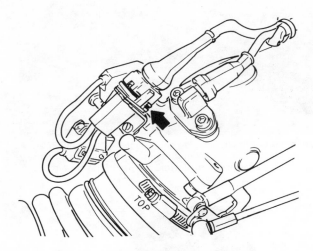

Fig. 4.27 Idle and full throttle switch wiring plug – arrowed (Sec 16)

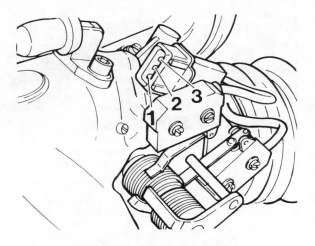

Fig. 4.28 Idle and full throttle switch socket terminal identification (Sec 16)

34 With the wiring plug still disconnected, check the resistance between terminals 2 and 3 in the wiring socket. There should be no reading shown on the ohmmeter scale. Now operate the throttle to activate the switch, and check that 0 ohms is shown on the ohmmeter. If these values are not obtained, have the full throttle switch adjustment checked by an Audi dealer, then repeat the checks. If the specified readings are still not obtained, renew the full throttle switch.
35 If the specified values are obtained, remove the cover over the ignition control unit, located in the right-hand side front footwell, and disconnect the wiring plug.
36 Check the continuity of the wiring by connecting the ohmmeter between terminal 1 on the idle and full throttle switch wiring plug, and terminal 20 on the control unit plug (Fig. 4.20). The specified reading should be 0 ohms. Now connect the ohmmeter between terminals 3 and 26 of the thorttle and control unit plugs respectively. The reading should again be 0 ohms. If the specified readings are not obtained, check for a fault in the wiring between the two plugs. If the readings are satisfactory, renew the ignition control unit.
37 Reconnect the wiring on completion of the tests.

Pick-up unit
38 Disconnect the central HT lead at the distributor cap (from coil terminal 4), and earth it with a bridging wire.
39 Disconnect the wiring plug at the pick-up unit on the side of the distributor (Fig. 4.29), and connect a voltmeter between the two outer terminals 1 and 3 (Fig. 4.30). Switch on the ignition, and check that at least 9 volts is indicated on the voltmeter, then switch off the ignition. If the specified valve is not obtained, check for a wiring fault in the lead to the pick-up unit.
40 If the readings are satisfactory, pull back the rubber grommet on the wiring plug and connect the voltmeter between terminals 1 and 2. With the voltmeter connected, refit the plug.
41 Remove the distributor cap, rotor arm and plastic cover, then using a spanner on the crankshaft pulley, turn the engine so that the rotor tooth openings are away from the pick-up unit (Fig. 4.31). Switch on the ignition and check that at least 4 volts are indicated on the voltmeter. Now turn the engine so that one of the rotor tooth openings is in line with the pick-up unit (Fig. 4.32), and check that the voltmeter reading is now between 0 and 0.5 volts. Switch off the ignition.
42 If the specified values are not obtained, renew the pick-up unit.
43 If the specified values are obtained, remove the cover over the ignition control unit, located in the right-hand side front footwell, and disconnect the wiring plug.
44 Check the continuity of the wiring by connecting an ohmmeter between terminal 1 of the pick-up unit wiring plug, and terminal 4 of the control unit wiring plug (Fig. 4.20). The specified reading should be 0 ohms. Now connect the ohmmeter between pick-up unit plug terminal 2, and control unit plug terminal 27, then pick-up plug terminal 3, and control unit plug terminal 25. The readings should again be 0 ohms in each case. If the specified values are not obtained,

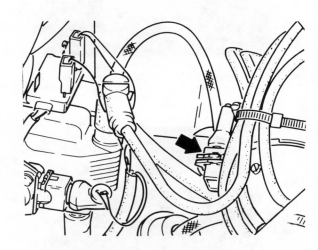

Fig. 4.29 Pick-up unit wiring plug (arrowed) on distributor (Sec 16)

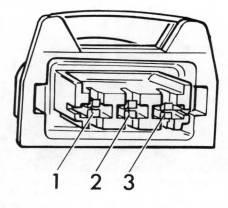

Fig. 4.30 Pick-up unit wiring plug terminal identification (Sec 16)

Fig. 4.31 Distributor rotor tooth openings positioned away from pick-up unit – arrowed (Sec 16)

Fig. 4.32 Distributor rotor tooth opening aligned with pick-up unit – arrowed (Sec 16)

check for a wiring fault between the two plugs. If the readings are satisfactory, renew the control unit.

45 Reconnect all wiring and components after completing the checks.

Ignition control unit

46 To check the supply voltage to the control unit, remove the control unit cover, located in the right-hand side front footwell, and disconnect the wiring plug.

47 Connect a voltmeter between wiring plug terminals 35 and 18, and 35 and 9 (Fig. 4.20), then switch on the ignition. The values indicated should be approximately 12 volts. Switch off the ignition.

48 Connect the voltmeter between terminals 32 and 9 in the wiring plug, switch on the ignition, and depress the brake pedal. Approximately 12 volts should be indicated on the voltmeter scale. If these values are not obtained, there is a wiring fault in the supply to the control unit, or the brake light switch is faulty. Switch off the ignition.

49 Reconnect the wiring plug on completion.

50 To check the control unit output signal to the fuel pump relay, pull the fuel pump relay out of socket 10 on the relay plate, and connect a voltmeter between terminals 46 and 47 in the plate (Fig. 4.33).

51 Briefly crank the engine on the starter motor, and check that approximately 9.5 volts is indicated on the voltmeter, then switch off the ignition.

52 If the specified voltage is not present, connect the voltmeter between terminal 46 and earth, then switch on the ignition. The reading should be approximately 12 volts. If this is not the case, there is a fault in the wiring to the relay plate. If the voltage is as specified, remove the cover over the ignition control unit in the right-hand front footwell and disconnect the wiring plug.

53 Using an ohmmeter, check for continuity between terminal 21 in the control unit plug (Fig. 4.20) and terminal 47 of socket 10 in the relay plate. The ohmmeter should indicate 0 ohms. If this is not the case, there is a fault in the wiring between the relay plate and control unit plug. If the specified value is obtained, renew the control unit.

54 Refit the relay and wiring plug on completion.

55 On manual transmission models, check the control unit output signal to the overrun cut-off valve as follows.

56 Ensure that the coolant temperature is at least 50°C (122°F), then accelerate the engine to at least 2000 rpm, and close the throttle abruptly. When the throttle is closed, the air intake elbow must visibly contract under negative pressure.

57 If the elbow does not contract, switch off the engine and disconnect the overrun cut-off valve wiring plug (Fig. 4.34).

58 Connect a voltmeter between the two terminals in the plug, start the engine and accelerate the engine to at least 2000 rpm once more. Close the throttle abruptly, and check that approximately 12 volts is shown on the voltmeter. If the specified value is obtained, and if the vacuum line is connected to the overrun cut-off valve, renew the valve.

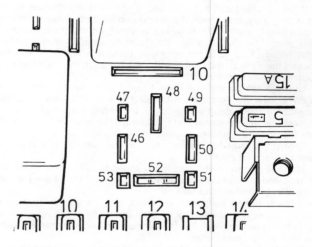

Fig. 4.33 Socket 10 terminal identification at the relay board (Sec 16)

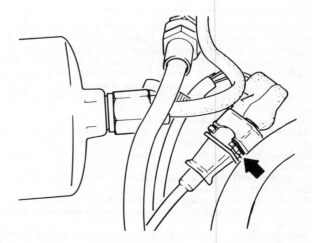

Fig. 4.34 Overrun cut-off valve wiring plug – arrowed (Sec 16)

If the specified reading is not obtained, check the idle switch as described earlier in this Section, then repeat the test. Switch off after checking.

59 If the specified reading is still not obtained, disconnect the ignition control unit wiring plug and, using an ohmmeter, check for continuity between terminal 1 in the cut-off valve wiring plug (Fig. 4.35), and terminal 14 in the control unit plug. (On 1985 onwards models the check is made between terminal 2 in the cut-off valve plug, and terminal 14 in the control unit plug). The ohmmeter reading should be 0 ohms. If this is not the case, there is a fault in the wiring between the cut-off valve and control unit plugs. If the reading is satisfactory, renew the control unit.

60 To check the control unit output signal to the two-way valve, first ensure that the coolant temperature is at least 80°C (176°F), then run the engine at idle.

61 Operate the full throttle switch by hand, and listen for an audible indication that the two-way valve is operating. If this is not the case, switch off the engine and disconnect the wiring plug at the two-way valve (Fig. 4.36).

62 Connect a voltmeter between the two plug terminals, and check that approximately 12 volts is indicated on the voltmetert scale. If the specified value is obtained, renew the two-way valve.

63 If the specified value is not obtained, connect the voltmeter between terminal 1 (blue/black wire) in the wiring plug, and earth. Switch on the ignition and check that approximately 12 volts is indicated, the switch off the ignition. If this figure is not obtained, check for a fault in the wiring to plug terminal 1.

64 If the specified value is obtained, disconnect the ignition control unit wiring plug, and check the wiring continuity between terminal 2 (yellow/black wire) in the two-way valve wiring plug, and terminal 8 of the control unit wiring plug. The ohmmeter should indicate 0 ohms. If the specified value is not obtained, there is a fault in the wiring between the control unit plug and the valve plug. If the specified value is obtained, renew the control unit.

65 To check the control unit output signal to the tachometer, remove the cover over the ignition control unit in the right-hand side front footwell. Pull back the rubber boot on the wiring plug, and connect a voltmeter between terminal 7 of the wiring plug, and earth (Fig. 4.38). Note that the plug remains connected for this test.

66 Connect a suitable tachometer to the engine following the manufacturer's instructions.

67 Start the engine, and increase the speed to 2000 rpm. Check that the indicated voltage is approximately 1.3 volts. If this is not the case, renew the ignition control unit.

68 If the specified voltage is obtained, but the vehicle tachometer does not agree with the test tachometer, there is a possible fault in the wiring from plug terminal 7 to the wiring plug in the instrument panel, or a fault in the tachometer.

69 Switch off the engine and reconnect the wiring on completion.

17 Ignition timing sender and rpm sender – removal and refitting

1   The ignition timing sender and rpm sender are located on the side of the cylinder block in line with the flywheel, and transmit information on engine speed and crankshaft position to the ignition control unit.

2   To remove either unit, disconnect its wiring plug at the wiring connector support bracket on the bulkhead (black plug for timing sender and grey plug for rpm sender – Fig. 4.21).

3   Using an Allen key, undo the retaining bolt, and remove the unit from its holder.

4   Refitting is the reversal of removal.

5   To check the fitted depth of the senders, as part of a test or fault diagnosis procedure, it will first be necessary to remove the transmission (Chapters 6 or 7) to gain access to the flywheel or driveplate.

6   Undo the bolts securing the sender unit mounting bracket, and remove the bracket and senders.

7   Turn the engine over using a spanner on the crankshaft pulley, until the pin on the flywheel or driveplate is centered in the sender opening (fig. 4.39).

8   Refit the sender bracket with senders and, using feeler gauges, measure the clearance between the end of the ignition timing sender and the pin on the flywheel (Fig. 4.10), and the clearance between the rpm sender and the flywheel ring gear teeth (Fig. 4.41). If the

measured clearances are outside the tolerance range given in the Specifications, check each unit for damage or distortion of the sensor end, and renew the unit as necessary. If the specified clearance still cannot be obtained, use packing shims to increase the clearance, or carefully file the sender bracket to decrease the clearance.

18 Spark plugs and HT leads – general

Refer to Section 9 of this Chapter.

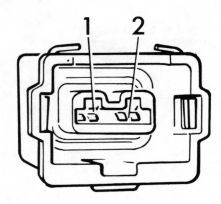

Fig. 4.35 Wiring plug terminal identification on 2-pin type (Sec 16)

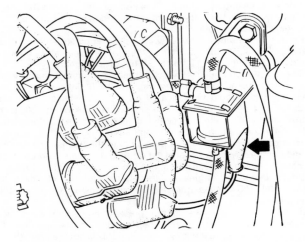

Fig. 4.36 Two-way valve wiring plug – arrowed (Sec 16)

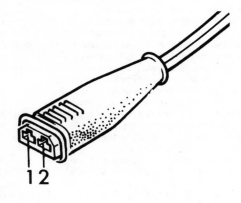

Fig. 4.37 Two-way valve wiring plug terminal identification (Sec 16)

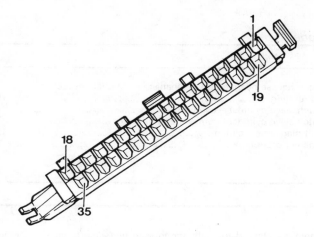

Fig. 4.38 Ignition control unit wiring plug terminal identification viewed from rear of plug (Sec 16)

Fig. 4.39 Flywheel pin centred in the ignition timing sender opening (Sec 17)

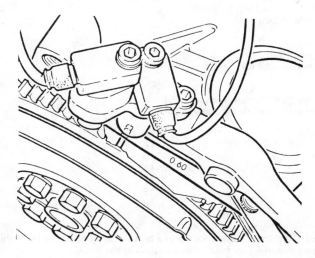

Fig. 4.40 Checking ignition timing sender-to-flywheel clearance (Sec 17)

Fig. 4.41 Checking rpm sender-to-flywheel ring gear clearance (Sec 17)

PART C – FAULT DIAGNOSIS

19 Fault diagnosis – ignition system

1   There are two distinct symptoms of ignition faults. Either the engine will not start or fire, or it starts with difficulty and does not run normally.
2   If the starter motor spins the engine satisfactorily, there is adequate fuel supply and yet the engine will not start, the fault is likely to be in the LT or primary side.
3   If the engine starts, but does not run satisfactorily, it is more likely to be an HT or secondary circuit fault.

Engine fails to start
4   If the starter motor spins the engine satisfactorily, but the engine does not start, first check that the fuel supply to the engine is in order, with reference to Chapter 3.
5   Check for obvious signs of broken or disconnected wires or wiring plugs, particularly those to the coil and distributor, and for damp distributor cap and HT leads.
6   For vehicles with transistorised coil ignition, follow the procedure described in Section 8. For vehicles with all-electronic ignition, follow the procedure described in Section 16, with particular emphasis on the ignition coil, pick-up unit, and ignition control unit.

Engine starts but misfires
7   Bad starting and intermittent misfiring can be caused by an LT fault, such as intermittent connection of either the distributor or coil LT wiring connections or plugs.
8   If these are satisfactory, look for signs of tracking or burning inside the distributor cap, then check the rotor arm, HT leads, spark plug caps, and plug insulators.
9   If the engine misfires regularly, it indicates that the fault is on one particular cylinder. This can often be confirmed by removing the spark plugs and checking to see if any are badly sooted or even wet, indicating that that particular spark plug is not firing. If this is the case, renew the HT lead, or try a lead known to be satisfactory. If the fault persists, check once again for tracking in the distributor cap. If these tests fail to cure the problem, there may be an internal engine fault on that cylinder, such as low cylinder compression.
10 If the misfire is of a more irregular nature, follow the test procedures described in Section 8 for vehicles with transistorised coil ignition, and Section 16 for vehicles with all-electronic ignition.
Warning: *When carrying out fault diagnosis tests or any checks on the ignition system, do not disconnect any wiring or leads (including spark plug HT leads) with the engine running or the ignition switched on.*

Chapter 5 Clutch

Refer to Chapter 13 for specifications on 1987 and later models

Contents

Specifications

Type .... Single dry plate, diaphragm spring with hydraulic or cable operation according to model

Clutch disc
Diameter .... 210 mm (8.27 in), 215 mm (8.47 in), 228 mm (8.98 in), or 240 mm (9.45 in) according to model

Maximum run-out .... 0.5 mm (0.020 in)

Pressure plate
Maximum distortion (inner edge to outer edge) .... 0.3 mm (0.012 in)
Maximum diaphragm spring finger scoring depth .... 0.3 mm (0.012 in)

Clutch adjustment
Free play (cable operated clutch) .... 15 mm (0.6 in) maximum at pedal
Pedal height (hydraulically operated clutch) .... 10 mm (0.4 in) above brake pedal

Torque wrench settings

	Nm	lbf ft
Pressure plate (clutch cover) retaining bolts	25	18
Clutch release lever clamp bolt (cable operated clutch)	25	18
Release shaft retaining bolt (cable operated clutch)	15	11
Release lever retainer (hydraulically operated clutch)	15	11
Master cylinder retaining bolts	25	18
Pedal mounting bracket retaining bolts	25	18

1 General description

All manual transmission models are equipped with a single dry plate diaphragm spring clutch. The unit consists of a steel cover which is bolted to the flywheel and contains the pressure plate and diaphragm spring.

The clutch disc is free to slide along the splined gearbox input shaft, and is held in position between the flywheel and the pressure plate by the pressure of the diaghragm spring. Friction lining material is riveted to the clutch disc, which has a spring cushioned hub to absorb transmission shocks and help ensure a smooth take-up of the drive.

Depending on vehicle specification, the clutch may be operated either mechanically by a cable or hydraulically by a master and slave cylinder. The clutch release mechanism consists of a release shaft on the cable operated type, or release lever on the hydraulically operated type, together with a release bearing, mounted in the clutch housing on the end of the gearbox.

2 Clutch – adjustment

1 The clutch operation and adjustment should be checked at the intervals given in Routine Maintenance using the following procedure according to clutch type.

Cable operated clutch

2 To check the adjustment, measure the free play at the clutch pedal which should be as given in the Specifications.
3 If adjustment is necessary, open the bonnet to gain access to the adjuster, which is either secured to a bracket attached to the left-hand engine mounting, or located midway along the cable.
4 Slacken the two locknuts, and turn the threaded cable ferrule in or out as necessary to achieve the specified free play. When the adjustment is correct, tighten the two locknuts (photo).

2.4 Clutch cable ferrule and end fitting

Hydraulically operated clutch

5 Remove the parcel shelf (see Chapter 11, Section 23) to gain access to the clutch master cylinder.
6 Release the locknut behind the clevis on the clutch master cylinder operating rod and turn the rod until the correct pedal height is achieved.
7 Depress the clutch pedal and then release it to ensure that the over-centre spring returns the pedal properly. After the pedal has returned, check that the pedal is clear of the pedal stop. If the pedal is against the pedal stop in the rest position, premature wear of the clutch facing will result.
8 When the operation of the pedal is satisfactory, tighten the clevis locknut and refit the parcel shelf.

3 Clutch cable – removal and refitting

1 Disconnect the battery negative terminal.
2 Remove the parcel shelf (see Chapter 11, Section 23) to gain access to the upper end of the clutch pedal.
3 Release the two locknuts on the clutch cable adjuster in the engine compartment and slide the cable assembly out of its anchorage.
4 Unhook the clutch cable connection from the hook on the upper end of the clutch pedal and from the hook on the end of the clutch operating lever.
5 Pull the clutch cable through the front bulkhead into the engine compartment and remove the assembly.
6 When fitting a new cable, fit the pedal end first and when installation has been completed, check and if necessary adjust the pedal freeplay.

4 Clutch pedal – removal and refitting

1 Disconnect the battery negative terminal.
2 Remove the parcel shelf (see Chapter 11, Section 23) to gain access to the pedal attachments.
3 On models equipped with a cable operated clutch, disconnect the cable at the pedal with reference to Section 3.
4 On models equipped with a hydraulically operated clutch, disconnect the master cylinder clevis pin at the pedal, then remove the master cylinder from its mounting bracket.
5 Disconnect the brake servo pushrod clevis pin at the brake pedal.
6 Disconnect the brake light switch wires, and any additional wiring or fittings according to model or optional equipment fitted.

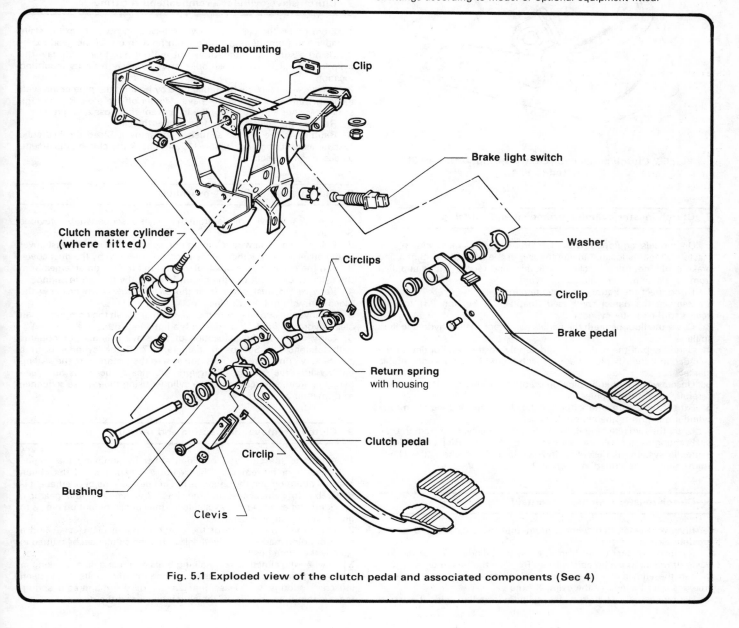

Fig. 5.1 Exploded view of the clutch pedal and associated components (Sec 4)

7   Undo the retaining nuts and bolts, and remove the pedal bracket assembly, complete with pedals, from the car.
8   Extract the circlips and clevis pins, and remove the clutch pedal over-centre spring. To facilitate removal and refitting of the over-centre spring, use tool 3117, or a suitable alternative made up from steel channel, to retain the over-centre spring in the compressed position.
9   Extract the pedal pivot circlip, release the brake pedal return spring, then remove the pivot and the two pedals. Recover the washers as the pedals are removed.
10 Where necessary, the pedal pivot bushes can be removed by punching them out with a drift, and pressing in new bushes between vice jaws.
11 Before reassembly, smear all contact surfaces with grease, and renew all locknuts and circlips. Reassemble and refit the pedals using the reverse sequence to removal. On completion check the clutch adjustment, as described in Section 2.

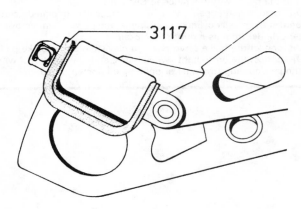

Fig. 5.2 Clutch pedal over-centre spring with tool 3117 fitted (Sec 4)

5   Clutch master cylinder – removal and refitting

On models equipped with a hydraulically operated clutch, the master cylinder is located inside the car, at the base of the clutch and brake pedal mounting bracket. Hydraulic fluid for the unit is supplied from the brake master cylinder reservoir.
1   Disconnect the battery negative terminal.
2   Remove the parcel shelf (see Chapter 11, Section 23) to gain access to the master cylinder.
3   Cover the floor beneath the pedals to protect against hydraulic fluid spillage.
4   Carefully pull the hydraulic fluid supply hose off the outlet on the cylinder, and quickly plug the hose with an old bolt or rod of suitable diameter.
5   Unscrew the hydraulic pipe union at the base of the cylinder, and carefully ease out the pipe.
6   Extract the circlip, and withdraw the clevis pin securing the master cylinder pushrod to the clutch pedal.
7   Undo the two retaining bolts, and remove the cylinder from the car.
8   Refitting is the reverse sequence to removal. Bleed the clutch hydraulic system, as described in Section 11, and check the clutch adjustment, as described in Section 2.

6   Clutch master cylinder – overhaul

1   Remove the master cylinder from the car, as described in the previous Section.
2   Remove the dust cover from the master cylinder then extract the pushrod retaining circlip and washer. Remove the pushrod.
3   Tap the end of the cylinder on a block of wood until the piston emerges from the end of the cylinder bore.
4   Withdraw the piston from the cylinder, together with the return

spring. Carefully remove the spring from the piston and recover the spring retainer.
5   Remove the primary and secondary cup seals from the piston, noting which way round they are fitted.
6   Wash all the components in clean hydraulic fluid, then wipe dry with a lint-free cloth.
7   Examine the cylinder bore and piston carefully for signs of scoring or wear ridges. If these are apparent, renew the complete master cylinder. If the condition of the components appears satisfactory, a new set of rubber seals must be obtained. Never re-use the old seals.
8   Begin reassembly by thoroughly lubricating the internal components and the cylinder bore, using clean hydraulic fluid.
9   Using fingers only, place the primary and secondary cup seals in position, with the lip of the seals facing towards the spring.
10 Place the spring retainer and spring in position over the piston, and carefully insert this assembly into the cylinder bore. Take care not to allow the lips of the seals to roll over as they are inserted.
11 Push the piston assembly down the cylinder bore using the pushrod, and refit the retaining circlip and washer.
12 Smear the inside of the dust cover with rubber grease, and place it in position over the end of the cylinder.

7   Clutch slave cylinder – removal and refitting

1   From under the car, withdraw the tensioning wire from the slave cylinder and from the retaining roll pin hole on top of the gearbox.
2   Using a suitable punch, drive out the roll pin, then withdraw the cylinder, complete with pushrod, rearwards away from its mounting location.
3   Unscrew the flexible hydraulic pipe by holding the pipe union with a spanner and unscrewing the slave cylinder off the pipe. Recover the sealing washer and plug the pipe to prevent fluid loss and dirt entry.
4   Remove the slave cylinder from under the car.
5   Refitting is the reverse sequence to removal. Bleed the hydraulic system, as described in Section 11, and check the clutch adjustment, as described in Section 2.

8   Clutch slave cylinder – overhaul

1   Remove the slave cylinder from the car, as described in the previous Section.
2   Release the small wire retaining ring securing the rubber dust cover to the pushrod, and withdraw the pushrod, followed by the dust cover.
3   Tap the cylinder on a block of wood until the piston emerges from the cylinder bore. Lift out the piston followed by the return spring.
4   Remove the dust cover from the bleed screw, then unscrew the bleed screw from the cylinder.
5   Remove the cup seal from the piston, then wash the components in clean hydraulic fluid. Wipe dry with a lint-free cloth.
6   Carry out a careful inspection of the slave cylinder components with reference to Section 6, paragraph 7. If the cylinder is in a satisfactory condition, fit a new cup seal to the piston, with the sealing lip towards the spring. Thoroughly lubricate the parts in clean hydraulic fluid, and reassemble the cylinder using the reverse sequence to dismantling.

9   Clutch – removal, inspection and refitting

1   Access to the clutch is obtained either by removing the engine (Chapter 1) or by removing the gearbox (Chapter 6). If the clutch requires attention and the engine is not in need of a major overhaul, it is preferable to gain access to the clutch by removing the gearbox, provided that either a pit is available, or the car can be put on ramps to give a good ground clearance.
2   Put a mark on the rim of the clutch pressure plate cover and a corresponding mark on the flywheel so that the clutch can be refitted in exactly the same position.
3   Slacken the clutch cover retaining bolts a turn at a time, working in diagonal pairs round the casing. When all the bolts have been loosened enough to release the tension of the diaphragm spring, remove the bolts and lift off the clutch cover and the disc.

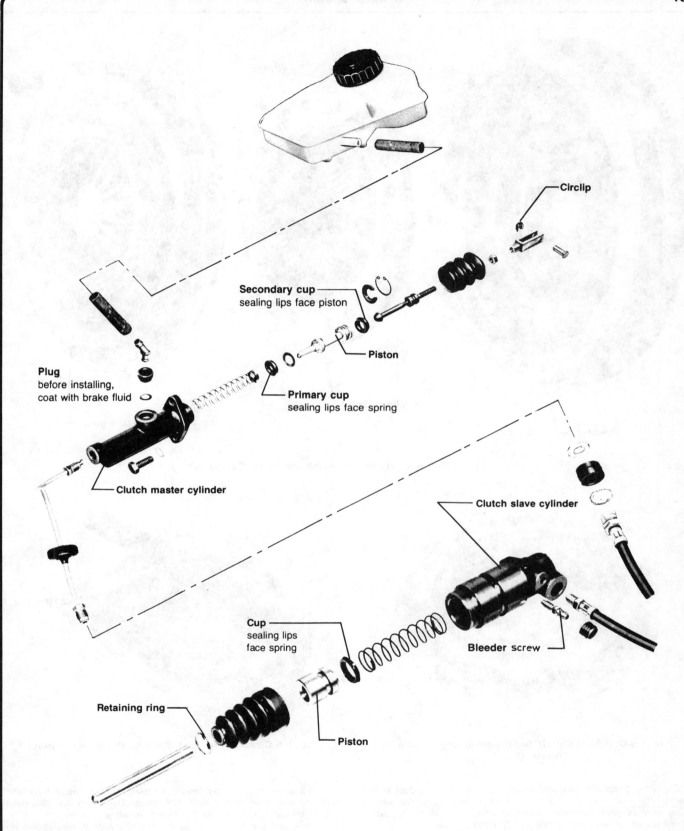

Circlip

Secondary cup
sealing lips face piston

Piston

Plug
before installing,
coat with brake fluid

Primary cup
sealing lips face spring

Clutch master cylinder

Clutch slave cylinder

Cup
sealing lips
face spring

Bleeder screw

Retaining ring

Piston

Fig. 5.3 Exploded view of the clutch master cylinder and slave cylinder – hydraulically operated clutch (Secs 6 and 8)

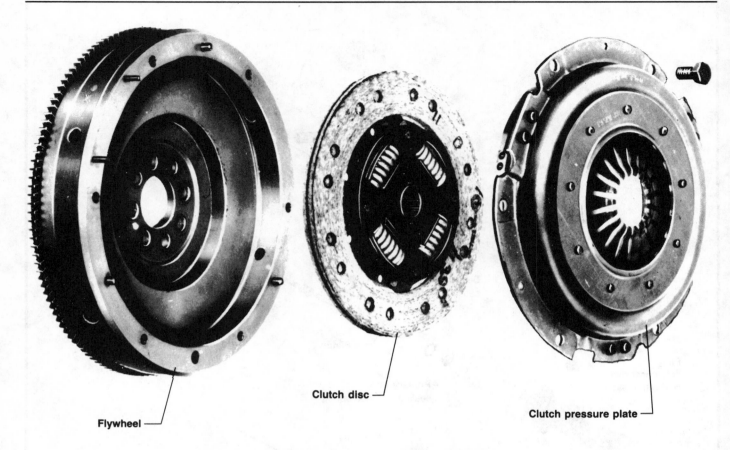

Fig. 5.4 Components of the clutch assembly (Sec 9)

Flywheel — Clutch disc — Clutch pressure plate

**Fig. 5.5 Checking clutch diaphragm spring fingers –
arrowed (Sec 9)**

**Fig. 5.6 Checking for distortion of the pressure plate
(Sec 9)**

4   Clean the parts with a damp cloth, ensuring that the dust is not inhaled. *Because the dust produced by the wearing of the clutch facing may contain asbestos, which is dangerous to health, parts should not be blown clean or brushed to remove dust.*

5   Examine the fingers of the diaphragm spring for signs of wear, or scoring. If the depth of any scoring exceeds 0.3 mm (0.012 in), a new cover assembly must be fitted.

6   Lay the clutch cover on its diaphragm spring end, place a steel straight-edge diagonally across the pressure plate and test for distortion of the plate (Fig. 5.6). If a 0.3 mm (0.012 in) feeler gauge can be inserted in any gap beneath the straight-edge, the clutch cover must be discarded and a new one fitted. The check for distortion should be made at several points round the plate.

7   Check that the pressure plate is not badly scored, and shows no signs of cracking, or burning.

8   Inspect the clutch disc and fit a new disc if the surface of the friction material left is approaching the level of the rivets. Discard the disc if the friction material has become impregnated with oil, or shows signs of breaking into shreds.

9   Examine the clutch disc splined hub for signs of damage, or wear.

Fig. 5.7 Checking clutch disc run-out (Sec 9)

Check that when the hub is on the gearbox input shaft, the hub slides smoothly along the shaft and that the radial clearance between the gearbox shaft and clutch hub is small.
10 If there is reason to suspect that the clutch hub is not running true, it should be checked by mounting the hub between centres and checking it with a dial gauge. Unless you have the proper equipment, get your local dealer to make this check.
11 Do not re-use any part which is suspect. Having gone to the trouble of dismantling the clutch, it is well worth ensuring that when reassembled it will operate satisfactorily for a long time. Check the flywheel for scoring and tiny cracks caused by overheating; refinish or renew as necessary.
12 Ensure that all the parts are clean, free of oil and grease and are in a satisfactory condition before reassembling.
13 Fit the clutch disc so that the torsion spring cages are towards the pressure plate (photo).
14 Fit the clutch cover to the flywheel ensuring (where applicable) that the marks made before dismantling are lined up, and insert all bolts finger tight to hold the cover in position (photo).
15 Centralise the clutch disc either by using a proprietary tool, or by making up a similar tool to hold the clutch disc concentric with the hole in the end of the crankshaft (photo).
16 With the centraliser holding the clutch disc in position, tighten all the clutch cover bolts a turn at a time in diagonal sequence until the specified torque is achieved.
17 Remove the centering tool and smear the hub splines with molybdenum disulphide grease.
18 Check the release bearing in the front of the gearbox for wear and smooth operation, and if necessary renew it, with reference to Section 10.
19 Refit the engine or gearbox with reference to Chapters 1 or 6.

10 Clutch release bearing and mechanism – removal, inspection and refitting

1 With the gearbox removed from the car, proceed as follows according to type.

Cable operated clutch

2 To remove the release bearing, either lift the release arm to disengage the forks from the spring clips, or extract the clips from each

9.13 Fit the clutch disc with the torsion springs toward the pressure plate ...

9.14 ... then fit the cover assembly

9.15 Using a proprietary tool to centralise the clutch disc

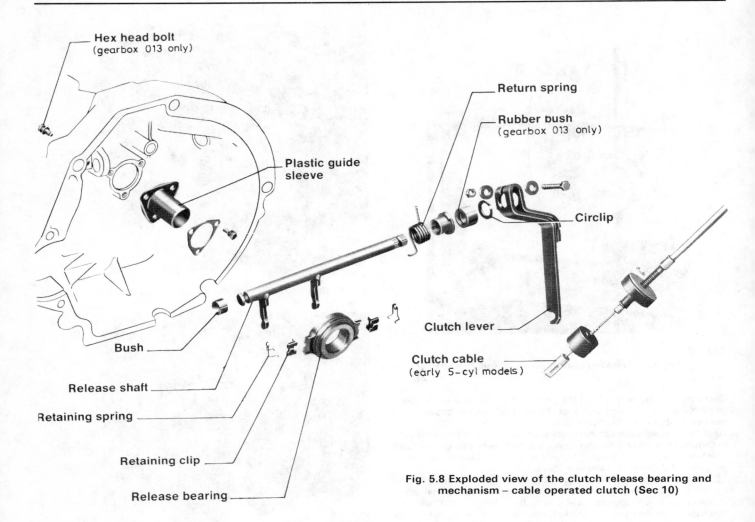

Fig. 5.8 Exploded view of the clutch release bearing and mechanism – cable operated clutch (Sec 10)

side of the bearing, noting how they are fitted (photos). The bearing can then be withdrawn from the guide sleeve.

3   Mark the release lever in relation to the shaft then unscrew the clamp bolt and withdraw the lever.

4   On four-cylinder models, remove the dowel bolt from the rear of the bellhousing. The bolt engages a groove in the end of the release shaft.

5   On all models, note the position of the release shaft return spring in relation to the ground projection cast in the bellhousing. The spring end fits either in the groove, or adjacent to it, according to gearbox type. Record the fitted position before removal.

10.2A Clutch release bearing and release shaft

10.2B Release bearing retaining clip fitment

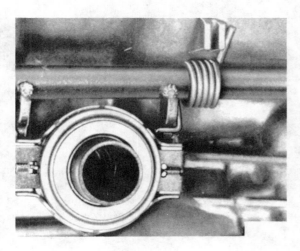

Fig. 5.9 Clutch release shaft return spring positioned adjacent to bellhousing cast projection (Sec 10)

10.6 Unhooking the release shaft return spring

6   Unhook the return spring from the release shaft fork (photo).
7   Extract the circlip from the splined end of the release shaft and prise out the rubber bush (where fitted) and the flanged bush (photo).
8   Turn the release shaft so that the forks are free of the guide sleeve, then remove the inner end from the bush and withdraw the shaft from inside the bellhousing (photo).
9   Clean the release bearing with a dry cloth. Do not wash the bearing in solvent, because this will cause its lubricant to be washed out. If the bearing is noisy, or has excessive wear, discard it and obtain a new one.
10 Inspect the release shaft and its bushes for wear. Do not remove the inner bush unless a new one has to be fitted. If a new inner bush is required, the old one will need a special extractor to remove it.
11 Before refitting the release shaft, coat the bearing surfaces with molybdenum disulphide grease and ensure that the return spring is fitted to the shaft.
12 Refitting is a reversal of removal. However, on four-cylinder models press in the release shaft until the rubber bush is compressed to approximately 18 mm (0.7 in) (photo) before inserting and tightening the dowel bolt. If a new release lever is being fitted, position it on the splined shaft as shown in Fig. 5.11 (photo). Coat all bearing surfaces with high melting-point grease, except for the plastic guide sleeve.

10.7 Removing the release shaft flanged bush

10.8 Removing the release shaft

Fig. 5.10 Inserting the dowel bolt (A) on four-cylinder models – press in the release shaft to compress the rubber bush to 18 mm (0.7 in) (Sec 10)

10.12A Checking the release shaft rubber bush dimension

10.12B Checking the release lever fitted dimension

Fig. 5.11 Release lever fitting dimension – cable operated clutch (Sec 10)

a = 185 mm (7.28 in)

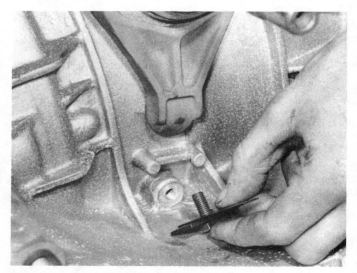

10.14 Removing the retainer and leaf spring

Hydraulically operated clutch

13   Remove the release bearing, as described in paragraph 2.

14   Unscrew and remove the bolt securing the clutch release lever retainer and leaf spring (photo). Remove the retainer and spring, then take out the clutch release lever.

15   Clean the release bearing, as described in paragraph 9. Coat the top of the ball cap inside the bellhousing and also all the working surfaces of the clutch operating lever with molybdenum disulphide grease and refit the arm and release bearing by reversing the removal procedure.

11 Clutch hydraulic system – bleeding

1   If any part of the hydraulic system is dismantled, or if air has accidentally entered the system, the system will need to be bled. The presence of air is characterised by the pedal having a 'spongy' feel (which lessens if the pedal is pumped a few times) and it results in difficulty in changing gear.

2   The design of the clutch hydraulic system does not allow bleeding to be carried out using the conventional method of pumping the clutch pedal. In order to remove all air present in the system, it is necessary to use pressure bleeding equipment. This is available from auto-accessory shops at relatively low cost.

3   The pressure bleeding equipment should be connected to the hydraulic system in accordance with the manufacturer's instructions. The system is normally bled through the bleed screw of the clutch slave cylinder, which is located at the top of the gearbox housing.

4   The system is bled until the fluid being ejected is free from air bubbles. The bleed screw is then closed and the bleeding equipment disconnected and removed.

5   Check the operation of the clutch to see that it is satisfactory. If air still remains in the system, repeat the bleeding operation.

6   Discard any fluid which is bled from the system, even if it looks clean. Hydraulic fluid absorbs water and its re-use can can cause internal corrosion of the master and slave cylinders, leading to excessive wear and failure of the seals.

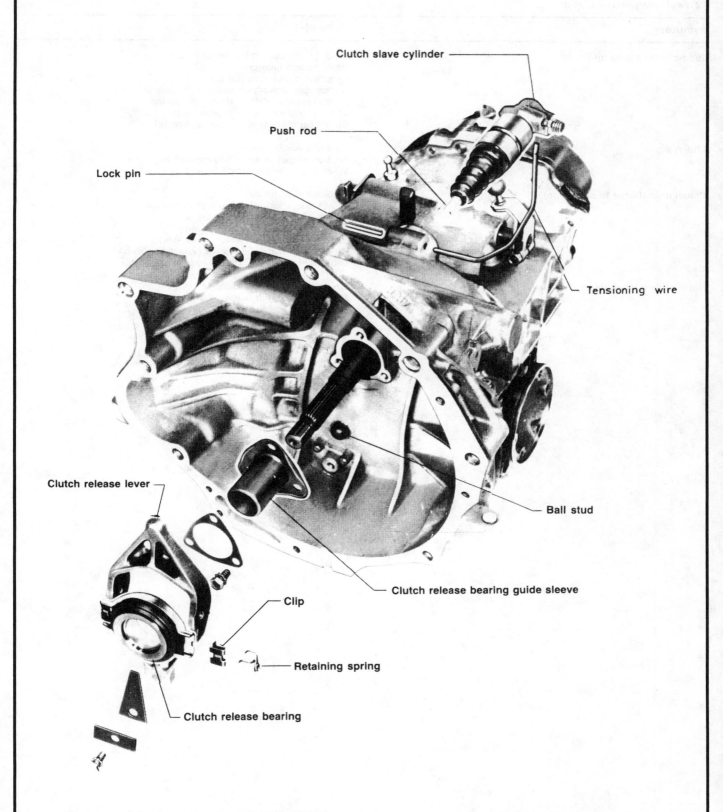

Clutch slave cylinder

Push rod

Lock pin

Tensioning wire

Clutch release lever

Ball stud

Clutch release bearing guide sleeve

Clip

Retaining spring

Clutch release bearing

Fig. 5.12 Exploded view of the clutch release bearing and mechanism – hydraulically operated clutch (Sec 10)

12 Fault diagnosis – clutch

Symptom	Reason(s)
Judder when taking up drive	Oil or grease contamination of friction linings Worn friction linings Excessive clutch disc run-out Clutch disc sticking on input shaft splines Faulty pressure plate or diaphragm spring Worn or broken engine/gearbox mountings Clutch cable sticking (where applicable)
Clutch slip	Incorrect adjustment Friction linings worn or contaminated Weak or broken diaphragm spring
Clutch drag (failure to disengage)	Incorrect adjustment Clutch disc sticking on input shaft splines Clutch disc sticking to flywheel Input shaft seized in spigot bearing Broken clutch cable (where applicable) Air in clutch hydraulic system (where applicable) Faulty clutch master cylinder (where applicable)
Noise evident when depressing clutch pedal	Dry or worn release bearing Dry clutch pedal or release shaft bushes Faulty clutch cable (where applicable)

Chapter 6 Manual gearbox

Contents

Specifications

Type .... Four or five forward speeds and reverse, with synchromesh on all forward speeds; integral final drive

Identification

Gearbox code number:

014	Four-speed gearbox fitted to 1.8 litre four-cylinder models
013	Five-speed gearbox fitted to 1.8 litre four-cylinder models
093	Five-speed gearbox fitted to 1.9 litre five-cylinder models
016	Five-speed gearbox fitted to UK 2.0, 2.2 and 2.3 litre five-cylinder models and all North American models

Ratios

Gearbox 014:

	QN	4X
Final drive	4.11 : 1	4.11 : 1
1st	3.46 : 1	3.46 : 1
2nd	1.79 : 1	1.79 : 1
3rd	1.07 : 1	1.07 : 1
4th	0.70 : 1	0.70 : 1
Reverse	3.17 : 1	3.17 : 1

Gearbox 013:

	3T	HE	HF
Final drive	4.11 : 1	4.11 : 1	4.11 : 1
1st	3.46 : 1	3.46 : 1	3.46 : 1
2nd	1.79 : 1	1.79 : 1	1.79 : 1
3rd	1.07 : 1	1.13 : 1	1.13 : 1
4th	0.78 : 1	0.83 : 1	0.83 : 1
5th	0.60 : 1	0.68 : 1	0.68 : 1
Reverse	3.17 : 1	3.17 : 1	3.17 : 1

Gearbox 093:

	3Q
Final drive	5.22 : 1
1st	2.84 : 1
2nd	1.52 : 1
3rd	0.90 : 1
4th	0.64 : 1
5th	0.48 : 1
Reverse	3.16 : 1

Gearbox 016:

	AAZ	3V	3K	5N	3U
Final drive	3.89 : 1	3.89 : 1	3.89 : 1	4.11 : 1	3.89 : 1
1st	3.60 : 1	3.60 : 1	3.60 : 1	3.60 : 1	3.60 : 1
2nd	2.13 : 1	2.13 : 1	2.13 : 1	2.13 : 1	1.88 : 1
3rd	1.46 : 1	1.46 : 1	1.36 : 1	1.36 : 1	1.19 : 1
4th	1.07 : 1	1.07 : 1	0.97 : 1	0.97 : 1	0.84 : 1
5th	0.86 : 1	0.83 : 1	0.78 : 1	0.73 : 1	0.64 : 1
Reverse	3.50 : 1	3.50 : 1	3.50 : 1	3.50 : 1	3.50 : 1

Synchro-ring wear limit

All gearboxes .... 0.5 mm (0.02 in)

Torque wrench settings

	Nm	lbf ft
Gearbox to engine	55	41
Gearbox mountings to subframe:		
013 and 014	45	33
093 and 016	40	30
Mounting brackets to gearbox (093 and 016)	40	30
Gearshift linkage sideplate bolt (014, 013 and 093)	30	22
Gearshift linkage adaptor lockbolt (014, 013 and 093)	20	15
Gearshift linkage support bar (014, 013 and 093)	25	18
Gearshift linkage shift rod clamp bolt (014, 013, 093 annd 016)	15	11
Shift rod to gearshift lever (014, 013, 093 and 016)	10	7
Gearshift lever housing to floor (014, 013, 093 and 016)	10	7
Gearshift lever stop, cover plate and lever bearing (014, 013, 093 and 016)	10	7
Pushrod clamp plate (016 later version)	20	15
Filler and drain plugs (014, 013, 093 and 016)	25	18
Final drive cover (014, 013, 093 and 016)	25	18
Drive flange bolts:		
014	20	15
013, 093 and 016	25	18
Pinion output shaft nut (014, 013 and 093)	100	74
Fifth speed driven and driving gear bolts (013, 093 and 016)	70	52
Gearshift housing and bearing carrier (014, 013, 093 and 016)	25	18
Selector shaft cover (016)	10	7
Reverse relay lever bolt (014, 013 and 093)	35	26

1 General description

The manual gearbox may be either a four-speed type or one of three variations of five-speed type, according to model.

The gearbox is bolted to the rear of the engine in conventional manner but, because of the front wheel drive configuration, drive is transmitted to a differential unit located at the front of the gearbox and then through the driveshafts to the front wheels. All forward gears incorporate synchromesh engagement, and reverse gear is obtained by engaging a spur type idler gear with the 1st/2nd synchro sleeve on the pinion shaft and a spur gear on the input shaft.

Gearshift is by means of a floor-mounted lever, and a single rod and linkage clamped to the selector rod which protrudes from the rear of the gearbox. The selector rod incorporates a finger which engages the other selector rods in the bearing carrier.

When overhauling the gearbox, due consideration should be given to the costs involved, since it is often more economic to obtain a service exchange or good secondhand gearbox rather then fit new parts to the existing gearbox. Repairs to the differential are not covered, as the special instrumentation required is not normally available to the home mechanic.

2 Maintenance and inspection

1 At the service interval given in Routine Maintenance at the beginning of this manual, inspect the gearbox joint faces and oil seals for any signs of damage, deterioration or oil leakage.

2 Also check and, if necessary, top up the gearbox oil. The filler plug is located on the left-hand side of the final drive housing and the oil level should be maintained up to the level of the filler plug orifice (photos). The oil drain plug is located just below the filler plug, but note that draining and refilling of the gearbox oil is not a service requirement.

2.2A Gearbox filler plug (A) and drain plug (B) (016 gearbox shown)

2.2B Topping-up the gearbox oil

3 Gearbox – removal and refitting

1   Position the front of the car over an inspection pit, or on ramps or axle stands and apply the handbrake firmly.

2   Disconnect the battery negative lead.

3   Unscrew and remove the upper bolts attaching the gearbox to the engine, noting the location of any brackets.

4   Disconnect the speedometer cable from the differential cover (photo).

5   On models equipped with a cable-operated clutch, detach the clutch cable from the gearbox with reference to Chapter 5.

6   On models equipped with a hydraulically-operated clutch, remove the slave cylinder from the gearbox, leaving the hydraulic hose attached, with reference to Chapter 5.

7   If working on the 016 type gearbox, refer to Chapter 3 and remove the air cleaner.

8   Remove the exhaust front pipe from the manifold and exhaust system, with reference to Chapter 3.

9   Disconnect the wiring to the econometer switch and remove the cable clip (photo). Disconnect any additional gearbox wiring where fitted.

10 On five-cylinder engine models, support the front of the engine with a hoist or bar arrangement similar to that shown in Fig. 6.1.

11 Unbolt and remove the gearbox front cover.

12 Remove the starter motor, as described in Chapter 12.

13 Disconnect the driveshafts from the drive flanges, with reference to Chapter 8, and tie them to one side.

14 Unscrew the lockbolt securing the selector adaptor to the selector rod on the rear of the gearbox (photo). Press the support rod from the balljoint and withdraw the adaptor from the selector lever. Remove the shift rod and, where fitted, the pushrod (016 gearbox).

Fig. 6.1 Support bar required when removing the gearbox on five-cylinder models (Sec 3)

15 If working on the 016 type gearbox, remove the guard plates from the subframe.

16 Support the gearbox with a trolley jack or stand.

17 Unscrew and remove the lower bolts attaching the gearbox to the engine.

18 If working on the 016 type gearbox remove the subframe rear mounting bolts (photo).

19 Undo the bolts securing the gearbox mountings to the subframe and where necessary remove the mounting brackets from the gearbox to clear the subframe (photo).

3.4 Speedometer cable attachment

3.9 Econometer switch wiring (016 gearbox shown)

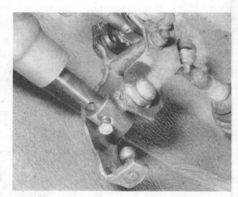

3.14 Disconnecting the selector linkage from the rear of the gearbox (013 gearbox shown)

3.18 Subframe rear mounting bolt (A) and gearbox mounting-to-subframe bolt (B) (016 gearbox shown)

3.19 Gearbox mounting bracket (arrowed) (016 gearbox shown)

20 With the help of an assistant, withdraw the gearbox from the engine; making sure that the input shaft does not hang on the clutch. Lower the gearbox to the ground and remove it from under the car.

21 Refitting is a reversal of removal, but lightly lubricate the input shaft splines and clutch release bearing front face with molybdenum disulphide grease and make sure that the engine/gearbox mountings are fitted free of strain. Adjust the gear lever and linkage if necessary, as described in the appropriate Sections of this Chapter. Check and if necessary top up the gearbox oil.

4 Gearbox (014) – dismantling into major assemblies

1   Remove the gearbox drain plug, drain out the oil and refit the plug. Clean away external dirt from the gearbox casing.

2   Remove the bolts from the gearshift housing. If necessary give the housing a light tap to separate it from the gear housing and then manoeuvre the gearshift housing off the gear housing. Remove the shim and gasket.

3   Carefully pull the 3rd/4th gear selector rod out of the casing until the small interlock plunger can be removed. Be careful not to pull the shaft out further than is absolutely necessary because the locking keys of the synchro-hub may fall out.

4   Having removed the plunger, push the shaft back into its neutral position. If the locking keys of the synchro-hub have fallen out it will not be possible to push the rod back in and the alternative method of removing the pinion nut will have to be used after removing the bearing carrier. This involves gripping the 4th gear in a soft-jawed vice, then unscrewing the pinion nut.

5   Pull the upper selector rod out to engage reverse gear and the lower one out to engage first gear. By engaging the two gears at once the shafts will be locked and the pinion nut can be undone.

6   Remove the circlip and thrust washer from the end of the input shaft.

7   If available, use the special puller to remove the input shaft bearing from the gear carrier housing, while supporting the front end of the input shaft with a bar bolted to the final drive housing. If not available, it will be necessary to remove the input shaft and pinion shaft simultaneously later.

8   Remove the bolts securing the bearing carrier and detach the bearing carrier with the input shaft and pinion shaft from the final drive housing.

9   Drive the dowel pins back until they are flush with the joint face.

10 Clamp the gearbox in a soft-jawed vice. Support the free end of the 3rd/4th gear selector shaft by jamming a block of hardwood under it and drive the roll-pin out of the selector shaft. If the free end of the shaft is not supported while the pin is driven out, the bore for the shaft in the gear carrier may be damaged.

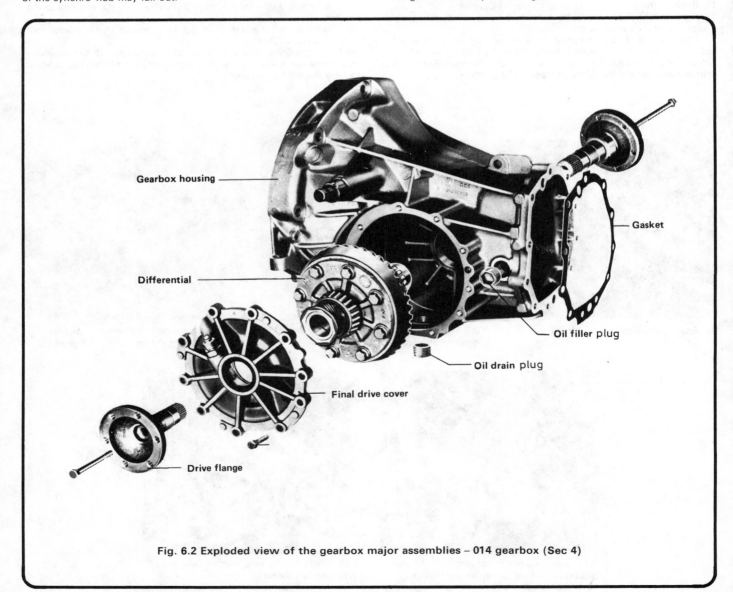

Fig. 6.2 Exploded view of the gearbox major assemblies – 014 gearbox (Sec 4)

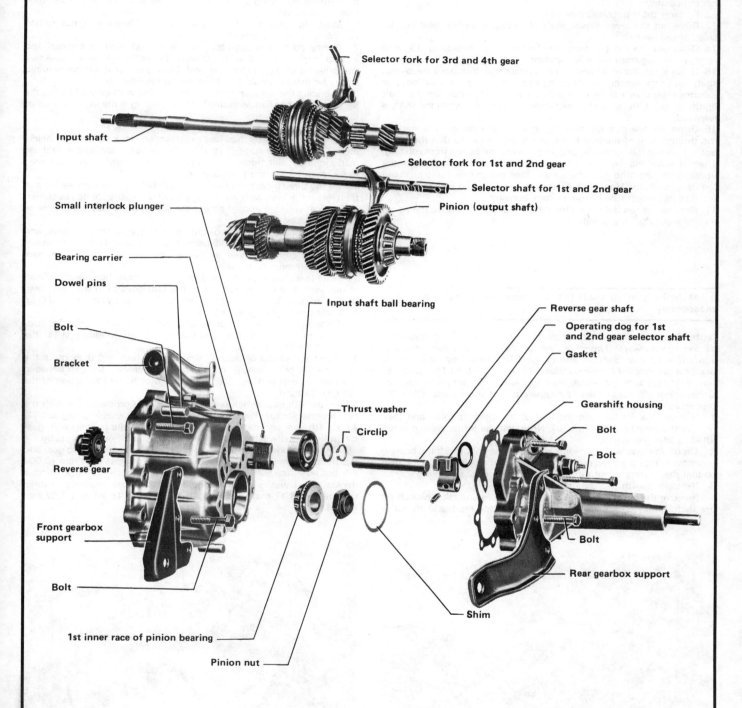

Selector fork for 3rd and 4th gear

Input shaft

Selector fork for 1st and 2nd gear

Selector shaft for 1st and 2nd gear

Pinion (output shaft)

Small interlock plunger

Bearing carrier

Dowel pins

Bolt

Bracket

Input shaft ball bearing

Reverse gear shaft

Operating dog for 1st and 2nd gear selector shaft

Gasket

Gearshift housing

Bolt

Bolt

Reverse gear

Thrust washer

Circlip

Front gearbox support

Bolt

Bolt

Rear gearbox support

Shim

1st inner race of pinion bearing

Pinion nut

Fig. 6.2 Exploded view of the gearbox major assemblies – 014 gearbox (Sec 4) (continued)

11 Pull out the 3rd/4th gear selector shaft until the 3rd/4th gear selector fork can be removed, and then push the shaft back to its neutral position.

12 Remove the input shaft assembly.

13 Drive out the reverse gear shaft and remove reverse gear and its selector segment (if fitted).

14 Drive out the roll-pin from the 1st/2nd gear operating dog and remove the dog from the selector shaft.

15 Using a soft-faced hammer, or a hammer and drift, drive the pinion shaft out of its bearing. While doing this, check that the 1st/2nd gear selector shaft does not become jammed, and if necessary tap the shaft lightly to free it. Recover the taper-roller bearing race when the shaft is removed.

16 Dismantle the gearbox housing as follows. First insert a suitable rod through one of the bolt holes of a drive flange, so that the rod is against one of the cover ribs and so prevents the flange from rotating. Then remove the bolt from the centre of the flange. Repeat the operation on the other drive flange and then use two levers to prise out the flanged shafts. Mark each shaft as it is removed to ensure that it is fitted to its correct side of the gearbox housing.

17 Remove the ten bolts from the differential cover, remove the cover, and take out the differential.

5   Mainshaft/input shaft (014) – dismantling and reassembly

Note: *The four and five-speed gearboxes have many fundamentally similar components. Therefore, whilst the photographic sequence applicable to this Section shows an 013 five-speed unit, for all practical purposes, it can be considered to illustrate the 014 four-speed unit. Any important differences are noted in the relevant photo caption. Other minor differences may be apparent, but should not affect the procedure described.*

1   Remove the circlip from the end of the shaft (photo) and then remove the thrust washer (photo). Note that the thrust washer is not fitted to later gearboxes.

2   Lift off 4th gear with its needle roller bearing (photo). If the bearing is removed from the gear, put a paint mark on the bearing and the gear so that the bearing is not turned end-for-end on reassembling.

3   Remove the 4th gear synchro-ring.

4   Remove the circlip retaining the synchro-hub and take the hub off the shaft. It may be possible to hold 3rd gear and tap the shaft out of

the synchro-hub, or it may be necessary to have the hub pressed off (photos).

5   Remove the 3rd gear synchro-ring, 3rd gear and its needle roller bearing (photos).

6   Mark the gear and bearing so that the bearing is not turned end-for-end on reassembly.

7   Before starting reassembly, ensure that all parts are clean and inspect them for signs of damage or excessive wear. Gearbox components are very expensive, and if any gears or shafts are required it may be more economic to fit an exchange gearbox.

8   Lubricate the 3rd gear needle roller bearing with gear oil and fit the bearing onto the shaft, ensuring that the bearing is the same way up as it was before removal.

9   Fit 3rd gear.

10 If the synchroniser has been dismantled, look for mating marks etched on the outer edge. If so, the hub must be assembled with these marks in line. Later models do not have mating marks and do not need to be reassembled in a particular position.

11 Fit the three locking keys into the hub before fitting the sleeve and then retain the keys with the springs, positioning the springs as shown in Fig. 6.4, with the angled end of the spring fitted into the hollow of the locking key.

12 Fit the 3rd gear synchro-ring onto the cone of the gear and measure the gap (a) in Fig. 6.5 using a feeler gauge. This gap must not exceed the amount given in the Specifications otherwise a new synchro-ring must be fitted.

13 Note that the splines on the bore of the synchro-hub are chamfered at one end. The chamfered end of the hub goes onto the shaft first, facing 3rd gear. The hub also has an additional groove at one end (Fig. 6.6) and this groove faces 4th gear.

14 Press the synchroniser on to the shaft, first turning the 3rd gear synchro-ring so that the grooves on it are aligned with the synchroniser locking keys.

15 Insert the circlip on top of the synchro-hub and then press the synchroniser back against the circlip. This increases the gap between the synchroniser and 3rd gear which ensures better lubrication of the 3rd gear bearing.

16 Fit the 4th gear synchro-ring, aligning the grooves in it with the synchroniser locking keys, then check its clearance, as in paragraph 12.

17 Fit 4th gear and its bearing, first lubricating the bearing with gear oil, fit the thrust washer (early models only) and finally the circlip.

18 On early models, measure the axial clearance between 4th gear and the thrust washer. This clearance should be at least 0.10 mm (0.004 in), but less than 0.40 mm (0.016 in). If it exceeds the upper limit, a thicker thrust washer must be fitted and these are available in three thicknesses, 3.47 mm (0.136 in), 3.57 mm (0.141 in) and 3.67 mm (0.144 in).

5.1A Remove the input shaft circlip ...

5.1B ... and thrust washer

5.2 Removing the 4th gear and needle roller bearing

5.4A Extract the circlip ...

5.4B ... and remove the 3rd/4th synchroniser

5.4C Using a puller to remove the 3rd/4th synchroniser

5.5A Removing 3rd gear

5.5B ... and the split needle roller bearing

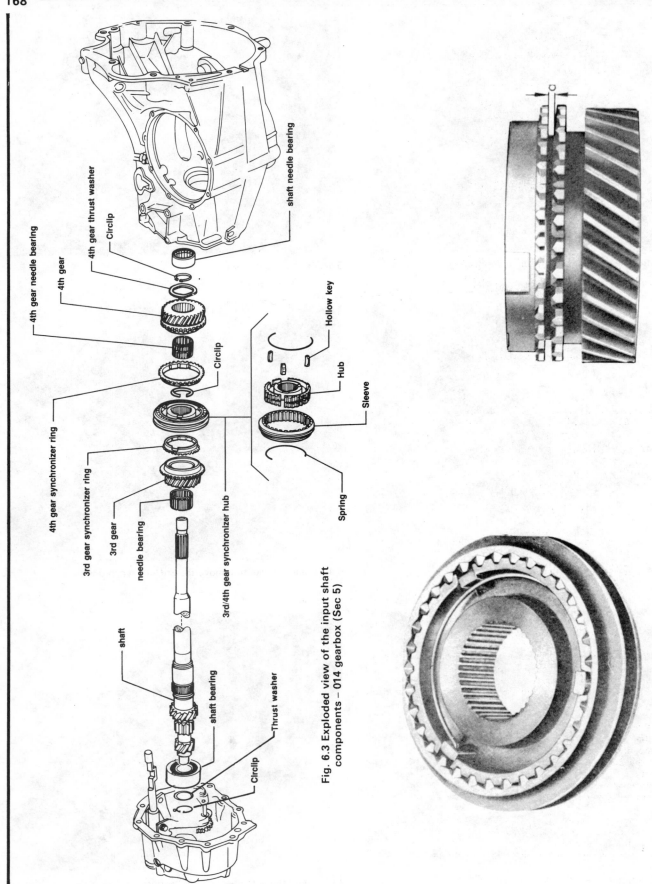

4th gear needle bearing

4th gear

4th gear thrust washer

Circlip

shaft needle bearing

4th gear synchronizer ring

Circlip

3rd gear synchronizer ring

3rd gear

needle bearing

3rd/4th gear synchronizer hub

Hollow key

Hub

Sleeve

Spring

shaft

shaft bearing

Thrust washer

Circlip

Fig. 6.3 Exploded view of the input shaft components – 014 gearbox (Sec 5)

Fig. 6.5 Synchro-ring wear gap 'a' (Sec 5)

Fig. 6.4 Correct fitting of synchro springs – 014 gearbox (Sec 5)

Fig. 6.6 Synchro-hub groove (white arrow) and chamfer (black arrow) – 014 gearbox (Sec 5)

6 Pinion shaft (014) – dismantling and reassembly

Note: *The four and five-speed gearboxes have many fundamentally similar components. Therefore, whilst the photographic sequence applicable to this Section shows an 013 five-speed unit, for all practical purposes, it can be considered to illustrate the 014 four-speed unit. Any important differences are noted in the relevant photo caption. Other minor differences may be apparent, but should not affect the procedure described.*

1 The depth of the pinion's engagement with the crownwheel is adjusted during manufacture to the optimum position for quiet running and long life. When components affecting the pinion engagement are changed, adjustments must be made to regain this optimum position. Before the pinion shaft is dismantled or replacement items fitted, the position of the pinion must be established by measurement. Because this requires the use of specialist measuring equipment the work should be entrusted to your Audi dealer. The components which affect the pinion engagement are the gearbox casing, the bearing carrier, the pinion bearings and the 1st gear needle roller bearing. The crownwheel and pinion must be renewed as a matched pair and the pinion engagement adjusted to the figure etched onto the crownwheel – a job for your Audi dealer.

2 Using a suitable puller, remove the bearing race and 1st gear, then remove the needle roller bearing and sleeve, keeping them identified for position (photos).

3 Lift off the 1st gear synchro-ring.

4 Using a puller with its legs placed beneath 2nd gear, draw off the gear and the 1st/2nd gear synchroniser assembly. Remove the 2nd gear synchro-ring.

5 Lift off the 2nd gear needle roller bearing and mark it to ensure correct refitting.

6 The 3rd and 4th gears are pressed and shrunk on to the shaft, and if they need to be removed the work should be entrusted to an Audi dealer.

7 Reassembly will commence with the pinion end bearing, 4th gear, 3rd gear and the circlip already on the pinion shaft; complete reassembly of the shaft as follows.

8 Lubricate the 2nd gear needle roller bearing with gear oil and fit it to the shaft.

9 Fit 2nd gear onto its bearing, then place the synchro-ring on the gear. Measure the gap, as in Fig. 6.5, if the gap exceeds the amount

6.2A From the pinion shaft remove the bearing ...

6.2B ... 1st gear ...

6.2C ... needle roller bearing ...

6.2D ... and bearing sleeve

given in the Specifications, a new synchro-ring must be fitted (photos).

10 If the synchroniser assembly has been dismantled, it must be reassembled in the following way. The sleeve and the hub may have matching marks, if so they must be assembled with these marks lined up. Fit the three locking keys into their slots and secure the keys with the circlips. The circlips should be spaced 120° apart and the angled end of the circlip should be engaged in the hollow of a locking key. If there are no matching marks on the hub and sleeve the two parts need not be assembled in any particular position, except that the grooves on the hub splines must face the 1st gear.

11 Fit the synchroniser assembly to the shaft, with the end of the sleeve having external teeth towards the pinion. Before pressing the hub down fully, turn the 2nd gear synchro-ring so that the slots in it are aligned with the locking keys in the synchroniser assembly (photo).

12 Fit the 1st gear synchro-ring, lining up its slots with the locking keys in the synchroniser assembly. Later models have a modified synchro-ring with a tooth missing at three points (Fig. 6.8). The tooth angle on these synchro-rings was altered from 120° to 110° to improve the engagement of 1st gear. This type of ring must only be used on 1st gear, and if the 1st gear ring is being renewed the 120° type having the

6.9A Fitting 2nd gear ...

6.9B ... and 2nd synchro-ring to the pinion shaft

6.9C Checking the synchro-ring wear with a feeler gauge

6.11 1st/2nd synchroniser fully installed (013 gearbox shown)

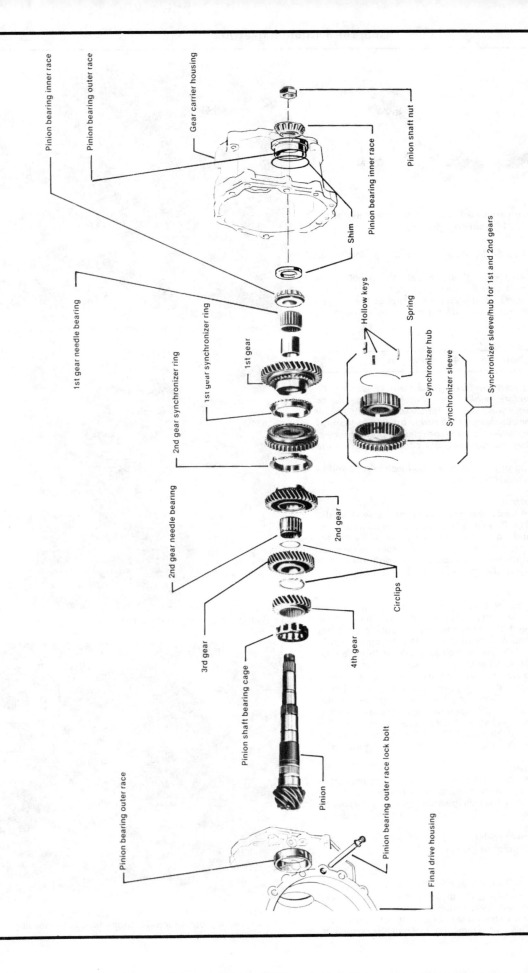

Pinion bearing inner race

Pinion bearing outer race

Gear carrier housing

Pinion shaft nut

Pinion bearing inner race

Shim

1st gear needle bearing

Hollow keys

Spring

1st gear synchronizer ring

1st gear

Synchronizer hub

2nd gear synchronizer ring

Synchronizer sleeve

Synchronizer sleeve/hub for 1st and 2nd gears

2nd gear needle bearing

2nd gear

Circlips

3rd gear

Pinion shaft bearing cage

4th gear

Pinion

Pinion bearing outer race

Pinion bearing outer race lock bolt

Final drive housing

Fig. 6.7 Exploded view of the pinion shaft components – 014 gearbox (Sec 6)

Fig. 6.8 Missing tooth (arrowed) on 110° 1st gear synchro ring – 014 gearbox (Sec 6)

full number of teeth should be fitted, as the modified ring is not available as a spare part.

13 Fit the 1st gear bearing sleeve, then lubricate the needle roller bearing with gear oil and fit it over the sleeve (photo).

14 Fit 1st gear and then press on the 2nd inner race of the tapered roller bearing. Use a metal tube to drive on the bearing if necessary (photo).

7 Gearbox/final drive housing (014) – servicing

Note: *The four and five-speed gearboxes have many fundamentally similar components. Therefore, whilst the photographic sequence applicable to this Section shows an 013 five-speed unit, for all practical purposes, it can be considered to illustrate the 014 four-speed unit. Any important differences are noted in the relevant photo caption. Other minor differences may be apparent, but should not affect the procedure described.*

1　The removal and refitting of the clutch release mechanism fitted in the gearbox housing is described in Chapter 5.

Input shaft needle bearing

2　Using a drift, or piece of hardwood dowel of suitable size, drive the bearing out from the clutch bellhousing end of the casing. Fit the new bearing so that the lettering on the bearing faces the drift used for installation. Enter the bearing into the bore squarely from the gearbox side of the casing and, using a drift or a piece of hardwood, knock it in until it is flush with the face of the casting (photo).

Pinion bearing

3　The outer track of the pinion bearing is secured by a pin which engages a depression in the outer circumference of the bearing (photo). Grip the grooved end of the pin and pull it out at least 3.2 mm (^{1}/8 in) so that the other end is clear of the bearing. Using a suitable drift, tap the outer race out of the end of the casing. When fitting a new outer track, line up the depression in the outer track with the pin, and then drive the track in flush with the face of the casting before tapping home the pin (the grooves on the end face of the bearing track should face towards the fitting tool). Renewing the roller assembly of the bearing is a job for an Audi agent; 3rd and 4th gears are shrunk onto the shaft and will require a substantial press tool to remove. On refitting the gears must be heated to 120°C (248°F) before being pressed into position (wide shoulder on each gear faces the pinion).

Driveshaft flange oil seals

4　The driveshaft oil seals in the gearbox housing and in the final drive cover may be prised out with a large screwdriver (photo).

5　Fit new seals with the lips of the seal inwards (photo). Take care to enter the seal squarely into the housing and drive it in fully using a hammer and a block of wood.

6　After fitting the seal, smear its lip with gear oil and fill the space between the lips with multi-purpose grease.

Input shaft oil seal

7　Remove the clutch release bearing, as described in Chapter 5.

8　Remove the three bolts attaching the guide sleeve to the housing and remove the guide sleeve and plate (photo).

9　Use a hooked lever to remove the oil seal, or prise it out with a short lever (photo). If the bush is also to be removed, this must be driven out

6.13 Fitting 1st synchro-ring and 1st gear needle roller bearing

6.14 Fitting the bearing to the pinion shaft

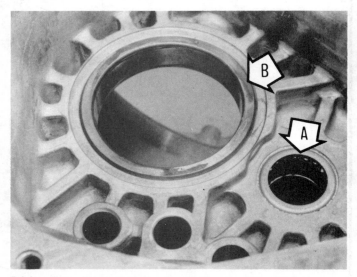

7.2 Location of input shaft needle roller bearing (A) and pinion shaft roller bearing outer race (B) in the final drive housing

7.3 Removing the pinion shaft bearing outer race retaining pin

7.4 Prising out a driveshaft flange oil seal

7.5 Installing a driveshaft flange oil seal

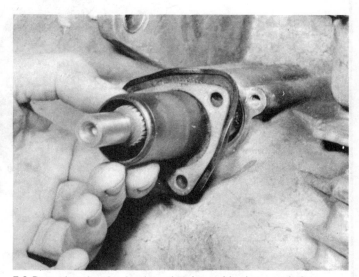

7.8 Removing the clutch release bearing guide sleeve and plate

7.9 Input shaft oil seal location in the final drive housing

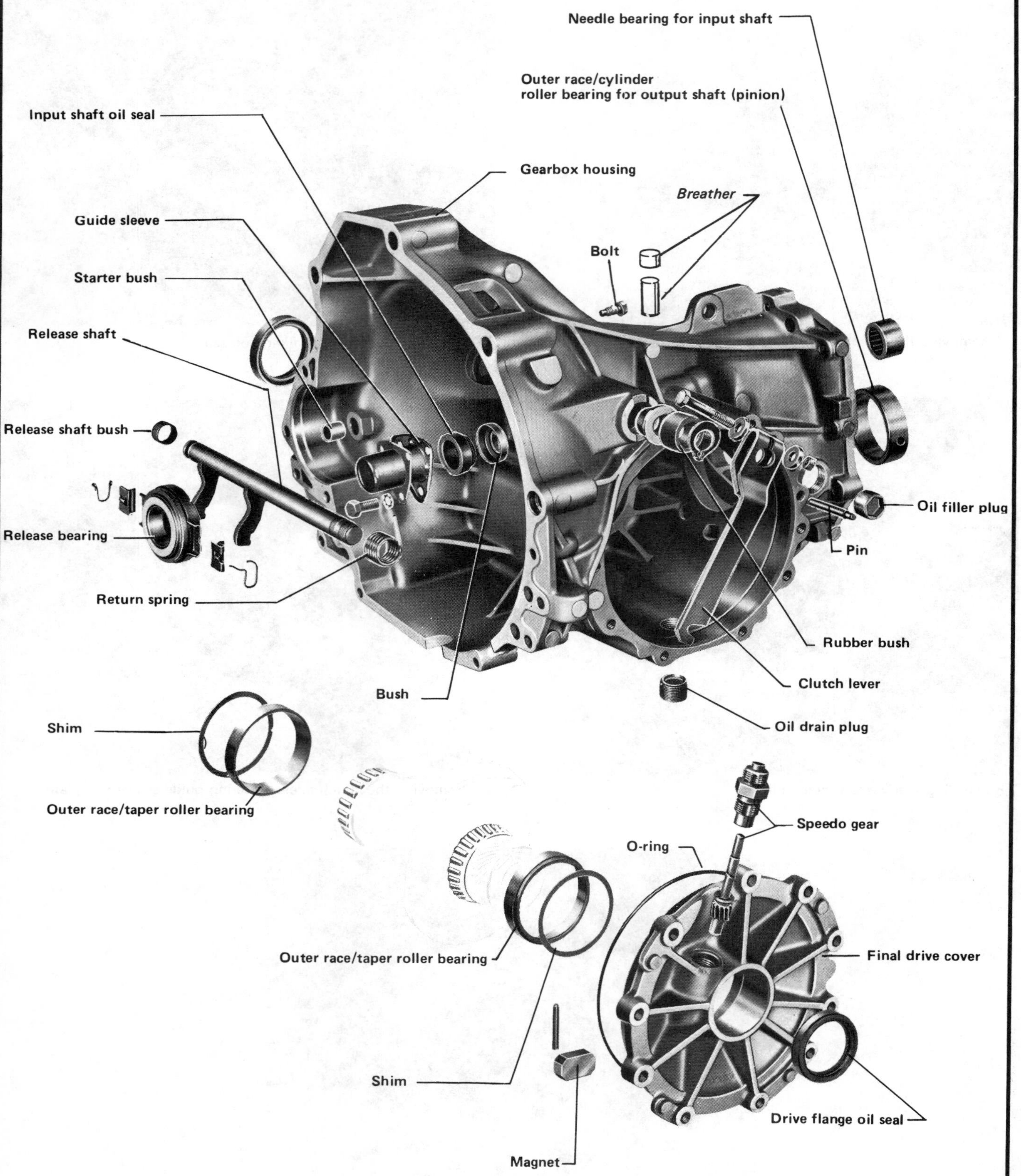

Needle bearing for input shaft

Outer race/cylinder
roller bearing for output shaft (pinion)

Input shaft oil seal

Gearbox housing

Breather

Bolt

Guide sleeve

Starter bush

Release shaft

Release shaft bush

Release bearing

Oil filler plug

Return spring

Pin

Rubber bush

Bush

Clutch lever

Oil drain plug

Shim

Outer race/taper roller bearing

Speedo gear

O-ring

Outer race/taper roller bearing

Final drive cover

Shim

Drive flange oil seal

Magnet

Fig. 6.9 Final drive housing components – 014 gearbox (Sec 7)

towards the bellhousing using a piece of tubing of suitable diameter which is long enough to extend into the gearbox housing. To renew the oil seal only, it is not necessary to dismantle the gearbox housing.
10   Drive the bush into the housing until the flat end of the bush seats against the bottom of the recess.
11   If the oil seal is being fitted with the input shaft in position, slide a piece of plastic sleeving over the splines of the input shaft, or wrap plastic tape round them before sliding the seal over the shaft. This will prevent the splines from damaging the seal. Fit the seal with its flat face outwards and oil the lips with gear oil before fitting it. Drive the seal in flush, using a hammer and a block of wood.
12   Fit the guide sleeve and plate and re-insert and tighten the fixing bolts. If the guide sleeve is plastic, it should be kept free from grease.

Starter bush

13   The starter bush is located in the bellhousing and if worn should be renewed. If an internal expanding removal tool is not available, it may be possible to force out the bush under hydraulic action by filling the bush with heavy grease then driving a tight fitting dowel rod into the bush.
14   Drive the new starter bush into the bellhousing until flush.

8   Bearing/gear carrier (014) – servicing

1   If the bearing carrier is being renewed, the meshing of the crownwheel and pinion is affected (see Section 6, paragraph 1). To ensure correct meshing, the pinion projection will need to be measured by an Audi dealer before and after the new carrier is fitted. They can then advise on the appropriate thickness of shim and gasket to be fitted between the new gear carrier and the gearbox housing to regain the original pinion projection.

Pinion bearing removal

2   The outer track of the bearing can be driven out of the case using a suitable drift, but the fitting of a new bearing and determining the correct thickness of shim needs to be done by an Audi dealer.

Gear detents – removal and refitting

3   Unscrew the pivot bolt and remove the reverse relay lever. Remove the pin from the reverse selector rod and pull the rod from the bearing carrier.
4   Pull the 3rd/4th gear selector rod out of the bearing carrier, taking care to recover the small interlock plunger within the rod.
5   To remove the detent plug at the top of the bearing carrier cut a 6 mm thread in the plug, screw a bolt into the plug and pull the bolt to extract the plug. With the plug removed, the spring and the detent can be removed.
6   The two detents in the side of the box are removed by driving in their plugs until the plugs can be removed from the gear selector rod bores. The detent, spring and sleeves can then be shaken out, together with the large interlock plungers.
7   Refitting is the reverse of removal. The correct position of the detents and interlock plungers is shown in Fig. 6.11.

Relay lever adjustment

8   It is not necessary to remove the selector rods in order to adjust the relay lever.

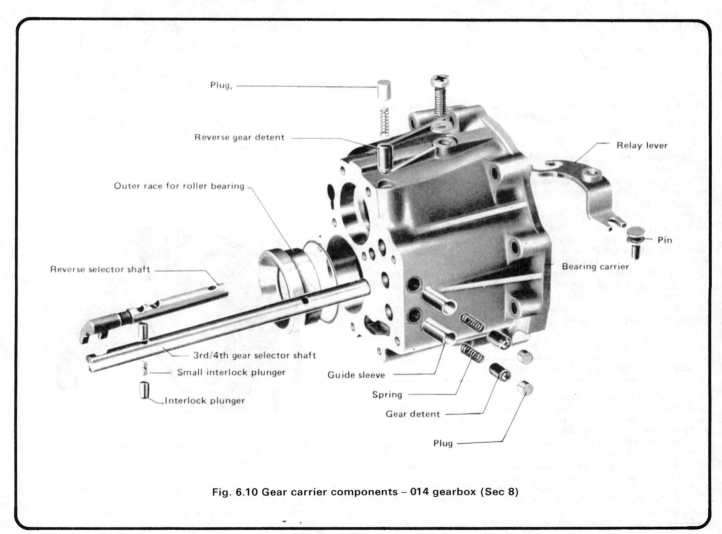

Fig. 6.10 Gear carrier components – 014 gearbox (Sec 8)

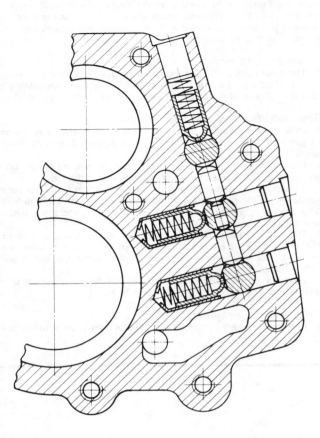

**Fig. 6.11 Cross-sectional view of the selector rod detents –
014 gearbox (Sec 8)**

9   Fit reverse gear and its shaft and then insert the relay lever and
selector link.
10   Fit the relay lever bolt and washer. Screw the bolt in until it touches
the relay lever, while the relay lever is being pressed in the direction of
the arrow (Fig. 6.12).
11   Press the relay lever against the end of the bolt and then screw in
the bolt until it just starts to engage the threads in the relay lever.
12   While still holding the relay lever in the same position, screw the
bolt in and tighten it to the torque given in the Specifications. The relay
lever should now be set at the correct distance from the gearcase.
13   Move the reverse gear selector rod to the reverse gear position
several times and check that the relay mechanism moves freely in all
positions.
14   If the relay lever has been adjusted with the selector rods removed,
reverse gear must be removed again before the selector rods can be
fitted.

9   Gearshift housing (014) – servicing

1   Pull out the selector rod and spring.
2   Before removing the rear bush, lever out the rear oil seal, and then
use a long drift to tap out the bush from the front end of the housing.
3   Enter the new bush squarely into the rear of the housing and tap it
home flush with the end of the casting, using a block of wood. In order
to drive the new bush in fully, rub the outside diameter of the *old* bush
with a piece of emery cloth to reduce its diameter enough to make it an
easy fit in the casting, then use this bush as a drift.
4   Fit a new oil seal, with the open end of the seal inwards, and using
a block of hardwood against the seal, drive it in until its face is flush
with the end of the casting.
5   The procedure for removing and fitting the front bush is similar,

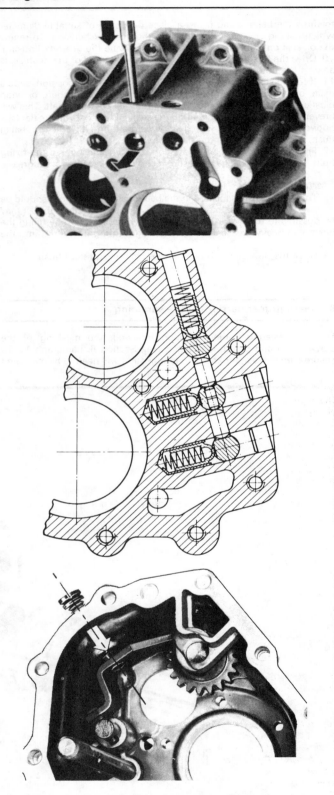

**Fig. 6.12 Press the reverse relay lever in direction of arrow
when fitting the pivot bolt – 014 gearbox (Sec 8)**

except that there is no oil seal and it is necessary to note which way
round the bush is fitted.
6   Lubricate the bushes and smear the lip of the oil seal with gear oil
before refitting the selector rod.

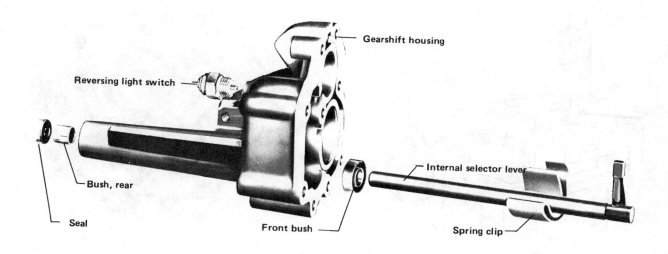

Fig. 6.13 Gearshift housing components – 014 gearbox (Sec 9)

10 Gearbox (014) – reassembly

1 If the selector rods have been removed from the bearing carrier, check that they have been inserted correctly and that the interlock plungers are in their proper places.

2 Fit the pinion assembly and the 1st/2nd gear selector fork into the bearing carrier.

3 Using a suitable piece of tubing as a drift, tap the outer part of the taper-roller bearing onto the end of the shaft, but while doing this make frequent checks to ensure that the 1st/2nd gear selector shaft has not jammed. If it has jammed, tap it lightly to free it.

4 Fit the 1st/2nd gear operating dog on the shift rod, line up its hole with the hole in the shift rod, then drive in the roll-pin.

5 Fit reverse gear and segment into the bearing carrier and then drive in the reverse gear shaft.

6 Fit the input shaft assembly loosely into the box without its bearing.

7 Pull back the 3rd/4th gear selector rod until the 3rd/4th gear selector fork can be fitted into the groove in the synchro-hub sleeve. Push the selector rod back to its neutral position and Line up the hole in the selector rod with the hole in the fork. Support the free end of the shaft in the same way as when removing the selector fork and drive in the roll-pin.

8 Fit a new gasket to the gearbox housing and fit the bearing carrier, with the input and pinion shaft assemblies, to the gearbox housing. Line up the holes and drive in the dowel pin. Insert and tighten the bolts.

9 Fit the input shaft ball-bearing squarely on to the end of its shaft, ensuring that the closed side of the bearing cage is towards the bearing carrier. Using a suitable tube, or a block of hardwood, drive the bearing in, taking care to see that it stays square to the shaft while also supporting the shaft on a block of wood.

10 Fit the thrust washer and circlip on top of the input shaft bearing.

11 Pull back the two selector rods until 1st and reverse gears are both engaged and the shafts are locked together. Fit the pinion shaft nut, tighten it to the specified torque and lock the nut to the shaft. Move the selector shafts back to their neutral position and check that both shafts are able to rotate freely.

12 The new operation requires great care if unecessary work is to be avoided. Very carefully pull out the 3rd/4th gear selector rod just enough for the small interlock plunger to be inserted. Smear grease on to the plunger, insert it into the hole and push the selector rod back in. If the rod is pulled out too far, the locking keys of the synchro-hub can come out and the gear assembly will have to be separated from the gearbox housing so that the locking keys can be re-inserted into the synchro-hub.

13 When refitting the gearshift housing to the bearing carrier, use a new gasket because the thickness of the gasket and the thickness of the shims control the position of the pinion.

14 If a new input shaft bearing or pinion bearing have been fitted it will be necessary to calculate the thickness of new shims required for fitting behind the bearing. To do this make sure the bearings are pressed fully onto their seats then measure the protrusion of each bearing from the end face of the bearing carrier (Fig. 6.14). Now measure the depth of the recesses in the gearshift housing for each bearing (Fig. 6.15). To determine the thickness of the shims required subtract the bearing protrusion from the depth of the recess plus 0.3 mm (0.0118 in). Having determined the thicknesses needed, new shims can be obtained from the range available.

15 When refitting the gearshift housing, first ensure that the shims are in place in the housing recess, with the recess in the shims towards the spring.

16 Fit the spring by first putting it over the internal selector lever. Compress the spring and slide it with the internal selector lever into the housing so that the end of the spring rests against the end of the housing and shim. Move the spring and the selector lever into the housing as far as they will go, and turn the selector lever so that the spring and selector lever are as shown in Fig. 6.16.

17 Insert the finger of the selector lever into the slots in the selector

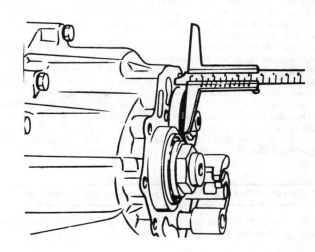

Fig. 6.14 Measuring bearing protrusion from the carrier end face – 014 gearbox (Sec 10)

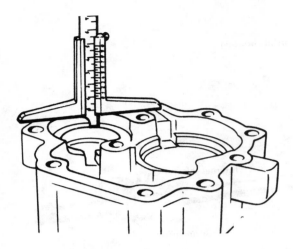

Fig. 6.15 Measuring depth of bearing recess in gearshift housing – 014 gearbox (Sec 10)

Fig. 6.16 Fitted position of selector lever spring in the gearshift housing – 014 gearbox (Sec 10)

rods and push the gearshift housing into place. Insert the bolts and tighten them to the specified torque.

18 Lower the differential into the final drive housing with the crownwheel teeth facing inward. Fit the O-ring to the cover and locate the cover on the housing. Insert the bolts and tighten them evenly in diagonal sequence to the specified torque.

19 Insert the drive flanges into each side of the differential and tighten the bolts while holding the flanges stationary with a rod through one of the bolt holes.

20 Fill the gearbox with oil.

11 Gearshift lever (014) – removal, refitting and adjustment

1   The adjustment of the gearshift linkage requires a special tool, so if the linkage is undone it is very important to mark the position of the shift rod in the shift finger before separating them.

2   Put a mark to show how far the shift rod is inserted into the clamp, and also mark a horizontal line on both the shift finger and the shift rod so that they can be reconnected without any rotational change.

3   Release the bolt on the clamp and separate the shift rod from the shift finger.

4   From inside the car, remove the centre console, as described in Chapter 11, undo the four nuts and washers securing the lever housing to the car floor and remove the gear lever assembly and shift rod.

5   To separate the shift rod from the gear lever, undo and remove the shift rod clevis bolt.

6   After refitting the gear lever, by reversing the removal operations, the basic setting of the linkage should be tested by engaging 1st gear and then moving the gear lever as far to the left as it will go. Hold the gear lever with one finger and allow it to spring back slowly to the pressure point. Measured at the gear lever knob the movement must be at last 5 to 10 mm (0.2 to 0.4 in). If the movement is insufficient, slacken the lever bearing retaining bolts and move the bearing to the right to reduce the gear lever movement, or to the left to increase it, then tighten the nuts. If gear selection is still unsatisfactory the adjustment should be checked by an Audi dealer.

12 Gearshift linkage (014) – dismantling and reassembly

1   The gearshift linkage consists of two principal parts, the shift rod coupling assembly and the lever assembly.

Gear lever assembly

2   Remove the gear lever, as described in Section 11.

3   Dismantle the assembly by unscrewing the gear knob, removing

the circlip from the gear lever and lifting off the washer and spring. The gear lever can then be pulled down out of the lever bearing assembly.

4   Before separating the lever bearing assembly from the lever housing, mark round the lever bearing plate with a scriber so that it can be returned to exactly the same position, then remove the two screws and washer from the plate.

5   Do not dismantle the bearing unless it is necessary to grease it. Push the rubber guide and locking ring (if fitted) down out of the housing plate, then prise the plastic shells apart and remove the ball halves and spring – the shells can then be removed from the rubber guide.

6   When reassembling, have the rubber guide with its shouldered end uppermost and press the two shells into it. Press the lower ball half into the shells, then the spring and finally press in the upper ball half, pushing the shells slightly apart if necessary.

7   After assembling the parts into the rubber guide, push the assembly up into the lever bearing plate, together with the locking ring, where fitted.

8   When inserting the lever into the bearing, note that the lever is cranked to the left, and when refitting the lever bearing plate to the housing, take care to line up the plate with the scribed mark made before dismantling.

Shift rod coupling

9   To dismantle the shift rod coupling, remove the bolt from the end of the support rod. Mark the position of the adaptor on the gearbox selector lever, then loosen the bolt and remove the shift rod coupling assembly.

10 Prise the ball coupling of the support off its mounting on the side plate. Remove the bolt which clamps the two side plates together and extract the shift finger and its bushes.

11 When reassembling the shift rod coupling, note that the adaptor should be fitted so that the hole for the clamp bolt is towards the front and the groove for the clamp bolt on the shift finger is on the left-hand side. Make sure that the holes in the two side plates are exactly in line, so that the coupling is assembled without any strain.

12 All the joints and friction surfaces of the shift rod coupling should be lubricated with special grease AOS 126 000 05.

13 Gearbox (013 and 093) – dismantling into major assemblies

Note: *Photo sequence shows 013 unit – some components of the 093 unit may differ slightly from those shown.*

1   Remove the drain plug, drain the oil and refit the plug. Clean away external dirt from the gearbox casing.

2   Pierce the cover plate with a screwdriver and prise it out – a new plate must be obtained for the reassembly procedure.

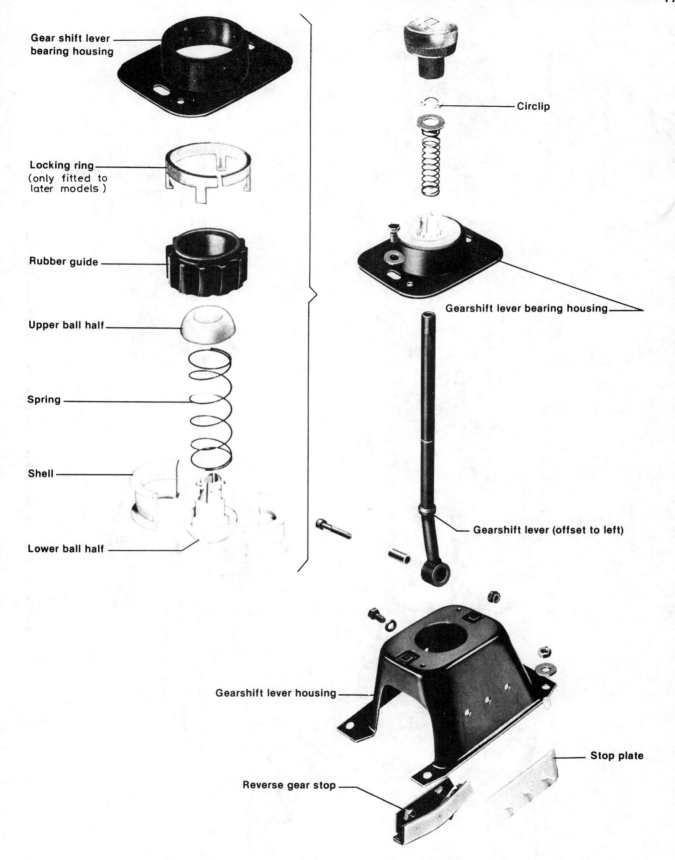

Gear shift lever bearing housing

Locking ring (only fitted to later models)

Rubber guide

Upper ball half

Spring

Shell

Lower ball half

Circlip

Gearshift lever bearing housing

Gearshift lever (offset to left)

Gearshift lever housing

Stop plate

Reverse gear stop

Fig. 6.17 Exploded view of the gearshift lever and linkage – 014 gearbox (Secs 11 and 12)

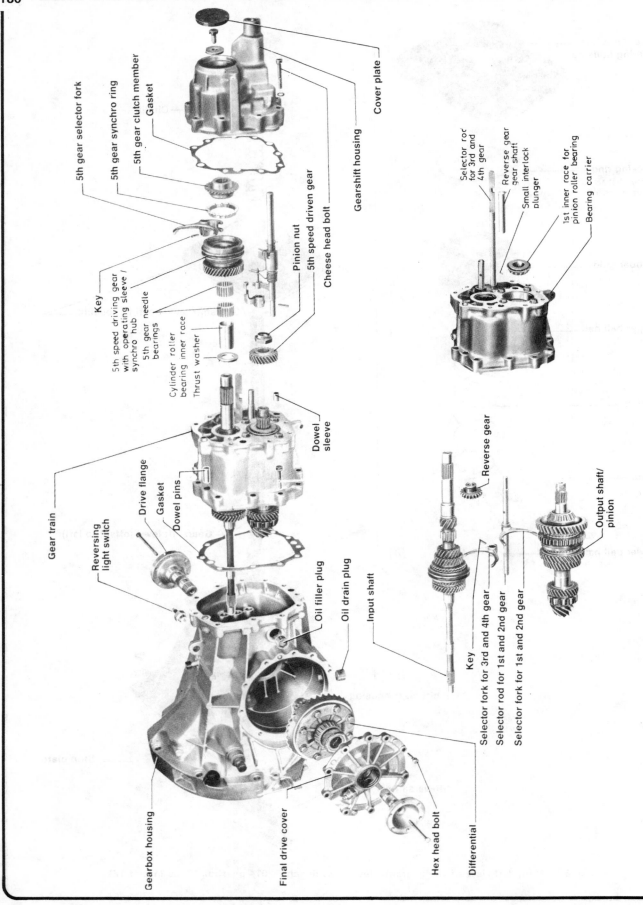

Fig. 6.18 Exploded view of the gearbox major assemblies – 013 gearbox (Sec 13)

5th gear selector fork

5th gear synchro ring

5th gear clutch member

Gasket

Gearshift housing

Cover plate

Key

5th speed driving gear with operating sleeve / synchro hub

5th gear needle bearings

Cylinder roller bearing inner race

Thrust washer

Pinion nut

5th speed driven gear

Cheese head bolt

Selector rod for 3rd and 4th gear

Reverse gear gear shaft

Small interlock plunger

1st inner race for pinion roller bearing

Bearing carrier

Gear train

Reversing light switch

Drive flange

Gasket

Dowel pins

Dowel sleeve

Oil filler plug

Oil drain plug

Input shaft

Reverse gear

Output shaft/ pinion

Key

Selector fork for 3rd and 4th gear

Selector rod for 1st and 2nd gear

Selector fork for 1st and 2nd gear

Differential

Gearbox housing

Final drive cover

Hex head bolt

3   Remove the reverse lamp switch wiring and unscrew the switch. Also unscrew the gear indicator switch (photo).
4   Remove the clutch release bearing and shaft, as described in Chapter 5.
5   Unscrew the drive flange centre bolts while holding the flange stationary with a rod inserted through a bolt hole. Mark each flange side for side, then withdraw them from the differential (photo).
6   On the 013 gearbox, unbolt and remove the differential cover and lift out the differential (photos). Although it is possible to remove the differential from the 093 gearbox at this stage, there is a likelihood of damage to the crownwheel and pinion teeth, and it is therefore recommended that the differential be removed after dismantling the remainder of the gearbox.
7   Unscrew the bolt from the end of the input shaft and remove the thick washer. The input shaft must be held stationary in order to unscrew the bolt – we used a nut splitter and block of wood (photo), but it is possible to make up a tool similar to that shown in Fig. 6.19 using an old clutch driven plate.
8   Using an Allen key, unscrew the bolts from the gearshift housing.
9   Pull the gearshift housing from the gear carrier and remove the gasket (photo). If the bearing is tight on the end of the input shaft a puller will be required.

13.3 Removing the reverse lamp switch

13.5 Removing a drive flange

13.6A Removing the differential cover ...

13.6B ... and differential (013 gearbox shown)

13.7 Using a nut splitter to hold the input shaft stationary

Fig. 6.19 Tool for holding the input shaft stationary – 013 and 093 gearboxes (Sec 13)

13.9 Removing the gearshift housing

10 Using a pin punch, drive the roll pin from the 1st/2nd selector dog and turn the dog anti-clockwise (photo).

11 Pull out the notched selector rod to engage 3rd gear, then turn the main selector rod anti-clockwise and extract it from the gear carrier (photo).

12 Remove the 1st/2nd selector dog and move the 3rd/4th selector rod to neutral (photo).

13 Using a pin punch, drive the roll pin fom the 5th gear selector fork while supporting the selector rod with a block of wood to prevent damage to the bore in the bearing carrier (photo).

14 Engage 5th gear by moving the synchro sleeve and 1st gear by pulling out the 1st/2nd selector rod. Both the input and pinion shafts are now locked to enable the nut to be unscrewed from the pinion shaft. After removing the nut return the gears to neutral.

15 Unscrew the bolts securing the gear carrier to the final drive housing, noting the location of any brackets.

16 Remove the gear carrier and gasket, and if necessary knock out the dowel pins (photo). To prevent unnecessary damage to the oil seal wrap adhesive tape around the input shaft splines before removing the gear carrier.

13.10 Removing the 1st/2nd selector dog roll pin

13.11 Removing the main selector rod

13.12 Removing the 1st/2nd selector dog

13.13 Removing the 5th gear selector fork roll pin

13.16 Removing the gear carrier

17 Using a puller beneath the 5th gear, pull off the 5th gear and synchro unit, 5th gear clutch member, and 5th selector fork. It may be possible to lever off these items, but this will depend on how tight the clutch member is on the input shaft.
18 Separate the clutch member and synchro-ring from the 5th gear and synchro unit (photo).
19 Remove the 5th gear needle roller bearings from the input shaft (photo).

20 Using a puller, remove the 5th driven gear from the pinion shaft.
21 Lever off the 5th gear thrust washer and inner race (photo). If the inner race is tight use a puller.
22 Using a pin punch, drive the roll pin from the 3rd/4th selector fork while supporting the selector rod with a block of wood to prevent damage to the bore in the bearing carrier (photo).
23 Pull the 3rd/4th selector rod out of the gear carrier. Remove the small interlock plunger from the rod and put it in a safe place (photo).

13.18 5th gear and synchro unit with the splined clutch member

13.19 Removing the 5th gear needle roller bearings

13.21 Removing the 5th gear thrust washer

13.22 Removing the 3rd/4th selector fork roll pin

13.23A Removing the 3rd/4th selector rod (arrowed)

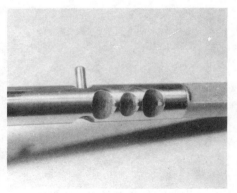

13.23B Interlock plunger location in the 3rd/4th selector rod

24 The pinion shaft must now be pushed through the tapered roller bearing inner race approximately 6 to 8 mm (0.24 to 0.32 in) to allow clearance for the input shaft to be removed. To do this, support the gear carrier and use a press, or alternatively use a plate (photo) and long bolts inserted into the bearing outer race retaining ring. If the latter method is used remove each bolt and insert the long bolts separately to prevent the ring from dropping.

25 Remove the input shaft, together with the 3rd/4th selector fork from the gear carrier (photo).

26 Set the selector rods to neutral.

27 Using a soft metal drift, drive out the reverse gear shaft and remove the reverse gear (photo).

28 Remove the pinion shaft, together with 1st/2nd selector rod and fork (photo).

29 Recover the interlock plungers from the gear carrier and put them in a safe place.

30 Remove the differential on the 093 gearbox, as necessary (see paragraph 6).

14 Mainshaft/input shaft (013 and 093) – dismantling and reassembly

Removal of the components from the front of the input shaft is identical to that for the 014 gearbox described in Section 5. The rear end of the input shaft is of course longer to accommodate 5th gear and incorporates the inner race of the rear roller bearing. To remove the race, insert a clamp beneath it and drive the input shaft through it. A long metal tube may be used to fit the race.

15 Pinion shaft (013 and 093) – dismantling and reassembly

The procedure is identical to that for the 014 gearbox, as described in Section 6. The rear end of the pinion shaft is of course longer to accommodate 5th gear. *However, note that when refitting the 1st/2nd*

13.24 Home-made plate for removing the pinion shaft

13.25 Removing the input shaft with 3rd/4th selector fork

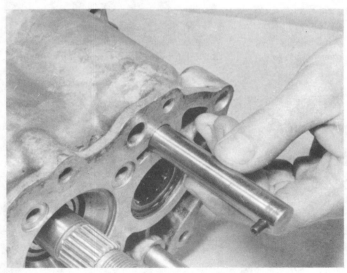

13.27 Removing the reverse gear shaft

13.28 Removing the pinion shaft with the 1st/2nd selector rod and fork

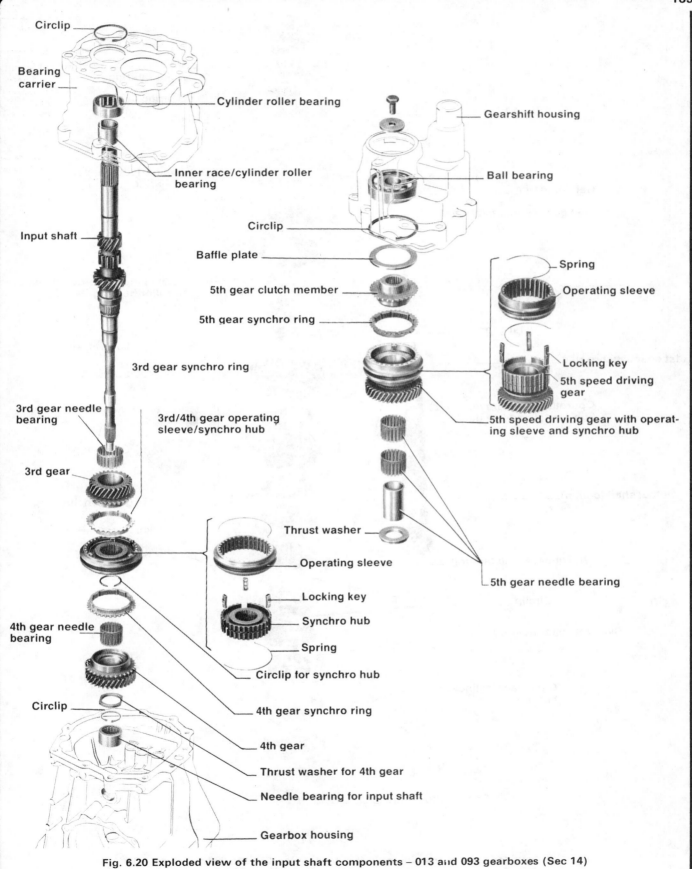

Fig. 6.20 Exploded view of the input shaft components – 013 and 093 gearboxes (Sec 14)

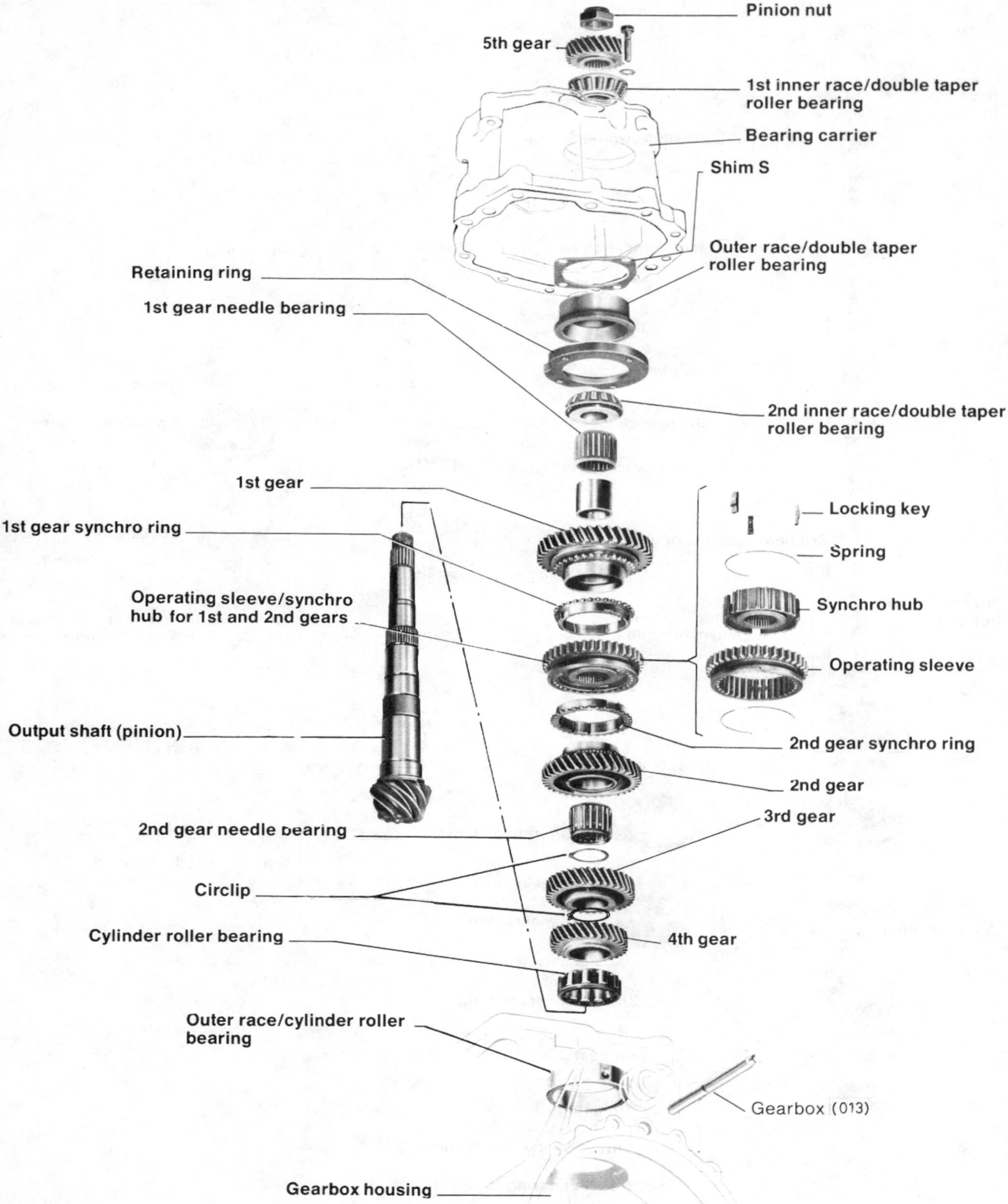

Fig. 6.21 Exploded view of the pinion shaft components – 013 and 093 gearboxes (Sec 15)

synchroniser the external teeth must be away from the pinion end of the shaft (ie the opposite way round to the 014 gearbox).

16 Gearbox/final drive housing (013 and 093) – servicing

The procedure is identical to that for the 014 gearbox with the following exceptions:

(a) *The pinion bearing outer track on the 093 gearbox is secured by a socket-headed bolt which must be removed with an Allen key*

(b) *The 093 gearbox does not incorporate an input shaft bush.*

The procedure for the 014 gearbox is described in Section 7.

17 Bearing/gear carrier (013 and 093) – servicing

Note: *Photo sequence shows 013 unit – some components of the 093 unit may differ slightly from those shown.*

The procedure is identical to that for the 014 gearbox given in Section 8 with the following exceptions.

Pinion bearing renewal

1   Unscrew the four bolts and remove the bearing outer race retaining ring, noting the location of the cut-outs (photos).
2   Using a metal tube, drive the outer race from the bearing carrier and remove the shim.
3   Refitting is a reversal of the removal procedure, but it will be

17.1A Remove the four bolts ...

17.1B ... and the pinion bearing outer race retaining ring

17.1C Pinion bearing outer race and shim

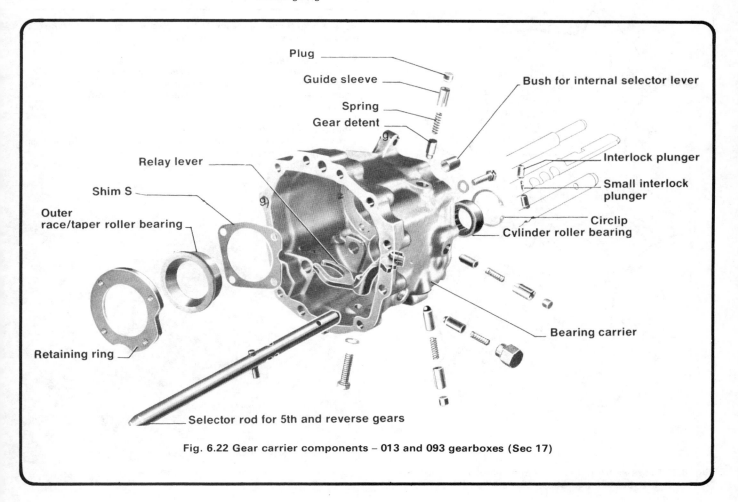

Fig. 6.22 Gear carrier components – 013 and 093 gearboxes (Sec 17)

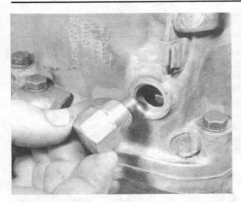

17.4A Removing the reverse detent from the bearing carrier

17.4B Location of the reverse relay lever and 5th/reverse selector rod in the bearing carrier

17.5 Selector rod detents in the bearing carrier

necessary for an Audi dealer to determine the correct thickness of shim to fit behind the race.

Gear detents – removal and refitting
4   Before removing the reverse relay lever, unscrew and remove the detent from the side of the bearing carrier. The relay lever is operated by a pin in the 5th/reverse selector rod (photos).
5   All the detents are removed using the 6 mm thread and bolt method (photo).

Main selector rod bush – removal
6   The bush can be removed and refitted using a soft metal drift. Drive the bush in flush when refitting.

Input shaft bearing – renewal
7   Extract the circlip then, using a metal tube, drive the bearing into the bearing carrier.
8   To fit the new bearing, first fit the circlip then, using the metal tube on the outer track, drive the bearing into the carrier until it contacts the circlip.

18 Gearshift housing (013 and 093) – servicing

Note: *Photo sequence shows 013 unit – some components of the 093 unit may differ slightly from those shown.*

Selector oil seal – renewal
1   Prise out the oil seal with a screwdriver (photo).
2   Insert the new oil seal and drive it in until flush using a block of wood, making sure that it is kept square to the housing.
3   Fill the space between the oil seal lips with multi-purpose grease.

Selector bush – renewal
4   Remove the oil seal and, using a suitable metal tube, drive the bush into the gearshift housing.
5   Drive the new bush into the housing from the same direction, then fit a new oil seal.

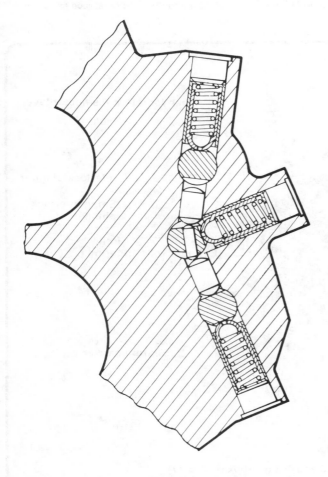

Fig. 6.23 Cross-sectional view of the selector rod detents – 013 and 093 gearboxes (Secs 17 and 20)

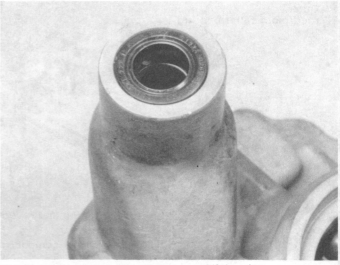

18.1 Main selector rod oil seal in the gearshift housing

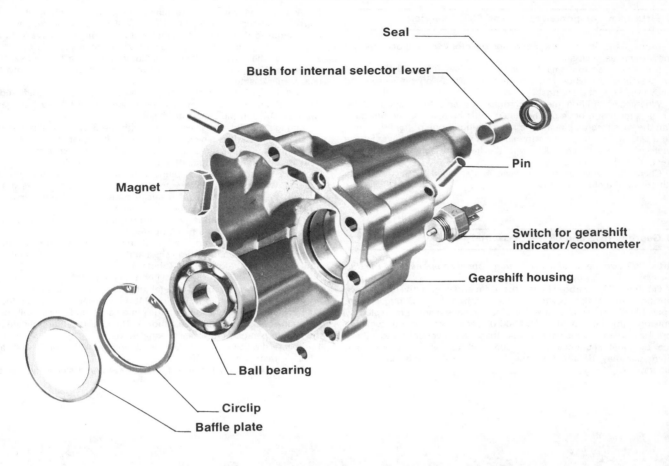

Fig. 6.24 Gearshift housing components – 013 and 093 gearboxes (Sec 18)

Input shaft ball-bearing – removal and refitting
6   Prise out the baffle plate from inside the gearshift housing. As the plate is peened into position it may be necessary to use a round file to remove the peening first.
7   Extract the circlip and, using a soft metal drift on the outer track,

drive the bearing into the housing (photo).
8   Drive the bearing fully into the housing using the metal tube on the outer track, then fit the circlip.
9   Press in the baffle plate and peen over the housing shoulder in three places to secure (photo).

18.7 Outer view of the input shaft bearing in the gearshift housing

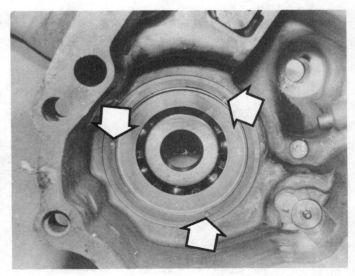

18.9 Peening points (arrowed) for securing the input shaft bearing baffle plate

19 Fifth gear components (013 and 093) – servicing

1   Examine the 5th gear and 5th driven gear for wear and damage and renew them, as necessary.

2   If it is required to dismantle the synchroniser, first mark the sleeve and gear hub in relation to each other, then slide off the sleeve and remove the keys and springs.

3   When reassembling the synchroniser observe the mating marks. The selector fork groove on the sleeve must be towards the 5th gear. With the keys inserted, locate the inner spring in one of the keys, then use a screwdriver to position the spring under the other keys. Fit the outer spring in a different key with the free end facing the opposite direction to the inner spring.

4   Check the synchro-ring for wear, as described in Section 5, by fitting it on the clutch member.

20 Gearbox (013 and 093) – reassembly

Note: *Photo sequence shows 013 unit – some components of the 093 unit may differ slightly from those shown.*

1   On the 093 gearbox lower the differential into the final drive housing and fit the cover, together with a new O-ring, where applicable. Where an O-ring is not used the cover should be sealed by applying a thin coat of AMV 188 000 02 sealing compound, available from Audi agents, to the cover flange. Insert the cover bolts and tighten in a diagonal sequence to the specified torque. If required the differential may be fitted to the 013 gearbox at this stage (see paragraph 28).

2   With the gear carrier on the bench, fit the interlock plungers in their correct positions as shown in Fig. 6.23. If the selector detents have been removed they can be fitted later. If a pen magnet is available the interlock plungers may be fitted as the work proceeds (photo).

3   Engage the 1st/2nd selector fork and rod with the 1st/2nd synchro sleeve on the output shaft, then lower them simultaneously into the gear carrier casing.

4   With the gear carrier on its side, insert the reverse gear shaft and at the same time locate the reverse gear between the relay lever jaws (photo). Drive in the shaft until flush.

5   Engage the 3rd/4th selector fork with the 3rd/4th synchro sleeve on the input shaft, then lower them into the gear carrier and into engagement with the pinion shaft gears. Take care to keep the synchro sleeves central in their hubs otherwise the keys may fall out.

6   Insert the small interlock plunger in the 3rd/4th selector rod and retain it with grease. Make sure that the interlock plungers are in position then insert the 3rd/4th selector rod into the gear carrier and through the selector fork.

7   Align the holes, then drive the roll pin into the fork end rod while supporting the rod with a block of wood.

8   Support the front ends of the shafts, then fit the tapered roller bearing inner race on the pinion shaft and drive it on using a metal tube until it contacts the outer race (photos).

9   Locate the 5th gear thrust washer on the input shaft, then drive on the 5th gear inner race using a metal tube (photo). The inner race can if necessary be pre-heated to 120°C (248°F) to ease the installation.

10   Locate the 5th driven gear on the pinion shaft and drive it fully onto the splines using a metal tube (photo). The gear may be preheated as the race in paragraph 9 to ease installation.

11   Locate the 5th gear needle roller bearings on the input shaft and lubricate them with gear oil.

12   Engage the 5th selector fork with the synchro sleeve on the 5th

20.2 Using a pen magnet to insert an interlock plunger

20.4 Fitting reverse gear shaft and reverse gear

20.8A Locate the bearing on the pinion shaft ...

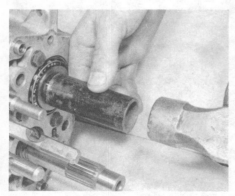

20.8B ... then drive it on with a metal tube

20.9 Installing the 5th gear inner race

20.10 Installing the 5th driven gear

20.12 Installing the 5th gear and synchro unit, together with the 5th selector fork

20.13 Fitting the 5th synchro-ring

gear and synchro unit, then locate the assembly over the input shaft and 5th/reverse selector rod (photo).

13 Fit the 5th synchro-ring to the synchroniser, making sure that the slots are aligned with the keys (photo).

14 Fit the clutch member and drive it fully onto the splines using a metal tube (photo). The member can if necessary be pre-heated to 120°C (248°F) to ease the installation.

15 Locate a new gasket on the final drive housing (photo).

16 To prevent damage to the oil seal, wrap adhesive tape around the input shaft splines (photo). Lower the gear carrier onto the final drive housing and insert the bolts, together with the mounting bracket.

17 Drive in the dowel pins until flush, then tighten the bolts in diagonal sequence to the specified torque. Remove the adhesive tape.

20.14 Installing the 5th gear clutch member

20.15 New gasket located on the final drive housing

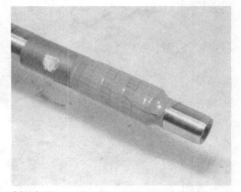

20.16 Wrap adhesive tape around the input shaft splines to prevent damage to the oil seal

20.19A Fit the nut to the pinion shaft ...

20.19B ... tighten the nut to the specified torque ...

20.19C ... and punch the collar onto the flat

18 Engage 5th gear by moving the synchro sleeve (ie leaving the 5th/reverse selector rod in neutral) and 1st gear by pulling out the 1st/2nd selector rod. Both the input and pinion shafts are now locked.

19 Fit and tighten the pinion shaft nut to the specified torque, and lock by punching the collar onto the shaft flat (photos). After tightening the nut, return the gears to neutral.

20 Align the holes, then drive the roll pin into the 5th gear selector fork and rod while supporting the rod with a block of wood.

21 Locate the 1st/2nd selector dog on its rod near its final position, but do not fit the roll pin at this stage.

22 Pull out the notched selector rod to engage 3rd gear, then insert the main selector rod by engaging the ends of the springs over the 3rd/4th selector rod, locating the finger in the notch, and pushing the main selector rod into the bush. When fitted, push the 3rd/4th selector rod into neutral (photos).

23 Align the holes, then drive the roll pin into the 1st/2nd selector dog and rod while supporting the rod with a block of wood.

24 Locate a new gasket on the gear carrier, then lower the gearshift

housing into position. If necessary, gently tap the inner race of the ball-bearing to locate it on the end of the input shaft.

25 Insert the bolts, together with the brackets, having first applied sealing compound to the bolt threads. Using an Allen key, tighten the bolts in diagonal sequence.

26 Insert the bolt and thick washer in the end of the input shaft, and tighten to the specified torque while holding the shaft stationary using the method described in Section 13, paragraph 7 (photo).

27 Clean the recess then press in a new cover plate (photo).

28 If not fitted yet, lower the differential into the final drive housing. Clean the cover and housing mating faces and apply a little sealing compound to them. Locate the cover on the housing, then insert and tighten the bolts in diagonal sequence to the specified torque. Note that the magnet on the cover should be positioned at the bottom (photo).

29 Insert the drive flanges into each side of the differential, and tighten the bolts while holding the flanges stationary with a rod through one of the bolt holes (photo).

20.22A Engage 3rd gear and fit the main selector rod ...

20.22B ... then engage neutral

20.26 Tightening the input shaft bolt

20.27 Fitting a new cover plate to the gearshift housing

20.28 The magnet on the differential cover must be at the bottom of the gearbox

20.29 Tightening a drive flange bolt

30 Refit the clutch release bearing and shaft, as described in Chapter 5.
31 Insert and tighten the reverse lamp switch, and clip the wiring into position.
32 Fill the gearbox with oil.

21 Gearshift lever (013 and 093) – removal, refitting and adjustment

1 The procedure is basically the same as that described for the 014 gearbox in Section 11. However, after checking the return distance in 1st gear, engage 5th gear and move the lever to the right as far as possible. Hold the gear lever with one finger and allow it to spring back slowly to the pressure point. The return distance should be the same as measured in the 1st gear position and, on these gearboxes, should be at least 5 mm (0.2 in). If the movement is not the same in both positions move the gear lever bearing within the travel allowed by its elongated holes: to the right for more movement in 5th gear or to the left for more movement in 1st gear. If gear selection is still unsatisfactory the adjustment should be checked by an Audi dealer.

22 Gearshift linkage (013 and 093) – dismantling and reassembly

The procedure is identical to that for the 014 gearbox described in Section 12. However, the bottom of the gear lever is not cranked and can therefore be fitted either way round.

23 Gearbox (016) – dismantling into major assemblies

1 Remove the gearbox drain plug, drain out the oil and refit the plug. Clean away external dirt from the gearbox casing.
2 Mark the position of the gear selector lever on its splines, then release the clamp bolt and pull the selector lever off.
3 Undo the selector shaft cover bolts, remove the cover and withdraw the selector shaft assembly.

4 Remove the bolts securing the bearing carrier to the gearbox housing and drive out the two dowel pins.
5 Push the selector shaft in as far as possible, so that it is disengaged from the dogs on the shift rods and then separate the bearing carrier with the gear assembly from the gearbox housing.
6 Remove the cover from the end of the bearing carrier. If a metal cover is fitted, tap the cover out with the drift and remove the O-ring. If a rubber plug is fitted, pierce the centre of the plug with a large screwdriver and lever the plug out. If the gearbox has a metal cover, a rubber plug must not be fitted, because it would block an oil hole.
7 Clamp the input shaft in a soft-jawed vice and unscrew and remove the hexagon bolt from the end of the shaft.
8 Support the gear (bearing) carrier housing then unscrew and remove the twelve retaining bolts. Withdraw the housing, tapping it free if necessary using a soft-faced mallet. Remove the ball-bearing inner race A (Fig. 6.26).
9 Using a suitable universal puller, pull free the 5th gear synchro-hub and the mainshaft bearing inner race, followed by the 5th gear synchroniser ring. Use a suitable pin punch and drive out the roll pin securing the 5th gear shift fork. When drifting the pin out, support the assembly to prevent damaging the selector rod or its bore in the carrier housing.
10 Extract the circlip securing 5th gear in position then withdraw 5th driving gear and its shift fork, leaving the 5th/reverse gear selector rod in the carrier housing.
11 Remove the selector rod stop screws then carefully clamp the 4th gear/pinion in a vice (fitted with soft jaws for protection). Unscrew and remove the pinion bolt.
12 To withdraw 5th driven gear you will probably need to use a puller. As the gear is removed retrieve its adjustment shim.
13 Support the free end of 1st/2nd selector fork shaft by jamming a block of wood under it and then drive out the roll pin securing the selector fork on the shaft. Rotate the selector (operator) so that it faces upwards.
14 Drive out the 3rd/4th selector fork roll pin (supporting the shaft as for 1st/2nd fork pin removal). Withdraw the 3rd/4th gear selector rod, but leave the selector fork engaged in its operating sleeve. Take care not to lose the interlock plunger.
15 Unscrew and remove the rocker lever bolt.
16 The pinion and input shaft must now be partially pulled out, and the input shaft, complete with 3rd/4th selector fork removed.
17 The reverse gear spring clip must now be unhooked on the pinion side and turned round to enable the pinion shaft to be withdrawn sufficiently to allow removal of the 1st/2nd selector fork and rod. Remove the pinion shaft.
18 Dismantle the gearbox housing as follows. First insert a suitable rod through one of the bolt holes of a drive flange so that the rod is

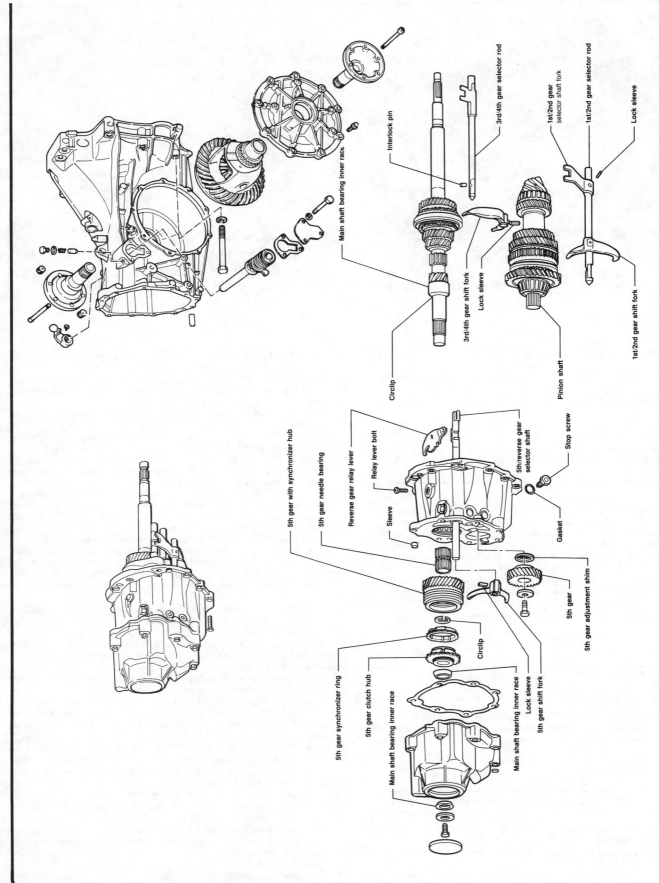

Main shaft bearing inner race

Interlock pin

3rd/4th gear selector rod

1st/2nd gear selector shaft fork

1st/2nd gear selector rod

Lock sleeve

3rd/4th gear shift fork

Lock sleeve

Circlip

Pinion shaft

1st/2nd gear shift fork

5th gear with synchronizer hub

5th gear needle bearing

Reverse gear relay lever

Relay lever bolt

Sleeve

5th/reverse gear selector shaft

Stop screw

Gasket

5th gear adjustment shim

5th gear

5th gear synchronizer ring

5th gear clutch hub

Circlip

Main shaft bearing inner race

Lock sleeve

5th gear shift fork

Fig. 6.25 Exploded view of the gearbox major assemblies – 016 gearbox (Sec 23)

Fig. 6.26 Removing the gear carrier housing and bearing inner race (A) – 016 gearbox (Sec 23)

Fig. 6.27 Removing the 5th gear synchro-hub and bearing inner race – 016 gearbox (Sec 23)

Fig. 6.29 Synchro-hub circlip removal – 016 gearbox (Sec 23)

Fig. 6.28 Using a pin punch to drive out the 5th gear shift fork roll pin – 016 gearbox (Sec 23)

Fig. 6.30 Removing the pinion bolt retaining 5th driven gear – 016 gearbox (Sec 23)

against one of the cover ribs and so prevents the flange from rotating, then remove the bolt from the centre of the flange. Repeat the operation on the other drive flange and then use two levers to prise out the flanged shafts. Mark each shaft as it is removed to ensure that it is fitted to its correct side of the gearbox housing.

19 Remove the bolts from the differential cover, remove the cover, and take out the differential.

Fig. 6.31 Using a pin punch to drive out the 1st/2nd selector fork roll pin – 016 gearbox (Sec 23)

24 Mainshaft/input shaft (016) – dismantling and reassembly

1   Remove the circlip from the end of the shaft and then remove the thrust washer (early models only).
2   Lift off 4th gear with its needle roller bearing. If the bearing is removed from the gear, put a paint mark on the bearing and the gear so that the bearing is not turned end-for-end on reassembling.
3   Remove the 4th gear synchro-ring.
4   Remove the circlip retaining the synchro-hub and take the hub off the shaft. It may be possible to hold 3rd gear and tap the shaft out of the synchro-hub, or it may be necessary to have the hub pressed off.
5   Remove the 3rd gear synchro-ring, 3rd gear and its needle roller bearing.
6   Mark the gear and bearing so that the bearing is not turned end-for-end on reassembly.
7   Before starting reassembly, ensure that all parts are clean and inspect them for signs of damage or excessive wear. Gearbox components are very expensive and if any gears or shafts are required it may be economic to fit an exchange gearbox.
8   Lubricate the 3rd gear needle roller bearing with gear oil and fit the bearing onto the shaft, ensuring that the bearing is the same way up as it was before removal.
9   Fit 3rd gear.
10 If the synchroniser has been dismantled, look for mating marks etched on the outer edge. If so, the hub must be assembled with these marks in line. Later models do not have mating marks, but are assembled with the hub groove and wide sleeve boss towards 4th gear.
11 Fit the three locking keys into the hub before fitting the sleeve and then retain the keys with the circlips, positioning the circlips as shown in Fig. 6.4, with the angled end of the spring fitted into the hollow of the locking key.
12 Fit the 3rd gear synchro-ring onto the cone of the gear and measure the gap a in Fig. 6.5 using a feeler gauge. This gap must not exceed the figure given in the Specifications otherwise a new synchro-ring must be fitted.
13 Note that the splines on the bore of the synchro-hub are chamfered at one end. The chamfered end of the hub goes onto the shaft first, facing 3rd gear. The hub also has an additional groove at one end (Fig. 6.32) and this groove faces 4th gear.
14 Press the synchroniser on to the input shaft, first turning the 3rd gear synchro-ring so that the grooves on it are aligned with the synchroniser locking keys.
15 Insert the circlip on top of the synchro-hub and then press the synchroniser back against the circlip. This increases the gap between the synchroniser and 3rd gear which ensures better lubrication of the 3rd gear bearing.

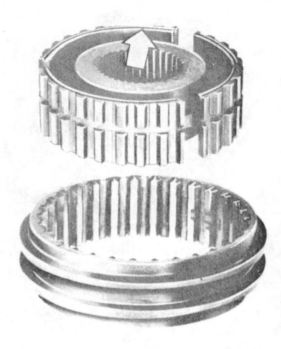

Fig. 6.32 Hub groove (arrowed) and wide boss on the sleeve of 3rd/4th synchroniser must be toward 4th gear – 016 gearbox (Sec 24)

16 Fit the 4th gear synchro-ring, aligning the grooves in it with the synchroniser locking keys, then check its clearance, as in paragraph 12.
17 Fit 4th gear and its bearing, first lubricating the bearing with gear oil, fit the thrust washer and finally the circlip.
18 Measure the axial clearance between 4th gear and the thrust washer. This clearance must be 0.20 to 0.35 mm (0.008 to 0.014 in), the smaller clearance the better. Circlips are available in three thicknesses to achieve the clearance, these being 1.65, 1.70 and 1.75 mm (0.065, 0.067 and 0.069 in). Note that on later gearboxes the shaft has been modified and a thrust washer is not fitted. A larger, single thickness circlip is used instead and the axial clearance is no longer adjustable.

25 Pinion shaft (016) – dismantling and reassembly

1   The depth of the pinion's engagement with the crownwheel is adjusted during manufacture to the optimum position for quiet running and long life. When components affecting the pinion engagement are changed, adjustments must be made to regain this optimum position. Before components are dismantled or replacement items fitted, the position of the pinion must be established by measurement. Because this requires the use of specialist equipment its work should be entrusted to your Audi dealer. The components which affect the pinion engagement are the gearbox casing, the bearing carrier, and the pinion shaft bearings.
2   Support the pinion shaft in a soft-jawed vice on the plain part between 3rd and 4th gear.
3   Using a puller, remove the bearing inner race with 1st gear.
4   Lift off the 1st gear needle bearing then fit the bearing back into the gear the same way round as when fitted to the shaft.
5   Remove the 1st gear synchro-ring and fit it to the gear.
6   Remove the circlip located against the synchro-hub.
7   Using a puller with its legs placed beneath 2nd gear, draw off 2nd gear and the 1st/2nd gear synchroniser assembly.
8   Lift off 2nd gear needle roller assembly and fit it inside the gear the same way round as when fitted to the shaft.

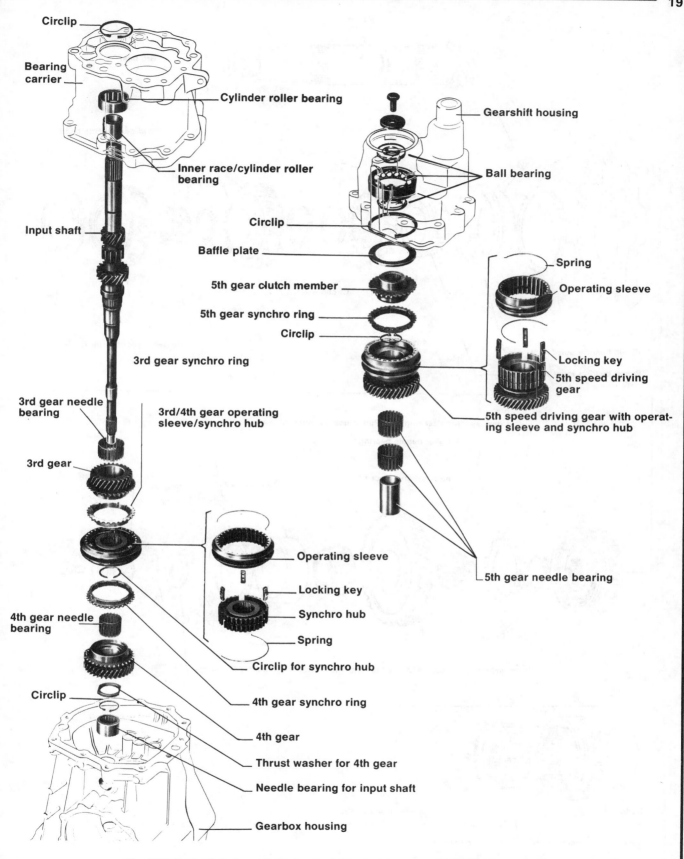

Circlip

Bearing carrier

Cylinder roller bearing

Gearshift housing

Inner race/cylinder roller bearing

Ball bearing

Input shaft

Circlip

Baffle plate

5th gear clutch member

Spring

Operating sleeve

5th gear synchro ring

Circlip

Locking key

3rd gear synchro ring

5th speed driving gear

5th speed driving gear with operating sleeve and synchro hub

3rd gear needle bearing

3rd/4th gear operating sleeve/synchro hub

3rd gear

Operating sleeve

Locking key

Synchro hub

Spring

Circlip for synchro hub

5th gear needle bearing

4th gear needle bearing

4th gear synchro ring

4th gear

Circlip

Thrust washer for 4th gear

Needle bearing for input shaft

Gearbox housing

Fig. 6.33 Exploded view of the input shaft components – 016 gearbox (Sec 24)

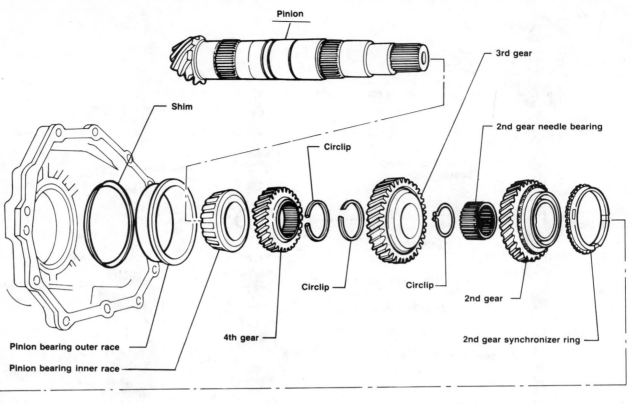

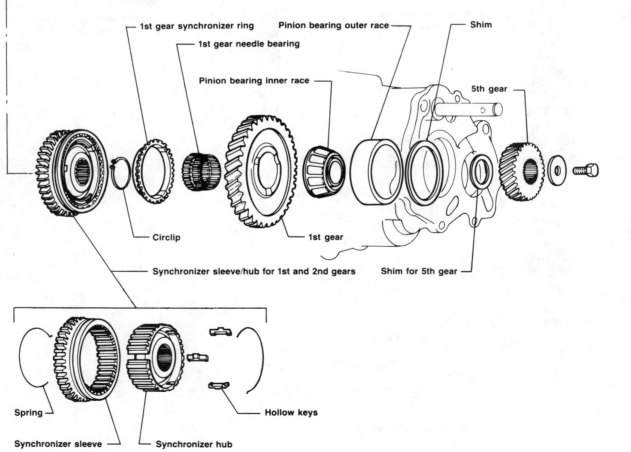

Fig. 6.34 Exploded view of the pinion shaft components – 016 gearbox (Sec 25)

Fig. 6.36 Checking 1st/2nd synchro-hub axial clearance – 016 gearbox (Sec 25)

18 Measure the distance between the teeth on the synchro-ring and the synchronising teeth on the gear as in paragraph 12 and fit a new synchro-ring if the gap exceeds 0.5 mm (0.020 in).
19 Tap the bearing inner race on to the end of the shaft, using a tubular drift, or a block of hardwood.

26 Bearing/gear carrier (016) – servicing

1 A general view of the bearing carrier and its components is shown in Fig. 6.37.
2 If the reverse idler gear assembly is to be dismantled for checking, extract the spring clip, unscrew the bolt then withdraw the retaining plate spring (noting orientation) and reverse gear synchroniser ring with baulk pins.
3 Disengage the reverse relay lever and retrieve the interlock plunger and spring. Remove the reverse idler gear.
4 To check the reverse idler gear and synchroniser for wear, hand press the synchroniser against the gear and check the clearance 'a' using a feeler gauge (Fig. 6.38). Renew the synchroniser if the clearance is in excess of the figure given.
5 Reassembly is a reversal of the dismantling procedure, but the relay lever must be adjusted. To do this fit the relay lever bolt and press the lever towards the middle of the housing. Continue tightening the bolt to the point where it seats on the lever recess.
6 It is important that the threaded bushing of the lever and the bolt are aligned correctly. To achieve this, press the lever against the bolt, loosen the bolt until its thread is just in contact with that of the bush. Tighten the bolt to the specified torque setting and then select reverse gear a few times to ensure that the relay lever movement is free in each direction. Also check that the interlock plunger is engaged correctly.
7 If the gear carrier housing is being renewed it is important that the correct pinion shaft bearing preload shim is used to suit the new housing. To select this, measure the depth of the old shim housing against that of the new (Fig. 6.40). Measure the thickness of the old shim and any difference measured can be allowed for by fitting a new shim of alternative thickness. If the new housing is deeper, a thicker shim will be required to make up the difference measured and vice versa if the housing depth is shallower.
8 The input shaft bearing outer race can be removed using a tube drift of suitable diameter. Press or drift the bearing out of its housing.
9 When fitting the new bearing outer race into position it is important that it is pressed in to the correct fitted depth ('a' in Fig. 6.41).

Gear detents – removal and refitting
10 The gear detents are removed by taking out the two socket-headed plugs on the side of the gearbox and tapping out the plungers and springs.
11 Refit the spring and then the plunger, but leave the plug until the appropriate shift rod has been fitted, then screw in the plug with a paper gasket beneath it.

Fig. 6.35 Removing the bearing inner race and 1st gear – 016 gearbox (Sec 25)

9 The 3rd and 4th gears are pressed and shrunk on to the shaft and if they need to be removed, or the pinion end bearing renewed, the work should be entrusted to an Audi dealer.
10 Reassembly will commence with the large bearing inner race, 4th gear, its circlip, 3rd gear and its circlip already on the shaft; complete reassembly of the shaft as follows.
11 Lubricate the 2nd gear needle roller bearing with gear oil and fit it to the shaft.
12 Fit 2nd gear onto its bearing, then place the synchro-ring on the gear. Measure the gap, as in Fig. 6.5. If the gap exceeds the figure given in the Specifications, a new synchro-ring must be fitted.
13 If the synchroniser assembly has been dismantled, it must be reassembled in the following way. Fit the three locking keys into their slots in the hub and secure the keys with circlips. The circlips should be spaced 120° apart and the angled end of the circlip should be engaged in the hollow of a locking key. Slide the operating sleeve over the synchro-hub, no special position of the sleeve relative to the hub is necessary.
14 Fit the synchroniser assembly to the shaft, the end of the sleeve having external teeth facing towards the pinion. Before pressing the hub down fully, turn the 2nd gear synchro-ring so that the slots in it are aligned with the locking keys in the synchroniser assembly.
15 Fit the circlip against the synchro-hub and, with the hub pressed down as far as possible, measure the clearance between the hub and the circlip (Fig. 6.36). The clearance should be between zero and 0.04 mm (0.002 in) and preferably nearer to the lower value. If the clearance exceeds the upper limit fit a new circlip of suitable thickness. The thicknesses available are 1.50, 1.55 and 1.60 mm (0.059, 0.061, 0.063 in).
16 Fit the 1st gear synchro-ring, lining up its slots with the locking keys in the synchroniser assembly. It may be found that the synchro-ring has a tooth missing at three points. This denotes a later modification when the tooth angle on the synchro-ring was altered from 115° to 110° to improve the engagement of 1st gear. This type of ring must only be used on 1st gear and if the 1st gear ring is being renewed, the 115° type, having the full number of teeth, should be fitted.
17 Lubricate the 1st gear needle roller bearing with gear oil and fit it to the shaft, then fit 1st gear.

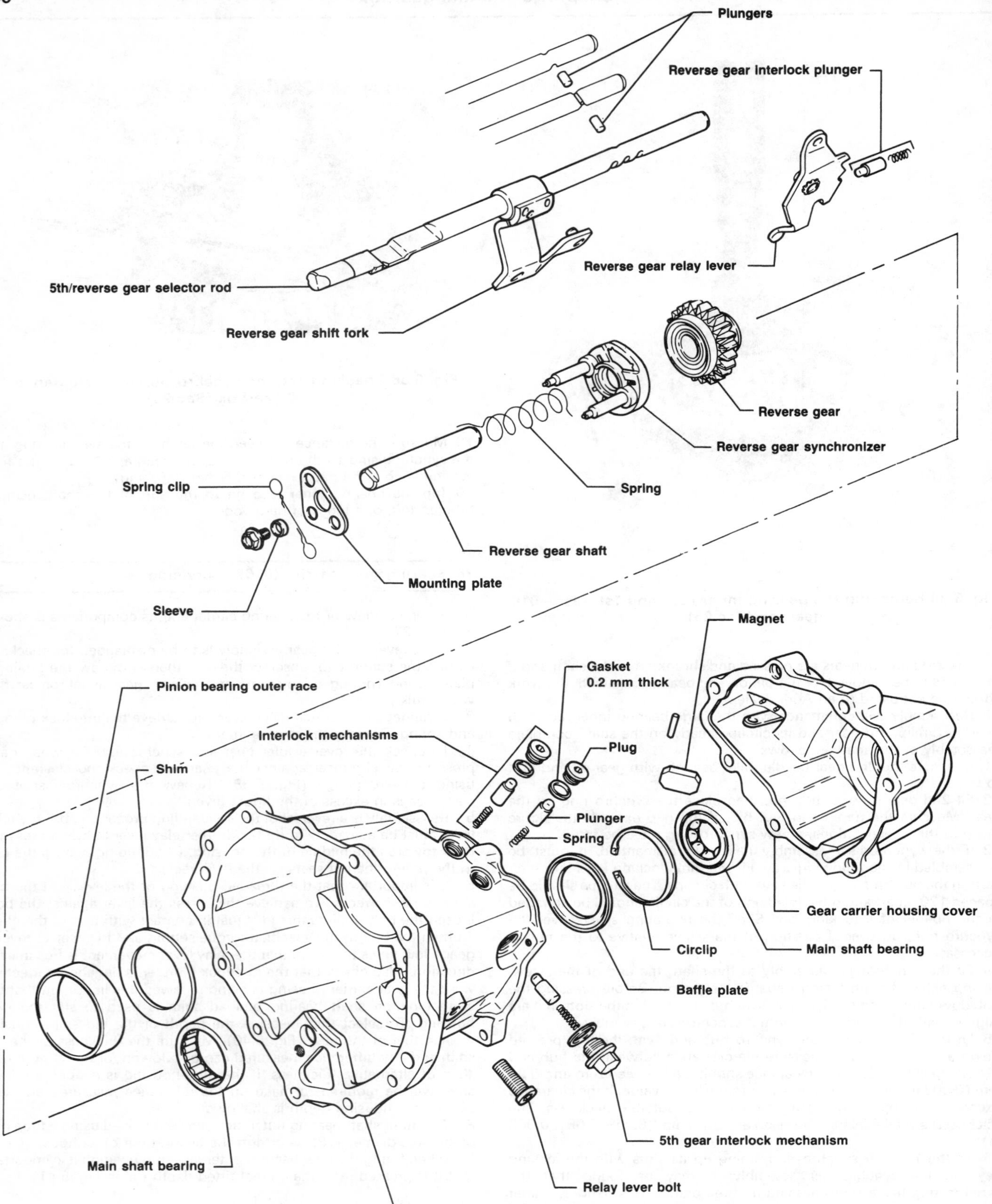

Plungers

Reverse gear interlock plunger

Reverse gear relay lever

5th/reverse gear selector rod

Reverse gear shift fork

Reverse gear

Reverse gear synchronizer

Spring clip

Spring

Reverse gear shaft

Mounting plate

Sleeve

Magnet

Pinion bearing outer race

Gasket
0.2 mm thick

Interlock mechanisms

Plug

Shim

Plunger

Spring

Gear carrier housing cover

Circlip

Main shaft bearing

Baffle plate

Main shaft bearing

5th gear interlock mechanism

Relay lever bolt

Gear carrier housing

Fig. 6.37 Bearing/gear carrier components – 016 gearbox (Sec 26)

Fig. 6.38 Checking reverse idler gear-to-synchroniser clearance – 016 gearbox (Sec 26)

Wear limit at a = 0.2 mm (0.008 in)

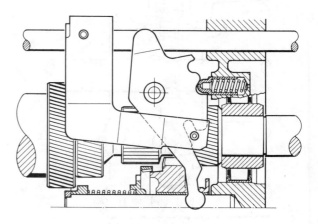

Fig. 6.39 Reverse gear detent assembly – 016 gearbox (Sec 26)

Fig. 6.40 Measuring gear carrier housing depth 'a' – 016 gearbox (Sec 26)

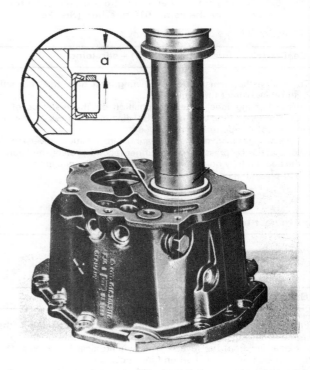

Fig. 6.41 Fitting the mainshaft bearing outer race – 016 gearbox (Sec 26)

Fitted depth 'a' must be 8.5 to 9.0 mm (0.33 to 0.35 in)

12 The detent operating the interlock plungers is beneath the hexagon-headed plug at the top rear of the casing. Remove the plug and tip out the spring and detent. It is likely that the interlock plungers will also fall out.

13 Refit the interlock plungers by holding them on a magnet and inserting them through the selector rod holes. Fit the selector rods and then insert the detent plunger and spring. Screw in the plug and tighten it.

14 If the plug is made of steel, it should have a sealing washer beneath it. If the plug is of aluminium it should be installed without any washer.

27 Gearbox/final drive housing (016) – servicing

1 The operations for servicing the gearbox housing are the same as those for the Type 014 gearbox described in Section 7 with the exception of the pinion bearing.

2 The outer track of the pinion bearing is flanged and is a shrink fit. It requires a special mandrel and a slide hammer to remove it and when fitting a new track either the complete gearbox housing, or the area round the bearing must be heated to 150°C (302°F). Shims are fitted between the bearing track and the gearbox housing to adjust the pinion engagement in the crownwheel and if the track is to be replaced it is a job for your Audi dealer (see Section 8, paragraph 1).

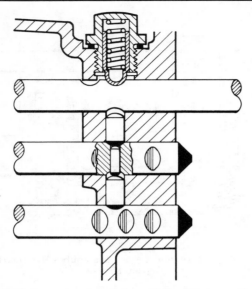

Fig. 6.42 Cross-sectional view of the 5th gear selector interlock mechanism – 016 gearbox (Sec 26)

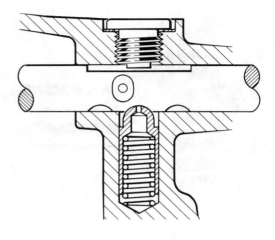

Fig. 6.43 Cross-sectional view of the 1st to 4th gear selector interlock mechanism – 016 gearbox (Sec 26)

28 Gear carrier housing cover (016) – servicing

1   To remove the mainshaft roller bearing, first prise free the baffle plate and then extract the circlip.
2   Fit the bearing inner race into position on the rear face of the bearing then use a tube drift of suitable diameter to press or drive the bearing out of its aperture in the cover.
3   Press the new mainshaft ball-bearing into position, reversing the removal process by pressing on the inner race to protect the bearing. With the bearing fully home in its aperture, locate the circlip to secure it and then press in a new baffle plate.

29 Fifth gear components (016) – servicing

Refer to Section 19 of this Chapter.

30 Gearbox (016) – reassembly

1   Fit the differential, as described in Section 20, paragraph 1, then move the reverse gear to the selected position and unhook the spring clip at one end from the reverse gear synchroniser baulk pins. Now partially insert the pinion shaft unit into position.
2   Insert the 1st/2nd gear selector rod and then fit the pinion shaft, pressing it home so that it is fully seated.
3   Reconnect the spring clip, temporarily unhooked from the reverse gear synchroniser baulk pin, disengaging reverse gear.
4   Locate the 3rd/4th selector fork engaging slot into the 5th/reverse gear selector rod.
5   If not already removed, remove the input shaft bearing inner race and circlip.
6   Partially refit the input shaft into position, then insert the 3rd/4th gear selector fork into the clutch sleeve and push home the input shaft. Check that it is fully seated.
7   Move each selector rod to its neutral position and then check that the interlock pins are located, as shown in Fig. 6.42.
8   Push the 3rd/4th gear selector rod into position and insert its interlock pin. Lubricate the pin with grease before fitting.
9   Lock the 3rd/4th gear selector fork in position by driving a new retaining roll pin into position. Support the shaft, as during pin removal, when driving the new one home.
10 Now secure the 1st/2nd gear selector rod with its key whilst supporting with a hammer or similar.

11 Fit the stop screws with new paper gaskets and tighten.
12 Grip the pinion shaft/4th gear in a soft-jawed vice, then calculate the 5th gear adjustment shim thickness requirement, measuring depth 'a' (Fig. 6.45). The shim thickness required will be as follows:

Depth measured	Shim thickness required
8.35 to 8.64 mm (0.328 to 0.340 in)	1.1 mm (0.043 in)
8.65 to 8.94 mm (0.341 to 0.351 in)	1.4 mm (0.055 in)
8.95 to 9.24 mm (0.352 to 0.363 in)	1.7 mm (0.066 in)
9.25 to 9.54 mm (0.364 to 0.375 in)	2.0 mm (0.078 in)
9.55 to 9.84 mm (0.376 to 0.387 in)	2.3 mm (0.090 in)

13 Having selected and fitted a shim you will need to heat up the 5th gear to a temperature of about 120°C (248°F) in order to allow it to be fitted into position on the shaft. Drive the gear home fully so that it seats against the sleeve and the collar faces towards the pinion. Fit the bolt and flat washer to secure, tightening the bolt to the specified torque setting. Note that on later models the bolt must be renewed on reassembly.
14 Now clamp the input shaft in the soft jaws of a vice so that the shafts are kept vertical.
15 Grease the input shaft bearing rollers and press the rollers outwards.
16 The inner race of the roller bearing must now be heated to 120°C (248°F) and fitted into position on the shaft, guiding it down through the rollers. Check that it is fully housed by driving the bearing down against the stop.
17 With the inner race in position it must be secured with a circlip of a suitable thickness. Select a circlip to provide an axial clearance not exceeding 0.05 mm (0.0019 in). Select the thickest possible circlip which will fit the groove and provide the correct axial clearance and fit it into position. The circlip thicknesses available are 1.35, 1.40 and 1.45 mm (0.053, 0.055 and 0.057 in).
18 Fit the 5th gear with its synchroniser hub, needle bearing and selector fork. When in position secure the fork on the shaft using a new roll pin. Support the shaft when driving in the roll pin.
19 Fit the circlip and then locate the 5th gear synchroniser ring.
20 To fit the clutch hub to 5th gear assembly it must be heated to about 120°C (248°F). If necessary drive it into position so that it is fully seated, then drive on and locate the inner race on the input shaft.
21 Locate a new gasket and then fit the gear carrier housing cover.
22 Locate the remaining input shaft bearing inner race, driving it down the shaft with a suitable sleeve drift.
23 When the inner race is fully fitted, the retaining bolt and flat washer

Fig. 6.44 Spring clip (arrowed) disconnected from reverse gear synchroniser baulk pins – 016 gearbox (Sec 30)

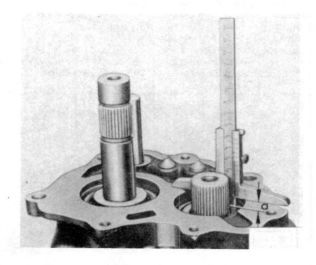

Fig. 6.45 Calculating 5th gear adjustment shim thickness by measuring depth 'a' – 016 gearbox (Sec 30)

can be installed and tightened to the specified torque setting. Note that on later models the bolt must be renewed.

24 Fit the gear carrier housing-to-housing cover bolts and tighten them to the specified torque. Fit the new cover cap into its aperture in the end of the cover.

25 Smear the gear carrier housing-to-gearbox/axle housing joint faces with sealant (sparingly), then assemble the gear carrier to the gearbox. Drive in the dowel locating pins, locate the securing bolts and tighten them to the specified torque setting.

26 Refit the selector lever, ensuring that it is fitted flush to the end of the serrations on the shaft.

27 On later models the selector lever and shaft assembly were modified. The selector shaft bearing on the shift finger side is integral in the gearcase, the small housing of the selector shaft being no longer fitted. The springs and washers compressing the lever into the 3rd/4th gear plane (and which prevent the possibility of a direct shift from 5th to reverse gear) are also modified.

28 The late type selector lever is secured to the shaft by a tapered bolt instead of being clamped as previously. The tapered bolt is a self locking type and must be renewed on reassembly.

Fig. 6.46 Fitting 5th gear, synchro-hub, bearing and selector fork – 016 gearbox (Sec 30)

31 Gearshift lever (016) – removal, refitting and adjustment

1 Two types of gearshift lever assembly and gearshift linkage are used on Audi models fitted with the 016 gearbox. The early type utilizes a single shift rod and is shown in Fig. 6.48. The later type utilizes a shift rod and also a pushrod to prevent movement of the engine/gearbox assembly from causing the gear lever to move. This later type is shown in Fig. 6.49. Although minor adjustment of the gearshift lever can be carried out without special tools, a setting gauge is needed to first establish a basic setting and this can only be done by an Audi dealer. For this reason it is very important to mark the fitted depth and angular position of the shift rods and, on later models, the pushrod before slackening any of the clamps.

2 To remove the early type gearshift lever first remove the centre console, as described in Chapter 11.

3 Undo the nut and bolt securing the shift rod to the gearshift lever and the four bolts securing the gear lever base to the car floor. Separate the shift rod and remove the gearshift lever assembly.

4 To remove the later type gearshift lever first remove the centre console, as described in Chapter 11.

5 Undo the nut and bolt securing the shift rod to the gearshift lever and the bolt and clamping plate securing the front and rear pushrods together.

6 Undo the four nuts and lift off the stop and cover plate. Disengage the rear pushrod bearing pin from the rubber mounting and withdraw the gearshift lever assembly.

Fig. 6.47 Locating the 5th gear clutch hub – 016 gearbox (Sec 30)

7   In both cases refitting is a reversal of the removal sequence, but on the later type adjust the position of the rear pushrod in the front push rod so that the bearing pin protrudes from the rear mounting by 17 mm (0.67 in), then tighten the clamping plate bolt.

8   To check the adjustment of the gearshift lever, engage 1st gear and then move the gearshift lever as far as it will go to the left. Hold the gearshift lever with one finger and allow it to spring back slowly to the pressure point. Measured at the lever knob the movement must be at

least 5 mm (0.2 in). Now engage 5th gear, move the lever to the right as far as possible and allow it to return as before. The measured movement should be approximately the same as the 1st gear movement, and at least 5 mm (0.2 in).

9   If the measured movement is not correct, slacken the four bolts securing the stop to the cover plate (photo) and move the stop, within its elongated holes, to the right for more movement in 5th gear or to the left for more movement in 1st gear. Tighten the stop retaining bolts and

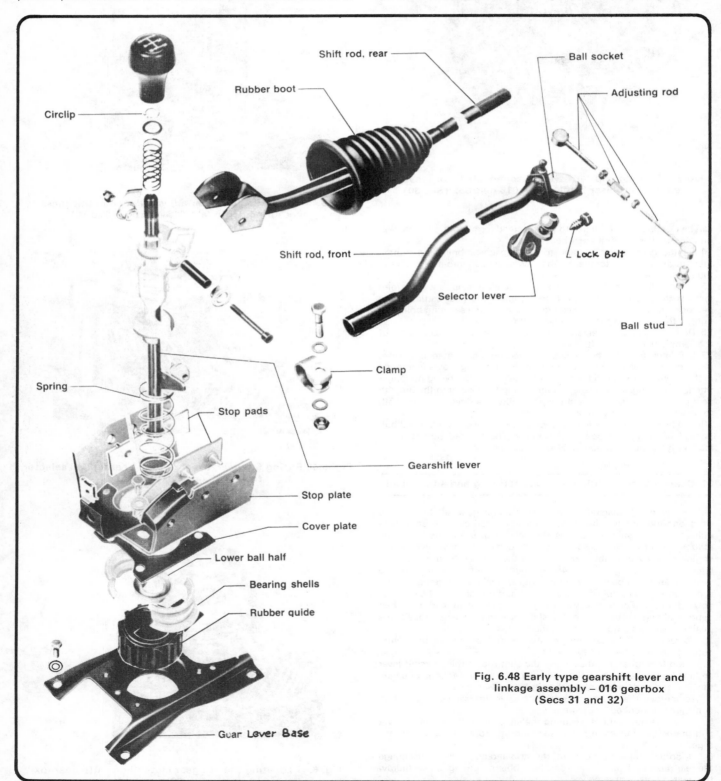

Fig. 6.48 Early type gearshift lever and linkage assembly – 016 gearbox (Secs 31 and 32)

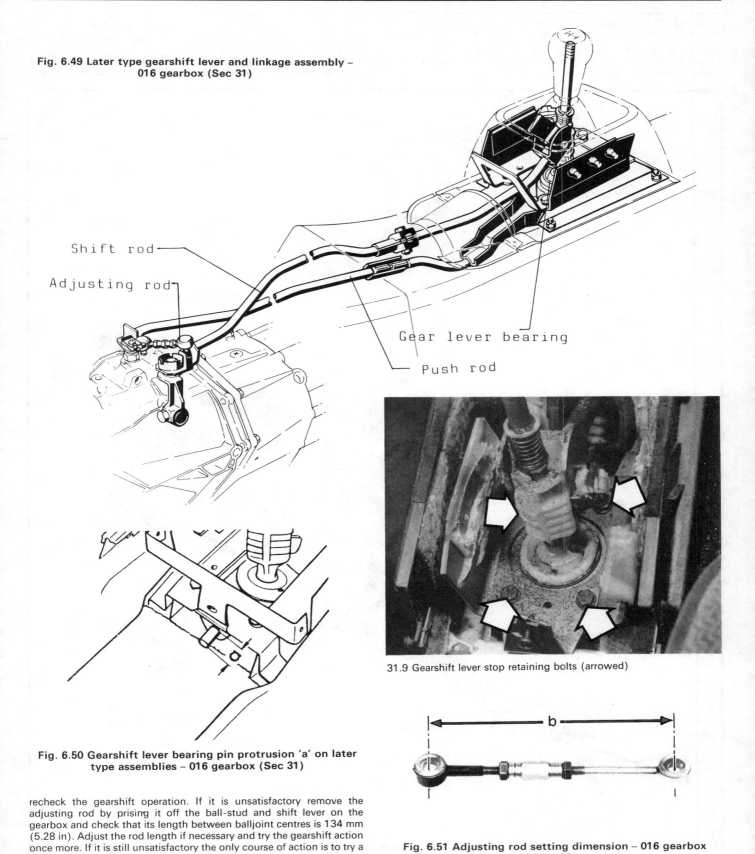

Fig. 6.49 Later type gearshift lever and linkage assembly –
016 gearbox (Sec 31)

Shift rod

Adjusting rod

Gear lever bearing

Push rod

31.9 Gearshift lever stop retaining bolts (arrowed)

Fig. 6.50 Gearshift lever bearing pin protrusion 'a' on later
type assemblies – 016 gearbox (Sec 31)

b

Fig. 6.51 Adjusting rod setting dimension – 016 gearbox
(Sec 31)

b = 134 mm (5.28 in)

recheck the gearshift operation. If it is unsatisfactory remove the adjusting rod by prising it off the ball-stud and shift lever on the gearbox and check that its length between balljoint centres is 134 mm (5.28 in). Adjust the rod length if necessary and try the gearshift action once more. If it is still unsatisfactory the only course of action is to try a long trial and error process by altering the position of the front and rear shift rods at the clamp or by having an Audi dealer adjust the linkage with the setting gauge.

32 Gearshift linkage (016) – dismantling and reassembly

Note: *before proceeding refer to Section 31, paragraph 1.*
1   The gearshift linkage consists of two principle parts, the gearshift lever assembly and the linkage rods.

Gearshift lever assembly
2   Remove the gearshift lever, as described in Section 31.
3   Unscrew the lever knob, remove the circlip and withdraw the spring from the gearshift lever.
4   On early versions mark the relationship of the stop to the cover plate then remove the four bolts and separate the stop, cover plate and

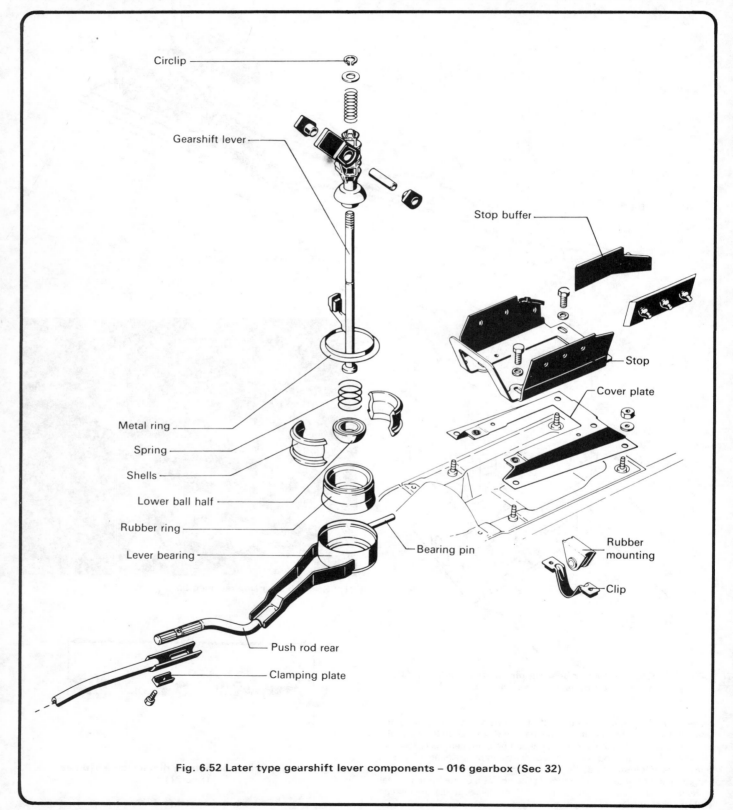

Circlip

Gearshift lever

Stop buffer

Stop

Cover plate

Metal ring

Spring

Shells

Lower ball half

Rubber ring

Lever bearing

Bearing pin

Rubber mounting

Clip

Push rod rear

Clamping plate

Fig. 6.52 Later type gearshift lever components – 016 gearbox (Sec 32)

gear lever base. Do not dismantle the lower bearing unless it is necessary to grease it. Push the rubber guide out of the gear lever base then prise the plastic shells apart and remove the gearshift lever and upper ball section and the lower ball section. On later versions it will be necessary to release the peening around the lower bearing then the metal ring and rubber guide can be removed and dismantled as previously described.

5   When reassembling, lubricate all the friction surfaces with special grease AOS 126 000 05.

6   When reassembling the rubber guide, position it with the shouldered end uppermost and press the two shells into it. Press the lower ball half into the shells then the spring and finally press in the upper ball half, pushing the shells apart if necessary.

7   Push the rubber gauge into the gear lever base or, on later versions, the rear pushrod. On later versions refit the metal ring and secure the assembly by peening in three places.

8   Reassemble the stop, cover plate and gear lever base, lining up the previously made marks.

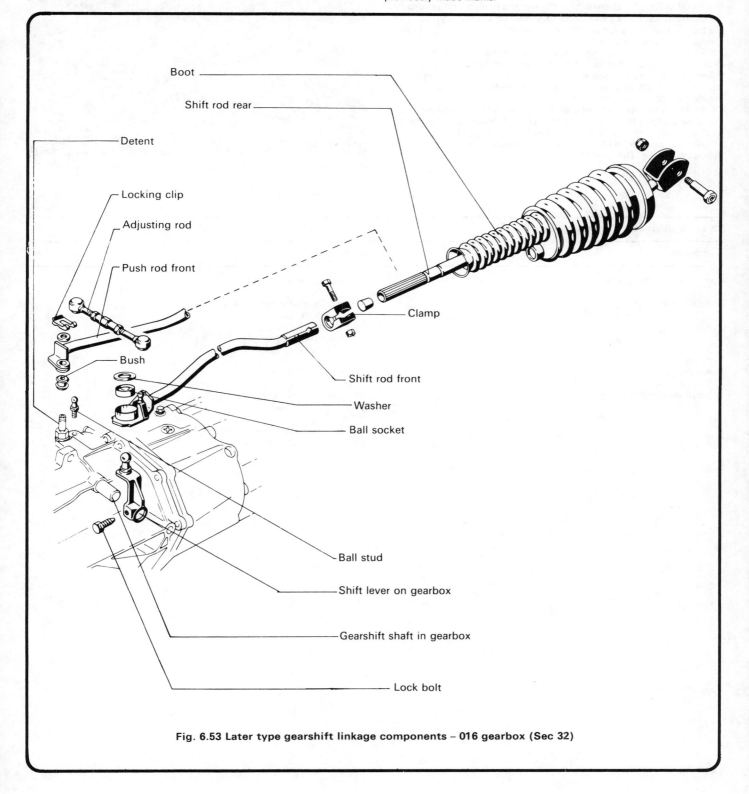

Fig. 6.53 Later type gearshift linkage components – 016 gearbox (Sec 32)

9 Refit the spring and circlip then screw on the gearshift knob.
10 Refit the gearshift lever assembly, as described in Section 31.

Linkage rods

11 To remove the front shift rod, prise the adjusting rod balljoint off
the shift rod then release the shift rod from the shift lever. Slacken the
clamp, withdraw the front shift rod from the rear shift rod (photo) and
remove from under the car. Refit in the reverse sequence to removal.
12 To remove the rear shift rod, remove the centre console, as
described in Chapter 11 then undo the nut and bolt securing the rod to
the gearshift lever. Slacken the clamp, withdraw the rear shift rod from
the front shift rod and remove the rod upwards and into the car. Refit in
the reverse sequence to removal.
13 To remove the adjusting rod, prise it off the front shift rod and
gearbox shift lever ball-studs then remove it from under the car.
Whenever the adjusting rod is removed, check its length which should
be 134 mm (5.28 in) and reset if necessary. Refit the adjusting rod by
pushing it back onto the ball-studs.
14 On later versions the front pushrod can be removed after removing
the locking clip at the gearbox and the clamp bolt and plate at the rear
pushrod attachment. Refit in the reverse sequence to removal.
15 The rear pushrod on later versions is removed in conjunction with
the gearshift lever (Section 31).

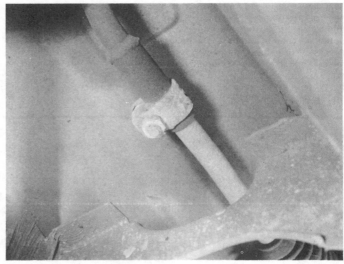

32.11 Front-to-rear shift rod clamp

33 Fault diagnosis – manual gearbox

Symptom	Reason(s)
Ineffective synchromesh	Worn synchro rings
Jumps out of gear	Weak or broken detent spring
	Worn selector forks or dogs
	Weak synchro springs
	Worn synchro unit or gears
	Worn bearings or gears
Noisy operation	Worn bearings or gears
Difficult engagement of gears	Worn selector components
	Worn synchro units
	Clutch fault
	Gearbox input shaft spigot bearing seized in end of crankshaft
	Incorrect gearshift adjustment

Chapter 7 Automatic transmission

Refer to Chapter 13 for information on 1987 and later models

Contents

Specifications

Type .... Three-speed planetary gearbox with hydrodynamic torque converter and integral final drive assembly

Identification

Transmission code number:
- 087 .... Fitted to five-cylinder models
- 089 .... Fitted to four-cylinder models

Ratios

	087	**089**
Final drive	3.08:1, 3.25:1 or 3.45:1 (according to model and engine)	3.42:1
1st	2.71:1	2.71:1
2nd	1.50:1	1.50:1
3rd	1.00:1	1.00:1
Reverse	2.43:1	2.43:1

Torque converter

Maximum diameter of bush	34.12 mm (1.34 in)
Maximum out-of-round of bush	0.03 mm (0.001 in)

Torque wrench settings

	Nm	**lbf ft**
Torque converter to driveplate	30	22
Transmission to engine	55	41
Mounting to transmission	40	30
Mounting to body	60	44
Oil pan bolts	20	15
Oil strainer cover	3	2
Selector cable clamp bolt	8	6

1 General description

The automatic transmission consists of three main assemblies, these being the torque converter, which is directly coupled to the engine; the final drive unit which incorporates the differential assembly; and the planetary gearbox with its hydraulically operated multi-disc clutches and brake bands. The gearbox also houses a rear mounted oil pump, which is coupled to the torque converter impeller, and this pump supplies automatic transmission fluid to the planetary gears, hydraulic controls and torque converter. The fluid performs a triple function by lubricating the moving parts, cooling the automatic transmission system and providing a torque transfer medium. The final

drive lubrication is separate from the transmission lubrication system, unlike the manual gearbox where the final drive shares a common lubrication system.

The torque converter is a sealed unit which cannot be dismantled. It is bolted to the crankshaft driveplate and replaces the clutch found on an engine with manual transmission.

The gearbox is of the planetary type with epicycle gear trains operated by brakes and clutches through a hydraulic control system. The correct gear is selected by a combination of three control signals; a manual valve operated by the gearshift cable, a manual valve operated by the accelerator pedal, and a governor to control hydraulic pressure. The gearshift cable and selector lever allow the driver to select a specific gear and override the automatic control, if desired. The accelerator control determines the correct gear for the desired rate of acceleration, and the governor determines the correct gear in relation to engine speed.

Because of the need for special test equipment, the complexity of some of the parts and the need for scrupulous cleanliness when servicing automatic transmissions, the amount which the owner can do is limited, but those operations which can reasonably be carried out are detailed in the following Sections. Repairs to the final drive differential are also not recommended.

2 Maintenance and inspection

1   At the intervals specified in Routine Maintenance the automatic transmission fluid level and the final drive differential oil level should be checked and if necessary topped up using the following procedures.
2   The fluid level should be checked when the transmission is at normal operating temperature (this will be reached after a journey of approximately 6 miles/10 km when starting from cold).
3   With the car standing on level ground and with the engine idling and the selector lever in the N (Neutral) position, withdraw the fluid dipstick and wipe it on a clean, lint-free rag. Reinsert the dipstick, withdraw it immediately and observe the fluid level which should be between the two marks.
4   If topping-up is necessary, switch off the engine and add the required quantity of the specified fluid through the dipstick tube. Take care not to overfill the transmission; noting that the difference between the upper and lower marks on the dipstick is 0.4 litre (0.75 Imp pt, 0.42 US quarts).
5   The final drive differential oil level is checked by means of the filler plug located just to the rear of the driveshaft flange on the left-hand side of the transmission. Access is easiest from below the car.
6   With the car level, unscrew the filler plug using a suitable hexagonal key and check that the level is up to the filler plug orifice.

7   If topping-up is necessary, add the specified lubricant through the filler orifice until the level is correct, then refit the plug.
8   At the less frequent intervals specified in Routine Maintenance the automatic transmission fluid should be drained and fresh fluid added, using the procedures described in Section 3. It is not necessary to drain and refill the final drive differential oil as part of the normal servicing procedures.

3 Automatic transmission fluid – draining and refilling

1   This job should not be attempted unless clean, dust free conditions can be achieved.
2   With the car standing on level ground, place a container of suitable capacity beneath the oil pan of the transmission. For working room beneath the car, jack it up and support it with axle stands, or use car ramps.
3   Unscrew the union nut securing the dipstick tube to the oil pan, pull out the tube and allow the fluid to drain out.
4   Remove the retaining screws and withdraw the oil pan. Remove the gasket.
5   Remove the screws and withdraw the cover, strainer, and gasket.
6   Clean the pan and strainer with methylated spirit and allow to dry.
7   Refit the strainer, cover and pan in reverse order using new gaskets and tightening the screws to the specified torque.
8   Insert the dipstick tube and tighten the union nut.
9   Wipe round the top of the dipstick tube, then remove the dipstick.
10 With the car on level ground, fill the transmission with the correct quantity and grade of fluid, using a clean funnel if necessary.
11 Start the engine and, with the handbrake applied, select every gear position once. With the engine idling and the transmission in N (Neutral), check the level of the fluid on the dipstick, and if necessary top up to the lower mark.
12 Road test the car for approximately 6 miles (10 km) then recheck the fluid level, as described in Section 2.

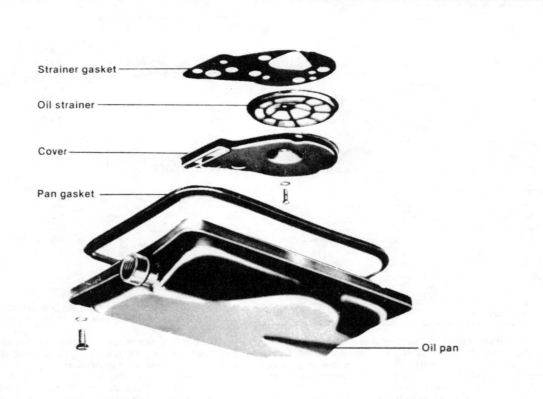

Fig. 7.1 Automatic transmission oil pan and strainer components (Sec 3)

4 Automatic transmission – removal and refitting

1 Position the car over an inspection pit or on car ramps or axle stands. Apply the handbrake and chock the wheels.
2 Disconnect the battery negative terminal.
3 Drain the cooling system, as described in Chapter 2.
4 Disconnect the two coolant hoses from the transmission fluid cooler.
5 Disconnect the speedometer cable at the transmission end.
6 Support the front of the engine using a hoist or support bar. Fig. 7.2 shows the Audi tool designed for this purpose and can be used as a guide for making up a similar aparatus if a hoist is not available.
7 Remove the starter motor, as described in Chapter 12.
8 Working through the starter aperture, unscrew the bolts securing the torque converter to the driveplate while holding the starter ring gear stationary with a screwdriver. It will be necessary to rotate the crankshaft to bring each bolt to an accessible position in the starter aperture.

9 Refer to Chapter 8 and separate the driveshaft inner constant velocity joints from the transmission drive flanges.
10 Remove the selector lever cable holder from the rear of the transmission. Extract the circlip and disconnect the selector lever cable from the transmission lever.
11 On the 087 transmission remove the accelerator linkage pushrod.
12 Disconnect the accelerator pedal cable and detach the cable at the transmission support bracket.
13 Place a suitable container beneath the transmission and unscrew the dipstick tube union nut at the oil pan. Withdraw the tube from the pan and allow the fluid to drain.
14 Unscrew and remove the upper engine-to-transmission bolts.
15 On the 089 transmission unscrew the throttle cable support bracket bolts, release the cable end locking clip and separate the cable and bracket from the transmission.
16 Support the transmission with a suitable trolley jack.
17 Unscrew and remove the lower engine-to-transmission bolts.
18 Remove the transmission mounting retaining bolts then remove the mounting supports.

Fig. 7.2 Using a special tool to support the front of the engine (Sec 4)

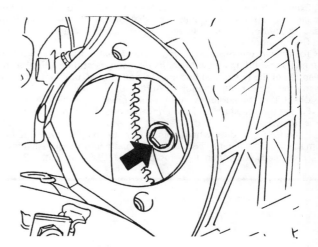

Fig. 7.3 A torque converter-to-driveplate bolt viewed through the starter aperture (Sec 4)

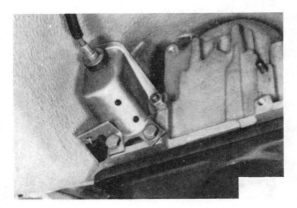

Fig. 7.4 Selector lever cable holder at the rear of the transmission (Sec 4)

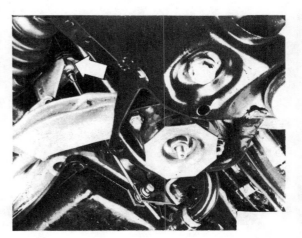

Fig. 7.5 Accelerator pedal cable attachment at the transmission support bracket (Sec 4)

19 With the help of an assistant, withdraw the transmission from the engine, making sure that the torque converter remains fully engaged with the transmission splines.

20 Lower the transmission and remove it from under the car.

21 Refitting is the reverse sequence to removal, bearing in mind the following points:

(a) Ensure that the torque converter is correctly positioned, and fully engaged with the pump shaft splines before installing the transmission

(b) Reconnect the driveshafts, with reference to Chapter 8, and refit the starter, with reference to Chapter 12

(c) Refill the cooling system, with reference to Chapter 2

(d) After refitting adjust the accelerator, throttle, selector lever and cables with reference to Sections 6 and 7, and fill the transmission with reference to Section 3

5 Torque converter – checking and draining

1 The torque converter is a welded unit and if it is faulty the complete unit must be replaced. Only the bush can be renewed.

2 Examine the bush for signs of scoring and wear. To check for wear requires an internal micrometer or dial gauge; if one is available measure the bore diameter to see if it exceeds the wear limit given in the Specifications.

3 To remove the bush requires a commercial extractor and a slide hammer. After fitting a new bush, its diameter must be within the limit given; if not the bush must be removed and another one fitted. For this reason the job is really one for an Audi agent.

4 Check that the cooling vanes on the converter are secure.

5 Fit the turbine shaft into the converter and check that the turbine turns freely.

6 If the fluid was dirty when drained from the oil pan, drain the fluid from the torque converter before the automatic transmission is refitted.

7 Have ready a container of about 2 litre (3.5 Imp pints, 2.1 US quarts) capacity, a plastic bottle and a piece of plastic tubing of not more than 8 mm (0.32 in) outside diameter.

8 Put the torque converter on the bench and support it so that it is tipped up slightly.

9 Cut one end of the plastic tube on an angle so that the end of the tube will not be blocked if it comes against a flat surface and push this end into the torque converter hub until it touches the bottom.

10 Connect the spout of the plastic bottle to the other end of the tube, hold the bottle below the level of the torque converter and squeeze the bottle. As the bottle expands again, fluid will be sucked into it; as soon as the fluid begins to syphon, pull the tube end off the bottle and rest the tube end in the larger container. Syphon as much fluid as possible from the torque converter. On reassembly and installation, the converter will fill with fluid as soon as the engine is started.

6 Accelerator pedal and linkage – adjustment

1 The accelerator linkage must be adjusted so that the operating lever on the transmission is at its idle position when the throttle is closed. If the adjustment is incorrect the shift speeds will be too high when the throttle is partially open and the main hydraulic pressure will be too high when the engine is idling.

087 transmission

2 Before carrying out any adjustments ensure that the engine is at normal operating temperature and that, on carburettor engines, the automatic choke is fully open.

3 Working in the engine compartment, disconnect the linkage pullrod and pushrod and, where fitted, the cruise control linkage.

4 Move the pullrod lever to its stop and check that the end fitting on the rod will fit easily on the ball-stud without opening the linkage. If necessary screw the pullrod end fitting in or out as necessary to achieve this condition.

5 Refit the pullrod and pushrod end fittings to the linkage.

Fig. 7.6 Checking the torque converter bush internal diameter with a dial gauge (Sec 5)

Fig. 7.7 Syphoning the fluid from the torque converter (Sec 5)

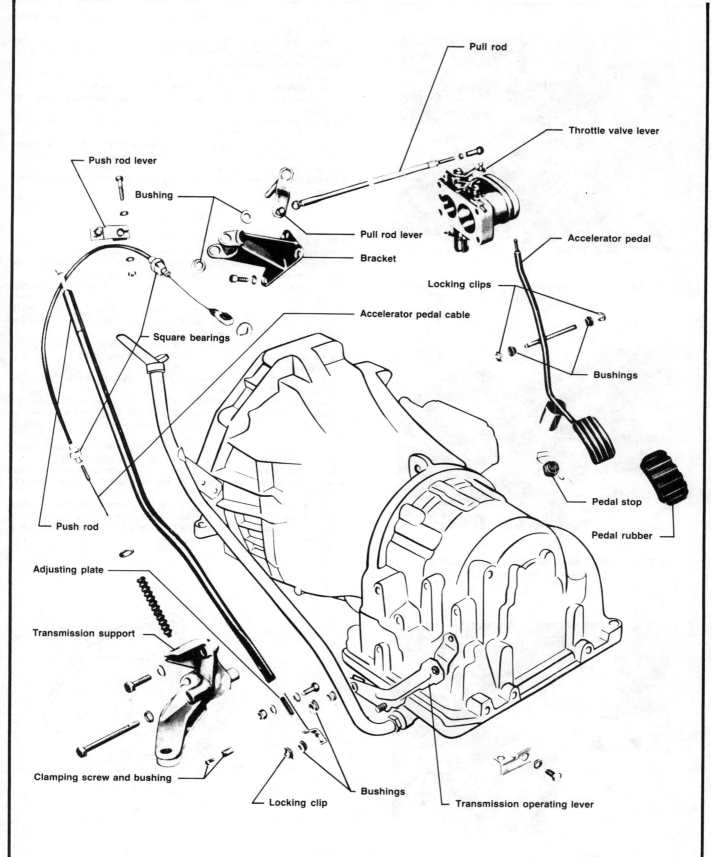

Pull rod

Throttle valve lever

Push rod lever

Bushing

Pull rod lever

Bracket

Accelerator pedal

Locking clips

Accelerator pedal cable

Bushings

Square bearings

Pedal stop

Pedal rubber

Push rod

Adjusting plate

Transmission support

Clamping screw and bushing

Bushings

Locking clip

Transmission operating lever

Fig. 7.8 Layout of the throttle and accelerator pedal cables on the 087 transmission (Sec 6)

Fig. 7.9 Pullrod end fitting adjustment – 087 transmission (Sec 6)

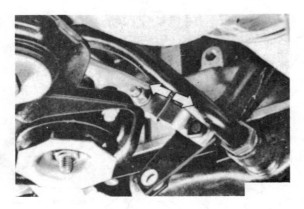

Fig. 7.10 Pushrod adjustment at the clamp bolt – 087 transmission (Sec 6)

6 From under the car slacken the clamp bolt at the transmission end of the pushrod.

7 With the transmission operating lever in contact with the no-throttle stop and the throttle lever in contact with the idle stop, tighten the pushrod clamp bolt.

8 Extract the locking clip and slip the pushrod end off the transmission operating lever. Unhook the return spring.

9 Have an assistant fully depress the accelerator pedal and hold it in this position.

10 Push the transmission operating lever against the kickdown stop and hold it in this position.

11 Slacken the accelerator pedal cable clamp bolt on the transmission operating lever, grip the cable end with pliers and pull the cable as shown in Fig. 7.11. Hold the cable end and tighten the clamp bolt.

12 Refit the pushrod to the operating lever and reconnect the return spring.

089 transmission

13 Note the adjustment criterion detailed in paragraph 2.

14 From under the car slacken the clamp bolt and disconnect the accelerator pedal cable from the transmission operating lever.

15 Slacken the two throttle cable adjusting nuts at the carburettor support bracket.

16 Hold the carburettor linkage closed and pull the outer cable through the bracket to eliminate all the free play. Hold the cable in this position and tighten the adjusting nuts.

17 At the transmission, unhook the operating lever return spring.

18 Have an assistant fully depress the accelerator pedal and hold it in this position.

19 Push the transmission operating lever against the kickdown stop and hold it in this position.

20 Slacken the accelerator pedal cable clamp bolt on the transmission operating lever, grip the cable end with pliers and pull the cable as shown in Fig. 7.15. Hold the cable end and tighten the clamp bolt.

21 Refit the return spring.

22 To check the adjustment, depress the accelerator pedal until resistance is felt at the full throttle position. Do not go into the kickdown position. Check that the throttle lever on the carburettor linkage is in contact with the full throttle stop and the kickdown spring is not compressed.

23 Now depress the accelerator pedal fully. Check that the transmission operating lever is in contact with the kickdown stop and the kickdown spring at the carburettor is compressed approximately 8 mm (0.32 in).

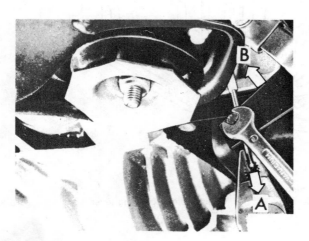

Fig. 7.11 Pull the accelerator pedal cable in direction A while pushing operating lever B against stop – 087 transmission (Sec 6)

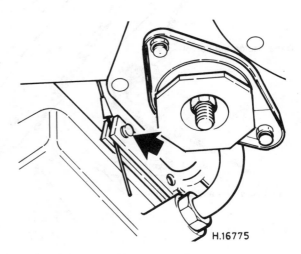

Fig. 7.12 Accelerator pedal cable attachment at transmission operating lever clamp bolt – 089 transmission (Sec 6)

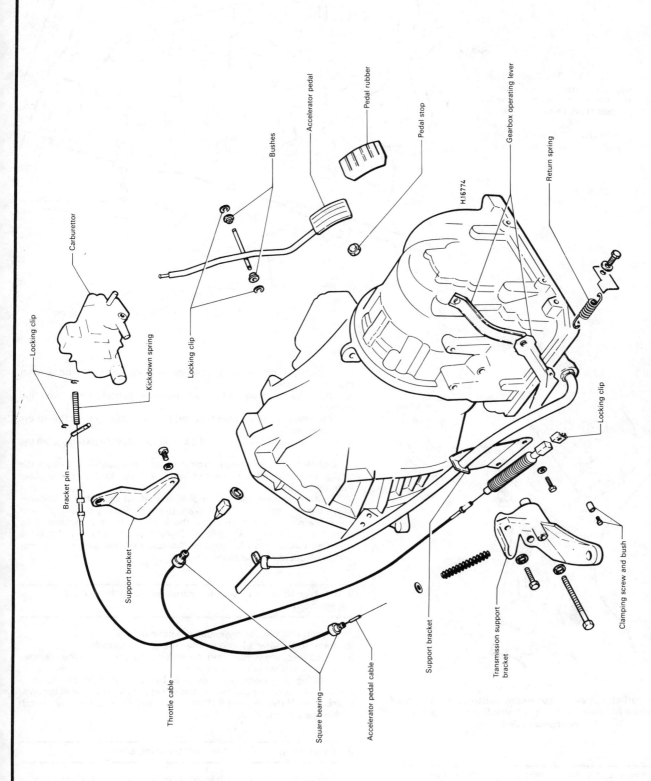

Carburettor

Locking clip

Kickdown spring

Bracket pin

Support bracket

Throttle cable

Square bearing

Accelerator pedal cable

Bushes

Accelerator pedal

Pedal rubber

Pedal stop

H.16774

Gearbox operating lever

Return spring

Locking clip

Locking clip

Support bracket

Transmission support bracket

Clamping screw and bush

Fig. 7.13 Layout of the throttle and accelerator pedal cables on the 089 transmission (Sec 6)

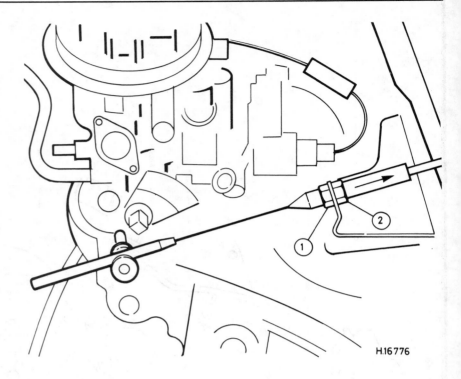

Fig. 7.14 Throttle cable adjusting nuts 1 and 2 at the carburettor support bracket – 089 transmission (Sec 6)

Pull outer cable in direction of arrow to eliminate free play

H.16776

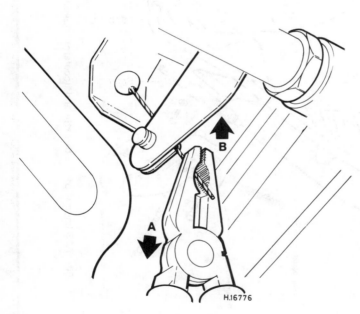

Fig. 7.15 Pull the accelerator pedal cable in direction of arrow A while holding operating lever B against stop – 089 transmission (Sec 6)

H.16776

7 Selector lever and cable – removal, refitting and adjustment

1   Disconnect the battery negative terminal.
2   If the selector lever or cable are to be removed, refer to Chapter 11 and remove the centre console. If adjustment only is being carried out, proceed to paragraph 8.

3   Disconnect the wiring from the starter inhibitor switch and selector illumination bulb.
4   Undo the retaining bolts and remove the console front mounting bracket.
5   Unscrew the cable clamp bolt and the nut securing the cable to the lever bracket.
6   Undo the bolts and remove the bracket and lever assembly from the floor.
7   Unbolt the cable bracket from the transmission, then extract the circlip and remove the cable end from the lever. Withdraw the cable from under the car.
8   Refitting is a reversal of removal, but adjust the cable as follows. Move the selector lever fully forward to the P (Park) position. Slacken the cable clamp bolt then move the lever on the transmission fully rearwards to the P (Park) position. Tighten the cable clamp bolt to the specified torque. Lightly lubricate the selector lever and cable pivots with molybdenum disulphide grease.

8 Starter inhibitor switch – removal, refitting and adjustment

1   Disconnect the battery negative terminal.
2   Refer to Chapter 11 and remove the centre console.
3   Disconnect the wiring from the starter inhibitor switch then remove the screws and withdraw the switch.
4   Refitting is a reversal of removal, but before fitting the console check that it is only possible to start the engine with the selector lever in positions N (Neutral) or P (Park). If necessary, reposition the switch within the elongated screw holes.

9 Fault diagnosis – automatic transmission

1   Before the automatic transmission is removed for repair of a suspected malfunction, it is imperative that the cause be traced and confirmed. To do this requires specialist experience and various tools and gauges not normally found in the DIY mechanic's workshop.
2   If any fault arises that cannot be cured by attention to the fluid level and the adjustments described in this Chapter, take the vehicle to an Audi dealer for diagnosis and repair.

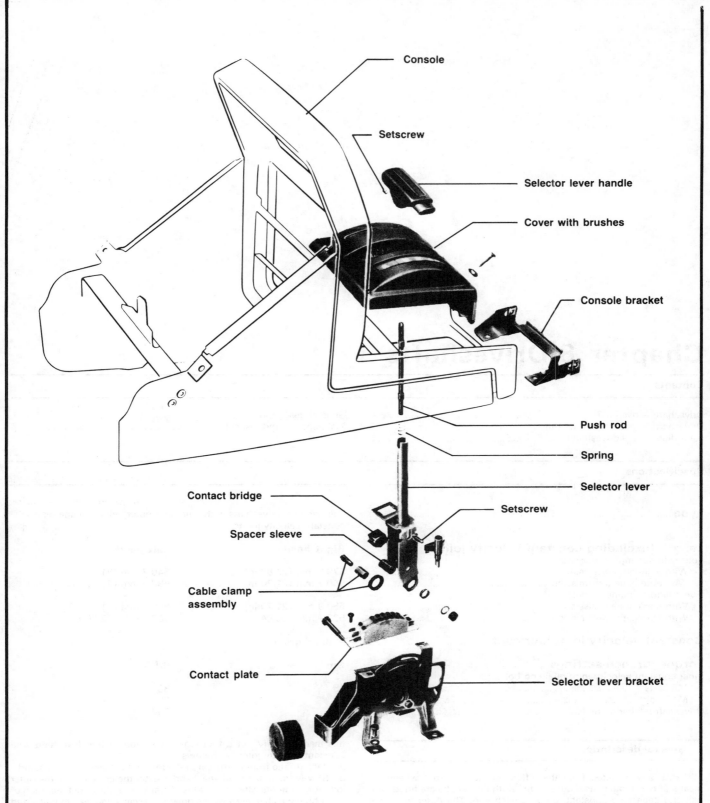

Fig. 7.16 Exploded view of the selector mechanism (Sec 7)

Chapter 8 Driveshafts

Contents

Specifications

Type .... Tubular steel driveshafts with inner and outer ball and cage type
constant velocity joints

Length (excluding constant velocity joints)
Four-cylinder engine models:

	Right-hand	Left-hand
With manual transmission	579.2 mm (22.82 in)	540.7 mm (21.30 in)
With automatic transmission	540.7 mm (21.30 in)	598.5 mm (23.58 in)
Five-cylinder engine models:		
With manual transmission	550.9 mm (21.70 in)	550.9 mm (21.70 in)
With automatic transmission	529.1 mm (20.84 in)	582.8 mm (22.96 in)

Constant velocity joint lubricant .... Audi G6 grease

Torque wrench settings

	Nm	lbf ft
Inner constant velocity joint retaining bolts:		
M8 bolts	45	33
M10 bolts	80	59
Driveshaft retaining nut	280	207

1 General description

Drive is transmitted from the differential to the front wheels by means of two tubular steel driveshafts. Both driveshafts are fitted with ball and cage type constant joints at each end. The outer joints are splined to accept the driveshaft and wheel hub while the inner joints are splined to accept the driveshaft and bolted to the differential drive flanges.

2 Maintenance and inspection

1 At the intervals given in Routine Maintenance at the beginning of this manual, carry out a thorough inspection of the driveshafts and constant velocity joints as follows.
2 Jack up the front of the car and support it securely on axle stands.
3 Slowly rotate the roadwheel and inspect the condition of the outer joint rubber boots. Check for signs of cracking, splits or deterioration of the rubber which may allow the grease to escape and lead to water and grit entry into the joint. Also check the security and condition of the retaining clamps. Repeat these checks on the inner constant velocity joints (photo). If any damage or deterioration is found, the joints should be attended to, as described in Section 4.
4 Continue rotating the roadwheel and check for any distortion or damage to the driveshafts. Check for any free play in the joints by holding the driveshaft firmly and attempting to rotate the wheel. Repeat this check whilst holding the differential drive flange. Any

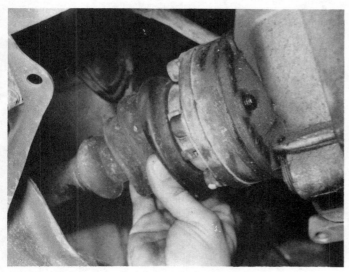

2.3 Checking the driveshaft inner joint rubber boot

noticeable movement indicates wear in the joints, wear in the driveshaft splines, or loose joint retaining bolts or hub nut.

5   Road test the car and check for any noticeable slackness in the driveline when changing from acceleration to overrun and *vice versa*, or for vibration felt through the car when accelerating. Problems of this nature usually indicate wear in the constant velocity joints.

3   Driveshafts – removal and refitting

Manual transmission models

1   Remove the wheel trim then unscrew the driveshaft retaining nut. This is tightened to a very high torque and no attempt to loosen it must be made unless the full weight of the car is on the roadwheels.
2   Loosen the four roadwheel retaining bolts.
3   Jack up the front of the car and securely support it on axle stands. Remove the roadwheel.
4   If working on the right-hand driveshaft, remove the exhaust front pipe, referring to Chapter 3 if necessary, and also the heat shield below the inner constant velocity joint.
5   Using a suitable multi-tooth socket bit, unscrew the inner constant

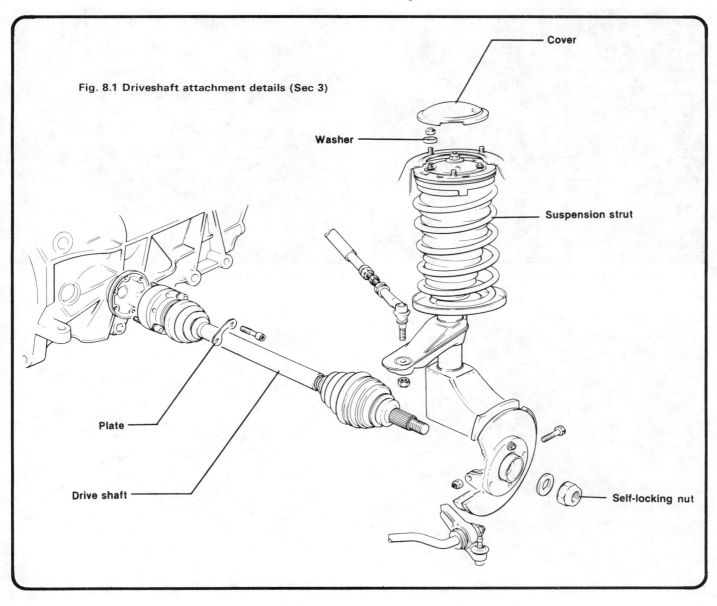

Fig. 8.1 Driveshaft attachment details (Sec 3)

Fig. 8.2 Driveshaft retaining nut – arrowed (Sec 3)

velocity joint retaining bolts then remove the bolts, together with the spreader plates (photo). Separate the inner constant velocity joint from the differential drive flange then angle the driveshaft upwards alongside the transmission.

6 Turn the steering onto full left lock if working on the left-hand driveshaft or right lock if working on the right-hand driveshaft.

7 Attach a suitable puller to the front hub using the roadwheel retaining bolts.

8 Using the puller, press the driveshaft out of the front hub then withdraw the shaft assembly from under the car (photo).

Automatic transmission models

9 Carry out the operations described in paragraphs 1 to 4 inclusive.

10 Undo the two bolts securing the anti-roll bar clamp to the crossmember on the side being worked on.

11 Undo the nut and remove the clamp bolt securing the track control arm balljoint to the suspension strut. Lever the track control arm downward and separate the balljoint from the strut (photo).

12 Using a suitable multi-tooth socket bit, unscrew the inner constant velocity joint retaining bolts then remove the bolts, together with the spreader plates. Separate the inner constant velocity joint from the differential drive flange.

3.5 Removing the inner joint retaining bolts

3.8A Press out the driveshaft using a puller ...

3.8B ... then remove it from the rear of the hub

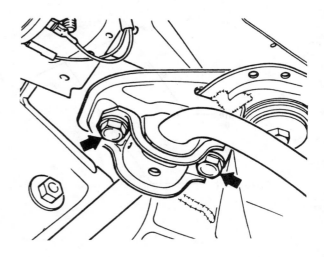

Fig. 8.3 Anti-roll bar clamp bolts – arrowed (Sec 3)

3.11 Track control arm balljoint clamp bolt

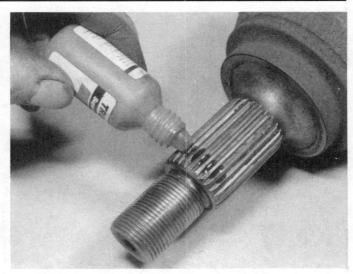

3.16A Applying locking compound to the constant velocity joint splines

13 Attach a suitable puller to the front hub using the roadwheel retaining bolts.
14 Move the suspension strut outwards at the bottom and press the driveshaft out of the front hub using the puller. Withdraw the driveshaft from under the car.

All models

15 Do not move the car with the driveshaft removed, otherwise the front wheel bearing will be damaged.
16 Refitting is the reverse sequence to removal, bearing in mind the following points:

(a) *Ensure that the splines and thread on the outer constant velocity joint are clean, then apply a locking compound in a 6 mm (0.25 in) band around the end of the splines before refitting the driveshaft (photo).*
(b) *Always use a new driveshaft retaining nut, inner joint-to-drive flange gasket, and where applicable control arm balljoint clamp bolt and nut.*
(c) *Tighten all nuts and bolts to the specified torque (photo).*

3.16B Tighten the driveshaft retaining nut with the car on its wheels

4 Driveshafts – overhaul

1   Remove the driveshaft from the car, as described in the previous Section.
2   To remove the inner constant velocity joint, remove the rubber boot retaining clamps and slide the boot down the shaft and off the joint.
3   Using a suitable drift, drive the protective cap off the constant velocity joint.
4   Extract the circlip from the end of the driveshaft (photo).
5   Support the underside of the ball cage and remove the driveshaft by pressing it out.
6   Withdraw the rubber boot and protective cap from the driveshaft, together with the dished washer, where fitted.
7   To remove the outer constant velocity joint, remove the two rubber boot retaining clamps and slide the boot down the shaft and off the joint (photo).
8   Spread the retaining circlip and tap the joint off the shaft using a soft metal drift against the inner edge of the hub (Fig. 8.6).
9   Withdraw the rubber boot from the driveshaft.
10 Before starting to dismantle the outer joint, mark the position of the hub in relation to the cage and housing. Because the parts are hardened this mark will either have to be done with a grinding stone, or with paint.

11 Swivel the hub and cage and take out the balls one at a time.
12 Turn the cage until the two rectangular openings align with the housing and then remove the cage and hub.
13 Turn the hub until one segment can be pushed into one of the rectangular openings in the cage and then swivel the hub out of the cage. The parts of the joint make up a matched set and no individual parts can be replaced. If there is excessive play in the joint which is noticeable when changing from acceleration to overrun, or *vice versa*, a new joint must be fitted, but do not renew a joint because the parts have been polished by wear and the track of the balls is clearly visible.
14 When reassembling the joint, clean off all the old grease and use a new circlip, rubber boot and clamps. Use only the special grease recommended by Audi for packing the joints – see Specifications.
15 Press half a sachet of grease (45 g. 1.6 oz) into the joint and then fit the cage and hub in to the housing, ensuring that it will be possible to line up the mating marks of the hub, cage, and housing after the balls have been inserted.
16 Press the balls into the hub from alternate sides, when all six have been inserted check that the mating marks on the hub, cage and housing are aligned.

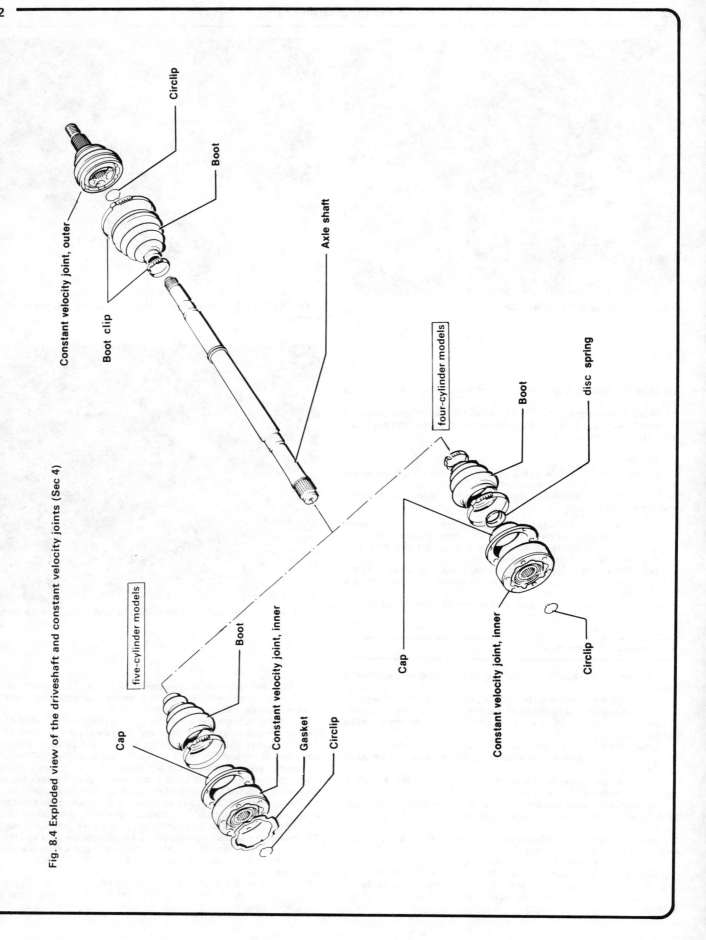

Fig. 8.4 Exploded view of the driveshaft and constant velocity joints (Sec 4)

Constant velocity joint, outer

Circlip

Boot

Boot clip

Axle shaft

four-cylinder models

Boot

disc spring

Constant velocity joint, inner

Cap

Circlip

five-cylinder models

Boot

Cap

Constant velocity joint, inner

Gasket

Circlip

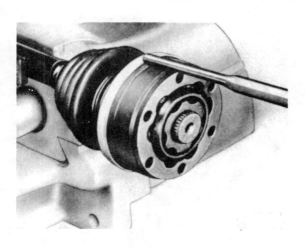

Fig. 8.5 Removing the protective cap from the inner joint (Sec 4)

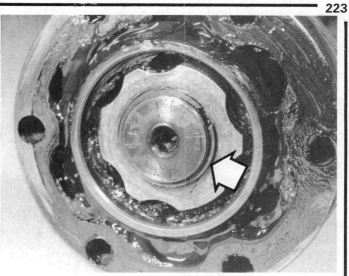

4.4 Constant velocity joint retaining circlip (arrowed)

4.7 Rubber boot retaining clamps (arrowed)

Fig. 8.6 Removing the outer constant velocity joint (Sec 4)

A Circlip
B Drive off the hub in the direction shown

Fig. 8.7 Removing the balls from the outer constant velocity joint (Sec 4)

Fig. 8.8 Removing the cage and hub from the outer constant velocity joint (Sec 4)

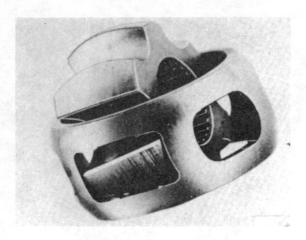

Fig. 8.9 Removing the outer constant velocity joint hub from the cage (Sec 4)

Fig. 8.10 Removing the inner constant velocity joint hub and cage (Sec 4)

17 Fit a new circlip into the groove in the hub and squeeze the remainder of the grease into the joint so that the total amount is 90 g (3.2 oz).

18 The inner joint is dismantled in a similar way. Pivot the hub and cage and press them out of the housing as shown in Fig. 8.10.

19 Press the balls out of the cage, then align two grooves and remove the hub from the cage (Fig. 8.11).

20 When reassembling the joint, press half the charge of grease into each side of the joint. Note that on 4-cylinder engine models the total amount of grease used in each inner joint is 90 g (3.2 oz) and on 5-cylinder engine models it is 120 g (4.2 oz). Ensure that the chamfer on the splined hub is towards the larger diameter side of the outer member. It will be necessary to pivot the joint hub when reassembling in order to align the balls with the grooves.

21 It is advisable to fit new rubber boots to the shaft; a defective boot will soon lead to the need to fit a new joint due to wear caused by grit entering the joint. Fit the boots to the shaft and put any residual grease into the boots.

22 Fit the dished washer, where applicable, to the inner end of the driveshaft and locate the protective cap on the boot. Note that the concave side of the dished washer must face the joint.

Fig. 8.11 Removing the inner constant velocity joint hub from the cage (Sec 4)

Arrows indicate grooves

Fig. 8.12 Reassembling the inner constant velocity joint (Sec 4)

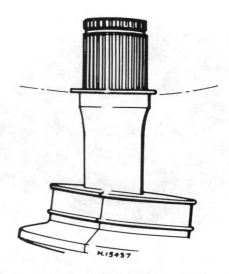

Fig. 8.13 Correct location of the dished washer on the inner end of the driveshaft (Sec 4)

23 Press the inner joint onto the shaft and secure it with a new circlip.
24 Tap the protective cap onto the outer member.
25 Place the outer joint in position against the end of the driveshaft and, using a mallet, drive it onto the shaft until the circlip engages the groove.
26 Fit new clamps to each end of the rubber boots, locate the boots over the joints and tighten the clamps. If the rubber boot fitted to the inner joint is of the type incorporating a breather hole, the inner (smaller) clamp should not be fitted.
27 Where applicable, fit a new gasket to the mating face of the inner joint by peeling off the protective film and sticking the gasket to the joint face.

5 Fault diagnosis – driveshafts

Symptom	Reason(s)
Vibration and noise on lock	Worn driveshaft joints
Noise on taking up drive or between acceleration and overrun	Worn driveshaft joints Worn front wheel hub and driveshaft splines Loose driveshaft bolts or nut

Chapter 9 Braking system

Refer to Chapter 13 for specifications and information on 1987 and later models

Contents

Specifications

System type .... Diagonally split, servo-assisted dual circuit hydraulic with pressure regulator in rear hydraulic circuit and cable-operated handbrake. Anti-lock braking system available on certain models

Front brakes

Type .... Disc with single piston sliding calipers
Make .... Girling or Teves
Disc diameter .... 256.0 mm (10.08 in)
Disc thickness:
    New .... 22.0 mm (0.866 in)
    Wear limit .... 20.0 mm (0.787 in)
Minimum disc thickness after machining .... 20.5 mm (0.807 in)
Maximum disc run-out .... 0.06 mm (0.002 in)
Minimum disc pad thickness .... 7.0 mm (0.27 in) including backing

Rear brakes

Type .... Single leading shoe drum, or disc with single piston sliding calipers
Drum brakes:
    Drum diameter:
        New .... 230.0 mm (9.055 in)
        Wear limit .... 231.0 mm (9.094 in)
    Maximum drum diameter after machining .... 230.5 mm (9.075 in)
    Maximum drum radial run-out .... 0.1 mm (0.004 in)
    Maximum drum lateral run-out at wheel contact face .... 0.2 mm (0.008 in)
    Brake shoe minimum lining thickness .... 2.5 mm (0.10 in)
    Wheel cylinder piston diameter .... 17.46 mm (0.687 in)
Disc brakes:
    Make .... Girling or Teves
    Disc diameter .... 245.0 mm (9.646 in)

Disc thickness:

New	10.0 mm (0.40 in)
Wear limit	8.0 mm (0.315 in)
Minimum disc thickness after machining	8.5 mm (0.335 in)
Maximum disc run-out	0.06 mm (0.002 in)
Minimum disc pad thickness	7.0 mm (0.27 in) including backing

Torque wrench settings

	Nm	lbf ft
Caliper guide pin bolts (Girling)	35	26
Caliper guide pins (Teves)	25	18
Front caliper carrier bracket to suspension strut	70	52
Rear caliper carrier bracket to rear axle	65	48
Rear brake backplate to stub axle (drum brakes)	30	22
Master cylinder to servo	25	18
Servo unit to bulkhead	25	18
Pressure regulator spring mounting	25	18

1 General description

The braking system is of the servo-assisted, dual circuit hydraulic type with disc brakes at the front and drum or disc brakes at the rear, according to model. A diagonally split dual circuit hydraulic system is employed in which each circuit operates one front and one diagonally opposite rear brake from a tandem master cylinder. Under normal conditions both circuits operate in unison; however, in the event of hydraulic failure in one circuit, full braking force will still be available at two wheels. A brake pressure regulator is incorporated in the rear brake hydraulic circuit. This unit regulates the pressure applied to each rear brake and reduces the possibility of the rear wheels locking under heavy braking.

The front disc brakes are operated by single piston sliding type calipers. On models equipped with rear drum brakes, leading and trailing brake shoes are operated by twin piston wheel cylinders and are self-adjusting by footbrake application. On models equipped with rear disc brakes, single piston sliding type calipers, similar to those used at the front, are employed. On all models a cable-operated handbrake provides an independent mechanical means of rear brake application.

The brake servo unit is of the conventional vacuum operated type on models with manual steering or hydraulically operated on models with power-assisted steering. System pressure for the hydraulic servo is generated by the power steering pump and contained in a pressure accumulator. This is then supplied to the hydraulic servo unit on demand to reduce pedal effort when the brakes are applied.

An anti-lock braking system (ABS) is also available as standard or optional equipment, according to model. Further information on this system will be found in the relevant Sections of this Chapter.
Warning: On models equipped with anti-lock braking systems (ABS) certain precautions must be observed when working on the braking system. Refer to Section 28 before carrying out any of the operations described in this Chapter.

2 Maintenance and inspection

1 At the intervals given in Routine Maintenance at the beginning of this manual the following service operations should be carried out on the braking system components.
2 Check the brake hydraulic fluid level and, if necessary, top up with the specified fluid to the MAX mark on the master cylinder reservoir (photos). Any need for frequent topping-up indicates a fluid leak somewhere in the system which must be investigated and rectified immediately.
3 Check the front disc pads and the rear disc pads or brake shoe linings, as applicable, and inspect the condition of the discs and drums. Details will be found in Sections 3, 10 and 7 respectively.
4 Check the condition of the hydraulic pipes and hoses, as described in Section 16. At the same time check the condition of the handbrake cables, lubricate the exposed cables and linkages (photo) and, if necessary, adjust the handbrake, as described in Section 19.
5 Renew the brake hydraulic fluid at the specified intervals by draining the system and refilling with fresh fluid, as described in Section 17.

2.2A Top up the master cylinder reservoir ...

2.2B ... until the level is up to the MAX mark (arrowed)

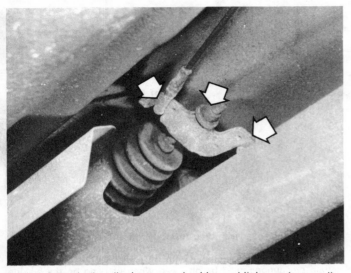

2.4 Lubricate the handbrake exposed cables and linkages (arrowed) with multi-purpose grease

3 Front disc pads – inspection and renewal

1 Jack up the front of the car and support it on stands. Remove both front roadwheels.
2 Check the thickness of the disc pads by viewing through the slot in the front of the caliper body. If the lining thickness on any of the pads is at, or below, the minimum specified thickness all four pads must be renewed as a complete set.

Girling caliper

3 Disconnect the pad wear indicator wiring connector and, using a suitable spanner, unscrew the lower guide pin bolt while holding the guide pin with a second spanner.
4 Pivot the caliper body upwards, withdraw the two disc pads and remove the piston heat shield. If the pads are to be re-used, suitably identify them so that they can be refitted in their original positions.
5 Brush the dust and dirt from the caliper, piston, disc and pads, but **do not inhale it,** as it is injurious to health.
6 Rotate the brake disc by hand and scrape away any rust and scale. Carefully inspect the entire surface of the disc and if there are any signs of cracks, deep scoring or severe abrasions, the disc must be renewed. Also inspect the caliper for signs of fluid leaks around the piston, corrosion, or other damage. Renew the piston seals or the caliper body as necessary.

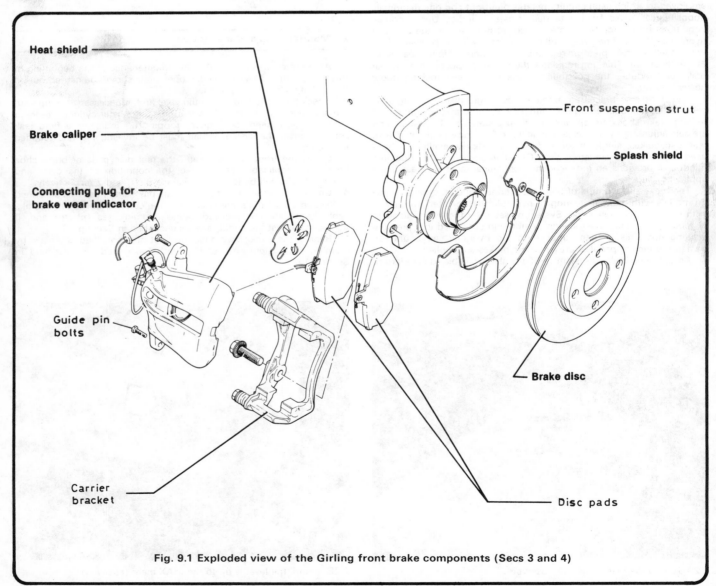

Heat shield

Brake caliper

Connecting plug for brake wear indicator

Guide pin bolts

Carrier bracket

Front suspension strut

Splash shield

Brake disc

Disc pads

Fig. 9.1 Exploded view of the Girling front brake components (Secs 3 and 4)

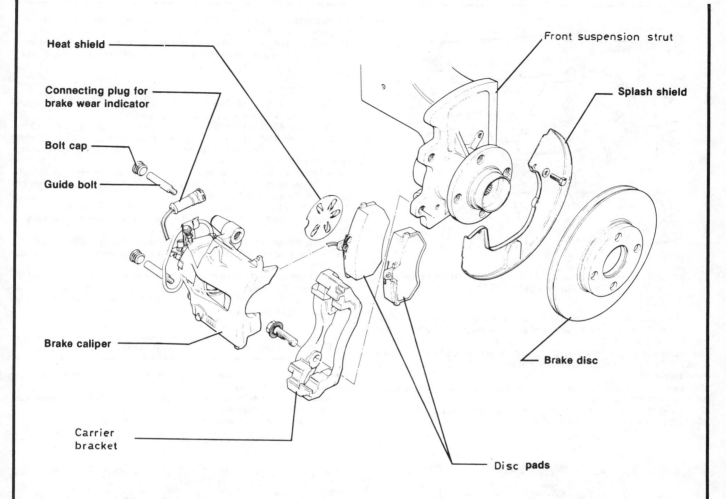

Heat shield

Connecting plug for brake wear indicator

Bolt cap

Guide bolt

Brake caliper

Carrier bracket

Front suspension strut

Splash shield

Brake disc

Disc pads

Fig. 9.2 Exploded view of the Teves front brake components (Secs 3 and 4)

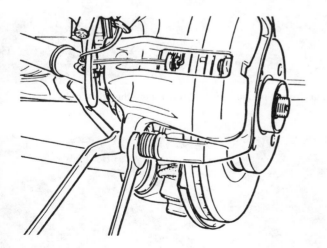

Fig. 9.3 Lower guide pin bolt removal – Girling caliper (Sec 3)

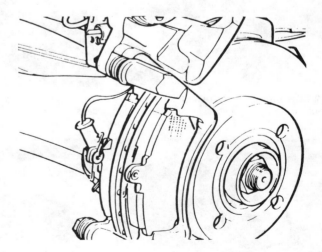

Fig. 9.4 Pivot the caliper body upwards to remove the pads – Girling caliper (Sec 3)

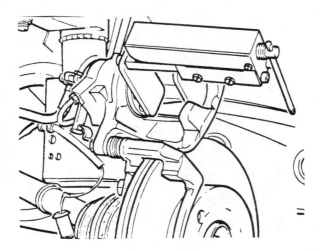

Fig. 9.5 Audi special tool being used to retract the caliper piston – Girling caliper (Sec 3)

7   If new pads are to be fitted, first push the piston back into its bore using a G-clamp or suitable blocks of wood as levers. While doing this, check that brake fluid will not overflow from the reservoir, and if necessary use a clean flexible plastic bottle to extract some fluid. **Note:** Brake fluid is poisonous and no attempt should be made to syphon the fluid by mouth.

8   Place a new heat shield on the piston then place the pads in position against the disc.

9   Swing the caliper body over the pads and secure using a new guide pin bolt tightened to the specified torque.

10 Reconnect the pad wear indicator wiring connector, refit the roadwheels and lower the car to the ground.

11 Depress the brake pedal several times to bring the piston into contact with the pads then check and, if necessary, top up the fluid in the master cylinder reservoir.

Teves caliper

12 Disconnect the pad wear indicator wiring connector then remove the plastic caps over the guide bolts (photos).

13 Using an Allen key, undo the upper and lower guide bolts and lift off the caliper body (photos). Suspend the caliper from a convenient place under the wheel arch using string or wire. Do not allow it to hang unsupported.

14 Withdraw the two disc pads from the carrier bracket (photos). If the pads are to be re-used, suitably identify them so that they can be refitted in their original positions.

15 Before refitting the pads refer to paragraphs 5, 6 and 7.

16 Place the pads in position on the carrier bracket and fit the caliper body.

17 Insert the guide bolts and tighten them to the specified torque.

18 Refit the guide bolt caps and reconnect the wear indicator wiring connector.

19 Refit the roadwheels and lower the car to the ground.

20 Depress the brake pedal several times to bring the piston into contact with the pads then check and, if necessary, top up the fluid in the master cylinder reservoir.

---

4   Front disc caliper – removed and refitting

Note: *On models equipped with an anti-lock braking system, refer to Section 28 before proceeding.*

1   Jack up the front of the car and support it on stands. Remove the appropriate front roadwheel.

2   Disconnect the pad wear indicator wiring connector.

3.12A Disconnect the warning light wiring connector ...

3.12B ... then remove the guide bolt plastic caps

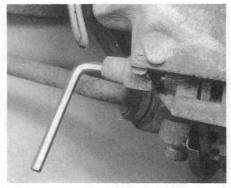

3.13A Unscrew the guide bolts ...

3.13B ... and lift off the caliper body

3.14A Withdraw the outer ...

3.14B ... and inner disc pads

3 Using a brake hose clamp, or self-locking wrench with protected jaws, clamp the flexible brake hose. This will minimise brake fluid loss during subsequent operations.

4 Unscrew the brake pipe-to-hose union at the caliper body then extract the retaining clip and lift away the hose.

Girling caliper

5 Using a suitable spanner, unscrew the lower guide pin bolt while holding the guide pin with a second spanner.

6 Unscrew the upper guide pin bolt in the same way then lift away the caliper leaving the pads and carrier bracket in place.

7 If necessary unbolt the carrier bracket and remove it, complete with pads, from the suspension strut.

Teves caliper

8 Remove the plastic caps then, using an Allen key, unscrew the upper and lower guide bolts.

9 Lift off the caliper leaving the pads and carrier bracket in place.

10 If necessary unbolt the carrier bracket and remove it, complete with pads, from the suspension strut.

Girling and Teves calipers

11 Refitting is the reversal of removal, but make sure all mating faces are clean and tighten the bolts and unions to the specified torque. Use new guide pin bolts on the Girling caliper.

12 Bleed the hydraulic system as described in Section 17, on completion.

5 Front disc caliper – overhaul

1 Remove the caliper, as described in Section 4, and clean it externally, taking care not to allow any foreign matter to enter the brake pipe aperture.

2 Use a foot pump, or a compressed air supply to blow the piston out

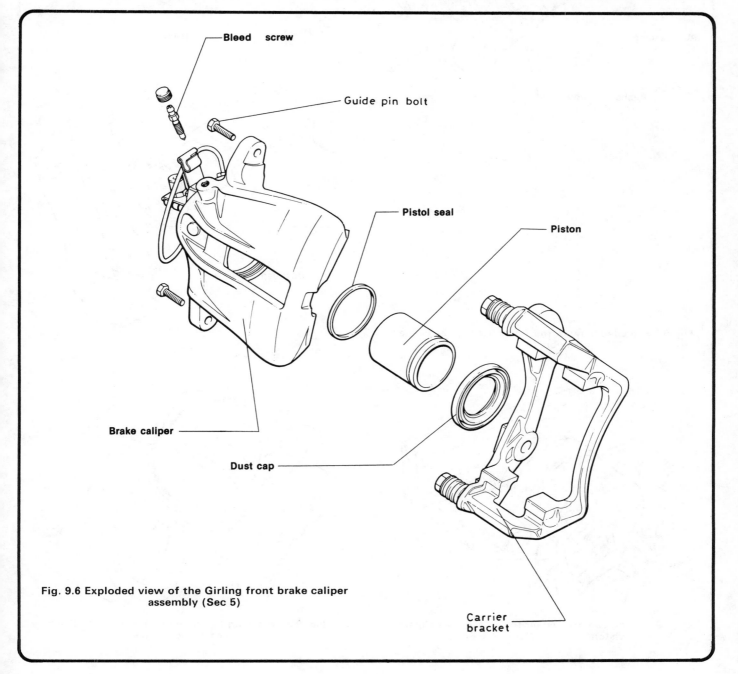

Fig. 9.6 Exploded view of the Girling front brake caliper assembly (Sec 5)

Bleed screw

Guide pin bolt

Pistol seal

Piston

Brake caliper

Dust cap

Carrier bracket

232

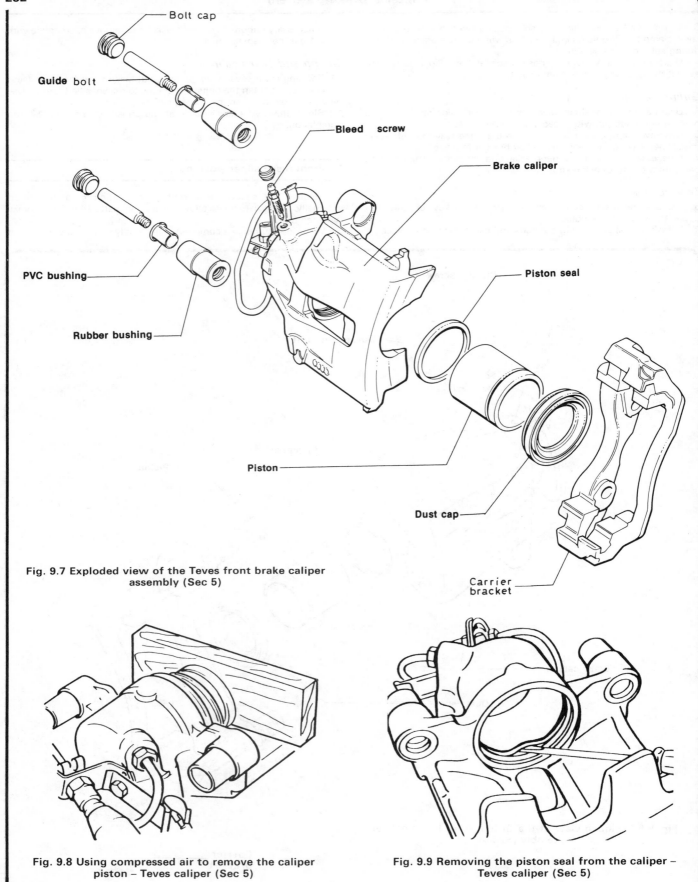

- Bolt cap
- Guide bolt
- Bleed screw
- Brake caliper
- PVC bushing
- Piston seal
- Rubber bushing
- Piston
- Dust cap
- Carrier bracket

Fig. 9.7 Exploded view of the Teves front brake caliper assembly (Sec 5)

Fig. 9.8 Using compressed air to remove the caliper piston – Teves caliper (Sec 5)

Fig. 9.9 Removing the piston seal from the caliper – Teves caliper (Sec 5)

Fig. 9.10 Fit the dust cap as shown before installing the piston – Teves caliper (Sec 5)

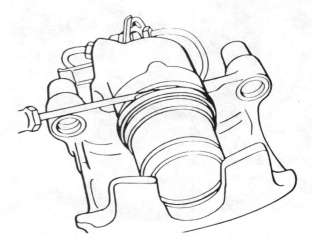

Fig. 9.11 Fitting the sealing lip of the dust cap into the cylinder bore – Teves caliper (Sec 5)

of the cylinder, but place a block of wood inside the frame to prevent damage to the piston. Remove the dust cap.

3   Use a blunt screwdriver to prise the seal out of the caliper bore, taking great care not to scratch the bore walls.

4   Clean the caliper components thoroughly with methylated spirit and allow to dry.

5   Inspect the piston and caliper bore for signs of damage, scuffing or corrosion and, if these conditions are evident, renew the caliper assembly. Also renew the guide pins and/or bushings if they show any sign of damage.

6   If the components are in a satisfactory condition a repair kit consisting of new seals and dust cap should be obtained.

7   Fit a new seal into the groove in the cylinder bore. Apply a thin coat of brake cylinder paste to the seal and to the cylinder.

8   Fit the dust cap on to the piston, as shown in Fig. 9.10, and then offer the piston up to the cylinder and fit the sealing lip of the dust cap into the groove of the cylinder bore using a screwdriver.

9   Smear brake cylinder paste over the piston and then press the piston into the cylinder until the outer lip of the dust cap springs into place in the piston groove.

6   Front brake disc – removal and refitting

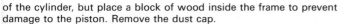

1   Jack up the front of the car and support it on stands. Remove the appropriate front roadwheel.

2   Rotate the disc and examine it for deep scoring or grooving. Light scoring is normal, but if excessive the disc should be removed and renewed, or ground by a suitably qualified engineering works. Use a micrometer in several positions to check the disc thickness.

3   To remove the disc, undo the two bolts securing the brake caliper carrier bracket to the suspension strut. Withdraw the caliper assembly, complete with pads, from the disc and place it to one side. Avoid straining the flexible brake hose.

4   Withdraw the disc from the hub flange.

5   Refitting is the reverse sequence to removal. Ensure that the mating face of the disc and hub flange are thoroughly clean and tighten all retaining bolts to the specified torque.

7   Rear brake shoes – inspection and removal

1   The thickness of the rear brake linings can be checked without removing the brake drums. Remove the rubber plug which is above the handbrake cable entry on the brake backplate. Use a flashlight to increase visibility and check the thickness of friction material remaining on the brake shoes. If the amount remaining is close to the minimum

given in the Specifications, a more thorough examination should be made by removing the brake drum.

2   Chock the front wheels, then jack up the rear of the car and support it on axle stands. Remove the rear wheels, and release the handbrake.

3   Remove the cap from the centre of the brake drum by tapping it on alternate sides with a screwdriver or blunt chisel.

4   Extract the split pin and remove the locking ring.

5   Unscrew the nut and remove the thrust washer.

6   Withdraw the brake drum, making sure that the outer wheel bearing does not fall out. If the brake drum binds on the shoes, insert a small screwdriver through a wheel bolt hole and lever up the wedged key in order to release the shoes.

7   Note the position of the brake shoes and springs and mark the webs of the shoes, if necessary, to aid refitting.

8   Using pliers, depress the spring retainer caps, turn them through 90° and remove them, together with the springs (photo).

9   Unhook the lower return spring from the shoes (photo).

10 Detach the bottom of the shoes from the bottom anchor, then release the top of the shoes from the wheel cylinder and swivel down to reveal the rear of the shoes (photo).

11 Disconnect the handbrake cable, then clamp the bottom of the shoes in a vice.

7.8 Remove the spring retainer caps and springs

7.9 Unhook the lower return spring (arrowed) from the brake shoes

7.10 Release the shoe upper locations from the wheel cylinder

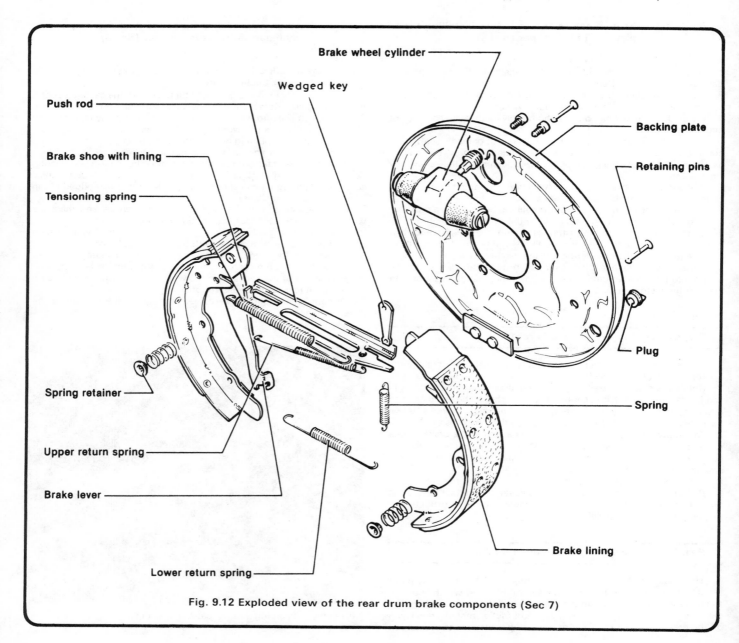

Brake wheel cylinder

Wedged key

Push rod

Brake shoe with lining

Tensioning spring

Backing plate

Retaining pins

Spring retainer

Upper return spring

Brake lever

Plug

Spring

Brake lining

Lower return spring

Fig. 9.12 Exploded view of the rear drum brake components (Sec 7)

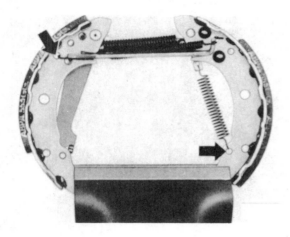

Fig. 9.13 Brake shoe upper return spring and wedged key spring removal (Sec 7)

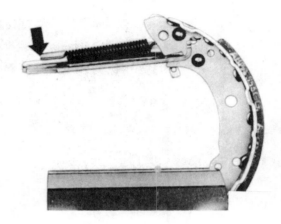

Fig. 9.14 Removal of tensioning spring end (arrowed) and pushrod from the leading brake shoe (Sec 7)

12 Unhook the upper return spring and the wedged key spring.
13 Separate the trailing shoe from the leading shoe and pushrod.
14 Unhook the tensioning spring and remove the pushrod from the leading shoe together with the wedged key.
15 Brush the dust from the brake drum, brake shoes, and backplate, but **do not inhale it,** as it is injurious to health.Scrape any scale or rust from the drum.
16 Measure the brake shoe lining thickness. If it is worn down to the specified minimum amount, renew all four rear brake shoes.
17 Clean the brake backplate. If there are any signs of loss of grease from the rear hub bearings, the oil seal should be renewed, with reference to Chapter 10. If hyraulic fluid is leaking from the wheel cylinder, it must be repaired or renewed, as described in Section 8. Do not touch the brake pedal while the shoes are removed. Position an elastic band over the wheel cylinder pistons to retain them.
18 Apply a little brake grease to the contact areas of the pushrod and handbrake lever.
19 Clamp the pushrod in a vice, then hook the tensioning spring on the pushrod and leading shoe and position the shoe slot over the pushrod.
20 Fit the wedged key between the shoe and pushrod.
21 Locate the handbrake lever on the trailing shoe in the pushrod, and fit the upper return spring.
22 Connect the handbrake cable to the handbrake lever, swivel the shoes upward and locate the top of the shoes on the wheel cylinder pistons.
23 Fit the lower return spring to the shoes, then lever the bottom of the shoes onto the bottom anchor.
24 Fit the spring to the wedged key and leading shoe (photo).
25 Fit the retaining springs and caps.
26 Press the wedged key upwards to give the maximum shoe clearance.
27 Fit the brake drum and adjust the wheel bearings, with reference to Chapter 10.
28 Depress the brake pedal once firmly in order to adjust the rear brakes.
29 Repeat the procedure on the remaining rear brake, then lower the car to the ground.

8 Rear wheel cylinder – removal, overhaul and refitting

1 Remove the brake shoes, as described in Section 7.
2 Remove the master cylinder reservoir filler cap and top up the reservoir fully. Place a piece of polythene over the filler neck and secure the polythene with an elastic band. This will minimise brake fluid loss during subsequent operations. Alternatively clamp the flexible brake hose between the rear axle and body using a brake hose clamp or self-locking wrench with protected jaws.

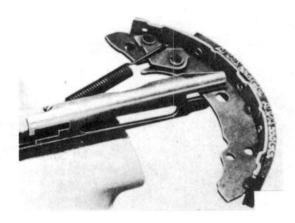

Fig. 9.15 Refitting the tensioning spring and leading brake shoe to the pushrod (Sec 7)

7.24 Brake shoe self-adjusting wedged key and spring (arrowed)

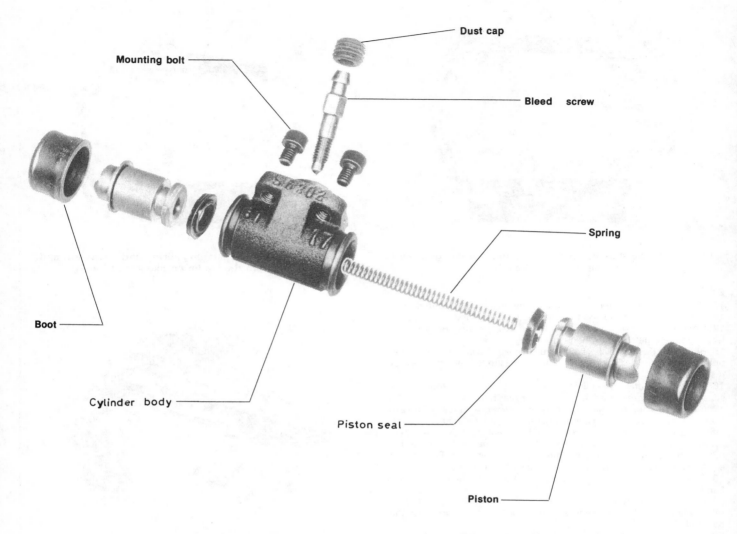

Fig. 9.16 Exploded view of the rear drum brake wheel cylinder (Sec 8)

3 Loosen the brake pipe union on the rear of the wheel cylinder.
4 Using an Allen key, unscrew the wheel cylinder mounting bolts.
5 Unscrew the brake pipe union and withdraw the wheel cylinder from the backplate. Plug the end of the hydraulic pipe, if necessary.
6 Clean the exterior of the wheel cylinder, taking care not to allow any foreign matter to enter the hydraulic pipe aperture.
7 Remove the rubber boots from the ends of the cylinder and extract the two pistons and the spring between them.
8 Inspect the cylinder bore for signs of scoring and corrosion and the pistons and seals for wear. If the cylinder is satisfactory a repair kit can be used; otherwise the cylinder should be discarded and a new complete assembly fitted. If servicing a cylinder, use all the parts in the repair kit. Clean all the metal parts, using methylated spirit if necessary, *but never petrol or similar solvents,* then leave the parts to dry in the air, or dry them with a lint-free cloth.
9 Apply brake cylinder paste to the seals and fit them so that their larger diameter end is nearest to the end of the piston.
10 Smear brake cylinder paste on to the pistons and into the bore of the cylinder. Fit a piston into one end of the cylinder and then the spring and other piston into the other end. Take care not to force the pistons into the cylinders because this can twist the seals.
11 Locate the rubber boots over the pistons and into the grooves of the wheel cylinder.
12 Refitting is a reversal of removal, but bleed the hydraulic system as described in Section 17.

9 Brake drum – inspection and renewal

1 Whenever the brake drums are removed, they should be checked for wear and damage. Light scoring of the friction surface is normal, but if it is excessive, or if the internal diameter exceeds the specified wear limit, the drum and hub assembly should be renewed.
2 After a high mileage the friction surface may become oval. Where this has occurred, it may be possible to have the surface ground true by a qualified engineering works. However, it is preferable to renew the drum and hub assembly.

10 Rear disc pads – inspection and renewal

1 Jack up the rear of the car and support it on stands. Remove both rear roadwheels.
2 Check the thickness of the disc pads by viewing through the slot in the caliper body. If the lining thickness on any of the pads is at, or below, the minimum specified thickness all four pads must be renewed as a complete set.

Girling caliper

3 Using a suitable spanner, unscrew the upper and lower guide pin bolts while holding the guide pins with a second spanner (photos).

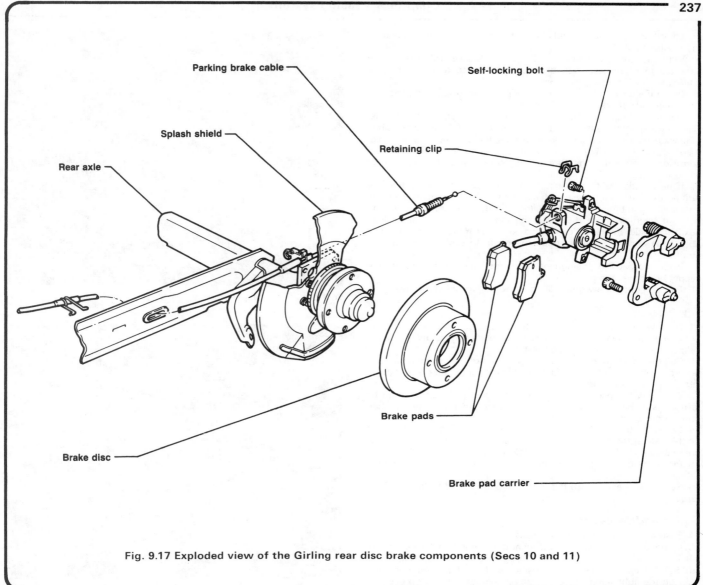

Parking brake cable

Self-locking bolt

Splash shield

Retaining clip

Rear axle

Brake pads

Brake disc

Brake pad carrier

Fig. 9.17 Exploded view of the Girling rear disc brake components (Secs 10 and 11)

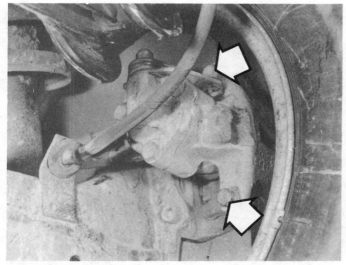

10.3A Rear caliper guide pin bolts (arrowed)

10.3B Removing the caliper upper guide pin bolt

4   Lift off the caliper body and place it to one side, but avoid straining the flexible brake hose (photo).

5   Withdraw the disc pads from the carrier bracket (photos). If the pads are to be re-used, suitably identify them so that they can be refitted in their original positions.

6   Brush the dust and dirt from the caliper, piston, disc and pads, but **do not inhale it,** as it is injurious to health.

7   Rotate the brake disc by hand and scrape away any rust and scale. Carefully inspect the entire surface of the disc and if there are any signs of cracks, deep scoring or severe abrasions, the disc must be renewed. Also inspect the caliper for signs of fluid leaks around the piston, corrosion, or other damage. Renew the piston seals or the caliper body as necessary.

8   If new pads are to be fitted, retract the piston into its bore by turning the piston clockwise with a suitable Allen key and at the same time pushing in firmly (photo). While doing this, check that brake fluid will not overflow from the reservoir, and if necessary use a clean flexible plastic bottle to extract some fluid. **Note:** Brake fluid is poisonous and no attempt should be made to syphon the fluid by mouth.

9   Place the pads in position on the carrier bracket then locate the caliper body over the pads.

10 Fit and tighten new guide pin bolts to the specified torque.

Teves caliper

11 Remove the plastic caps over the guide bolts then unscrew the bolts using an Allen key. Only unscrew the bolts sufficiently to free the caliper; do not remove them completely.

12 Pull the caliper body away from the centre of the car, then swivel it rearwards and lift it off the pads. Place the caliper to one side but avoid straining the flexible brake hose.

13 Withdraw the pads from the carrier bracket. If the pads are to be re-used, suitably identify them so that they can be refitted in their original positions.

14 Before refitting the pads, refer to paragraphs 6, 7 and 8. Note that on this caliper the piston is retracted by simply pushing it back into its bore using a G-clamp or suitable block of wood as a lever.

15 Place the pads in position on the carrier bracket followed by the caliper.

16 Secure the caliper with the guide bolts tightened to the specified torque, then refit the plastic caps.

Girling and Teves calipers

17 Ensure that the handbrake is released.

18 Using a screwdriver, pull the handbrake operating lever on the left-hand caliper so that the lever rests against its stop peg (Figs. 9.22 and 9.23). Hold the lever in this position and check that the operating lever on the right-hand caliper is also resting against its stop peg.

10.4 Lift off the caliper body

10.5A Remove the outer ...

10.5B ... and inner disc pads

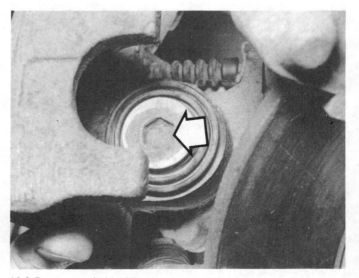

10.8 Engage a suitable Allen key in the piston hexagonal slot then turn clockwise to retract the piston

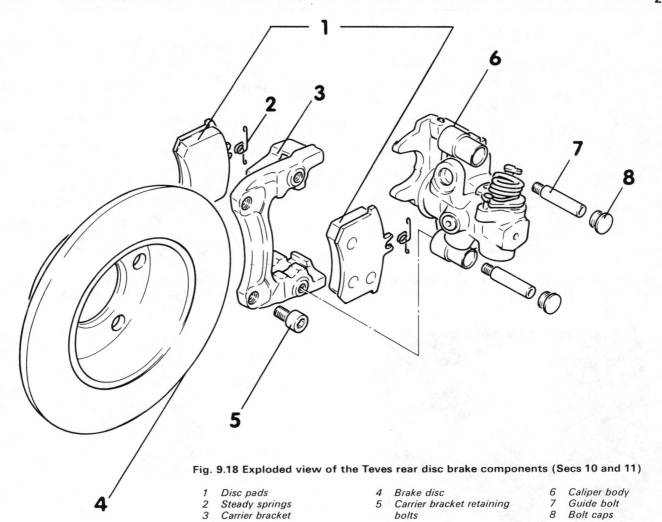

Fig. 9.18 Exploded view of the Teves rear disc brake components (Secs 10 and 11)

1   Disc pads
2   Steady springs
3   Carrier bracket

4   Brake disc
5   Carrier bracket retaining
    bolts

6   Caliper body
7   Guide bolt
8   Bolt caps

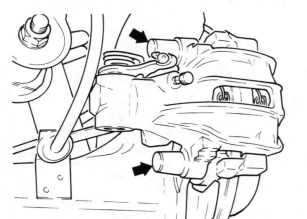

Fig. 9.19 Guide bolt plastic caps (arrowed) – Teves caliper (Sec 10)

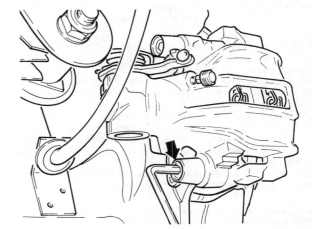

Fig. 9.20 Lower guide bolt removal using an Allen key (arrowed) – Teves caliper (Sec 10)

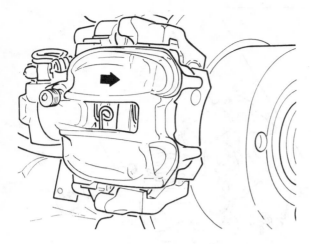

Fig. 9.21 Pull the caliper in the direction of the arrow, swivel rearwards and remove – Teves caliper (Sec 10)

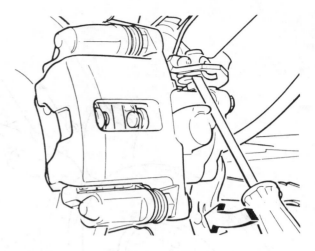

Fig. 9.22 Press the handbrake operating lever on the caliper against its stop using a screwdriver (Sec 10)

Fig. 9.23 Handbrake operating lever stop peg (arrowed) on rear caliper (Sec 10)

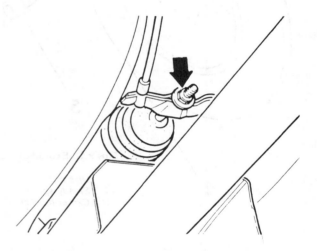

Fig. 9.24 Handbrake cable adjusting nut – arrowed (Sec 10)

19 If the right-hand lever is pulled away from its stop during this procedure, slacken the handbrake cable adjusting nut (Fig. 9.24) until both levers rest against their stops.

20 Insert a screwdriver of at least 6 mm (0.25 in) between the brake pressure regulator operating spring and the roller on the rear axle (Fig. 9.25).

21 With the engine switched off, pump the brake pedal approximately 40 times using moderate pressure then check that both rear discs are free to turn with the pedal released. If this is not the case repeat the procedure in paragraphs 18 to 21 but slacken the handbrake cable adjusting nut further.

22 On completion, remove the screwdriver from the regulator, refit the roadwheels then lower the car to the ground.

11 Rear disc caliper – removal and refitting

Note: *On models equipped with an anti-lock braking system, refer to Section 28 before proceeding.*

1   Jack up the rear of the car and support it on stands. Remove the appropriate rear roadwheel.

2   Extract the clip securing the handbrake cable to the caliper body, release the cable end from the operating lever and move the cable to one side.

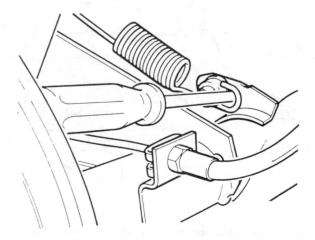

Fig. 9.25 Screwdriver inserted between brake pressure regulator spring and spring mounting roller (Sec 10)

3   Using a brake hose clamp, or self-locking wrench with protected jaws, clamp the flexible brake hose. This will minimise brake fluid loss during subsequent operations.

4   Slacken but do not remove the brake hose-to-caliper union.

Girling caliper

5   Using a suitable spanner, unscrew the upper and lower guide pin bolts while holding the guide pins with a second spanner.

6   Lift away the caliper, hold the brake hose and unscrew the caliper from the hose.

7   If necessary unbolt the carrier bracket and remove it, complete with pads, from the rear axle.

Teves caliper

8   Remove the plastic caps over the guide bolts then unscrew the two guide bolts using an Allen key. Only unscrew the guide bolts sufficiently to free the caliper; do not remove them completely.

9   Pull the caliper body away from the centre of the car then swivel it to the rear and lift it off the pads. Hold the brake hose and unscrew the caliper from the hose.

10   If necessary unbolt the carrier bracket and remove it, complete with pads, from the rear axle.

Girling and Teves calipers

11   Refitting is the reversal of removal, but make sure all mating faces are clean and tighten the bolts and unions to the specified torque. Use new guide pin bolts on the Girling caliper.

12   Bleed the hydraulic system, as described in Section 17, then carry out the rear brake basic adjustment procedure described in Section 10, paragraphs 17 to 22 inclusive.

12   Rear disc caliper – overhaul

1   Remove the caliper, as described in Section 11, and clean it externally, taking care not to allow any foreign matter to enter the brake hose aperture.

Girling caliper

2   Using a suitable Allen key, unscrew the piston from the cylinder and remove the piston dust cap.

3   Use a blunt screwdriver to prise the seal out of the cylinder bore, taking great care to avoid scratching the bore walls.

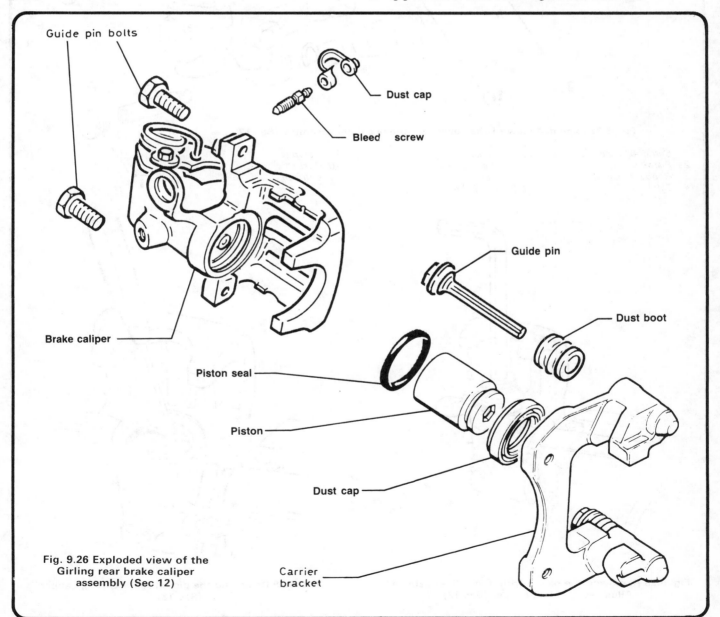

Fig. 9.26 Exploded view of the Girling rear brake caliper assembly (Sec 12)

Guide pin bolts

Dust cap

Bleed   screw

Guide pin

Dust boot

Brake caliper

Piston seal

Piston

Dust cap

Carrier bracket

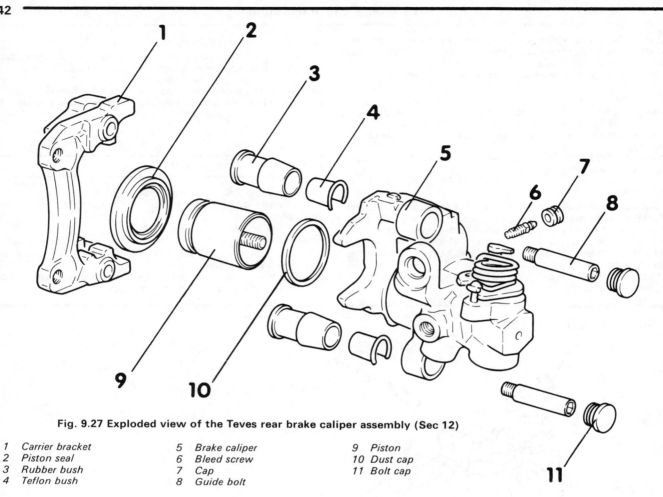

Fig. 9.27 Exploded view of the Teves rear brake caliper assembly (Sec 12)

1	Carrier bracket	5	Brake caliper	9	Piston
2	Piston seal	6	Bleed screw	10	Dust cap
3	Rubber bush	7	Cap	11	Bolt cap
4	Teflon bush	8	Guide bolt		

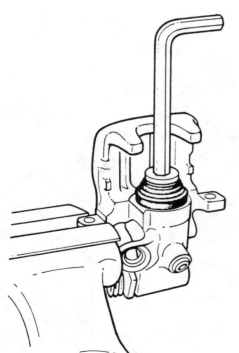

Fig. 9.28 Removing the piston from the caliper using an Allen key – Girling caliper (Sec 12)

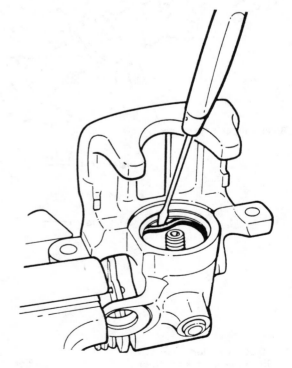

Fig. 9.29 Removing the piston seal – Girling caliper (Sec 12)

4   Clean the caliper components thoroughly with methylated spirit and allow to dry.

5   Inspect the piston and caliper bore for signs of damage, scuffing or corrosion and, if these conditions are evident, renew the caliper assembly. Also renew the guide pins and dust boots if they show any sign of damage.

6   If the components are in a satisfactory condition a repair kit consisting of new seals and dust cap should be obtained.

7   Fit a new seal into the groove in the cylinder bore. Apply a thin coat of brake cylinder paste to the seal and to the cylinder.

8   Fit the dust cap on to the piston as shown in Fig. 9.30 and then offer the piston up to the cylinder. Fit the sealing lip of the dust cap into the groove of the cylinder bore using a screwdriver.

9   Smear brake cylinder paste over the piston and screw the piston into the cylinder while pressing down firmly. With the piston screwed in as far as possible engage the outer lip of the dust cap with the piston groove.

Teves caliper

10 Use a foot pump or compressed air supply to blow the piston out of the cylinder, but place a block of wood inside the frame to prevent damage to the piston.

11 Remove the piston dust cap.

12 Use a blunt screwdriver to prise the seal out of the cylinder bore, taking great care to avoid scratching the bore walls.

13 Clean the caliper components thoroughly with methylated spirit and allow to dry.

14 Carry out a careful inspection of the parts as described in paragraphs 5 and 6 but additionally inspect, and if necessary renew, the rubber and Teflon guide pin bushes.

15 Fit a new seal into the groove in the cylinder bore.

16 Using a screwdriver inserted through the threaded insert in the caliper, push the insert back against its stop. Ensure that the threaded insert is free to turn.

17 Fit the dust cap on the piston, as shown in Fig. 9.3 then apply a thin coat of brake cylinder paste to the piston, seal and cylinder bore.

18 Offer the piston up to the cylinder and fit the sealing lip of the dust cap into the groove of the cylinder bore using a screwdriver.

19 Turn the piston slightly so that the thread engages with the threaded insert. Push the piston into the cylinder using a G-clamp or by levering with a block of wood. Ensure that the piston is pushed back squarely to avoid damaging the automatic adjuster mechanism. As the piston is pushed back, engage the outer lip of the dust cap with the piston groove.

13 Rear brake disc – removal and refitting

1   Jack up the rear of the car and support it on stands. Remove the appropriate rear road wheel.

2   Rotate the disc and examine it for deep scoring or grooving. Light scoring is normal, but if excessive the disc should be removed and renewed, or ground by a suitably qualified engineering works. Use a micrometer in several positions to check the disc thickness.

3   To remove the disc, refer to Section 11 and remove the rear disc caliper and carrier bracket. However, do not disconnect the flexible brake hose – suspend the caliper by string or wire from a convenient place under the wheel arch.

4   Withdraw the disc from the hub flange.

5   Before refitting, ensure that the mating faces of the disc and hub flange are thoroughly clean then place the disc in position.

6   Refit the caliper assembly, as described in Section 11, but note that it will not be necessary to bleed the hydraulic system.

14 Master cylinder – removal and refitting

Note: *The master cylinder is a sealed unit and cannot be dismantled for repair or overhaul. In the event of master cylinder failure the unit must be renewed as a complete assembly. On models equipped with an anti-lock braking system, refer to Section 28 before proceeding.*

1   Remove the reservoir filler cap and draw off the fluid using a syringe or flexible plastic bottle. Take care not to spill fluid on the car paintwork – if some is spilled, wash it off immediately with copious amounts of cold water.

Fig. 9.30 Correct positioning of dust cap prior to fitting piston – Girling caliper (Sec 12)

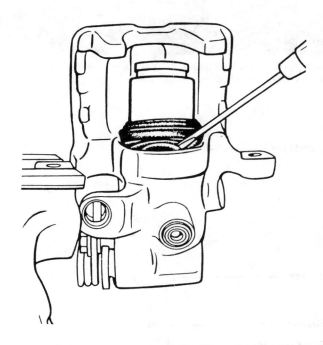

Fig. 9.31 Inserting the dust cap sealing lip into the cylinder bore groove – Girling caliper (Sec 12)

Fig. 9.32 Ensure that the threaded insert is pushed back to its stop – Teves caliper (Sec 12)

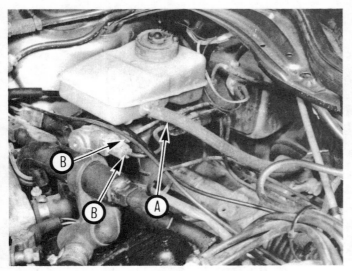

14.3 Clutch hydraulic fluid hose (A) and brake pipe connections (B) on left-hand side of master cylinder

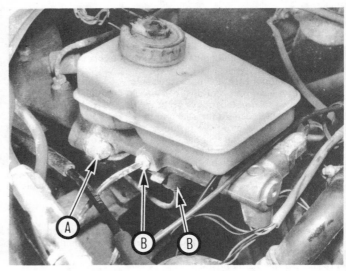

14.4 Master cylinder retaining bolt (A) and right-hand side brake pipe connections (B)

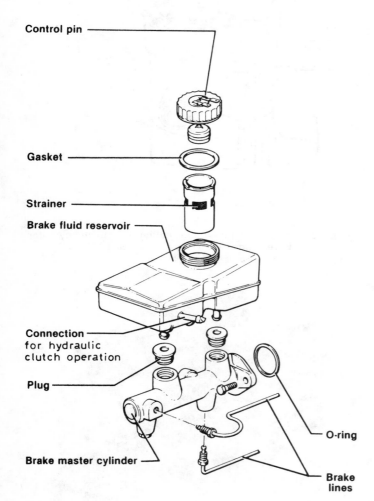

Control pin

Gasket

Strainer

Brake fluid reservoir

Connection for hydraulic clutch operation

Plug

Brake master cylinder

O-ring

Brake lines

Fig. 9.33 Brake master cylinder and reservoir components (Sec 14)

2   Refit the filler cap, but disconnect the warning light wiring connector.
3   Where applicable, detach the clutch hydraulic fluid hose from the side of the reservoir (photo).
4   Place some rags beneath the cylinder then unscrew the brake pipe union nuts and pull the pipes just clear of the master cylinder (photo).
5   Unscrew the mounting bolts and withdraw the master cylinder from the servo unit. Recover the O-ring seal. Do not depress the brake pedal with the master cylinder removed.
6   Refitting is the reversal of removal, but always fit a new O-ring seal. Bleed the hydraulic system, as described in Section 17, after fitting.

15 Brake pressure regulator – testing and adjustment

Note: *On models equipped with an anti-lock braking system, refer to Section 28 before proceeding*

1   The brake pressure regulator is located on the left-hand side of the rear axle, and is controlled by the up-and-down movement of the rear axle.
2   To test the operation of the regulator, have an assistant depress the footbrake firmly then release it quickly. With the weight of the car on the suspension the arm on the regulator should move, indicating that the unit is not seized.
3   To test the regulator for leakage, pressure gauges must be connected to the left-hand front caliper and right-hand rear wheel cylinder or caliper. As the equipment will not normally be available to the home mechanic, this work should be entrusted to an Audi dealer. However, an outline of the procedure is as follows. Depress the brake pedal so that the pressure in the left-hand front caliper is 100 bar (1450 lbf/in²). Hold this pressure for 5 seconds and check that the pressure in the right-hand rear wheel cylinder or caliper varies by no more than 10 bar (145 lbf/in²).
4   To adjust the regulator, the pressure gauges must be connected as described in paragraph 3, and the car must be at kerb weight with a full fuel tank and driver. Bounce the rear suspension several times, then depress the brake pedal so that the pressure in the left-hand front caliper is 50 bar (725 lbf/in²) – the pressure in the rear wheel cylinder or caliper should be 32.5 to 42.5 bar (471 to 616 lbf/in²). With the front caliper pressure at 100 bar (1450 lbf/in²) the rear wheel cylinder or caliper pressure should be 54.0 to 71.5 bar (783 to 1037 lbf/in²).
5   If the rear wheel cylinder or caliper pressure is too high, loosen the spring mounting on the rear axle and move the mounting forwards to release the tension. If the pressure is too low, move the mounting rearwards to increase the tension (photo).

15.5 Pressure regulator spring mounting (arrowed)

16 Hydraulic brake pipes and hoses – removal and refitting

Note: *On models equipped with an anti-lock braking system, refer to Section 28 before proceeding.*
1   Before removing a brake pipe or hose unscrew the master cylinder reservoir filler cap and top up the reservoir fully. Place a piece of polythene over the filler neck and secure with an elastic band. This will minimise brake fluid loss during subsequent operations.
2   To remove a rigid brake pipe, unscrew the union nuts at each end, prise open the support clips and withdraw the pipe. Refitting is a reversal of removal.
3   To remove a flexible brake hose, unscrew the union nut securing the rigid brake pipe to the end of the flexible hose while holding the hose end stationary. Remove the retaining clip and withdraw the hose from the bracket. Unscrew the remaining end from the component or rigid pipe, according to position, release any retaining clips or brackets and remove the hose from the car. Refitting is a reversal of removal (photo).

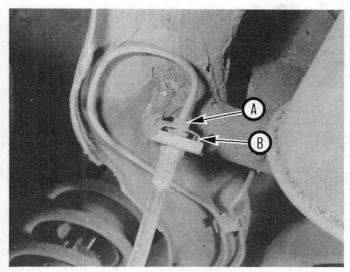

16.3 Brake hose pipe union nut (A) and retaining clip (B)

4   Bleed the hydraulic system as described in Section 17, after fitting a rigid pipe or flexible hose, and whenever a pipe or hose union is disconnected.

17 Hydraulic system – bleeding

Note: *On models equipped with an anti-lock braking system, refer to Section 28 before proceeding*
1   The correct functioning of the brake hydraulic system is only possible after removal of all air from the components and circuit; this is achieved by bleeding the system. Note that clean unused brake fluid which has remained unshaken for at least 24 hours must be used.
2   If there is any possibility of incorrect fluid being used in the system, the brake lines and components must be completely flushed with uncontaminated fluid and new seals fitted to the components.
3   *Never reuse* brake fluid which has been bled from the system.
4   During the procedure, do not allow the level of brake fluid to drop more than halfway down the reservoir.
5   Before starting work, check that all pipes and hoses are secure, unions tight and bleed screws closed. Take great care not to allow brake fluid to come into contact with the car paintwork, otherwise the finish will be seriously damaged. Wash off any spilled fluid immediately with cold water.
6   There are a number of one-man, do-it-yourself, brake bleeding kits currently available from motor accessory shops. Always follow the instructions supplied with the kit. It is recommended that one of these kits is used wherever possible, as they greatly simplify the bleeding operation and also reduce the risk of expelled air and fluid being drawn back into the system. If one of these kits is not available, it will be necessary to gather together a clean jar and a suitable length of clear plastic tubing which is a tight fit over the bleed screw, and also to engage the help of an assistant.
7   If brake fluid has been lost from the master cylinder due to a leak in the system, ensure that the cause is traced and rectified before proceeding further.
8   If the hydraulic system has only been partially disconnected and suitable precautions were taken to prevent further loss of fluid it should only be necessary to bleed that part of the system.
9   If the complete system is to be bled then it should be done in the following sequence:

(1)   Right-hand rear wheel cylinder or brake caliper
(2)   Left-hand rear wheel cylinder or brake caliper
(3)   Right-hand front brake caliper
(4)   Left-hand front brake caliper

Note: *If the system is being bled after removal and refitting of the master cylinder it will also be necessary to bleed the clutch system on models with a hydraulically operated clutch. This should be done* **first**, *as described in Chapter 5.*
10   To bleed the system, first clean the area around the bleed screw and fit the bleed tube. If necessary, top up the master cylinder reservoir with brake fluid.
11   If the system incorporates a vacuum servo, destroy the vacuum by giving several applications of the brake pedal in quick succession.

Bleeding – two-man method

12   Gather together a clean jar and a length of rubber or plastic tubing which will be a tight fit on the brake bleed screws.
13   Engage the help of an assistant.
14   Push one end of the bleed tube onto the first bleed screw and immerse the other end in the jar which should contain enough hydraulic fluid to cover the end of the tube.
15   Open the bleed screw one half turn and have your assistant depress the brake pedal fully then slowly release it. Tighten the bleed screw at the end of each pedal downstroke to obviate any chance of air or fluid being drawn back into the system.
16   Repeat this operation until clean hydraulic fluid, free from air bubbles, can be seen coming through into the jar.
17   Tighten the bleed screw at the end of a pedal downstroke and remove the bleed tube. Bleed the remaining screws in a similar way.

Bleeding – using a one-way valve kit

18   There are a number of one-man, one-way brake bleeding kits available from motor accessory shops. It is recommended that one of

these kits is used wherever possible as it will greatly simplify the bleeding operation and also reduce the risk of air or fluid being drawn back into the system, quite apart from being able to do the work without the help of an assistant.

19 To use the kit, connect the tube to the bleed screw and open the screw one half turn.

20 Depress the brake pedal fully and slowly release it. The one-way valve in the kit will prevent expelled air from returning at the end of each pedal downstroke. Repeat this operation several times to be sure of ejecting all air from the system. Some kits include a translucent container which can be positioned so that the air bubbles can be seen being ejected from the system.

21 Tighten the bleed screw, remove the tube and repeat the operations on the remaining brakes.

22 On completion, depress the brake pedal. If it still feels spongy repeat the bleeding operations, as air must still be trapped in the system.

Bleeding – using a pressure bleed kit

23 These kits are also available from motor accessory shops and are usually operated by air pressure from the spare tyre.

24 By connecting a pressurised container to the master cylinder fluid reservoir, bleeding is then carried out by simply opening each bleed screw in turn and allowing the fluid to run out, rather like turning on a tap, until no air is visible in the expelled fluid.

25 By using this method, the large reserve of hydraulic fluid provides a safeguard against air being drawn into the master cylinder during bleeding which often occurs if the fluid level in the reservoir is not maintained.

26 Pressure bleeding is particularly effective when bleeding 'difficult' systems or when bleeding the complete system at the time of routine fluid renewal.

All methods

27 When bleeding is completed, check and top up the fluid level in the master cylinder reservoir.

28 Check the feel of the brake pedal. If it feels at all spongy, air must still be present in the system and further bleeding is indicated. Failure to bleed satisfactorily after a reasonable repetition of the bleeding operations may be due to worn master cylinder seals.

29 Discard brake fluid which has been expelled. It is almost certain to be contaminated with moisture, air and dirt making it unsuitable for futher use. Clean fluid should always be stored in an airtight container as it is hygroscopic (absorbs moisture readily) which lowers its boiling point and could affect braking performance under severe conditions.

18 Brake pedal – removal and refitting

1 The clutch and brake pedals share a common bracket assembly and pivot shaft. Removal and refitting procedures for both pedals are given in Chapter 5.

19 Handbrake – adjustment

1 Due to the self-adjusting action of the rear brakes, adjustment of the handbrake should only be necessary after renewal of the brake shoes or pads, or after removal and refitting of any of the handbrake components.

2 To adjust the handbrake, jack up the rear of the car and support it on stands.

Rear drum brake models

3 Release the handbrake fully.

4 From under the car, slacken the handbrake cable adjusting nut at the cable compensator (photo).

5 Depress the brake pedal firmly once then release it.

6 Pull the handbrake lever up to the third notch of the ratchet.

7 Tighten the cable adjusting nut until both rear brakes are dragging, but can still just be turned by hand.

8 Release the handbrake and check that the rear drums are free to turn.

9 Lubricate the adjusting nut threads and compensator with multi-purpose grease then lower the car to the ground.

Rear disc brake models

10 Remove both rear roadwheels then ensure that the handbrake is released fully.

11 From under the car tighten the handbrake cable adjusting nut at the cable compensator (photo 19.4) until the handbrake operating levers on both rear calipers just move off their stop pegs (Fig. 9.23).

12 Now slacken the handbrake adjusting nut two complete turns.

13 Using a screwdriver, pull the handbrake operating lever on the left-hand caliper so that the lever rests against its stop peg (Figs. 9.22 and 9.23). Hold the lever in this position and check that the operating lever on the right-hand caliper is also resting against its stop peg. If this is not the case, slacken the cable adjusting nut further until both levers rest against their stops.

14 Lubricate the adjusting nut threads and compensator with multi-purpose grease, refit the roadwheels and lower the car to the ground.

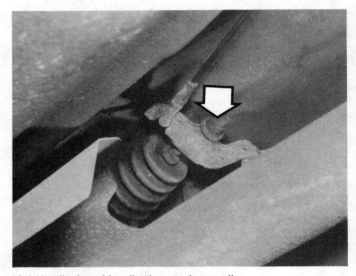

19.4 Handbrake cable adjusting nut (arrowed)

20 Handbrake lever – removal and refitting

1 Chock the front wheels, jack up the rear of the car and support it on stands. Release the handbrake.

2 From under the car, unscrew the handbrake cable adjusting nut (photo 19.4), remove the washer and slide the compensator off the adjusting rod.

3 From inside the car, slide up the gaiter to gain access to the lever mechanism.

4 Disconnect the warning light wiring at the lever switch.

5 Extract the circlip, withdraw the pivot bolt and remove the lever assembly.

6 If necessary, the ratchet may be dismantled by grinding off the rivet heads and removing the internal parts (Fig. 9.34).

7 Refitting is the reversal of removal, but lubricate the pivots and compensator with multi-purpose grease. Finally adjust the handbrake, as described in Section 19.

21 Handbrake cable – removal and refitting

1 Chock the front wheels, jack up the rear of the car and support it on stands. Remove the appropriate rear roadwheel then release the handbrake fully.

2 Slacken the handbrake cable adjusting nut at the cable compensator then remove the cable end from the compensator arm.

3 On models with rear drum brakes, remove the brake drum, as described in Section 7, slip the cable end off the brake shoe lever and withdraw the cable from the backplate.

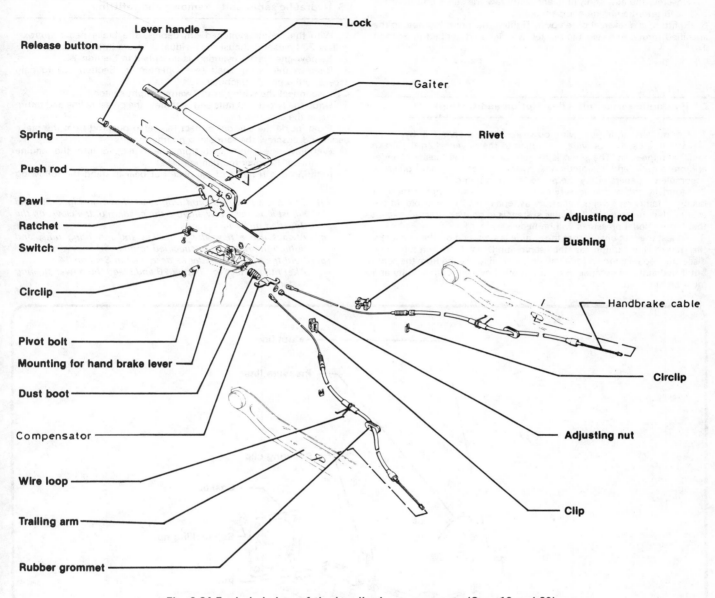

Fig. 9.34 Exploded view of the handbrake components (Secs 19 and 20)

Labels on figure: Release button, Lever handle, Lock, Gaiter, Spring, Rivet, Push rod, Pawl, Ratchet, Switch, Adjusting rod, Bushing, Circlip, Handbrake cable, Pivot bolt, Mounting for hand brake lever, Dust boot, Circlip, Compensator, Adjusting nut, Wire loop, Trailing arm, Clip, Rubber grommet

4 On models with rear disc brakes, extract the clip securing the handbrake cable to the caliper body then release the cable end from the operating lever.

5 On all models, withdraw the cable and grommet from the trailing arm, release the retaining clips and wire loop then remove the cable from under the car.

6 Refitting is the reversal of removal, but adjust the cable as described in Section 19 on completion.

22 Vacuum servo unit – description and testing

1 The vacuum servo unit is located between the brake pedal and the master cylinder and provides assistance to the driver when the brake pedal is depressed. The unit operates by vacuum from the inlet manifold, and on some models, the vacuum is increased by incorporating a vacuum booster in the vacuum supply.

2 The unit basically comprises a diaphragm and non-return valve. With the brake pedal released, vacuum is channelled to both sides of the diaphragm, but when the pedal is depressed, one side is opened to the atmosphere. The resultant unequal pressures are harnessed to assist in depressing the master cylinder pistons.

3 Normally, the vacuum servo unit is very reliable, but if the unit becomes faulty, it should be renewed. In the event of a failure, the hydraulic system is in no way affected, except that higher pedal pressures will be necessary.

4 To test the vacuum servo unit, depress the brake pedal several times with the engine switched off to dissipate the vacuum. Apply moderate pressure to the brake pedal then start the engine. The pedal should move down slightly if the servo unit is operating correctly.

23 Vacuum servo unit – removal and refitting

1 Remove the master cylinder, as described in Section 14.

2 Remove the parcel shelf (see Chapter 11, Section 23) to gain access to the pedal attachments.

3 Disconnect the servo pushrod from the brake pedal, but note in which of the two holes in the pushrod the clevis pin is inserted.

4 From within the engine compartment, pull the non-return valve and vacuum hose from the servo unit body.

5   Unscrew the mounting nuts and withdraw the servo unit from the bulkhead into the engine compartment.
6   Refitting is a reversal of removal. Tighten the mounting nuts to the specified torque and refit the master cylinder as described in Section 14.

24 Hydraulic servo unit – description and testing

1   On models equipped with power-assisted steering a hydraulic servo unit is used to provide assistance to the driver when the brake pedal is depressed. The servo is located between the master cylinder and brake pedal and operated under hydraulic pressure from a pressure accumulator, generated by the power steering pump.
2   Normally the hydraulic servo unit is very reliable, but if the unit becomes faulty renewal is necessary as repairs are not possible. In the event of failure the brake hydraulic system is in no way affected, except that higher pedal pressures will be necessary.
3   To test the unit ensure that the engine is switched off then unscrew the return line union at the servo unit. With the return line disconnected it is normal for a few drops of oil to escape from the servo but if hydraulic oil escapes in a continuous flow, the unit is faulty and must be renewed.

25 Hydraulic servo unit – removal and refitting

1   With the engine switched off, depress the brake pedal approximately 20 times to exhaust the residual pressure in the system.
2   Remove the master cylinder, as described in Section 14.
3   Remove the parcel shelf (see Chapter 11, Section 23) to gain access to the pedal attachments.
4   Disconnect the wiring at the warning light switch.
5   Undo the two union nuts and withdraw the pressure line and return line from the servo unit.
6   From inside the car, disconnect the servo pushrod from the brake pedal and unscrew the four servo mounting nuts.
7   Withdraw the servo unit from the bulkhead into the engine compartment. Recover the flange gasket.
8   Refitting is a reversal of removal, but bear in mind the following points:

   (a) Check the servo pushrod length, as shown in Fig. 9.36, and adjust if necessary by altering the position of the clevis on the threaded pushrod.
   (b) Always use a new flange gasket and mounting nuts, and tighten the nuts to the specified torque.
   (c) Refit the master cylinder as described in Section 14.
   (d) After fitting, refer to Chapter 10 and bleed the power steering system

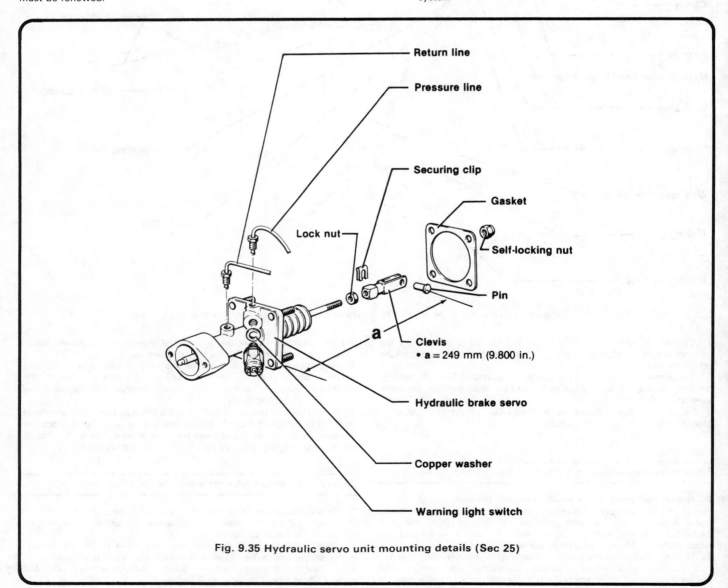

Fig. 9.35 Hydraulic servo unit mounting details (Sec 25)

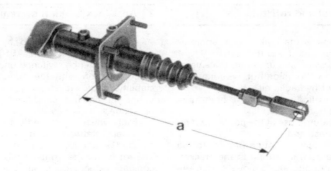

Fig. 9.36 Hydraulic servo pushrod setting dimension (Sec 25)

a = 249 mm (9.800 in)

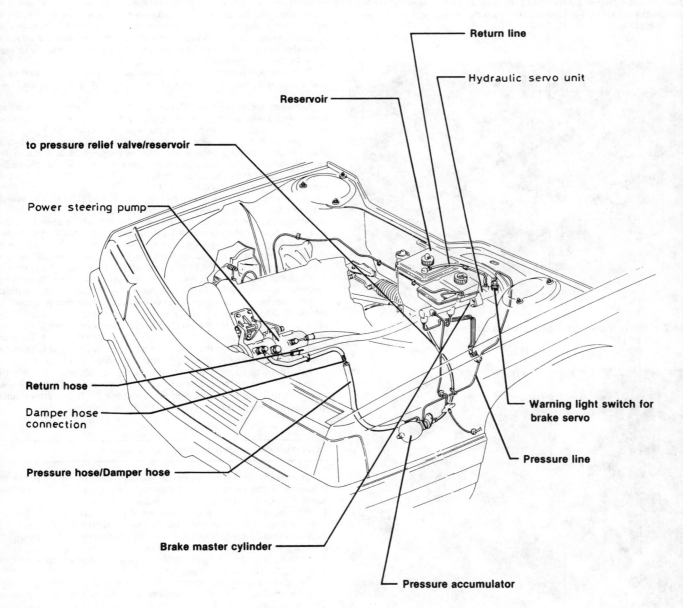

Fig. 9.37 Hydraulic servo unit and pressure accumulator layout (Secs 25 and 26)

26 Pressure accumulator – removal and refitting

1   With the engine switched off, depress the brake pedal approximately 20 times to exhaust the residual pressure in the system.
2   Wipe clean the area around the pressure line union on the side of the accumulator body (photo). Unscrew the union nut, withdraw the pipe and plug its end to prevent loss of hydraulic oil.
3   Unscrew the damper hose at the in-line pipe-to-hose union just below the power steering pump. Plug both hose ends.
4   Slacken the clamp and detach the return hose at the connection on the end of the accumulator. Plug the hose end.
5   Unscrew the two nuts securing the rear mounting bracket to the body and slacken the nut securing the front mounting to the bracket. Withdraw the accumulator from its mounting and remove it from the engine compartment (photo).
6   Refitting is the reverse sequence to removal, but refer to Chapter 10 and bleed the power steering system on completion. If the pressure accumulator has been renewed, render the old unit safe before discarding by drilling a 3 mm (0.12 in) hole in the accumulator body to release the pressure. Take great care when doing this and always wear safety glasses.

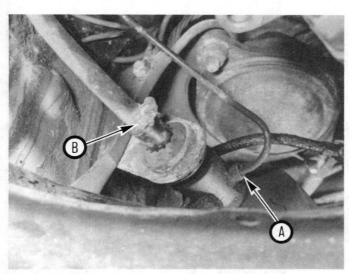

26.2 Pressure accumulator pressure line union (A) and return hose (B)

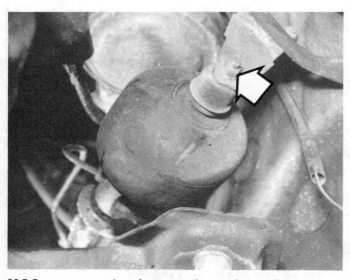

26.5 Pressure accumulator front mounting nut (arrowed)

27 Anti-lock braking system – description and operation

Certain models covered by this manual are equipped with an anti-lock braking system (ABS) as standard or optional equipment. The system can be switched on or off under driver control and is used in conjunction with the normal braking system to provide greater stability, improved steering control and shorter stopping distances under all braking conditions. A brief description of the system operation is as follows.

Each wheel is provided with a wheel speed sensor which monitors the wheel rotational speed. The sensor consists of a magnetic core and coil and is mounted at a predetermined distance from a toothed rotor. The rotors for the front wheels are pressed onto the driveshaft outer constant velocity joints and the rotors for the rear wheels are pressed onto the rear hubs. When each hub turns it alters the magnetic field of the sensor thus inducing an alternating voltage, the frequency of which varies according to wheel speed.

Signals from the wheel speed sensors are sent to an electronic control unit which can accurately determine whether a wheel is accelerating or decelerating in relation to a reference speed. Information from the electronic control unit is sent to the hydraulic modulator which contains four solenoids, each operating one inlet and one exhaust valve for one brake, and all working independently of each other in three distinct phases:

Pressure build-up phase: The solenoid inlet valves are open and brake pressure from the master cylinder is applied directly to the brake calipers.

Constant pressure phase: The solenoid inlet and exhaust valves are closed and brake pressure at the calipers is maintained at a constant level even though master cylinder pressure may increase.

Pressure reduction phase: The solenoid inlet valve is closed to prevent further brake pressure reaching the caliper and, in addition, the exhaust valve is open to reduce existing pressure and release the brake. Fluid is returned to the master cylinder in this phase via the return pump in the hydraulic modulator.

The braking cycle for one wheel is therefore as follows and will be the same for all four wheels, although independently.

Wheel rotational speed is measured by the wheel speed sensors and processed by the electronic control unit. By comparing the signals received from each wheel the control unit can determine a reference speed, and detect any variation from this speed, which would indicate a locking brake. Should a lock-up condition be detected the control unit initiates the constant pressure phase and no further increase in brake pressure is applied to the affected brake. If the lock-up condition is still detected the pressure reduction phase is initiated to allow the wheel to turn. The control unit returns to the constant pressure phase until the wheel rotational speed exceeds a predetermined value then the cycle repeats with the control unit re-initiating the pressure build-up phase. This control cycle is continuously and rapidly repeated until the brake pedal is released or the car comes to a stop.

Additional circuitry within the electronic control unit monitors the functioning of the system and informs the driver of any fault condition by means of a warning light. Should a fault occur, the system switches off allowing normal braking, without ABS, to continue.

28 Anti-lock braking system – precautions

Due to the complex nature of the anti-lock braking system the following precautions must be observed when carrying out maintenance and repair work to cars so equipped.
1   Whenever the battery terminals are disconnected ensure that the terminal clamps are securely tightened when refitting.
2   Disconnect the electronic control unit wiring plug before using any electric welding equipment on the car.
3   Ensure that the battery earth terminal is disconnected before removing the hydraulic modulator.
4   Avoid subjecting the electronic control unit to prolonged high temperatures such as those experienced in a paint spray oven. Maximum acceptable temperatures are 95°C (203°F) for very short periods or 85°C (185°F) for up to two hours.
5   After any general maintenance or simple repair operation such as brake pad renewal, brake disc renewal, handbrake cable adjustment or renewal, or any work not directly involving the ABS components, road

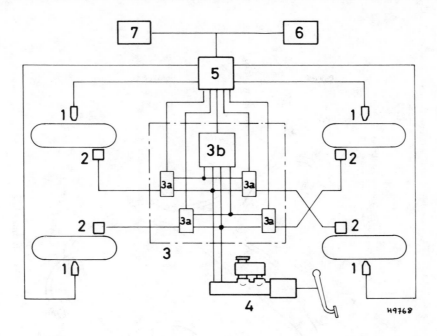

Fig. 9.38 Diagrammatic layout of the anti-lock braking system (Sec 27)

1	Wheel speed sensors	3a	Solenoid valves
2	Brake calipers	3b	Return pump
3	Hydraulic modulator		

4	Brake master cylinder	6	Indicator light
5	Electronic control unit	7	ABS switch

test the car and check that the ABS warning light does not come on when the vehicle reaches a speed of 4 mph (6 kph). If the warning light illuminates there is a fault in the system and the advice of an Audi dealer should be sought.

6   If it is necessary to bleed the brake hydraulic system after a repair operation the system must be bled using a pressure bleeding device (see Section 17). It will also be necessary to have the complete system checked by a suitably equipped Audi dealer if the repair work involved disturbing any of the ABS components.

29 Anti-lock braking system components – removal and refitting

Note: *Before proceeding refer to Section 28*

Hydraulic modulator

1   Disconnect the battery earth terminal.

2   To remove the modulator control relays undo the screw and lift off the plastic cover. Remove the relays by pulling them out of their location. The large relay controls the solenoid valve operation and the small relay controls the return pump operation. Refitting is the reversal of removal.

3   To remove the complete modulator unit remove the relay cover, unscrew the cable clamp and disconnect the modulator wiring. Disconnect the earth lead on the modulator body.

4   Mark each brake pipe and its location as an aid to refitting. Unscrew each brake pipe union, withdraw the pipe and immediately plug its end and the modulator orifice.

5   Undo the modulator mounting nuts and retainers and remove the unit from its location. Do not attempt to dismantle the modulator as it is a sealed unit and no repairs are possible.

6   Refitting is the reverse sequence to removal. Bleed the hydraulic system with reference to Sections 17 and 28.

Electronic control unit

7   Disconnect the battery earth terminal.

8   Remove the rear seat, as described in Chapter 11. The control unit is located under the seat on the left-hand side.

9   Disconnect the control unit wiring plug by depressing the spring tag at the cable end, lift the plug up at the cable end then disengage the tab at the other end.

10 Undo the retaining nuts and withdraw the control unit from its location.

11 Refitting is the reverse sequence to removal, but ensure that the wiring plug engages securely and with an audible click from the spring tag.

Front wheel speed sensor

12 Jack up the front of the car and support it on stands. Remove the appropriate front roadwheel.

13 Using an Allen key, undo the retaining bolt and withdraw the sensor from the front suspension strut.

14 Release the cable grommets from the support clips on the suspension strut and under the wheel arch.

15 From within the engine compartment, release the wiring connector from its holder and separate the connector. The left-hand connector is located just to the rear of the radiator expansion tank, and the right-hand connector is located behind the windscreen washer reservoir.

16 Pull the wiring through to the wheel arch and remove the speed sensor assembly.

17 Refitting is the reverse sequence to removal. When refitting the sensor to the suspension strut carefully push it in as far as it will go so that the tip just touches the rotor on the constant velocity joint. Hold the sensor in this position and tighten the retaining bolt. Ensure that all grommets are located in their support clips.

Rear wheel speed sensor

18 Jack up the rear of the car and support it on stands. Remove the appropriate rear roadwheel.

19 Press the handbrake cable spacer off the rear axle flange to gain access to the sensor.

20 Using an Allen key, undo the retaining bolt and withdraw the sensor from the rear axle flange.

21 Undo the retaining bolts and release the sensor wiring harness from the trailing arm.

22 Remove the rear seat, as described in Chapter 11.

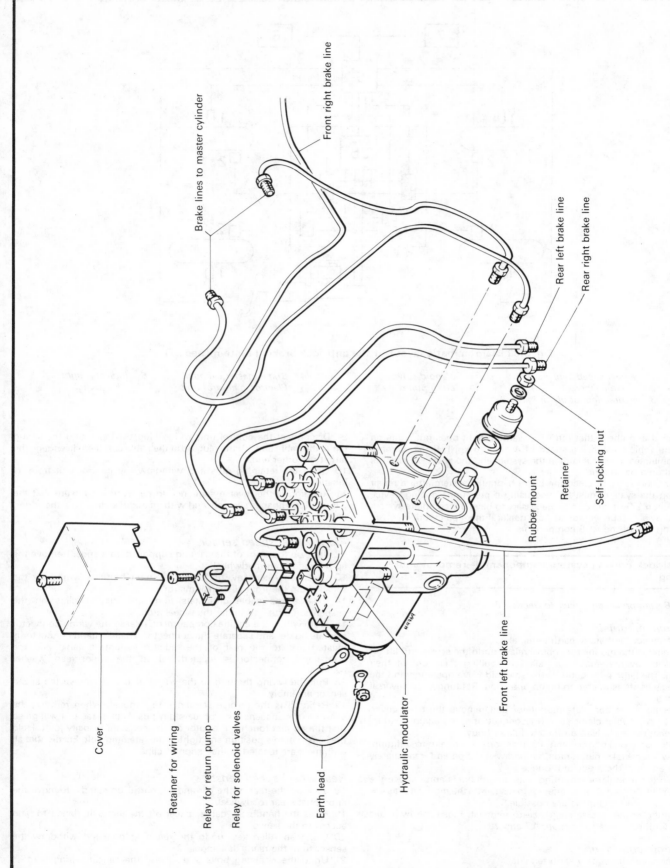

Front right brake line

Brake lines to master cylinder

Rear left brake line

Rear right brake line

Self-locking nut

Retainer

Rubber mount

Front left brake line

Hydraulic modulator

Earth lead

Relay for solenoid valves

Relay for return pump

Retainer for wiring

Cover

Fig. 9.39 Hydraulic modulator and related component details (Sec 29)

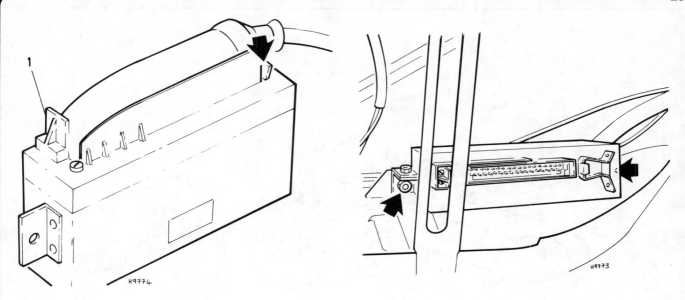

Fig. 9.40 Electronic control unit wiring plug spring tag (arrowed) and locating tab (1) (Sec 29)

Fig. 9.41 Electronic control unit retaining screws – arrowed (Sec 29)

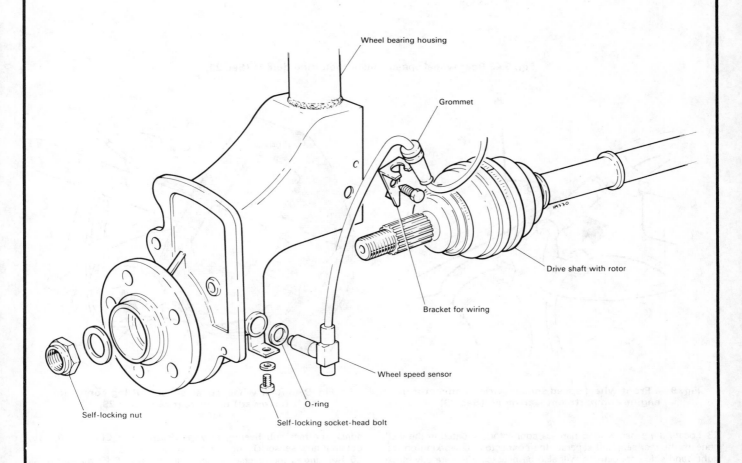

Wheel bearing housing

Grommet

Drive shaft with rotor

Bracket for wiring

Wheel speed sensor

Self-locking nut

O-ring

Self-locking socket-head bolt

Fig. 9.42 Front wheel speed sensor mounting details (Sec 29)

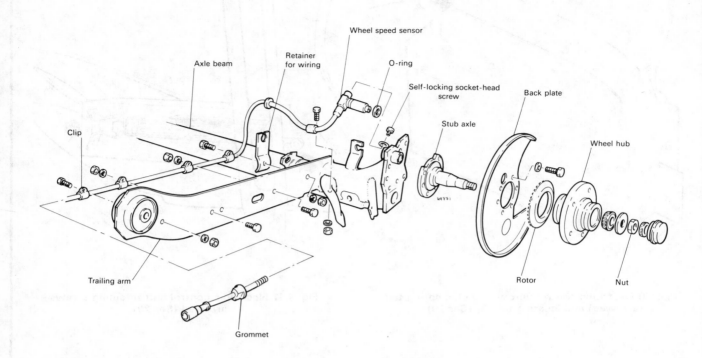

Fig. 9.43 Rear wheel speed sensor mounting details (Sec 29)

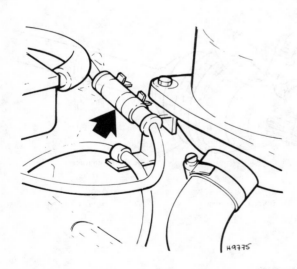

Fig. 9.44 Front wheel speed sensor wiring connector in engine compartment – arrowed (Sec 29)

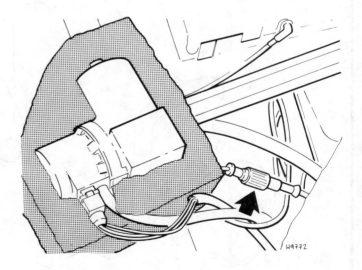

Fig. 9.45 Rear wheel speed sensor wiring connector (arrowed) under rear seat (Sec 29)

23 Locate the sensor wiring harness connectors, situated in the well beneath the rear seat and separate the connectors. If working on the right-hand side connector, it will also be necessary to carefully move aside the underseat padding and the pump assembly for the central door locking system to gain access to the connector.

24 Release the grommets and pull the wiring through the floor then remove the sensor from under the car.

25 Before refitting the wheel speed sensor check and, if necessary,

adjust the rear hub bearing play, as described in Chapter 10. Also obtain a new sensor O-ring seal.

26 Refitting is the reverse sequence to removal. Coat the sensor all round with brake cylinder paste then push it into its location as far as it will go so that the tip just touches the rotor on the rear hub. Hold the sensor in this position and tighten the retaining bolt. Ensure that all wiring clips and grommets are correctly located on the trailing arm and in the floor panel.

Wheel speed sensor rotor

27 The rotors for the front wheel speed sensors are an integral part of the driveshaft outer constant velocity joint and cannot be renewed separately. If the rotor is in any way unserviceable a new outer joint must be fitted (see Chapter 8).

28 To remove the rear wheel speed sensor rotors, refer to Chapter 10 and remove the rear hub assembly.

29 Mount the hub in a vice and knock off the rotor using a punch inserted through the holes in the hub.

30 Press on a new rotor then refit the hub assembly, as described in Chapter 10.

---

30 Fault diagnosis – braking system

Note: *Fault diagnosis on the anti-lock braking system (where fitted) should be entrusted to a suitably equipped Audi dealer due to the need for special gauges and test equipment*

Symptom	Reason(s)
Excessive pedal travel	Rear brake self-adjust mechanism inoperative Air in hydraulic system Faulty master cylinder
Brake pedal feels spongy	Air in hydraulic system Faulty master cylinder
Judder felt through brake pedal or steering wheel when braking	Excessive run-out or distortion of discs or rear drums Brake pads or linings worn Brake backplate or disc caliper loose Wear in suspension or steering components or mountings – see Chapter 10
Excessive pedal pressure required to stop car	Faulty servo unit Wheel cylinder(s) or caliper piston seized Brake pads or brake shoe linings worn or contaminated Brake shoes incorrectly fitted Incorrect grade of pads or linings fitted Primary or secondary hydraulic circuit failure
Brakes pull to one side	Brake pads or linings worn or contaminated Wheel cylinder or caliper piston seized Seized rear brake self-adjust mechanism Brake pads or linings renewed on one side only Tyre, steering or suspension defect – see Chapter 10
Brakes binding	Wheel cylinder or caliper piston seized Handbrake incorrectly adjusted Faulty master cylinder

Chapter 10 Suspension and steering

Refer to Chapter 13 for specifications on 1987 and later models

Contents

Specifications

Front suspension
Type .... Independent, with coil spring struts incorporating telescopic shock absorbers, lower track control arm and anti-roll bar

Rear suspension
Type .... Transverse torsion axle incorporating trailing arms, Panhard rod and coil spring struts with telescopic shock absorbers. Self-levelling facility fitted to certain models

Steering
Type .... Manual or power-assisted rack-and-pinion. Steering damper fitted to manual steering models

Front wheel alignment
Toe setting .... $0° +5'$ (toe-in) $-10'$ (toe-out)
Camber .... $-30' \pm 30'$
Maximum camber difference between sides .... $30'$
Castor:
    Manual steering models .... $-15' \pm 40'$
    Power-assisted steering models without self-levelling
    suspension .... $+50' \pm 40'$
    Power-assisted steering models with self-levelling suspension ...... $+1°5' \pm 40'$
Maximum castor difference between sides .... $1°$

Rear wheel alignment
Camber .... $-40' \pm 30'$
Maximum camber difference between sides .... $30'$
Toe setting at each wheel:
    Up to Chassis No EA 085 288 or EA 082 448 (UK models) or
    EN 096 669 (North American models) .... $+15' \pm 10'$ (toe-in)
    All other models .... $+10' \pm 5'$ (toe-in)

Wheels
Type .... Pressed steel or light alloy
Size .... 5^1/2J x 14, 6J x 14, 6J x 15

Tyres
Size:
    UK models .... 165 SR 14, 185/70 SR 14, 185/70 HR 14, 205/60 VR 15
    North American models .... 185/70 SR 14, 185/65 HR 15, 205/60 HR 15
Pressures .... Refer to handbook or pressure data sticker inside fuel tank flap for
pressures according to model and territory

Torque wrench settings

	Nm	lbf ft
Front suspension		
Strut upper mounting to body	30	22
Strut piston retaining nut	60	44
Shock absorber screw cap	180	133
Suspension balljoint to strut	65	48
Track control arm to subframe	85	63
Subframe mounting to subframe	20	15
Subframe mounting to body	110	81
Anti-roll bar to track control arm	110	81
Rear suspension		
Panhard rod	90	66
Trailing arm to body	95	70
Shock absorber to rear axle	90	66
Shock absorber to body	20	15
Shock absorber upper retaining nut	20	15
Stub axle to rear axle	30	22
Self-levelling suspension linkage nuts	10	7
Self-levelling suspension reservoir	20	15
Steering		
Steering wheel retaining nut	40	30
Flange tube to steering gear pinion	25	18
Steering column clamp to safety bracket	35	26
Steering gear to body	25	18
Damper to steering gear and body	40	30
Tie-rods to steering gear and suspension strut	60	44
Tie-rod adjuster locknuts	40	30
Power-assisted steering pump mounting and adjustment nuts:		
Four-cylinder engine	25	18
Five-cylinder engine	20	15
Power-assisted steering pump pulley nuts (four-cylinder engine)	20	15
Wheels		
Wheel bolts	110	81

1 General description

The front suspension is of independent type, incorporating coil spring struts and lower track control arm. The struts are fitted with telescopic shock absorbers, and both front suspension units are mounted on a subframe. An anti-roll bar is fitted to the track control arms and also provides fore and aft location of each strut assembly.

The rear suspension comprises a transverse torsion axle with trailing arms rubber bushed to the body. The axle is attached to the lower ends of the rear shock absorber which act as struts, since they incorporate mountings for the coil springs. Side-to-side movement of the axle is controlled by a Panhard rod. A self-levelling system is used on certain models which utilizes gas and hydraulic pressure acting on the rear struts to keep the car at the same height irrespective of load.

The steering is of rack and pinion type mounted on the engine compartment bulkhead. The tie-rods are attached centrally to a common bracket which is itself bolted to the steering rack. Power assistance is used on certain models and a steering damper is used on those versions with manual steering.

2 Maintenance and inspection

1 At the intervals given in Routine Maintenance at the beginning of this manual a thorough inspection of all suspension and steering components should be carried out using the following procedure as a guide.

Front suspension and steering
2 Apply the handbrake, jack up the front of the car and support it securely on axle stands.
3 Visually inspect the lower balljoint dust covers and the steering rack and pinion gaiters for splits, chafing, or deterioration. If the balljoint dust covers are damaged they can be renewed separately, as described in Section 7. If the rack-and-pinion gaiters require attention, refer to Section 23.
4 Grasp the roadwheel at the 12 o'clock and 6 o'clock positions and try to rock it. Very slight free play may be felt, but if the movement is appreciable further investigation is necessary to determine the source. Continue rocking the wheel while an assistant depresses the footbrake. If the movement is now eliminated or significantly reduced, it is likely that the hub bearings are at fault. If the free play is still evident with the footbrake depressed, then there is wear in the suspension joints or mountings. Pay close attention to the lower balljoint and track control arm mounting bushes. Renew any worn components, as described in the appropriate Sections of this Chapter.
5 Now grasp the wheel at the 9 o'clock and 3 o'clock positions and try to rock it as before. Any movement felt now may again be caused by wear in the hub bearings or the steering tie-rod inner or outer balljoints. If the movement is eliminated with the footbrake depressed the tie-rod joints are suspect. Removal and refitting of the tie-rod assemblies is described in Section 20.
6 Using a large screwdriver or flat bar check for wear in the anti-roll bar mountings and track control arm mountings by carefully levering against these components. Some movement is to be expected, as the mountings are made of rubber, but excessive wear should be obvious. Renew any bushes that are worn.

7 With the car standing on its wheels, have an assistant turn the steering wheel back and forth about one eighth of a turn each way. There should be no lost movement whatever between the steering wheel and roadwheels. If this is not the case, closely observe the joints and mountings previously described, but in addition check the steering column joints for wear and also the rack-and-pinion steering gear itself. Any wear should be visually apparent and must be rectified, as described in the appropriate Sections of this Chapter.

8 On models equipped with power-assisted steering, check the hydraulic oil level in the reservoir. Carry out this check with the vehicle unladen and with the engine running and the steering in the straight-ahead position. If necessary add the specified hydraulic oil, to bring the level up to the MAX mark (photo). Check the condition of the power steering pump drivebelt and renew it or adjust its tension, where necessary, as described in Section 27.

Rear suspension

9 Chock the front wheels, jack up the rear of the car and support it securely on axle stands.

10 Visually inspect the rear suspension components, attachments and linkages for any visible signs of wear or damage.

11 Grasp the roadwheel at the 12 o'clock and 6 o'clock positions and try to rock it. Any excess movement here indicates maladjusted hub bearings which should be checked, as described in Section 12.

Wheels and tyres

12 Carefully inspect each tyre, including the spare, for signs of uneven wear, lumps, bulges or damage to the sidewalls or tread face. Refer to Section 30 for further details.

13 Check the condition of the wheel rims for distortion, damage and excessive run-out. Also make sure that the balance weights are secure with no obvious signs that any are missing. Check the torque of the wheel bolts and check the tyre pressures.

Shock absorbers

14 Check for any signs of fluid leakage around the shock absorber body or from the rubber boot around the piston rod. Should any serious fluid leak be noticed the shock absorber is defective internally and renewal is necessary.

15 The efficiency of the shock absorber may be checked by bouncing the car at each corner. Generally speaking the body will return to its normal position and stop after being depressed. If it rises and returns on a rebound, the shock absorber is probably suspect. Examine also the shock absorber upper and lower mountings for any sign of wear. Renewal procedures are contained in Sections 4 and 10.

---

3 Front suspension strut – removal and refitting

1 Remove the wheel trim, then unscrew the driveshaft retaining nut. This is tightened to a very high torque and no attempt to loosen it must be made unless the full weight of the car is on its roadwheels.

2 Loosen the four roadwheel retaining bolts.

3 Jack up the front of the car and securely support it on stands. Remove the roadwheel.

4 Remove the brake caliper and carrier bracket, with reference to Chapter 9, but do not disconnect the hydraulic hose. Support the caliper without straining the hose.

5 Detach the brake pad wear warning light wire from the strut (photo) and, where fitted, the wheel speed sensor and wiring for the anti-lock braking system (see Chapter 9).

6 Unscrew and remove the suspension balljoint clamp bolt and nut (photo) noting that its head faces rearwards.

7 Using a balljoint separator tool, as described in Section 20, unscrew the nut and disconnect the tie-rod end from the suspension strut.

8 Unscrew the driveshaft nut then lever the track control arm down to release the balljoint from the strut.

9 Attach a suitable puller to the front hub using the roadwheel retaining bolts and press the driveshaft out of the hub assembly.

10 From within the engine compartment, lift off the plastic cover over the strut upper mounting (photo).

11 Support the suspension strut from below and unscrew the three outer nuts securing the strut upper mounting to the body (photo).

12 Lower the strut and remove it from under the wheel arch.

2.8A Fill the reservoir with hydraulic oil up to the MAX mark (arrowed) ...

2.8B ... through the reservoir filler neck

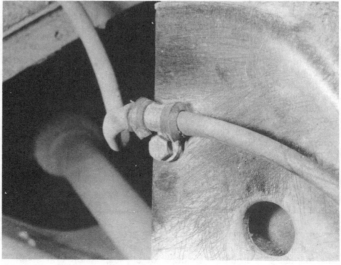

3.5 Brake pad warning light wire attachment on front strut

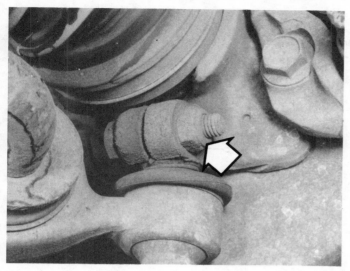

3.6 Remove the suspension balljoint clamp bolt and nut (arrowed)

Fig. 10.1 Levering the track control arm down to release the balljoint from the strut (Sec 3)

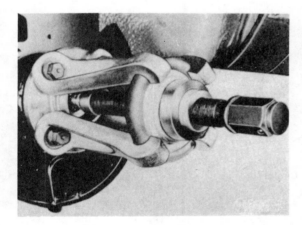

Fig. 10.2 Using a puller to release the driveshaft from the hub (Sec 3)

3.10 Lift off the cover over the strut upper mounting ...

13 Refitting is the reverse sequence to removal. Refer to Chapter 8 when installing the driveshaft, and Chapter 9 when installing the brake caliper. Tighten all nuts and bolts to the specified torque. If the strut has been dismantled the front camber angle must be checked, as described in Section 29.

4 Front suspension strut – dismantling and reassembly

1 Do not attempt to dismantle the suspension strut unless a spring compressor has been fitted over the coils of the spring. If such a tool is not available take the strut to a suitably equipped garage for dismantling.
2 With the spring compressor in place on the spring, mount the strut assembly in a vice.
3 Compress the spring until the upper spring retainer is free of tension then remove the nut and washer from the top of the piston.
4 Pull off the bearing plate, complete with strut bearing, upper spring retainer, protective ring and damping ring. **Do not** loosen the nuts

3.11 ... then unscrew the strut upper mounting retaining nuts (arrowed)

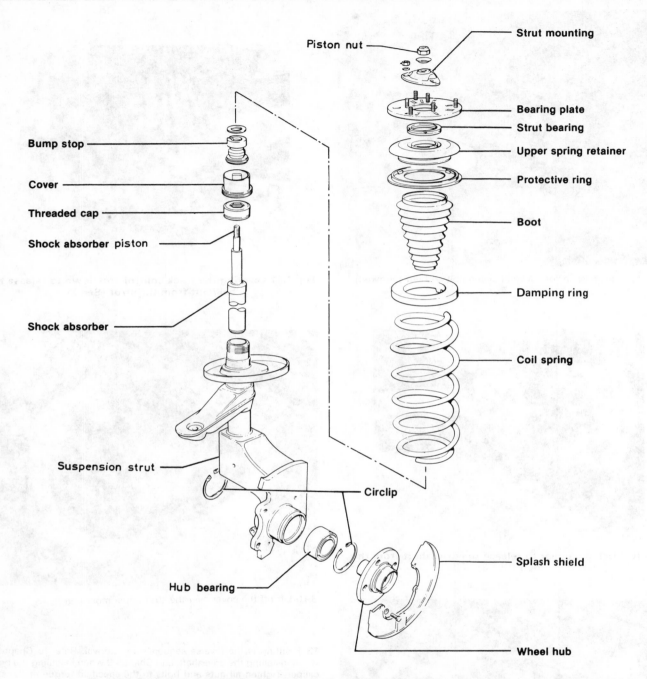

Piston nut

Strut mounting

Bump stop

Bearing plate

Strut bearing

Cover

Upper spring retainer

Threaded cap

Protective ring

Shock absorber piston

Boot

Shock absorber

Damping ring

Coil spring

Suspension strut

Circlip

Splash shield

Hub bearing

Wheel hub

Fig. 10.3 Exploded view of the front suspension strut and hub bearings (Secs 3, 4 and 5)

securing the strut mounting to the bearing plate, otherwise the camber setting will be lost.

5   With the compressor still in place, remove the spring, boot and cover, followed by the bump stop.

6   Unscrew and remove the screw cap which retains the shock absorber in the suspension strut and pull out the shock absorber.

7   With the shock absorber removed, examine it for oil leaks and obvious signs of damage. Hold the shock absorber vertically and check its operation by pulling the piston rod out fully, then push it in fully by hand several times. Resistance should be even and the movement smooth over the entire stroke. If a shock absorber has not been in use for a long time, it may require pumping up and down several times before it becomes effective.

8   If there has been excessive leakage of oil from the shock absorber it

may be ineffective on the rebound stroke, but if there is only a slight oil seepage it may be refitted.

9   Clean out the bore of the suspension strut before fitting the shock absorber, so that the shock absorber slides in easily. Do not drive the shock absorber into the strut.

10 Refit the screw cap and tighten to the specified torque.

11 Reassemble the spring and mounting using a reversal of the dismantling procedure. If a new damping ring is being fitted note that the underside of the ring has either one, two or three projections moulded in which denote the ring thickness (Fig. 10.4). Ensure that the new ring has the same number of projections as the old one unless the spring has been changed, or there is a difference in ride height between the right and left-hand sides of the car which is being corrected.

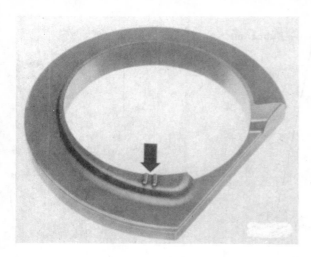

Fig. 10.4 Damping ring identification projections – arrowed (Sec 4)

Fig. 10.5 Using a puller to remove the hub bearing inner race (Sec 5)

5 Front hub bearings – removal and refitting

1 Remove the front suspension strut, as described in Section 3.
2 Remove the brake disc from the hub.
3 Remove the screws and withdraw the splash guard.
4 Support the suspension strut with the hub facing downward, and press or drive out the hub using a suitable mandrel. The bearing inner race will remain on the hub, and therefore, once removed, it is not possible to re-use the bearing. Use a puller to remove the inner race from the hub.
5 Extract the circlips, then, while supporting the suspension strut press or drive out the bearing, using a mandrel on the outer race.
6 Clean the recess in the housing, then smear it with a little general purpose grease.
7 Fit the outer circlip, then support the strut and press or drive in the new bearing, using a metal tube *on the outer race only*.
8 Fit the inner circlip making sure that it is correctly seated.
9 Position the hub with its bearing shoulder facing upward, then press or drive on the bearing and housing, using a metal tube *on the inner race only*.

10 Refit the splash guard and brake disc, then refit the front suspension strut, as described in Section 3.

6 Anti-roll bar – removal and refitting

1 If the anti-roll bar is distorted, or damaged, it must not be straightened, but a new one must be fitted.
2 Remove the two bolts from each of the two brackets which secure the anti-roll bar to the subframe and remove the brackets (photo).
3 Remove the nut and washer from each end of the anti-roll bar (photo).

6.2 Anti-roll bar bracket attachments (arrowed) ...

6.3 ... and end mounting at track control arm (arrowed)

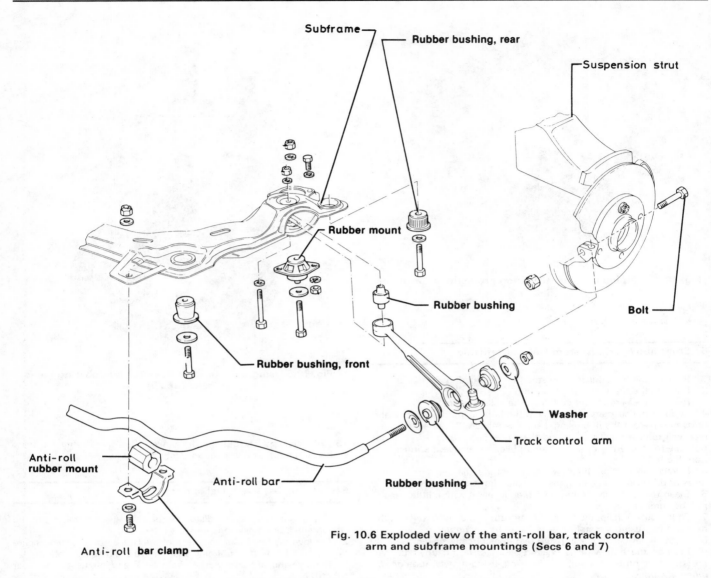

Fig. 10.6 Exploded view of the anti-roll bar, track control arm and subframe mountings (Secs 6 and 7)

4   Bounce the front suspension up and down with the vehicle standing on its wheels, at the same time pulling the anti-roll bar out of the bushes on the track control arms.

5   Refitting is the reverse of removal, The front suspension should be bounced up and down while inserting the anti-roll bar into the bushes of the track control arms. Tighten the mountings to the specified torque.

7   Front track control arm – removal and refitting

1   Remove the anti-roll bar, as described in Section 6.

2   Jack up the front of the car and support it on stands. Remove the appropriate front roadwheel.

3   Unscrew and remove the suspension balljoint clamp bolt and nut, noting that the bolt head faces rearwards.

4   Lever the track control arm down to release the balljoint from the suspension strut.

5   Undo and remove the inner mounting nut and bolt, then withdraw the track control arm from the subframe.

6   To renew the inner mounting rubber bush, press the bush out using suitable mandrels and press in a new bush until flush. The outer balljoint is an integral part of the track control arm and if worn a new arm must be obtained. The dust cover may, however, be obtained separately.

7   Refitting is the reverse sequence to removal, but tighten all nuts and bolts to the specified torque. Refit the anti-roll bar, as described in Section 6.

8   Rear axle – removal and refitting

1   Jack up the rear of the car and support it with axle stands positioned beneath the underbody. Chock the front wheels and remove the rear wheels.

2   Remove the brake master cylinder filler cap, place a piece of polythene over the reservoir filler neck and secure the polythene with an elastic band. This will minimise brake fluid loss during subsequent operations.

3   Slacken the handbrake cable adjusting nut and slip the two cable ends off the compensator.

4   Prise the handbrake cable guide bushes from the underbody brackets and remove the cables from the rear brackets.

5   Unhook the brake pressure regulator spring from the rear axle.

6   Disconnect both rear flexible brake hoses at their unions with the rigid brake pipes. Plug the pipes and hoses after disconnection.

7   On cars fitted with an anti-lock braking system, remove the rear wheel speed sensors and wiring from the rear axle and trailing arms, as described in Chapter 9.

8   On cars equipped with self-levelling suspension, disconnect the regulator valve linkage at the rear axle.

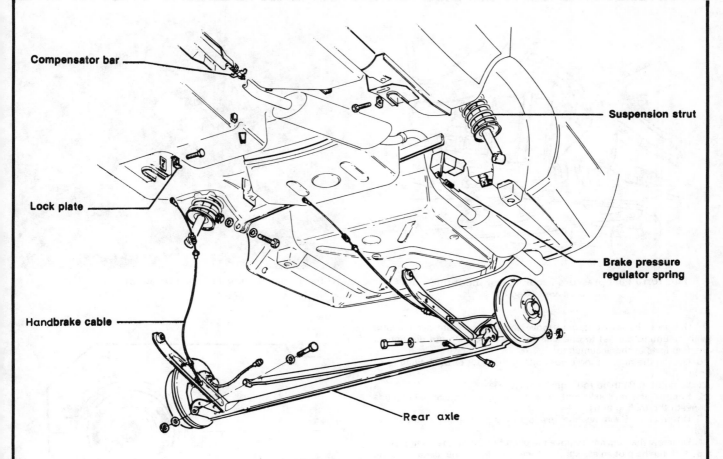

Compensator bar

Suspension strut

Lock plate

Brake pressure
regulator spring

Handbrake cable

Rear axle

Fig. 10.7 Rear axle removal details (Sec 8)

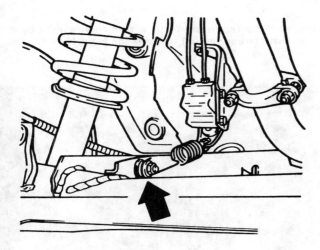

Fig. 10.8 Detach the brake pressure regulator spring
(arrowed) at the rear axle (Sec 8)

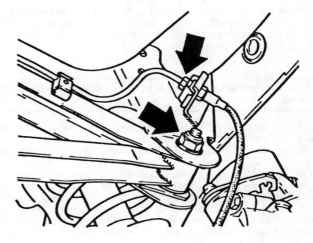

Fig. 10.9 Brake pipe-to-hose union and Panhard rod
mounting – arrowed (Sec 8)

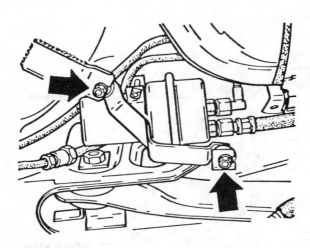

Fig. 10.10 Fuel pressure accumulator mounting nuts –
arrowed (Sec 8)

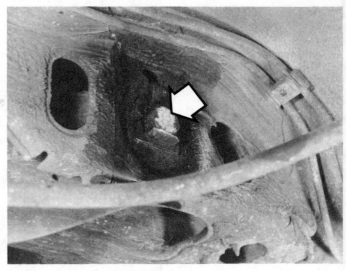

8.10 Trailing arm pivot bolt location (arrowed)

9   Unscrew the two nuts and move the fuel pressure accumulator
with mounting bracket to one side (where fitted). Do not disconnect
the fuel lines at the accumulator.
10 Loosen the nuts on the pivot bolts at the front of the trailing arms
(photo).
11 Unbolt the Panhard rod from the rear axle.
12 Support the rear axle with a trolley jack, and place axle stands
beneath the trailing arms.
13 Unscrew and remove the rear shock absorber lower mounting
bolts.
14 Unscrew the nuts and remove the pivot bolts from the trailing arms.
15 With the help of an assistant, if necessary, lower the rear axle to the
ground.
16 If necessary, remove the stub axles, also remove the brake lines and
handbrake cables, if required. The pivot bushes may be renewed using
a long bolt and nut, metal tube, and packing washers, but make sure
that the bush gaps are in line with the trailing arms and with the larger
bush gap at the front, then press the bushes in flush.
17 Refitting is a reversal of removal, but delay tightening the rear axle,
shock absorber and Panhard rod mounting bolts until the weight of the
car is on the suspension. Bleed the hydraulic system and adjust the
handbrake cable, as described in Chapter 9.

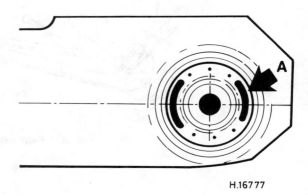

H.16777

Fig. 10.11 Correct positioning of trailing arm pivot bush
with larger gap (A) towards the front (Sec 8)

9   Rear suspension strut/shock absorber – removal and refitting

1   Jack up the rear of the car and support it on stands. Chock the front
wheels and remove the appropriate rear wheel.
2   Place a jack beneath the rear axle on the side being worked on and
just take the weight of the axle.
3   On cars with self-levelling suspension locate the three-way
connector in the hydraulic pressure line to the rear suspension
reservoirs (Fig. 10.20). Attach a suitable hose to the bleed screw on
the three-way connector and place the other end of the hose in a
container. Open the bleed screw to release the pressure then close it
again and remove the hose. Disconnect the hydraulic pipe union at the
strut unit.
4   Unscrew the nut and remove the bolt securing the shock absorber
lower mounting (photo).
5   Undo the three upper mounting nuts and remove the suspension
strut/shock absorber from under the wheel arch (photo).
6   Refitting is the reverse sequence to removal, but tighten all nuts
and bolts to the specified torque. On cars with self-levelling
suspension top up the power steering reservoir to the MAX mark with
the engine running and the steering in the straight-ahead position. If,
however, the reservoir was allowed to run dry when the strut was
removed, refer to Section 25 for filling and bleeding procedures.

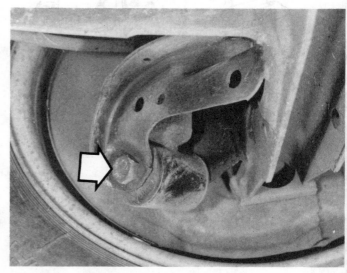

9.4 Strut/shock absorber lower mounting (arrowed)

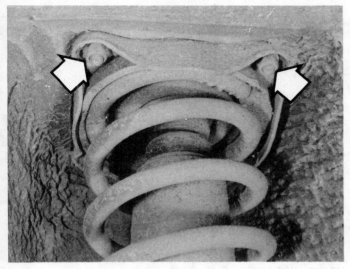

9.5 Two of the strut/shock absorber upper mounting nuts (arrowed)

10 Rear suspension strut/shock absorber – dismantling and reassembly

1   Do not attempt to dismantle the suspension strut unless a spring compressor has been fitted over the coils of the spring. If such a tool is not available take the strut to a suitably equipped garage for dismantling.

2   With the spring compressor in place on the spring, mount the strut assembly in a vice.

3   Compress the spring until the upper spring retainer is free of tension then hold the piston rod and unscrew the upper self-locking retaining nut.

4   Withdraw the rubber bearing, upper spring retainer and damper ring.

5   On cars with self-levelling suspension pull the hydraulic connector off the piston rod.

6   Withdraw the spring, with the compressor still in place, followed by the bump stop and sleeve, protection cap and lower spring retainer.

7   With the shock absorber removed, examine it for oil leaks and obvious signs of damage. Hold the shock absorber vertically and check its operation by pulling the piston rod out fully, then push it in fully by hand several times. Resistance should be even and the movement smooth over the entire stroke. If a shock absorber has not been in use

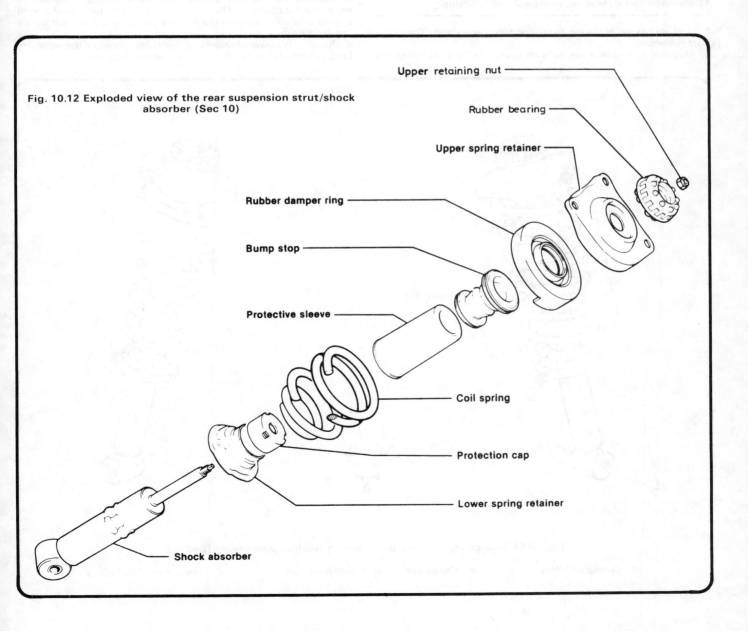

Fig. 10.12 Exploded view of the rear suspension strut/shock absorber (Sec 10)

Upper retaining nut

Rubber bearing

Upper spring retainer

Rubber damper ring

Bump stop

Protective sleeve

Coil spring

Protection cap

Lower spring retainer

Shock absorber

for a long time, it may require pumping up and down several times before it becomes effective.

8   If there has been excessive leakage of oil from the shock absorber it may be ineffective on the rebound stroke, but if there is only a slight oil seepage, it may be refitted. Defective shock absorbers normally make a rumbling sound when the car is driven and this can also be used as a guide to the serviceability of the unit.

9   Obtain new parts, as necessary, then reassemble the strut using the reverse sequence to dismantling with regard to the following.

10 If a new rubber damper ring is being fitted note that the underside of the ring may or may not have a small moulded in projection which identifies the thickness of the ring. Rings with a projection are thicker than those without, and it is necessary to obtain replacements of similar thickness (Fig. 10.13).

11 Note the fitted positions of the coil spring and upper spring retainer when reassembling, as shown in Fig. 10.14.

12 On cars with self-levelling suspension, push the hydraulic connector onto the piston rod so that the threaded connection faces the hole in the upper spring retainer. Do not turn the connector once it is in place on the piston rod.

13 Apply talcum powder to the damper ring before fitting and tighten a new upper self-locking retaining nut to the specified torque.

---

11 Panhard rod – removal, overhaul and refitting

1   Jack up the rear of the car and support it on axle stands. Chock the front wheels.

2   Unscrew and remove the bolts attaching the Panhard rod to the

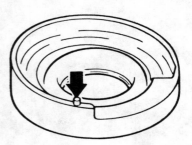

Fig. 10.13 Rubber damping ring identification projection – arrowed (Sec 10)

underbody and rear axle, noting which way round the bolts are fitted (photos). Withdraw the Panhard rod.

3   Examine the rod and bushes for damage and deterioration. If necessary, the bushes can be renewed, using a long bolt together with a metal tube and washers – dip the new bushes in soapy water before installing them.

4   Refitting is a reversal of removal, but delay tightening the mounting bolts until the weight of the car is on the suspension.

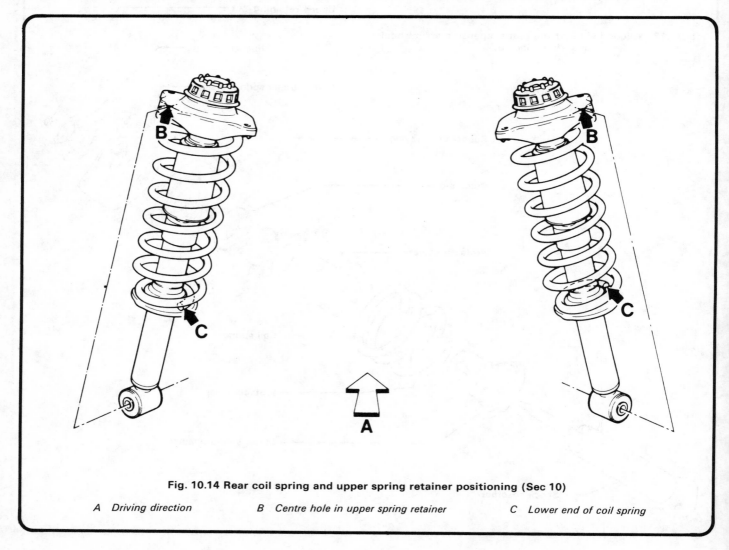

Fig. 10.14 Rear coil spring and upper spring retainer positioning (Sec 10)

A   Driving direction   B   Centre hole in upper spring retainer   C   Lower end of coil spring

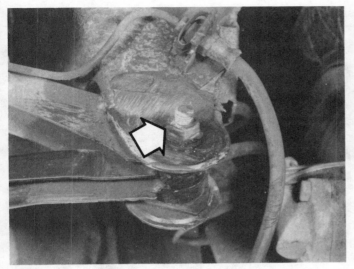

11.2A Panhard rod to body mounting (arrowed) ...

11.2B ... and attachment to rear axle (arrowed)

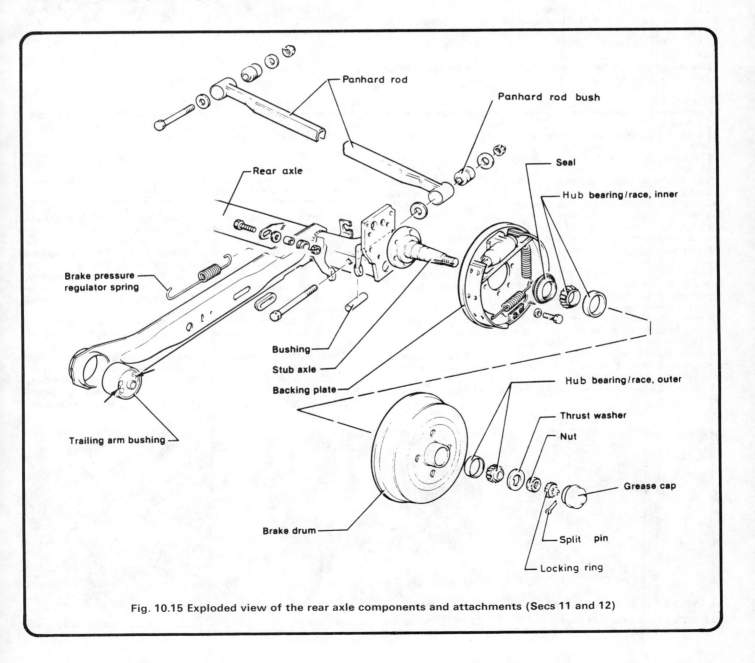

Fig. 10.15 Exploded view of the rear axle components and attachments (Secs 11 and 12)

12 Rear hub bearings – removal, refitting and adjustment

1   Chock the front wheels, then jack up the rear of the car and support it on stands. Remove the appropriate rear roadwheel and release the handbrake.

Rear drum brake models

2   Remove the cap from the centre of the brake drum by tapping it on alternate sides with a screwdriver or blunt chisel.
3   Extract the split pin and remove the locking ring.
4   Unscrew the nut and remove the thrust washer.
5   Withdraw the brake drum, making sure that the outer bearing does not fall out. If the brake drum binds on the shoes, insert a small screwdriver through a wheel bolt hole and lever up the wedged key in order to release the shoes – refer to Chapter 9, if necessary.

Rear disc brake models

6   Remove the brake caliper and carrier bracket, with reference to Chapter 9, but do not disconnect the hydraulic hose. Support the caliper without straining the hose.
7   Withdraw the brake disc from the hub.
8   Remove the cap from the centre of the hub by tapping it on alternate sides with a screwdriver or blunt chisel (photo).
9   Extract the split pin and remove the locking ring (photo).
10   Unscrew the nut and remove the thrust washer.
11   Withdraw the hub, making sure that the outer bearing does not fall out.

All models

12   Remove the outer bearing inner race and rollers from the brake drum/hub.
13   Lever the oil seal from the inner side of the brake drum/hub and withdraw the inner bearing inner race and rollers.
14   Using a soft metal drift, drive the outer races from each side of the brake drum/hub.
15   Clean the bearings and brake drum/hub with paraffin, and also wipe the stub axle clean. Examine the tapered rollers, inner and outer races, brake drum/hub, and stub axle for wear and damage. If the bearing surfaces are pitted, renew them. Obtain a new oil seal.
16   Pack the bearing cages and tapered rollers with a lithium based grease, and also pack the grease into the brake drum/hub inner cavity.
17   Using a length of metal tube, drive the outer races fully into the brake drum/hub.
18   Insert the inner bearing inner race and rollers, then locate the oil seal with the sealing lip facing inwards, and drive it in with a block of wood until flush. Smear a little grease on the oil seal lip then wipe clean the outer face of the seal.
19   Locate the brake drum/hub on the stub axle and fit the outer wheel bearing, followed by the thrust washer and nut (photo).
20   Tighten the nut firmly while turning the drum/hub, then back off the nut until the thrust washer can *just* be moved by pressing on it with a screwdriver. Do not lever or twist the screwdriver in an attempt to move the thrust washer (photo).
21   Fit the locking ring without moving the nut, and install a new split pin.

12.8 Remove the cap from the centre of the hub ...

22   Tap the grease cap onto the drum/hub.
23   Where applicable refit the disc followed by the caliper assembly, with reference to Chapter 9.
24   Refit the roadwheel and lower the car to the ground.

13 Self-levelling suspension – general description

The self-levelling system is hydraulically operated and keeps the rear of the car at a constant ride height irrespective of load.

The power steering pump is used to provide hydraulic pressure to a regulator valve which controls the pressure applied to the two rear suspension strut units. The struts perform the same function as shock absorbers, but with the addition of the variable ride height capability. The regulator valve is connected to the rear axle by an adjustable linkage and a gas charged suspension reservoir is provided between the regulator valve and each strut unit.

As the load on the rear axle varies the hydraulic pressure in the strut units is increased, or decreased, thus raising or lowering the rear of the car.

The hydraulic operation of the system is such that pressure gauges and special test equipment are required when undertaking most repair, overhaul or fault diagnosis operations. Apart from the procedures described in the following Sections, all other repair operations should be entrusted to an Audi dealer suitably equipped to carry out the work.

12.9 ... then extract the split pin and locking ring

12.19 Fitting the rear hub outer bearing

12.20 Checking the hub bearing adjustment

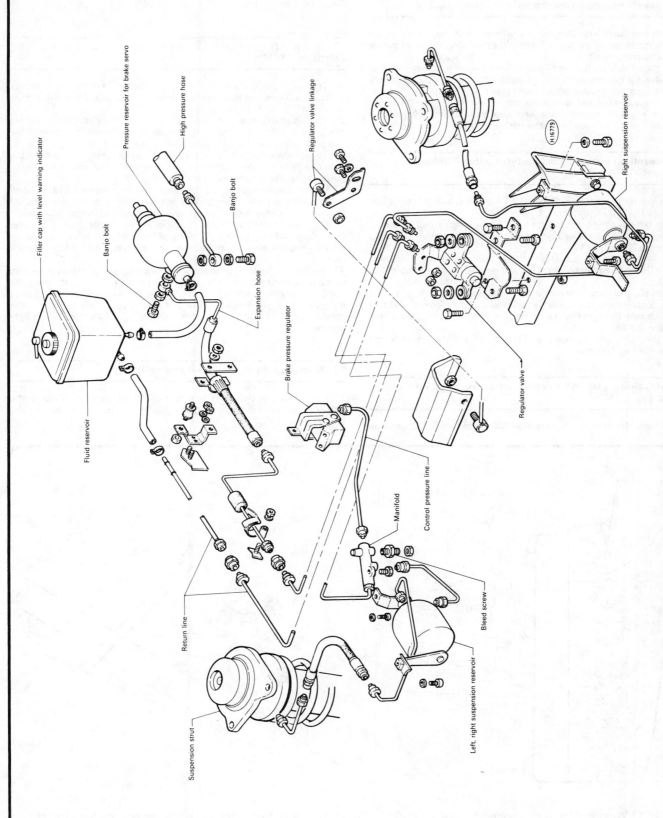

Filler cap with level warning indicator

Pressure reservoir for brake servo

High pressure hose

Banjo bolt

Banjo bolt

Regulator valve linkage

Right suspension reservoir

H16779

Expansion hose

Brake pressure regulator

Fluid reservoir

Regulator valve

Manifold

Control pressure line

Return line

Bleed screw

Suspension strut

Left, right suspension reservoir

Fig. 10.16 Exploded view of the self-levelling suspension components and layout (Secs 13 to 17)

14 Self-levelling suspension regulator valve – testing

1   With the vehicle standing on its wheels, and with the engine running at idling speed, measure the height above the ground of the sill at the rear jacking point.
2   Load the vehicle by having two people sit on the rear seat and after waiting about a minute so that the system has time to operate, check the height from the ground at the same point.
3   Unload the vehicle and, after allowing the same time interval, check the height again to see that the levelling system has lowered the suspension system to counteract the rise caused by unloading.

15 Self-levelling suspension regulator valve – linkage adjustment

1   Cut two wooden blocks 309 mm (12.17 in) long from a piece of 50 x 50 mm (2.0 x 2.0 in) timber.
2   If possible have the vehicle over a pit, or on ramps to make access to the regulator valve easier and place the blocks at the measuring points shown in Fig. 10.17.
3   Load the luggage compartment so that the measuring points only just touch the ends of the blocks. This will require a load of about 100 kg (220 lb).
4   Loosen the two clamp bolts on the regulator linkage (Fig. 10.18) and then set the regulator valve by pushing a short piece of welding rod, or thick wire through the hole in the arm and into the locating hole on the valve body.
5   With the valve set, tighten the clamp bolts and then remove the wire from the locating hole.

16 Self-levelling suspension strut units – removal and refitting

1   Apart from the hydraulic connection the procedure is the same as

for conventional suspension and the procedures are covered in Sections 9 and 10, but refer to Fig. 10.19.

17 Self-levelling suspension reservoirs – removal and refitting

1   The suspension reservoirs are gas pressurised and a loss of gas pressure will result in heavy knocks from the rear axle when the vehicle is driven.
2   Testing of the reservoirs is carried out with them in position on the car, but it is not a job which can be done by the home mechanic. If the gas pressure is low the reservoir must be renewed.
3   To replace a reservoir which is known to be defective, remove the dust cap from the bleed screw on the pipe connector and fit a piece of plastic tube over the screw (Fig. 10.20).
4   With the open end of the tube in a jar to catch the expelled oil, open the bleed screw until the residual pressure has been released and oil flow ceases. Close the screw, remove the pipe and fit the dust cap.
5   Disconnect the two hydraulic pipes from the reservoir and cover their open ends to prevent the entry of dirt and loss of oil.
6   Remove the two mounting nuts and washers and lift the reservoir clear.
7   Refitting is the reverse sequence to removal, but fill the system with hydraulic oil using the procedure described in Section 25. If a reservoir has been renewed, render the old unit safe before discarding by drilling a 3 mm (0.12 in) diameter hole in the reservoir body to release the residual pressure. Take care when doing this and always wear safety glasses.

18 Steering wheel – removal and refitting

1   Pull the horn bar from the centre of the steering wheel – the retainers are quite strong and quite an effort is required to release the bar (photo).

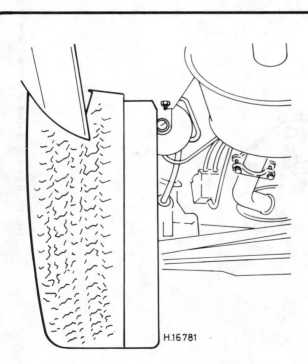

Fig. 10.17 Wooden blocks positioned for self-levelling suspension regulator valve linkage adjustment (Sec 15)

Fig. 10.18 Regulator valve linkage adjustment (Sec 15)

Linkage clamp bolts and wire rod in locating hole arrowed

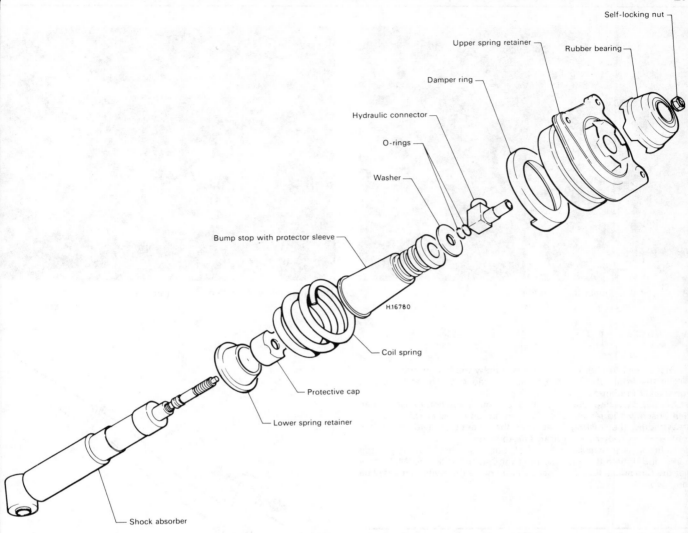

Self-locking nut

Upper spring retainer

Rubber bearing

Damper ring

Hydraulic connector

O-rings

Washer

Bump stop with protector sleeve

H.16780

Coil spring

Protective cap

Lower spring retainer

Shock absorber

Fig. 10.19 Exploded view of the self-levelling suspension strut (Sec 16)

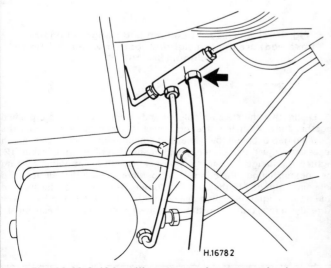

H.16782

Fig. 10.20 Self-levelling suspension reservoir pipe
connector (arrowed) with hose attached to bleed screw
(Sec 17)

18.1 Pull the horn bar from the centre of the steering wheel ...

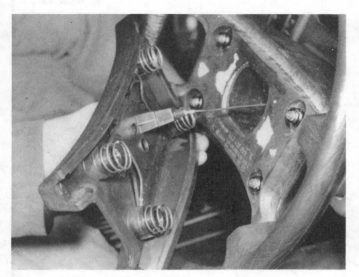

18.2 ... and disconnect the horn wiring

18.4 Steering wheel retaining nut (arrowed)

2   Disconnect the horn wiring and withdraw the bar (photo).
3   Set the front wheel in the straight-ahead position, and the turn signal lever in neutral.
4   Mark the steering wheel and inner column in relation to each other, then unscrew and remove the retaining nut and washer (photo).
5   Withdraw the steering wheel from the inner column splines. If it is tight, ease it off by rocking from side to side.
6   Refitting is a reversal of removal, but align the previously made marks, and tighten the retaining nut to the specified torque. Make sure that the turn signal lever is in neutral, otherwise the switch arm may be damaged.

19 Steering column – removal, overhaul and refitting

1   Disconnect the battery negative terminal.
2   Remove the steering wheel, as described in Section 18, then refer to Chapter 12 and remove the steering column combination switch and the instrument panel.
3   Where necessary, remove the parcel shelf and air duct below the facia to gain access to the steering column/flange tube connection.
4   Slacken the clamp securing the flange tube to the steering gear pinion and move the flange tube upwards to separate it from the steering column.
5   Remove the shear-bolt securing the steering column lock/ignition switch by drilling off the head and unscrewing the bolt with a stud remover tool. Access is just possible through the instrument panel aperture. Pull the lock/ignition switch housing out of the steering column.
6   Undo the nuts and remove the bolts securing the steering column clamps to the safety bracket.
7   Withdraw the column tube, column clamp and steering column upwards and remove it from the car.
8   Pull the column out of the column tube and withdraw the tube from the clamp.
9   Examine the components for wear, damage or distortion – paying particular attention to the bushes at the base of the steering column and the support bush inside the column tube. The bushes at the base of the column can be removed and refitted by hand. If the column tube requires renewal, tubes of suitable diameter can be used to tap out the bush and fit a new one. Ensure that the bush is flush with the end of the column tube.
10   Reassembly and refitting is the reversal of the foregoing procedures but note the following.

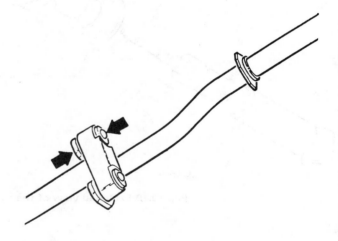

Fig. 10.21 Ensure that column and flange tube joint (arrowed) are pushed tightly together when refitting column (Sec 19)

11   Ensure that the steering column and flange tube joint are pushed together fully. With the steering wheel in place make sure that the specified gap between the wheel and combination switch exists and if necessary adjust the switch position, as described in Chapter 12. Tighten the flange tube-to-steering gear pinion clamp while holding the column/flange tube connection together. Ensure that all nuts and bolts are tightened to the specified torque. In the case of the steering column lock/ignition switch make sure that the switch and lock work correctly before tightening the new shear-bolt until the head breaks off.

20 Tie-rod – removal and refitting

1   Apply the handbrake, jack up the front of the car, and support it on axle stands. Remove the roadwheel.

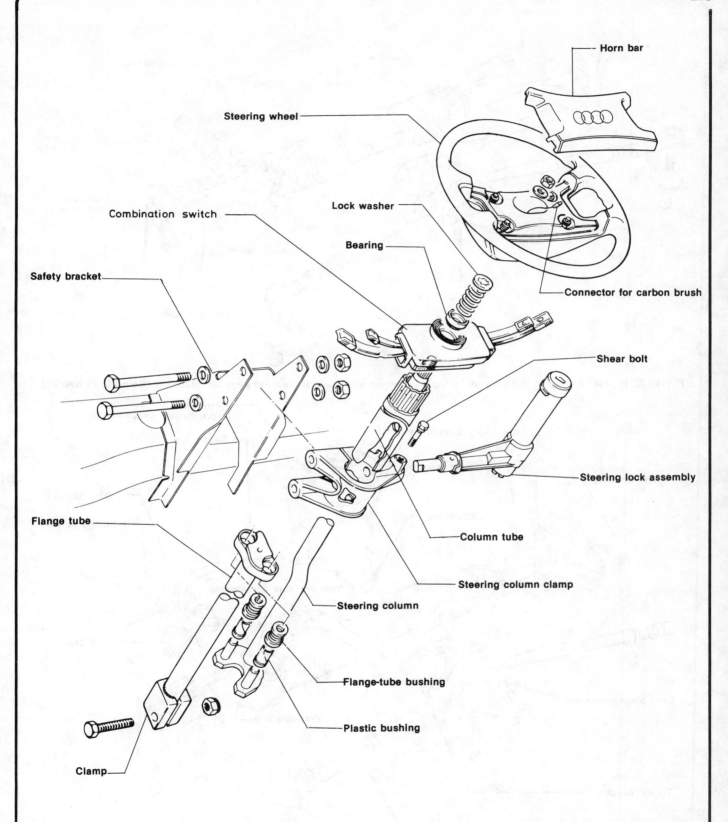

Horn bar

Steering wheel

Combination switch

Lock washer

Bearing

Safety bracket

Connector for carbon brush

Shear bolt

Steering lock assembly

Column tube

Steering column clamp

Flange tube

Steering column

Flange-tube bushing

Plastic bushing

Clamp

Fig. 10.22 Exploded view of the steering column assembly (Sec 19)

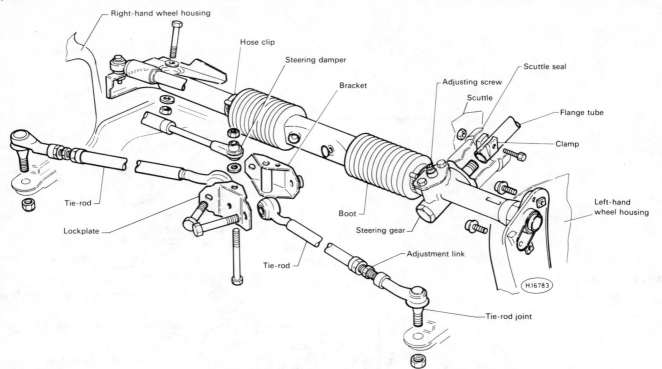

Fig. 10.23 Exploded view of the tie-rods, steering damper and manual steering gear attachments (Secs 20, 21 and 22)

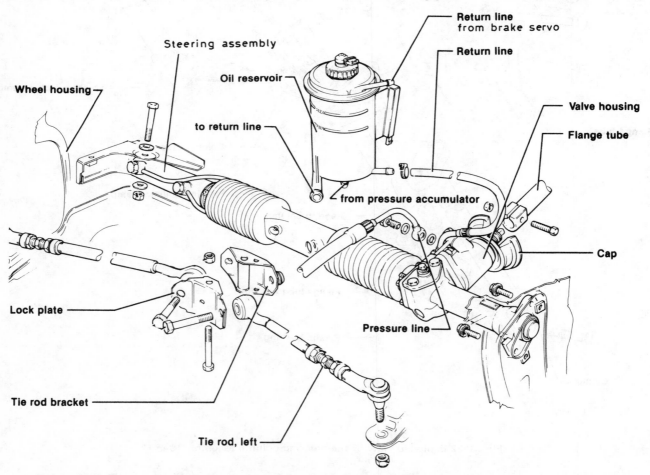

Fig. 10.24 Exploded view of the tie-rods and power-assisted steering gear attachments (Secs 20 and 21)

20.2 Using a separator tool to detach the tie-rod balljoint

2 Unscrew the balljoint nut from the outer end of the tie-rod, and use a separator tool to detach the tie-rod from the strut (photo).
3 At the inner end of the tie-rod, flatten the lockplate, unscrew the bolt and withdraw the tie-rod. If the remaining tie-rod is to be removed as well, refit the removed bolt first, otherwise it will be difficult to refit the bolts.
4 If renewing the end of a tie-rod, measure the distance between the two ends before screwing the old tie-rod end out, and then screw in the new one to the same dimension, otherwise the front wheel alignment will be disturbed.
5 Refitting is a reversal of removal, but renew the lockplate. Tighten the nuts and bolts to the specified torque, but delay tightening the tie-rod inner mountings until the weight of the car is on the suspension. Lock the bolts by bending the lockplate onto one flat. Check and, if necessary, adjust the front wheel alignment, as described in Section 29.

21 Steering gear – removal and refitting

1 Apply the handbrake, jack up the front of the car, and support it on axle stands. Remove the roadwheels.
2 Disconnect the inner ends of the tie-rods with reference to Section 20, paragraph 3.
3 Where applicable, remove the bolt securing the steering damper to the tie-rod bracket.
4 Unscrew and remove the clamp bolt securing the flange tube to the steering gear pinion, then, using a soft metal drift, drive the flange tube off the pinion.
5 On models equipped with power-assisted steering, place a suitable container beneath the steering gear, then unscrew the union nut and bolt, and detach the hydraulic feed and return lines. Recover the washers.
6 Unscrew the mounting bolts, and withdraw the steering gear through the aperture in the side panel.
7 Refitting is a reversal of removal, but use a new lockplate when refitting the tie-rod bolts. Tighten all nuts and bolts to the specified torque and, if power-assisted steering gear is fitted, fill or top up the hydraulic reservoir, as described in Section 25.

22 Steering damper – testing, removal and refitting

1 A steering damper is fitted to models which do not have power-assisted steering, and it is connected btween the tie-rod bracket and the side of the engine compartment.

2 Repair of the steering damper is not possible. If the steering is sensitive to road shocks, remove the damper and check its operation. The damper is attached by a bolt at each end.
3 Test the damper by moving the piston rod in and out by hand, over the whole range of its travel. If the movement is not smooth and with a uniform resistance, fit a new damper.

23 Steering gear gaiter – renewal

1 Remove the steering gear, as described in Section 21.
2 On power-assisted steering gear, remove the two hydraulic pipe banjo unions on the end of the steering gear and recover the washers.
3 Release the gaiter retaining clips, remove the tie-rod bracket and slide the gaiter off the end of the steering gear.
4 Fit a new gaiter using the reversal of this procedure. On manual steering gear types position the gaiter 200 mm (7.88 in) from the end of the rack then secure with the clip.

24 Steering gear – adjustment

1 If there is any undue slackness in the steering gear, resulting in noise or rattles, the steering gear should be adjusted as follows, with reference to Fig. 10.25.
2 With the wheels in the straight-ahead position, turn the adjusting bolt clockwise approximately 20°.
3 Road test the car and check that the steering still self-centres and is not unduly stiff. If the steering does not self-centre, slacken the bolt slightly (anti-clockwise). If the steering still rattles tighten the bolt further.

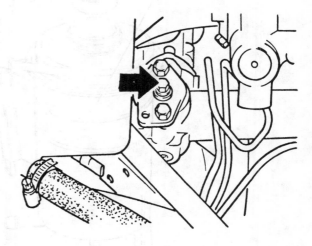

Fig. 10.25 Steering gear adjusting bolt – arrowed (Sec 24)

25 Power-assisted steering gear – bleeding

1 The power-assisted steering gear utilizes hydraulic oil for its operation contained in a reservoir mounted on the engine compartment bulkhead.
2 The power steering pump is also the central hydraulic pump for all other hydraulic systems on the car such as the braking system, anti-lock braking system and self-levelling suspension. If the hydraulic connections of any of these systems have been disturbed the following procedure should be used to fill and bleed the system.
3 If the system is only being topped up, and the oil level in the reservoir has not fallen below the MIN mark, set the steering in the straight-ahead position and, with the vehicle unladen, start the engine. Add the specified hydraulic oil to the reservoir to bring the level up to the MAX mark then refit the filler cap and switch off the engine.

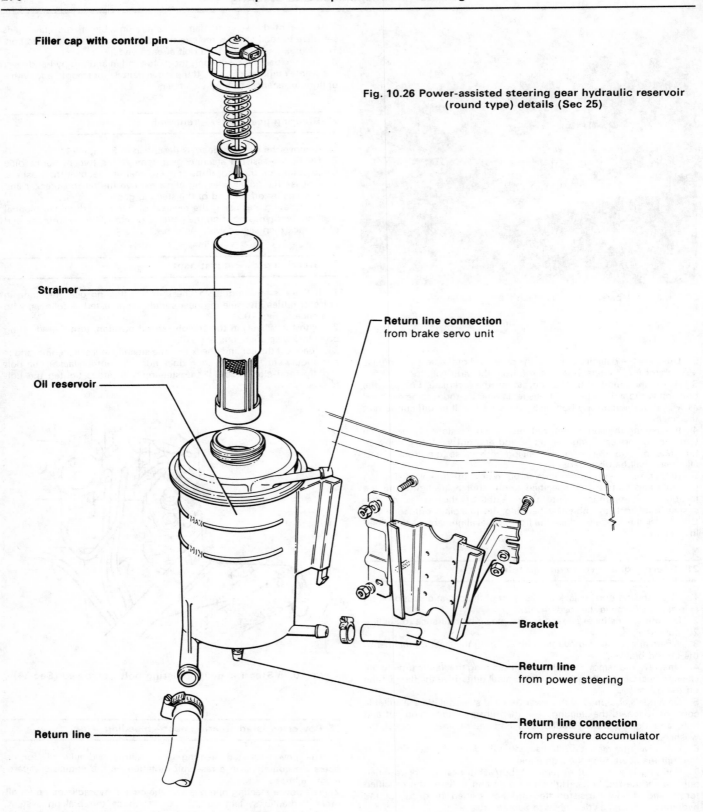

Filler cap with control pin

Fig. 10.26 Power-assisted steering gear hydraulic reservoir (round type) details (Sec 25)

Strainer

Return line connection from brake servo unit

Oil reservoir

Bracket

Return line from power steering

Return line connection from pressure accumulator

Return line

4   If the system is being refilled after a repair operation, or if the level in the reservoir has fallen below the MIN mark, first remove the oil strainer from the filler cap assembly and clean it in petrol. Dry the strainer and refit it to the cap.
5   Jack up the front of the car so that the wheels are just clear of the ground and support it on stands.
6   Fill the reservoir with the specified oil to the MAX mark and, with the engine switched off, turn the steering quickly from lock to lock several times.
7   Top up the reservoir to the MAX mark once more.
8   Start the engine and continue adding oil until the level remains constant and no more bubbles appear when the steering is turned.
9   Switch off the engine, check the oil level once more then refit the filler cap and lower the car to the ground.

26 Power-assisted steering gear – checking for leaks

1 With the engine running, turn the steering to full lock on one side and hold it in this position to allow maximum pressure to build up in the system.

2 With the steering still at full lock, check all joints and unions for signs of leaks, and tighten if necessary. To check the steering rack seal, remove the inner end of the rack gaiter from the steering gear, and pull it back to reveal the seal.

3 Turn the wheel to full lock on the other side and again check for leaks.

27 Power-assisted steering pump drivebelt – removal, refitting and adjustment

Four-cylinder engine models

1 Jack up the front of the car and support it on stands.

2 Undo the three pump pulley retaining nuts and remove the outer shims and the pump pulley outer half.

3 Remove the drivebelt from the pump and crankshaft pulley.

4 Examine the belt for cracks, fraying or other signs of deterioration and renew it if worn.

5 To refit and adjust the belt, first place all the original shims together with the pulley inner half over the pump flange studs.

6 Fit the drivebelt to the crankshaft pulley and over the shims on the pump pulley then place the pulley outer half over the studs.

7 Place the spare shims over the studs and refit the three pulley retaining nuts.

8 Tighten the nuts while turning the pulley so that the belt does not jam between the two pulley halves.

9 Apply moderate thumb pressure to the belt midway between the crankshaft and pump pulleys. When the belt is correctly adjusted the deflection should be approximately 10 mm (0.4 in). If the belt is slack, remove the pulley outer half, take out a shim, refit the outer half and check the deflection again. Repeat until the tension is correct. If the belt is too tight, add a shim between the pulley halves using one of the spare shims. Store the spare shims between the pulley outer half and the retaining nuts.

10 After adjustment lower the car to the ground.

Five-cylinder engine models

11 If the drivebelt is to be renewed, refer to Chapter 12 and remove the alternator drivebelt.

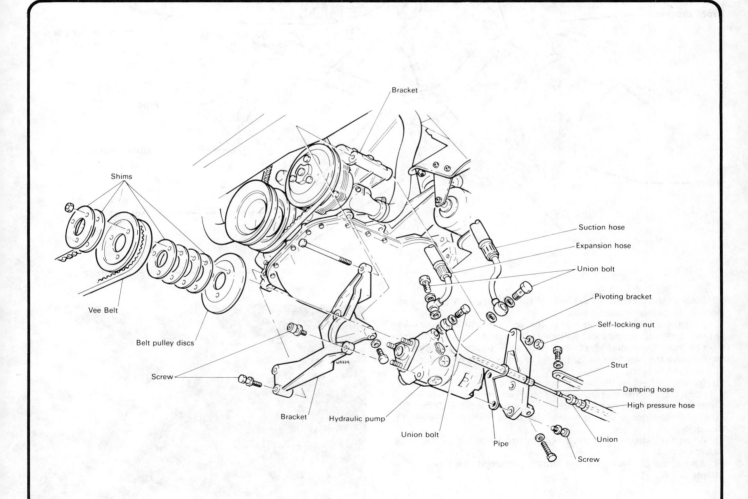

Fig. 10.27 Power-assisted steering pump drivebelt adjustment and pump mounting details – four-cylinder engines (Sec 27 and 28)

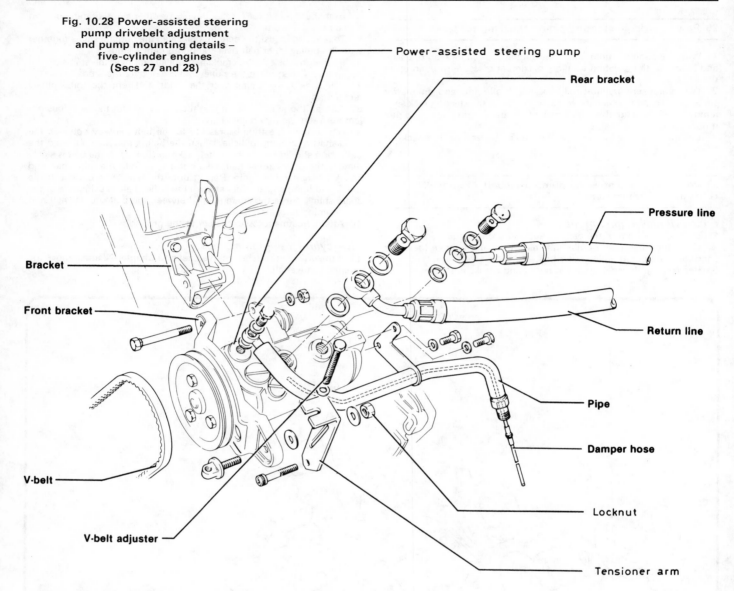

Fig. 10.28 Power-assisted steering pump drivebelt adjustment and pump mounting details – five-cylinder engines (Secs 27 and 28)

Power-assisted steering pump

Rear bracket

Pressure line

Bracket

Front bracket

Return line

Pipe

Damper hose

V-belt

Locknut

V-belt adjuster

Tensioner arm

12 Slacken the locknut on the side of the adjuster arm (photo) and slacken the pump mounting bolt.
13 Turn the adjuster bolt on top of the adjuster arm anti-clockwise until the belt is slack and can be slipped off the pump pulley. Withdraw the belt from the crankshaft pulley and remove it from the engine.
14 Examine the belt for cracks, fraying or other signs of deterioration and renew it if worn.
15 To refit and adjust the belt, slip it into place over the two pulleys then turn the adjuster bolt clockwise to tension the belt. The tension is correct when the belt can be deflected by approximately 10 mm (0.4 in) under moderate thumb pressure at a point midway between the two pulleys.
16 When the tension is correct, tighten the locknut and the pump mounting bolt.
17 Where applicable refit the alternator drivebelt, as described in Chapter 12.

28 Power-assisted steering pump – removal and refitting

Four-cylinder engine models
1   Jack up the front of the car and support it on stands.
2   Place a container beneath the pump to catch the hydraulic oil then unscrew the fluid hose banjo unions on the pump body. Recover the sealing washers.

27.12 Pump adjuster arm locknut (A) and adjuster bolt (B)

3   Undo the three pump pulley retaining bolts, lift off the pump pulley outer half and slip off the drivebelt. Remove the adjustment shims and the pulley inner half.
4   Undo the pump front and rear mounting bolts, move the hose support bracket clear and remove the pump from under the car.
5   Refitting is the reversal of removal, but renew the hydraulic pipe union sealing washers. Tighten all nuts and bolts to the specified torque and adjust the drivebelt tension, as described in Section 27. Fill and bleed the hydraulic system, as described in Section 25.

Five-cylinder engine models
6   Place a container beneath the pump to catch the hydraulic oil then unscrew the three fluid hose banjo unions on the pump body. Recover the sealing washers.
7   Remove the hose support bracket and any retaining clips then move the hoses to one side.
8   Slacken the drivebelt adjuster, as described in Section 27, and slip the belt off the pump pulley.
9   Unscrew the bolt securing the adjuster arm to the engine, remove the pump mounting bolt and lift away the pump.
10 Refitting is the reversal of removal, but renew the hydraulic pipe union sealing washers. Tighten all nuts and bolts to the specified torque and adjust the drivebelt tension, as described in Section 27. Fill and bleed the hydraulic system, as described in Section 25.

29 Front wheel alignment and steering angles

1   Accurate front wheel alignment is essential to provide positive steering and prevent excessive tyre wear. Before considering the steering/suspension geometry, check that the tyres are correctly inflated, the front wheels are not buckled and the steering linkage and suspension joints are in good order, without slackness or wear.
2   Wheel alignment consists of four factors:
Camber is the angle at which the front wheels are set from the vertical when viewed from the front of the car. 'Positive camber' is the amount (in degrees) that the wheels are tilted outward at the top from the vertical.
Castor is the angle between the steering axis and a vertical line when viewed from each side of the car. 'Positive castor' is when the steering axis is inclined rearward.
Steering axis inclination is the angle (when viewed from the front of the car) between the vertical and an imaginary line drawn between the suspension strut upper mounting and the lower suspension arm balljoint.

Toe setting is the amount by which the distance between the front inside edges of the roadwheels (measured at hub height) differs from the diametrically opposite distance measured between the rear inside edges of the front roadwheels.
3   Castor and steering axis inclination are set in production and cannot be altered.
4   Camber is adjustable by slackening the three suspension strut top mounting nuts and moving the strut within the limits of the elongated mounting plate holes. Without special gauges adjustment should not be attempted, but left to a dealer.
5   Two methods are available to the home mechanic for checking the toe setting. One method is to use a gauge to measure the distance between the front and rear inside edges of the roadwheels. The other method is to use a scuff plate in which each front wheel is rolled across a movable plate which records any deviation, or scuff, of the tyre from the straight-ahead position as it moves across the plate. Relatively inexpensive equipment of both types is available from accessory outlets to enable these checks, and subsequent adjustments, to be carried out at home.
6   If, after checking the toe setting using whichever method is preferable, it is found that adjustment is necessary, proceed as follows.
7   Slacken the two nuts on each tie-rod and turn the threaded adjusters as necessary to achieve the desired setting (photo). Turn both adjusters by equal amounts, but only approximately one quarter of a turn each time, then recheck the setting using the gauges or scuff plate. Tighten the clamps when the setting is correct.

30 Wheels and tyres – general care and maintenance

Wheels and tyres should give no real problems in use provided that a close eye is kept on them with regard to excessive wear or damage. To this end, the following points should be noted.
Ensure that tyre pressures are checked regularly and maintained correctly. Checking should be carried out with the tyres cold and not immediately after the vehicle has been in use. If the pressures are checked with the tyres hot, an apparently high reading will be obtained owing to heat expansion. Under no circumstances should an attempt be made to reduce the pressures to the quoted cold reading in this instance, or effective underinflation will result.
Underinflation will cause overheating of the tyre owing to excessive flexing of the casing, and the tread will not sit correctly on the road surface. This will cause a consequent loss of adhesion and excessive wear, not to mention the danger of sudden tyre failure due to heat build-up.

Fig. 10.29 Suspension strut upper mounting bolts for camber adjustment – arrowed (Sec 29)

29.7 Tie-rod locknuts (A) and threaded adjuster (B)

Overinflation will cause rapid wear of the centre part of the tyre tread coupled with reduced adhesion, harsher ride, and the danger of shock damage occurring in the tyre casing.

Regularly check the tyres for damage in the form of cuts or bulges, especially in the sidewalls. Remove any nails or stones embedded in the tread before they penetrate the tyre to cause deflation. If removal of a nail *does* reveal that the tyre has been punctured, refit the nail so that its point of penetration is marked. Then immediately change the wheel and have the tyre repaired by a tyre dealer. Do *not* drive on a tyre in such a condition. In many cases a puncture can be simply repaired by the use of an inner tube of the correct size and type. If in any doubt as to the possible consequences of any damage found, consult your local tyre dealer for advice.

Periodically remove the wheels and clean any dirt or mud from the inside and outside surfaces. Examine the wheel rims for signs of rusting, corrosion or other damage. Light alloy wheels are easily damaged by 'kerbing' whilst parking, and similarly steel wheels may become dented or buckled. Renewal of the wheel is very often the only course of remedial action possible.

The balance of each wheel and tyre assembly should be maintained to avoid excessive wear, not only to the tyres but also to the steering and suspension components. Wheel imbalance is normally signified by vibration through the vehicle's bodyshell, although in many cases it is particularly noticeable through the steering wheel. Conversely, it should be noted that wear or damage in suspension or steering components may cause excessive tyre wear. Out-of-round or out-of-true tyres, damaged wheels and wheel bearing wear/maladjustment also fall into this category. Balancing will not usually cure vibration caused by such wear.

Wheel balancing may be carried out with the wheel either on or off the vehicle. If balanced on the vehicle, ensure that the wheel-to-hub relationship is marked in some way prior to subsequent wheel removal so that it may be refitted in its original position.

General tyre wear is influenced to a large degree by driving style – harsh braking and acceleration or fast cornering will all produce more rapid tyre wear. Interchanging of tyres may result in more even wear, but this should only be carried out where there is no mix of tyre types on the vehicle. However, it is worth bearing in mind that if this is completely effective, the added expense of replacing a complete set of tyres simultaneously is incurred, which may prove financially restrictive for many owners.

Front tyres may wear unevenly as a result of wheel misalignment. The front wheels should always be correctly aligned according to the settings specified by the vehicle manufacturer.

Legal restrictions apply to the mixing of tyre types on a vehicle. Basically this means that a vehicle must not have tyres of differing construction on the same axle. Although it is not recommended to mix tyre types between front axle and rear axle, the only legally permissible combination is crossply at the front and radial at the rear. When mixing radial ply tyres, textile braced radials must always go on the front axle, with steel braced radials at the rear. An obvious disadvantage of such mixing is the necessity to carry two spare tyres to avoid contravening the law in the event of a puncture.

In the UK, the Motor Vehicles Construction and Use Regulations apply to many aspects of tyre fitting and usage. It is suggested that a copy of these regulations is obtained from your local police if in doubt as to the current legal requirements with regard to tyre condition, minimum tread depth, etc.

31 Fault diagnosis – suspension and steering

Note: *More detailed fault diagnosis on the power-assisted steering gear and self-levelling suspension (where fitted) entails the use of special test equipment. Apart from the general references listed below, faults on these systems should be referred to an Audi dealer*

Symptom	Reason(s)
Excessive play in steering	Worn steering gear Worn tie-rod end balljoints Worn tie-rod bushes Incorrect rack adjustment Worn suspension balljoints
Wanders, or pulls to one side	Incorrect wheel alignment Worn tie-rod end balljoints Worn suspension balljoints Uneven tyre pressures Weak shock absorber Broken or weak coil spring
Heavy or stiff steering	Seized steering or suspension balljoint Incorrect wheel alignment Low tyre pressures Leak of lubricant in steering gear Power steering faulty (where applicable) Power steering pump drivebelt broken (where applicable)
Wheel wobble and vibration	Roadwheels out of balance Roadwheels damaged Weak shock absorbers Worn hub bearings
Excessive tyre wear	Incorrect tyre pressures Roadwheels out of balance

Chapter 11 Bodywork

For modifications, and information applicable to later models, see Supplement at end of manual

Contents

1 General description

The body is of unitary all-steel construction, and incorporates computer calculated impact crumple zones at the front and rear, with a central safety cell passenger compartment. During manufacture the body is undersealed and treated with cavity wax injection. In addition all open box members are sealed.

There are two body styles, the four-door Saloon and the five-door Avant, and there are a number of trim options on the Saloon version.

2 Maintenance – bodywork and underframe

The general condition of a vehicle's bodywork is the one thing that significantly affects its value. Maintenance is easy but needs to be regular. Neglect, particularly after minor damage, can lead quickly to further deterioration and costly repair bills. It is important also to keep watch on those parts of the vehicle not immediately visible, for instance the underside, inside all the wheel arches and the lower part of the engine compartment.

The basic maintenance routine for the bodywork is washing – preferably with a lot of water, from a hose. This will remove all the loose solids which may have stuck to the vehicle. It is important to flush these off in such a way as to prevent grit from scratching the finish. The wheel arches and underframe need washing in the same way to remove any accumulated mud which will retain moisture and tend to encourage rust. Paradoxically enough, the best time to clean the underframe and wheel arches is in wet weather when the mud is thoroughly wet and soft. In very wet weather the underframe is usually cleaned of large accumulations automatically and this is a good time for inspection.

Periodically, except on vehicles with a wax-based underbody protective coating, it is a good idea to have the whole of the underframe of the vehicle steam cleaned, engine compartment included, so that a thorough inspection can be carried out to see what minor repairs and renovations are necessary. Steam cleaning is available at many garages and is necessary for removal of the accumulation of oily grime which sometimes is allowed to become thick in certain areas. If steam cleaning facilities are not available, there are one or two excellent grease solvents available which can be brush applied. The dirt can then be simply hosed off. Note that these methods should not be used on vehicles with wax-based underbody protective coating or the coating will be removed. Such vehicles should be inspected annually, preferably just prior to winter, when the underbody should be washed down and any damage to the wax coating repaired. Ideally, a completely fresh coat should be applied. It would also be worth considering the use of such wax-based protection for injection into door panels, sills, box sections, etc, as an additional safeguard against rust damage where such protection is not provided by the vehicle manufacturer.

After washing paintwork, wipe off with a chamois leather to give an unspotted clear finish. A coat of clear protective wax polish will give added protection against chemical pollutants in the air. If the paintwork sheen has dulled or oxidised, use a cleaner/polisher combination to restore the brilliance of the shine. This requires a little effort, but such dulling is usually caused because regular washing has been neglected. Care needs to be taken with metallic paintwork, as special non-abrasive cleaner/polisher is required to avoid damage to the finish. Always check that the door and ventilator opening drain holes and pipes are completely clear so that water can be drained out. Bright work should be treated in the same way as paint work. Windscreens and windows can be kept clear of the smeary film which often appears by the use of a proprietary glass cleaner. Never use any form of wax or other body or chromium polish on glass.

3 Maintenance – upholstery and carpets

Mats and carpets should be brushed or vacuum cleaned regularly to keep them free of grit. If they are badly stained remove them from the vehicle for scrubbing or sponging and make quite sure they are dry before refitting. Seats and interior trim panels can be kept clean by wiping with a damp cloth. If they do become stained (which can be more apparent on light coloured upholstery) use a little liquid detergent and a soft nail brush to scour the grime out of the grain of the material. Do not forget to keep the headlining clean in the same way as the upholstery. When using liquid cleaners inside the vehicle do not over-wet the surfaces being cleaned. Excessive damp could get into the seams and padded interior causing stains, offensive odours or even rot. If the inside of the vehicle gets wet accidentally it is worthwhile taking some trouble to dry it out properly, particularly where carpets are involved. *Do not leave oil or electric heaters inside the vehicle for this purpose.*

4 Minor body damage – repair

The photographic sequences on pages 286 and 287 illustrate the operations detailed in the following sub-sections.
Note: *For more detailed information about bodywork repair, the Haynes Publishing Group publish a book by Lindsay Porter called The Car Bodywork Repair Manual. This incorporates information on such aspects as rust treatment, painting and glass fibre repairs, as well as details on more ambitious repairs involving welding and panel beating.*

Repair of minor scratches in bodywork

If the scratch is very superficial, and does not penetrate to the metal of the bodywork, repair is very simple. Lightly rub the area of the scratch with a paintwork renovator, or a very fine cutting paste, to remove loose paint from the scratch and to clear the surrounding bodywork of wax polish. Rinse the area with clean water.

Apply touch-up paint to the scratch using a fine paint brush; continue to apply fine layers of paint until the surface of the paint in the scratch is level with the surrounding paintwork. Allow the new paint at least two weeks to harden; then blend it into the surrounding paintwork by rubbing the scratch area with a paintwork renovator or a very fine cutting paste. Finally, apply wax polish.

Where the scratch has penetrated right through to the metal of the bodywork, causing the metal to rust, a different repair technique is required. Remove any loose rust from the bottom of the scratch with a penknife, then apply rust inhibiting paint to prevent the formation of rust in the future. Using a rubber or nylon applicator fill the scratch with bodystopper paste. If required, this paste can be mixed with cellulose thinners to provide a very thin paste which is ideal for filling narrow scratches. Before the stopper-paste in the scratch hardens, wrap a piece of smooth cotton rag around the top of a finger. Dip the finger in cellulose thinners and then quickly sweep it across the surface of the stopper-paste in the scratch; this will ensure that the surface of the stopper-paste is slightly hollowed. The scratch can now be painted over as described earlier in this Section.

Repair of dents in bodywork

When deep denting of the vehicle's bodywork has taken place, the first task is to pull the dent out, until the affected bodywork almost attains its original shape. There is little point in trying to restore the original shape completely, as the metal in the damaged area will have stretched on impact and cannot be reshaped fully to its original contour. It is better to bring the level of the dent up to a point which is about ⅛ in (3 mm) below the level of the surrounding bodywork. In cases where the dent is very shallow anyway, it is not worth trying to pull it out at all. If the underside of the dent is accessible, it can be hammered out gently from behind, using a mallet with a wooden or plastic head. Whilst doing this, hold a suitable block of wood firmly against the outside of the panel to absorb the impact from the hammer blows and thus prevent a large area of the bodywork from being 'belled-out'.

Should the dent be in a section of the bodywork which has a double skin or some other factor making it inaccessible from behind, a different technique is called for. Drill several small holes through the metal inside the area – particularly in the deeper section. Then screw

long self-tapping screws into the holes just sufficiently for them to gain a good purchase in the metal. Now the dent can be pulled out by pulling on the protruding heads of the screws with a pair of pliers.

The next stage of the repair is the removal of the paint from the damaged area, and from an inch or so of the surrounding 'sound' bodywork. This is accomplished most easily by using a wire brush or abrasive pad on a power drill, although it can be done just as effectively by hand using sheets of abrasive paper. To complete the preparation for filling, score the surface of the bare metal with a screwdriver or the tang of a file, or alternatively, drill small holes in the affected area. This will provide a really good 'key' for the filler paste.

To complete the repair see the Section on filling and re-spraying.

Repair of rust holes or gashes in bodywork

Remove all paint from the affected area and from an inch or so of the surrounding 'sound' bodywork, using an abrasive pad or a wire brush on a power drill. If these are not available a few sheets of abrasive paper will do the job just as effectively. With the paint removed you will be able to gauge the severity of the corrosion and therefore decide whether to renew the whole panel (if this is possible) or to repair the affected area. New body panels are not as expensive as most people think and it is often quicker and more satisfactory to fit a new panel than to attempt to repair large areas of corrosion.

Remove all fittings from the affected area except those which will act as a guide to the original shape of the damaged bodywork (eg headlamp shells etc). Then, using tin snips or a hacksaw blade, remove all loose metal and any other metal badly affected by corrosion. Hammer the edges of the hole inwards in order to create a slight depression for the filler paste.

Wire brush the affected area to remove the powdery rust from the surface of the remaining metal. Paint the affected area with rust inhibiting paint; if the back of the rusted area is accessible treat this also.

Before filling can take place it will be necessary to block the hole in some way. This can be achieved by the use of aluminium or plastic mesh, or aluminium tape.

Aluminium or plastic mesh is probably the best material to use for a large hole. Cut a piece to the approximate size and shape of the hole to be filled, then position it in the hole so that its edges are below the level of the surrounding bodywork. It can be retained in position by several blobs of filler paste around its periphery.

Aluminium tape should be used for small or very narrow holes. Pull a piece off the roll and trim it to the approximate size and shape required, then pull off the backing paper (if used) and stick the tape over the hole; it can be overlapped if the thickness of one piece is insufficient. Burnish down the edges of the tape with the handle of a screwdriver or similar, to ensure that the tape is securely attached to the metal underneath.

Bodywork repairs – filling and re-spraying

Before using this Section, see the Sections on dent, deep scratch, rust holes and gash repairs.

Many types of bodyfiller are available, but generally speaking those proprietary kits which contain a tin of filler paste and a tube of resin hardener are best for this type of repair. A wide, flexible plastic or nylon applicator will be found invaluable for imparting a smooth and well contoured finish to the surface of the filler.

Mix up a little filler on a clean piece of card or board – measure the hardener carefully (follow the maker's instructions on the pack) otherwise the filler will set too rapidly or too slowly.   Using the applicator apply the filler paste to the prepared area; draw the applicator across the surface of the filler to achieve the correct contour and to level the filler surface. As soon as a contour that approximates to the correct one is achieved, stop working the paste – if you carry on too long the paste will become sticky and begin to 'pick up' on the applicator. Continue to add thin layers of filler paste at twenty-minute intervals until the level of the filler is just proud of the surrounding bodywork.

Once the filler has hardened, excess can be removed using a metal plane or file. From then on, progressively finer grades of abrasive paper should be used, starting with a 40 grade production paper and finishing with 400 grade wet-and-dry paper. Always wrap the abrasive paper around a flat rubber, cork, or wooden block – otherwise the surface of the filler will not be completely flat. During the smoothing of the filler surface the wet-and-dry paper should be periodically rinsed in water. This will ensure that a very smooth finish is imparted to the filler at the final stage.

At this stage the 'dent' should be surrounded by a ring of bare metal, which in turn should be encircled by the finely 'feathered' edge of the good paintwork. Rinse the repair area with clean water, until all of the dust produced by the rubbing-down operation has gone.

Spray the whole repair area with a light coat of primer – this will show up any imperfections in the surface of the filler. Repair these imperfections with fresh filler paste or bodystopper, and once more smooth the surface with abrasive paper. If bodystopper is used, it can be mixed with cellulose thinners to form a really thin paste which is ideal for filling small holes. Repeat this spray and repair procedure until you are satisfied that the surface of the filler, and the feathered edge of the paintwork are perfect. Clean the repair area with clean water and allow to dry fully.

The repair area is now ready for final spraying. Paint spraying must be carried out in a warm, dry, windless and dust free atmosphere. This condition can be created artificially if you have access to a large indoor working area, but if you are forced to work in the open, you will have to pick your day very carefully. If you are working indoors, dousing the floor in the work area with water will help to settle the dust which would otherwise be in the atmosphere. If the repair area is confined to one body panel, mask off the surrounding panels; this will help to minimise the effects of a slight mis-match in paint colours. Bodywork fittings (eg chrome strips, door handles etc) will also need to be masked off. Use genuine masking tape and several thicknesses of newspaper for the masking operations.

Before commencing to spray, agitate the aerosol can thoroughly, then spray a test area (an old tin, or similar) until the technique is mastered. Cover the repair area with a thick coat of primer; the thickness should be built up using several thin layers of paint rather than one thick one. Using 400 grade wet-and-dry paper, rub down the surface of the primer until it is really smooth. While doing this, the work area should be thoroughly doused with water, and the wet-and-dry paper periodically rinsed in water. Allow to dry before spraying on more paint.

Spray on the top coat, again building up the thickness by using several thin layers of paint. Start spraying in the centre of the repair area and then, using a circular motion, work outwards until the whole repair area and about 2 inches of the surrounding original paintwork is covered. Remove all masking material 10 to 15 minutes after spraying on the final coat of paint.

Allow the new paint at least two weeks to harden, then, using a paintwork renovator or a very fine cutting paste, blend the edges of the paint into the existing paintwork. Finally, apply wax polish.

Plastic components

With the use of more and more plastic body components by the vehicle manufacturers (eg bumpers, spoilers, and in some cases major body panels), rectification of damage to such items has become a matter of either entrusting repair work to a specialist in this field, or renewing complete components. Repair by the DIY owner is not really feasible owing to the cost of the equipment and materials required for effecting such repairs. The basic technique involves making a groove along the line of the crack in the plastic using a rotary burr in a power drill. The damaged part is then welded back together by using a hot air gun to heat up and fuse a plastic filler rod into the groove. Any excess plastic is then removed and the area rubbed down to a smooth finish. It is important that a filler rod of the correct plastic is used, as body components can be made of a variety of different types (eg polycarbonate, ABS, polypropylene).

If the owner is renewing a complete component himself, he will be left with the problem of finding a suitable paint for finishing which is compatible with the type of plastic used. At one time the use of a universal paint was not possible owing to the complex range of plastics encountered in body component applications. Standard paints, generally speaking, will not bond to plastic or rubber satisfactorily. However, it is now possible to obtain a plastic body parts finishing kit which consists of a pre-primer treatment, a primer and coloured top coat. Full instructions are normally supplied with a kit, but basically the method of use is to first apply the pre-primer to the component concerned and allow it to dry for up to 30 minutes. Then the primer is applied and left to dry for about an hour before finally applying the special coloured top coat. The result is a correctly coloured component where the paint will flex with the plastic or rubber, a property that standard paint does not normally possess.

5 Major body damage – repair

Where serious damage has occurred, or large areas need renewal due to neglect, it means that the complete new panels will need welding in, and this is best left out professionals. If the damage is due to impact, it will also be necessary to check completely the alignment of the bodyshell, and this can only be carried out accurately by an Audi dealer using special jigs. If the body is left misaligned, it is primarily dangerous as the car will not handle properly, and secondly, uneven stresses will be imposed on the steering, suspension and possibly transmission, causing abnormal wear, or complete failure, particularly to such items as the tyres.

6 Door inner trim panel – removal and refitting

1 Undo the screws and lift off the door front pillar trim (photos). Unscrew the door lock button.

6.1A Door pillar trim retaining screw (arrowed)

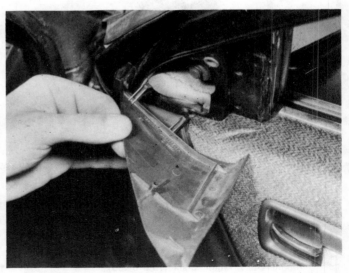

6.1B Removing the door pillar trim

6.2A Remove the trim over the door pull ...

6.2B ... then undo the screws and remove the door pull

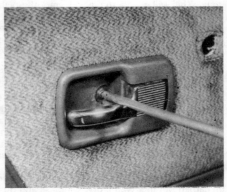

6.3 Removing the interior handle trim plate

2   Carefully prise off the door pull trim then undo the screws and remove the handle (photos).
3   Undo the interior handle trim plate screw and remove the trim plate (photo).
4   Where manually-operated windows are fitted, prise off the window crank handle trim, undo the screw and remove the handle. On later models the crank handle trim is removed by pressing the retaining lug at the knob end with a screwdriver, then pulling off (Fig. 11.1).
5   Undo the two upper screws at each end of the trim panel and the screw accessible through the door pull opening (photos).
6   Using a suitable flat tool, carefully prise the trim panel off the door, then pull the panel up and remove it from the door (photo). Where power windows are fitted, disconnect the wiring connector at the operating switch (photo).
7   To remove the inner insulation panel, remove the upper clips and lift the panel off the door (photo).
8   Refitting is a reversal of removal.

7   Door locks – removal and refitting

1   Remove the door inner trim panel, as described in Section 6.
2   Undo the two screws on the edge of the door securing the interior handle cable support (photo).

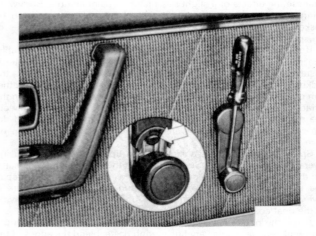

Fig. 11.1 Removal of the later type window crank handle trim by depressing lug (arrowed) with screwdriver (Sec 9)

6.5A Trim panel upper retaining screw (arrowed)

6.5B Trim panel retaining screw accessible through the door pull opening

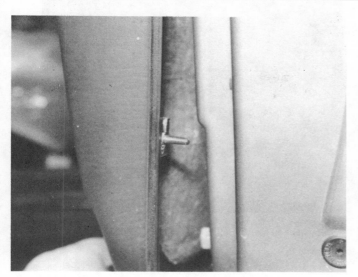

6.6A Remove the trim panel ...

6.6B ... and disconnect the power window switch wiring (where applicable)

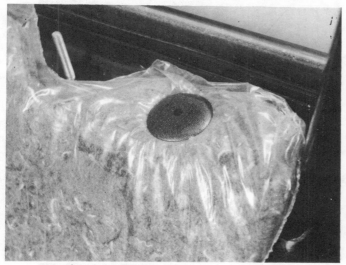

6.7 Insulation panel retaining clip

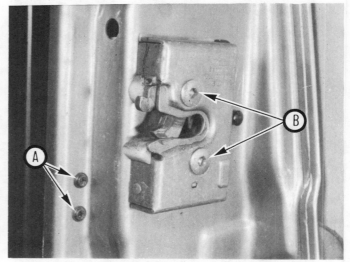

7.2 Interior handle cable support screws (A) and lock retaining screws (B)

3   Undo the two door lock retaining screws using an Allen key.
4   Disconnect the operating rods and cable then withdraw the lock from the door.
5   Refitting is a reversal of removal.

8   Door exterior handle – removal and refitting

1   Remove the door inner trim panel, as described in Section 6.
2   Carefully prise off the plastic insert using a screwdriver.
3   Disconnect the operating rods, undo the two screws and withdraw the handle from the door (photo).
4   Refitting is a reversal of removal.

9   Doors – dismantling and reassembly

1   Remove the inner trim panel, door lock and door exterior handle, as described in Sections 6, 7 and 8.
2   Disconnect the wiring connector on models with power windows.

8.3 Door exterior handle retaining screw

This photo sequence illustrates the repair of a dent and damaged paintwork. The procedure for the repair of a hole is similar. Refer to the text for more complete instructions

After removing any adjacent body trim, hammer the dent out. The damaged area should then be made slightly concave

Use coarse sandpaper or a sanding disc on a drill motor to remove all paint from the damaged area. Feather the sanded area into the edges of the surrounding paint, using progressively finer grades of sandpaper

The damaged area should be treated with rust remover prior to application of the body filler. In the case of a rust hole, all rusted sheet metal should be cut away

Carefully follow manufacturer's instructions when mixing the body filler so as to have the longest possible working time during application. Rust holes should be covered with fiberglass screen held in place with dabs of body filler prior to repair

Apply the filler with a flexible applicator in thin layers at 20 minute intervals. Use an applicator such as a wood spatula for confined areas. The filler should protrude slightly above the surrounding area

Shape the filler with a surform-type plane. Then, use water and progressively finer grades of sandpaper and a sanding block to wet-sand the area until it is smooth. Feather the edges of the repair area into the surrounding paint.

Use spray or brush applied primer to cover the entire repair area so that slight imperfections in the surface will be filled in. Prime at least one inch into the area surrounding the repair. Be careful of over-spray when using spray-type primer

Wet-sand the primer with fine (approximately 400 grade) sandpaper until the area is smooth to the touch and blended into the surrounding paint. Use filler paste on minor imperfections

After the filler paste has dried, use rubbing compound to ensure that the surface of the primer is smooth. Prior to painting, the surface should be wiped down with a tack rag or lint-free cloth soaked in lacquer thinner

Choose a dry, warm, breeze-free area in which to paint and make sure that adjacent areas are protected from over-spray. Shake the spray paint can thoroughly and apply the top coat to the repair area, building it up by applying several coats, working from the center

After allowing at least two weeks for the paint to harden, use fine rubbing compound to blend the area into the original paint. Wax can now be applied

3 Refer to Fig. 11.2 and undo the four bolts securing the inner door panel to the outer door panel. Note the adjusting spacers on two lower bolts.

4 Withdraw the complete inner door panel with the glass and frame from the outer door panel.

5 Undo the bolts securing the window regulator to the door panel (photos), and the clip securing the regulator slide to the window glass. Withdraw the regulator from the inner door panel.

6 Remove the window glass by sliding it down and out of the guide channels.

7 Refitting is a reversal of removal, but adjust the window glass as follows before refitting the inner door panel to the outer door panel.

8 Move the window to its lowest position using the regulator handle or by temporarily reconnecting the power window wiring.

9 View down the guide channel and check that the lower guide pin is located in the centre of the guide. If not, slacken the regulator retaining bolts and move the regulator within the elongated holes until the guide pin is centralised.

10 Raise the window and adjust the regulator frame upper mounting so that the glass contacts the seal evenly at the points indicated in Fig. 11.5. It may also be necessary to turn the stop screw on the regulator slide as required (Fig. 11.6).

Fig. 11.2 Inner door panel retaining bolts (arrowed) (Sec 9)

9.5A Window regulator retaining nuts ...

9.5B ... and regulator frame upper ...

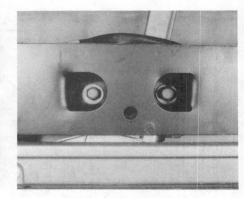

9.5C ... and lower retaining bolts

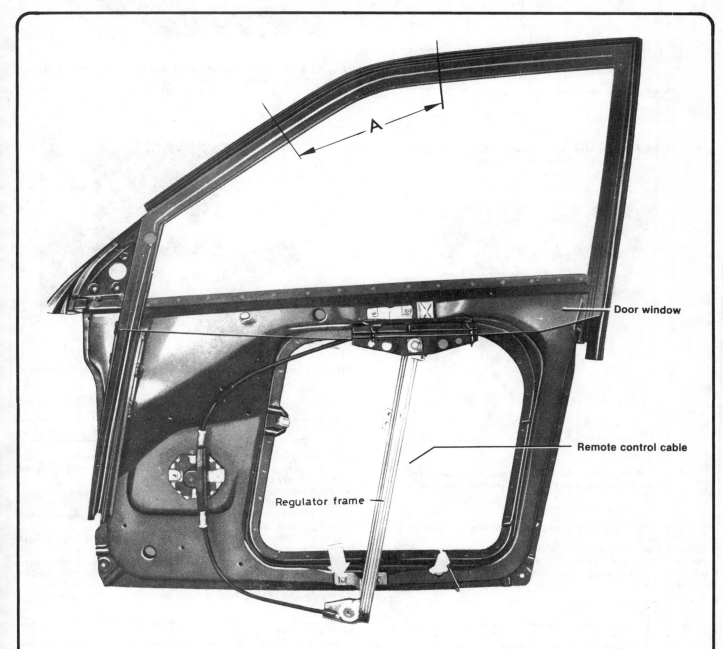

A

Door window

Remote control cable

Regulator frame

Fig. 11.3 Window regulator with lower mounting (arrowed) as viewed from inside the inner door panel (Sec 9)

A Door-to-body critical sealing area

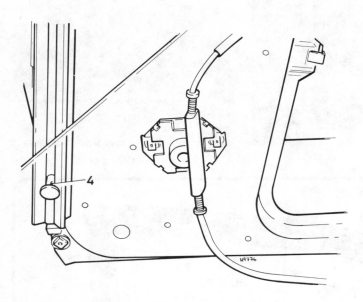

Fig. 11.4 Adjust window regulator so that guide pin (4) is central in guide (Sec 9)

Fig. 11.5 Adjust the regulator frame upper mounting (6) so that the glass contacts the seal evenly at the points indicated (Sec 9)

Fig. 11.6 Regulator slide stop screw (arrowed) for additional adjustment of glass position (Sec 9)

Fig. 11.7 Door inner panel lower mounting spacer location – arrowed (Sec 9)

10 Doors – removal and refitting

1   Remove the inner trim panel, as described in Section 6.
2   If the same door is being refitted, mark round the hinges on the door to simplify realignment.
3   Disconnect the electrical and vacuum connections inside the door, as applicable, and remove the wiring and hoses from the door.
4   Drill off the lower part of the door check strap retaining rivet then remove the rivet using a drift.
5   Support the door, undo the hinge retaining bolts (photo) and remove the door from the car.
6   Refitting is a reversal of removal, but peen over the bottom of a new check strap rivet to retain it in place. Adjust the striker, as described in Section 11, and adjust the inner door panel, as described in Section 9, if a satisfactory fit of the door cannot be achieved at the striker.

11 Door striker – adjustment

1   Mark round the door striker (photo) with a pencil, or a fine ballpoint pen.
2   Fit a spanner to the hexagon on the striker and unscrew the striker about one turn so that the striker moves when tapped with a soft-headed hammer.

11 With the inner and outer door panels assembled, adjust the inner panel as follows.
12 Check the closure of the door and the fit of the door in the door aperture. If adjustment is necessary, slacken all four bolts securing the inner panel to the outer panel. Move the panel as necessary noting the following:

   (a) *The elongated holes in the upper mountings allow height adjustment*
   (b) *The elongated holes in the lower mountings allow height and side adjustment*
   (c) *By changing the thickness of the spacers at the lower mountings (two thicknesses available) lateral adjustment of the panel at the top of the window frame is allowed*
   (d) *The most critical sealing area of the door is midway along the window frame at the top (Fig. 11.3) and attention should be paid to the fit and adjustment of the door in this area.*

10.5 Door hinge retaining bolt

11.1 Front door striker pin

3 Tap the striker towards the inside of the car if the door rattles, or towards the outside of the car if the door fits too tightly, but be careful to keep the striker in the same horizontal line, unless it also requires vertical adjustment. Only move the striker a small amount at a time; the actual amount moved can be checked by reference to the pencil mark made before the striker was loosened.

4 When a position has been found in which the door closes firmly, but without difficulty, tighten the striker.

5 If a satisfactory adjustment cannot be achieved at the striker, check the adjustment of the inner door panel, as described in Section 9.

12 Bonnet – removal, refitting and adjustment

1 Support the bonnet in its open position and place some rags in the corners by the hinges.

2 Disconnect the windscreen washer hose and detach the engine compartment light wiring from the washer hose (photos). Disconnect the wiring at the connector in the plenum chamber.

3 Mark around the hinges to facilitate realignment when refitting.

4 Extract the retaining clips from the support strut upper retaining pins (photo) and withdraw the pins.

12.2A Windscreen washer hose connector ...

12.2B ... and engine compartment light wiring clipped to hose

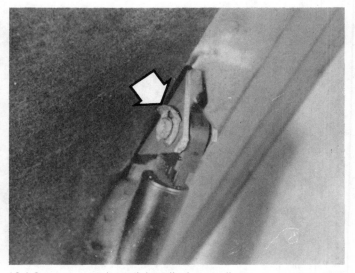

12.4 Support strut pin retaining clip (arrowed)

5   Undo the four bonnet hinge retaining bolts and, with the help of an assistant, lift the bonnet off the car (photo).
6   Refitting is a reversal of removal, but adjust the hinges to their original positions so that the bonnet edge gap remains constant. If necessary adjust the two strikers on the front of the bonnet to achieve satisfactory closure.

13 Bonnet support strut – removal and refitting

1   Support the bonnet in the open position.
2   Extract the retaining clip from the support strut upper retaining pin and withdraw the pin.
3   If the strut lower mounting is of the plastic ball socket type, withdraw the retaining clip approximately 4.0 mm (0.15 in) using a screwdriver and pull the strut lower mounting off the ball-stud. Do not remove the clip fully or it will be damaged.
4   If the lower mounting is of the metal ball socket type, pull out the retaining pin using pliers and remove the strut lower mounting from the ball-stud.
5   Refitting is a reversal of removal.

14 Bonnet lock cable – removal, refitting and adjustment

1   Remove the radiator grille, as described in Section 22.
2   Undo the clamp bolt and disconnect the cable end from the nipple.
3   Release the cable from the locking levers, sleeves and cable clips in the engine compartment.
4   Undo the two screws securing the cable release lever assembly inside the car, pull the cable through the bulkhead and remove it from inside the car.
5   Refitting is a reversal of removal, but adjust the cable to take up the free play at the nipple without tensioning the locking levers.

15 Boot lid – removal, refitting and adjustment

1   Support the boot lid in its open position, and place some rags beneath the corners by the hinges.
2   Disconnect the wiring loom and vacuum hose, as necessary, then mark the location of the hinges with a pencil (photo).
3   With the help of an assistant, unscrew the nuts and withdraw the boot lid from the car.
4   Refitting is a reversal of removal, but adjust the hinges to their original positions so that the boot lid is level with the surrounding bodywork.

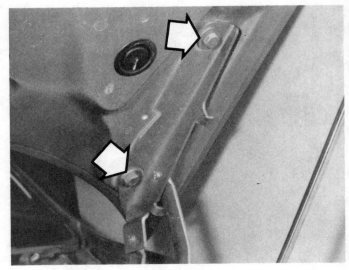

12.5 Bonnet hinge retaining bolts (arrowed)

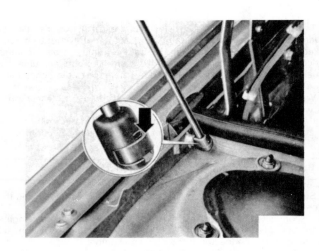

Fig. 11.8 Retaining clip (arrowed) on bonnet support strut with plastic ball socket (Sec 13)

Fig. 11.9 Retaining pin (arrowed) on bonnet support strut with metal ball socket (Sec 13)

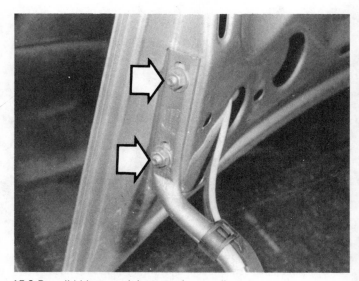

15.2 Boot lid hinge retaining nuts (arrowed)

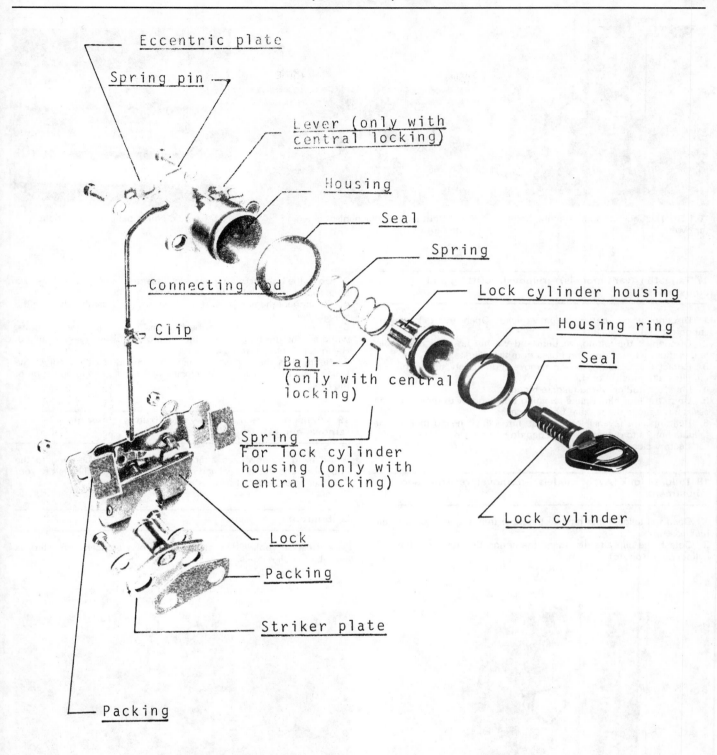

Fig. 11.10 Exploded view of the boot lid lock components (Sec 16)

16 Boot lid lock – removal, refitting and adjustment

1   Open the boot lid, undo the two bolts and withdraw the lock cylinder from the boot lid (photo).
2   Twist the lock to release it from the connecting rod and remove it from the car.

3   Undo the two nuts and withdraw the lock mechanism off the studs (photo). Recover the packing, where fitted.
4   Disconnect the connecting rod and remove the lock from the car.
5   Refitting is a reversal of removal, but adjust the closure of the boot lid and the operation of the lock by adjusting the striker plate as necessary (photo).

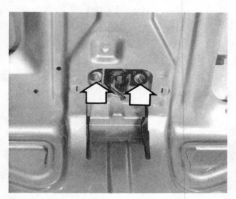

16.1 Boot lid lock cylinder retaining bolts (arrowed)

16.3 Boot lid lock mechanism retaining nuts (arrowed)

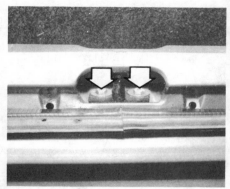

16.5 Boot lid striker plate retaining bolts (arrowed)

17 Tailgate (Avant models) – removal, refitting and adjustment

1   Disconnect the battery negative lead. Open the tailgate and support it.
2   Disconnect the wiring, vacuum and washer hose, as applicable, and withdraw the wiring and hoses from the tailgate.
3   Extract the locking clip and remove the support struts from the tailgate ball-studs (photo).
4   Mark the outline of the tailgate hinges.
5   Undo the four hinge plate retaining bolts and, with the help of an assistant, remove the tailgate from the car.
6   Refitting is a reversal of removal, but adjust the position of the tailgate hinges to provide an even gap down both sides, together with satisfactory closing.

18 Tailgate lock (Avant models) – removal, refitting and adjustment

1   Open the tailgate and remove the inner trim to gain access to the lock assemblies.
2   Detach the clip and disengage the connecting rod from the lock cylinder arm (photo).

3   Undo the bolt securing the lock cylinder to the tailgate and the two bolts securing the lock carrier plate to the tailgate.
4   Disconnect the two pullrods and remove the assembly through the tailgate aperture.
5   To remove the two lock mechanisms undo the retaining bolts, withdraw the mechanism into the tailgate and disengage the pullrod. Remove the lock from the car.
6   Refitting is the reversal of removal, but if necessary adjust the striker plate to give satisfactory closure of the tailgate and operation of the lock.

19 Windscreen, rear window and fixed window glass – removal and refitting

All fixed windows are attached by direct flush bonding to the bodywork, and the removal and refitting of glass should be left to your Audi dealer or a specialist glass replacement company.

20 Sunroof – general

A steel sunroof, either mechanically or electrically operated, is available on all models.

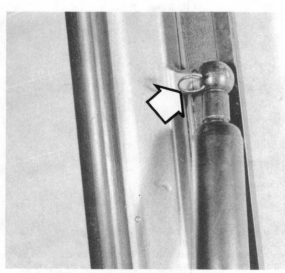

17.3 Tailgate support strut locking clip (arrowed)

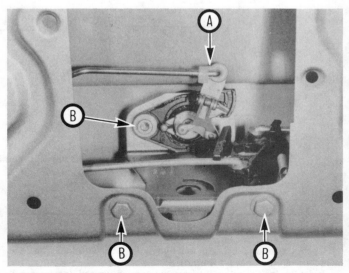

18.2 Tailgate lock connecting rod clip (A) and retaining bolts (B)

The sunroof is maintenance-free, but any adjustment or removal and refitting of the component parts should be entrusted to a dealer due to the complexity of the unit and the need to remove much of the interior trim and headlining to gain access. The latter operation is involved, and entails the use of special tools.

21 Bumpers – removal and refitting

Front bumper

1 Where fitted, remove the front foglights and/or direction indicators from the bumper, as described in Chapter 12.
2 Lever off the edging strip along the top edge of the bumper below the headlights.
3 Undo the screws below the radiator grille securing the centre trim strip, then carefully lever up the strip at both ends (photo) and remove it.
4 Refer to Section 22 and remove the radiator grille and ventilation grille.

5 Undo the two upper and one lower bolt on each side (photos) and pull the bumper forwards slightly.
6 Detach the headlamp washer hose, where applicable, then pull the bumper forwards out of the side guides and remove it from the car.
7 Refitting is a reversal of removal.

Rear bumper

8 From within the luggage compartment, undo the two bolts each side securing the bumper mounting brackets, pull the bumper rearwards out of the side guides and remove it from the car.
9 Refitting is a reversal of removal.

22 Radiator grille and ventilation grille – removal and refitting

1 Open the bonnet and undo the radiator grille centre retaining screw (photo).
2 Release the catches on each side of the grille and pull it forwards (photo).

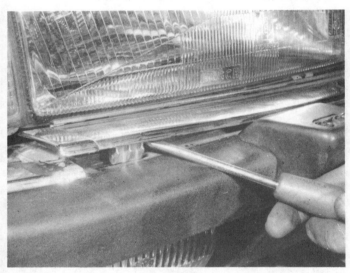

21.3 Removing the bumper centre trim strip (Audi 100 shown)

21.5A Front bumper upper right-hand retaining bolts

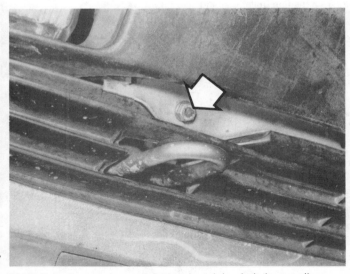

21.5B Front bumper lower right-hand retaining bolt (arrowed)

22.1 Removing the radiator grille centre retaining screw

22.2 Releasing the radiator grille side retaining catches

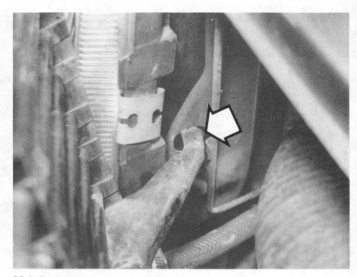

22.3 Radiator grille lower retaining lug (arrowed)

3   Disengage the lower lugs and remove the radiator grille from the car (photo).
4   To remove the ventilation grille below the bumper, undo the screws each side (photo) and withdraw the grille.
5   Refitting is a reversal of removal.

23 Facia – removal and refitting

Audi 100 and Audi 5000S models
1   Remove the steering wheel, as described in Chapter 10.
2   Remove the combination switch and instrument panel, as described in Chapter 12.
3   Remove the centre console, as described in Section 24 of this Chapter.
4   Undo the four screws at the side of the heater control panel and lower the panel.
5   Undo the four screws at the side of the upper switch and vent panel (photo), withdraw the panel and disconnect the wiring at the rear after labelling the connectors. Remove the panel.

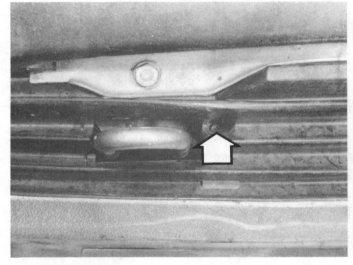

22.4 Ventilation grille retaining screw (arrowed)

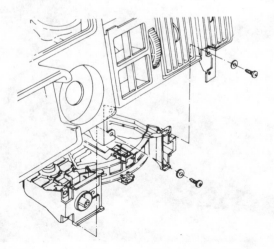

Fig. 11.11 Heater control panel attachments at the facia – Audi 100 and Audi 5000S (Sec 23)

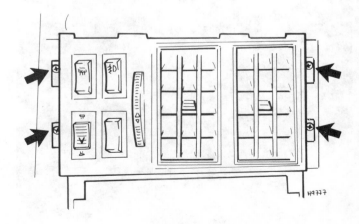

Fig. 11.12 Switch and vent panel retaining screws (arrowed) – Audi 100 and Audi 5000S (Sec 23)

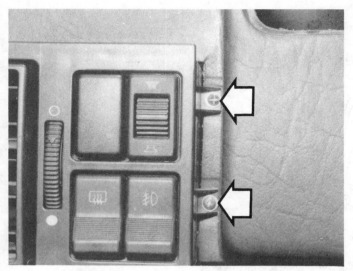

23.5 Upper switch and vent panel retaining screws (arrowed)

6   Undo the parcel shelf retaining screws on the driver's side, lower the shelf and detach it from its guides. Remove the shelf (photo).
7   Undo the parcel shelf retaining screws on the passenger's side, lower the shelf and detach it from its guides. Remove the shelf.
8   Disconnect the air ducts at the heater blower under the facia.
9   Undo the two screws each side (photo) and one through the instrument panel aperture securing the facia to its brackets. Detach the

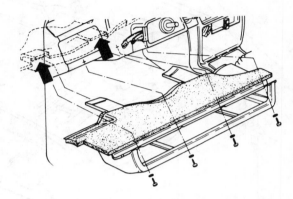

Fig. 11.13 Driver's side parcel shelf attachments – Audi 100 and Audi 5000S (Sec 23)

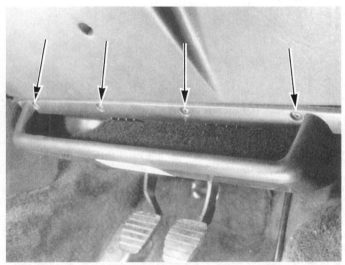

23.6 Driver's side parcel shelf retaining screws (arrowed)

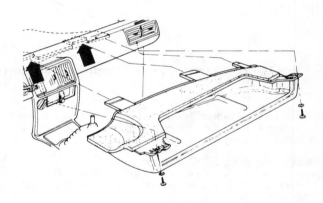

Fig. 11.14 Passenger's side parcel shelf attachments – Audi 100 and Audi 5000S (Sec 23)

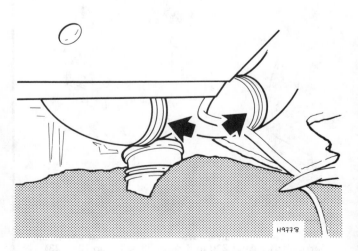

Fig. 11.15 Air duct attachments beneath the facia (arrowed) – Audi 100 and Audi 5000S (Sec 23)

23.9 Facia right-hand side retaining screws

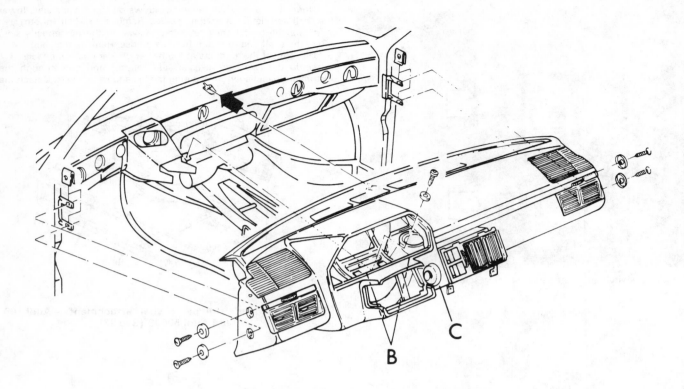

Fig. 11.16 Facia retaining screw locations, cable clip (B) and cable binder (C) locations – Audi 100 and Audi 5000S (Sec 23)

wiring harness at the cable clips and cable binder, and pull the facia out of its location. Remove the facia from the car.
10 Refitting is a reversal of removal.

Audi 200 and Audi 5000 Turbo models
11 Remove the steering wheel, as described in Chapter 10.
12 Remove the combination switch and instrument panel, as described in Chapter 12.

13 Undo the screw securing the left-hand hinge of the glove compartment to the facia. Disengage the glove compartment from the right-hand hinge and remove it from the facia.
14 Press out the side moulding lower clip, undo the three screws and remove the side moulding by lowering it to disengage the upper tags (Fig. 11.18).
15 Undo the screws, disengage the tags and remove the cover under the facia on the driver's side.

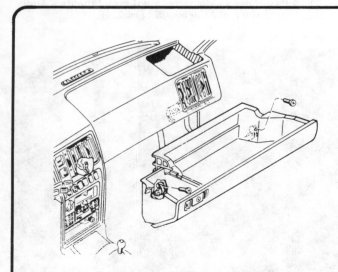

Fig. 11.17 Glove compartment removal – Audi 200 and Audi 5000 Turbo (Sec 23)

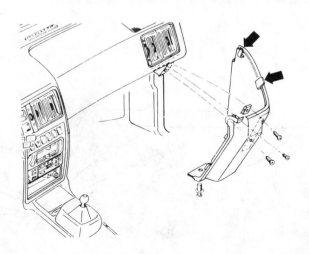

Fig. 11.18 Side moulding retaining screws and upper tags (arrowed) – Audi 200 and Audi 5000 Turbo (Sec 23)

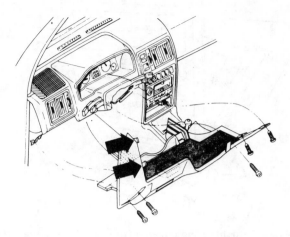

Fig. 11.19 Driver's side cover under facia retaining
screws and tags (arrowed) – Audi 200 and Audi 5000
Turbo (Sec 23)

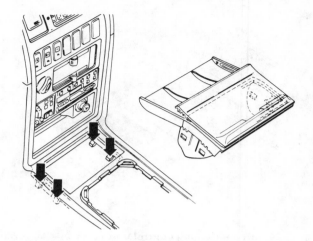

Fig. 11.20 Ashtray insert retaining tabs (arrowed) – Audi
200 and Audi 5000 Turbo (Sec 23)

16 Remove the gear lever knob or selector lever handle then
disengage the gear lever or selector lever trim from the clips by pulling
it upwards.

17 Press the ashtray insert retaining tabs outwards and press out the
ashtray insert through the gear lever trim aperture in the console.

18 Undo the screws and disengage the clips then withdraw both
console side panels downwards to remove.

19 Undo the screws securing the facia inner covers and disconnect
the wiring at the adjacent control units. Remove the covers and control
units.

20 Pull off the heater control knobs, undo the heater control faceplate
screw and remove the faceplate.

21 Undo the heater control panel retaining screws, disconnect the
wiring and lower the control panel.

22 On cars with automatic climate control/air conditioning, pull off
the trim plate, undo the screws and withdraw the control unit.
Disconnect the wiring and remove the control unit.

23 Refer to Chapter 12 if necessary and remove the radio/cassette
player.

24 Press out all the facia switches and disconnect the wiring after
labelling the connectors.

25 Remove the on-board computer after disconnecting and labelling
the wiring connectors.

26 Detach the wiring harness, plug connectors and auxiliary relay
panel from the facia and console.

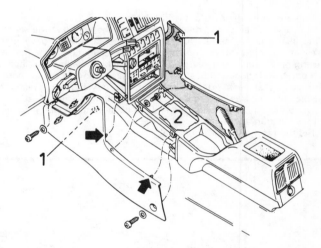

Fig. 11.21 Centre console side panel removal – Audi 200
and Audi 5000 Turbo (Sec 23)

1   Upper retaining clips   2   Inner retaining screw

Side retaining clip locations arrowed

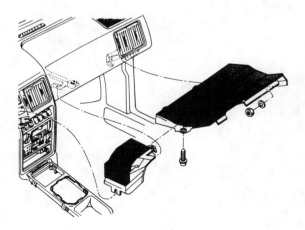

Fig. 11.22 Facia inner cover removal – Audi 200 and Audi
5000 Turbo (Sec 23)

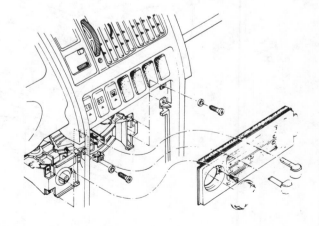

Fig. 11.23 Heater control panel faceplate removal – Audi 200
and Audi 5000 Turbo (Sec 23)

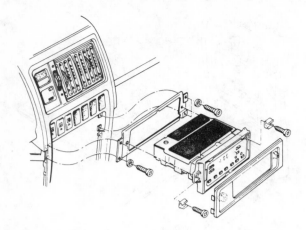

Fig. 11.24 Air conditioning control unit removal – Audi 200 and Audi 5000 Turbo (Sec 23)

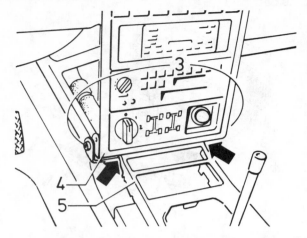

Fig. 11.25 Detaching the console from the front panel frame – Audi 200 and Audi 5000 Turbo (Sec 23)

3   *Retaining screws*   5   *Console*
4   *Front panel*

Console to front panel retaining tags arrowed

27 Pull the wiring harness out of the facia.
28 On cars with air conditioning, disconnect the wiring at the sensor in the centre of the facia. Disconnect the air conditioning vacuum hoses at the plug connectors near the on-board computer, heater housing on the right, and instrument panel. Detach the lower air hoses from the rear air duct and heater housing then remove the front panel frame screws at each side, press the frame forwards and press the console cover downwards to disengage the retainers (Fig. 11.25).
29 Undo the screws securing the facia to its mountings, pull the facia from its location and remove it from the car.
30 Refitting is a reversal of removal.

24 Centre console – removal and refitting

Audi 100 and Audi 5000S models
1   Disconnect the battery negative lead.
2   Remove the gear lever knob then undo the screw at the rear and remove the cover trim (photo).

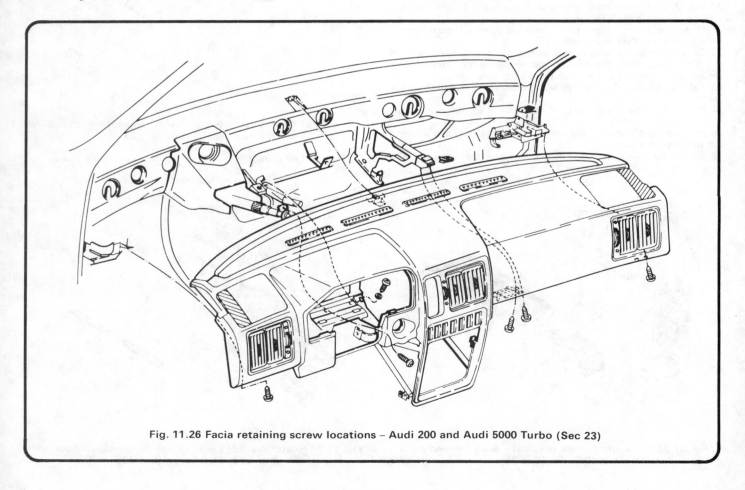

Fig. 11.26 Facia retaining screw locations – Audi 200 and Audi 5000 Turbo (Sec 23)

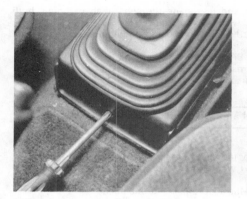

24.2 Removing the centre console cover trim retaining screw (arrowed)

24.3 Console trim surround rear retaining screw (arrowed)

24.4 Console trim surround front retaining screw (arrowed)

3   Undo the two rear screws securing the console trim surround (photo).
4   Remove the ashtray and undo the two screws at the front accessible through the ashtray aperture (photo).
5   Lift the trim surround up at the rear, disengage it from the retaining tags and remove it from the console (photo).
6   Remove the radio/cassette player, as described in Chapter 2, or the trim over the radio aperture if a radio/cassette player is not fitted.
7   Pull off the heater control knobs (photos), then undo the screw securing the heater control panel and remove the panel (photos).

24.5 Removing the console trim surround

24.7A Pull off the heater control rotary ...

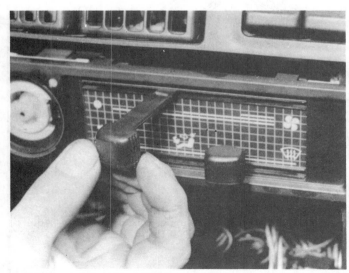

24.7B ... and sliding control knobs ...

24.7C ... undo the control panel retaining screw (arrowed)

24.7D ... and remove the control panel

8   If switches are fitted below the radio aperture, push them out and disconnect the wiring after noting their locations and labelling the wiring.
9   Disconnect the wiring at the cigarette lighter.
10 Undo the console retaining screws and withdraw the console from its location.
11 Refitting is a reversal of removal.

Audi 200 and Audi 5000 Turbo models
12 Disconnect the battery negative lead.
13 Remove the gear lever knob or selector lever handle. Remove the trim around the handle or lever by pulling up to disengage the clips.
14 Remove the ashtray by pressing the retaining tabs outwards then press out the ashtray insert through the gear or selector lever aperture (Fig. 11.20).

15 Undo the screws and disengage the clips, then withdraw both console side panels downwards to remove (Fig. 11.21).
16 Undo the screws, disengage the clips and withdraw both rear side panels.
17 Undo the screws, disconnect the wiring and withdraw the console upper section rearwards to remove.
18 Refitting is a reversal of removal.

25 Seats – removal and refitting

Front seat
1   Push the seat fully forward.
2   Remove the screw where fitted, then pull the trim piece from the seat runner.
3   Pull the cap from the seat runner side-member.
4   At the front of the seat unscrew the stop nut.
5   Pull up the lever and slide the seat off the rear of the runners. Remove the seat through the door aperture.
6   Where electrically-operated front seats are fitted, disconnect the battery negative lead, disconnect the wiring and undo the bolts securing the seat frame to the floor (see also Chapter 12).
7   Refitting is a reversal of removal.

Rear seat
8   To remove the cushion, remove the two screws, one each side below the front edge, lift up the cushion at the front and pull it upwards and out.
9   To remove the seat back on Saloon models, remove the cushion then undo the two screws at the bottom of the seat back, lift it up and out to remove.
10 To remove the seat back on Avant models, remove the trim as necessary to gain access to the hinges.
11 Undo the hinge retaining bolts and remove the seat back from the car.
12 Refitting is a reversal of removal.

26 Central door locking system – general

1   Certain models are equipped with a central door locking system which automatically locks all doors and the rear boot lid/tailgate in unison with the manual locking of either front door. The system is

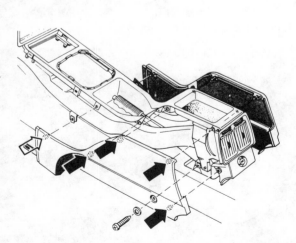

Fig. 11.27 Centre console rear side panel removal – Audi 200 and Audi 5000 Turbo (Sec 24)

Retaining clip locations arrowed

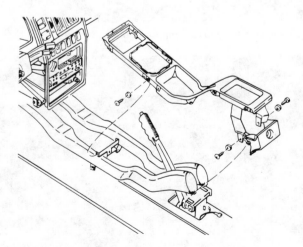

Fig. 11.28 Centre console upper section removal – Audi 200 and Audi 5000 Turbo (Sec 24)

vacuum-operated, and the vacuum for the system is generated by an electric pump located under the rear seat.

2   Any fault in the system is most likely to be caused by a leak in one of the hoses, in which case the hose and connection should be checked and repaired as necessary. Access to the relevant actuator is straightforward after removal of the appropriate trim panel (photo). Removal and refitting of the actuator entails disconnecting the vacuum hose and operating rod, then undoing the retaining screws. Refitting is a reversal of removal. If a fault develops on the vacuum pump repair should be entrusted to an Audi dealer, but first check that a fuse has not blown.

27 Power operated windscreen – general

1   Certain models are equipped with power (electric) operated windows which can be raised or lowered when the ignition is switched on.
2   If a fault develops, first check that the system fuse has not blown.
3   Access to the electric motors and regulator mechanism is gained by removing the door panels, as described in Section 9.

28 Heater unit (without air conditioning) – removal and refitting

1   Disconnect the battery negative lead.
2   Drain the cooling system, as described in Chapter 2.
3   Disconnect the heater hoses at the engine compartment bulkhead.
4   Refer to Section 24 or Section 23 and remove the centre console or facia components, as applicable, sufficiently to release the heater controls from their attachments, and the air ducts and wiring from the heater and facia.
5   Remove the black plastic cover over the plenum chamber in the engine compartment.
6   Undo the screw and free the heater retaining strap (photo).
7   Withdraw the heater upwards from its location and remove it, complete with heater controls and wiring loom, from the engine compartment.
8   Refitting is a reversal of removal, but renew the self-adhesive seals on the heater assembly before installing.

29 Heater blower motor (without air conditioning) – removal and refitting

1   Disconnect the battery negative lead.
2   Remove the black plastic cover over the plenum chamber in the engine compartment.
3   Disconnect the wiring plug on the end of the blower motor and extract the motor ventilating hose elbow from the motor and heater case.
4   Extract the circlip, retaining washer and grommet from the end of the motor.
5   At the other end of the heater unit, withdraw the intake duct and air flap then pull the motor and fan out of the heater case.
6   Refitting is a reversal of removal.

30 Heater controls (without air conditioning) – removal and refitting

1   Disconnect the battery negative lead.
2   Refer to Section 24 or Section 23 and remove the centre console or facia components, as applicable, sufficiently to release the heater controls from their attachments.
3   Release the clips securing the control cables to the control unit then disconnect the cable ends from the operating levers. Remove the control unit.
4   If the cables are to be removed, disconnect them at the heater then pull through the bulkhead to remove.
5   Refitting is a reversal of removal. To adjust the cables, connect them to the heater first then pull the inner cables out as far as they will go. Attach the inner cables to the control unit levers, set the levers and

rotary knob in their end positions and secure the outer cables with the retaining clips.

31 Air conditioning – precautions and maintenance

1   Never disconnect any part of the air conditioner refrigeration circuit unless the system has been discharged by your Audi dealer or a qualified refrigeration engineer.
2   Where the compressor or condenser obstruct other mechanical operations such as engine removal, then it is permissible to unbolt their mountings and move them to the limit of their flexible hose deflection, but not to disconnect the hoses. If there is still insufficient room to carry out the required work then the system must be discharged before disconnecting and removing the assemblies.
3   The system will, of course, have to be recharged on completion.
4   Regularly check the condenser for clogging with flies or dirt. Hose clean with water or compressed air.
5   Check the drivebelt condition and if necessary adjust the belt tension, as described in Section 32.

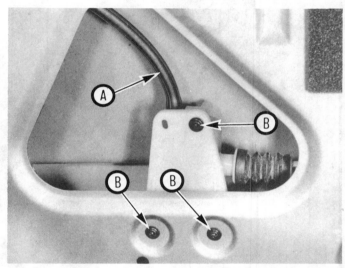

26.2 Central locking actuator vacuum hose (A) and retaining screws (B) in the Avant tailgate

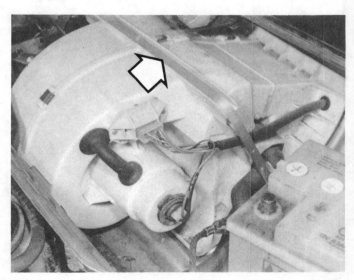

28.6 Heater unit retaining strap (arrowed)

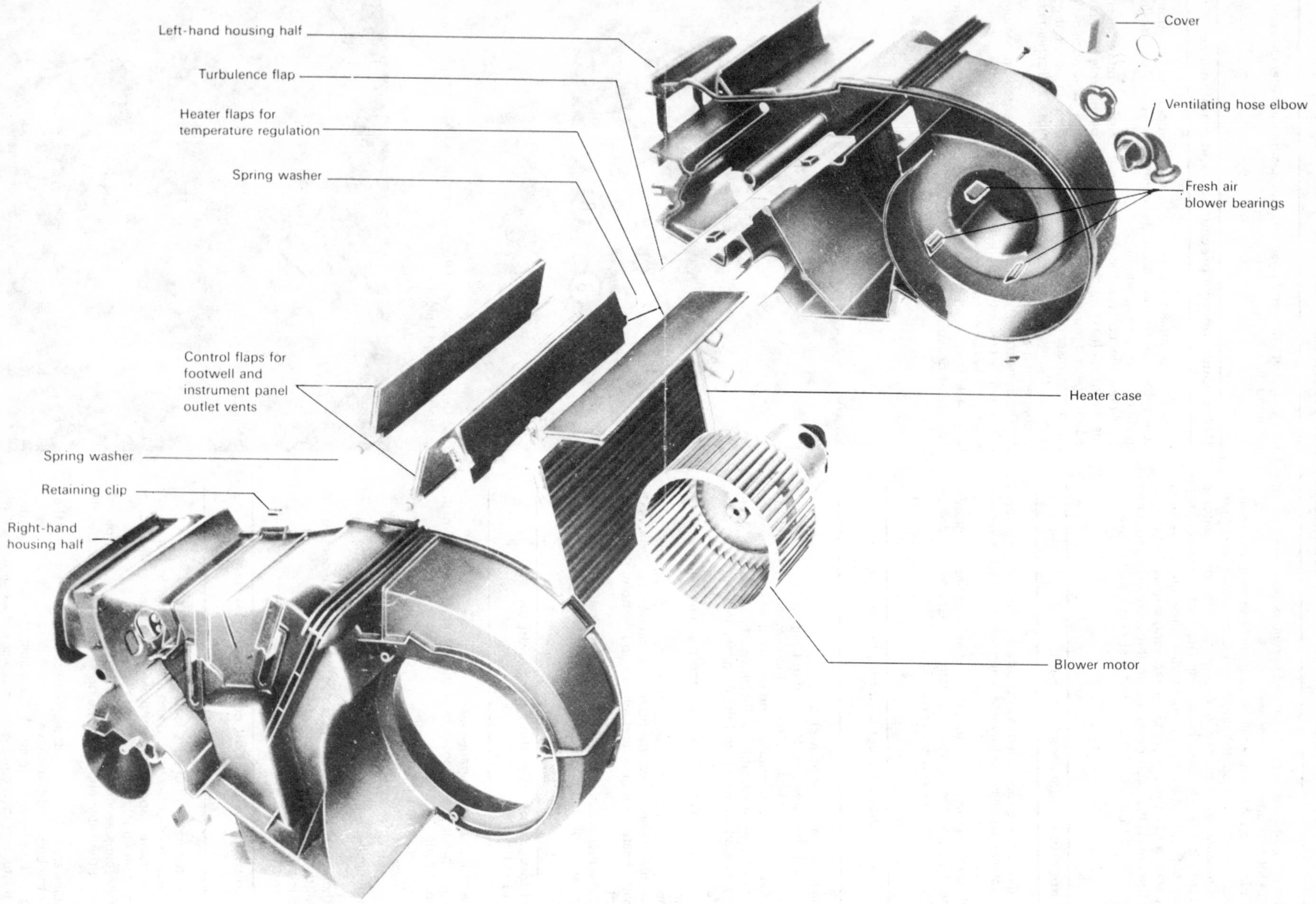

Cover

Ventilating hose elbow

Fresh air blower bearings

Heater case

Blower motor

Left-hand housing half

Turbulence flap

Heater flaps for temperature regulation

Spring washer

Control flaps for footwell and instrument panel outlet vents

Spring washer

Retaining clip

Right-hand housing half

Fig. 11.29 Exploded view of the heater unit components on models without air conditioning (Sec 28)

32 Air conditioner drivebelt – removal, refitting and adjustment

1 Remove the alternator and/or power-assisted steering pump drivebelt, as necessary, to allow removal of the drivebelt.
2 Slacken the compressor mounting and adjustment nuts, move the compressor in towards the engine and slip the drivebelt off the pulleys.
3 Fit a new belt over the pulleys and tension the belt by levering the compressor away from the engine until it is just possible to deflect the belt by 10 mm (0.4 in) under thumb pressure at a point midway between the pulleys. Hold the compressor in this position and tighten the adjustment and mounting nuts.

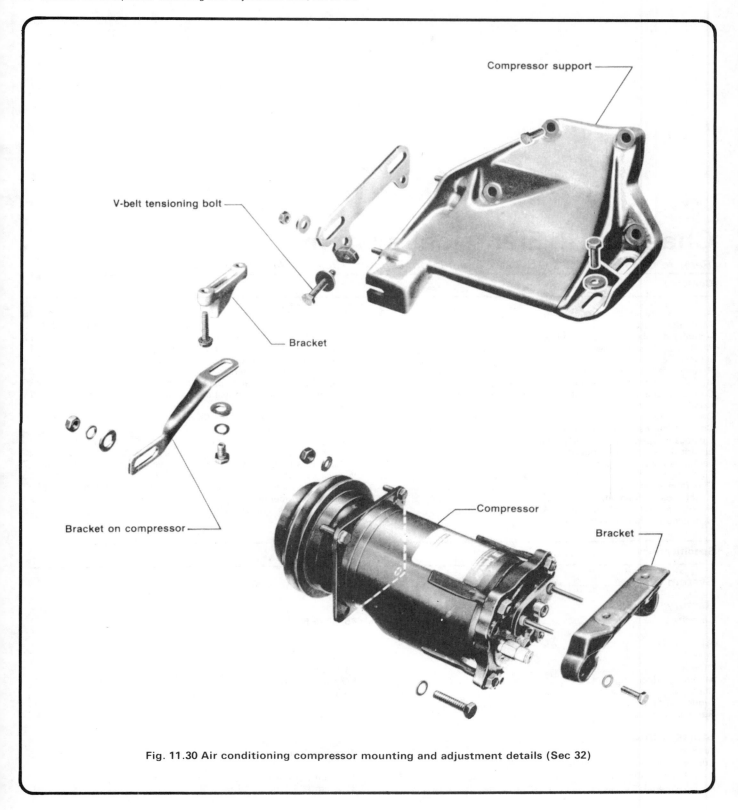

Fig. 11.30 Air conditioning compressor mounting and adjustment details (Sec 32)

Chapter 12 Electrical system

Refer to Chapter 13 for specifications and information on 1987 and later models

Contents

Specifications

System type .... 12 volt negative earth

Battery
Capacity .... 45, 54 or 63 Ah

Alternator
Type .... Bosch
Output .... 65 or 90 amp
Minimum brush length .... 5.0 mm (0.2 in)
Stator winding resistance .... 0.1 ohm maximum
Diode resistance .... 50 to 80 ohm
Rotor winding resistance .... 3.0 to 4.0 ohm

Starter motor
Type .... Bosch pre-engaged, 0.95 or 1.1 kw rating
Commutator minimum diameter:
  0.95 kw starter .... 33.5 mm (1.32 in)
  1.1 kw starter .... 31.2 mm (1.23 in)

Commutator maximum run-out	0.03 mm (0.001 in)
Commutator insulation undercut	0.5 to 0.8 mm (0.02 to 0.03 in)
Armature axial play:	
0.95 kw starter	0.1 to 0.3 mm (0.004 to 0.012 in)
1.1 kw starter	0.05 to 0.4 mm (0.002 to 0.016 in)
Minimum brush length:	
0.95 kw starter	11.5 mm (0.45 in)
1.1 kw starter	8.0 mm (0.32 in)

Fuses

Fuse	Function	Rating (amps)
1	Front and rear fog lights (UK models)	15
2	Hazard warning lights, air conditioner	15
3	Horn, brake lights	25
4	Interior lights, courtesy lights, luggage compartment light, front cigarette lighter, or on-board computer, radio	15
5	Vacant	
6	Right-hand tail and parking lights	5
7	Left-hand tail and parking lights	5
8	Right-hand headlight main beam, main beam warning light	10
9	Left-hand headlight main beam	10
10	Right-hand headlight dipped beam	10
11	Left-hand headlight dipped beam	10
12	Instruments, reversing lights, Auto-check system	15
13	Electric fuel pump	15
14	Number plate light, glovebox light, engine compartment light, heater controls, ashtray lighting	5
15	Direction indicators, windscreen wipers/washers	25
16	Rear window heater, on-board computer lights, clock	30
17	Fresh air blower	30
18	Electric sliding roof (UK models) rear window wiper/ washer, electrically heated seats (North American models)	30
19	Central locking system, electric mirrors	10
20	Electrically heated seats (UK models)	30
21	Rear cigarette lighter	25
22	Vacant	

Additional fuses on fusebox inside wall

23	Passenger's seat adjustment, seat memory control unit	30
27	Electric sliding roof (North American models)	20

Bulbs

	Wattage
Headlamps	55/60
Front foglights/additional driving lights	55
Sidelights	4
Direction indicators	21
Rear foglights	21
Brake lights	21
Tail lights	5 and 10
Reversing lights	21
Number plate light	5
Interior lights	10
Ashtray illumination	1.2
Heater control illumination	1.2
Instrument panel illumination	3
Instrument panel warning lights	1.2 and 2
Glovebox light	2
Engine compartment light	10
Luggage compartment light	5
Reading lights	5
Vanity mirror light	3

Torque wrench settings

	Nm	lbf ft
Alternator mounting bolts	35	26
Alternator adjustment bolts	20	15
Alternator pulley nut	35	26
Starter motor to engine	60	44
Windscreen wiper arm to spindle	16	12
Wiper frame	7	5
Wiper motor	4	3
Wiper motor crankarm nut	5	4

1 General description

The electrical system is of the 12 volt negative earth type, and consists of a 12 volt battery, alternator, starter motor and related electrical accessories, components and wiring. The battery is charged by an alternator which is belt-driven from the crankshaft pulley. The starter motor is of the pre-engaged type incorporating an integral solenoid. On starting, the solenoid moves the drive pinion into engagement with the flywheel ring gear before the starter motor is energised. Once the engine has started, a one-way clutch prevents the motor armature being driven by the engine until the piston disengages from the flywheel.

Further details of the major electrical systems are given in the relevant Sections of this Chapter.

Caution: *Before carrying out any work on the vehicle electrical system, read through the precautions given in Safety First! at the beginning of this manual and in Section 2 of this Chapter.*

2 Electrical system – precautions

It is necessary to take extra care when working on the electrical system to avoid damage to semi-conductor devices (diodes and transistors), and to avoid the risk of personal injury. In addition to the precautions given in Safety First! at the beginning of this manual, observe the following items when working on the system.

1 *Always remove rings, watches, etc before working on the electrical system.* Even with the battery disconnected, capacitive discharge could occur if a component live terminal is earthed through a metal object. This could cause a shock or nasty burn.

2 *Do not reverse the battery connections.* Components such as the alternator or any other having semi-conductor circuitry could be irreparably damaged.

3 If the engine is being started using jump leads and a slave battery, connect the batteries *positive to positive,* and *negative to negative.* This also applies when connecting a battery charger.

4 Never disconnect the battery terminals, or alternator wiring when the engine is running.

5 The battery leads and alternator wiring must be disconnected before carrying out any electric welding on the car.

6 Never use an ohmmeter of the type incorporating a hand cranked generator for circuit or continuity testing.

7 Always ensure that the battery negative lead is disconnected (photo) when working on the electrical system.

3 Maintenance and inspection

1 At regular intervals (see Routine Maintenance) carry out the following maintenance and inspection operations on the electrical system components.

2 Check the operation of all the electrical equipment, ie wipers, washers, lights, direction indicators, horn etc. Refer to the appropriate Sections of this Chapter if any components are found to be inoperative.

3 Visually check all accessible wiring connections, harnesses and retaining clips for security, or any signs of chafing or damage. Rectify any problems encountered.

4 Check the alternator drivebelt for cracks, fraying or damage. Renew the belt if worn or, if satisfactory, check and adjust the belt tension, as described in Section 7.

2.7 Battery with negative terminal disconnected

3.7A Top up the windscreen washer reservoir ...

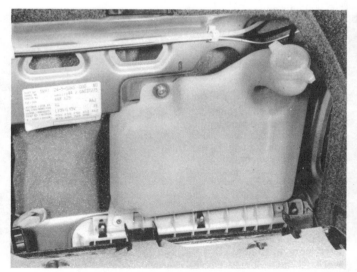

3.7B ... and the rear window washer reservoir on Avant models

5   Check the condition of the wiper blades and if they are cracked or show signs of deterioration, renew them, as described in Sections 23 and 26. Check the operation of the windscreen rear window and headlamp washers (if fitted). Adjust the nozzles using a pin, if necessary.

6   Check the battery terminals, and if there is any sign of corrosion disconnect and clean them thoroughly. Smear the terminals and battery posts with petroleum jelly before refitting the plastic covers. If there is any corrosion on the battery tray, remove the battery, clean the deposits away and treat the affected metal with an anti-rust preparation. Repaint the tray in the original colour after treatment.

7   Top up the washer reservoirs and check the security of the pump wires and water pipes (photos).

8   Check the electrolyte level in the battery by viewing the side of the translucent case. Maintain the level between the MIN and MAX marks by adding distilled or de-ionized water as necessary.

9   It is advisable to have the headlight aim adjusted using optical beam setting equipment.

10 While carrying out a road test check the operation of all the instruments and warning lights, and the operation of the direction indicator self-cancelling mechanism.

4.2 Battery negative terminal (A), positive terminal (B), vent hose (C) and clamp bolt (D)

4   Battery – removal and refitting

1   The battery may be located at the rear of the engine compartment under a black plastic cover or under the rear seat bench according to model.

2   Slacken the negative terminal clamp and disconnect the lead (photo).

3   Slacken the positive terminal clamp and disconnect the lead.

4   Detach the battery vent hose.

5   Unscrew the bolt and remove the battery holding clamp.

6   Lift the battery out of its location taking care to keep it upright.

7   Refitting is a reversal of removal, but make sure that the polarity is correct before connecting the leads and do not overtighten the clamps.

4   Special rapid 'boost' charges, which are claimed to restore the power of the battery in 1 to 2 hours, can be dangerous unless they are thermostatically controlled, as they can cause serious damage to the battery plates through overheating.

5   While charging the battery, ensure that the temperature of the electrolyte never exceeds 37.8°C (100°F) and loosen the vent caps (where applicable).

5   Battery – charging

1   In winter when a heavy demand is placed on the battery, such as when starting from cold and using more electrical equipment, it is a good idea to have the battery fully charged occasionally from an external source at a rate of 10% of the battery capacity (ie 6.3 amp for a 63 Ah battery). It is advisable to disconnect the battery leads when charging.

2   Continue to charged the battery until no further rise in specific gravity is noted over a four hour period.

3   Alternatively, a trickle charger, charging at a rate of 1.5 amp can be safely used overnight.

6   Alternator – removal and refitting

1   Disconnect the battery negative lead.

2   On five-cylinder engines undo the nuts and remove the cover plate from the rear of the alternator (photo). On some models it will first be necessary to remove the cooling air hose.

3   Slacken the alternator mounting and adjustment bolts and slip the drivebelt off the pulley (photo).

4   Note the location of the wiring then disconnect it from the rear of the alternator (photo).

5   Undo the mounting and adjustment bolts and remove the alternator from the engine.

6   Refitting is a reversal of removal, but adjust the drivebelt as described in Section 7.

6.2 Alternator rear cover plate on five-cylinder engines

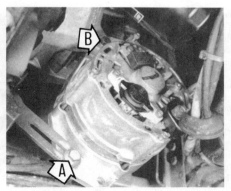

6.3 Alternator adjustment bolt (A) and mounting bolt (B) on five-cylinder engines

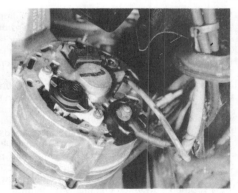

6.4 Wiring connections at the rear of the alternator on five-cylinder engines

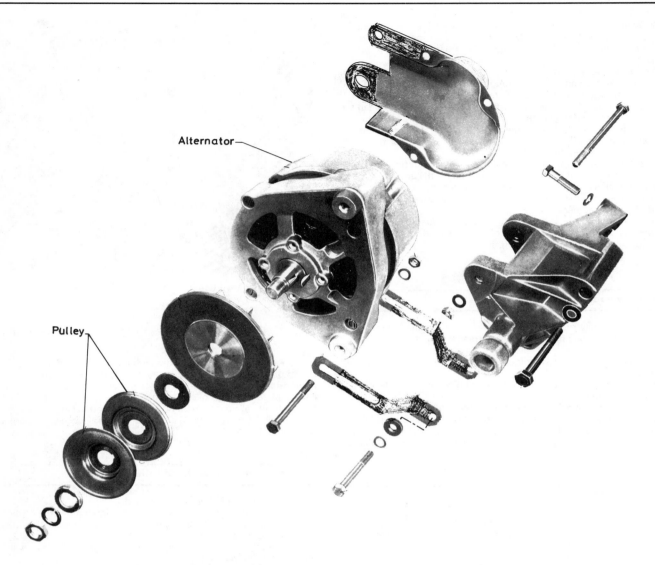

Fig. 12.1 Alternator pulley and mounting details – five-cylinder engines (Sec 6)

7 Alternator drivebelt – removal and adjustment

1   At the intervals specified in Routine Maintenance the drivebelt should be checked for condition and re-tensioned. If there are any signs of cracking or deterioration, the drivebelt should be renewed.
2   To remove the drivebelt, first remove the air conditioner drivebelt (Chapter 11) and/or power-assisted steering pump drivebelt (Chapter 10) as necessary.
3   Slacken the alternator mounting and adjustment arm bolts so that the alternator is free to move, then push the unit towards the engine. Slip the drivebelt off the pulleys and remove it from the engine.
4   Slip the new drivebelt over the pulleys then lever the alternator from the engine until it is just possible to deflect the belt under moderate thumb pressure by 10 to 15 mm (0.4 to 0.6 in) at a point midway between the âlternator and crankshaft pulleys (photo). Hold the alternator in this position and tighten the mounting and adjustment bolts. Note that on later models the adjustment bolt incorporates an inner toothed nut which engages with teeth in the adjustment arm in the form of a rack and pinion arrangement. Turn the nut using a spanner or socket until the tension is correct then tighten the adjusting bolt.

Fig. 12.2 Drivebelt adjustment point – four-cylinder engines (Sec 7)

a Specified drivebelt deflection

7.4 Using a screwdriver to tension the alternator drivebelt on five-cylinder engines

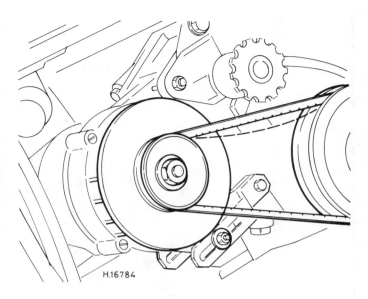

H.16784

Fig. 12.3 Drivebelt adjustment point – five-cylinder engines (Sec 7)

5   Refit the other belts, where applicable, as described in the relevant Chapters, then run the engine for several minutes. Switch off then recheck the tension and adjust if necessary.

8   Alternator – servicing

Note: *The voltage regulator and brushes can be removed without removing the alternator. However, the following complete dismantling procedure assumes that the alternator is on the bench.*

1   Clean the exterior of the alternator.
2   Remove the screws and withdraw the voltage regulator and brushes. If the brushes are worn below the specified minimum length, they must be renewed, complete with the voltage regulator, as an assembly.
3   Mark the end housings and stator in relation to each other.
4   Grip the pulley in a vice then unscrew the nut and withdraw the washer, pulley and fan, together with any spacers. Prise out the key.
5   Unscrew the through-bolts and tap off the front housing, together with the rotor.
6   Using a mallet or puller, remove the rotor from the front housing and remove the spacers.
7   Remove the screws and retaining plate. Drive the bearing from the front housing with a soft metal drift.
8   Using a suitable puller, remove the bearing from the slip ring end of the rotor, but take care not to damage the slip rings.
9   Remove the screw, disconnect the lead, and withdraw the suppressor condenser from the rear housing.
10 Unscrew the terminal nut(s), then remove the washers, and remove the insulator from the rear housing.
11 Carefully separate the stator from the rear housing without straining the wires. Identify each wire for location, then unsolder them using the minimum of heat to avoid damage to the diodes. Long-nosed pliers may be used as a heat sink.
12 Remove the screws and separate the diode plate from the rear housing.
13 Remove the wave washer from the rear housing.
14 Check the stator windings for a short to ground by connecting an ohmmeter or test bulb between each wire and the outer ring. Check that the internal resistance between the wires is as given in the Specifications using an ohmmeter between wires 1 and 2, then 1 and 3, and 2 and 3 – the numbering of the wires is of no importance.
15 Using the ohmmeter check that the resistance of each diode is as given in the Specifications when the ohmmeter is connected across

Fig. 12.4 Later type alternator adjustment components (Sec 7)

A   *Toothed adjustment arm*   B   *Toothed adjusting nut*

the diode in one direction. Reverse the wires and check that there is now no resistance.
16 Check the rotor windings for a short to ground by connecting an ohmmeter or test bulb between each slip ring and the winding core. Check that the internal resistance of the winding is as given in the Specifications using an ohmmeter between the two slip rings.
17 Clean all the components and obtain new bearings, brushes etc, as required.
18 Reassembly is a reversal of dismantling, but when fitting the bearing to the front housing, drive it in using a metal tube *on the outer race* making sure that the open end of the bearing faces the rotor. When fitting the rear bearing to the rotor, drive it on using a metal tube *on the inner race,* making sure that the open end of the bearing faces the rear housing.

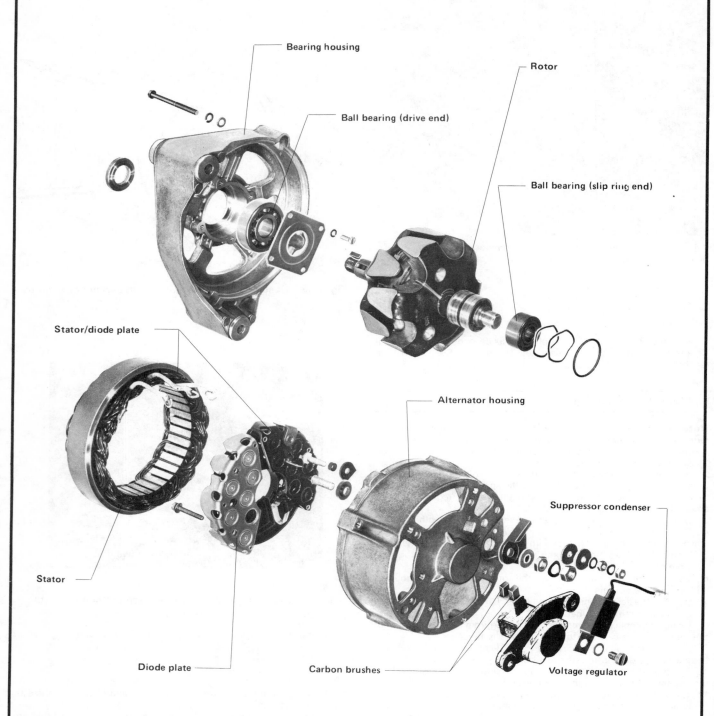

Bearing housing

Rotor

Ball bearing (drive end)

Ball bearing (slip ring end)

Stator/diode plate

Alternator housing

Suppressor condenser

Stator

Diode plate

Carbon brushes

Voltage regulator

Fig. 12.5 Exploded view of the alternator (Sec 8)

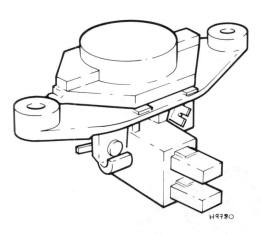

Fig. 12.6 Alternator voltage regulator with integral brushes (Sec 8)

10.2 Wiring connections at the starter solenoid

9 Starter motor – testing in the car

1 If the starter motor fails to respond when the starter switch is operated, first check that the fault is not external to the starter motor.
2 Connect a test lamp between chassis earth and the large terminal on the starter solenoid, terminal 30. This terminal is connected directly to the battery and the test lamp should light whether or not the ignition switch is operated.
3 Remove the test lamp connection from the large terminal (30) and transfer it to the smaller terminal (50) on the solenoid. The lamp should light only when the starter switch is in its *Start* position.
4 If both these tests are satisfactory the fault is in the starter motor.
5 If the starter motor is heard to operate, but the engine fails to start, check the battery terminals, the starter motor leads and the engine-to-body earth strap for cleanliness and tightness.

10 Starter motor – removal and refitting

1 Disconnect the battery negative lead.
2 Note the location of the wires on the starter solenoid, then disconnect them (photo).
3 Unscrew the mounting bolts and withdraw the starter motor (photo).
4 Refitting is a reversal of removal, but make sure that the mating faces are clean and tighten the mounting bolts to the specified torque.

10.3 Starter motor lower mounting bolt (arrowed)

11 Starter motor – overhaul

1 Mark the housings and mounting bracket (where fitted) in relation to each other.
2 Remove the nuts and washers and withdraw the end support plate (where fitted).
3 Remove the screws and withdraw the small end cover and gasket, then extract the circlip and remove the shims. Note the exact number of shims, as they determine the shaft endfloat.
4 Unscrew the through-bolts and remove the commutator end bearing housing.
5 Unscrew the nut and disconnect the field wire at the solenoid.
6 Note the position of the brush holder plate and withdraw the plate from the field winding housing and armature.
7 Unscrew the three bolts and remove the solenoid from the drive end housing. Unhook the solenoid from the actuating lever.
8 Prise out the actuating lever cover pad from the drive end housing.
9 On the 1.1 kw starter, withdraw the armature from the reversing gear assembly.

10 Remove the armature on 0.95 kw starters, or the reversing gear assembly on 1.1 kw starters, from the drive end housing and disengage the actuating lever from the pinion.
11 Using a metal tube, drive the stop ring off the circlip, then extract the circlip and pull off the stop ring.
12 Withdraw the pinion drive from the armature or reversing gear.
13 Clean all the components in paraffin and wipe dry, then examine them for wear and damage. Check the pinion drive for damaged teeth and make sure that the one-way clutch only rotates in one direction. If the shaft bushes are worn they can be removed using a soft metal drift and new bushes installed. However, the new bushes must first be soaked in hot oil for approximately five minutes. Clean the commutator with a rag moistened with a suitable solvent. Minor scoring can be removed with fine glasspaper, but deep scoring will necessitate the commutator being skimmed in a lathe and then being undercut. Commutator refinishing is a job which is best left to a specialist. On the 1.1 kw starter do not dismantle the reversing gear assembly, but renew it as a unit if it was rough or noisy in operation.
14 Measure the length of the brushes. If less than the minimum given in the Specifications, renew the brush holder plate as an assembly. To

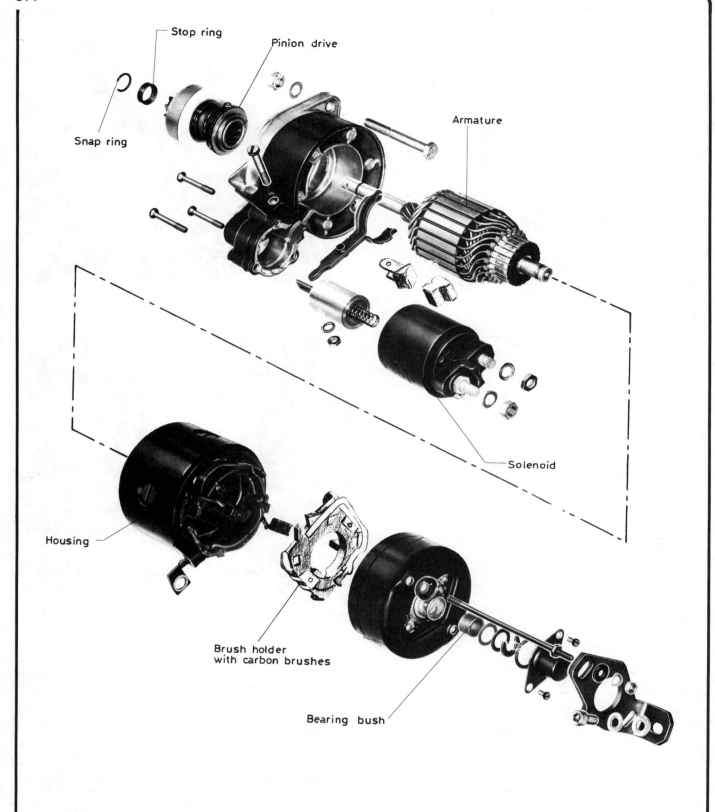

Stop ring

Pinion drive

Snap ring

Armature

Solenoid

Housing

Brush holder
with carbon brushes

Bearing bush

Fig. 12.7 Exploded view of the Bosch 0.95 Kw starter motor (Sec 11)

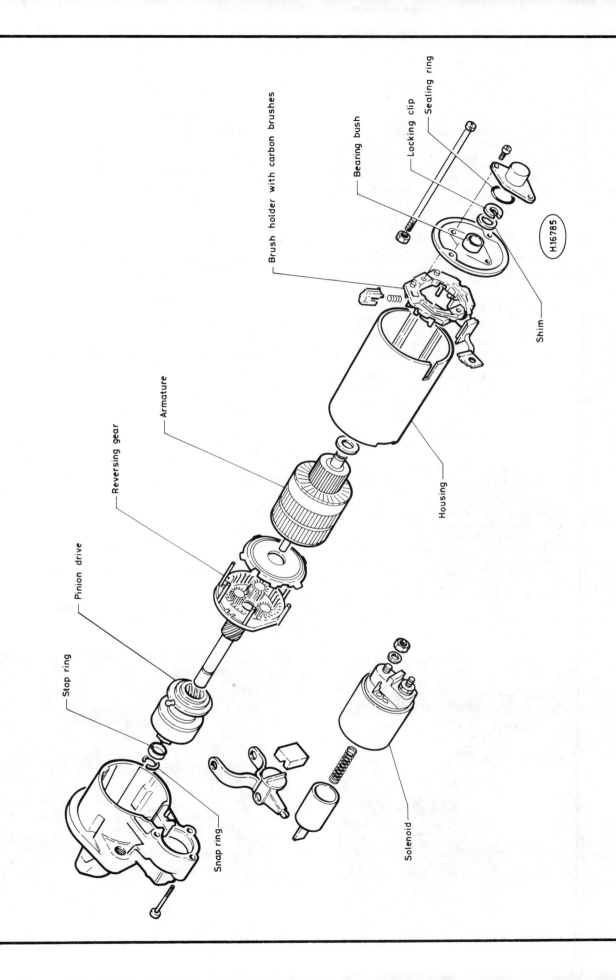

Sealing ring

Locking clip

Bearing bush

Brush holder with carbon brushes

Shim

H.16785

Armature

Reversing gear

Housing

Pinion drive

Stop ring

Solenoid

Snap ring

Fig. 12.8 Exploded view of the Bosch 1.1 Kw starter motor (Sec 11)

do this on the 0.95 kw starter, cut off the copper braid next to the brush holder and solder it to the new holder.

15 Reassembly is a reversal of the dismantling procedure, but note the following. To fit the brush assembly over the commutator, either hook the brush springs on to the edge of the brush holder, or bend pieces of wire to hold the springs off the brushes until the brush assembly has been fitted. As soon as this has been done, release the brush springs and position them so that they bear on the centres of the brushes. Apply a little molybdenum disulphide grease to the splines of the pinion drive. Fit a new circlip to the pinion end of the shaft and ensure that the circlip groove is not damaged. Any burrs on the edges of the groove should be removed with a fine file. During reassembly apply sealing compound to the points indicated in Figs. 12.9 and 12.10.

12 Fuses, relays and control units – general

Fuses

1   The fusebox is situated at the rear of the engine compartment on the right or left-hand side of the plenum chamber – according to model. To gain access to the fuses, release the fusebox cover from its clips and lift off. The fuse locations, current rating and circuits protected are listed on the inside of the cover (photo). Each fuse is colour-coded and has its rating stamped on it (photo).
2   To remove a fuse from its location, hook it out using the small plastic removal tool provided. This is located, together with the spare fuses, in the fusebox tray. Hook the tool over the fuse and pull up to remove. Refit the fuse by pressing it firmly into its location.
3   Always renew a fuse with one of an identical rating. Never renew a fuse more than once without finding the cause of the trouble.

Relays and control units

4   The main relays are located alongside the fuses in the fusebox and there is an additional relay carrier located under the left-hand side of the facia.
5   The relays can be removed by simply pulling them from their respective locations. If a system controlled by a relay becomes inoperative, and the relay is suspect, operate the system and if the relay is functioning it should be possible to hear it click as it is energised. If this is the case, the fault lies with the components of the system. If the relay is not being energised then the relay is not receiving a main supply voltage, a switching voltage or the relay itself is faulty.
6   Control units for the various systems will be found situated throughout the car; depending on equipment and options fitted, and territory of export. The control unit locations are shown in Figs. 12.11, 12.12 and 12.13.

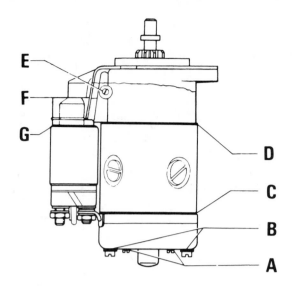

Fig. 12.9 Sealing points on the 0.95 Kw starter motor (Sec 11)

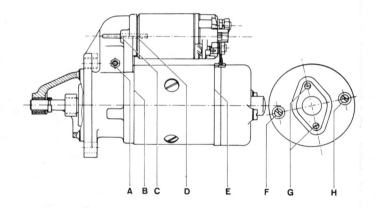

Fig. 12.10 Sealing points on the 1.1 Kw starter motor (Sec 11)

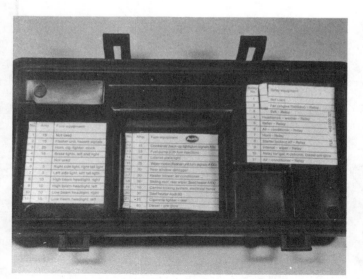

12.1A Fuse and relay positions shown on the inside of the fusebox cover

12.1B Fuses and relays in the fusebox

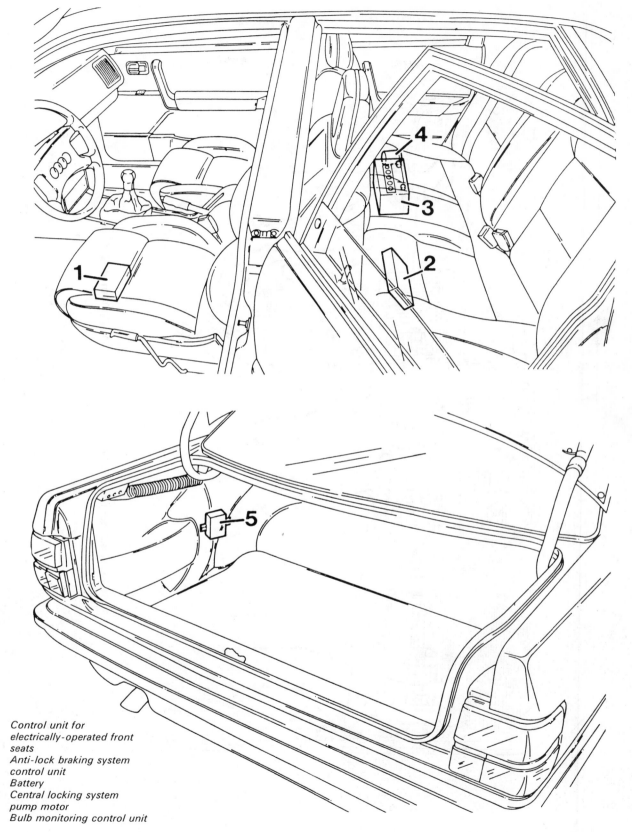

1 Control unit for
   electrically-operated front
   seats
2 Anti-lock braking system
   control unit
3 Battery
4 Central locking system
   pump motor
5 Bulb monitoring control unit

Fig. 12.11 Control unit locations in the car interior and luggage compartment (Sec 12)

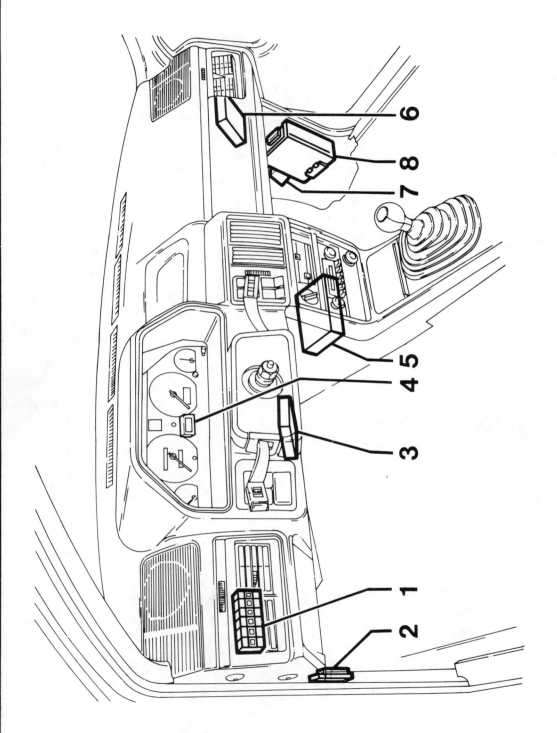

Fig. 12.12 Relay and control unit location at the facia – Audi 100 models (Sec 12)

1 Additional relay carrier
2 Transistorized coil ignition control unit (alternative position)
3 Control unit for cruise control system
4 Direction indicator relay
5 Main control unit for Auto-check system
6 Air conditioning control unit and regulator
7 Altitude sensor
8 Control unit for KE-Jetronic fuel injection system

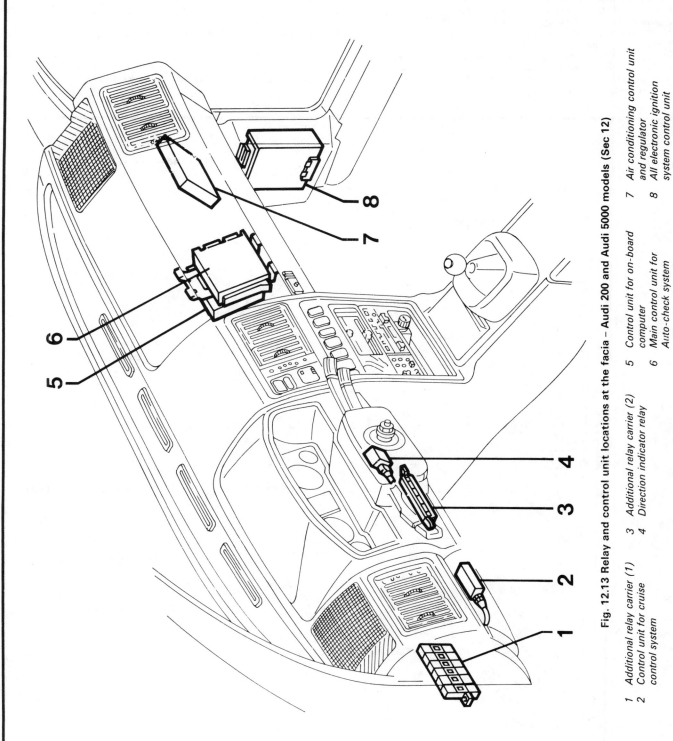

Fig. 12.13 Relay and control unit locations at the facia – Audi 200 and Audi 5000 models (Sec 12)

1 Additional relay carrier (1)
2 Control unit for cruise
   control system
3 Additional relay carrier (2)
4 Direction indicator relay
5 Control unit for on-board
   computer
6 Main control unit for
   Auto-check system
7 Air conditioning control unit
   and regulator
8 All electronic ignition
   system control unit

13 Ignition system/steering column lock – removal and refitting

1   Remove the instrument panel, as described in Section 17.
2   Working through the instrument panel aperture, disconnect the wiring plug at the rear of the ignition switch.
3   Scrape away the paint over the retaining screw, undo the screw and withdraw the ignition switch.
4   Refit the switch with the hole in the housing and switch aligned, then refit the screw and seal with paint.
5   To remove the steering column lock, first remove the combination switch, as described in Section 14.

6   Using a 2.5 mm diameter drill bit, drill out the lock housing shear-bolt then remove the remains of the shear-bolt with a stud extractor.
7   Undo the two nuts and remove both steering column upper mounting bolts.
8   Remove the trim under the facia and the air ducting sufficiently to allow the column to be lowered.
9   Push the steering column down and withdraw the lock housing from the column.
10 Using a 3 mm diameter drill, drill into the lock housing at the point shown in Fig. 12.18. Take care when doing this otherwise the drill will damage the lock once it penetrates the lock housing wall.

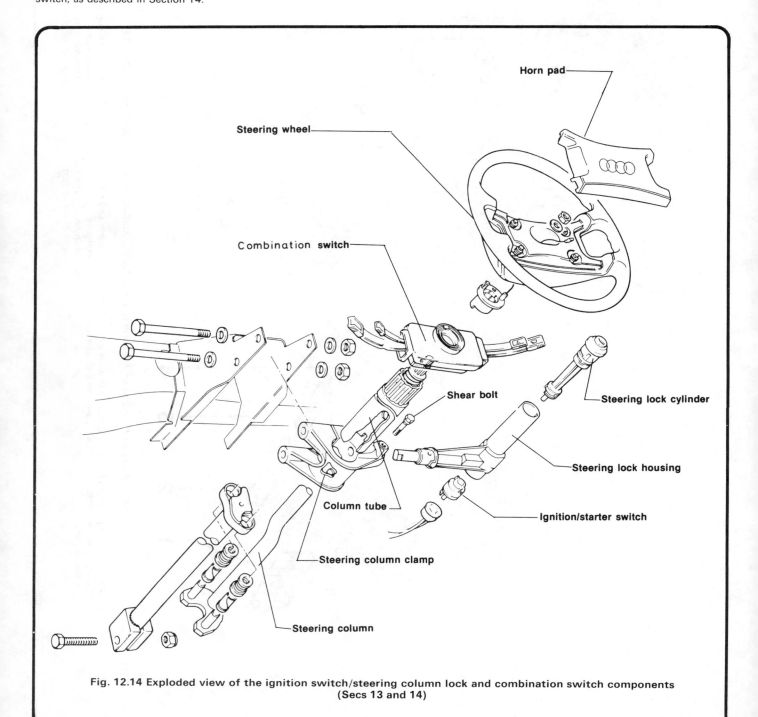

Fig. 12.14 Exploded view of the ignition switch/steering column lock and combination switch components (Secs 13 and 14)

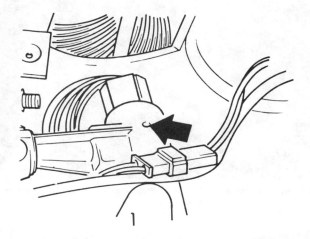

Fig. 12.15 Ignition switch retaining screw location – arrowed (Sec 13)

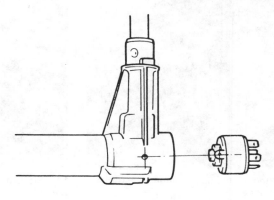

fig. 12.16 Alignment of ignition switch and housing locating holes (Sec 13)

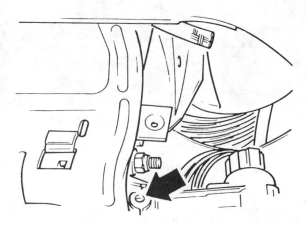

Fig. 12.17 Lock housing shear-bolt location – arrowed (Sec 13)

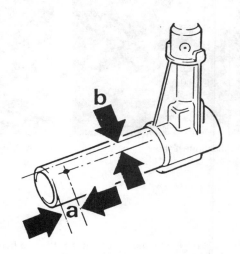

Fig. 12.18 Lock housing drilling point for lock removal (Sec 13)

a = 12.5 mm (0.5 in)   b = 8.0 mm (0.3 in)

11 Depress the retaining pin through the drilled hole and withdraw the lock from the lock housing.
12 Refit the lock by pushing it into the housing until the pin springs into the hole.
13 Refit the lock housing to the column using a new shear-bolt. Check the operation of the lock before tightening the shear-bolt until the head breaks off.
14 The remainder of refitting is a reversal of removal. Refit the instrument panel, as described in Section 17, and the combination switch, as described in Section 14.

14 Combination switch – removal and refitting

1 Disconnect the battery negative lead.
2 Remove the steering wheel, as described in Chapter 10.
3 Withdraw the trim end cappings from the combination switch stalks (photo).
4 Insert a screwdriver through the opening under the switch and slacken the switch clamp screw (photo).
5 Withdraw the switch assembly from the steering column, disconnect the wiring connectors and remove the combination switch (photos).

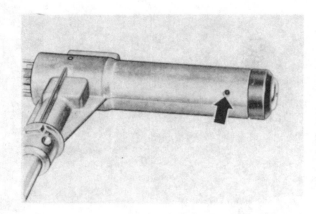

Fig. 12.19 Depress the pin (arrowed) and withdraw the lock from the housing (Sec 13)

14.3 Withdraw the combination switch trim end cappings

14.4 Slacken the combination switch clamp screw

14.5A Withdraw the combination switch assembly ...

14.5B ... and disconnect the wiring connectors

15.4A Withdraw the facia plate ...

15.4B ... then push out the console switches

6   Refitting is a reversal of removal. Check that the gap between the switch and steering wheel is 3 mm (^{1}/8 in), if necessary adjust the switch position.

15 Centre console and facia switches – removal and refitting

1   The number of switches fitted, their type and position will vary according to model and options fitted, but the procedure is similar for all versions.
2   Disconnect the battery negative terminal.
3   Refer to Chapter 11 and remove the centre console cover trim.
4   Withdraw the facia plate over the lower switches and withdraw the switches from the console (photos). The switches can be released from their opening by carefully prising out with a screwdriver or, if access permits, by pushing out the switch from behind.
5   Disconnect the switch wiring plug and remove the switch.
6   The upper console and facia switches are removed by carefully prising them out at the top then withdrawing from their location (photo). Disconnect the wiring plug and remove the switch.
7   Refitting is a reversal of removal.

16 Courtesy light switches – removal and refitting

1   Disconnect the battery negative lead.
2   Undo the screw securing the switch in position (photos), withdraw the switch and disconnect the wiring.
3   Refitting is a reversal of removal.

17 Instrument panel – removal and refitting

1   Disconnect the battery negative lead.
2   Refer to Chapter 10 and remove the steering wheel.

15.6 Facia switch removal

16.2A Interior courtesy light switch on door pillar

16.2B Luggage compartment light switch on boot lid

17.3 Instrument panel retaining screws (arrowed)

17.5 Instrument panel removal

3   Undo the two screws securing the instrument panel to the facia hood (photo) and pull the instrument out slightly.
4   Reach behind the panel and disconnect the speedometer cable (bayonet fitting) then withdraw the panel.
5   Mark the location of the wiring connectors and vacuum hose then disconnect them from the rear of the panel (photo). Remove the instrument panel from the car.
6   Refitting is a reversal of removal.

18 Instruments – removal, testing and refitting

1   Remove the instrument panel, as described in Section 17.
2   Remove the relevant instrument, component or printed circuit with reference to Figs. 12.20, 12.21 and 12.22.
3   Much of the instrument testing entails the use of an Audi tester, but the following can be carried out without the use of specialist equipment.
4   To test the voltage stabilizer, reconnect the instrument wiring plugs and reconnect the battery negative lead.
5   Connect a voltmeter between the voltage stabilizer positive connection and earth (Fig. 12.23) (photo). Switch on the ignition and

18.5 Voltage stabilizer connections (arrowed) on the instrument panel

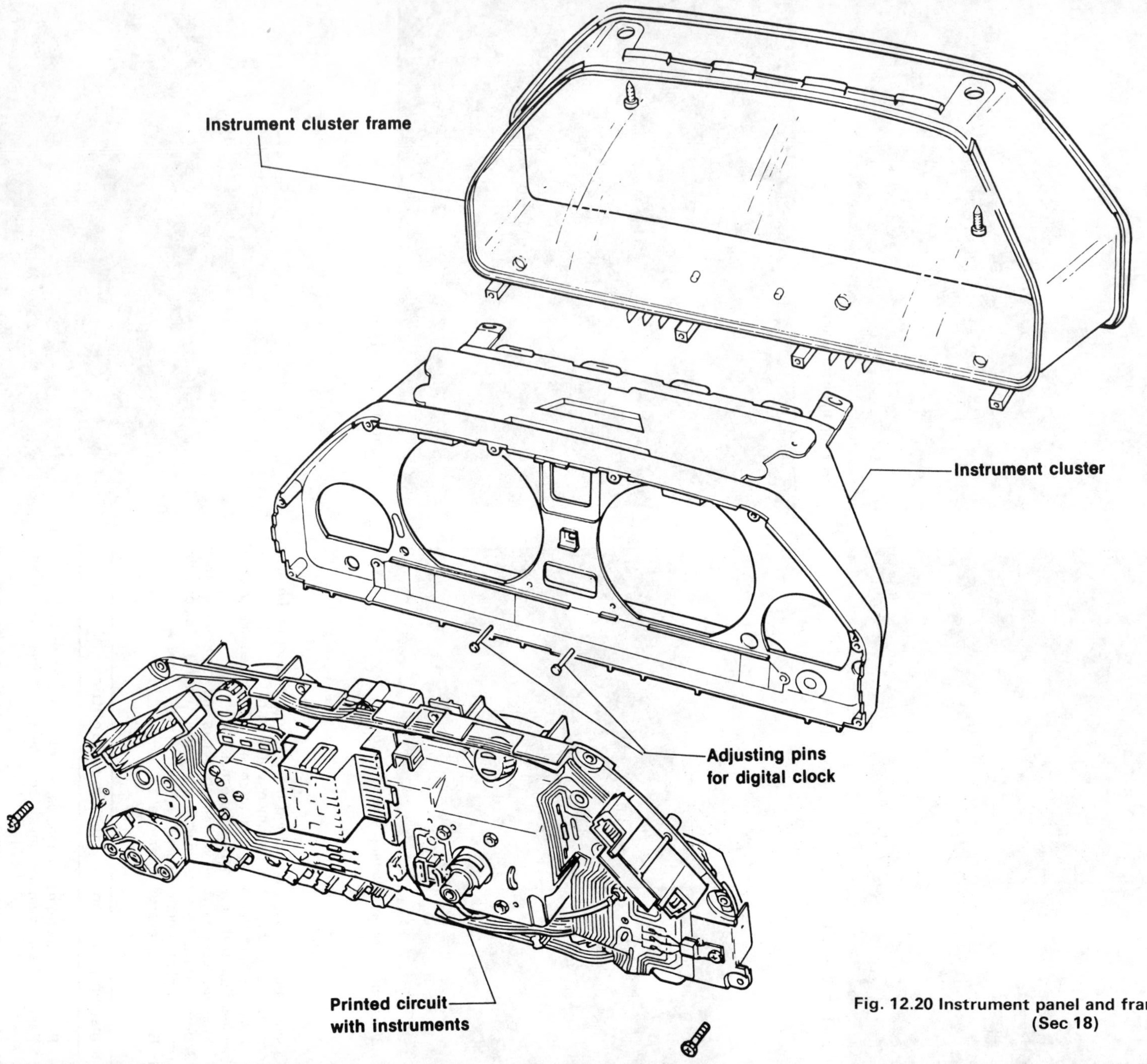

Instrument cluster

Instrument cluster frame

Adjusting pins
for digital clock

Printed circuit
with instruments

Fig. 12.20 Instrument panel and frame components
(Sec 18)

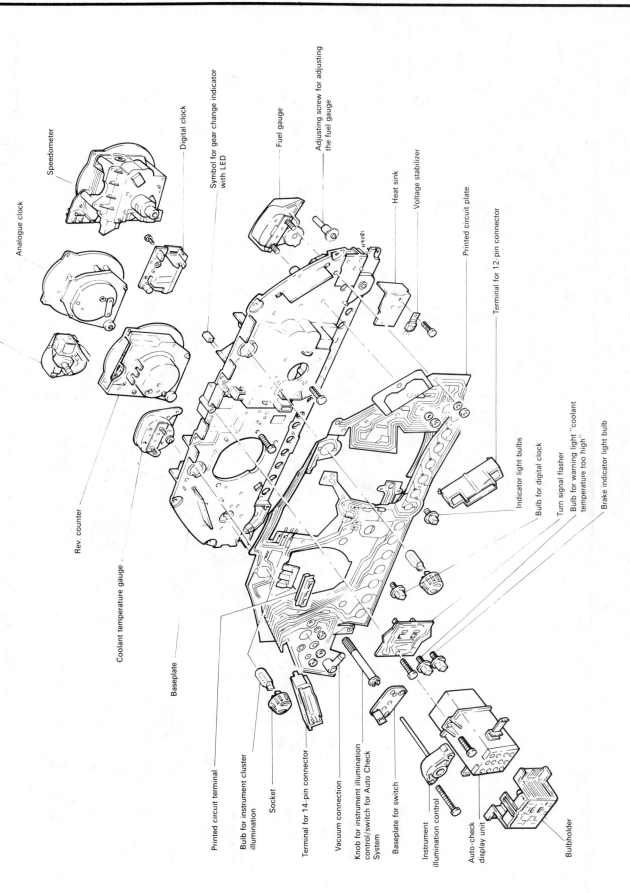

Speedometer

Analogue clock

Econometer

Rev. counter

Coolant temperature gauge

Baseplate

Printed circuit terminal

Bulb for instrument cluster illumination

Socket

Terminal for 14-pin connector

Vacuum connection

Knob for instrument illumination control/switch for Auto Check System

Baseplate for switch

Instrument illumination control

Auto-check display unit

Bulbholder

Digital clock

Symbol for gear change indicator with LED

Fuel gauge

Adjusting screw for adjusting the fuel gauge

Heat sink

Voltage stabilizer

Printed circuit plate

Terminal for 12-pin connector

Indicator light bulbs

Bulb for digital clock

Turn signal flasher

Bulb for warning light "coolant temperature too high"

Brake indicator light bulb

Fig. 12.21 Exploded view of the instrument panel fitted to UK models (Sec 18)

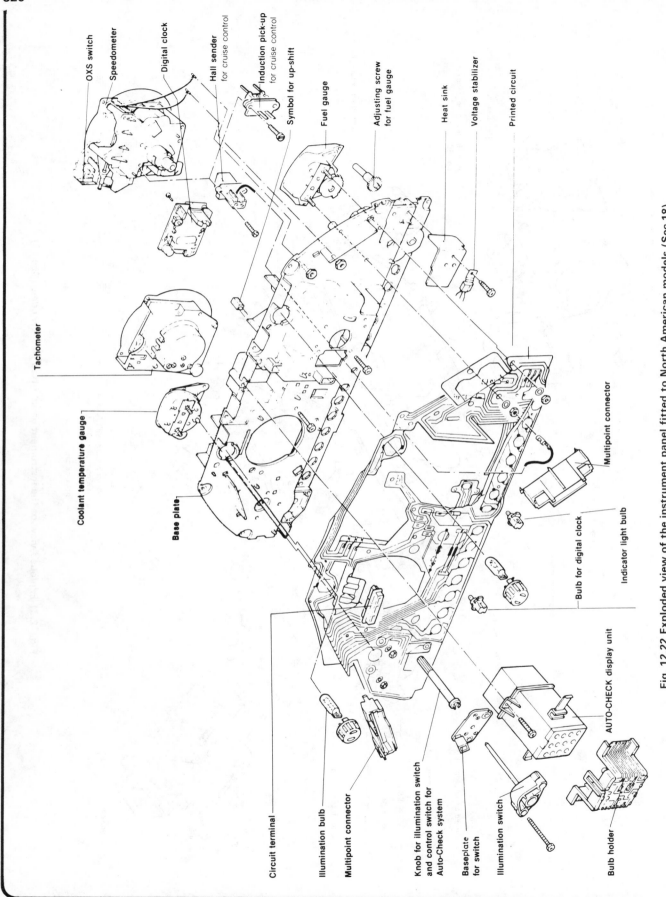

OXS switch

Speedometer

Digital clock

Hall sender
for cruise control

Induction pick-up
for cruise control

Symbol for up-shift

Fuel gauge

Adjusting screw
for fuel gauge

Heat sink

Voltage stabilizer

Printed circuit

Tachometer

Coolant temperature gauge

Base plate

Multipoint connector

Bulb for digital clock

Indicator light bulb

AUTO-CHECK display unit

Circuit terminal

Illumination bulb

Multipoint connector

Knob for illumination switch
and control switch for
Auto-Check system

Baseplate
for switch

Illumination switch

Bulb holder

Fig. 12.22 Exploded view of the instrument panel fitted to North American models (Sec 18)

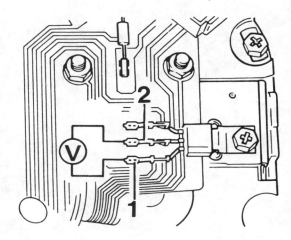

Fig. 12.23 Checking voltage stabiliser supply voltage (Sec 18)

1 Positive supply connection *2 Earth*

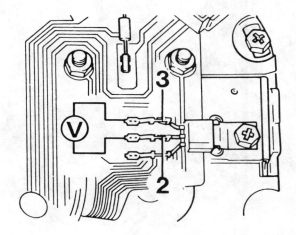

Fig. 12.24 Checking voltage stabiliser output voltage (Sec 18)

2 Earth *3 Positive output connection*

check that approximately battery voltage is shown on the voltmeter. If not, check for a wiring fault in the feed to the stabilizer.

6 Check the stabilizer output voltage by connecting the voltmeter between connection 3 (positive output) and 1 (earth), as shown in Fig. 12.24. With the ignition switched on a voltage of between 9.75 and 10.25 volts should be indicated. If not, renew the voltage stabilizer. Switch off the ignition after completing the checks.

7 The accuracy of the fuel gauge can be checked after removing all fuel from the tank by syphon or hand pump (ensure a well ventilated area is available for this) then filling with exactly 12.0 litres (2.64 Imp gal/3.17 US gal) of fuel.

8 Switch on the ignition and wait two minutes for the gauge reading to stabilize. After this time the needle should be aligned with the upper edge of the red reserve zone. If necessary turn the adjusting screw below the gauge to correct the reading.

9 Reassembly of the instrument panel is the reverse of removal.

19 Speedometer cable – removal and refitting

1 Disconnect the battery negative lead.
2 Remove the two screws and withdraw the instrument panel just sufficiently to allow the speedometer cable to be disconnected from behind (bayonet fitting).
3 Working in the engine compartment disconnect the speedometer cable from the transmission.
4 Withdraw the speedometer cable through the bulkhead into the engine compartment.
5 Detach the cable from the retaining clips and remove it from the car.
6 Refitting is a reversal of removal.

20 Headlamp and headlamp bulbs – removal and refitting

UK models
1 To remove the bulb, open the bonnet and remove the bulb cover by turning it anti-clockwise on the Audi 100 (photo), or by disengaging the wire clip on the Audi 200.
2 Disconnect the wiring plug from the bulb (photo).
3 Depress the ends of the bulb retaining wire clip and swing it to one side on the Audi 100 (photo), or turn the retaining ring anti-clockwise on the Audi 200.
4 Withdraw the bulb from the lens unit (photo). Take care not to touch the bulb glass with your fingers; if touched clean the bulb with methylated spirit.
5 To remove the headlamp unit, remove the front direction indicator

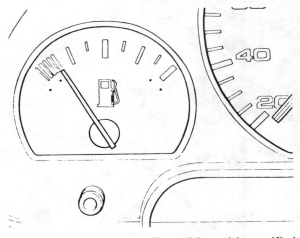

Fig. 12.25 Fuel gauge needle position with specified quantity of fuel in the tank (Sec 18)

Fig. 12.26 Bulb locations in the headlamp unit – Audi 200 models (Sec 20)

A Headlamp bulb *C Additional driving lamp*
B Sidelight bulb

20.1 Remove the headlamp bulb cover (Audi 100 shown)

20.2 Disconnect the wiring plug from the bulb

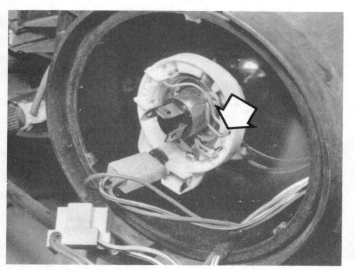

20.3 Release the bulb retaining wire clip – arrowed (Audi 100 shown)

20.4 Withdraw the bulb from the lens unit

(Audi 100), or the additional driving lamp (Audi 200), and the sidelight bulb, as described in Section 22.

6   Remove the radiator grille, as described in Chapter 11.

7   Carefully prise up the bumper upper trim strip (photo) and remove it.

8   Undo the two upper and two lower retaining screws and withdraw the unit from the car (photos).

9   Refitting the bulb and headlamp unit is a reversal of removal.

North American models

10 To remove the sealed beam headlamp bulb, open the bonnet and disconnect the wiring plug at the rear of the bulb.

11 Remove the side marker lamp bulbholder.

12 Remove the two trim surround retaining screws (Fig. 12.27) push out the trim and withdraw it from the guides.

13 Remove the four screws securing the headlamp bulb retainer, withdraw the retainer and take out the sealed beam bulb.

14 To remove the headlamp support frame, remove both sealed beam bulb units on the side to be removed.

15 Undo the four mounting frame retaining screws and withdraw the frame from the car.

16 Refitting the sealed beam bulbs and mounting frame is a reversal of removal.

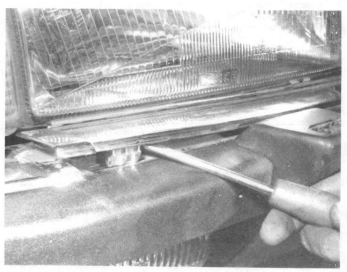

20.7 Remove the bumper upper trim strip (Audi 100 shown)

20.8A Headlamp unit upper ...

20.8B ... and lower retaining screws (Audi 100 shown)

Fig. 12.27 Headlamp trim surround retaining screws (arrowed) – North American models (Sec 20)

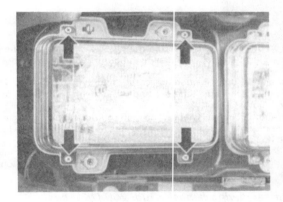

Fig. 12.28 Headlamp bulb retainer screws (arrowed) – North American models (Sec 20)

21 Headlamps – alignment

1   At the intervals specified in Routine Maintenance the headlamp aim should be checked and, if necessary, adjusted.
2   Due to the light pattern of the homofocal headlamp lenses fitted, optional beam setting equipment must be used to achieve satisfactory aim of the headlamps. It is recommended, therefore, that this work is entrusted to an Audi dealer.

22 Bulbs and lamp units – removal and refitting

Front sidelights – UK models
1   From within the engine compartment, remove the cover at the rear of the headlamp by turning it anti-clockwise (photo).
2   Withdraw the sidelight bulbholder from the headlamp then push and twist the bulb to remove it (photo).

Front side marker lights – North American models
3   From within the engine compartment, remove the rubber boot and bulb holder from the side marker light.
4   Push and turn the bulb to remove it.

22.1 Remove the headlamp bulb cover ...

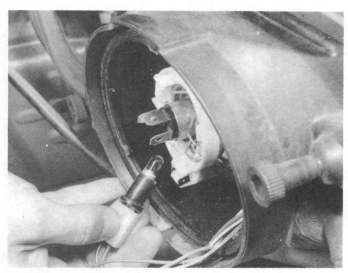

22.2 ... and remove the sidelight bulb and holder (Audi 100 shown)

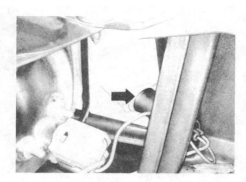

Fig. 12.29 Front side marker light bulbholder (arrowed) –
North American models (Sec 22)

Front direction indicator – UK models

5   On Audi 100 models, turn the bulb holder at the rear of the lamp unit anti-clockwise and withdraw it (photo). Push and twist the bulb to renew it.

6   To remove the direction indicator lamp unit on the Audi 100, depress the plastic tag on the side and withdraw the unit forwards from the car (photos).

7   On Audi 200 models, renew the bulb by undoing the two screws at the front of the lens and removing the lens. Push and twist the bulb to remove it.

8   To remove the lamp unit, disconnect the wiring at the connector, undo the retaining screws at the rear and remove the unit from the bumper.

Additional driving lamps – Audi 200 UK models

9   From within the engine compartment, disengage the cover retaining clip, swing the clip upwards and remove the cover.

10 Pull the wiring plug off the bulb, disengage the bulb retaining clip and remove the bulb.

Front foglamp – UK models

11 Withdraw the trim surround (where fitted) from the front of the lamp unit (photo).

12 Undo the two retaining screws and pull out the lamp unit (photo).

Fig. 12.30 Front direction indicator lamp lens – Audi 200
models (Sec 22)

13 Disengage the wire retaining clip at the rear of the bulb(photo), then lift the bulb holder out of the lamp unit (photo).

14 Remove the bulb by pulling it out of the holder.

Rear lamp cluster

15 Working in the luggage compartment, undo the two knurled nuts and remove the cover at the rear of the lamp cluster.

16 Depress the catches on each side of the bulb plate and withdraw the bulb plate from the lamp cluster (photo).

17 Push and twist the bulbs to remove (photo).

22.5 Front direction indicator bulb and holder (Audi 100 shown)

22.6A Depress the plastic tag ...

22.6B ... and remove the direction indicator lamp unit (Audi 100 shown)

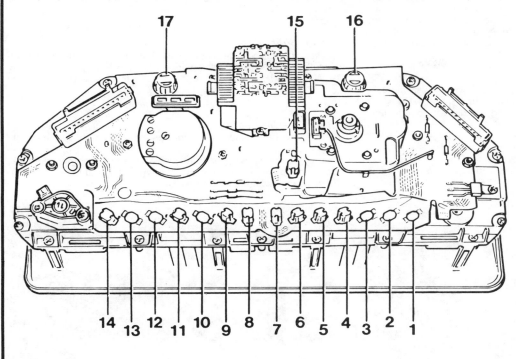

Fig. 12.31 Bulb locations at the rear of the instrument panel (Sec 22)

1   Anti-lock braking system warning light (UK only)
2   Seat belt warning light (UK only)
3   Cold coolant temperature warning light (UK only)
4   Handbrake warning light
5   Alternator charge warning light
6   Oil pressure warning light (UK)/OXS system warning light (North America)
7   Trailer turn signal warning light (UK)/left direction indicator light (North America)
8   Hazard light indicator (UK)/right direction indicator light (North America)
9   Headlamp mainbeam warning lamp
10 Rear foglight warning lamp
11 Heated rear window warning lamp
12 Heated front seat warning lamp
13 Direction indicator warning lamp (UK only)
14 Seat belt warning lamp (North America only)
15 Digital clock illumination
16 Instrument panel right-hand illumination
17 Instrument panel left-hand illumination

Additional for certain UK models, not shown on illustration – brake warning lamp and hot coolant temperature warning lamp – located in the centre of the panel

22.11 Withdraw the foglamp trim surround

22.12 Undo the two foglamp retaining screws (arrowed)

22.13A Disengage the wire retaining clip ...

22.13B ... and lift out the bulb and bulb holder

22.16 Rear lamp cluster bulb plate

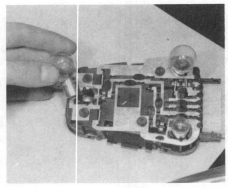

22.17 Rear lamp cluster bulb renewal

18 To remove the lamp cluster, undo the four retaining nuts and washers then carefully prise the unit off the body (photo). The unit will be found stuck quite firmly in place, due to the mastic sealing, and considerable effort is needed to initially break the seal. When refitting, ensure that the mastic sealant is spread evenly around the groove in the lamp cluster (photo).

Boot lid/trunk lid/tailgate lights
19 Open the boot/trunk/tailgate and, using a screwdriver, carefully prise off the trim panel at the rear of the light unit (photos).
20 Turn the bulb holder anti-clockwise and withdraw it from the light unit (photo).
21 Push and twist the bulbs to remove.

Number plate/licence plate light
22 Open the boot/trunk/tailgate and undo the two screws securing the lens cover (photo).

23 Withdraw the lens and lamp unit then remove the bulb by pushing and twisting (photo).

Interior light
24 Press the clip on the edge of the light lens opposite the switch carefully inwards, using a screwdriver.
25 Withdraw the lens and remove the festoon type bulb from the contacts (photo).

Interior reading light
26 Pull down the handle and undo the two screws above the handle hinges (photo).
27 Using a screwdriver, carefully prise off the cap over the coat hook.
28 Undo the coat hook screw and withdraw the bulb holder (photo).
29 Push and twist the bulb to remove.

22.18A Removing the rear lamp cluster lens assembly

22.18B Sealing mastic evenly spread in lamp cluster groove

22.19A Removing the boot lid trim cover on Saloon models ...

22.19B ... and the tailgate trim panel on Avant models

22.20 Removing the bulbholder from the boot lid

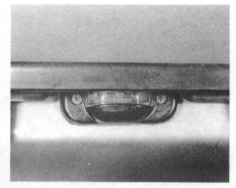
22.22 Number plate light retaining screws

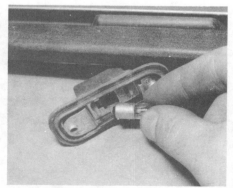
22.23 Number plate light bulb renewal

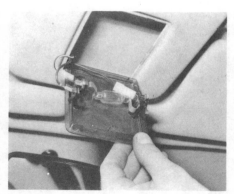
22.25 Removing the interior light lens and bulb

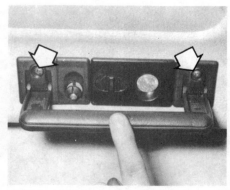
22.26 Interior grab handle and light retaining screws (arrowed)

22.28 Interior light lens and bulb

22.33A Removing an instrument panel illumination bulb ...

22.33B ... and warning light bulb

Luggage compartment light

30 Using a screwdriver, carefully prise out the bulb holder and lens.
31 Withdraw the festoon type bulb from the contacts.

Instrument panel lamps

32 Remove the instrument panel, as described in Section 17.
33 Turn the bulb holder through 90° and remove it from the instrument panel (photos).
34 Pull out the wedge type bulb.

Glovebox lamp

35 Open the glovebox and prise out the switch/bulbholder.
36 Push and twist the bulb to remove it.

All lamp units

37 Refitting is a reversal of removal.

23 Windscreen wiper blades and arms – removal and refitting

Wiper blades

1 Lift the wiper blade and arm from the windscreen.
2 Depress the plastic clip and lift the blade from the hooked end of the arm (photo).
3 Insert the new blade, making sure the plastic clip is engaged.

Wiper arms

4 Prise the trim button off the top of the arm (photo).
5 Unscrew the nut securing the arm to the spindle (photo).

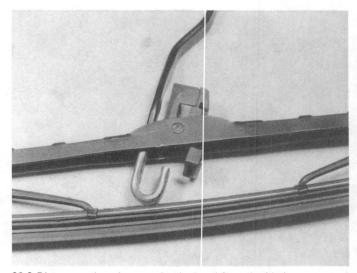

23.2 Disengage the wiper arm hooked end from the blade

23.4 Remove the wiper arm trim button ...

23.5 ... then unscrew the retaining nut

23.6 Lock the wiper arm in the closed position using a bolt or dowel prior to removal from the spindle

6   Insert a dowel rod or bolt into the hole on the edge of the arm to retain the arm locked against spring pressure (photo).
7   Carefully lever off the wiper arms.
8   Refitting is a reversal of removal, but install the arm so that the blade is parallel and approximately 20 mm (0.78 in) below the black edging of the windscreen when the wipers are parked.

24 Windscreen wiper linkage and motor – removal and refitting

1   Disconnect the battery negative lead.
2   Remove the wiper arms, as described in Section 23.
3   Remove the black plastic cover trim over the plenum chamber at the rear of the engine compartment.
4   Disconnect the wiring plug at the wiper motor.
5   Undo the bolts securing the wiper linkage frame and wiper motor to the body (photo) then remove the linkage and motor assembly from the plenum chamber.
6   Detach the linkage arms from the motor and remove the motor.
7   Refitting is a reversal of removal.

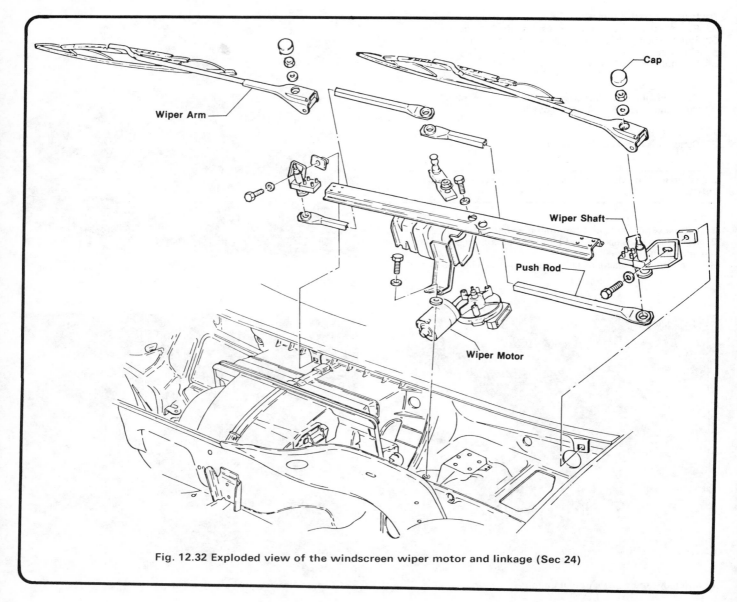

Fig. 12.32 Exploded view of the windscreen wiper motor and linkage (Sec 24)

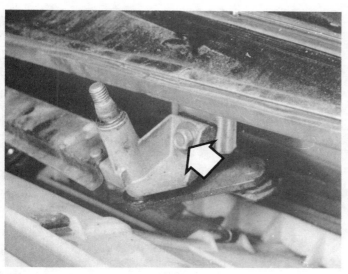
24.5 Wiper linkage frame left-hand retaining bolt (arrowed)

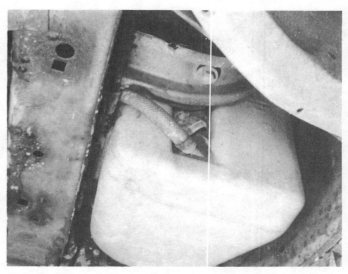
25.2 Windscreen washer reservoir, pump and mounting

25 Windscreen washer system – removing, refitting and adjustment

1   The windscreen washer reservoir is located at the front right-hand side on UK models and at the rear of the engine compartment on North American models. The washer pump is attached to the reservoir on all models except those for the UK with headlamp washers, in which case it is remotely sited. On UK models with headlamp washers the reservoir serves both systems, and the pump attached to the reservoir is for the headlamp system.
2   To remove the reservoir, lift it out of its retaining bracket or remove the retaining screws (photo).
3   The pump is a push-fit in the reservoir and can be removed by carefully prising out. The pump is a sealed unit and cannot be repaired.
4   If the washer jets require cleaning, do not use a needle or piece of wire because this will damage the orifice. Jets can be cleaned without damage by using a brush bristle or a piece of nylon line.
5   Adjust the jets to give the spray pattern shown in Fig. 12.33.

26 Tailgate wiper blades and arm (Avant models) – removal and refitting

Wiper blades
1   The procedure is the same as for the windscreen wiper blades described in Section 23.

Wiper arm
2   Flip up the cover and unscrew the arm retaining nut.
3   Carefully lever the arm off the spindle.
4   Refitting is a reversal of removal, but position the arm as near as possible to the bottom edge of the window with the wiper motor in the park position.

27 Tailgate wiper motor (Avant models) – removal and refitting

1   Disconnect the battery negative lead.
2   Remove the wiper arm, as described in Section 26.
3   Carefully prise off the trim cover around the motor from inside the tailgate and lift out the wiring connector (photo).
4   Separate the halves of the wiring connector.
5   From outside, undo the spindle retaining nut and remove the washers and seals; noting their arrangement.

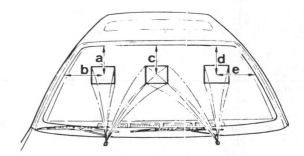
Fig. 12.33 Windscreen washer jet aiming diagram (Sec 25)

a = 160 mm (6.3 in)   d = 160 mm (6.3 in)
b = 220 mm (8.6 in)   e = 220 mm (8.6 in)
c = 120 mm (4.7 in)

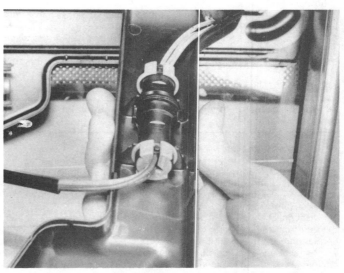
27.3 Remove the wiper motor trim cover and wiring connector

27.6A Wiper motor mounting frame right-hand retaining screw ...

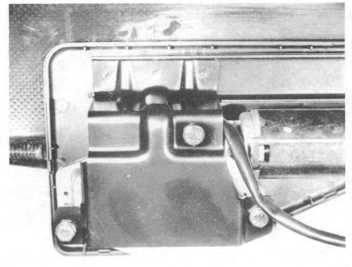

27.6B ... and motor securing bolts

6   From inside, undo the screw and bolts securing the motor to the mounting frame and withdraw the motor from the tailgate (photos).
7   Refitting is a reversal of removal.

28 Horn – removal and refitting

1   The horns are located beneath the left-hand side of the engine compartment (photo).
2   Disconnect the battery negative lead.
3   Disconnect the wiring from the relevant horn and unbolt it from the bracket.
4   Refitting is a reversal of removal.

29 Headlamp washers – removal and refitting

1   Carefully prise out the edge trim over the front bumper.
2   Undo the two nuts securing the washer assembly to the bumper (photo).
3   Withdraw the washer assembly and disengage the hose valve from the grommet.
4   Refitting is a reversal of removal. Adjust the jets so that the water strikes the headlamp glass at two points roughly equidistant from the centre of the glass and with the outer water jet slightly lower than the inner water jet.

30 Radio/cassette player and speakers – removal and refitting

1   Disconnect the battery negative lead.
2   Refer to Chapter 11 and remove the centre console cover trim.
3   Remove the control knobs and front facia plate (photo).
4   According to equipment type fitted, either remove the retaining screws, or wire retaining clips, and withdraw the radio from the console (photo).
5   Disconnect the relevant wiring at the rear of the radio and remove the unit from the car.
6   Refitting is a reversal of removal.
7   Removal and refitting of the speakers simply entails undoing the retaining screws and removing the relevant speaker after first removing the covers and wiring. The arrangement of the audio system is shown in Fig. 12.34.

28.1 Horn mountings and wiring connections

29.2 Headlamp washer retaining nuts (arrowed)

30.3 Remove the radio facia plate (Audi 100 shown)

30.4 Radio removal (Audi 100 shown)

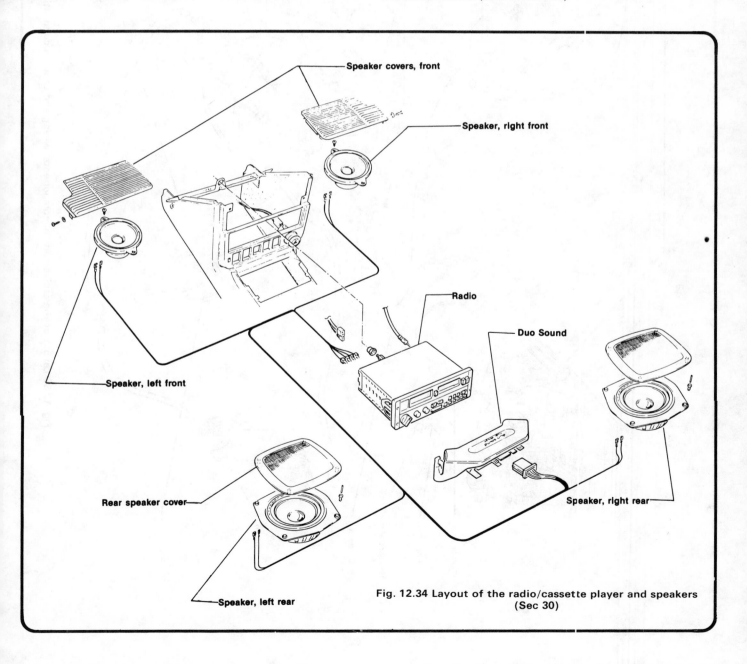

Speaker covers, front

Speaker, right front

Radio

Duo Sound

Speaker, left front

Rear speaker cover

Speaker, right rear

Speaker, left rear

Fig. 12.34 Layout of the radio/cassette player and speakers
(Sec 30)

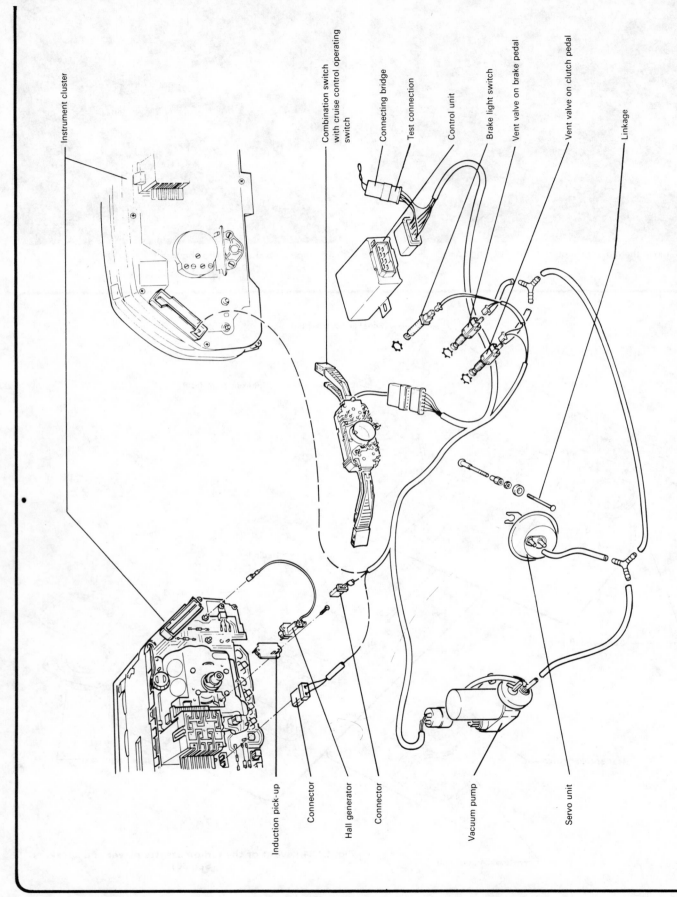

Instrument cluster

Combination switch with cruise control operating switch

Connecting bridge

Test connection

Control unit

Brake light switch

Vent valve on brake pedal

Vent valve on clutch pedal

Linkage

Induction pick-up

Connector

Hall generator

Connector

Vacuum pump

Servo unit

Fig. 12.35 Layout of the cruise control components, wiring and vacuum connections (Sec 31)

31 Cruise control system – removal and refitting of components

The cruise control system automatically maintains a desired speed when actuated above approximately 22 mph (35 km/h). When engaged, the system controls the position of the throttle linkage by means of a vacuum-operated servo unit, and maintains a constant road speed. The servo unit is controlled by an electronic control unit which in turn receives information from various sensors. The system can be overridden by the driver by means of the function switch or whenever the clutch or brake pedal are depressed.

Control unit – removal and refitting
1 Disconnect the battery negative lead.
2 On Audi 100 models, remove the trim under the facia on the driver's side. On Audi 200 and Audi 5000 models, remove the cover and trim below the facia on the driver's side and take out the parcel shelf.
3 Disconnect the wiring, remove the retaining screws and remove the control unit.
4 Refitting is a reversal of removal.

Control switch – removal and refitting
5 The control switch is part of the steering column combination switch and removal and refitting procedures are contained in Section 14.

Clutch/brake pedal vent valves
6 Disconnect the battery negative lead.
7 Remove the facia trim or parcel shelf, as necessary, to gain access to the clutch and brake pedals.
8 Disconnect the wiring and vacuum hose to the relevant vent valve then prise the unit out of its holder. Audi tool 2041 is available for removal of the valves, but even with the special tool the valves must be discarded after removal as the threads will be damaged.
9 To fit new valves, place them in position and push them into their holders as far as they will go using a 10 mm socket.
10 Pull up on the clutch or brake pedal as far as it will go to set the valve adjustment.
11 Refit the trim and reconnect the battery.

Vacuum servo unit – removal and refitting
12 Disconnect the throttle linkage at the servo unit.
13 Detach the vacuum hose.
14 Undo the retaining nut and remove the servo unit.
15 Refitting is the reversal of removal.
16 To adjust the linkage, check the clearance at the point where the linkage rod contacts the servo bushing, with the throttle at rest (photo). The clearance should be 0.1 to 1.0 mm (0.004 to 0.04 in). If necessary, adjust at the adjusting nut in the centre of the linkage rod.

Vacuum pump – removal and refitting
17 Remove the cooling system expansion tank retaining screws and move the tank clear.
18 Disconnect the vacuum hoses and wiring connector then undo the screws and remove the pump.
19 Refitting is the reversal of removal.

32 On-board computer – general

An on-board computer is available as standard or optional equipment on certain models. The computer provides the driver with information on fuel consumption, average speed, cruising range, journey time, time of day and ambient temperature; sequentially controlled by a function switch. On models having the display incorporated in the lower part of the tachometer, the computer module is located behind the instrument panel. On models having a separate display on the centre console, the computer module is located behind the glove compartment.

Fault diagnosis and repair of the system can only be carried out using Audi test equipment and all work on the system must be entrusted to an Audi dealer.

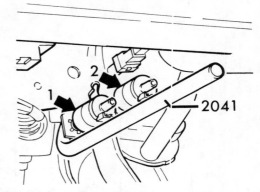

Fig. 12.36 Removal of the clutch pedal vent valve (1) using tool 2041 (Sec 31)

2 Brake pedal vent valve

31.16 Cruise control linkage rod to servo bushing contact point (A) and adjusting nut (B)

33 Auto-check system – general

Certain models are equipped with an Auto-check system which monitors various components and functions and provides the driver with an audible and visual warning in the event of a fault being detected.

The system is controlled by an electronic control unit located at the front of the centre console on Audi 100 models, or behind the glove compartment on Audi 200 and Audi 5000 models.

Fault finding and repair must be left to an Audi dealer as special test equipment is required for all checking and repair operations.

34 Electrically-operated front seats – general

Certain models are available with electrically-operated front seats; incorporating a position memory on the driver's seat.

The seat positions are infinitely variable for height, rake, fore-and-aft position, and backrest adjustment by means of electric motors and actuators. Switches in the door armrest control the operation of the various motors.

Fault diagnosis entails the use of Audi test equipment and removal and refitting of many of the components entails the removal and separation of the seat upholstery. For this reason any repairs required should be entrusted to an Audi dealer. An exploded view of the main components is shown in Fig. 12.37 for reference purposes.

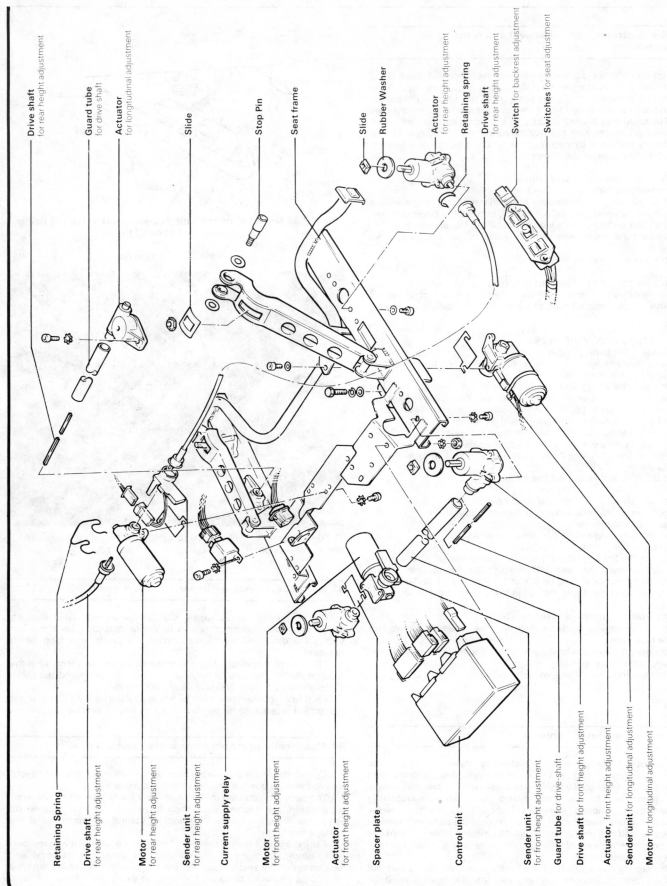

Drive shaft for rear height adjustment

Guard tube for drive shaft

Actuator for longitudinal adjustment

Slide

Stop Pin

Seat frame

Slide

Rubber Washer

Actuator for rear height adjustment

Retaining spring

Drive shaft for rear height adjustment

Switch for backrest adjustment

Switches for seat adjustment

Retaining Spring

Drive shaft for rear height adjustment

Motor for rear height adjustment

Sender unit for rear height adjustment

Current supply relay

Motor for front height adjustment

Actuator for front height adjustment

Spacer plate

Control unit

Sender unit for front height adjustment

Guard tube for drive-shaft

Drive shaft for front height adjustment

Actuator, front height adjustment

Sender unit for longitudinal adjustment

Motor for longitudinal adjustment

Fig. 12.37 Exploded view of the electrically-operated front seat components (Sec 34)

35 Wiring diagrams – description

1   The wiring diagrams included at the end of this Chapter are of the current flow type where each wire is shown in the simplest line form without crossing over other wires.
2   The fuse/relay panel is at the top of the diagram and the combined letter/figure numbers appearing on the panel terminals refer to the multi-plug connector in letter form and the terminal in figure form.
3   Internal connections through electrical components are shown by a single line.
4   The encircled numbers along the bottom of the diagram indicate the earthing connecting points as given in the key.

36 Fault diagnosis – electrical system

Symptom	Reason(s)
Starter fails to turn engine	Battery discharged or defective Battery terminal and/or earth leads loose Starter motor connections loose Starter solenoid faulty Starter brushes worn or sticking Starter commutator dirty or worn Starter field coils earthed Starter armature faulty
Starter turns engines very slowly	Battery discharged Starter motor connections loose Starter brushes worn or sticking
Starter noisy	Pinion or ring gear teeth badly worn Mounting bolts loose
Battery will not hold charge	Plates defective Electrolyte level too low Alternator drivebelt slipping Alternator or regulator faulty Short in electrical circuit
Ignition light stays on	Alternator faulty Alternator drivebelt broken
Ignition light fails to come on	Warning bulb blown Warning light open circuit Alternator faulty
Instrument readings increase with engine speed	Voltage stabilizer faulty
Fuel or temperature gauge gives no reading	Wiring open circuit Sender unit faulty
Fuel or temperature gauge gives maximum reading all the time	Wiring short circuit Sender unit or gauge faulty
Lights inoperative	Bulb blown Fuse blown Switch faulty Wiring open circuit Connection corroded
Failure of component motor	Commutator dirty or burnt Armature faulty Brushes sticking or worn Armature shaft bearings seized Field coils faulty Fuse blown Wiring loose or broken
Failure of an individual component	Wiring loose or broken Fuse blown Switch faulty Component faulty

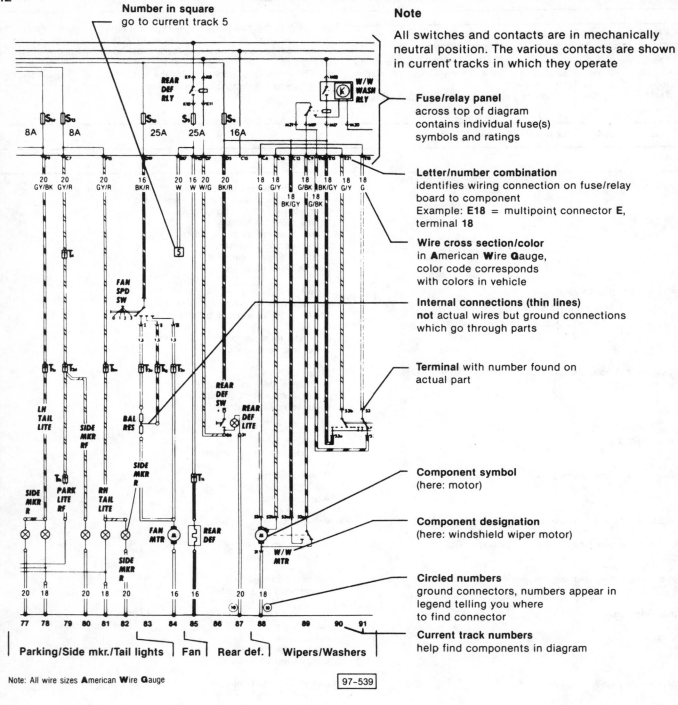

Number in square
go to current track 5

Note

All switches and contacts are in mechanically neutral position. The various contacts are shown in current tracks in which they operate

Fuse/relay panel
across top of diagram
contains individual fuse(s)
symbols and ratings

Letter/number combination
identifies wiring connection on fuse/relay board to component
Example: **E18** = multipoint connector **E**, terminal **18**

Wire cross section/color
in **A**merican **W**ire **G**auge,
color code corresponds
with colors in vehicle

Internal connections (thin lines)
not actual wires but ground connections which go through parts

Terminal with number found on actual part

Component symbol
(here: motor)

Component designation
(here: windshield wiper motor)

Circled numbers
ground connectors, numbers appear in legend telling you where
to find connector

Current track numbers
help find components in diagram

Parking/Side mkr./Tail lights | Fan | Rear def. | Wipers/Washers

Note: All wire sizes **A**merican **W**ire **G**auge

97-539

Sample legend

Description	Current Track
Parking light, right front	79
Rear window defogger element	85
Rear window defogger indicator light	87
Rear window defogger relay	85
Rear window defogger switch	86
Sidemarker, right front	80
Sidemarker, rear	77, 82
Tail light, right	81
Windshield wiper intermittent switch	68
Windshield wiper motor	88, 89

Where to find a wire connector on car

Wire Connectors	Current Track
T2d — double, behind dash	79
T2e — double, behind dash	83, 84
10 — Ground connector, instrum. clstr.	87, 88
11 — Ground connector, body	

Fig. 12.38 Instructions for using current flow diagrams

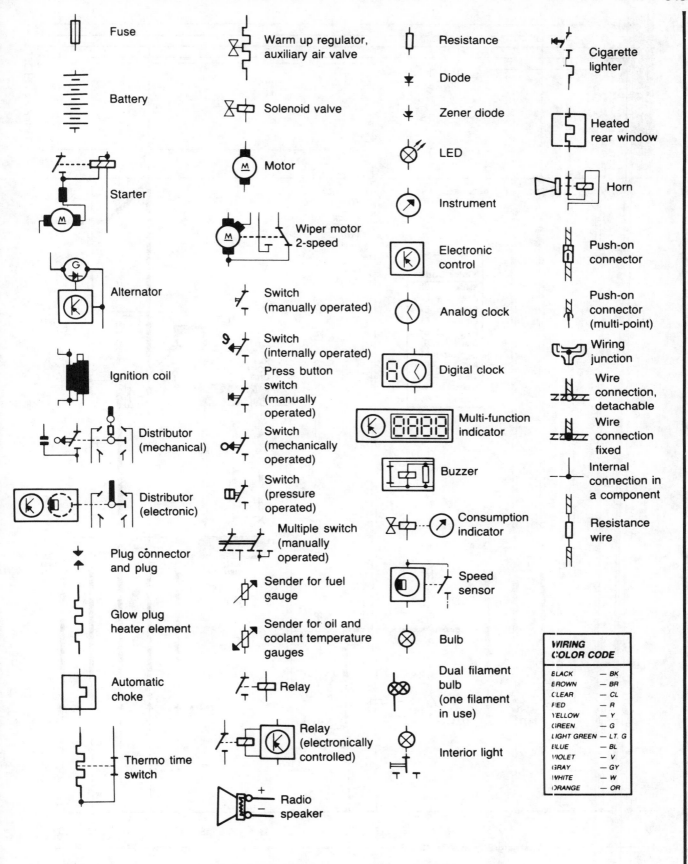

Fuse

Battery

Starter

Alternator

Ignition coil

Distributor (mechanical)

Distributor (electronic)

Plug connector and plug

Glow plug heater element

Automatic choke

Thermo time switch

Warm up regulator, auxiliary air valve

Solenoid valve

Motor

Wiper motor 2-speed

Switch (manually operated)

Switch (internally operated)

Press button switch (manually operated)

Switch (mechanically operated)

Switch (pressure operated)

Multiple switch (manually operated)

Sender for fuel gauge

Sender for oil and coolant temperature gauges

Relay

Relay (electronically controlled)

Radio speaker

Resistance

Diode

Zener diode

LED

Instrument

Electronic control

Analog clock

Digital clock

Multi-function indicator

Buzzer

Consumption indicator

Speed sensor

Bulb

Dual filament bulb (one filament in use)

Interior light

Cigarette lighter

Heated rear window

Horn

Push-on connector

Push-on connector (multi-point)

Wiring junction

Wire connection, detachable

Wire connection fixed

Internal connection in a component

Resistance wire

WIRING COLOR CODE

BLACK	— BK
BROWN	— BR
CLEAR	— CL
RED	— R
YELLOW	— Y
GREEN	— G
LIGHT GREEN	— LT. G
BLUE	— BL
VIOLET	— V
GRAY	— GY
WHITE	— W
ORANGE	— OR

Fig. 12.39 Symbols used in the wiring diagrams

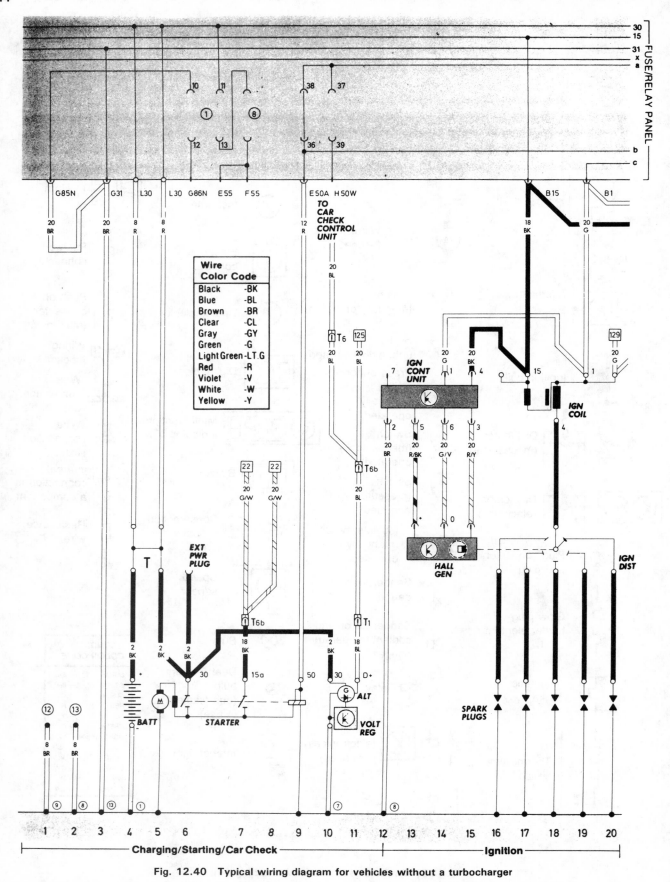

Fig. 12.40 Typical wiring diagram for vehicles without a turbocharger

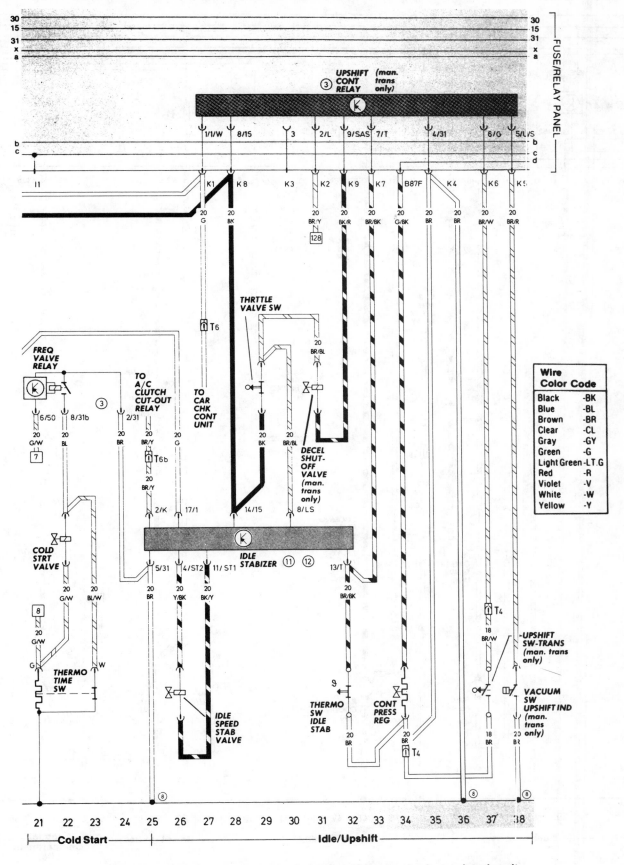

Fig. 12.40 Typical wiring diagram for vehicles without a turbocharger (continued)

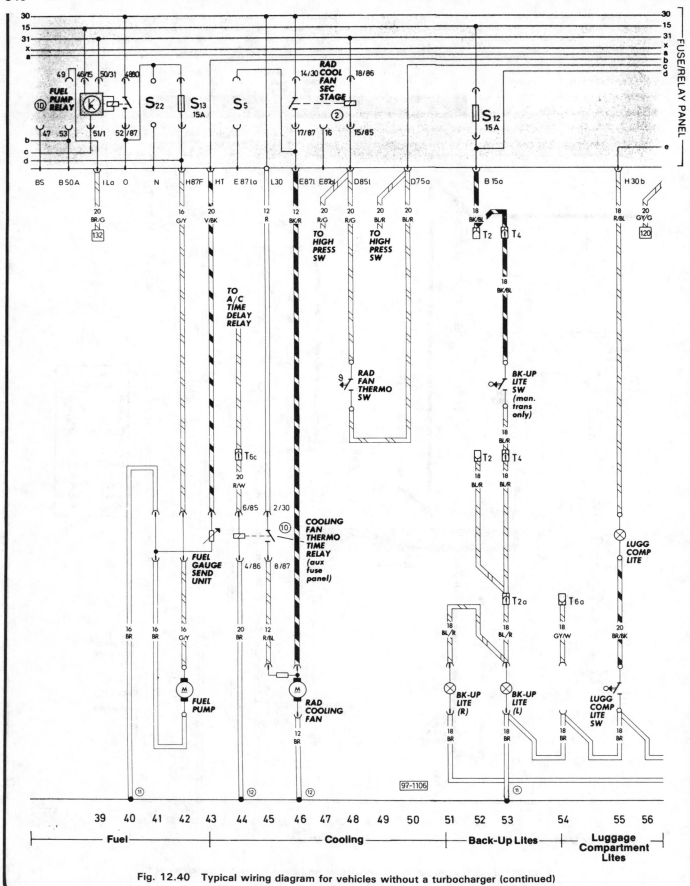

Fig. 12.40   Typical wiring diagram for vehicles without a turbocharger (continued)

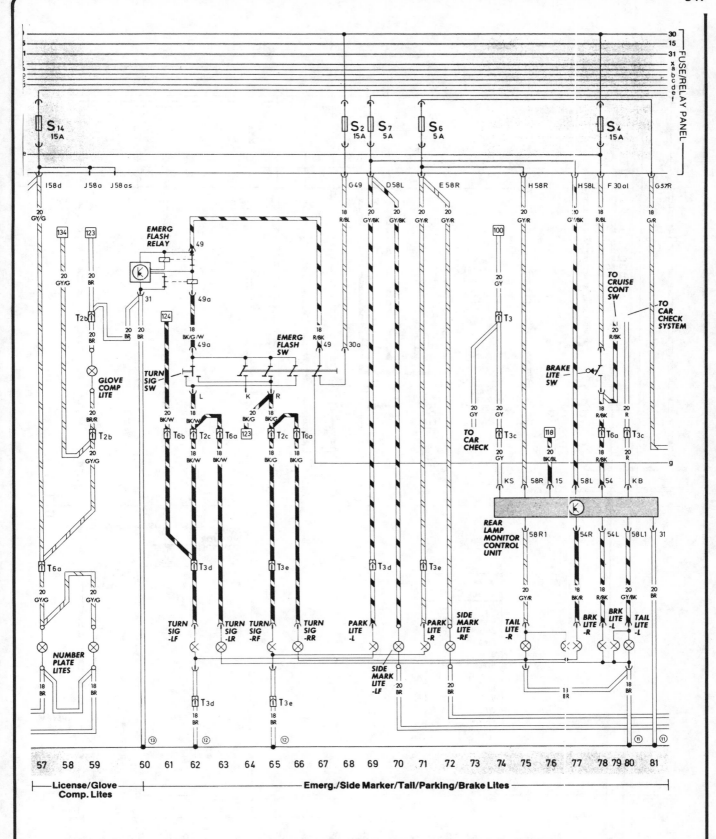

Fig. 12.40 Typical wiring diagram for vehicles without a turbocharger (continued)

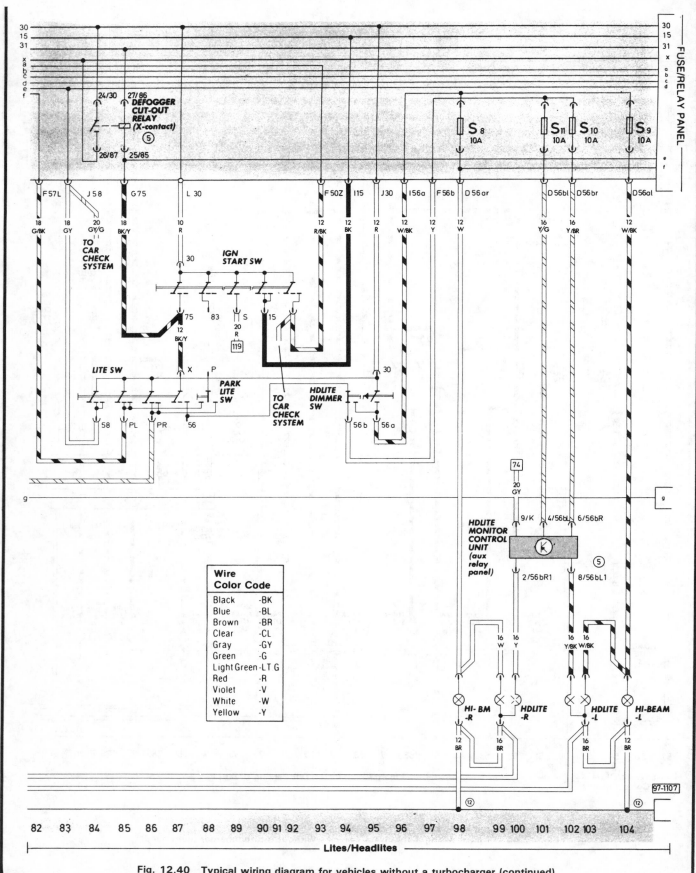

Fig. 12.40 Typical wiring diagram for vehicles without a turbocharger (continued)

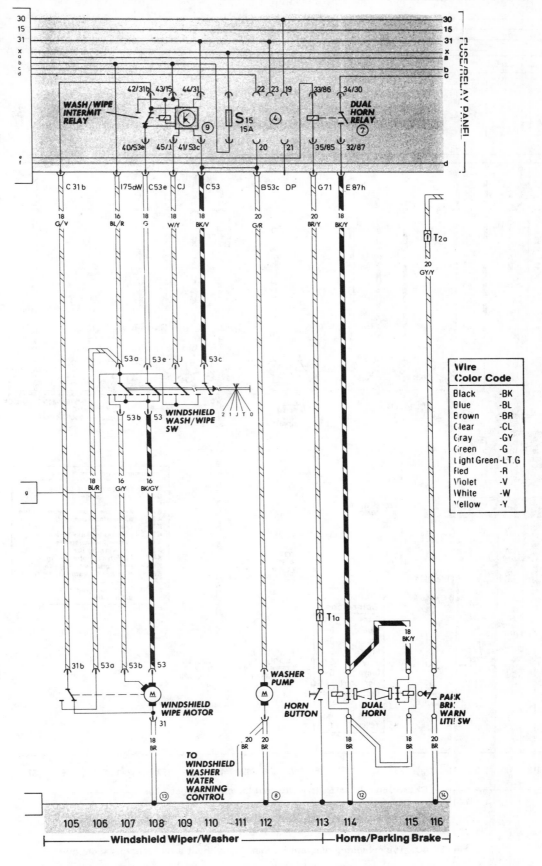

Fig. 12.40 Typical wiring diagram for vehicles without a turbocharger (continued)

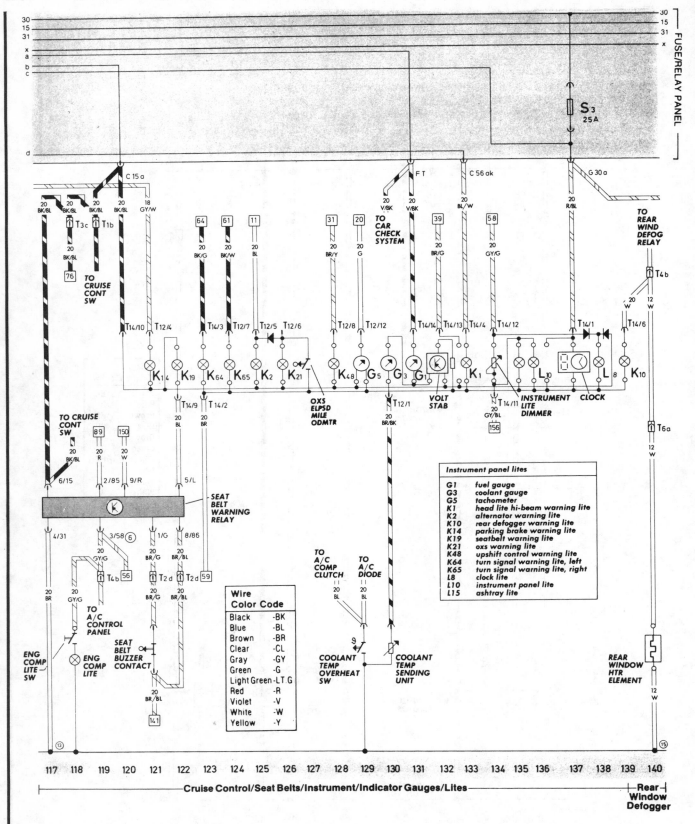

Fig. 12.40 Typical wiring diagram for vehicles without a turbocharger (continued)

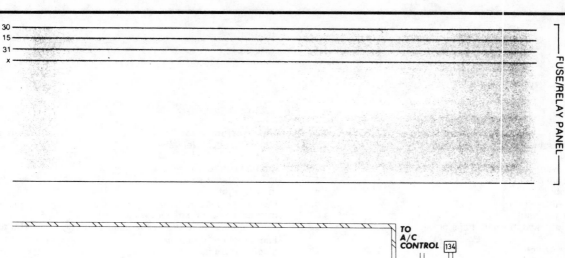

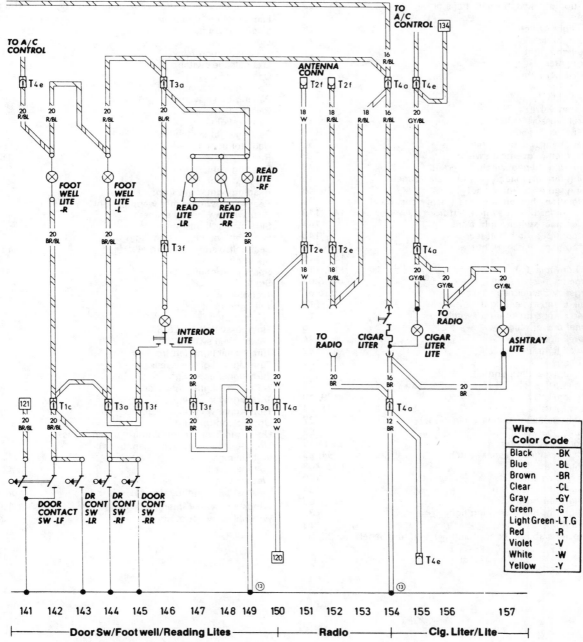

Note: All wire sizes American Wire Gauge

Fig. 12.40   Typical wiring diagram for vehicles without a turbocharger (continued)

Key to Fig. 12.40

Description	Current track	Description	Current track
A/C compressor clutch cut-out relay	25	Idle speed stabilizer valve	26
Alternator	11	Ignition oil	17, 18
Alternator warning light	125	Ignition distributor	18
Antenna connection	151, 152	Ignition/starter switch	87, 92
Ashtray light	157	Interior light	146
Back-up light, left	53	Instrument panel light	135, 136
Back-up light, right	51	Instrument panel dimmer switch	154
Back-up light switch (man. trans only)	53	Lamp monitor unit, front (aux. relay panel) ⑤	100 to 102
Battery	4	Lamp monitor unit, rear	74 to 81
Brake light switch	78	License plate light	57, 59
Brake light, left	78	Light switch	84 to 87
Brake light, right	77	Load reduction relay ⑤	
Cigar lighter	155	Oxs mileage switch	127
Cigar lighter light	154	Oxs warning light	126
Clock	137	Parking brake warning light	121
Clock light	138	Parking brake warning light switch	116
Cold start valve	22	Parking light, right	71
Control pressure regulator	34	Parking light, left	69
Coolant temp. gauge	130	Parking light switch	88
Coolant temp. sending unit	130	Radiator cooling fan	46
Coolant temp. overheat switch	129	Radio	151, 152
Cooling fan thermoswitch	48	Reading light, left rear	147
Cooling fan relay stage ⑩ (aux. relay panel)	44, 45	Reading light, right rear	148
Cooling fan relay 2nd stage ②	46, 48	Reading light, right front	149
Deceleration shut-off solenoid (man. trans. only)	31	Rear window defogger warning light	139
Door contact/buzzer switch, left front	141, 142	Rear window heater element	140
Door contact switch, right front	144	Side marker lights, front	70, 72
Door control switch, left rear	143	Seat belt warning system light	122
Door contact switch, right rear	145	Seat belt warning system relay ⑥	117, 122
Dual horn	114, 115	Spark plugs	16 to 20
Dual horn relay ⑦	113, 114	Spark plug connectors	16 to 20
Emergency flasher switch	64 to 67	Starter	5 to 9
Emergency flasher relay	60 to 62	Tachometer	129
Engine compartment light	118	Tail light, right	75, 77
Engine compartment light switch	118	Tail light, left	79, 80
External power plug	6	Thermo-switch for I.S.S.	32
Footwell light, left	144	Thermotime switch	21, 23
Footwell light, right	142	Turn signal light, left front	62
Fuel gauge	131	Turn signal light, left rear	63
Fuel gauge sending unit	43	Turn signal light, right front	65
Fuel pump	42	Turn signal light, right rear	66
Fuel pump relay ⑩	39, 40	Turn signal warn light, left	123
Frequency valve relay	21, 24	Turn signal warn light, right	124
Gearshift indicator switch (man. trans)	37	Upshift control light	128
Glove compartment light	59	Upshift indicator control unit ③ (man. trans)	27 to 38
Hall ignition generator	13 to 15	Upshift vacuum switch (man. trans)	38
Headlight dimmer/flasher switch	94, 95	Voltage regulator	11
Headlight, left	102, 103	Voltage stabilizer	132
Headlight, right	99, 100	Washer pump	112
Headlight, hi-beam, left	104	Wash/wipe intermit. relay ⑨	108 to 110
Headlight, hi-beam, right	98	Windshield wiper intermit. switch	107, 110
Headlight, hi-beam warning light	133	Windshield wiper motor	105, 108
Horn button	113		
Idle speed stabilizer control unit ⑪ ⑫ (aux. panel)	25, 52		

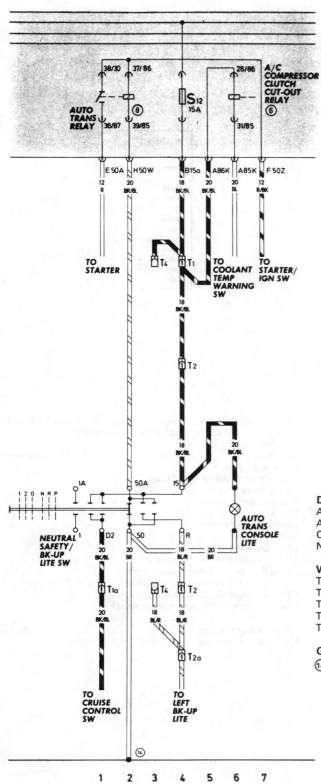

Wire Color Code	
Black	-BK
Blue	-BL
Brown	-BR
Clear	-CL
Gray	-GY
Green	-G
Light Green	-LT.G
Red	-R
Violet	-V
White	-W
Yellow	-Y

Fig. 12.41 Additional wiring diagram – automatic transmission

Description	Current track
Automatic transmission relay	8
Automatic transmission console light	6
Compressor clutch cut out relay	6
Neutral safety/back-up light switch	1

Wire connectors

T1	single, behind dashboard
T1a	single, behind dashboard
T2	double, behind dashboard
T2a	double, behind dashboard
T4	four point, engine compartment, right

Ground connector

⑭ near parking brake lever

Note: All wire sizes American Wire Gauge

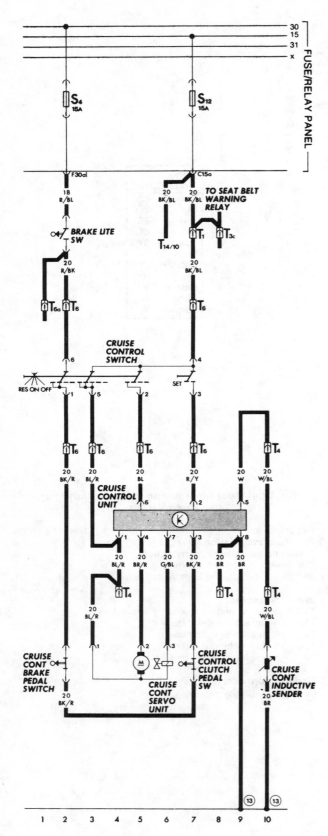

Wiring Color Code

Black	– BK
Brown	– BR
Clear	– CL
Red	– R
Yellow	– Y
Green	– G
Light Green	– LT.G
Blue	– BL
Violet	– V
Gray	– GY
White	– W

Fig. 12.42 Additional wiring diagram – cruise control on manual gearbox models

Description	Current track
Brake light switch	2
Cruise control brake pedal switch	2
Cruise control clutch pedal switch	7
Cruise control induction sender	10
Cruise control unit	4-9
Cruise control switch	2-7

Wire Connectors

T1	single, behind dashboard
T4	four point, behind dashboard (test connection for production only)
T6	six point, behind dashboard
T14	fourteen point, instrument panel

Ground connector

(13) wiring harness, dashboard

Note: All wire sizes American Wire Gauge

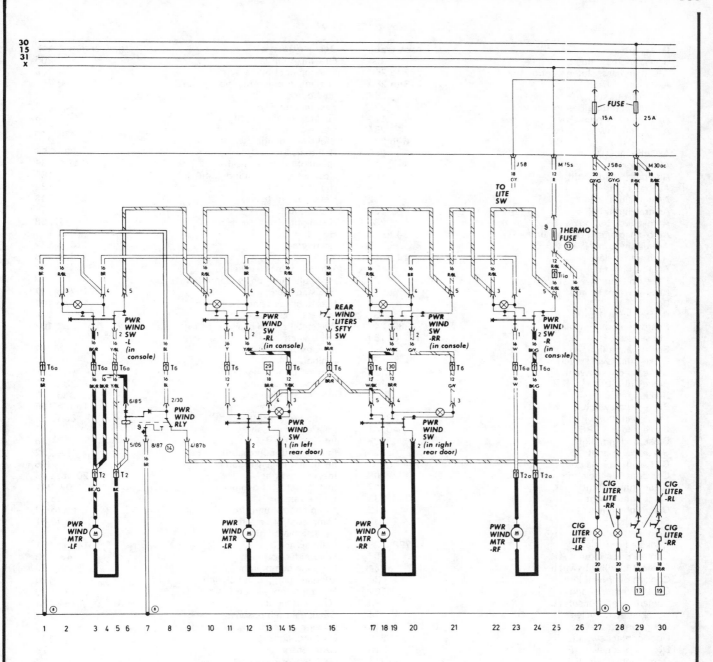

Fig. 12.43 Additional wiring diagram – power windows

Description	Current track	Description	Current track
Cigarette lighter, left rear	29	Power window switch, (in left rear door)	11 to 13
Cigarette lighter, right rear	30	Power window switch, left rear (in console)	10 to 20
Cigarette lighter light, left rear	27	Power window switch (in right rear door)	17 to 20
Cigarette lighter light, right rear	28	Thermofuse (location 13 on additional relay panel)	–
Fuses on fuse/relay panel (S14.S21)	–	To light switch	23
Rear window/lighter safety switch	16		
Power window motor, left front	3	**Wire connectors**	
Power window motor, right front	23	T2 double, left door (front)	
Power window motor, left rear	12	T2a double, right door (front)	
Power window motor, right rear	18	T6 six point, behind dash	
Power window relay (in 14 on fuse/relay panel)	6 to 8	T6a six point, behind dash	
Power window switch, left (in console)	2 to 6		
Power window switch, left (in console)	2 to 6	**Ground connector**	
Power window switch, right (in console)	22 to 25	(8) behind dash	

Key to Fig. 12.44

Description	Current track	Description	Current track
A/C compress. clutch	254	Fuel inj. cool fan	205
A/C compress. clutch control unit	252 to 258	Fuel inj. cool fan relay	203
A/C control head	273 to 280	Fuel inj. cool fan thermo-switch	203
A/C cut-out switch	258	Fuel pump	62
A/C evaporator air temp. sensor	272	Fuel pump relay	66 to 73
A/C refrig. hi-press. sw	114	Fuel reserve ind. light	28
A/C refrig. low press. sw.	254	Glove comp. light	239
A/C reg. unit	266 to 271	Glove comp. light sw.	239
A/C thermostat	259	Hall generator	93 to 95
Alternator	15	Headlight dimmer/flasher	157, 158
Alternator warn. light	193	Headlight, hi-beam ind. light	189
Ashtray light	249	Headlight, hi-beam, L	139
Ashtray light, LR	232	Headlight, hi-beam, R	143
Ashtray light, RR	231	Headlight, L	54, 55
Auto-check button	237	Headlight, R	57, 58
Auto-check main control unit	24 to 42	Horn button	175
Auto trans console light	23	Horn relay	174 to 177
Auto trans relay	14 to 17	Horns	176 to 178
Back-up light, L	20	Hydraulic fluid level sw.	36
Back-up light, R	21	Hydraulic fluid press. control sw	37
Back-up light switch	17 to 20	Idle stabilizer	102 to 107
Battery	10	Idle stabilizer control unit	102 to 107
Battery warn. light	31	Idle stabilizer valve	104
Board computer display	239, 240	Idle stabilizer valve sw.	107
Boost gauge	182 to 184	Idle switch	72
Boost gauge light	210	Ignition booster	96, 97
Brake fluid level switch	35	Ignition coil	100
Brake fluid level warn. light	25	Ignition control light	195
Brake light, L	50	Ignition control unit	78 to 92
Brake light, R	46	Ignition distributor	98 to 102
Brake light switch	176	Ign/start switch	150 to 155
Brake pad ind., LF	38, 39	Ignition timing sensor	80 to 82
Brake pad ind., RF	40, 41	Inlet air temp. sender	83
Brake pad ind., light	33	Interior light	226
Brake warn. light	31	Interior light control unit	217, 222
CAT elapsed mile counter	194 to 196	Inside temp. sensor fan	266
Charcoal filter solenoid valve	72, 208	Inst. panel light	203 to 209
Cigar lighter, front	247	Inst. panel light dimmer	202, 241
Cigar lighter light	248, 233	Knock sensor	86 to 88
Cigar lighter, rear	212	Lamp control unit, front	55 to 57
Clock light	242, 238	Lamp control unit, rear	45 to 51
Cold start valve	65	License plate light	118
Console light relay	228, 229	Light switch	148 to 151
Control press regulator	207	Load reduction relay	148, 149
Coolant low level switch	34	Luggage comp. light	120
Coolant over heat light	30	Luggage comp. light switch	120
Coolant temp. gauge	200	Neutral safety switch	17 to 20
Coolant temp. sensor	89	"OK" ind. light	34
Decel. shut-off valve	74	Outside air temp. sensor	277
Door contact sw., LF	217, 218	Outside air temp. sw.	260
Door contact sw., LR	216	OXS ind. light	194
Door contact sw., RF	215	OXS sensor	78
Door contact sw., RR	214	OXS sensor heater	77
Door warn. light	191	Park brake ind. light	180
Electronic thermo-switch	31, 32	Park brake warn. light sw.	180
Emerg. flash. relay	122 to 124	Park light, LF	136
Emerg. flash, switch	126 to 131	Park light, RF	141
Emerg. flash. warn. light	181	Park light switch	152
Eng. compart. light	116	Passenger compart. temp sensor	274
Eng. oil press. sw., 0.3 bar	25	Rad. cool fan	112
Eng. oil press. sw., 1.8 bar	26	Rad. cool fan relay, 1st stage	108, 109
Eng. oil press. warn. light	32	Rad. cool fan relay, 2nd stage	110 to 114
Footwell light, LF	251	Rad. cool fan relay, 3rd stage	112, 113
Footwell light, RF	250	Rad. cool fan series resistance	109, 110
Fresh air fan	263	Rad. cool fan thermo-switches	113
Fresh air fan control unit	261 to 265	Radio connections	244, 245
Fresh air fan thermo-switch	278	Read light, LF	216
Frequency valve	71	Read light, LR	219
Fuel economy sender	183	Read light, RF	224
Fuel enrichment switch	73	Read light, RR	222
Fuel gauge	201	Read light relay	214 to 217
Fuel gauge sender	183	Rear window defog. element	283

Key to Fig. 12.44 (continued)

Description	Current track
Rear window defog. relay	281 to 283
"Red triangle" warn. light	36
Resistor wire	71
RPM sender	83 to 85
Seatbelt switch, LF	186
Seatbelt warn. light	188
Seatbelt warn. relay	185 to 190
Side marker lights, front	135, 140
Spark plug connectors	98 to 102
Spark plugs	98 to 102
Speedometer	185, 186
Speedometer sending unit	186, 187
Starter	11 to 14
Tachometer	187
Tail light ind. light	26
Tail light, LR	18, 51, 52
Tail light, RR	22, 44, 45
Turbo cooling pump	202
Turbo cool pump relay	196 to 199
Turbo cool pump thermo-switch	201
Turn sig., LF	123
Turn sig., LR	43
Turn sig., RF	126
Turn sig., RR	53
Turn sig. switch	124
Turn sig. ind. light, L	196
Turn sig. ind. light, R	197
Voltage regulator	16
Voltage stabilizer	198 to 199
Washer fluid level ind.	29
Washer fluid level switch	27
Washer pump	173
Washer/wiper intermit. relay	169 to 171
Washer/wiper intermit. switch	166 to 170
Wastegate solenoid	73
Windshield wiper motor	165 to 169

Wire connectors

T	wire distributor
T1	single, behind instrument panel
T1a	single, engine compartment, right
T1b	single, behind instrument panel
T1c	single, slip ring connection
T1d	single, green, behind instrument panel
T1e	single, behind instrument panel
T1f	single, behind instrument panel
T1g	single, behind instrument panel, ABS connection
T2	double, behind console
T2a	double, behind instrument panel
T2b	double, behind instrument panel
T2c	double, yellow, behind instrument panel
T2d	double, engine compartment, behind intake pipe
T2e	double, behind instrument panel
T2f	double, behind instrument panel
T2g	double, behind instrument panel
T2h	double, engine compartment right
T3	three point, behind instrument panel
T3a	three point, gray, engine compartment
T3b	three point, black, engine compartment
T3c	three point, red, engine compartment

T3d	three point, behind instrument panel
T3e	three point, spring strut right
T3f	three point, spring strut left
T3g	three point, engine compartment right
T3h	three point, engine compartment left
T3j	three point, engine compartment
T3k	three point, throttle valve body
T4	four point, behind instrument panel
T4a	four point, green, behind instrument panel
T4b	four point, yellow, behind instrument panel
T4c	four point, yellow, behind instrument panel
T4d	four point, behind instrument panel
T4e	four point, green, behind instrument panel
T4f	four point, behind instrument panel
T4g	four point, green, behind instrument panel
T4h	four point, red, behind instrument panel
T4j	four point, black, behind instrument panel
T4k	four point, behind instrument panel
T4l	four point, behind instrument panel
T6	six point, yellow, behind instrument panel
T6a	six point, green, behind instrument panel
T6b	six point, brown, behind instrument panel
T6d	six point, blue, behind instrument panel
T6e	six point, behind instrument panel
T6e/	six point, indicator unit, Auto-check system
T6f	six point, white, behind instrument panel
T6g	six point, yellow, behind instrument panel
T8	eight point, indicator unit, Auto-check system
T9	nine point, behind instrument panel
T12	twelve point, behind instrument panel
T14/	fourteen point, instrument cluster
T14a	fourteen point, instrument cluster
T35	wire distributor, terminal 15
T36	wire distributor, terminal 30
T37	wire distributor, terminal 58

Ground Connector

①	strap, battery to body
⑦	strap, alternator to engine
⑧	behind instrument panel
⑨	engine compartment left
⑩	engine compartment right
⑪	luggage compartment
⑫	wiring harness left front
⑬	wiring harness instrument panel
⑭	under rear seat
⑮	package shelf rear window
⑯	near parking brake lever
⑱	near interior light
⑲	wiring harness right front
㉗	wiring harness electronic ignition

Plus (+) Connections

Ⓒ	terminal 15, wiring harness electronic ignition
Ⓕ	terminal 30 al, wiring harness instrument panel
Ⓖ	terminal 87a, wiring harness electronic ignition

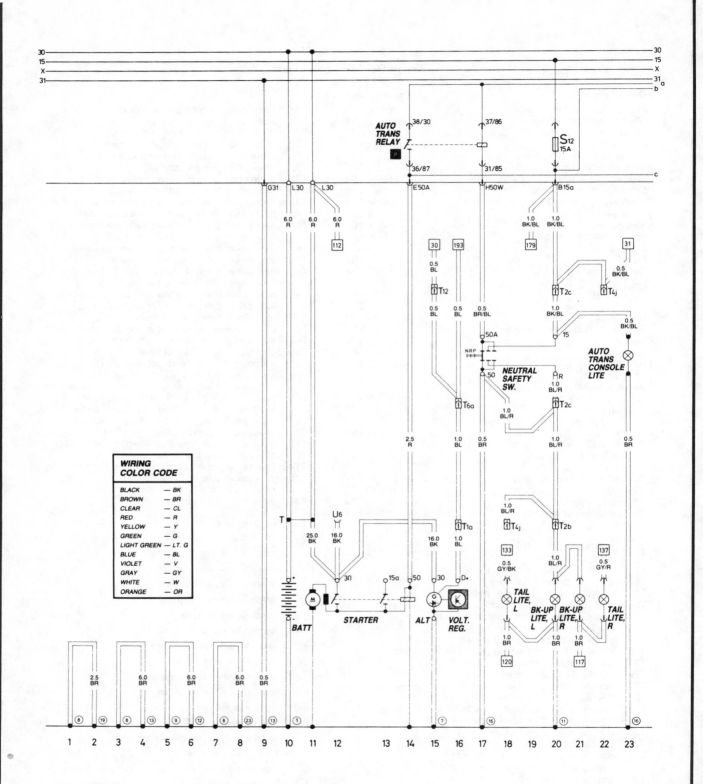

Fig. 12.44   Typical wiring diagram for vehicles with a turbocharger

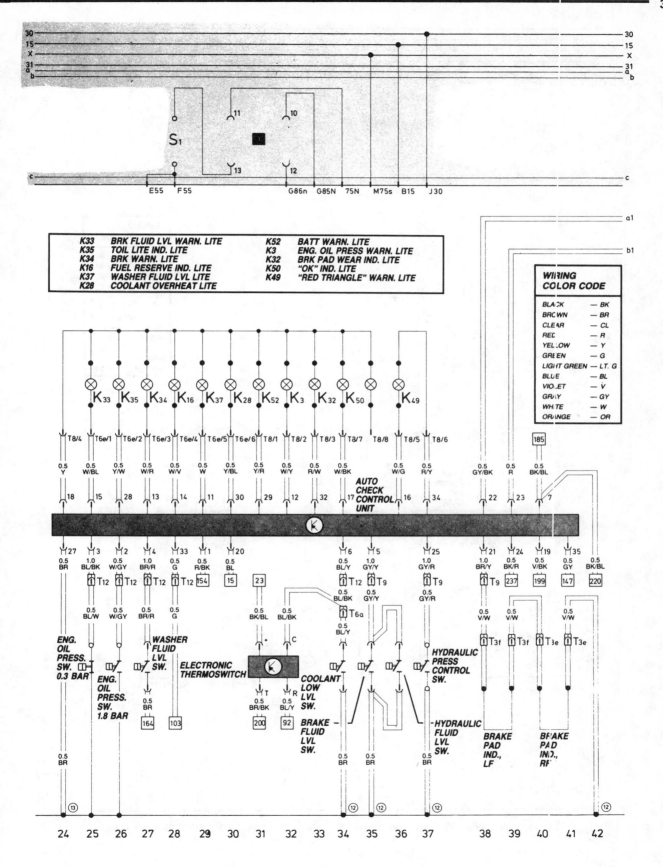

Fig. 12.44 Typical wiring diagram for vehicles with a turbocharger (continued)

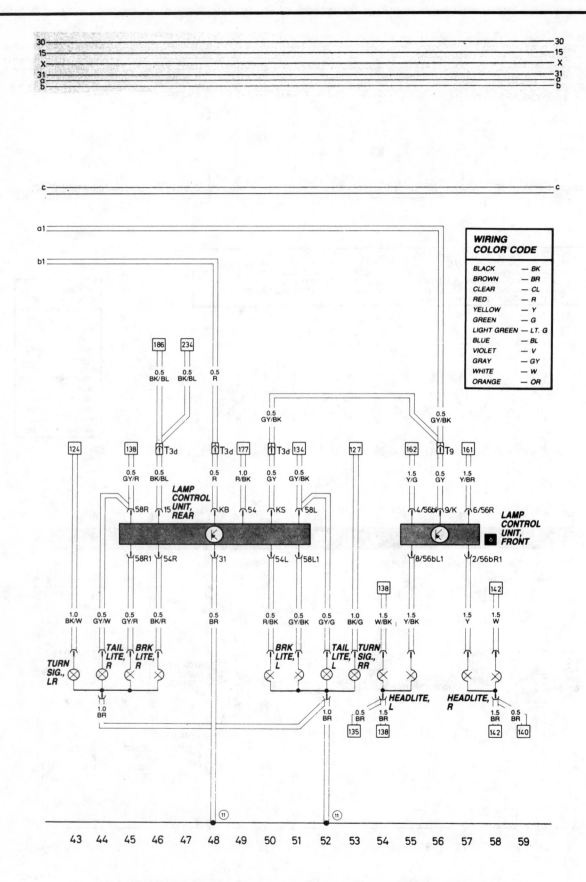

Fig. 12.44 Typical wiring diagram for vehicles with a turbocharger (continued)

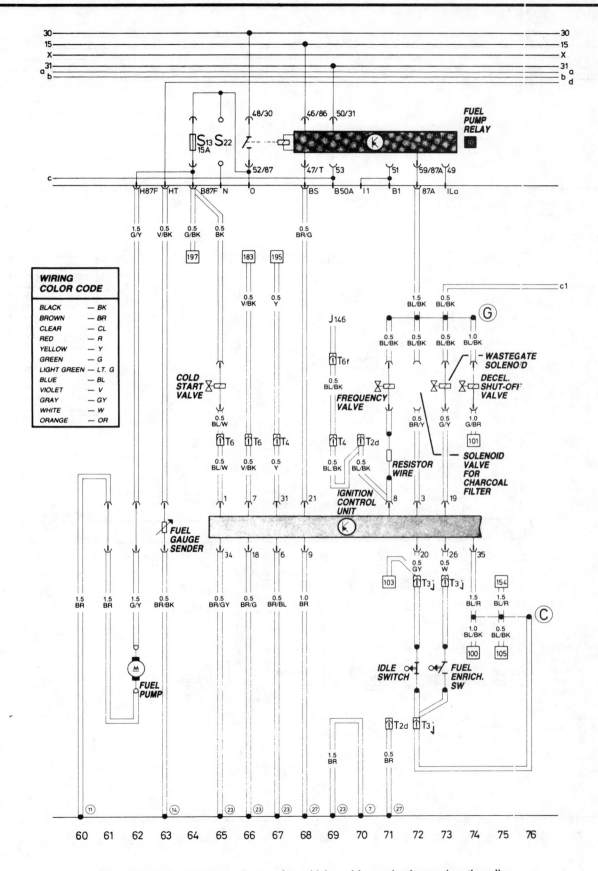

Fig. 12.44 Typical wiring diagram for vehicles with a turbocharger (continued)

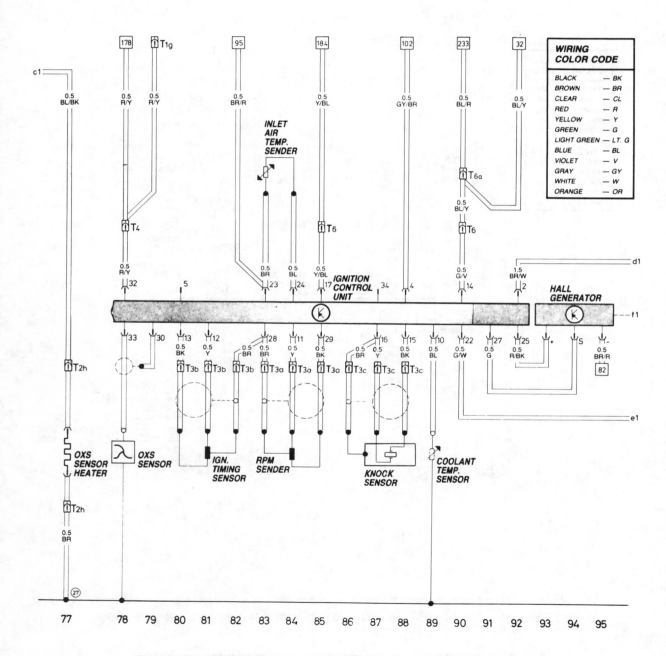

Fig. 12.44   Typical wiring diagram for vehicles with a turbocharger (continued)

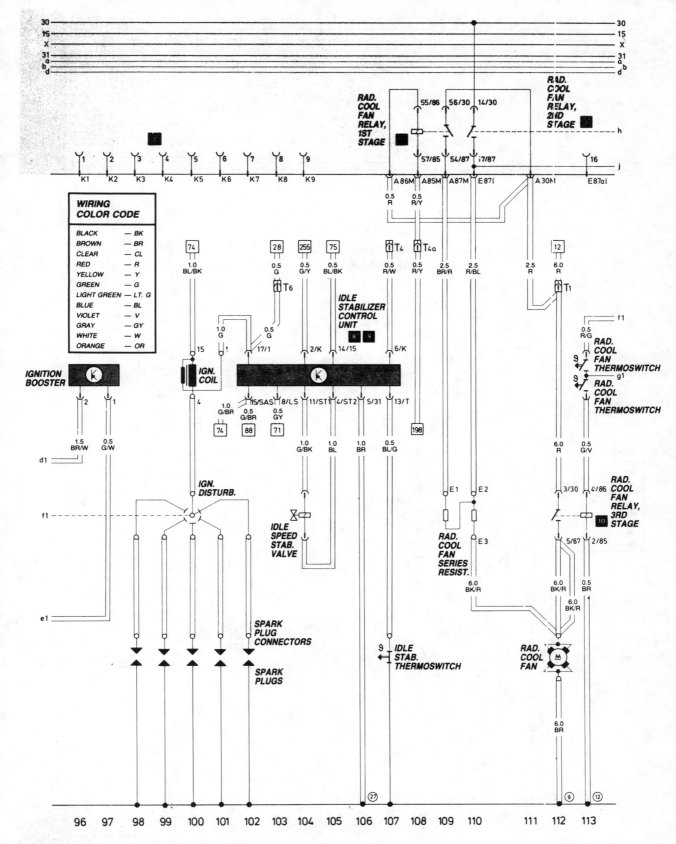

Fig. 12.44 Typical wiring diagram for vehicles with a turbocharger (continued)

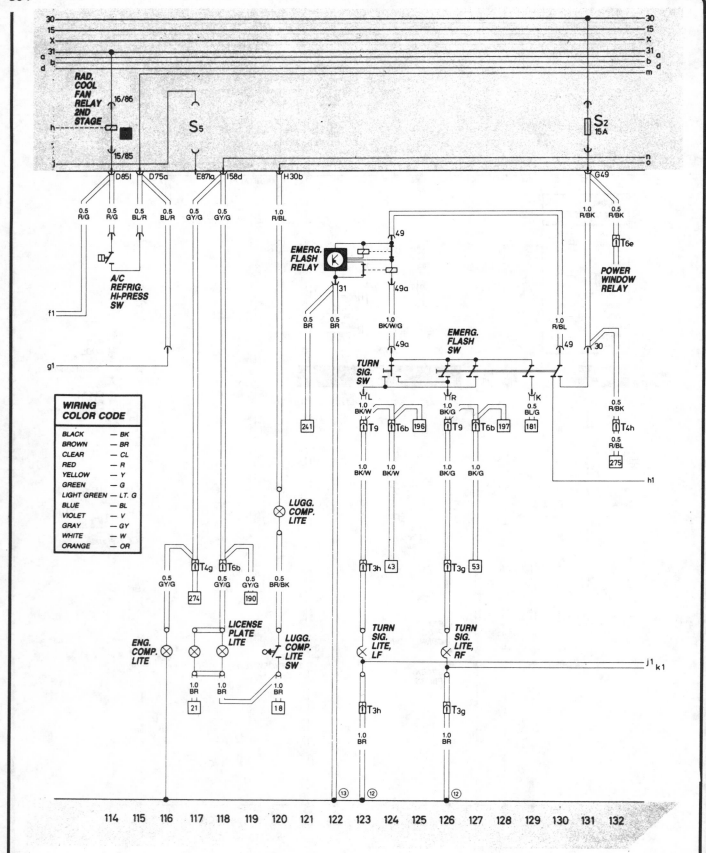

Fig. 12.44 Typical wiring diagram for vehicles with a turbocharger (continued)

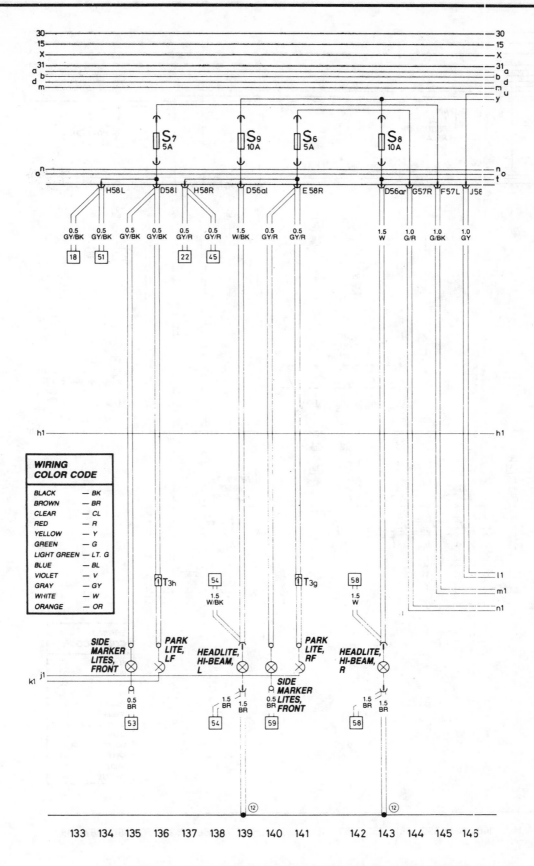

Fig. 12.44 Typical wiring diagram for vehicles with a turbocharger (continued)

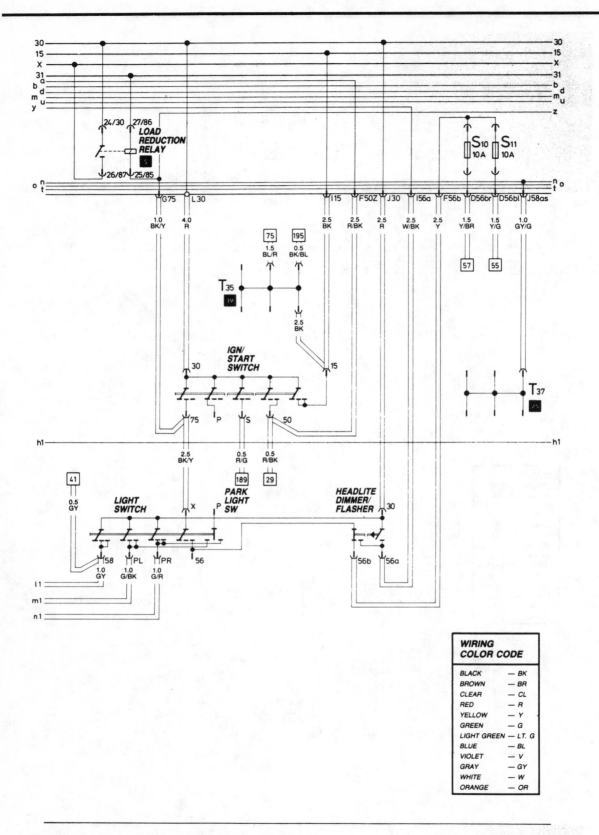

Fig. 12.44 Typical wiring diagram for vehicles with a turbocharger (continued)

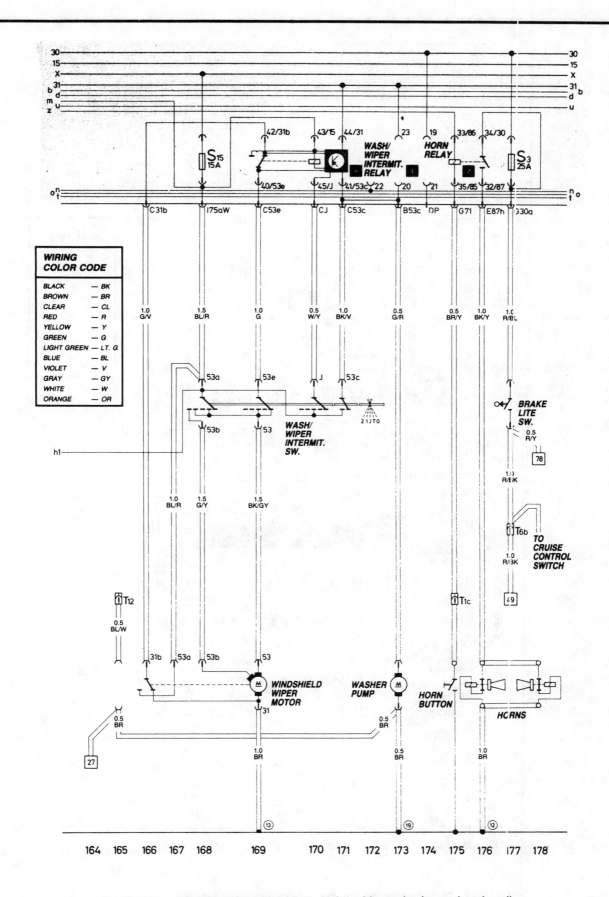

Fig. 12.44 Typical wiring diagram for vehicles with a turbocharger (continued)

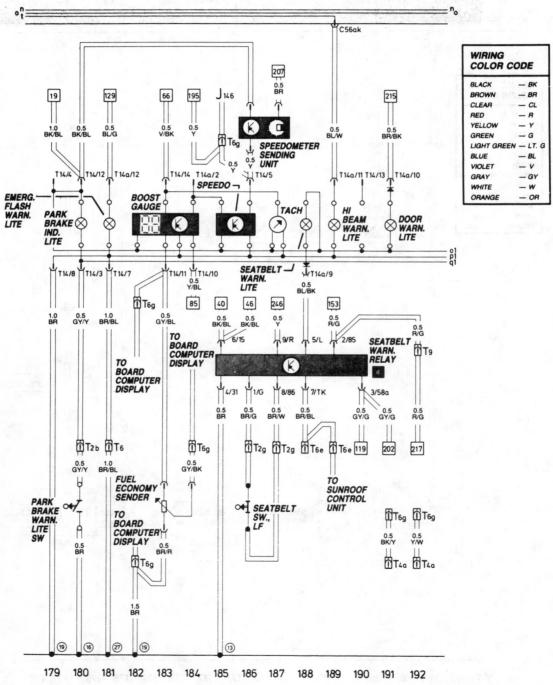

Fig. 12.44 Typical wiring diagram for vehicles with a turbocharger (continued)

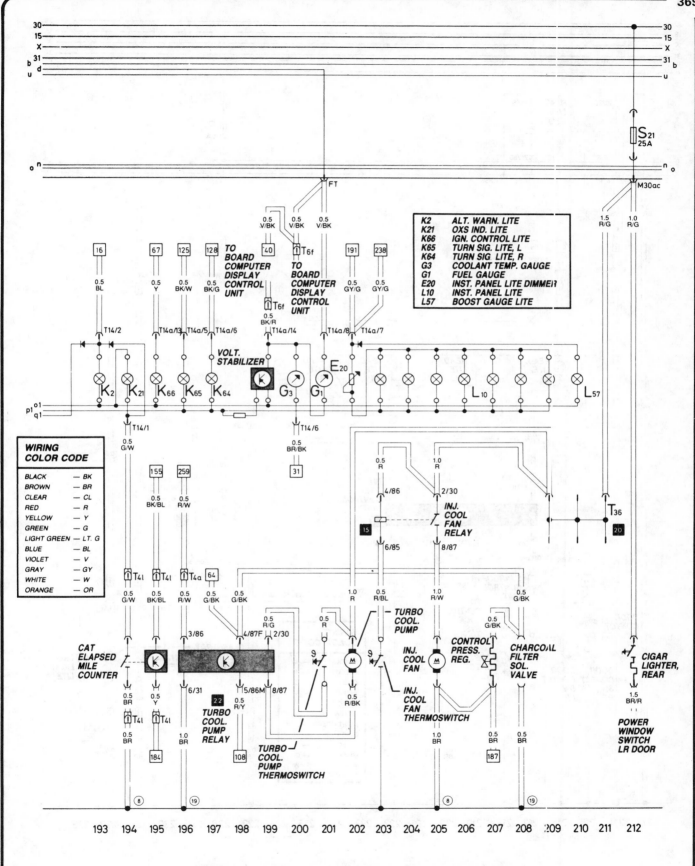

Fig. 12.44 Typical wiring diagram for vehicles with a turbocharger (continued)

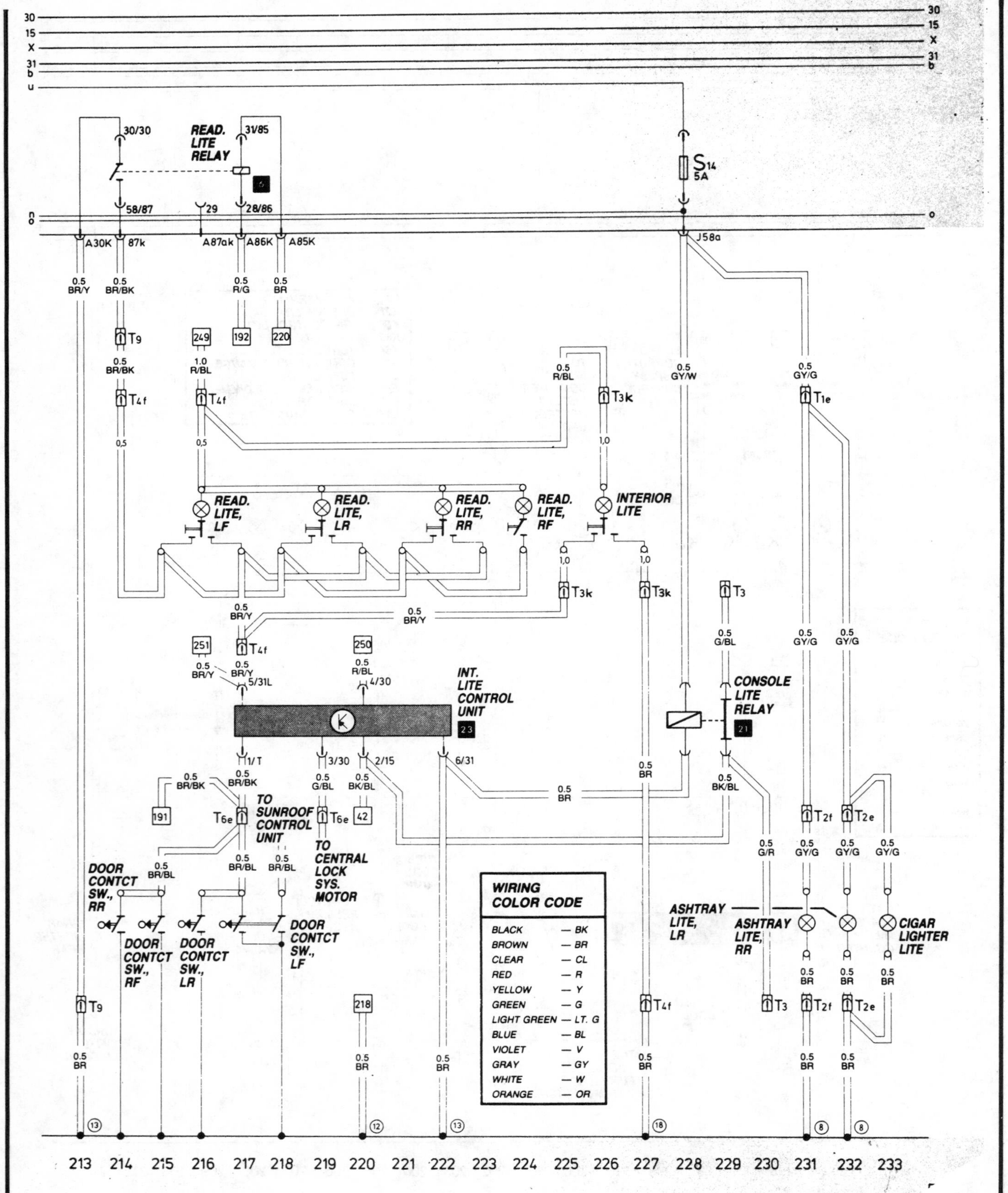

Fig. 12.44 Typical wiring diagram for vehicles with a turbocharger (continued)

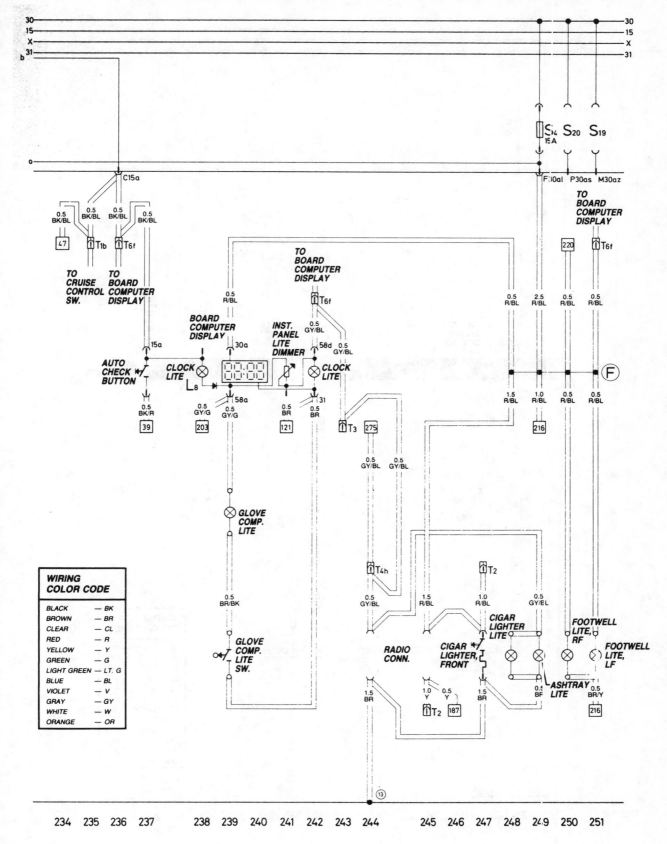

Fig. 12.44 Typical wiring diagram for vehicles with a turbocharger (continued)

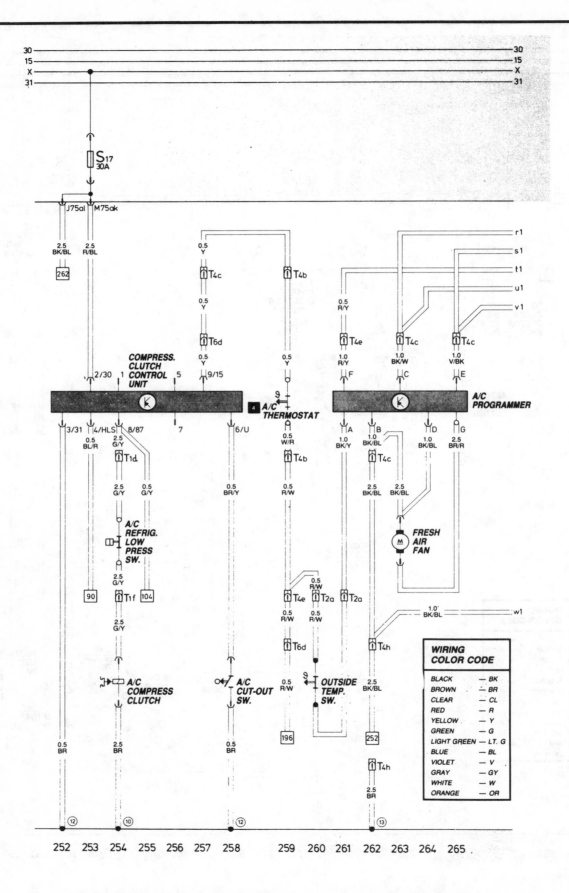

Fig. 12.44 Typical wiring diagram for vehicles with a turbocharger (continued)

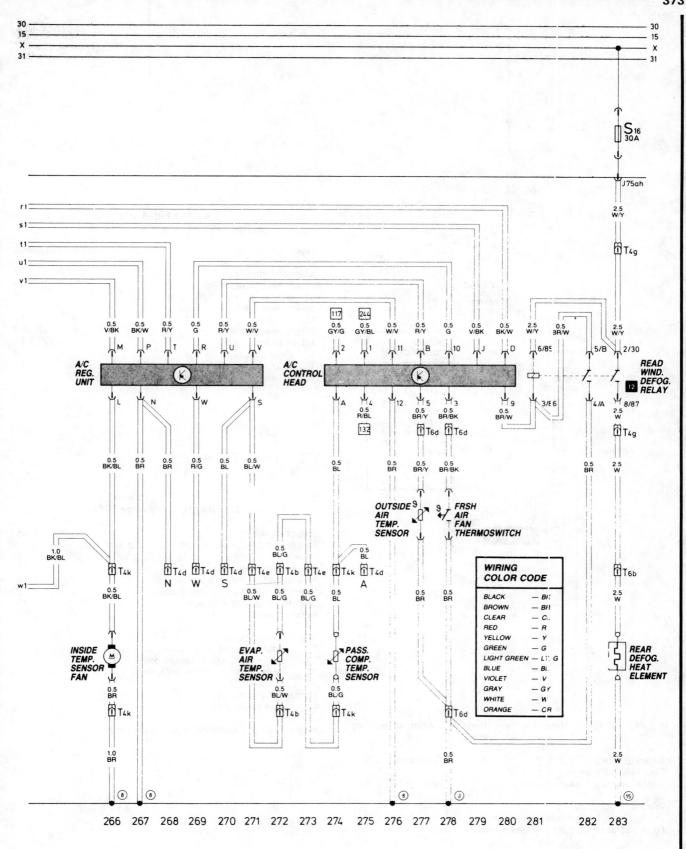

Fig. 12.44 Typical wiring diagram for vehicles with a turbocharger (continued)

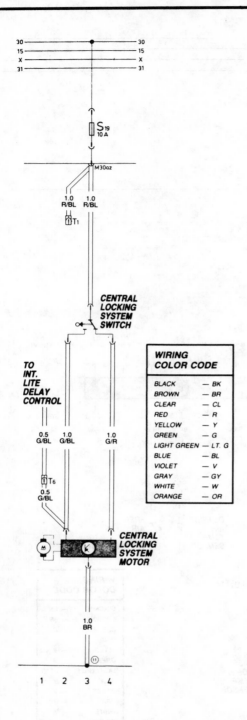

Fig. 12.45 Additional wiring diagram – central locking system

WIRING COLOR CODE	
BLACK	— BK
BROWN	— BR
CLEAR	— CL
RED	— R
YELLOW	— Y
GREEN	— G
LIGHT GREEN	— LT. G
BLUE	— BL
VIOLET	— V
GRAY	— GY
WHITE	— W
ORANGE	— OR

Description	Current track
Central locking system motor	1, 2
Central locking system switch	1, 2

Wire connectors
T1   single, behind instrument panel
T6   six-point, behind instrument panel

Ground Connector
⑪   under rear seat

Key to Fig. 12.46
(for diagram see opposite page)

Description	Current track
Magnetic clutch, left	8
Magnetic clutch, right	17
Mirror heat element, left	9
Mirror heat element, right	9
Mirror motor, left	5
Mirror motor, right	14
Mirror switch, left	3 to 8
Mirror switch, right	12 to 17
To central lock. sys. switch	3
To rear defog. switch	11
To rear wind. heater element	9

Key to Fig. 12.47
(for diagram see page 376)

Description	Current track
Power window/sunroof control unit (in aux. relay panel)	6-8
Sunroof motor	13
Sunroof relay	8-15
Sunroof stop switch (closed pos.)	8
Sunroof stop switch (open pos.)	11
Sunroof switch	2-5

Wire connectors
T1   single, behind instrument panel
T1a   single, behind instrument panel
T3   three point, near sunroof switch

Ground Connector
⑱   near sunroof switch

Note: Fuse S-43 located in aux. relay panel

R

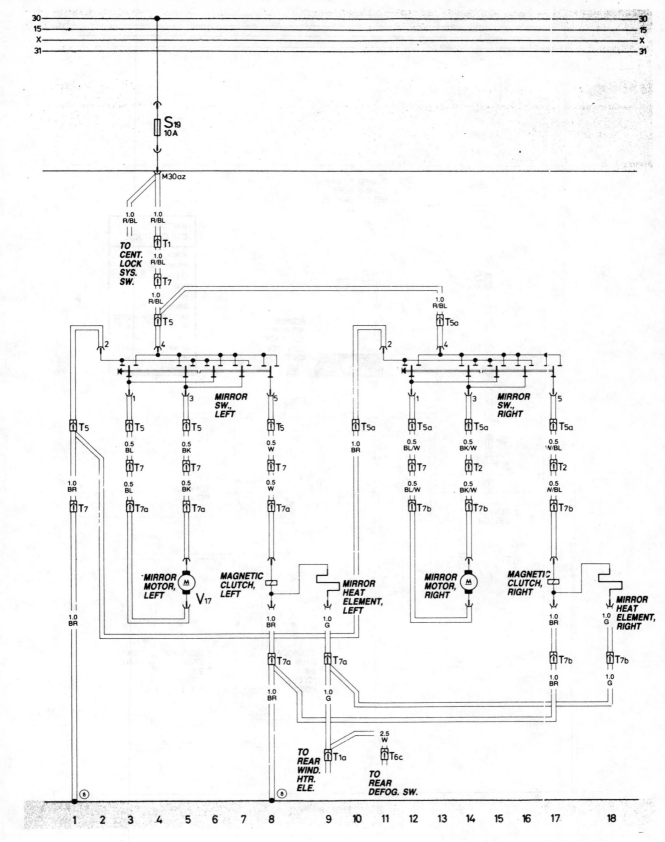

Fig. 12.46 Additional wiring diagram – power mirrors

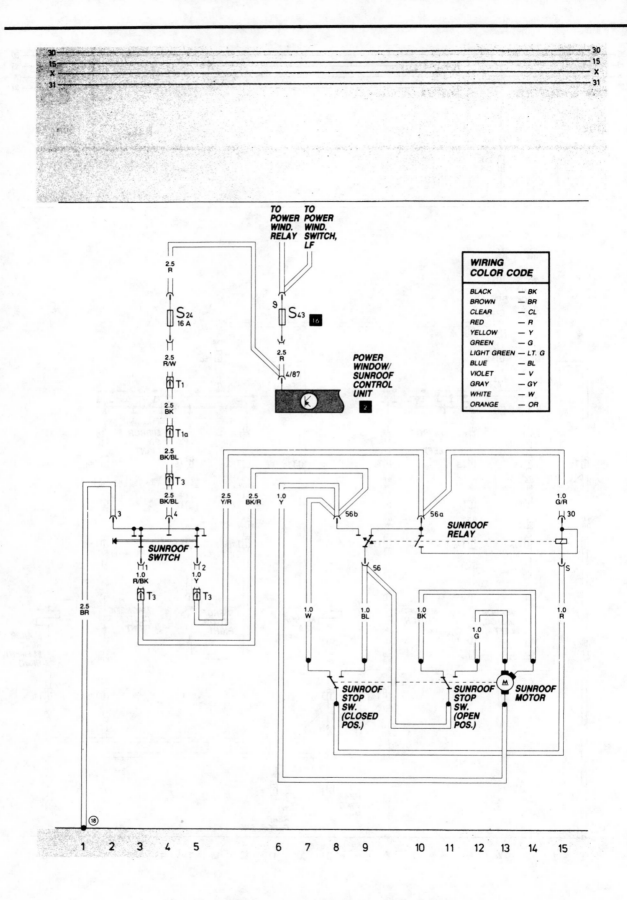

Fig. 12.47 Additional wiring diagram – electric sunroof

Chapter 13 Supplement: Revisions and information on 1987 and later models

Contents

1 Introduction

This Supplement contains Specifications and service procedure changes that apply exclusively to Audi 5000 models manufactured in 1987 and 1988. Also included is information related to previous models that was not available at the time of original publication of this manual.

Where no differences (or very minor differences) exist between 1986 models and later models, no information is given. In those instances, the original material included in Chapters 1 though 12, pertaining to 1986 models, should be used.

Before beginning a service or repair procedure, check this Supplement for new specifications and procedure changes. Make note of the supplementary information and be sure to include it while following the original procedure in Chapters 1 through 12.

2 Specifications

Note: *The following specifications are revisions of or supplementary to those listed at the beginning of each Chapter of this manual. The original specifications apply unless alternative information is included here.*

Engine

General

Code letters
    2.2 liter (turbo) . . . . MC
    2.3 liter . . . . NF
Capacity
    MC . . . . 2.22 liter (136 cu in)
    NF . . . . 2.30 liter (141 cu in)
Power output
    MC . . . . 162 bhp
    NF . . . . 130 bhp
Bore
    MC . . . . 81.0 mm (3.19 in)
    NF . . . . 82.5 mm (3.25 in)
Stroke (MC and NF) . . . . 86.4 mm (3.40 in)
Compression ratio
    MC 7.8:1
    NF 10.1:1

Pistons and rings

Piston diameter

MC engine

Standard	80.98 mm
1st oversize	81.23 mm
2nd oversize	81.48 mm

NF engine

Standard	82.48 mm
1st oversize	82.74 mm
2nd oversize	82.98 mm

Bore diameter

MC engine

Standard	81.01 mm
1st oversize	81.26 mm
2nd oversize	81.51 mm

NF engine

Standard	82.51 mm
1st oversize	82.76 mm
2nd oversize	83.01 mm

Valves

Valve head diameter (NF engine)

Intake	40.0 mm (1.575 in)
Exhaust	33.0 mm (1.299 in)

Valve timing at 1.0 mm lift/0 mm clearance (NF and MC engines)

Inlet opens before TDC	0°
Inlet closes before BDC	41.1°
Exhaust opens before BDC	40.0°
Exhaust closes before TDC	1.1°

Torque wrench settings	Nm	lbf ft
Flywheel/driveplate mounting bolts		
With shoulder on bolt	100	74
Without shoulder on bolt	75	54

Fuel, exhaust and emission control systems

General — MC engine

System type	CIS with turbocharger
System pressure	5.8 to 6.6 bar (84.1 to 95.7 psi)

General — NF engine

System type	CIS E-III
System pressure (with pressure gauge shut-off in closed position)	6.1 to 6.5 bar (88.5 to 94.0 psi)

Adjustment data — MC engine

Idle speed

Manual transmission	750 to 850 rpm
Automatic transmission	670 to 870 rpm
Fuel octane rating	95 RON unleaded

Adjustment data — NF engine

Idle speed	Regulated by the CIS-E III control unit

Ignition system

Turbo engine (MC)

Ignition timing	TDC

Spark plug type

Bosch	WR7DS or W7DTC
Beru	RS35 or 14-7DTU
Champion	N8GY or N9BYC
Spark plug gap	0.6 to 0.8 mm (0.024 to 0.032 in)
Firing order	1-2-4-5-3

Non-turbo engine (NF)

Spark plug type

Bosch	W7DTC
Beru	14-7DTU
Spark plug gap	0.7 to 0.9 mm (0.027 to 0.035 in)
Firing order	1-2-4-5-3

Clutch

Torque wrench settings	Nm	lbf ft
Flywheel/driveplate mounting bolts		
With shoulder on bolt	100	74
Without shoulder on bolt	75	54

Braking system

Double piston caliper front brakes
Disc

Diameter	276 mm (10.866 in)
Thickness	25 mm (0.984 in)
Wear limit	23 mm (0.905 in)
Maximum runout	0.03 mm (0.001 in)

Torque wrench settings	Nm	lbf ft
Double piston caliper		
Self-locking bolt	35	26
Brake pad carrier	125	92

Suspension and steering

Torque wrench settings	Nm	lbf ft
Axle nut (self-locking)	280	207

Electrical system
Alternator drivebelt deflection (alternators without "toothed" adjustment arm)

Total belt length UNDER 1000 mm (39.4 in)	
New belt	2 mm (5/64 in)
Used belt	5 mm (3/16 in)
Total belt length OVER 1000 mm (39.4 in)	
New belt	10 mm (3/8 in)
Used belt	15 mm (19/32 in)

Alternator drivebelt deflection (alternators with "toothed" adjustment arm)

New belt	4 mm (5/32 in)
Used belt	8 mm (19/64 in)

Torque wrench settings	Nm	lbf ft
Alternator pulley nut		
With Woodruff key	35	26
Without Woodruff key	50	37

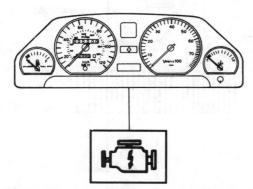

Fig. 13.1 The two-digit engine code (arrow) will appear on the Vehicle Data Sticker located on the inside of the truck lid (Sec 3)

Fig. 13.2 The CIS E-III engine control system has a dashboard warning lamp to indicate to the driver that a system fault has been detected (Sec 5)

3 Engine

Engine identification

Throughout the Specifications and procedures in this Supplement, and in Chapters 1 through 12, are references to engine code letters (MC, NF, etc.). The engine code is included as part of the Vehicle Data Sticker, which is attached to the inside of the trunk lid (see Fig. 13.1).

4 Cooling system

Water pump — removal and installation

Note that during the manufacture of water pumps, it may have been necessary to resurface and enlarge the O-ring groove in the water pump housing. An oversized (5 mm) gasket O-ring must be installed on these units, as the standard 4 mm O-ring will not seal properly. Water pumps which have been resurfaced to the larger size can be identified by a "5" stamped on the mounting flange area.

5 Fuel, exhaust and emission control systems

General description

1   All vehicles with engine code NF come equipped with a new fuel injection system called CIS E-III.
2   While most of the components of the CIS E-III system are similar to the previous CIS system, the new fuel injection system has a very sophisticated diagnosis capability which allows a mechanic to extract fault codes in the event of a problem.
3   A fault lamp indicator is incorporated in the instrument cluster (see Fig. 13.2) to warn the driver that the system has detected a problem. If the lamp comes on while driving, reduce the vehicle speed and drive, with reduced power, to an Audi dealer to have the malfunction corrected.

Fuel injectors and lines

4   With the CIS E-III system, the opening pressure of the fuel injectors has been raised to allow a higher residual pressure.

5   Also, the fuel injectors have a finer thread for the fuel line connections.

6   The fuel lines are also exposed to higher pressure and are steel armored.

7   When replacing any CIS E-III components, use replacement parts of the same design and quality.

Vacuum hose routing

8   A number of changes are reflected in the vacuum hose routing on later models. The accompanying illustrations (Fig. 13.3 and 13.4) show the vacuum hoses and the various components they connect.

6   Ignition system

General description

1   Later models equipped with a turbocharged engine feature an ignition system very similar to earlier models as outlined in Chapter 4, Part B.

2   The ignition system on non-turbocharged models (engine code NF) is an integral part of the CIS E-III control system as described in Section 5 above. Although most of the components are similar in design to other models, the ignition system is controlled by an electronic knock sensor and ignition control unit mounted on the driver's side kick panel (see Fig. 13.5).

3   Like the fuel system, the ignition system of the CIS E-III features

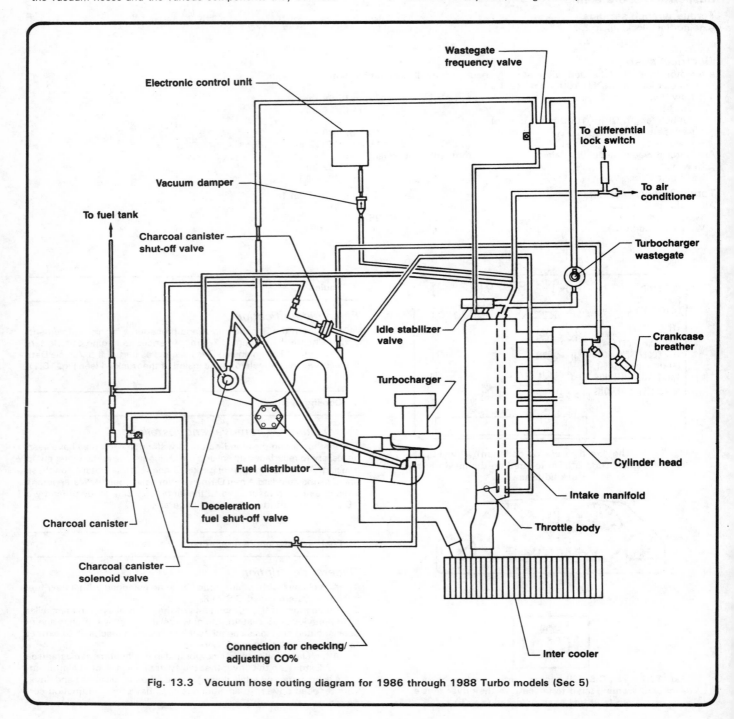

Fig. 13.3   Vacuum hose routing diagram for 1986 through 1988 Turbo models (Sec 5)

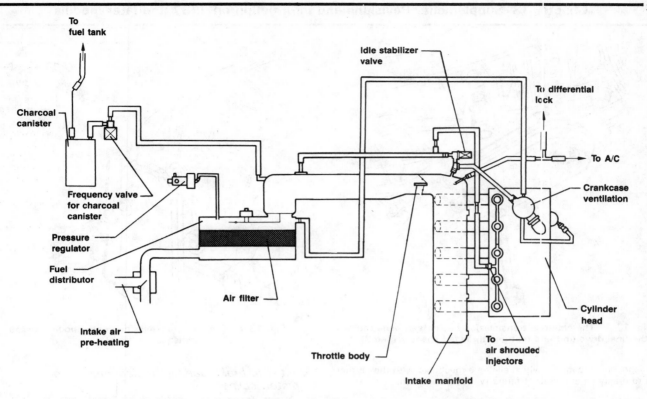

Fig. 13.4 Vacuum hose routing diagram for all late models with CIS E-III system (Sec 5)

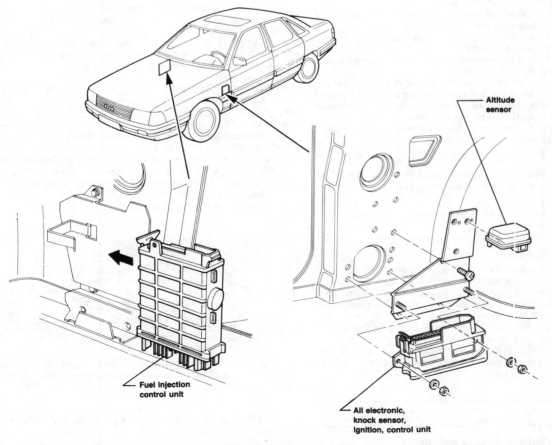

Fig. 13.5 The CIS E-III system has two control units — one for the fuel injection components and one for the ignition components (Sec 6)

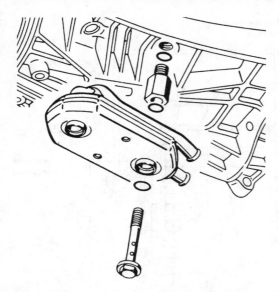

Fig. 13.6   The old-style transmission cooler is attached to the final drive unit and features threaded spacers (Sec 7)

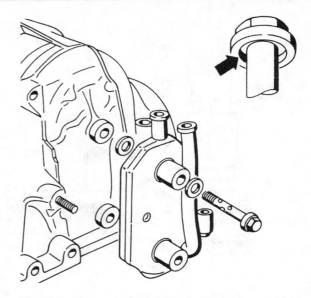

Fig. 13.7   The new transmission cooler mounts to the transmission (Sec 7)

self-diagnostic capability, which allows a mechanic with the correct tools to diagnose and correct faults within the system.

CIS E-III ignition system precautions

4   In addition to the precautions in Section 12 of Chapter 4, the following safety guidelines must be followed:
   a) Do not touch or disconnect ignition cables when the engine is running or the starter is being operated.
   b) Connect and disconnect tester leads to the ignition system only when the ignition is switched off.
   c) Do not connect any suppressor condensers or test lamps to terminal 1 of the coil.
   d) When the high tension cable (terminal 4 from the coil) is disconnected from the distributor, always connect it directly to ground with a jumper wire. Otherwise the engine must not be cranked with the starter (such as during a compression test).
   e) The battery must be completely disconnected when using arc, spot or electrical welding equipment.
   f) Do not wash the engine while it is running or if the ignition is switched on.
   g) High tension cables must be suppressed with at least 2 K-ohms of resistance (with 1 K-ohm at the rotor arm).

7   Automatic transmission

Transmission fluid cooler

1   The cooler for the automatic transmission fluid (ATF) has been redesigned and mounted in a different location on later models.
2   On previous models, the cooler was installed in the "return" line, bolted to the final drive unit and incorporating two spacer sleeves and union bolts (see Fig. 13.6).
3   The new type cooler is mounted on the transmission and is connected to the "supply" line (see Fig. 13.7).
4   Removal and installation of the coolers, regardless of type is essentially the same. Be sure to use new O-rings (where applicable) and do not overtighten the union bolts.

8   Braking system

Anti-lock brake system — precautions

In additon to the precautions included in Section 28 of Chapter 9, due to the difference in tire circumference, mini-spare tires should not be installed on a vehicle equipped with anti-lock brakes.

Front disc brake pads — replacement (single piston caliper)

1   Newly designed heat protection plates are available to help eliminate front disc brake squeal or noise. They are rubber coated to help eliminate vibration and noise during braking.
2   The new plates can be installed in earlier models in place of the existing heat protection plates. See an Audi dealer for the necessary parts.
3   The procedure for front disc brake pad replacement is unchanged from the one in Chapter 9 and the steps included there can be used to replace the heat protection plates as well.

Front disc brake pads — replacement (double piston caliper)

4   A new double piston caliper has been installed on some later models (see Fig. 13.8).
5   The new caliper is very similar to the Girling brake caliper as shown in Chapter 9, and most of the procedures for the Girling system will apply. Note, however, that there are no heat protection plates on the double piston caliper and it will be necessary to press both pistons back into the caliper bores to make room for the new pads.
6   Also, some vehicles are equipped with an outer pad retaining spring on the rear side of the brake pad (see Fig. 13.9).

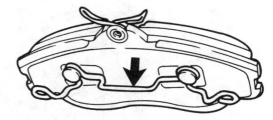

Fig. 13.9   Some double piston caliper pads come equipped with an outer pad retaining spring (Sec 8)

Front disc brake caliper — overhaul (double piston caliper)

7   The overhaul of the double piston caliper (see Fig. 13.10) is very similar to the procedure for single piston calipers found in Chapter 9 and all steps there will apply.
8   During piston removal, remove only one piston at a time by using

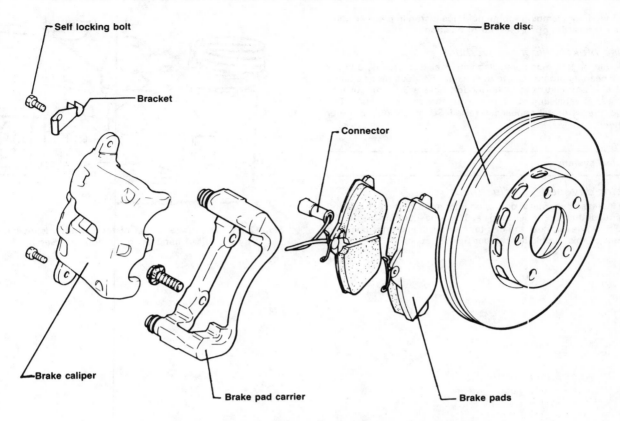

Fig. 13.8   Double piston brake caliper and pad mounting details (Sec 8)

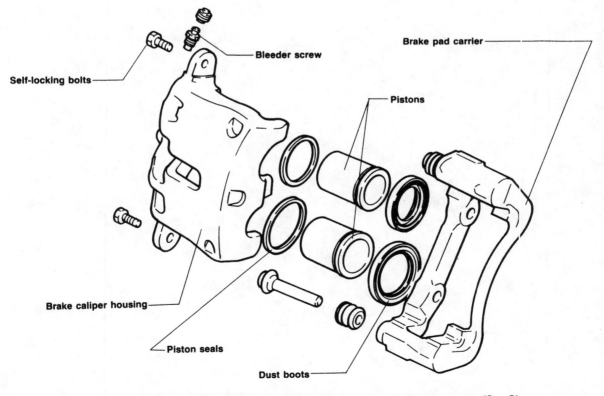

Fig. 13.10   Exploded view of the double piston brake caliper components (Sec 8)

a block of wood or clamping tool to hold one piston in place as compressed air forces the other one out of position.

Rear disc brake caliper — overhaul

9   Note that on late model vehicles with rear disc brakes, a larger piston has been incorporated into the design. Previous models had a 36.0 mm diameter piston and later models have a 38.0 mm piston. Make sure that replacement parts are for the correct caliper. The diameter of the piston will appear as a raised '36' or '38' on the caliper body (see Fig. 13.11).

9   Electrical system

Alternator drivebelt — adjustment

Due to increased alternator output on later models, the belt tension is more critical than on earlier models. The procedure in Chapter 12 is still valid. However, note the belt tension specifications appearing at the front of this Supplement under Specifications.

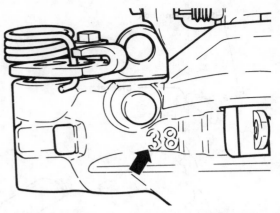

Fig. 13.11   The brake caliper piston diameter is indicated by the raised number on the housing (Sec 8)

Index

HAYNES AUTOMOTIVE MANUALS

NOTE: New manuals are added to this list on a periodic basis. If you do not see a listing for your vehicle, consult your local Haynes dealer for the latest product information.

ALFA-ROMEO
531	Alfa Romeo Sedan & Coupe '73 thru '80

AMC
694	Jeep CJ – see JEEP (412)
	Mid-size models, Concord, Hornet,
934	Gremlin & Spirit '70 thru '83
	(Renault) Alliance & Encore '83 thru '87

AUDI
162	100 '69 thru '77
615	4000 '80 thru '87
428	5000 '77 thru '83
1117	5000 '84 thru '88
207	Fox '73 thru '79

AUSTIN
049	Healey 100/6 & 3000 Roadster '56 thru '68
	Healey Sprite – see MG Midget Roadster (265)

BLMC
260	1100, 1300 & Austin America '62 thru '74
527	Mini '59 thru '69
*646	Mini '69 thru '88

BMW
276	320i all 4 cyl models '75 thru '83
632	528i & 530i '75 thru '80
240	1500 thru 2002 exceptTurbo '59 thru '77
348	2500, 2800, 3.0 & Bavaria '69 thru '76

BUICK
	Century (front wheel drive) – see GENERAL MOTORS A-Cars (829)
*1627	Buick, Oldsmobile & Pontiac Full-size (Front wheel drive) '85 thru '90 Buick Electra, LeSabre and Park Avenue; Oldsmobile Delta 88 Royale, Ninety Eight and Regency; Pontiac Bonneville
*1551	Buick Oldsmobile & Pontiac Full-size (Rear wheel drive) Buick Electra '70 thru '84, Estate '70 thru '90, LeSabre '70 thru '79, Oldsmobile Custom Cruiser '70 thru '90, Delta 88 '70 thru '85, Ninety-eight '70 thru '84 Pontiac Bonneville '70 thru '86, Catalina '70 thru '81, Grandville '70 thru '75, Parisienne '84 thru '86
627	Mid-size all rear-drive Regal & Century models with V6, V8 and Turbo '74 thru '87 Skyhawk – see GENERAL MOTORS J-Cars (766)
552	Skylark all X-car models '80 thru '85

CADILLAC
	Cimarron – see GENERAL MOTORS J-Cars (766)

CAPRI
296	2000 MK I Coupe '71 thru '75
283	2300 MK II Coupe '74 thru '78
205	2600 & 2800 V6 Coupe '71 thru '75
375	2800 MK II V6 Coupe '75 thru '78
	Mercury in-line engines – see FORD Mustang (654)
	Mercury V6 & V8 engines – see FORD Mustang (558)

CHEVROLET
*1477	Astro & GMC Safari Mini-vans '85 thru '90
554	Camaro V8 '70 thru '81
*866	Camaro '82 thru '89
	Cavalier – see GENERAL MOTORS J-Cars (766)
	Celebrity – see GENERAL MOTORS A-Cars (829)
625	Chevelle, Malibu & El Camino all V6 & V8 models '69 thru '87
449	Chevette & Pontiac T1000 '76 thru '87
550	Citation '80 thru '85
*1628	Corsica/Beretta '87 thru '90
274	Corvette all V8 models '68 thru '82
*1336	Corvette '84 thru '89
704	Full-size Sedans Caprice, Impala, Biscayne, Bel Air & Wagons, all V6 & V8 models '69 thru '90
319	Luv Pick-up all 2WD & 4WD '72 thru '82
626	Monte Carlo all V6, V8 & Turbo '70 thru '88
241	Nova all V8 models '69 thru '79
*1642	Nova & Geo Prizm front wheel drive '85 thru '90
*420	Pick-ups '67 thru '87 – Chevrolet & GMC, all V8 & in-line 6 cyl 2WD & 4WD '67 thru '87
*1664	Pick-ups '88 thru '90 – Chevrolet & GMC all full-size (C and K) models, '88 thru '90
*831	S-10 & GMC S-15 Pick-ups '82 thru '90
*345	Vans – Chevrolet & GMC, V8 & in-line 6 cyl models '68 thru '89
208	Vega except Cosworth '70 thru '77

CHRYSLER
*1337	Chrysler & Plymouth Mid-size front wheel drive '82 thru '88
	K-Cars – see DODGE Aries (723)
	Laser – see DODGE Daytona (1140)

DATSUN
402	200SX '77 thru '79
647	200SX '80 thru '83
228	B-210 '73 thru '78
525	210 '78 thru '82
206	240Z, 260Z & 280Z Coupe & 2+2 '70 thru '78
563	280ZX Coupe & 2+2 '79 thru '83 300ZX – see NISSAN (1137)
679	310 '78 thru '82
123	510 & PL521 Pick-up '68 thru '73
430	510 '78 thru '81
372	610 '72 thru '76
277	620 Series Pick-up '73 thru '79
235	710 '73 thru '77
	720 Series Pick-up – see NISSAN Pick-up (771)
376	810/Maxima all gasoline models '77 thru '84
124	1200 '70 thru '73
368	F10 '76 thru '79 Pulsar – see NISSAN (876) Sentra – see NISSAN (982) Stanza – see NISSAN (981)

DODGE
*723	Aries & Plymouth Reliant '81 thru '88
*1231	Caravan & Plymouth Voyager Mini-Vans '84 thru '89
699	Challenger & Plymouth Saporro '78 thru '83
236	Colt '71 thru '77
419	Colt (rear wheel drive) '77 thru '80
610	Colt & Plymouth Champ (front wheel drive) '78 thru '87
*556	D50 & Plymouth Arrow Pick-ups '79 thru '88
234	Dart & Plymouth Valiant all 6 cyl models '67 thru '76
*1140	Daytona & Chrysler Laser '84 thru '88
*545	Omni & Plymouth Horizon '78 thru '89
*912	Pick-ups all full-size models '74 thru '90
*349	Vans – Dodge & Plymouth V8 & 6 cyl models '71 thru '89

FIAT
080	124 Sedan & Wagon all ohv & dohc models '66 thru '75
094	124 Sport Coupe & Spider '68 thru '78
087	128 '72 thru '79
310	131 & Brava '75 thru '81
038	850 Sedan, Coupe & Spider '64 thru '74
479	Strada '79 thru '82
273	X1/9 '74 thru '80

FORD
*1476	Aerostar Mini-vans '86 thru '88
788	Bronco and Pick-ups '73 thru '79
*880	Bronco and Pick-ups '80 thru '90
014	Cortina MK II except Lotus '66 thru '70
295	Cortina MK III 1600 & 2000 ohc
268	Courier Pick-up '72 thru '82
789	Escort & Mercury Lynx all models '81 thru '90
560	Fairmont & Mercury Zephyr all irr-line & V8 models '78 thru '83
334	Fiesta '77 thru '80
754	Ford & Mercury Full-size, Ford LTD & Mercury Marquis ('75 thru '82); Ford Custom 500, Country Squire, Crown Victoria & Mercury Colony Park ('75 thru '87); Ford LTD Crown Victoria & Mercury Gran Marquis ('83 thru '87)
359	Granada & Mercury Monarch all in-line, 6 cyl & V8 models '75 thru '80
773	Ford & Mercury Mid-size, Ford Thunderbird & Mercury Cougar ('75 thru '82); Ford LTD & Mercury Marquis ('83 thru '86); Ford Torino, Gran Torino, Elite, Ranchero pick-up, LTD II, Mercury Montego, Comet, XR-7 & Lincoln Versailles ('75 thru '86)
*654	Mustang & Mercury Capri all in-line models & Turbo '79 thru '90
*558	Mustang & Mercury Capri all V6 & V8 models '79 thru '89
357	Mustang V8 '64-1/2 thru '73
231	Mustang II all 4 cyl, V6 & V8 models '74 thru '78
204	Pinto '70 thru '74
649	Pinto & Mercury Bobcat '75 thru '80
*1026	Ranger & Bronco II gasoline models '83 thru '89
*1421	Taurus & Mercury Sable '86 thru '90
*1418	Tempo & Mercury Topaz all gasoline models '84 thru '89
1338	Thunderbird & Mercury Cougar/XR7 '83 thru '88
*344	Vans all V8 Econoline models '69 thru '90

GENERAL MOTORS
*829	A-Cars – Chevrolet Celebrity, Buick Century, Pontiac 6000 & Oldsmobile Cutlass Ciera '82 thru '89
*766	J-Cars – Chevrolet Cavalier, Pontiac J-2000, Oldsmobile Firenza, Buick Skyhawk & Cadillac Cimarron '82 thru '89
*1420	N-Cars – Pontiac Grand Am, Buick Somerset and Oldsmobile Calais '85 thru '87; Buick Skylark '86 thru '87

GEO
	Tracker – see SUZUKI Samurai (1626)
	Prizm – see CHEVROLET Nova (1642)

GMC
	Safari – see CHEVROLET ASTRO (1477)
	Vans & Pick-ups – see CHEVROLET (420, 831, 345, 1664)

HONDA
138	360, 600 & Z Coupe '67 thru '75
351	Accord CVCC '76 thru '83
*1221	Accord '84 thru '89
160	Civic 1200 '73 thru '79
633	Civic 1300 & 1500 CVCC '80 thru '83
297	Civic 1500 CVCC '75 thru '79
*1227	Civic except 16-valve CRX & 4 WD Wagon '84 thru '86
*601	Prelude CVCC '79 thru '89

HYUNDAI
*1552	Excel '86 thru '89

ISUZU
*1641	Trooper & Pick-up all gasolime models '81 thru '89

JAGUAR
098	MK I & II, 240 & 340 Sedans '55 thru '69
*242	XJ6 all 6 cyl models '68 thru '86
*478	XJ12 & XJS 12 cyl models '72 thru '85
140	XK-E 3.8 & 4.2 all 6 cyl models '61 thru '72

JEEP
*1553	Cherokee, Comanche & Wagoneer Limited '84 thru '89
412	CJ '49 thru '86

LADA
*413	1200, 1300, 1500 & 1600 all models including Riva '74 thru '86

LANCIA
533	Lancia Beta Sedan, Coupe & HPE '76 thru '80

LAND ROVER
314	Series II, IIA, & III 4 cyl gasoline models '58 thru '86
529	Diesel '58 thru '80

MAZDA
648	626 Sedan & Coupe (rear wheel drive) '79 thru '82
*1082	626 & MX-6 (front wheel drive) '83 thru '90
*267	B1600, B1800 & B2000 Pick-ups '72 thru '90
370	GLC Hatchback (rear wheel drive) '77 thru '83
757	GLC (front wheel drive) '81 thru '86
109	RX2 '71 thru '75
096	RX3 '72 thru '76
460	RX-7 '79 thru '85
*1419	RX-7 '86 thru '89

MERCEDES-BENZ
*1643	190 Series all gasoline '84 thru '88
346	230, 250 & 280 Sedan, Coupe & Roadster all 6 cyl sohc models '68 thru '72
983	280 123 Series all gasoline models '77 thru '81
698	350 & 450 Sedan, Coupe & Roadster '71 thru '80
697	Diesel 123 Series 200D, 220D, 240D, 240TD, 300D, 300CD, 300TD, 4- & 5-cyl incl. Turbo '76 thru '85

MERCURY
See FORD Listing

MG
475	MGA '56 thru '62
111	MGB Roadster & GT Coupe '62 thru '80
265	MG Midget & Austin Healey Sprite Roadster '58 thru '80

MITSUBISHI
	Pick-up – see Dodge D-50 (556)

MORRIS
074	(Austin) Marina 1.8 '71 thru '80
024	Minor 1000 sedan & wagon '56 thru '71

NISSAN
*1137	300ZX all Turbo & non-Turbo '84 thru '86
*1341	Maxima '85 thru '89
*771	Pick-ups/Pathfinder gas models '80 thru '88
*876	Pulsar '83 thru '86
*982	Sentra '82 thru '90
*981	Stanza '82 thru '90

OLDSMOBILE
	Custom Cruiser – see BUICK Full-size (1551)
658	Cutlass all standard gasoline V6 & V8 models '74 thru '88
	Cutlass Ciera – see GENERAL MOTORS A-Cars (829)
	Firenza – see GENERAL MOTORS J-Cars (766)
	Ninety-eight – see BUICK Full-size (1551)
	Omega – see PONTIAC Phoenix & Omega (551)

OPEL
157	(Buick) Manta Coupe 1900 '70 thru '74

PEUGEOT
161	504 all gasoline models '68 thru '79
663	504 all diesel models '74 thru '83

PLYMOUTH
425	Arrow '76 thru '80
	For all other PLYMOUTH titles, see DODGE listing.

PONTIAC
	T1000 – see CHEVROLET Chevette (449)
	J-2000 – see GENERAL MOTORS J-Cars (766)
	6000 – see GENERAL MOTORS A-Cars (829)
1232	Fiero '84 thru '88
555	Firebird all V8 models except Turbo '70 thru '81
*867	Firebird '82 thru '89 Full-size Rear Wheel Drive – see Buick, Oldsmobile, Pontiac Full-size (1551)
551	Phoenix & Oldsmobile Omega all X-car models '80 thru '84

PORSCHE
*264	911 all Coupe & Targa models except Turbo '65 thru '87
239	914 all 4 cyl models '69 thru '76
397	924 including Turbo '76 thru '82
*1027	944 including Turbo '83 thru '89

RENAULT
141	5 Le Car '76 thru '83
079	8 & 10 with 58.4 cu in engines '62 thru '72
097	12 Saloon & Estate 1289 cc engines '70 thru '80
768	15 & 17 '73 thru '79
081	16 89.7 cu in & 95.5 cu in engines '65 thru '72
598	18i & Sportwagon '81 thru '86 Alliance & Encore – see AMC (934)
984	Fuego '82 thru '85

ROVER
085	3500 & 3500S Sedan 215 cu in engines '68 thru '76
*365	3500 SDI V8 '76 thru '85

SAAB
198	95 & 96 V4 '66 thru '75
247	99 including Turbo '69 thru '80
*980	900 including Turbo '79 thru '88

SUBARU
237	1100, 1300, 1400 & 1600 '71 thru '79
*681	1600 & 1800 2WD & 4Wd '80 thru '88

SUZUKI
1626	Samurai/Sidekick and Geo Tracker '86 thru '89

TOYOTA
*1023	Camry '83 thru '90
150	Carina Sedan '71 thru '74
229	Celica ST, GT & liftback '71 thru '77
437	Celica '78 thru '81
*935	Celica except front-wheel drive and Supra '82 thru '85
680	Celica Supra '79 thru '81
1139	Celica Supra in-line 6-cylinder '82 thru '86
201	Corolla 1100, 1200 & 1600 '67 thru '74
361	Corolla '75 thru '79
961	Corolla (rear wheel drive) '80 thru '87
*1025	Corolla (front wheel drive) '84 thru '88
*636	Corolla Tercel '80 thru '82
230	Corona & MK II all 4 cyl sohc models '69 thru '74
360	Corona '74 thru '82
*532	Cressida '78 thru '82
313	Land Cruiser '68 thru '82
200	MK II all 6 cyl models '72 thru '76
*1339	MR2 '85 thru '87
304	Pick-up '69 thru '78
*656	Pick-up '79 thru '90
787	Starlet '81 thru '84

TRIUMPH
112	GT6 & Vitesse '62 thru '74
113	Spitfire '62 thru '81
028	TR2, 3, 3A, & 4A Roadsters '52 thru '67
031	TR250 & 6 Roadsters '67 thru '76
322	TR7 '75 thru '81

VW
091	411 & 412 all 103 cu in models '68 thru '73
036	Bug 1200 '54 thru '66
039	Bug 1300 & 1500 '65 thru '70
159	Bug 1500 all basic, sport & super (curved windshield) models '70 thru '74
110	Bug 1600 Super (flat windshield) '70 thru '72
238	Dasher all gasoline models '74 thru '81
*884	Rabbit, Jetta, Scirocco, & Pick-up all gasoline models '74 thru '89 & Convertible
451	Rabbit, Jetta & Pick-up all diesel models '77 thru '84
082	Transporter 1600 '68 thru '79
226	Transporter 1700, 1800 & 2000 all models '72 thru '79
084	Type 3 1500 & 1600 '63 thru '73
1029	Vanagon all air-cooled models '80 thru '83

VOLVO
203	120, 130 Series & 1800 Sports '61 thru '73
129	140 Series '66 thru '74
244	164 '68 thru '75
*270	240 Series '74 thru '90
400	260 Series '75 thru '82
*1550	740 & 760 Series '82 thru '88

SPECIAL MANUALS
1479	Automotive Body Repair & Painting Manual
1654	Automotive Electrical Manual
1480	Automotive Heating & Air Conditioning Manual
482	Fuel Injection Manual
299	SU Carburetors thru '88
393	Weber Carburetors thru '79
300	Zenith/Stromberg CD Carburetors thru '76

See your dealer for other available titles

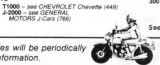

* Listings shown with an asterisk (*) indicate model coverage as of this printing. These titles will be periodically updated to include later model years — consult your Haynes dealer for more information.

Over 100 Haynes motorcycle manuals also available

6-1-90

Haynes Publications Inc., P.O. Box 978, Newbury Park, CA 91320 ● (818) 889-5400 ● (805) 498-6703